ML

The
BOOKER T. WASHINGTON
Papers

The
BOOKER T. WASHINGTON
Papers

VOLUME 10

1909–11

Louis R. Harlan
and
Raymond W. Smock
EDITORS

Geraldine McTigue
and
Nan E. Woodruff
ASSISTANT EDITORS

University of Illinois Press
URBANA · CHICAGO · LONDON

The BOOKER T. WASHINGTON *Papers*
is supported by
The National Endowment for the Humanities
The National Historical Publications and Records Commission
The University of Maryland

Library of Congress Cataloging in Publication Data

Washington, Booker Taliaferro, 1856–1915.
  The Booker T. Washington papers.

  Vol. 10   edited by L. R. Harlan and R. W. Smock.
  Geraldine McTigue and Nan E. Woodruff, assistant editors.
  Includes bibliographies.
  CONTENTS: v. 1. The autobiographical writings.
—v. 2.   1860–89.—[etc.]—v. 10.   1909–11.
  1. Washington, Booker T., 1856–1915.
  2. Afro-Americans—History—1863–1877—Sources.
  3. Afro-Americans—History—1877–1964—Sources.
  4. Afro-Americans—Correspondence. I. Harlan,
Louis R. II. Smock, Raymond W.
E185.97.W274   301.45′19′6073024   75–186345
ISBN 0–252–00800–6 (v. 10)

To the Students of Tuskegee Institute
1881-1915

CONTENTS

Contents

Contents

CONTENTS

Contents

CONTENTS

CONTENTS

Contents

xix

INTRODUCTION

DURING THE PERIOD covered by this volume, from January 1909 to March 1911, Booker T. Washington remained the most powerful figure in black America. The inauguration of William Howard Taft as President of the United States early in 1909, however, somewhat weakened Washington's political alliance, and later in the same year the founding of the National Association for the Advancement of Colored People brought together the black opponents of Washington's racial leadership and northern white liberals who had earlier supported him. Washington's credibility as a racial peacemaker also suffered as race riots, lynchings, and discriminatory laws punctuated the troubled race relations of the segregation era.

Though his public utterances remained unfailingly optimistic, Washington spent much of his energies on rear-guard action against change. He declined Oswald Garrison Villard's invitation to the conference which formed the NAACP, but received assurances that the white liberals would prevent the efforts of Du Bois, Trotter, and other blacks to use the NAACP to attack him. Washington's friend Robert R. Moton undertook behind the scenes to reconcile the two black factions, but these efforts came to naught because of a public attack on Washington by Du Bois and other blacks using stationery of the National Negro Committee, the original name of the NAACP. Washington showed his irreconcilability by opposing appointment of Du Bois to the faculty of Howard University, hounding Professor William Pickens of Talladega College for signing the National Negro Committee appeal, and encouraging newspapers to publish scandalous articles on white officers of the

NAACP. Washington's private conduct in this regard was in sharp contrast to his public show of indifference to his critics.

President Theodore Roosevelt had proven to be no champion of black civil rights, but he had been personally loyal to his adviser Booker T. Washington. Though Washington had supported Taft in 1908 despite the Brownsville affair, and though Roosevelt urged Taft to continue Washington as a presidential adviser, Taft began as soon as he entered office to dismantle Washington's black patronage machine. He kept Washington as an adviser, and even overruled Washington's appointment to the Liberian Commission on the ground that he needed him in the country for consultation. Washington's first assignment, however, was to persuade Collector William D. Crum of the port of Charleston to resign before Taft fired him. Taft adopted a policy of removal of southern black officeholders wherever whites objected to them. Furthermore, he denied Washington a monopoly of federal black appointments by making a man who had no obligations to Washington, Henry Lincoln Johnson, recorder of deeds of the District of Columbia. On the other hand, Taft strengthened Washington's hand in the northern black communities by appointing northern blacks to federal offices, most notably William H. Lewis as assistant attorney general.

The Liberian Commission, established largely through Washington's urging, included his private secretary Emmett J. Scott and two white men. On its recommendation the United States established a protectorate over Liberia that included customs supervision and training of its frontier forces, but unfortunately not economic aid or educational development.

In an energetic effort to promote better race relations and improvement of black educational and economic opportunity, Washington made whirlwind speaking tours of Mississippi, South Carolina, Virginia, and Tennessee in 1909 and North Carolina in 1910. The magic of his name drew large crowds of both races as perhaps no other person could have, and he handled these crowds successfully with a combination of lecture and entertainment, concession and appeal, realism and optimistic dream.

Washington in this period took a stand on several social issues of the day. His conservative views on woman suffrage, published in the New York *Times*, raised an outcry from feminists. He took every opportunity to support prohibition of alcoholic beverages as a deterrent to black crime. By serving as a trustee of both Howard and Fisk and through an article in a national magazine, he sought to lay to rest the frequent charge that he opposed higher education for blacks. He championed privately the legal cases of two black farmers, Alonzo Bailey and Pink Franklin, who ran afoul of unconstitional peonage statutes. He aided efforts to save the homes of Frederick Douglass and Joel Chandler Harris. He wrote for publication tributes to the southern white moderate Edgar Gardner Murphy, the black explorer Matthew Henson, the oil millionaire H. H. Rogers, Mark Twain, Robert C. Ogden, and Bert Williams. Washington's popular history of his race, *The Story of the Negro*, appeared in two volumes in 1909. It is not included here because of its length, and because parts of it appeared in Volume 1 of this series. Furthermore, it did not represent his best work and much of it was ghostwritten by Robert E. Park. He was also at work on two other books, *My Larger Education* (1911), a sequel to *Up from Slavery*, and *The Man Farthest Down* (1912), a study of the working classes of Europe.

That events at Tuskegee play but a small part in this volume is the result of the wealth of documents on Washington's national role. He continued to watch every detail of the daily routine of the campus and the surrounding black community, a concern abetted by changes in the board of trustees. Seth Low as chairman of the board showed an obsessive interest in management efficiency and cost accounting of the school's agricultural and industrial departments. Under this pressure Tuskegee's most distinguished faculty member, George Washington Carver, was tested and found wanting as an administrator. Washington narrowed Carver's duties to research and teaching, despite Carver's threat to resign. Other changes in this period were the establishment of nurse training and extension work in agriculture and education.

This volume, like earlier ones, owes much to the meticulous work of Sadie M. Harlan. We thank also our secretaries, Denise P. Moore, Susan M. Valenza, and Linda E. Waskey.

The National Endowment for the Humanities, the National Historical Publications and Records Commission, and the University of Maryland have continued their generous support and encouragement of this project. The editors thank them and hope that their faith has been justified by the present volume and the promise of three more to come.

SYMBOLS AND ABBREVIATIONS

STANDARD ABBREVIATIONS for dates, months, and states are used by the editors only in footnotes and endnotes; textual abbreviations are reproduced as found.

DOCUMENT SYMBOLS

1. A — autograph; written in author's hand
   H — handwritten by other than signator
   P — printed
   T — typed

2. C — postcard
   D — document
   E — endorsement
   L — letter
   M — manuscript
   W — wire (telegram)

3. c — carbon
   d — draft
   f — fragment
   p — letterpress
   t — transcript or copy made at much later date

4. I — initialed by author
   r — representation; signed or initialed in author's name
   S — signed by author

Among the more common endnote abbreviations are: ALS — autograph letter, signed by author; TLpI — typed letter, letterpress copy, initialed by author.

REPOSITORY SYMBOLS

Symbols used for repositories are the standard ones used in *Symbols of American Libraries Used in the National Union Catalog of the Library of Congress*, 10th ed. (Washington, D.C., 1969).

ATT	Tuskegee Institute, Tuskegee, Ala.
DHU	Howard University, Washington, D. C.
DLC	Library of Congress, Washington, D.C.
DNA	National Archives, Washington, D.C.
InU	Indiana University, Bloomington, Ind.
KyBB	Berea College, Berea, Ky.
MH	Harvard University, Cambridge, Mass.
MiU-H	University of Michigan, Michigan Historical Collection, Ann Arbor.
NcU	University of North Carolina, Chapel Hill.
NNC	Columbia University, NYC.

OTHER ABBREVIATIONS

BTW	Booker T. Washington
Con.	Container
NNBL	National Negro Business League
RG	Record Group

Documents, 1909–11

From William Holcombe Thomas

Montgomery, Ala. [ca. Jan. 5, 1909]

Personal

Dear Dr: I am in receipt of a letter from Prof Charles Richmond Henderson[1] of the University of Chicago in which he says the following: "Professor Daenell[2] of University of Kiel" (Germany) "& I have already agreed to meet on the evening of January 7th at the same place," (in Montgomery,) ["] and the following morning early go out to see Mr Booker T. Washington's famous school,[3] returning in time for my address in the evening." He speaks here as you see from clipping at night.

Confidentially I had letter from Ray Stannard Baker replying to my letter with following: "How much would it take for a final appeal of the Bailey Case. How much can be raised down there? It is possible that one or two friends of mine might be willing to help a little in the matter. Also would you make a clear statement in a few words of just what the issue is — & its importance, so that in making suggestions to my friends I can give them your own statement of the case."

I also had letter from you can read & return to me.[4] I am going to do my best to get help for the new appeal. I did not want it taken up on *habeas corpus* but had to allow Mr Watts[5] to have his way as he began the case and is a nephew of my opponent and political enemy so Mr Ball[6] came into the case by consent as you know. Ball is anxious to go on with it if we can get some one now to pay this expense. He desires no fee. The one paying the expense of the lost appeal could hardly stand the additional financial burden I should think. However if several contributed it could easily be made up and no one known in the matter for Mr Ball would again have his guaranty Company make the bond for costs and damages. I also hand you copy of letter to Mr Abbott[7] you will return to me. I am doing what I can to keep the matter in shape for second appeal if desired and financial help is found. I am   Yours Truly

William H. Thomas

ALS Con. 900 BTW Papers DLC.

[1] Charles Richmond Henderson (1848–1915), a Baptist clergyman from 1873 to

3

1892, received a Ph.D. from the University of Leipzig (1901) and began a second career as professor of sociology at the University of Chicago. A specialist in social work and criminology, he was president of the National Conference of Charities (1898–99), member of the International Prison Commission (1909), president of the International Prison Congress (1910), and president of the United Charities of Chicago (1913). He was the author of numerous books on theology and social work.

2 Ernst R. Daenell, born in Stettin in 1872 and educated at the University of Leipzig (Ph.D. 1897), was a professor of history at the University of Kiel from 1899 to 1907. In 1908 he became an exchange professor at the University of Chicago and in 1910–11 was exchange professor at Columbia University. In 1914 he became a professor at the University of Münster.

3 Henderson and Daenell visited Tuskegee Institute on Jan. 8, and Henderson gave a short lecture to an agriculture class. He showed special interest in two faculty members who had been his students at the University of Chicago, John W. Hubert and Monroe N. Work. His tour of the South was for the purpose of promoting greater interest in prevention of crime and pauperism through training for useful labor. (*Tuskegee Student*, 20 [Jan. 16, 1909], 4.)

4 Thus in original.

5 Edward Seabrook Watts (1882–1916), born in Montgomery, Ala., graduated from the law department of the University of Alabama in 1904 and did postgraduate study at Columbia University Law School (1904–5). Practicing in Montgomery, Ala., he was county attorney from 1908 until his resignation in 1911. He was elected city attorney in 1913.

6 Fred Samuel Ball (1866–1942), born in Portsmouth, Ohio, and a law graduate of Ohio State University, began his practice of law in Montgomery, Ala., in 1891. From 1902 to 1912 he was secretary of the Alabama Child Labor Committee. At one time he was W. H. Thomas's law partner.

7 Lawrence Fraser Abbott.

To James Jenkins Dossen

[Tuskegee, Ala.] Jan. 7, 1909

Personal and Confidential

My dear Vice President Dossen: Your letter of November 29th has just been received. I shall await further information from you regarding the boy to be sent here to be educated by the lady in New York.[1]

By this time you must have received the information which I have already sent to you stating the terms on which we will admit a number of young Liberians to the Tuskegee Institute. If you have not received this information please let me know and I will repeat it.

Since I last wrote you, I have been in Washington several times, and in addition to that the Ambassador from Great Britain, Mr. Bryce, together with Sir Harry Johnston, have both spent two days here as my guests at Tuskegee. After talking with both of those gentlemen and giving them a chance to express themselves rather freely, I am convinced that so far as they are concerned they have no wish to do anything to disturb the integrity and independence of Liberia. Of course, they may not speak of nor know about the designs of those higher in authority than they are.

Now, will you be kind enough to let me know as speedily as possible just what further demands England has made upon your country, and what you think I can do in order to help.

Before taking up another point, let me say that judging from all I can see and hear, anything that you can get Germany to do in the way of showing interest and activity will not hurt, but will help; in fact, I think what you have already done in that direction has been wise and helpful to your cause.

I have, as stated, been in Washington two or three times since I last wrote you, and had conferences with Secretary Root and Secretary Bacon, and during one of my recent visits to Washington I had a conference with Ambassador Bryce. During my last visit to Washington I saw Secretary Root, Secretary Bacon and Ambassador Bryce at the State Department at the same time and we spent an hour discussing Liberian conditions. Mr. Root, as he always is, was very frank with the British Ambassador, he told him rather plainly that Liberia feared the further encroachments on the part of England. In the presence of all Mr. Bryce repeated that his country had no selfish designs on Liberia.

Now, to the main point. The decision has about been reached that the United States Government will send a commission consisting of three people to Liberia. The object of this commission is three-fold.

1st. To make a demonstration that will let the rest of the world know that the U.S. has not lost interest in Liberia and that it means in some way to re-awaken and strengthen its former interest and connection.

2d. To be of any service in the way of suggesting improvements and reforms in the government of Liberia.

3d. To help strengthen the educational work in your country.

I have been asked to become a member of this commission. I am not sure that I can do so. I am trying to feel my way. Much depends upon the method of transportation and the length of time it would take me and the other members of the commission to look into conditions and make the journey to and fro. I presume something will be decided definitely within a few days. The only danger I can see in carrying out this plan and the further helping of Liberia is the change of administration which means a new Secretary of State. I am hoping that Mr. Knox, who will succeed Mr. Root, will take as much interest as Mr. Root has. I have already been over the matter, at Secretary Root's suggestion, with President-elect Taft, and he is in hearty sympathy with the plans of the commission. I will keep you informed as to further developments. Now, of course, it will be very embarrassing to me if the information that this commission is to be sent should come back to the State Department or should in any way become public before it has been announced by the U.S. Government. Please guard this information most carefully.

Whether or not the commission will go if I cannot personally go I am not sure, but my impression is the commission will go at any rate whether I am a member of it or not. I am trying to select high types of men. I think, perhaps, it is just as well to state that the other members of the commission are likely to be white men of high standing.

In regard to your dispatching a second commission to the United States, I hardly think it well for you to move in this direction until the United States has sent a commission to Liberia. If the commission goes from here, that would lay the basis, it seems to me, for another commission being sent to this country from Liberia.

If you will let me know very definitely just what encroachments England and any other country have made recently, I shall be able to help you better.

I shall be glad to hear from you as often as possible. Yours very truly,

Booker T. Washington

TLpS Con. 369 BTW Papers DLC.

1 Olivia Egleston Phelps Stokes.

From Annie Nathan Meyer[1]

New York. Jan. 7 [1909]

My dear Dr. Washington, I have been hoping ever since I read it to get time to thank you for the admirably expressed, calm, restrained words on the question of Woman Suffrage.[2]

I know that the new League for the Civic Education of Women of which I am an Hon. V. Pres. is greatly encouraged. I want you to tell me at once if Tuskegee loses any financial support because of your declaration in the Times.

Of course the feeling among the Suffragists is very bitter and some may be small enough to try to make you eat your words. But perhaps you remember last summer I wrote you after reading your helpful book "Working with the Hands." I knew you could not be a suffragist — your vision is too clear. I want you to read Appleton's for Feb. "Some Problems of Enfranchisement" by me[3] in which I show how your example is needed among workers — to set about doing the work of the *past* more effectively — not seeking *new* spheres. I want you to read it as my tribute to you is most sincere. I don't know if you read the mawkish — at bottom — insincere letter to Prof Du Bois in Jan. American.[4] I shall answer it some day — full of real sex antagonism — & a reluctance to accept the differentiations of sex.

A few words from you after reading Appleton's will be appreciated by me deeply, and take the precaution please to mark "*Confidential*" if you prefer I should not make use of it. If you do *not* mind, I should like perhaps to use it in one way or another. Or you may mark *part* confidential, in which case — if you know who I am — you will have no doubt that *no one* will ever lay eyes on it.

I give you my town address — tho' at the moment I am at Saratoga where my husband Dr. Alfred Meyer[5] is trying to recover from his breakdown occasioned by his hard work in connection with the Tuberculosis Congress & Exhibit. Cordially

Annie Nathan Meyer
(Mrs. Alfred Meyer)

ALS Con. 896 BTW Papers DLC.

[1] Annie Nathan Meyer (1867–1951) was a leading opponent of woman suffrage, despite activities in behalf of broader professional careers for women. After writing

many articles on higher education for women, she helped establish Barnard College in 1889 and raised most of its operating funds in its first year. Her novel, *Helen Brent, M.D.* (1892), centered on the dilemma of choice between career and marriage. She also wrote a number of plays on social themes and an autobiography.

2 For BTW's statement see BTW to Charles Monroe Lincoln, Dec. 14, 1908, above, 9:700–701.

3 Annie Nathan Meyer, "The Problem before Women," *Appleton's Magazine*, 13 (Feb. 1909), 194–97, drew an analogy between the post-emancipation problems of blacks and women. Meyer praised BTW for his stress on the value and dignity of labor, and urged women leaders to follow his example by restoring to dignity the traditional women's occupations of home-making and child-rearing.

4 *American Magazine*, 67 (Jan. 1909), 288–90, contained an open letter entitled "The Problem of the Intellectual Woman," addressed to the American Negro in care of W. E. B. Du Bois. The letter drew parallels between the kinds of discrimination faced by blacks and women.

5 Alfred Meyer (1854–1950), a graduate of Columbia College and the College of Physicians and Surgeons of Columbia University, practiced medicine on Park Avenue in New York City beginning in 1880. In 1887 he married Annie Nathan. Meyer was perhaps the leading figure in developing an awareness in New York City that tuberculosis was a social disease. As director of the National Tuberculosis Association he helped in the development of state sanitoriums.

To William Holcombe Thomas

[Tuskegee, Ala.] January 9, 1909

Personal

My dear Sir: I have your kind letter of some days ago.

Prof. Charles R. Henderson of the University of Chicago has written us of his intention of coming to Tuskegee from Montgomery.

I am very glad to learn of Mr. Ray Stannard Baker's interest in the matter about which you write and, also, of Mr. Lawrence Abbott's interest in the matter.

I have just read the second editorial review of the Bailey case, which appeared in The Outlook. It may be that with Mr. Baker's help and Mr. Abbott's interest, as well as Mr. Peabody's,[1] you may be able to command funds sufficient to litigate the case a second time.

I return the within to you, as per your request. Yours truly,

Booker T. Washington

TLpSr Con. 900 BTW Papers DLC.

1 George Foster Peabody.

A Sunday Evening Talk

[Tuskegee, Ala.] January 10, 1909

Strength in Simplicity

There is one lesson, among many others, that cannot be too much impressed upon students and any other class of people, who are starting out in life. I refer especially just now to the strength there is in simplicity, in naturalness.

It is especially valuable, it seems to me, for students to keep that in mind, not only while they are in school, but more important for them to keep it in mind as they go out for their life work. Let me repeat, there is strength in one's being simple and natural.

A person never gains anything in real power, in real lasting influence except as he remains always himself, always natural, always simple — and whenever he departs from that attitude, yielding to the temptation to imitate somebody else, or something else, to be that which he is not, in that same degree he loses his influence, he loses his power, and his strength.

A great many people, especially those who have been through a course of training, make the mistake of feeling that they gain certain power and certain influence and attract certain attention by being unnatural in their language, in their use of words. You will find that the best educated people, the most influential people — if you will study their writings, study their conversation — are the most simple people, the people who use the shortest words. Never use a long word, if you can find a shorter one that will express the same meaning.

So often is it true that students having gone through a course at an institution, make themselves not ridiculous in the sight of those whom they would serve, but lose their power and influence by forgetting that the way to show their education, the way to let people know they have been in school, is not by the use of long words, is not by studying the dictionary in order to find unused words that are not in the vocabulary of their own common language, or the language of the community they are in, but by the use of the shortest and simplest words. In making a public address or in private conversation, the way to let people know you have got education is not to get into the habit of using long, involved and almost mean-

9

ingless sentences, but to grow into the habit of using the shortest, the most direct, the most simple sentences. And so, as day by day, you are learning to write various forms of composition, do not make the mistake of feeling that because you are a student, because you are learning something, you have got to write long sentences, for with long sentences, you are likely not to understand what they mean and no one else may understand them. Use the very fewest words in your sentences that will express your meaning. Have your sentences just as short, just as crisp as possible.

We have just been reading some beautiful words taken from the Bible. There is not a single person in this room who cannot understand every sentence we have read — simple, direct, the best English. You understand them because the sentences are short, simple and direct and so when you write and speak, cut out all your long sentences. If you are in the habit, as some students are, of writing letters home and expressing yourself in long sentences, just cut out all that: let your parents understand what you mean and your friend understand what you mean.

When you go away from here, if you are called upon to teach Sunday school, if you are called upon to give any kind of public address, do so, as I said a few minutes ago, in the shortest words, in the fewest and most direct, simple sentences. In that way, you will show the people that you have real education.

Also, our people might learn that there is great power in simple titles and simple names. I was glad to have our friend, Mr. Carroll, who is here from South Carolina, when I addressed him as Dr. Carroll, say to me, "I am not to be addressed as Doctor." That was very refreshing. If a man is a doctor, it is all right to be called so. I saw a letter from a man who was trying to borrow enough money to pay his way home on the train and he wrote A.B., A.M., after his name. That kind of a thing, so far from helping a person, makes a person ridiculous in the sight of people who have real education, who have real culture. If persons have received titles legitimately, it is all right for them to use them, and to be proud of them on legitimate occasions, but the habit in many sections of the country we have fallen into using and stringing out a long line of letters after a name is most disgusting and does not help people. If a person has education, has power, these elements will manifest themselves, and no long string of titles is going to help him one bit.

I do not say you should not use them, should not possess them, should not crave them, but do not make the mistake of feeling that titles are going to help you, unless you have got strength aside from the title. No amount of titles will put brains into a person's head, if the brains are not there before. Simplicity in titles, simplicity in name gives strength. Nobody would ever speak of Abraham Lincoln as LL.D., or anything of the kind. You could not add a single element of strength to his name by giving him all the titles you could conjure. I hope you will study his life as you have never studied it before. He had that power, that lasting influence that at all times, on all occasions, he was simply natural and direct.

No amount of flattery, no amount of power, no amount of exaltation could swerve him from that simplicity which was at the bottom of his strength. If you will read, as I hope you will, the life of Abraham Lincoln, his speeches — especially that great speech, which will live longer than perhaps any other speech ever uttered in the English language, the speech at Gettysburg — read it for its simplicity of language, the shortness of its words and the directness of its sentences, the nobility and inspiring character of it, and you will see in it all and through it all, that Lincoln was great, that he was powerful, because in every movement, in every word, in every utterance, he was a simple, direct, natural human being.

In the matter of dress, as you go out from here, remember the same thing, that there is great power in simplicity of dress. The best dressed person is the person whose dress does not attract attention. Whenever a student is so dressed that his dress attracts attention, then he is not well dressed. He is over-dressed. The same is true of a woman. Whenever she is so dressed that her hat or her ribbons or anything about her apparel attracts special attention, she is not well dressed.

Now, I do not mean to say that people should not be neat, should not wear costly and good clothes, if they are able to pay for them, but whenever students get to the point where their dress attracts more attention than they do themselves, then they make a mistake. Modesty and simplicity give strength.

In all these matters I want to impress upon you in these few sentences the importance of setting a good example to the people among whom you shall mingle. Remember this sentence: try always to be more than you seem to be. Try in all things to be more

11

than you seem to be, and if you have got anything in you, in your head, in your dress, in your character, the world will find it out sooner or later without your trying to exhibit your possessions either through your spoken words, or through your dress.

Go out from here resolved that on the school grounds, and as you go out into the world, at all times, that you will be simple, natural and yourself, and you will carry with you a strength and power and influence that you cannot otherwise get.

Tuskegee Student, 20 [21] (Jan. 23, 1909), 1, 2. Stenographically reported.

From Mary W. Allen

Cambridge Mass. Jan. 10, 1909

Dear Sir   I was much disappointed and even pained at seeing your name yesterday in a list of the college presidents who were opposed to equal rights for women.

Most of the more thoughtful persons of your race and of my sex are trying to win rights, self respect and opportunities for usefulness and self help for their weaker fellows. I think we should sympathise with each other's efforts to rise. From my babyhood I was brought up to feel the deepest sympathy with your race, and it cuts me to feel that you, their leader, should use your influence, so justly great, against woman suffrage. I feel that the wage earning women need the vote to help control the conditions under which they work, and those who are better off need it in their philanthropic work. The more I read and study the subject the stronger this conviction becomes. It is almost too much to ask you to study anything beyond the interests of Tuskegee, but will you not keep an open mind and not let prejudice sway your mind against justice to any human being?

Excuse my breaking in upon the time of an overworked man and believe me, with sincere regard, yours very truly,

Mary W. Allen

ALS   Con. 888   BTW Papers   DLC.

To Annie Nathan Meyer

[Tuskegee, Ala.] January 15, 1909

Personal

My dear Mrs. Meyer: I have your kind letter of some days ago, and thank you for writing me respecting my note which appeared in the New York Times, on the "Women's Suffrage Movement." I have had but one expression of an adverse nature regarding it.

I shall try to secure a copy of Appleton's for February, so as to read the article to which you refer.

Thanking you again for your kind letter, which I cordially appreciate, I am, Yours very truly,

Booker T. Washington

TLpSr   Con. 896   BTW Papers   DLC.   Signed in Emmett J. Scott's hand.

An Appeal in Behalf of the
Frederick Douglass Home

Tuskegee Institute, Ala., January 15, 1909

Under date of March 20, 1908, I had the honor to submit an Appeal to the Negro people of the United States reading in part as follows:

"Some two or three years ago the suggestion was made at a banquet of the Pen and Pencil Club of Washington, D.C., that something should be done to assist the efforts that were at that time being made to preserve and transmit as a legacy to the Negro people of this country the home of Frederick Douglass at Anacostia, District of Columbia.

"The custom of celebrating the anniversary of Frederick Douglass' death is already widespread among our people, but it seemed to those of us who were present at the dinner of the Pen and Pencil Club, given in honor and memory of Frederick Douglass, that the time had come when his memory should be preserved in something less perishable than after-dinner speeches, however eloquent. It seemed to us that the time had come when we could properly appeal to the masses of our people to assist in preserving the Douglass Home, with all its memories and traditions and make it a permanent memorial not only of our great leader but to the Negro people of the United States, as well.

13

"An association, known as the Frederick Douglass Memorial and Historical Association, has been formed to effect this purpose. I have been asked by the officers of the Memorial Association to assist in securing the comparatively small sum of money amounting to some $5,400 and interest necessary to clear off the mortgage on the property and so secure the property for all time to the Association and the Negro people of the United States."

February 14th is generally celebrated as the birthday of Frederick Douglass. I wish to emphasize the above statement and ask that Negro fraternal organizations, churches and Sunday schools throughout the country set aside this day in celebration of Mr. Douglass' devoted services in behalf of his race. The $4,800 still remaining unpaid should be raised this year.

I want to especially urge upon those in charge of the above named organizations that properly arranged programs be followed and that systematic collections be taken to the end that we may wipe out this indebtedness of $4,800 and make Cedar Hill a Mecca for our people as Mount Vernon is to the white people of the country. The masses of the people, if properly appealed to will be sure to respond and liberally. Amounts, however small, will be greatly appreciated, and may be forwarded to me at Tuskegee Institute, Alabama, or to any of the officers of the Frederick Douglass Memorial and Historical Association.

BOOKER T. WASHINGTON

PDSr Con. 794 BTW Papers DLC. The original includes a photograph of Douglass and one of his home.

To Theodore Roosevelt

Tuskegee Institute, Alabama   Jan. 18, 1909

Personal

My dear Mr. President: Ever since you mentioned the matter to me I have been intending to write extending my special thanks to you for what you said regarding speaking to Mr. Taft about my relations to your administration and what I have attempted to do. I had not expected any such consideration on your part, but it is in keeping with all the generous and fine things that you have done and are constantly doing. If I can be of any service to Mr. Taft, I shall be more than glad.

I shall hope to see you while in Washington on the 25th and 26th at the meeting for dependent children.[1] Yours very truly,

Booker T. Washington

TLS   William Howard Taft Papers   DLC.   A press copy is in Con. 7, BTW Papers, DLC.

[1] See An Address before the White House Conference on the Care of Dependent Children, Jan. 25, 1909, below.

To William G. Humphreys[1]

[Tuskegee, Ala.] January 19, 1909

Dear Sir: I have delayed much longer than I had intended, sending you the enclosed Ten Dollars to be used in connection with the monument to the late Mr. Joel Chandler Harris.

It was my pleasure to know him personally. He was one of the best and most helpful friends that my race ever had anywhere in the country. Yours truly,

Booker T. Washington

TLpS   Con. 894   BTW Papers   DLC.

[1] William G. Humphreys was vice-president of an investment firm, Robinson-Humphreys Co., and an Atlanta city councilman in 1911.

Theodore Roosevelt to William Howard Taft

The White House   Washington   January 20, 1909

Dear Will: The enclosed letter explains itself.[1] I send it to you simply to remind you of our conversation about Booker T. Washington. There is not a better or truer friend of his race than Booker

Washington; and yet he is so sane and reasonable that following his advice never gives cause for just criticism by the white people. Ever yours,

Theodore Roosevelt

TLS William Howard Taft Papers DLC. A copy is in Con. 48, BTW Papers, DLC.

1 See BTW to Theodore Roosevelt, Jan. 18, 1909, above.

To William Burns Paterson

[Tuskegee, Ala.] January 22, 1909

Personal and Confidential.

My dear Prof. Paterson: Without using my name in connection with this information, I am writing you to say that Mr. Carnegie has just made a gift of a library to an institution somewhat similarly situated as your own, without any condition, and I believe if you will approach him, say, in February or March, he will take off the condition, so far as your institution is concerned.

I shall take for granted, as I have said, that you will not use my name in connection with this information. Yours very truly,

Booker T. Washington

TLpS Con. 897 BTW Papers DLC.

Timothy Thomas Fortune to Emmett Jay Scott

Red Bank, N.J., Jan 23, 1909

Dear Mr. Scott: I enclose a letter for the Wizard the subject matter of which I wish you would discuss with him *before* he becomes committed to others. I want to be one of the Liberian Commission because I believe I am competent, because I want to see Europe and Africa and because I need the emoluments of the position. I believe I can rely upon you and the Wizard to serve me in this matter because of past good relationships.

You will be glad to know that Mrs. Fortune and I have reached a good understanding and that *I have recovered my senses but not my cents.*

With love for you and yours, Yours sincerely,

T. Thos. Fortune

ALS Con. 45 BTW Papers DLC.

An Address before the White House Conference on the Care of Dependent Children[1]

[Washington, D.C., Jan. 25, 1909]

DESTITUTE COLORED CHILDREN OF THE SOUTH

Mr. Chairman, I have been listening with a great deal of interest to what has been said, both this afternoon and this evening, and I find that most, if not all, of what you have said will apply in some degree to my own race. In fact, as I have heard these addresses I thought of a little experience that I witnessed some time ago in Montgomery, Ala.

It used to be the custom there, as I think it is now, that when the trains start out in the morning, bound for New York, it is the duty of the Pullman car porter to stand near the head of the train and call out the various stations through which the train will pass. So one morning they put on a new porter, and the old porter at the head of the train yelled out: "This train will pass through Atlanta, Charlotte, Danville, Lynchburg, Charlottesville, Washington, and New York." The new porter, not being able to remember all of those places, yelled out: "Just the same at this end, too." [Laughter.]

Now, as to most of what has been said and the main principles laid down, I think I can say with that new Pullman car porter in regard to my race: "Just the same at this end, too."

I shall speak to you for a few minutes mainly concerning the members of my race, in relation to this subject, as it relates to them in the southern portion of the United States, where the great body of our people live. It is to be kept in mind that the negro of the South is, for the most part, a rural population. I think I am safe in saying that 85 per cent of our people in the Southern States are to be found outside of the larger cities and towns.

While the negro has his vices and his disappointments, he also has his virtues and his encouragements. In studying the negro as a race, especially as you find him in his normal, regular life in the rural districts of the South, you will find that the negro, for the most part, is not a degraded human being. He may be an ignorant human being so far as books are concerned; but there is a great difference between degradation and pure simple ignorance. [Applause.]

From that point of view the problem is, in a large degree, encouraging. You will find, too, if you have studied the negro and noticed his life, that, as a rule, he is not a beggar. It is very seldom that, in the South or in the North, and especially is it true in the South, that you find a black hand reached out from the corner of the street asking for charity from anybody; and wherever you find a negro asking for alms in the Southern States, in nine cases out of ten you will find him on the highway of travel between the North and Florida, where somebody has spoiled him in that respect. The negro does not often beg, and neither does he starve. [Laughter.] You have heard of starving Russians, and starving Armenians, and starving Japanese, and starving Jews; but nobody ever heard of a starving black man in America. He is a peculiar individual in that respect. He lives and can live in more climes and circumstances and in more climates and under more different conditions than any other human being that exists.

But I find, in studying his condition carefully, that the negro, for the most part, is best off in the country districts, and best off in the country districts of our southern country. [Applause.]

Growing largely out of the reasons to which I have referred, you will be surprised to know that the number of dependents among my own race in America is relatively small as compared with the number of dependents among the white population.

I heard a gentleman state a few moments ago that the State of Massachusetts alone pays over $600,000 annually toward the care and support of the dependents in that State. Why, my friends, I guarantee that the most careful and rigid examination into the facts would reveal that which I think is true — that that is more money than is spent for the dependent negro children in the whole southern country.

I think you will find that the latest statistics show that in the whole United States there are about 31,000 negro dependent children in institutions of all kinds. The total negro population of Alabama is about 900,000, and out of the total population of 900,000 I find that, according to our most recent reports in Alabama, there are 301 children in institutions for the care of the dependent — 301 out of a total population of about 900,000.

In fact, this subject of the care of dependent children with us who reside in the rural districts of the South is so new and so little discussed that I confess I never looked into it very carefully from your point of view until after I received the invitation to come to this meeting. When I received the invitation I said at once that I would look about me and see what was going on in my own county — in Macon County — which is largely a rural and farming county. On making an examination I found that there were 23,000 people of my race in that county. I went at once to an institution about 9 miles from our institute, for the care of dependents of both races in that county, and I made an examination. I went to the superintendent, who had been in charge of that institution for eight years, and got what information I could from him.

In the first place, I found that during the past four years there had been an average of only six dependents of any age in this institution of my race — only six in four years of any age. I found, when I made my visit last week, that there was not a single negro dependent of any age in that institution.

The county authorities there will admit the members of my race fairly and they will extend to them the same care in Macon County that they will extend to the people of their own race. The dependents of my race are not kept out by reason of any special discrimination against them or because they are not wanted. I will explain to you later why they are not there.

I found, further, that not only was there not a single dependent there at the present time, but I found by investigating the record that during the past eight years there had been in that institution only one negro child, and the superintendent told me that this child went there because his grandmother was taken there and the little fellow cried and he was humored to the extent of being taken there with her. As soon as his grandmother died the superintendent said that some strange woman came there and begged the privilege of taking that child home and making him a part of her family. Since that time we have not had a negro dependent in that institution. Remember, that is out of a total negro population of 23,000 in our county.

You may suggest that this is an unusual condition, existing perhaps by reason of the influence of the Tuskegee Institute. That may have something to do with it; but very little, I think. I hope that our good friend who is the leader of this movement in Alabama will speak to you about this subject, and I am quite sure that he will bear out the statements I am trying to emphasize.

You will find that in other counties where there is no Tuskegee Institute much the same conditions prevail.

This condition exists because, as you will find, the negro, in some way, has inherited and has had trained into him the idea that he must take care of his own dependents, and he does it to a greater degree than is true, perhaps, of any other race in the same relative stage of civilization. Why, my friends, in our ordinary southern communities we look upon it as a disgrace for an individual to be permitted to be taken from that community to any kind of an institution for dependents. [Applause.]

I do not know of any case in my own experience where the parents of children have died but what within a few hours, almost before the breath has passed from the body of the parent, one neighbor, sometimes two, three, and sometimes half a dozen have appeared on the scene and begged the privilege of taking this child and that child into their own families. You will find the same to be true in reference to sick people and to the unfortunate of all classes. They are cared for by individuals in the community. They are cared for through their churches. We have not got so far along yet in civilization that we do not think it is a part of the duty of the church to take care of the sick people of the community. [Applause.] They are cared for more largely in recent years through the various secret organizations, of which we have so many.

You hear a great deal about these secret organizations, but you do not know how many we have. I spent a week or ten days in Mississippi recently, and if there is a negro man, woman, or child in the whole State of Mississippi who does not belong to one or more secret organizations I did not find him. These organizations have their humorous side, perhaps, and their useless side; but they also have their valuable side, that of teaching our people how to take care of the dependents of their own race, among others.

It is only as the negro is brought into contact with an artificial civilization and newer surroundings, as he leaves his normal, regular, and best life in the South, in my opinion, and comes into contact with the artificial life of the city and especially with the artificial life of your northern cities, that this condition is changed.

Charity workers — I do not like the word. I am not a charity worker. I am in business the same as anybody else, and I do not like anybody to call me a charity worker, because I do not beg, even. I ask people if they have got money to invest, and talk to them as though they were investing money in the Pennsylvania Railroad, or any other corporation that is to help the country.

But, my friends, those of you who have the privilege and opportunity, and many of you will have the privilege and opportunity, of observing my race and the children of my race, I beg of you to exert that influence in keeping the negro on the soil, in keeping him close in touch with Mother Earth, in keeping him out of contact with the temptations and complications and the artificial influences of your large-city life. Just in proportion as that is done you will find that many of these problems you are discussing in such an interesting manner will not disturb you so far as the negro race is concerned.

The very minute a negro leaves the South and comes to a place like Washington, Baltimore, or New York he hears, in some roundabout way, that there is a fund somewhere, which grows in importance and amounts up into the thousands of dollars. He gets the idea that this fund is meant to support all the poor people, and the hard-working people, and every person who gets into trouble, and he usually gets his part of that fund. He knows how to get it, and in proportion as he is brought into contact with this artificial life, this new life, in that proportion he loses the spirit of simplicity, the spirit of helpfulness which he had before he came into the city environments.

I repeat that, in the negro's present condition of inexperience and lack of strength in many matters, that you should use your influence, wherever you can, to keep him on the soil in the rural districts, and especially in the rural districts of our southern country.

As I have suggested, the negro has been putting into practice the very ideas you have been emphasizing all through this afternoon and evening. He has been putting into practice more largely than any other race in America in the same relative stage of civilization, the principles which you have been talking about to-day.

Now as to the influence of institutional life upon the negro: I strongly advocate, as I have already suggested, the keeping of the individual negro child in the individual family. I have had some experiences in connection with asylums of various kinds and with institutions that are organized for the care of dependent children of my race, and my observation and experience, so far as it concerns my people, is this: I find that in many cases the child would be better off if left to chance to get into some home than he is in the average orphan asylum. We have at Tuskegee many individuals and many students who come to us from the orphan asylums. We used to have more than we have now; but we have learned something in recent years that we did not know then, so that we have still fewer now. We have looked with suspicion upon any boy or girl that comes to us from an orphan asylum. In fact, I happen to know of a case with reference to one of our most widely advertised orphan asylums. One morning, when I happened to be in this institution, I learned that a previous night a number of the boys had got together and broken open the cupboard and got out the pies; the pies had disappeared overnight. The next morning the good woman — she was one of these good-hearted creatures — called these boys in and had special prayer with them. [Laughter.]

The difficulty is that the large proportion of the people who organize these institutions for the care of negro children are wanting in executive business ability. They are good people, sentimental people, and the best people on earth, and they want to do everything for everybody. Those are the people who usually start an orphan asylum first of all. In many other cases I have found that many of these institutions are started, primarily, with a view to finding a job for a superintendent or somebody else, and not with a view to helping the negro child. [Applause.]

And so in this way or that way I have learned, my friends, to become very suspicious of the average orphan asylum, organized and built up for the support of the members of my race. It pays far better to use our time and our influence and our money, if we have it, to keep the negro in the country, in the natural environment, until he gets the strength and experience which has made your race great and strong and useful.

My friends, I heard one speaker refer to-day to the sacrifice that such people as compose this gathering are making. I am not a very old man; but the longer I live and the more experience I have in life, the more I am convinced that the only thing that is worth living for and worth dying for, if necessary, is the opportunity and privilege of making some human being more happy and more useful. I have never made a sacrifice in my life. Some people refer to me as making sacrifices for my race; but I have never made a sacrifice for my race, for any race. I always pity, from the bottom of my heart, the man who has learned to live for himself, and I envy the man who has learned to live for somebody else. The further down we can reach in the saving of these little human beings, these dependent children, the higher up are we ourselves lifted into the Christ atmosphere. [Applause.]

Proceedings of the Conference on the Care of Dependent Children Held at Washington, D.C., January 25, 26, 1909, 60th Cong., 2nd Sess., Senate Doc. no. 721 (Washington, D.C., 1909), 113–17.

1 BTW spoke at the New Willard Hotel in the evening of the first day of the conference. He was the last of a series of speakers, including Jane Addams and Rabbi Emil G. Hirsch. That afternoon the conference was opened at the White House by President Theodore Roosevelt.

From Maud Nathan[1]

[New York City] Jan. 28–09

My dear Mr. Washington. It has recently been stated publicly that you are opposed to Woman Suffrage, as this seems inconsistent in one holding your ideas generally, I would be glad to hear from you if this is true, and if so what are your reasons for not believing in Equal Suffrage?

Hoping to hear from you, I am, Very truly yours —

(Mrs. Frederick) Maud Nathan

ALS Con. 896 BTW Papers DLC. Docketed in Emmett J. Scott's hand: "Here's another."

[1] Maud Nathan (1862–1946), sister of the anti-suffragist Annie Nathan Meyer, was herself a leading advocate of woman suffrage. Married to her first cousin Frederick Nathan, a stockbroker, she became interested in the working conditions of shop girls and in 1890, with Josephine Shaw Lowell, founded the Consumers' League of New York. She also served on the national executive committee and as vice-president of the Consumers' League. She was chairman of the industrial commission of the General Federation of Women's Clubs in 1902–4. Her lobbying efforts in Albany convinced her that voteless women were powerless, and she became an officer of the Equal Suffrage League of New York. In 1912 she was active in the Progressive party. In 1936 she attacked Frankin D. Roosevelt for his tax policies and alleged betrayal of his class.

To Timothy Thomas Fortune

New York. Jan. 29, 1909

My dear Mr. Fortune: I have received your kind letter, also the information which you requested Dr. Scott[1] to send to me. I shall give the whole matter careful consideration. As yet there is nothing certain regarding the Liberian matter. In the first place, the bill has to pass Congress, and with all the changes that are going on at Washington both in the State Department and in the White House, no one can predict with accuracy just what is likely to take place.

So far, it seems to be the policy of the State Department to try to find people for the commission who have had actual experience in rebuilding and reorganizing countries and governments such as has been done in the Philippines, Porto Rico, Cuba, San Domingo. Liberia is in a pretty bad way, worse, I fear, than has got into the public print, and it will take some pretty hard, serious work to save it and get it upon its feet. This is the problem that the Department of State at Washington is facing, but, as I have said, your letter will have very careful consideration.

I am glad to hear that your health is improving and that you and Mrs. Fortune are at Red Bank. Yours very truly,

[Booker T. Washington]

TLc   Con. 45   BTW Papers   DLC.

1 Isaiah Benjamin Scott.

To Maud Nathan

[Tuskegee, Ala.] February 2, 1909

My dear Mrs. Nathan: In reply to your letter of January 28th, I am enclosing you a copy of a statement recently made by me in the New York Times.

I did not realize, when I ventured to express this opinion, that I was getting into something dangerously like a political controversy or even that I was "opposing woman suffrage." If I had done so, I should perhaps have hesitated to express an opinion upon a matter which, it seems to me must be left in the last analysis to the decision of women themselves. Yours very truly,

Booker T. Washington

TLpSr   Con. 896   BTW Papers   DLC.   Signed in Emmett J. Scott's hand.

To Emmett Jay Scott

Mt. Pleasant, Mich. February 5, 1909

Dear Mr. Scott: In your own way, I think it might not be a bad plan for you to advise Mr. Rucker to stick pretty closely to Clark Howell. I have an idea that it is a possible thing that he may go into Mr. Taft's cabinet, although no one has told me so directly. Yours truly,

B. T. W.

TLI   Con. 587   BTW Papers   DLC.

To James R. B. Van Cleave[1]

[Hotel Manhattan, New York City] February 9, 1909

My dear Sir: It is a matter of keen regret to me that, owing to a long standing promise to speak in New York on the occasion of the one hundredth anniversary of the birth of Abraham Lincoln, I find myself unable to accept your generous invitation to speak in his home city on that day. There is no spot in America where it would have given me greater satisfaction to have spoken my word than in Springfield, the city that he loved and the city where his body rests.

There are many lessons which can and will be drawn from the life of our great hero, but there is one above all others at this moment that I deem fitting to call attention to on this occasion. Among other reasons, I do so because of recent occurrences in this city of Lincoln's adoption.

When Lincoln freed my race there were four millions. Now there are ten millions. Naturally, more and more this increase means that they will scatter themselves through the country, North as well as South. A large element already is in the North. If my race would honor the memory of Lincoln and exhibit their gratitude for what he did, it can do so in no more fitting manner than by putting into daily practice the lessons of his own life. Mr. Lincoln was a simple, humble man, yet a great man. Great men are always simple. No matter where members of my race reside, we should resolve from this day forward that we shall lead sober, industrious, frugal, moral lives, and that while being ambitious we shall at the same time be patient, law-abiding and self-controlled as Lincoln was. These are the elements that will win success and respect, no matter where we live.

Every member of my race who does not work, who leads an immoral life, dishonors the memory and the name of Lincoln. Every one, on the other hand, who leads a law-abiding, sober life is justifying the faith which the sainted Lincoln placed in us.

In every part of the country I want to see my race live such high and useful lives that they will not be merely tolerated, but that they shall actually be needed and wanted because of their usefulness in the community. The loafer, the man who tries to live by his wits, is never wanted anywhere.

Many white people in the North who are now honoring the memory of Lincoln, are coming into contact with the race that Lincoln freed for the first time. I have spoken of the patience and self-control needed on the part of my race. With equal emphasis I wish to add, that no man who hallows the name of Lincoln will inflict injustice upon the Negro because he is a Negro or because he is weak. Every act of injustice, of law breaking, growing out of the presence of the Negro, seeks to pull down the great temple of justice and law and order which he gave his life to make secure. Lawlessness that begins when a weak race is the victim, grows by what it feeds upon and soon spreads till it involves all races. It is easy for a strong man or a strong race to kick down a weak man or a weak race. It is ignoble to kick down; it is noble to lift up as Lincoln sought to do all through his life.

Just in the degree that both races, while we are passing through this crucial period, exhibit the high qualities of self-control and liberality which Lincoln exhibited in his own life, will we show that in reality we love and honor his name, and will both races be lifted into a high atmosphere of service to each other. Yours truly,

[Booker T. Washington]

TL Copy Con. 821 BTW Papers DLC. A draft in BTW's hand, dated Jan. 29, 1909, on letterhead of the Hotel Manhattan, is also in Con. 821. The letter appeared in the Springfield (Ill.) *News*, Feb. 13, 1909.

1 James R. B. Van Cleave was president of the Lincoln Bank in Springfield, Ill., from 1907 to 1909. From 1912 to 1915 he was treasurer of the Hal M. Smith Co., which dealt in wholesale notions, groceries, and sundries.

To William Burns Paterson

Hotel Manhattan, New York. February 10, 1909

My dear Professor Paterson: This, of course, is confidential. I had a good talk with Mr. Bertram about you and your need for a library this afternoon. Curious enough, he mentioned the fact as soon as I mentioned your name that he had been discussing you and your history only the night before at his house.

Mr. Carnegie is going South to be gone three weeks. At the end of this time I feel rather sure that if you could come here and see Mr. Bertram again perhaps with me that we could arrange matters. Yours very truly,

[Booker T. Washington]

TLc   Con. 897   BTW Papers   DLC.

To Harry Hamilton Johnston

Hotel Manhattan, New York. February 10, 1909

My dear Sir Harry: Your letter of January 19th from Kingston has been received. I did not cable you for two reasons. First, when I received your letter I was in the West and could not cable you conveniently; and secondly, there was nothing very definite which I could have said in a cable.

The matter so far as Liberia is concerned stands as follows: The bill which I enclose, is now before Congress with the prospect, I think, of its passing before the 4th of March. The Secretary of State[1] has asked me to become a member of this commission and to assist him also in selecting the other members. You will note that the bill provides that the commission go on a naval vessel.[2] If this plan carries it will preclude our going by way of England; in fact, the only plan by which I could go is for such arrangement to be made as would enable the commission to go direct to Liberia and return, losing just as little time as possible in travel. This would have the further advantage of enabling us to spend the greater part of the time on the ground studying the situation instead of en route. I have not definitely given a promise to go, altho our Trustees have given me permission. I hope to be able to arrange my affairs so as to make the trip.

Enclosed I send you a rather interesting document sent me by

T. McCants Stewart. On the face of it, it seems to sound pretty well.

As to the make-up of the commission. It is the present wish of the State Department that the commission be composed of one person who has had experience in reorganizing and rebuilding governments such as in the Philippines, Porto Rico, San Domingo and Cuba. That another member be one who has had experience in reorganizing the finances and customs such as was done recently in San Domingo. And the third be one able to help them in their educational matters. This is what we have been aiming at. Of course, there are few colored people who have had experience in such matters. I hope in some way that Mr. Banks, of Mound Bayou, may be made a member of the commission. What do you think of that? At any rate, I am quite sure there will be one if not two members of the commission white people.

I am very glad that you have given me information concerning the best time to visit Liberia. It may be that the trip will have to be postponed until November.

I shall be very glad to hear your opinion of Haiti. I am deeply interested in the future of that country.

The New York Sun a few days ago had a very fine editorial on your letters concerning the South in the London Times. Will you not tell me how I can get hold of all of these letters? Yours very truly,

[Booker T. Washington]

TLc Con. 894 BTW Papers DLC.

1 Robert Bacon.

2 BTW had doubted the wisdom of his acceptance of this appointment and eventually decided against it. There are also indications that officials in the Roosevelt administration were uncertain. On Feb. 15, 1909, Secretary Bacon asked the White House military aide Archibald Butt for his advice, and Butt wrote to his sister-in-law that he had replied: "I agree with you, Mr. Secretary, that the government of Liberia should be preserved for the Negroes, and also that Booker Washington should go on any commission which is sent there. I also believe that a navy vessel should be anchored off the coast, but I do not believe that a navy vessel should be used to convey Booker Washington there. The people will understand why he ought to go, and will not hesitate to endorse it, but they will make a hue and cry against such a marked distinction in sending him on a government vessel. They will not forgive the President for doing it, either." And Butt cautioned Bacon, "As you love the President and hope for his renomination some day don't hamper him now with another incident with Booker Washington." (Butt, Letters, 341–42.)

To William Tecumseh Vernon

New York. February 11, 1909

Personal and Confidential

My dear Mr. Vernon: I am writing you regarding a matter which I think I ought to mention. I think always the best way to show one's friendship to an individual is to be perfectly frank on all matters.

I very much fear that some of your friends are hurting you by the kind of matter that is being sent out from Washington and appearing simultaneously in different journals in various parts of the country. The matter, in the opinion of several, seems to bear the stamp of being sent out by the same individual in a concerted way which tends to emphasize the fact that all the other people holding office in Washington are against you and that all the others are likely to be put out of office except yourself, and more of this kind of stuff. I do not believe that that kind of thing helps one. In my experience and it is to this policy I owe whatever success I have attained, is this: It pays best to emphasize in public print and elsewhere the accomplishments of one, leaving aside all matters of comparison. I always tell my friends if they want to injure me they can do so in no more surer way than by trying to defend me. I ask them not to defend me or make any comparisons but to state wherever they please and as often as they please just what I have accomplished for the good of mankind. That kind of advertising does more in the long run than any other kind. Please excuse me for being so frank but, as I have said, that is the only way to deal with a friend.

You will find in Washington that there are any number of people who will be willing to put you in an awkward position before the public in order that they may use you to feather their nests. In the last analysis they are not thinking about your interests but are thinking about their own. I never permit such people to use me knowingly.

You are troubled with the same kind of little people, I know, that trouble me and others. There are always fellows hanging around Washington who want to write something about you in order to obligate you to them and in the end they expect to get something out of you for it. As I have stated, in each case they are thinking more about themselves than they are about you, in a word, they are simply using you to serve their own selfish interests.

It has been one of the satisfactions of President Roosevelt's administration that he has had a high type of clean colored men holding office in Washington under him, men who have risen above petty jealousies and have served the administration and the country in a clean, first class manner, and I am very anxious, as all of our people are that the high tone of President Roosevelt's official family will be in no degree lowered by petty jealousies, and that the same high tone will be maintained throughout President Taft's administration. All this can be done by individuals rising above petty selfishness and jealousies which in the long run never pay. I seldom ever go to Washington but some little fellow does not try to pour into my ears some petty little stuff concerning yourself. I pay no attention to this. I know in nine cases out of ten the fellow is simply trying to use me to promote his own interests. Yours very truly,

[Booker T. Washington]

TLc   Con. 399   BTW Papers   DLC.

From Maud Nathan

[New York City] February 11, 1909

My dear Mr. Washington, Your letter of February second enclosing a copy of your statement published in the *New York Times* was received. I am surprised that you should feel that the question of equal suffrage should be left entirely to the judgment of the women. I think very strongly, that it is a question that concerns men quite as much as it does the women of the country.

I am also surprised that you feel that *indirect* influence can exert a more beneficent influence than *direct*. In the matter of legislation, no pressure can be brought to bear upon the legislators except from their constituents. They are sensitive to criticism which would affect their careers but they are not sensitive to criticism which does not threaten to replace them, at the following election, with other candidates.

The privilege of the franchise which your race would not give up was not bestowed upon you because there was a great demand on their part for it — it was given from a sense of justice, and with the view of developing them and making them feel responsibilities as citizens, and to feel that they had a real participation in this democracy. These same reasons hold for the enfranchisement of women. The suffrage would not only develop the women but would be better for the American people as a whole. Yours very truly,

Maud Nathan

ALS   Con. 896   BTW Papers   DLC.

From Grace Lathrop Dunham Luling

Fox Holm, Cobham, Surrey. February 12th–1909

Dear Sir — A few years ago I wrote to you on behalf of my friend Mr E. B. Sargant, enclosing a list of questions to which he was anxious to have your answer. Mr Sargant was then about to go out to South Africa, where he had been appointed by Lord Milner[1] to organize a system of Public School education among the natives.

Mr Sargant has successfully accomplished this work, & has now returned to England.

He has asked me to forward to you the enclosed report,[2] which he thinks may be of interest to you.

Believe me, with kind regards, Yours very truly,

Grace L. Luling
(Mrs Theodore Luling)

ALS   Con. 895   BTW Papers   DLC.

[1] Alfred, Viscount Milner (1854–1925), active in the Liberal party, became governor of Cape Colony and High Commissioner for South Africa after the Jameson Raid in 1895. During and after the Boer War, he sought to reconstruct the two Boer republics into a union with the British settlement colonies, employing able young Oxford graduates ("Milner's Kindergarten") to reform not only the government, but also the mines, railroads, educational system, and other institutions.

Self-government was restored in 1906 along federal lines that marked a transition from centralized colonial concepts of British rule toward the idea of commonwealth.

2 Edmund Beale Sargant's published report on education in South Africa. (BTW to Luling, Feb. 25, 1909, Con. 895, BTW Papers, DLC.)

An Address on Abraham Lincoln
before the Republican Club of New York City

New York City, February 12, 1909

Mr. Chairman, Ladies and Gentlemen: You ask that which he found a piece of property and turned into a free American citizen to speak to you tonight on Abraham Lincoln. I am not fitted by ancestry or training to be your teacher tonight for, as I have stated, I was born a slave.

My first knowledge of Abraham Lincoln came in this way: I was awakened early one morning before the dawn of day, as I lay wrapped in a bundle of rags on the dirt floor of our slave cabin, by the prayers of my mother, just before leaving for her day's work, as she was kneeling over my body earnestly praying that Abraham Lincoln might succeed, and that one day she and her boy might be free. You give me the opportunity here this evening to celebrate with you and the nation the answer to that prayer.

Says the Great Book somewhere, "Though a man die, yet shall he live." If this is true of the ordinary man, how much more true is it of the hero of the hour and the hero of the century — Abraham Lincoln! One hundred years of the life and influence of Lincoln is the story of the struggles, the trials, ambitions, and triumphs of the people of our complex American civilization. Interwoven into the warp and woof of this human complexity is the moving story of men and women of nearly every race and color in their progress from slavery to freedom, from poverty to wealth, from weakness to power, from ignorance to intelligence. Knit into the life of Abraham Lincoln is the story and success of the nation in the blending of all tongues, religions, colors, races into one composite nation, leaving each group and race free to live its own separate social life, and yet all a part of the great whole.

If a man die, shall he live? Answering this question as applied

33

to our martyred President, perhaps you expect me to confine my words of appreciation to the great boon which, through him, was conferred upon my race. My undying gratitude and that of ten millions of my race for this and yet more! To have been the instrument used by Providence through which four millions of slaves, now grown into ten millions of free citizens, were made free would bring eternal fame within itself, but this is not the only claim that Lincoln has upon our sense of gratitude and appreciation.

By the side of Armstrong and Garrison, Lincoln lives today. In the very highest sense he lives in the present more potently than fifty years ago; for that which is seen is temporal, that which is unseen is eternal. He lives in the 32,000 young men and women of the Negro race learning trades and useful occupations; in the 200,000 farms acquired by those he freed; in the more than 400,000 homes built; in the forty-six banks established and 10,000 stores owned; in the $550,000,000 worth of taxable property in hand; in the 28,000 public schools existing, with 30,000 teachers; in the 170 industrial schools and colleges; in the 23,000 ministers and 26,000 churches.

But, above all this, he lives in the steady and unalterable determination of ten millions of black citizens to continue to climb year by year the ladder of the highest usefulness and to perfect themselves in strong, robust character. For making all this possible, Lincoln lives.

But, again, for a higher reason he lives tonight in every corner of the republic. To set the physical man free is much. To set the spiritual man free is more. So often the keeper is on the inside of the prison bars and the prisoner on the outside.

As an individual, grateful as I am to Lincoln for freedom of body, my gratitude is still greater for freedom of soul — the liberty which permits one to live up in that atmosphere where he refuses to permit sectional or racial hatred to drag down, to warp and narrow his soul.

The signing of the Emancipation Proclamation was a great event, and yet it was but the symbol of another, still greater and more momentous. We who celebrate this anniversary should not forget that the same pen that gave freedom to four millions of African slaves at the same time struck the shackles from the souls of twenty-seven millions of Americans of another color.

In any country, regardless of what its laws say, wherever people act upon the idea that the disadvantage of one man is the good of another, there slavery exists. Wherever in any country the whole people feel that the happiness of all is dependent upon the happiness of the weakest, there freedom exists.

In abolishing slavery, Lincoln proclaimed the principle that, even in the case of the humblest and weakest of mankind, the welfare of each is still the good of all. In reestablishing in this country the principle that, at bottom, the interests of humanity and of the individual are one, he freed men's souls from spiritual bondage; he freed them to mutual helpfulness. Henceforth no man of any race, either in the North or in the South, need feel constrained to fear or hate his brother.

By the same token that Lincoln made America free, he pushed back the boundaries of freedom everywhere, gave the spirit of liberty a wider influence throughout the world, and reestablished the dignity of man as man.

By the same act that freed my race, he said to the civilized and uncivilized world that man everywhere must be free, and that man everywhere must be enlightened, and the Lincoln spirit of freedom and fair play will never cease to spread and grow in power till throughout the world all men shall know the truth, and the truth shall make them free.

Lincoln in his day was wise enough to recognize that which is true in the present and for all time: that in a state of slavery and ignorance man renders the lowest and most costly form of service to his fellows. In a state of freedom and enlightenment he renders the highest and most helpful form of service.

The world is fast learning that of all forms of slavery there is none that is so harmful and degrading as that form of slavery which tempts one human being to hate another by reason of his race or color. One man cannot hold another man down in the ditch without remaining down in the ditch with him. One who goes through life with his eyes closed against all that is good in another race is weakened and circumscribed, as one who fights in a battle with one hand tied behind him. Lincoln was in the truest sense great because he unfettered himself. He climbed up out of the valley, where his vision was narrowed and weakened by the fog and miasma, onto the mountain top, where in a pure and unclouded atmosphere he could see the truth which enabled him to rate all men at their true worth. Growing out of this anniversary season and atmosphere, may there crystallize a resolve throughout the nation that on such a mountain the American people will strive to live.

We owe, then, to Lincoln physical freedom, moral freedom, and yet this is not all. There is a debt of gratitude which we as individuals, no matter of what race or nation, must recognize as due Abraham Lincoln — not for what he did as chief executive of the nation, but for what he did as a man. In his rise from the most abject poverty and ignorance to a position of high usefulness and power, he taught the world one of the greatest of all lessons. In fighting his own battle up from obscurity and squalor, he fought the battle of every other individual and race that is down, and so helped to pull up every other human who was down. People so often forget that by every inch that the lowest man crawls up he makes it easier for every other man to get up. Today, throughout the world, because Lincoln lived, struggled, and triumphed, every boy who is ignorant, is in poverty, is despised or discouraged, holds his head a little higher. His heart beats a little faster, his ambition to do something and be something is a little stronger, because Lincoln blazed the way.

To my race, the life of Abraham Lincoln has its special lesson at this point in our career. In so far as his life emphasizes patience, long suffering, sincerity, naturalness, dogged determination, and courage — courage to avoid the superficial, courage to persistently seek the substance instead of the shadow — it points the road for my people to travel.

As a race we are learning, I believe, in an increasing degree that the best way for us to honor the memory of our Emancipator is by seeking to imitate him. Like Lincoln, the Negro race should seek to be simple, without bigotry and without ostentation. There is great power in simplicity. We as a race should, like Lincoln, have moral courage to be what we are, and not pretend to be what we are not. We should keep in mind that no one can degrade us except ourselves; that if we are worthy, no influence can defeat us. Like other races, the Negro will often meet obstacles, often be sorely tried and tempted; but we must keep in mind that freedom, in the broadest and highest sense, has never been a bequest; it has been a conquest.

In the final test, the success of our race will be in proportion to the service that it renders to the world. In the long run, the badge of service is the badge of sovereignty.

With all his other elements of strength, Abraham Lincoln possessed in the highest degree patience and, as I have said, courage. The highest form of courage is not always that exhibited on the battlefield in the midst of the blare of trumpets and the waving of banners. The highest courage is of the Lincoln kind. It is the same kind of courage, made possible by the new life and the new possibilities furnished by Lincoln's Proclamation, displayed by thousands of men and women of my race every year who are going out from Tuskegee and other Negro institutions in the South to lift up their fellows. When they go, often into lonely and secluded districts, with little thought of salary, with little thought of personal welfare, no drums beat, no banners fly, no friends stand by to cheer them on; but these brave young souls who are erecting school-houses, creating school systems, prolonging school terms, teaching the people to buy homes, build houses, and live decent lives are fighting the battles of this country just as truly and bravely as any persons who go forth to fight battles against a foreign foe.

In paying my tribute of respect to the Great Emancipator of my race, I desire to say a word here and now in behalf of an element of brave and true white men of the South who, though they saw in Lincoln's policy the ruin of all they believed in and hoped for, have loyally accepted the results of the Civil War, and are today working with a courage few people in the North can understand to uplift the Negro in the South and complete the emancipation that Lincoln began. I am tempted to say that it certainly required as high a degree of courage for men of the type of Robert E. Lee and John B. Gordon to accept the results of the war in the manner and spirit in which they did, as that which Grant and Sherman displayed in fighting the physical battles that saved the Union.

Lincoln also was a Southern man by birth, but he was one of those white men, of whom there is a large and growing class, who resented the idea that in order to assert and maintain the superiority of the Anglo-Saxon race it was necessary that another group of humanity should be kept in ignorance.

Lincoln was not afraid or ashamed to come into contact with the lowly of all races. His reputation and social position were not of

37

such a transitory and transparent kind that he was afraid that he would lose them by being just and kind, even to a man of dark skin. I always pity from the bottom of my heart any man who feels that somebody else must be kept down or in ignorance in order that he may appear great by comparison. It requires no courage for a strong man to kick a weak one down.

Lincoln lives today because he had the courage which made him refuse to hate the man at the South or the man at the North when they did not agree with him. He had the courage as well as the patience and foresight to suffer in silence, to be misunderstood, to be abused, to refuse to revile when reviled. For he knew that, if he was right, the ridicule of today would be the applause of to-morrow. He knew, too, that at some time in the distant future our nation would repent of the folly of cursing our public servants while they live and blessing them only when they die. In this con-nection I cannot refrain from suggesting the question to the mil-lions of voices raised today in his praise: "Why did you not say it yesterday?" Yesterday, when one word of approval and gratitude would have meant so much to him in strengthening his hand and heart.

As we recall tonight his deeds and words, we can do so with grate-ful hearts and strong faith in the future for the spread of righteous-ness. The civilization of the world is going forward, not backward. Here and there for a little season the progress of mankind may seem to halt or tarry by the wayside, or even appear to slide backward, but the trend is ever onward and upward, and will be until someone can invent and enforce a law to stop the progress of civilization. In goodness and liberality the world moves forward. It goes forward beneficently, but it moves forward relentlessly. In the last analysis the forces of nature are behind the moral progress of the world, and these forces will crush into powder any group of humanity that resists this progress.

As we gather here, brothers all, in common joy and thanksgiving for the life of Lincoln, may I not ask that you, the worthy repre-sentatives of seventy millions of white Americans, join heart and hand with the ten millions of black Americans — these ten millions who speak your tongue, profess your religion — who have never lifted their voices or hands except in defense of their country's honor and their country's flag — and swear eternal fealty to the memory and the traditions of the sainted Lincoln? I repeat, may we not join with your race, and let all of us here highly resolve that justice, good will, and peace shall be the motto of our lives? If this be true, in the highest sense Lincoln shall not have lived and died in vain.

And, finally, gathering inspiration and encouragement from this hour and Lincoln's life, I pledge to you and to the nation that my race, in so far as I can speak for it, which in the past, whether in ignorance or intelligence, whether in slavery or in freedom, has always been true to the Stars and Stripes and to the highest and best interests of this country, will strive to so deport itself that it shall reflect nothing but the highest credit upon the whole people in the North and in the South.

Ernest Davidson Washington, ed., *Selected Speeches of Booker T. Washington* (Garden City, N.Y.: Doubleday, Doran and Co., 1932), 190–99. A typescript is in Con. 959, BTW Papers, DLC.

From Ellen A. Craft Crum

Charleston, S.C. Feb. 13–09

Personal

Dear Mr. Washington: I hope you will pardon this intrusion, but I am writing from the fullness of my heart, and am entirely convinced you can evolve some satisfactory solution for this most crushing problem.[1]

I am not unmindful of the possible effect of this most unexpected Waterloo, on my husband, all I have.

To circumvent the necessity of making the Crum case a test, and thereby meeting a possible defeat of the hopes of the Negro, it seems to me a compromise would be the best thing under the circumstances. This has been suggested by others. This compromise, in order that the Negroe's side may appear in the best possible light, and with the least appearance of failure, should come from or be advanced by the Negro himself.

The principle Mr. Roosevelt set forth has been entirely vindicated and the good judgment of those who recommended to him the applicant, have been made good. During the five years or his entire incumbency, no patron, at any time, has made complaint against him, nor has the Government at any time found fault with the management of affairs.

What ever is Mr. Taft's attitude on this subject it might serve our best interests as a race, to procrastinate the finding out, instead of forcing the issue.

There is a great deal at stake and a passing thought should be given the "I told you so" element. I refer to Mr. Du Boise, Bishop Walters &c.

It would serve as a beacon light for their ref[e]rence.

It has been suggested by the Southern press, to give the person in question, a position at the seat of the general government or elsewhere, and I think that would be a happy solution.

This would leave the "door of hope" still open to the Negro and give Mr. Taft an opportunity to look about him for a while.

There is only one person in my opinion, who can bring this about, and that is, the acknowledged leader of our race in America and that is also my reason for writing to you.

With kindest wishes for yourself and Mrs. Washington and again asking your indulgence I remain   Very Sincerely

Ellen A. Crum

ALS   Con. 890   BTW Papers   DLC.

[1] Clippings enclosed with the letter (New York *Sun*, Feb. 10, 1909; Charleston *News and Courier*, n.d.) indicated that the Senate probably would not confirm William D. Crum's reappointment as collector of customs at Charleston, and suggested that Taft was unenthusiastic about continuing Roosevelt's appointment of a black man to a major southern patronage position.

To Robert Bacon

[Tuskegee, Ala.] Feb. 16, 1909

Think I could be ready to start by time vessel is gotten ready and other commissioners chosen. Find can get away with less injury to work here now than later provided trip can be shortened going and coming in every way possible so as to permit of all time in Liberia possible and so as to get back here early in spring before close of school year. Very much prefer going and returning on same naval vessel and without any change of vessels. In that case can keep up much valuable work on vessel which I usually do here. Would prefer to arrange to live on vessel while there so commission can keep in good physical shape to do good work. If neither Mr. Ogden nor Dr. Frissell can go have another man to suggest. My feeling is that appearance of man of war will have fine effect not only on Liberians but upon other countries that are interested. In order to know how to plan here, please let me know soon as you find out probable time required going and coming, leaving three weeks to be spent in active work there.

Booker T. Washington

TWpSr   Con. 895   BTW Papers   DLC.

To Seth Low

[Tuskegee, Ala.] February 16, 1909

My dear Mr. Low: I had a long conference with the Secretary of State Bacon and with the Assistant Secretary Sunday night. The Liberian matter is practically reduced to the following point. The people in the State Department say they think I can save Liberia by going. If I do not go, they fear that the independence and usefulness of the country will be lost. The Department is so impressed with the importance of my going at once that it is willing to use an emergency fund for expenses, either to defray the expenses of the entire commission of three or for me to go alone. Under the circumstances, using the permission granted me by the Board of Trustees, I have placed myself in the hands of the State Department. It seemed to me that this was the only thing to do as it was a clear case of duty. I have a feeling that if the Department carries out its present plan to have the commission go on a man of war that the time required will not be very great and that I can get back here in time to do a great deal of valuable work before the close of our financial year.

In going over our financial condition, in order to come out clear at the end of the year I find that we shall have to raise by that time $113,000 aside from assured income. I think I can do this. I shall have to put in a good deal of time on ship board in writing letters. I shall keep you informed.

Troubles in Liberia are both internal and external. The British Government has marched troops into Monrovia and will keep them there until the American Commission arrives. Yours very truly,

Booker T. Washington

TLpS   Con. 45   BTW Papers   DLC.

To James Jenkins Dossen

[Tuskegee, Ala.] February 19, 1909

My dear Vice-President: I have been delayed in answering your kind letter of December 31st, for the reason that I have been away from home.

I am very sorry to hear of developments in your country since your letter was written. I hope that by the present time matters are quieting down. I have been to the State Department several times recently, and am keeping in close touch with developments.

Certainly, I can say to you that the visit of the Liberian Envoys has had the result of deepening and quickening the interest of this country in Liberia, in a way that nothing has done in recent years.

It is the present intention of the State Department to send a Commission to Liberia at an early date, and I have been asked to go as a member of this Commission. I am trying to see my way clear to do so. If the present intention of having a man go directly to Liberia and return, for the accommodation of the Commission, is carried out, I think I shall go.

You can depend upon this, that whoever does go will be high-minded people of large influence and capable of service. I think that Mr. Robert C. Ogden, Mr. John Wanamaker's partner in New York and Philadelphia, is likely to be one of the members of the Commission.

I shall try to write you more in detail later. Yours truly,

Booker T. Washington

TLpS   Con. 891   BTW Papers   DLC.

From Robert Heberton Terrell

Washington, D.C., Feb. 19, 1909

My dear Doctor Washington, I greatly appreciate your telegram of congratulations. I am glad that this honor has come to us at this time when so many people are depressed over the Crum affair. It is very gratifying to me to have the cordial and unanimous endorsement of the bar association of the District of Columbia. The southern men are as hearty in their commendation as the northern men.

So far as this promotion is a personal honor I am wholly indebted to you. You are the Alpha and Omega of my judicial life. I have tried to justify the confidence you reposed in my character and in my ability. I believe that in some respects I have not disappointed your expectations.

I am the first man born in slavery who has ever held a judicial position of this nature.

I am receiving letters from all parts of the country touching my elevation.

With kindest regards for Mrs. W. and Mr. Scott I am, yours faithfully,

Robert H Terrell

P.S. Please tell Mr. Hunt that his letter with enclosure came to-day. Thanks.

ALS   Con. 399   BTW Papers   DLC.

To the Editor[1] of *The Delineator*

[Tuskegee, Ala.] February 20, 1909

Dear Sir: You ask me to name the book that has most influenced my life.[2] This is not a difficult task. The book that has had the greatest influence in shaping my motives and actions is the Bible. From my earliest childhood, even while I was a slave, I was taught to listen reverently to the words of the Bible. As I grew older, and

43

I had the opportunity of attending a public school, the Bible was always read the first thing in the morning at the opening exercises.

All this made a big impression upon me. Later when I went to Hampton Institute, Virginia, where I was a pupil for a period of several years, I was fortunate in meeting there a good woman by the name of Nathalie Lord, who took special pains in giving me extra lessons in the Bible.

My daily contact with the practical affairs of life, in nearly all parts of the country, has served to deepen my impression of the value of the Bible in shaping the life of any man. No matter how busy I am, no matter how perplexing the problems, or no matter how pressing the work upon me, I have made it a rule, from which I very seldom ever depart, to read a chapter in my Bible before I leave my room for the task of the day. I have found this practice of value in shaping my life from several points of view.

No book that I have ever studied has helped me more than the Bible in putting my thoughts before the world, whether on the platform or through the printed page, in a concise, and clear, and emphatic manner. I find as I write or speak that without reflection I am likely to quote directly from the Bible, and in some way my sentences are influenced or shaped by what I have read in that great and good Book. I very seldom ever write an article for a magazine or paper, or prepare an important speech for the public that I do not find myself quoting directly or indirectly from the Bible, and such quotations, I notice, invariably attract the attention of the audience. One can get many apt illustrations from the Scriptures to liven up or to awaken the interest of an audience in almost any subject.

Sometime ago I heard a gentleman, who has had experience in speaking before the public, say that it used to be his custom to get his stories or illustrations from newspapers and magazines, but he found that when he would begin to tell these stories, a smile would pass over the audience, which indicated that the story was an old one or chestnut. After that he changed his plan and got his stories or illustrations from the Bible. These he said were effective because they were new to the audience. I do not know whether he was right about these stories being new, but I agree with him that they were effective.

Fortunately or unfortunately, I was taught in my youth to believe pretty thoroughly in the moral and spiritual teachings of the Bible, and I have never had cause to regret it. There are a great many people who, of course, do not believe in the Bible, and have failed to follow its moral and spiritual teachings, but there are very few people who can claim that they have ever been injured by reading and following the Bible or by following its moral teachings. There are millions who have been hurt by not following in spirit, at least, the teachings of the Bible. Yours truly,

Booker T. Washington

TLpS   Con. 896   BTW Papers   DLC.

[1] Theodore Dreiser (1871–1945) was editor of *The Delineator*, a women's fashion magazine, and of other Butterick publications from 1907 to 1910. It was Charles Hanson Towne, however, *The Delineator*'s literary editor, who had asked BTW to write on the book that had most influenced him. (Towne to BTW, Feb. 15, 1909, Con. 896, BTW Papers, DLC.)

[2] The magazine did not publish BTW's response in its article in August 1909.

From William Henry Lewis

Boston   February 20, 1909

Dear Mr. Washington: I enclose copy of an article in the Herald[1] which is important, if true, and should be looked into. If this is to be the President's policy, it seems to me he ought not to announce it. It will not help in the South, and will hurt us in the North. No good can come out of it. Personally I much prefer that the President should say nothing upon the race question whatever — just let it alone.

Believe me, Sincerely yours,

William H Lewis

TLS   Con. 393   BTW Papers   DLC.

[1] The clipping reported that Taft would announce in his inaugural address that he would appoint no Negroes to federal office in places where the white community objected. (Boston *Herald*, Feb. 20, 1909, 1.)

From Fred Warner Carpenter

Washington, D.C., February 22, 1909

My dear Dr. Washington: I have your telegram of the 20th instant, and am reserving two seats on the reviewing stand in front of the White House for your son-in-law and daughter, Mr. and Mrs. W. S. Pittman.

Mr. Taft's allotment of seats on the stand at the Capitol is so limited that there will scarcely be enough to accommodate the members of his and Mr[s]. Taft's immediate families and relatives, so that it would not be possible for him to give you seats for the exercises there. He is glad however to grant this request. Very sincerely yours,

Fred W Carpenter

TLS Con. 44 BTW Papers DLC.

To Emmett Jay Scott

New York, [Feb.] 23d [1909]

Just had hours undisturbed frank talk with Mr. T.[1] Did not go into details of Washington address but notwithstanding had sent it to office Associated Press, New York, had it recalled and going to read me whole document tomorrow. He strongly opposes my going to L.[2] Says am needed here too much.

W.

TWIr Con. 587 BTW Papers DLC.

[1] William Howard Taft.
[2] Liberia.

To Emmett Jay Scott

New York, Feb. 23d. 190[9]

Forgot to state in other telegram that friend here[1] had most frank talk regarding relations between himself and other friend.[2] Says enemies tried to disturb matters but now everything settled. He means to stand by him and carry out his policies far as possible.

W.

TWIr Con. 587 BTW Papers DLC. Addressed to BTW at the Hotel Manhattan, New York City.

1 William Howard Taft.
2 Theodore Roosevelt.

From Emmett Jay Scott

[Tuskegee, Ala.] February 23, 1909

Am happy to learn of interview. It is all most encouraging. Lewis in letter received today calls attention to disturbing dispatch which appeared Boston Herald twentieth. He and others are writing hoping our friend will leave whole subject undiscussed if attitude is to be as stated.

E. J. Scott

TWSr Con. 587 BTW Papers DLC.

Extracts from an Address at Carnegie Hall

[New York City] February 23, 1909

I wish to express not only the gratitude of the Hampton Institute, but the obligation that the Negro race throughout this country feels to President-elect William H. Taft, for his presence, and for his words at this meeting tonight. It seems a great deal, not only for the Hampton Institute, but for the cause of education and higher civilization, for my race throughout this country, that the President-elect of the United States should turn aside from his many duties and serious responsibilities, at the present time, to lend his presence and his words to further the cause of education among the millions of my race in this country. Judging from what he has said, and by what he has done throughout his career, I feel safe in stating that the Negro race and the white race in the South will have no truer and wiser friend than President Taft. I feel sure, further, that he will inspire us with the same confidence, and will exhibit the same inflexible determination to deal justly with all sections and with all races as his great predecessor has done. As he enters upon his new duties and responsibilities, no group of people in or out of America will pray more earnestly and constantly that he may be guided and inspired by an All-wise Providence than will be true of the black millions scattered through America.

Not only does the Hampton Institute but the thousands of graduates of that institution as well as the Negro race and the nation owe a deep debt of gratitude to Dr. Hollis B. Frissell for the magnificent way in which he is continuing and perpetuating the influence and work of Gen. S. C. Armstrong; in supporting and holding up his hands, people will be helping not only the Negro race but our whole country. A few months ago it was my privilege to return to the old farm in Virginia upon which I was born, and spent my early years as a slave. I had been absent for forty years, and it was my first visit since the days of slavery. I met on this farm one of the grandsons of my former owner, who was made the executor of my former master's estate. Among other interesting things, he showed me the inventory of the estate, which had been entrusted to him. As I read the items, I found, so many acres of land, valued at so many dollars; so many houses, valued at so many dollars; so many horses valued at so many dollars; so many cows valued at so many dollars; further down I found the word "Booker" valued at $400. If during the years that have passed, I have been able to make my mind and body worth more than $400. to the cause of civilization, it is all due to the influence and the work of the Hampton Institute, where I was educated, and where I received the inspiration that led me to devote my life to the cause of education in the Southern States. I could not help but recall, when this gentleman handed me the inventory, that the same proclamation which made me free, also made him free, and, so two races instead of one, are now free in the South; free to sympathize with each other, to help each other to work, and bear the daily burdens and responsibilities that confront us in our communities.

Upon this platform tonight you see a practical exhibit of the work that the Hampton Institute stands for in teaching farming, mechanics, and housekeeping. I call your attention to the fact that the exhibit is made in a Northern city, but the Southern states furnish the opportunity for the Negro, in a larger degree than any other section of our country, where he can put his knowledge and his skill into practical effect. The North is a good place to make the exhibition, but the South is the best place to do the actual work. In the Southern States we have the advantage of touching and rubbing up against, in our daily life, the real problems of humanity.

I do not pity a race that is up against the real problems of life. The only question to be considered is, is progress being made. So far from being at a disadvantage, the race that is up against the problem every day of acquiring land, cultivating that land, of getting good out of the soil, the problem of securing shelter; the problem of building schoolhouses; prolonging the school term; of building churches and securing good ministers and teachers; such a race is not to be pitied, if progress is being made, because out of such experiences one gets a ruggedness of character that can be secured in no other way.

Recently I have had two experiences, that have convinced me that in meeting and solving these practical problems of daily life, that the Negro is succeeding, and the best type of white people in the South are helping him to succeed.

I spent a good part of the month of October in travelling through the States of Mississippi and Arkansas where I could see for myself the progress that the race is making in all these vital matters; where I could see for myself something of the wisdom, the dignity, determination and patience with which the Negro is meeting the fundamental and primary problems of securing land, building houses, going into business, establishing schools, and church[es].

I have had more recent experience within the last few days of witnessing at Tuskegee, the presence of some two thousand Negro farmers, who had come there from all sections of the South to attend our Annual Tuskegee Negro Conference. If there are those who doubt the future success of the Negro race, and doubt our ability as a nation to solve what is known as the race problem, I wish that they could have witnessed the proceedings of this Conference at Tuskegee for two days. I wish that you could have heard the marvelous stories told by the men and women who were present. I wish you could have heard the individuals tell, how in many cases they had begun in the most abjected poverty and ignorance, how in some way they have secured a cow for the cultivation of the soil, how later they have secured a mule, then two mules, and then half a dozen mules, how later they have secured a horse and then a dozen horses, and then within a period of twelve or fifteen years they had struggled up to the point where at the present time, in some cases, they own as much as 500 acres of land, which is well tilled; how now they live in decent and comfortable cottages, have money in the bank; have entered into business of their own; and have spent and are spending a portion of their earnings in building schoolhouses and prolonging school terms; in erecting churches, and paying the ministers. I wish you might have heard these marvelous stories of sacrifice, of progress, and triumph, and during the two days, I did not hear a single word of bitterness uttered against a single white man in America. I wish, in other words, you might have heard them express their deep gratitude to the white people by whom they were surrounded, for the encouragement, for the guidance, and for the practical aid which these white people had rendered to them in bettering their material condition, their educational, moral, and religious life.

The white man of whom we heard at this Conference, who in Macon County, Alabama, made a contribution in cash of $100. within recent months to help build a Negro schoolhouse in his community, made a contribution to the cause of education that, when we consider it, is equal to perhaps $10,000 given by somebody else whose circumstances were far different from that of this white citizen.

In all these matters relating to the uplift of the Negro, we must bear in mind that there are two classes of white people in the South; one class that expresses itself as not believing in the education of the Negro; there is another class, a growing class, a cultured and important class that believes in the education of the Negro, and while you do not hear a great deal from them in the public prints, or on the public platform, they are, nevertheless, in their daily lives manifesting their interests in the most practical form. They are far seeing, and understand the fundamental truth that wherever, in any part of the world, one race is down, the other race, to a degree is also down.

We must not, however, let our optimism overshadow the actual facts. Conditions are improving, but there is much to be done for this generation, much for the succeeding generations before the life of the Negro in the South will be placed upon a plane where it will not hinder or retard the progress of the remaining portion of America. In his material life, in his educational and moral life tremendous work yet remains to be done. In some communities in the South, we have not yet gotten to the point where the average salary paid the Negro teacher is more than $15. for five months' teaching. This condition means ignorance; this condition means immorality; this condition means a lack of producing power. Immorality, ignorance, slothfulness and poverty draw no color line. The influences of these hurtful elements show themselves in the life of all people.

Some of the real heroes of America at the present time, are the men and the women who are going out from such institutions as Hampton, Tuskegee, Fisk, Atlanta, Talladega, Spelman, and other educational centers, to give their lives, in a plain, simple courageous manner in showing the masses of our people how to get land, how to build decent homes, how to erect schoolhouses and to improve their moral and religious lives. In many cases, these young men and women go into lonely, desolate districts with little hope of getting salaries, where there are little personal comforts or the evidences of living, and give themselves, in this beautiful manner to the uplift of our people.

Just in proportion as such work as that which is being done at Hampton is encouraged and supported by practical gifts, just in the same degree will we be able to send out more such leaders; will we be able to help the white South in its efforts to uplift the Negro in education and otherwise.

To be more practical and pointed, Hampton needs at the present moment to have its endowment fund increased by at least $2,000,000. It needs in the meantime a larger number of generous friends who will pay $70 a year for the education of individual students. Without the payment of $70 by a friend to help me through Hampton so far as my tuition was concerned, it would not have been possible for me to have received the education which I secured at that institution.

Every man whose mind we can make intelligent, whose body we

can make useful, whose soul we can make purer, clears the way for the spread of intelligence, of usefulness, and righteousness among all the people, regardless of race, in our Southern communities. It makes our progress as a nation safer and easier.

Perhaps it has not occurred to many people in America, that while many predicted at the time Abraham Lincoln set us free, that as a race the Negro would starve for want of food, or die for want of shelter or clothing, that from the very day that Lincoln emancipated us we have taken care of ourselves, so far as our bodily and personal needs are concerned, except in the case of some special or local calamity. The Negro has not called upon the nation to furnish him with land, to furnish him with a home, to furnish him with shelter or clothing except in cases of special calamity. The only call, in forty years, that he has made upon the American people for assistance has been in the direction of education, of morality, of religious uplift. We will take care of our own personal and material needs; having done that, we believe that we have a right, when we consider all that has taken place in the past, and all the service that we have rendered to America in slavery and in freedom, to have her assist us to improve our educational, moral and religious life.

TM Con. 959 BTW Papers DLC. An account of the occasion, including Taft's speech, is in the *Tuskegee Student*, 21 (Mar. 6, 1909), 1–4.

To William Demosthenes Crum

[New York City] Feb. 24, 1909

Meet me ticket office Broad street station, Philadelphia, five oclock Friday afternoon.[1] Important. Let no one know you are making trip. Answer Fifth Avenue Bank, New York.

W.

TWpIr Con. 389 BTW Papers DLC.

1 Crum agreed to meet BTW at this time and place. (Crum to BTW, Feb. 25, 1909, Con. 389, BTW Papers, DLC.) They may have changed the meeting until the next day in New York City, or met a second time, since BTW wrote to Taft that he saw Crum on Feb. 27. (See BTW to Taft, Feb. 28, 1909, below.)

To Emmett Jay Scott

New York City [ca. Feb. 24, 1909]

Friend[1] here will not reappoint Dr. C.[2] What do you think of wisdom of getting him to get initiative of resigning? Answer.

W.

TWIr Con. 587 BTW Papers DLC.

1 William Howard Taft.
2 William Demosthenes Crum.

To Emmett Jay Scott

New York, Feb. 24 190[9]

Think well for you attend Inauguration. Had two more long conferences with friend. Read document fully. He permitted me to make whatever changes I desired. Newspaper reports exaggerated contents, but Anderson, Major Moton and I went through it carefully and guarded it from misinterpretation. On the whole it is all right. He notified Bacon today will not permit me to leave. Says wants to depend on me in all important matters as other friend did.

W.

TWIr Con. 587 BTW Papers DLC.

From Emmett Jay Scott

[Tuskegee, Ala., ca. Feb. 24, 1909]

It will be strategic racial mistake to resign, but if do so would earnestly urge he give out statement that he does so to relieve embarrassment at beginning of administration. Will strengthen him personally but action will be severely criticised as relieving a situation not created by reason of any fault of his own.

E. J. Scott

TWSr Con. 587 BTW Papers DLC.

Emmett Jay Scott to William Henry Lewis

[Tuskegee, Ala.] February 24, 1909

My dear Mr. Lewis: I telegraphed yesterday the substance of your letter of February 20th to Dr. Washington at Hotel Manhattan, New York.

I think it would mean a great deal if you and other friends would on your personal responsibility write to Mr. Taft showing the general feeling of our people with regard to the suggested "innovations." A series of such letters would accomplish great good, I am sure. Yours very truly,

[Emmett J. Scott]

TL Copy   Con. 393   BTW Papers   DLC.

To Emmett Jay Scott

Hotel Manhattan, New York. February 25, 1909

Dear Mr. Scott: I received your telegram in regard to Dr. C. Nothing whatever can be gained by his holding on with a view of being renominated. Mr. Taft positively will not renominate him. The only question is, whether he can serve his own interests by getting out gracefully or by being forced out. Mr. Taft feels most kindly toward him and is going to do his best to provide him something else, but he will feel more kindly to him if he gets out in the way suggested, that is, by resigning. Further than this, I find that people everywhere, even among our best friends, are tired of the Crum case. They feel that enough effort has already been made to keep him in this position. Mr. Taft says that his case has placed the whole Southern situation in an awkward position in that it makes people feel that the South is full of Negro office holders when in fact there [are] but very few, and but for this fact he would not feel it was necessary to treat the subject of office holding at all in the South by Negroes.

There is absolutely nothing in the report that the relations between Mr. Taft and Mr. Roosevelt are not pleasant.

I have had three or four conferences with Mr. Taft since I have been here, and all have been of the most cordial character. He is even more cordial than before the election. In the last interview he suggested that he did not want me to wait until he asked me for advice, but wanted me to come to him and speak to him frankly regarding any subject that I thought he ought to be spoken to about. He said that he meant to lean on me heavily during his administration. Yours very truly,

B. T. W.

TLI   Con. 587   BTW Papers   DLC.

To Margaret James Murray Washington

New York, Feb. 25 [1909]

Mr. Taft absolutely refuses consent me go to Liberia because he needs me here. Tell Mr. Scott says will appoint him in my place if he consents provided commission does not go before he becomes president — have asked him appoint Mr. Scott — show this telegram to Mr. Scott.[1]

W.

TWIr   Con. 591   BTW Papers   DLC.

[1] Scott expressed the belief that the movement to rescue Liberia would "lose its significance and its hope of success with you out of it." He also felt "altogether unworthy" of appointment to the commission and unenthusiastic about making the trip. (Scott to BTW, Feb. 26, 1909, Con. 588, BTW Papers, DLC.)

To George Washington Albert Johnston

Hotel Manhattan, New York. February 25, 1909

My dear Albert: I have received your letter from Nashville, and you do not realize how very grateful I am to you for what you have done. I appreciate it all thoroughly. I shall be writing you more fully later.

Please tell Mr. Thompson confidentially that Mr. Taft has gone over with me the whole of his inaugural address, and I think he will find it a strong and helpful document. What it says regarding the South and the colored people is on the whole sound and guarded. I find that many of the sensational stories that have been sent out regarding what he is going to do in reference to the South and the Negro are without foundation.

You can also tell Mr. Thompson that Mr. Taft absolutely refuses to let me go to Liberia for the reason that he says he needs my services in this country especially just now. Your uncle,

[Booker T. Washington]

TLc   Con. 45   BTW Papers   DLC.

From Emmett Jay Scott

Tuskegee Institute, Alabama   February 27, 1909

My dear Mr. Washington: It has been a very great pleasure to find out from your letter of February 25th and from your telegrams that, under the new administration, you are to be even closer than you were to the Roosevelt administration. Mr. Taft will never know just how much he really owes to you and I am very glad that he is at the very start giving evidence of his appreciation of that fact.

With reference to Dr. Crum. From a personal point of view, I can see altogether how much better it will be for him to resign. I think I said this in my letter to you, but from the point of view of the race, you can see what a mistake it will be for him to voluntarily solve a situation involving what is a straightout principle. He can very graciously retire with the statement that he did not wish to embarrass the new administration at the very beginning. This, also, is in accordance with what I telegraphed you. Yours very truly,

Emmett J. Scott

TLS   Con. 46   BTW Papers   DLC.

William Demosthenes Crum to Theodore Roosevelt

Charleston, S.C. [ca. Feb. 27, 1909]

Dear Sir: I hereby resign the position of Collector of the Port of Charleston, S.C., to take effect March 4th next.

In doing so I wish to thank you most heartily not only for appointing me to this office (blank) years ago, but for renominating me to fill the same office for a second term.

Ever since I have held this position I have striven diligently to justify the confidence imposed in me. During all the years that I have occupied this position, so far as I know not a single charge has been brought against my moral character or a single adverse criticism made in regard to the performance of my official duties. I wish further to add that those employed in this office under me composed of both races have been at all times courteous, kind and interested, and we have all worked together to make the office work successful and satisfactory.

When I became Collector of the Port (blank) years ago the annual receipts were $[*blank*]. I am glad to state that the receipts have gradually increased until at the close of the last fiscal year they amounted to $[*blank*]. Of course I cannot claim credit for all of this increase in receipts; much of it would have been brought about through the natural growth of business, but I have striven in every way possible to increase the usefulness of the office and the position which I hold.

Before closing I think I ought to add that during all the years I have held this position I have been treated kindly by all the people outside of my immediate office force who have had official business with my office, and I have had no unpleasant contact with any one in the city.

In closing permit me to thank you again for the trust imposed and to wish you as you end your official career a hearty Godspeed and long life.[1] Yours truly,

[William D. Crum]

TLd Con. 389 BTW Papers DLC. Apparently BTW prepared this draft for Crum, for there is a correction of the date of resignation in BTW's hand.

1 Roosevelt accepted the resignation, thanking Crum for his admirable performance of duty. "You have amply justified the confidence I placed in you," he wrote. (Roosevelt to Crum, Mar. 1, 1909, Theodore Roosevelt Papers, DLC.)

To William Howard Taft

Hotel Manhattan, New York. February 28, 1909

Personal

My dear Mr. Taft: I am writing according to promise. I saw Dr. C. here yesterday and went over the whole situation with him. He took it in good spirit and went back home immediately to consult with his wife. I believe he is going to act in a sensible manner.

You asked me to remind you to see Mr. Goethals[1] concerning Panama. I might say that incidentally I mentioned the Panama position to him,[2] but he did not take kindly to it. I do not believe he would go, but it may be worth while to make an opening there for some other good colored doctor. I prefer to talk to you about Dr. C. and the whole colored situation before any move is made. Yours very truly

[Booker T. Washington]

TLc   Con. 48   BTW Papers   DLC.

[1] George Washington Goethals (1858–1928), chief engineer of the Panama Canal Commission (1907–14) and acting quartermaster general of the U.S. Army in World War I.

[2] William Demosthenes Crum.

To Harry Hamilton Johnston

[Hotel Manhattan, New York City] February 28, 1909

My dear Sir Harry Johnston: Since I last wrote you there have been so many new phases bobbing up in connection with the Liberian situation that I am hardly able to keep up with them. I review them very briefly for your information.

Secretary Root definitely decided to send a commission composed of three persons to Liberia, two white and one colored. A bill was introduced into Congress asking for the money and also for permission to send a naval vessel for the use of the commission. All this was done on the heels of the adjourning of Congress. The bill has not yet passed Congress but it may pass before it adjourns. In the meantime matters in Liberia grew, as you know, so serious that the Secretary of State telegraphed me last week to come to Washington for an interview and said that he was ready to send the commission without authority of Congress, that is using an emergency fund, as he felt that the situation justified his doing that. I was urged to consent to go as a member of this commission, or if I thought best, to go alone. In the meantime President Roosevelt was approached on the matter, and he rather felt that he would like to get the bill through Congress before sending the commission. This held the matter up for several days. In the meantime Mr. Root went out of office and was succeeded by Secretary Bacon. Matters stood in this condition for a few days, when President-elect Taft was approached concerning the commission, and especially my being a member of it. He at once objected to my leaving this country especially at this time, stating that he needed my services here during the first few months, especially, of his administration. He said that he would take all the responsibility of changing and explaining the whole matter to the Secretary of State. It is unfortunate that the whole matter came up just on the eve of three changes, the change in the office of Secretary of State, the adjournment of Congress, and the change of Presidents. My present belief is that nothing definite will be done until the new administration has taken charge and settled down to business. It may be that later on President Taft will change his opinion concerning my going. I have had three interviews with him on the subject, and in each case he definitely and strongly objected to my leaving this country.

We are trying to get some strong men for the commission. It may interest you to know that Mr. Robert C. Ogden, the partner of John Wanamaker, has virtually consented to go as a member of the commission if appointed. Who the other member or members will be I am not sure.

The Secretary of State told me that he was going to try to arrange with Mr. Bryce for you to be present in Liberia when the commission reaches there.

I have written you thus hastily what the conditions are. I am sorry they are not more satisfactory.

I have seen all the dispatches from Liberia and from our Ambassador in London. Conditions seem to be serious in Liberia.

The plan is to have the commission go and return on a man of war. Yours very truly,

[Booker T. Washington]

TLc   Con. 894   BTW Papers   DLC.

An Article in *World's Work*

February 1909

A CHEERFUL JOURNEY THROUGH MISSISSIPPI

WHICH SHOWED THE RAPID PROGRESS OF THE NEGRO RACE IN EDUCATION, IN ACQUIRING LAND, IN BUILDING UP BUSINESS, AND IN BECOMING FINANCIALLY INDEPENDENT AND THRIFTY

Some months ago, I was invited by the Negro Business League of Mississippi to make a rather extended journey through that state for the purpose of learning something at first-hand of the progress that the members of my race are making there; to say a word of encouragement and advice; and, if possible, to make some suggestions that would help to improve the relations between the races.

Before I attempt to say anything about the results of my observations, however, I want to add something more definite about the circumstances under which the journey was made. When I first came into Alabama, some twenty-seven years ago, to begin my work at Tuskegee, I made it a practice to go out into the country districts whenever I had an opportunity, in order to visit the people in their homes, on the farms, and on the plantations. On these trips, I frequently stayed overnight with some of the colored farmers. On such occasions, in the evening, after supper, we would usually sit around the fire until a late hour at night, and discuss the condition, difficulties, hopes, and ambitions of the colored people in that part of the country. I inquired about the schools and about the churches, and I learned a great deal also about the personal histories, the struggles, the failures, and the successes of the individual men and women whom I met. In this way and in others I got to know the people in their daily lives.

Usually, when I visited a community, I was called upon at some time during my stay to make an address to the people. In these "lectures," as the country people called them, I tried to say something that would have a direct, practical bearing on the difficulties that they were meeting in their schools or in their churches. Incidentally, I told them about the school we had started in Tuskegee; I explained to them the kind of education that I proposed to give there, and tried to make clear to them in what way I hoped that this education would meet the actual needs of the people, by fitting the children to take up and carry on the work that their fathers and mothers had begun.

In making these visits, I had a double purpose: I wanted to find out the actual condition of the people in the country districts, so that I could make the work of the school fit into the lives of the people; and, at the same time, I wanted to popularize the idea of this kind of education among the masses of the people. I wanted to make the fathers and mothers of our pupils realize and thoroughly understand that a real education, whether it was "high" or "low," whether it was education in the book or in the field, must somewhere touch the earth and change the conduct, the character, and the condition of the people.

As years went by, the circle of my journeys widened, and so I have been able to speak to members of my race in all parts of the country in a way to impress them not merely with the value of industrial education but with the importance of getting property, of building homes, of thrift, industry, and those other fundamental things which are essential to the success of any race and any class of people.

In 1900, in Boston, in company with a number of other colored men, I succeeded in organizing what is known as the National Negro Business League, of which there are now more than four hundred local organizations in different parts of the country. These organizations have done much, not merely to encourage the economic progress of the masses of the colored people, but to extend and emphasize the idea that is back of the movement for industrial education among the colored people of the South.

I mention these facts here because they illustrate the purpose of my visit to Mississippi, and because they indicate that the work of the National Negro Business League is very clearly related to the work of education that we are carrying on at Tuskegee Institute.

As an indication of the general interest in the purpose and the success of my visit, I ought to say that, while the journey was made under the direction of the Negro Business League of Mississippi, representatives of nearly every important interest among Negroes in the state either accompanied the party for a portion of the journey or assisted in making the meetings successful at the different places at which we stopped. For instance, as I remember, there were not less than eight presidents of Negro banks and many other successful business men who were members of the party at some time in the course of the eight-day trip. Among them were Charles Banks, president of the Negro Business League of Mississippi, and one of the most influential colored men of the state. It was he who was more directly responsible than anyone else for organizing and making a success of our journey. Not only the business men, but the representatives of different religious denominations and of the secret organizations, which are particularly strong in Mississippi, united with the members of the Business League to make the meetings which we held in the different parts of the state as successful and as influential as it was possible to make them.

It is a matter of no small importance to the success of the people of my race in Mississippi that business men, teachers, and the members of the different religious denominations are uniting disinterestedly in the effort to give the colored children of the state a proper and adequate education, and that they are using their influence to encourage the masses of the people to get property and build homes.

Dr. E. C. Morris, for instance, who was a member of the party, represents the largest Negro organization of any kind in the world — the National Baptist Convention, which has a membership of more than two millions; J. W. Strauther,[1] as a member of the Finance Committee of the Negro Pythians, represented an organization of about seventy thousand persons, owning about three hundred and twenty-two thousand dollars' worth of property. "The African Methodist Episcopal Review," of which Dr. H. T. Kealing is editor, is probably the best-edited and one of the most influential periodicals published by the Negro race. It has been in existence now for more than twenty-five years.

I have mentioned the names of these men and have referred to their positions and influence among the Negro people as showing how widespread at the present time is the interest in the moral and material upbuilding of the race.

I had heard a great deal, indirectly, before I reached Mississippi of the progress that the colored people were making there. I had also heard a great deal through the newspapers of the difficulties under which they were laboring. There are some portions of Mississippi, for instance, where a large part of the colored population has been driven out as a result of white-capping organizations. There are other portions of the state where the white people and the colored people seem to be getting along as well if not better than in any other portion of the Union.

After leaving Memphis, the first place at which we stopped was Holly Springs, in Marshall County. Holly Springs has long been an educational centre for the colored people of Mississippi. Shortly after the war, the Freedman's Aid and Southern Educational Society of the Methodist Church established here the Rust University. Until a few years ago, the State Normal School for Training Negro Teachers was in existence in Holly Springs, when it was finally abolished by Governor Vardaman. The loss of this school was a source of great disappointment to the colored people of the state, as they felt that, in vetoing the appropriation, the governor was making an attack upon the Negro education of the state. Under the leadership of Bishop Cottrell, a new industrial school and theological seminary has grown up to take the place of the Normal Training School and do its work. During the last two years, Bishop Cottrell has succeeded in raising more than seventy-five thousand dollars, largely from the colored people of Mississippi, in order to erect the two handsome modern buildings which form the nucleus of the new school. He is now at work in the hope of raising $50,000, during the coming year and from the same sources, with which to erect a new central building for the school. In this city there has also been recently established a Baptist Normal School, which is the contribution of the Negro Baptists of the state in response to the abolition of the State Normal School.

The enthusiasm for education that I discovered at Holly Springs is merely an indication of the similar enthusiasm in every other part of the state that I visited. At Utica, Miss., I spoke in the assembly-room of the Utica Institute, founded October 27, 1903, by William H. Holtzclaw, a graduate of Tuskegee. After leaving Tuskegee, he determined to go to the part of the country where it seemed to him that the colored people were most in need of a school that could be conducted along the lines of Tuskegee Institute. He settled in Hinds County, where there are forty thousand colored people, thirteen thousand of whom can neither read nor write. In the community in which this school was started the Negroes outnumber the whites seven to one. He began teaching out in the forest. From the very first, he succeeded in gaining the sympathy of both races for the work that he was trying to do. In the five years since the school started, he has succeeded in purchasing a farm of fifteen hundred acres. He has erected three large and eleven small buildings of various kinds for schoolrooms, shops, and homes. On the farm, there are one large plantation house and about thirty farmhouses. He tells me that a conservative estimate of the property which the school now owns would make the valuation something more than seventy-five thousand dollars. In addition to this, he has already started an endowment-fund in order to make the work that he is doing there permanent, and to give aid by means of scholarships to worthy students who are not fully able to pay their own way.

At Jackson, Miss., there are two colleges for Negro students. Campbell College was founded by the African Methodist Episcopal Church; Jackson College, which has just opened a handsome new building for the use of its students, was established and is supported by the Baptist denomination. At Natchez, I was invited to take part in the dedication of the beautiful new building erected by the Negro Baptists of Mississippi at a cost of about twenty thousand dollars.

Perhaps I ought to say that, while there has been considerable rivalry among the different Negro churches along theological lines, it seems to me that I can see that, as the leaders of the people begin to realize the seriousness of the educational problem, this rivalry is gradually dying out in a disinterested effort to educate the masses of the Negro children irrespective of denominations. The so-called denominational schools are merely a contribution of the members of the different sects to the education of the race.

Nothing indicates the progress which the colored people have made along material lines so well as the number of banks that have been started by colored people in all parts of the South. I have made a special effort recently to learn something definite of the success and something of the influence of these institutions upon the mass of the colored people. At the present time, there are no less than forty-five Negro banks in the United States. All but one or two of them are in the Southern States. Of these forty-five banks, eleven are in the State of Mississippi. Not infrequently I have found that Negro banks owe their existence to the secret and fraternal organizations. There are forty-two of these organizations, for example, in the State of Mississippi, and they collected $708,670 last year, and paid losses to the amount of $522,757. Frequently the banks have been established to serve as depositories for the funds of these institutions. They have then added a savings department, and have done banking business for an increasing number of stores and shops of various kinds that have been established within the last ten years by Negro business men.

A special study of the city of Jackson, Miss., shows that there are ninety-three businesses conducted by Negroes in that city. Of this number, forty-four concerns do a total annual business of about three hundred and eighty-eight thousand dollars a year. But, of this amount of business, one contractor alone did one hundred thousand dollars' worth. As near as could be estimated, about 73 per cent. of the colored people own or are buying their own homes. It is said that the Negroes, who make up one-half of the population, own one-third of the area of the city of Jackson. The value of this property, however, is only about one-eleventh of the taxable value of the city.

As nearly as can be estimated, Negroes have on deposit in the various banks of the city almost two hundred thousand dollars. Of this amount, more than seventy thousand is in the two Negro banks of the city. I said that most of these businesses have been started in the last ten years, but as a matter of fact one of the oldest business men in Jackson is a colored man with whom I stopped during my visit to that city. H. T. Risher is the leading business man in his particular line in Jackson. He has had a bakery and restaurant in that city, as I understand, for more than twenty years. He has one of the handsomest of the many beautiful residences of colored people in the city, which I had an opportunity to visit on my journey through the state.

Among the other business enterprises that especially attracted my attention during my journey was the drug store and offices of Dr. A. W. Dumas,[2] of Natchez. His store is located in a handsome two-story brick block, and although there are a large number of Negro druggists in the United States, I know of no store which is better kept and makes a more handsome appearance.

According to the plan of our journey, I was to spend seven days in Mississippi; starting from Memphis, Tenn., going thence to Holly Springs, Utica, Jackson, Natchez, Vicksburg, Greenville, Mound Bayou; and then, crossing the Mississippi, to spend Sunday in the city of Helena, Ark. As a matter of fact, we did stop, and I had an opportunity to speak to audiences of colored people and white people at various places along the railroad, the conductor kindly holding the train for me to do this at several points, so that I think it is safe to say that I spoke to forty or fifty thousand people during the eight days of our journey. Everywhere, I found the greatest interest and enthusiasm among both the white people and colored people for the work that we were attempting to do. In Jackson, which for the last ten years has been the centre of agitation upon the Negro question, there was some opposition expressed to the white people of the town attending the meeting, but I was told that among the people in the audience were Governor Noel;[3] Lieutenant-Governor Manship;[4] Major R. W. Millsaps,[5] who is said to be the wealthiest man in Mississippi; Bishop Charles B. Galloway, of the Methodist Episcopal Church (South); United States Marshal Edgar S. Wilson; the postmaster of Jackson, and a number of other prominent persons.

At Natchez, the white people were so interested in the object of the meeting that they expressed a desire to pay for the opera-house in which I spoke, provided that the seating-capacity would be equally divided between the two races. At Vicksburg, I spoke in a large building that had been used for some time for a roller-skating rink. I was informed that hundreds of people who wished to attend the meeting were unable to find places. At Greenville, I delivered an address in the court-house; and there were so many people who were unable to attend the address that, at the suggestion of the sheriff, I delivered a second one from the steps of the court-house.

The largest and most successful meeting of the trip was held at Mound Bayou, a town founded and controlled entirely by Negroes. This town, also, is the centre of a Negro colony of about three thousand people. Negroes own thirty thousand acres of land in direct proximity to the town. Mound Bayou is in the centre of the Delta district, where the colored people outnumber the whites frequently as much as ten to one; and there are a number of Negro settlements besides Mound Bayou in which no white man lives. My audience extended out in the surrounding fields as far as my voice could reach. I was greatly impressed with the achievements and possibilities of this town, where Negroes are giving a striking example of successful self-government and business enterprise.

From what I was able to see during my visit through Mississippi, and from what I have been able to learn from other sources, I am tempted to believe that more has been accomplished by the colored people of that state during the last ten years than was accomplished by them during the whole previous period since the Civil War. To a large extent, this has been due to the fact that the colored people have learned that in getting land, in building homes, and in saving their money they can make themselves a force in the communities in which they live. It is generally supposed that the colored man, in his efforts to rise, meets more opposition in Mississippi than anywhere else in the United States, but it is quite as true that there, more than anywhere else, the colored people seem to have discovered that, in gaining habits of thrift and industry, in getting property, and in making themselves useful, there is a door of hope open for them which the South has no disposition to close.

As an illustration of what I mean, I may say that while I was in Holly Springs I learned that, though the whites outnumbered the blacks nearly three to one in Marshall County, there had been but one lynching there since the Civil War. When I inquired of both white people and colored people why it was that the two races were able to live on such friendly terms, both gave almost exactly the same answer. They said that it was due to the fact that in Marshall County so large a number of colored farmers owned their own farms. Among other things that have doubtless helped to bring about this result is the fact that the treasurer of the Odd Fellows of Mississippi, who lives in Holly Springs, frequently has as much as two hundred thousand dollars on deposit in the local banks.

I have long been convinced that the most important work that we have been able to do at Tuskegee and through Tuskegee, during the years that the school has been in existence, has not been in the educating of six or seven thousand students to the point where they are able to do good work, but that it has been in turning the attention of the masses of the people in the direction of those fundamental things in which the interest and the desire of both races in the South are in harmony; in teaching the people the dignity of labor; and in emphasizing the importance of those simple, common, homely things which make the life of the common people sweet and wholesome and hopeful.

If circumstances would permit, I would like to carry the campaign begun in Mississippi into every state in the South.

World's Work, 17 (Feb. 1909), 11278–82.

[1] John W. Strauther, an undertaker of Greenville, Miss., spoke at the NNBL meeting in 1904 on "Fraternal Insurance."

[2] A graduate of Illinois Medical College in 1899, Dumas later operated a sanitarium.

[3] Edmund Favor Noel (1856–1927), governor of Mississippi from 1908 to 1912.

[4] Luther Manship.

[5] Reuben Webster Millsaps (1833–1916), a graduate of Harvard Law School (1858), was a major in the Confederate Army and afterward a successful cotton broker and banker in Jackson, Miss. As an active Methodist layman he helped to found Millsaps College and gave it financial support.

From Louis Bronislavovich Skarzynski[1]

New York   March 6th, 1909

Dear Mr. Washington: You were so kind as to promise me a written answer to the questions which puzzle me regarding the liquor problem in America. I should be glad to have an explanation of the subject from one so experienced as yourself in social problems.

1. Do you think that the liquor problem has any part (and if so, what part), in the solution of the entire Negro problem in the United States?

2. Do you think that the Negro race has more inclination to the abuse of liquors that [than] the white, as is claimed by some people? or that it is only the economical position of the Negros which drives them to drink?

3. Do you think that Prohibition laws are the best way to stop drinking among colored people? and do you not fear that Prohibition laws will result in secret manufacturing and secret trade of liquor?

4. Will the enforcement of the Prohibition laws not lead to the demoralisation of the police by means of bribery from those desiring to deal secretly in liquor?

5. Is the use of intoxicating liquors regarded by the Negros, as it is among certain religious denominations of the Whites, as being a violation of the laws of God? And, if so does not the sense of degradation which is felt by [a] respectable man, who has yielded to liquor, cause him to become a social outcast?

6. As prohibition laws ruin flourishing industries upon which thousands of people are dependent, do you not think that there is a lack of compensation to those who find themselves without their usual means of support?

7. Do you think that such industries can be ruined without compensation also being made to the owners of the industries?

8. The Temperance papers and the messages of several governors assert that there is an undoubted improvement in social conditions, as the result of Prohibition. Meanwhile, the consumption of liquor in the United States is increasing; how do you explain this?

9. Do you think that the Prohibition laws when made general throughout the United States will stop the consumption of liquor; if so by what new tax do you think that the Federal Government will be compensated for the loss of Doll 260,000,000 of the internal revenue?

You will oblige me very much by answering these questions, and I would ask you also to be so kind as to allow me to make use in my work of your very valuable views of this subjects.

With kindly regards yours respectfully

Count Louis Skarzynski

ALS Con. 398 BTW Papers DLC.

1 Louis Bronislavovich Skarzynski, a Polish count interested in social welfare and social reform, had formerly worked under Sergei Witte, the Russian minister of

finance (1893–1903), when Witte established the government monopoly on the manufacture and sale of alcohol.

To Warren Logan

[Hotel Manhattan, New York City] March 7, 1909

Have bricks bought in town put in foundation so bricks showing above ground will be those made by students and of uniform character. Greatly astonished at what Mr. Wheeler did.

B. T. W.

TWcIr Con. 594 BTW Papers DLC.

To Warren Logan

Hotel Manhattan, New York. March 7, 1909

Dear Mr. Logan: Your letter of March 3d has been received. I am astounded at what Mr. Wheeler has done in regard to buying bricks in town. He not only has manifested a disposition in this matter to go contrary to the policy of the school, but is evidently lacking in common sense. No matter what authority was given him in my letter, and no matter how he interpreted my letter, if he had used ordinary sense he certainly would have consulted with you and the other officers there on the grounds before entering into such a contract. I would not hesitate to ask him to give up all work on account of this action but for the fact that he could spread the news in town that he had been dismissed because of patronizing people in the town of Tuskegee. We have always boasted that we have made our own bricks, and it certainly [is] discouraging at this point to begin buying bricks from the outside when, as you say, the bricks on the grounds have not been used and when we have already begun manufacturing bricks. Yours truly,

[Booker T. Washington]

TLc Con. 594 BTW Papers DLC.

To Theodore Roosevelt

Hotel Manhattan, New York. March 9, 1909

My dear Mr. Roosevelt: If you cannot say "yes" do not say "no" in answer to this letter, but simply keep the matter in mind until your return from Africa, unless you want to decide favorably before going to Africa.

We are very anxious to have you consent to go on our Board of Trustees at Tuskegee. We have our principal meetings in New York. There is real work to be done in the South in connection with such a board, and I am sure you will enjoy it. We have a fine board of Trustees, among them Mr. Seth Low, Mr. George Foster Peabody, Mr. Robert C. Ogden, Mr. Wm. Jay Schieffelin, etc. We want to add your name.

I shall be at this hotel for several days. Yours very truly,

[Booker T. Washington]

TLc BTW Papers ATT.

To Louis Bronislavovich Skarzynski

Hotel Manhattan, New York. March 11, 1909

My dear Count Skarzynski: I just have opportunity to send a reply to your letter of March 6th. Replying thereto I would say:

1. The masses of the Negro people in the South are, as you perhaps know, a class corresponding in a way to the peasant classes of Europe. I believe that the prohibition laws as enacted in the South will not only be a great help to the Negro people themselves, but to the whites as well. This is amply borne out by the records in the police courts of such cities as Birmingham and Atlanta. The cases of one kind and another growing out of drunkenness for which heretofore large numbers of Negro men, and in some cases women, were arrested have been reduced from 60 to 75 per cent. I think that the money which formerly went for liquor, etc., is now more satisfactorily used.

2. Taken as a whole, I do not think that the Negro people have any more inclination to the use of liquor than other races. Of course the contrary claim is often made, but my opinion is as stated.

3. I do not believe that, taken as a whole, the Negro people will be found secretly promoting traffic in liquor. I believe in the Southern States, as a whole, that the prohibition laws are being honestly enforced. Whenever I have had opportunity I have urged our people as strongly as I could to see that the liquor laws are enforced. I hand you herewith some declarations of a Conference recently held at Tuskegee in which reference is made to this matter of enforcing the prohibition laws.

4. I am unable to make any statement regarding your fourth inquiry.

5. I think that the more thoughtful classes of Negroes quite sincerely deprecate the use of liquor among the masses of our people, as we have some knowledge of the demoralizing degradation which its use has wrought among us.

I am unable to submit any statements with reference to numbers 6 and 7.

8. I am unable to account for the increase in the consumption of liquor, if this is true. I do know, however, that in the South there is not such consumption of liquor as was true before the prohibition laws were passed.

9. Congress is to meet in special session March 15th. I do not know just what special action will be undertaken to make up the loss in dollars because of the decrease from internal revenue taxes. It has been suggested that an inheritance tax or a tax on proprietary medicines, on bank checks, stocks, bonds, telegrams, etc., may be resorted to to make up the deficit.

I have the honor to enclose herewith several letters of introduction in accordance with my promise. Yours very truly,

[Booker T. Washington]

TLc   Con. 398   BTW Papers   DLC.

From Theodore Roosevelt

New York, March 12th, 1909

My dear Dr. Washington: Doubtless I shall accept, but do not ask me to make a definite promise until I get back from Africa. Sincerely yours,

Theodore Roosevelt

TLSr Copy BTW Papers ATT.

To James Hardy Dillard

Greenville, S.C. March 20, 1909

My dear Dr. Dillard: Your kind letter of March 12th has been received, and I note what you say regarding the executive committee meeting later on. I agree with your plan. The Tuskegee trustees meet in New York sometime during the latter part of June. Several of our trustees are members of the executive committee. Would it be agreeable to have the executive committee meeting either the day before or the day following our trustee meeting?

I think you are right in the policy of moving slowly but in constructive directions.

I am spending this week traveling through the state of South Carolina speaking at meetings three and four times a day on education. I am simply amazed at the interest manifested. Wherever I have gone, as large a proportion of white people have attended as colored people, I mean in proportion to the population. For example, yesterday in Sumter I must have spoken to 300 white men and women, the same being true last night in Florence. I wish you could hear some of the addresses delivered by mayors and leading white citizens where I have gone. The white Baptist minister who introduced me in Sumter said the time had come when Southern white people must stop lying about the Negro, stop lying and deceiving themselves and face the facts.

I am very, very glad that you are finding such good fields for

73

effective work in Virginia and North Carolina. South Carolina is full of promise. Yours very truly,

[Booker T. Washington]

TLc   Con. 44   BTW Papers   DLC.

James A. Cobb to Emmett Jay Scott

Washington, D.C. March 22, 1909

Dear Emmett: I wish very much that at your earliest convenience you would have the Dr. drop a line to the Pres., calling his attention to Judge Terrell and myself in order that he may know who is interested in us when our cases come before him. Personally, I have no fears, if Mr. Taft adheres to his rule, namely, only efficiency will count in the department of Justice, but I prefer to be on the safe side. There are so many rumors afloat as to candidates, especially for the judge's place, I think that we ought to get busy. Baker[1] says that he will give me a clean bill of health, but as you know he is white, and while I believe that he prefers me over any other colored man, he would probably have no hesitancy in sacrificing me for a white man. I dislike very much to bother you and the Dr. further but it is so much easier to attend to such matters before than afterwards.

Kindly let me hear from you and let me know how you feel about the matter. If all I hear be true there will be a vacancy in the recordership. Sincerely,

Jim

ALS   Con. 44   BTW Papers   DLC.

1 Daniel W. Baker, born in Maryland, was a U.S. attorney with the U.S. circuit and district courts of the District of Columbia. Four years earlier BTW wrote him urging the appointment of Cobb as an assistant in his office, apparently with success. (Dec. 13, 1905, Con. 2, BTW Papers, DLC.)

Emmett Jay Scott to J. Frank Wheaton[1]

[Tuskegee, Ala.] March 23, 1909

My dear Friend: Will you not, in your own way, put this matter before Mr. Jack Johnson.[2] Tell him that I write to him, as I do, simply and only because as a fellow Texan, I am not only interested in his achievements, but proud of him as well; and because I want him to do the absolutely proper and dignified thing. I am not at all disposed to have him think that I am inclined to meddle in any of his affairs, but I think it would be well for him to take counsel of those who have nothing to gain and who are interested only because they want to see him continue to succeed. The point of my letter is this:

I very much hope that Johnson will give as few interviews to the newspapers as possible, and that he will refrain from anything resembling boastfulness in his interviews. We all believe that he can defeat Jeffries,[3] but I think it would be much better for him not to boast about what he is going to do in that particular, but simply stand on his record and on the statement that "he would fight any living man for the Heavy Weight Championship of the World."

And then, too, if there is any possible way for him to again bring it about, I wish that he might again get the services of Sam Fitzpatrick[4] as manager. I am sure, he will have much to gain and practically nothing to lose from Fitzpatrick's management. I was just a bit disturbed by Fitzpatrick's statement that Johnson was hard to manage after winning a fight, simply and only because I do not like white men to feel that Negroes cannot stand large prosperity.

You can talk these matters over with Johnson in your own way, and can write to me whenever you can find the time to do so. Yours very truly,

[Emmett J. Scott]

TLp Con. 48 BTW Papers DLC.

[1] J. Frank Wheaton was a black criminal lawyer in New York City and was active in civic and civil rights actions in Harlem. Born in 1866 in Hagerstown, Md., he studied law at Howard University and received an LL.B. degree from the University of Minnesota in 1894. He began to practice law in Hagerstown in 1893, and was clerk of the municipal court of Minneapolis from 1895 to 1899. He served as a Republican in the Minnesota House of Representatives in 1898–1900 and was a delegate to Republican national conventions in 1888, 1896, and 1900. Establishing the law

firm of Wheaton and Curtis in New York City about 1901, Wheaton was successful in a number of murder trials in that city. He was a co-founder in 1911 of the Equity Congress, a civic organization which financed suits challenging restrictive covenants, fought the spread of vice in the neighborhood, and encouraged blacks to patronize black businesses.

2 John Arthur Johnson (1878–1946), better known as Jack Johnson, was born in Galveston, Tex. He began prizefighting in 1899 and became the first black heavyweight champion on Dec. 26, 1908, when he defeated Tommy Burns in a fight held in Australia. Johnson's colorful and flamboyant style, his penchant for fine clothes and expensive jewelry, and his private life, which included three marriages to white women, made him one of the most controversial boxers of all time.

In 1912 Johnson was accused of violation of the Mann Act and fled to Europe, where he lived in exile for eight years. In 1915 he lost his title to Jess Willard in a twenty-six round bout in Havana, Cuba. Johnson returned to the United States in 1920 and served his jail sentence of a year and a day. After his release from prison he resumed boxing at exhibitions and in cabarets until the late 1920s. He was killed in an automobile accident in Raleigh, N.C., in 1946. (See Farr, *Black Champion;* Gilmore, *Bad Nigger!*)

BTW's attitude toward Johnson was rather ambivalent. Probably not unlike Emmett J. Scott in the above letter, BTW was proud that there was a black champion, but sorry it had to be someone as controversial and unconventional as Johnson. Before Johnson's famous fight with James Jeffries on July 4, 1910, BTW turned down an offer of $1,000 and all expenses paid to attend the fight as a reporter for the Denver *Post*. (Frederick G. Bonfils to BTW, Apr. 25, May 21, 1910, Con. 402, BTW Papers, DLC; BTW to Bonfils, May 17, May 23, 1910, Con. 402, BTW Papers, DLC.) BTW was interested in the fight, however, and at Tuskegee a special assembly room was set aside to receive telegraphic reports of the Reno, Nev., fight while it was in progress. (Charles H. Fearing to E. J. Scott, May 10, 1910, Con. 596, BTW Papers, DLC.)

It was Emmett J. Scott who had direct correspondence with Johnson, and there is some evidence that Scott's wife was a former schoolmate of Johnson's in Texas. (P. M. Ashburn to Scott, ca. July 5, 1910, Con. 401, BTW Papers, DLC.) John H. Washington, Jr., BTW's nephew, acted as an emissary to Johnson's California training camp before the Jeffries fight and reported to Scott on Johnson's lavish style of living and his disapproval of Johnson's wife. Young Washington wrote to Scott that the boxer had "ruined himself when he married in to the other world." (May 24, 1910, Con. 414, BTW Papers, DLC.) At the time of Johnson's indictment for violation of the Mann Act, BTW issued a statement condemning the crime Johnson was accused of, but reserving any condemnation of the champion until the courts had spoken. The statement was actually prepared at Tuskegee in BTW's absence by Scott and Robert E. Park. (See A Statement on Jack Johnson for the United Press Association, Oct. 23, 1912, below, vol. 11; BTW to Scott, Oct. 24, 1912, Con. 619, BTW Papers, DLC.)

3 James J. Jeffries (1875–1953), world heavyweight champion (1899–1905), returned from retirement in 1910 to fight Jack Johnson, who defeated him.

4 Sam Fitzpatrick was Jack Johnson's manager until Johnson won the heavyweight title in late 1908, when the two men parted company.

To William Howard Taft

New York, March 25, 1909

Dr. Frissell finds it impossible to go to Liberia. Think it important that white man with wide and successful experience in working with colored people at the south be selected as third man if possible. Will communicate with you later regarding such man.

Booker T. Washington

TWSr   William Howard Taft Papers   DLC.

To Jesse Edward Moorland

New York City. March 25, 1909

Personal

My dear Dr. Moorland: This is confidential of course. Enclosed I send you a copy of a letter which I have just written to President Thirkield. This is the second or third time that I have received this kind of notice, and I think the time has come to end this kind of business.

It is my opinion that the real business which the trustees should look after is being attended to by the executive committee and sub-committees. I think that the trustees should do the business of the institution and not parcel it out in so large a degree to the executive committee or any sub-committee. Sending out notices of this character enables two or three people to do whatever they wish to do regarding the institution, and if I stay on the board a change will have to be made in this method of doing business. Yours very truly,

Booker T. Washington

TLS   Jesse Edward Moorland Collection   DHU.

To Wilbur Patterson Thirkield

Hotel Manhattan, New York. March 25, 1909

My dear Dr. Thirkield: Your letter dated March 17th notifying me of a meeting of the Building Committee on March 18th has been received. Of course a notice written on the 17th notifying me of a meeting to take place on the following day means absolutely nothing so far as my attendance is concerned. It seems to me that if the attendance of members is desired, that such meetings should be planned for some distance ahead — at least a week — otherwise it is impossible for anybody to arrange to attend who has business of his own. I should like to attend such meetings whenever it is possible, but it is not possible for me to do so unless I have proper notice. In the case of our own trustees at Tuskegee, I always see to it that they are not only notified ahead of the meetings, but whenever possible I consult their convenience as to when they can attend meetings. I believe this would be a good policy for Howard to pursue. Yours very truly,

[Booker T. Washington]

TLc   Jesse Edward Moorland Collection   DHU.

From William James

Cambridge [Mass.]. March 28. 09

Dear Mr. Washington   I have been steeling my heart against the appeals of all institutions for money in the past 2 or 3 years, for such very heavy burdens have come on me in the way of helping individuals, not all of whom are blood relatives, that I have said "let other men take care of institutions, I can do no more." Nevertheless I have such a sentiment towards *you* and towards the gospel work you are doing for both the black and the white people, that I must send you a paltry $50.00, and sorrowfully say at the same time that I can't do it next year.

How any multimillionaire, after reading "Up from Slavery," can refrain from opening his bank account to your draughts freely,

I have never been able to understand. The colored people of this land have now perhaps the greatest opportunity ever put in reach of a people to build up a tribal life, so to speak, based on the moral realities & simplicities, and divorced from the shams and vanities, that are eating into the heart of the wealthy white civilization around them. Could large numbers of them but see it, and identify their race with those ideals, they would be missionaries in our midst, in the end, and be a precious saving element in our whole civilization, setting patterns for the sounder whites to follow. Already your methods of industrial education have set such patterns. It is all in the lap of God, who will preserve you, I trust, dear Mr. Washington, for many a long year yet to be one of our most precious citizens and a ferment of social rightness for our entire population.

With best regards to Mrs Washington, believe me most sincerely yours,

Wm James

Some paragraphs in your Lincoln address were *splendid.*

ALS   Con. 735   BTW Papers   DLC.

To Edgar Gardner Murphy

[Tuskegee, Ala.] April 1, 1909

My dear Mr. Murphy: I am so glad to know that you are again in Alabama.

No program has so far been printed for the exercises on the 4th but they take place at half past two o'clock. We shall be very glad to have you present. Mr. Ogden is to be present and speak.

I do hope you can come here before I go North again. I shall be here until the 7th. On that day I go to Nashville to speak before the Theological Department of Vanderbilt University. I spoke there three years ago to both the students and the ministers of the town and I felt quite sure that great good was accomplished.

I was simply amazed at the reception which was accorded me throughout the state of South Carolina. There are some of the finest and best white men and women in that state that I know of.

They did everything possible to make our work profitable and pleasant while in the state. In Anderson, S.C., the richest white people in the town gave us their carriages with their coachmen to use for the day. The railroad conductors went out of their way to be kind, stopping the trains wherever we wished them to be stopped in order that we might speak to the people at the stations. This is the real kind of work that I wish I could devote a large part of my life to.

I shall be very glad to read the proof of your book,[1] or any part of it, after I get settled for the summer.

I think that after my visit to Nashville I shall be returning here for a stay of several days.

One thing that struck me regarding South Carolina so far as the education of the Negro is concerned is the matter of ignorance on the part of the white people as to just what conditions are. When I told the white audiences, as I did, about the Negro school in their state in the country being in session only two or three months, they seemed shocked. In some way we must let the white people in the South know just what we are trying to do in the way of education, just what we hope to accomplish and what conditions are.

I am very sorry to hear that you have had another bad turn. I hope you are now well. Yours very truly,

Booker T. Washington

TLpS Con. 47 BTW Papers DLC.

[1] *The Basis of Ascendancy: A Discussion of Certain Principles of Public Policy Involved in the Development of the Southern States* (1909).

From Emmett Jay Scott

Washington: April first, 1909

Dear Mr. Washington: I beg to report as I have already wired you: 1. That Judge Hundley has seen the Attorney General[1] twice (once yesterday & once today — after he had seen the President[)]. The latter asked him to put before the Attorney General an explanation he had made in respect to certain additional charges brought against him. He considers the interviews with the Attorney General as most satisfactory but the President did not commit himself. He only listened to him in the way of a hearing. I have not succeeded in seeing Mr. Wickersham.

2. Cohen & Kuntz[2] went first to see Mr Hitchcock. He saw them Tuesday. The whole situation as you understand it was explained to him and he wound up by saying their concessions were entirely fair & considerate & that they ought to get together along the lines of Cohen's suggestion. He also said they had been most patient. They went to see the President who told them on Wednesday he c'd not talk quite as satisfactorily as they desired & asked them to come back today. They went back with this result: They first of all (at my suggestion) explained how anxious they were not to embarrass the administration at the beginning by squabbling, but that the other fellows would listen to no effort to get them together & were going ahead making recommendations for office before the reorganization was perfected. He asked them whom the lily whites were recommending & took the names of both of them. He asked Kuntz & Cohen if they objected & their reply was simply that Mr Roosevelt had refused to appoint Beehan[3] to the Post office & that the other man was a rank *lily white.* He asked them (Cohen & Kuntz) whom they wanted in these places & they replied they had not come to annoy him about patronage (but about the reorganization) & were not yet ready to submit any names. He asked them to let him know *whom they wanted* & went further to [and] told Cohen he deserved recognition & that he wanted *him* (Cohen) to write him regularly & let him know of conditions in the South, & especially in Louisiana. He spoke of the poor showing of the lily whites in La — & also told Cohen as he had told you of his intention to reappoint him — & when Cohen mentioned about the pay of the place he said the consolidated office sh'd be located at *New Orleans* & that Cohen ought to receive a satisfactory salary. They express themselves as being overjoyed at the success of their *interviews* & of the hearty way the President received them. Capers was in & *near* them when the President told Cohen he meant to continue him in office. The President was pleased with the letters from white business men asking Cohen's reappointment, & had already told Senator Foster[4] (of La) he intended recognizing colored men in that state.

3. Banks of Miss. & 11 (eleven) others from that State saw the Pres-

ident also today. I dont consider the trip a success in the light of the expense they went to in coming here, but *Banks* seems pleased. They read a memorial (which I suggested they get in The Star) & introduced the party & told the President what they *each* stand for. He was jovial in receiving them & when Banks handed him a newspaper clipping saying all colored postmasters are to be removed, He said pay no attention to these reports.

4. The State Dept. is in communication with Dr Buttrick trying to get in touch with Dr Sale.[5] Shall know tomorrow if he is reached.

May go on King Luise[6] Steamer Apr 10 — making effort to that end. Yours truly

Emmett J. Scott

ALS   Con. 46   BTW Papers   DLC.

[1] George Woodward Wickersham (1858–1936) was U.S. Attorney General from 1909 to 1913.

[2] Emile Kuntz was a white investment banker in New Orleans and a leader of Walter Cohen's black-and-tan faction of Louisiana Republicans.

[3] William J. Behan.

[4] Murphy James Foster (1849–1921), a Democrat, was an anti-lottery governor of Louisiana (1892–1900), U.S. senator (1901–13), and collector of the port of New Orleans (1914–21).

[5] George Sale (1856–1911), born and educated in Canada, was president of Atlanta Baptist College from 1890 to 1906. He then became superintendent of education for the Baptist Home Missionary Society. Sale was one of the three U.S. commissioners to Liberia in 1909. BTW was relieved when Sale accepted the post. "From the very first," he wrote Sale, "yours was among the names that I wanted to have the President consider." In late March, BTW, Wallace Buttrick, and Hollis B. Frissell called on President Taft to urge Sale's appointment. (BTW to Sale, Apr. 2, 1909, Con. 398, BTW Papers, DLC.) Fred R. Moore, in a letter to the New York *Times*, praised Sale as being "most free from racial prejudice." Moore said that Sale would not object to serving on a commission with a black man since he had eaten at the same table and slept in the same building with blacks for years. (Fred R. Moore to the editor of the New York *Times*, Apr. 19, 1909, Con. 396, BTW Papers, DLC.)

[6] The *Koenigin Luise.*

Timothy Thomas Fortune to Emmett Jay Scott

Maple Hall   Red Bank, N.J., April 1, 1909

My dear Mr. Scott: In reply to your letter of the 23rd. ult., permit me to say that after further consideration of the matter, and in light of developments in the Liberian Commission appointments, in which my application was turned down in each of the three compositions of the Commission, I think it just and prudent to make a return of my letters to Dr. Washington a condition of my return of his to you.[1] Very respectfully

T. Thos. Fortune

ALS Con. 45 BTW Papers DLC.

[1] BTW agreed to return the letters. (See BTW to Fortune, May 11, 1909, below.)

To George Foster Peabody

[Tuskegee, Ala.] April 2, 1909

My dear Mr. Peabody: I am thinking very seriously of using the principal instead of the interest only of the Ten Thousand Dollars, which Miss Jeanes placed in my hands sometime before she died. I am quite sure that Miss Jeanes meant that I use my judgement in the use of this money, either using the principal or the interest. Just now however, I am actuated by two motives:

First, you will note by the enclosed statement that we have gotten into quite a considerable tangle on account of having used more of the interest from the $200,000 than we should have used. This came about by reason of the fact that Hampton was slow in beginning to use this money and we went ahead, using more than we should have used. The result is, we shall have to wait a good many months before Hampton catches up. In the meantime, we have seriously obligated ourselves to people who have been erecting schoolhouses on condition that if they raised so much, they would get so much from us. You can see how awkward the conditions are. My experience and observation convince me that a small amount of money spent now in the erection of a schoolhouse will do more good than much money spent in the future in some other direction. I find that when the people get a good schoolhouse in their midst, that it settles a lot of other problems. In the first place, it means a better teacher, a longer school term and the schoolhouse becomes a social center for the neighborhood. In a word, I believe that for the present and for the future, I could help the race much better by using of [up?] this money for the building of schoolhouses than by merely spending the small interest which accrues each year.

Another consideration is this. At my death, I should not care to have any question about the ownership and use of this fund. As it is now, it is a personal matter, but the main point is in connection with the tangle in which we have gotten, and if we do not get money to meet our obligations, we will be seriously crippled and the work generally hurt.

I am glad to hear that your health continues to improve. Yours very truly,

Booker T. Washington

TLpS   Con. 47   BTW Papers   DLC.

To Richard Olney[1]

[Tuskegee, Ala.] April 2, 1909

Personal

My dear Sir: I understand that a meeting is to be held sometime in May at which time the Peabody Fund will be distributed among institutions in the South.

I am writing to ask you to keep in mind the claims of the Tuskegee Normal and Industrial Institute in the final distribution of this fund.

In connection with our application, I think you will find that there is an erroneous impression existing in the minds of some concerning the wealth of this institution. We are not wealthy, but our needs are constant and pressing. While we have more in the way of equipment and endowment than some other institutions, our expenses are much larger. We have, however, this advantage: I think we have a plant and an organization that can spend money to the best advantage. We also have a board of trustees that I think will command the confidence of the Peabody Board.

You may not think it, but nevertheless it is true, the colored people in the South at the present time receive a very small proportion of the public school money. I am sure that where $12 is spent for the education of a white child in the South, only $1 is spent for the education of a black child. That is about the present ration.

The colored people feel that in the final distribution of this fund they should have a generous share. Yours very truly,

Booker T. Washington

TLpS   Con. 897   BTW Papers   DLC.

[1] Olney was a trustee of the Peabody Education Fund, which was then considering the distribution of its principal among white and black schools in the South. BTW sent the same letter to William C. Doane, George Peabody Wetmore, Joseph H. Choate, and William Lawrence.

From William Henry Lewis

Boston, Mass. April 3rd, 1909

PERSONAL:

Dear Mr. Washington: Recalling my conversation with the President, you will remember that I told you he said he intended to see that I was taken care of and suggested that there were positions open to attorneys in the Department of Justice. I told the President if I could have my heart's desire I would like to be appointed an Assistant Attorney General of the United States. The President said that those places were few but stated that I might submit any endorsements which I might obtain to the Attorney General — the Honorable George W. Wickersham. I enclose copies of the endorsements which I have received to date for your information. The originals of these letters I have sent to the Attorney General through Senator Crane.

I feel that the President would make the appointment if Mr. Wickersham would suggest it.

I know that you are perfectly willing and ready to help in any way you can — the method I leave to you. I thought I might suggest this, however, that if there are any attorneys in New York City, who presumably would know Mr. Wickersham, and whom you could interest in me, it would be a great help.

I feel confident that if I can obtain the appointment, by hard work I shall be able to make good and to give entire satisfaction. Believe me, Sincerely yours, etc.

William H. Lewis

TLS Con. 393 BTW Papers DLC. Fourteen letters of recommendation of Lewis were enclosed.

To William Henry Lewis

[Tuskegee, Ala.] April 5, 1909

Personal

My dear Mr. Lewis: I thank you very much for the letter which you have sent me together with the enclosures. It seems to me that you are proceeding on right lines. When the proper time comes in my own way I shall endeavor to do what I can to assist you. Please keep me informed of any new developments. Those endorsements would reflect credit upon any man in the state of Massachusetts, and they are from people who would not say what they do unless they felt it.

While I am writing, I must call your attention to one other matter. There is a fellow in New York whose name I need not call,[1] who is very active just now trying to get a certain office. This man plays on every side of every question and is constantly unfriendly to our forces. No man was more bitter in condemnation of President Taft and President Roosevelt than he was; in fact he led the fight, as you know, in the attempt to break up the Florida convention when it tried to endorse President Taft. He claims you, as one of his friends and one of his supporters. I think he exhibits one of your letters and makes use of it as showing your friendship and states that you always look him up when you come to New York. My own experience is that the best way is to make these fellows play straight, and the only way to make them play straight is to make them come out as our friends or our foes. Yours very truly,

Booker T. Washington

TLpS Con. 393 BTW Papers DLC.

[1] J. Douglas Wetmore.

To William Loeb, Jr.

[Tuskegee, Ala.] April 6, 1909

Personal and Confidential.

My dear Mr. Loeb: A little fellow, J. Douglas Wetmore, whom I think you will remember as trying to embarrass the President when he introduced him in Jacksonville, Florida and who has been rather pestiferous ever since, is trying to be appointed Assistant District Attorney under Mr. Wise[1] in New York. Wetmore was one of the most persistent and dirty of President Roosevelt's abusers during the latter months of his administration and this same Wetmore was the man who went from New York to Augusta, Ga. to break up the convention there and thus prevent it from endorsing Mr. Taft.

I wish you would, if you have not already done so, call Charles W. Anderson in and get his full history from Mr. Anderson. It would be a great pity for a man of this type to receive any recognition at the hands of the national administration. Yours sincerely,

Booker T. Washington

TLpS Con. 45 BTW Papers DLC.

[1] Henry Alexander Wise (b. 1874), U.S. attorney for the southern district of New York from 1909 to 1913.

To Charles William Anderson

[Tuskegee, Ala.] April 10, 1909

Personal and Confidential.

My dear Mr. Anderson: Enclosed, I return the Stewart letter,[1] which I have read with interest. It seems to me that the situation is pretty well taken care of now, though we shall have to watch it. When I get to New York, I will try to have a talk with Moore and see if I cannot have him start out in the direction you suggest. If he were to punch Bennet[2] up, it would do good.

I have said nothing to the President about only having one Negro on the Liberian Commission. The fact was, the State Department, months ago, decided itself that it would have only one Negro on the Liberian Commission. Yours very truly,

Booker T. Washington

TLpS   Con. 43   BTW Papers   DLC.

1 Anderson had written on Apr. 4, 1909, enclosing a letter of Gilchrist Stewart urging the appointment of J. Douglas Wetmore as assistant U.S. attorney in New York. Anderson's Colored Republican Club of the City of New York, however, endorsed Theodore E. Hill for the post. (Con. 43, BTW Papers, DLC.)

2 William Stiles Bennet (1870–1962), Republican congressman from New York City (1905–11, 1915–17). In 1920 he moved to Chicago and resumed practice as a corporation lawyer. Bennet was one of Wetmore's supporters, and Anderson had written BTW: "Moore ought to be instructed to sail into these fellows, who are white men socially, and Negroes for profit." He urged also that Moore should explain to such Republican leaders as Bennet that Wetmore and Stewart had been "violently anti-Taft before the convention." (Apr. 4, 1909, Con. 43, BTW Papers, DLC.)

To Ray Stannard Baker

[Tuskegee, Ala.] April 13, 1909

My dear Mr. Baker: I regret that owing to the want of time I cannot answer your letter regarding liquor as satisfactorily as I should like. My own view of the case is this. Prohibition helps the Negro throughout the South immensely. True, some get liquor, but my observation in a general way convinces me that where one man gets liquor ten are prevented from getting it. I also note that since prohibition came into effect that our people are saving money, are working harder, but I have not the time to back these statements up with detailed information of a convincing character. I do not believe that our people are wasting money in other ways that they formerly spent for whiskey. They are putting it into the bank and are beginning to buy property. Yours very truly,

Booker T. Washington

TLpS   Con. 387   BTW Papers   DLC.

To Susan Helen Porter

New York, April 18th, 1909

My dear Miss Porter: I did not have time to answer your letter[1] before leaving Tuskegee, and then again I wanted time to fully consider what you had said.

Of course in the final analysis, you of yourself will have to be the judge; I can only suggest and advise. My own belief is that there is no reason for your resigning. I do think as the years go on that you will get suggestions and information from experience that will help you in several directions, as all of us have to be helped. I think as a rule you take matters most too seriously, that is to say that you keep yourself keyed up to too high a nervous tension. This I think you can overcome by experience. I think too, as I stated to you, that as the years go on that one accomplishes his purpose more effectually and more speedily by working with people, rather than seeming to do that which opposes their inclinations and wishes.

In dealing, of course, with untrained young people there is to be a lot of opposing and a lot of negative work. But gradually one learns to make the constructive and positive work so great and impressive that the negative side is minimized. I think you will get a great deal of help by leaving aside many of the little details that now take your time and strength, and give yourself a large amount of time, in fact a number of hours each day for careful constructural work. You ought to have several hours each day that you could give in an undisturbed manner in talking with teachers and students in getting hold of their views and their wishes. A very large proportion of the mere routine office work, merely telling students what they can and what they cannot do I think can be given to somebody else, leaving you for the larger and more important work of devising and constructing plans for the higher development of the girls. Suppose you let the whole matter stand over until I return to Tuskegee.[2] Yours truly,

[Booker T. Washington]

TLc Con. 594 BTW Papers DLC.

[1] She offered her resignation on account of "too many unfavorable criticisms con-

cerning my work," and asked for a letter of recommendation. (Porter to BTW, Apr. 15, 1909, Con. 594, BTW Papers, DLC.)

[2] She remained as dean of the women's department, taking a year's leave of absence in 1912–13 but returning to her position until after BTW's death.

To W. C. Buckner[1]

[Hotel Manhattan, New York City] April Nineteenth, 1909

Dear Sir: In reply to your letter of April 3,[2] let me say that the Negro plantation hymns to which you refer are only a small part of the music that was produced by the plantation Negroes during the period of slavery. In those days these songs were about the only means the Negro had of pouring out his feelings. In the morning, going to work; and in the evening twilight, coming back to "quarters"; or whenever there was anything that tended to heighten his feelings, the Negro expressed those feelings in a song.

These songs have, in my opinion, played a great part in the life of the members of my race. They helped to lighten their labors; and to relieve their minds from the feelings of sorrow and despair that would have left them embittered, if they had not found expression and relief in this way. These songs have enabled the Negro in all his trials to retain his cheerfulness, and this has permitted him to live where other primitive peoples have died out.

The plantation hymns, that is the songs that were and are still sung in the churches, are the only documents we have for studying and understanding the inner life of the Negro during the long period before he had the opportunity or ability to express himself in a literary form.

I am glad to know that you are making a study of these songs. I suggest to you that you study the words as well as the music for you will find in these words many flashes of imagination; many picturesque and exceedingly condensed expressions, which show genuine literary quality. Very truly yours,

[Booker T. Washington]

TLc Con. 388 BTW Papers DLC.

[1] W. C. Buckner, a white man, was manager of "The Original Dixie Jubilee Concert Company and the Columbia Tennessean Jubilee Singers."

[2] Buckner to BTW, Apr. 3, 1909, Con. 388, BTW Papers, DLC.

To James A. Cobb

New York. Apr. 21, 1909

My dear Mr. Cobb: I meant to have begged your pardon for making the suggestion when we were in the President's room yesterday that I wanted to talk with him alone. The fact is that the big fellow is getting down to brass tacks now on you fellows and he wanted to ask me some important questions. Yours very truly,

[Booker T. Washington]

TLc   Con. 44   BTW Papers   DLC.

To William Howard Taft

[Hotel Manhattan, New York City] April 23, 1909

My dear Mr. President: When I was in Washington a few days ago, I meant to have told to you in effect the same thing which I told President Roosevelt in regard to Mr. Cohen of Louisiana because I think you ought to know all the facts. Some years ago before he was put into office, Mr. Cohen led rather a fast and unbecoming life, but I am in a position to state unhesitatingly that during all the time that he has been holding office and for some time before he has led a clean, upright life, and I know no man of our race at the present time whose life is more faultless than is the case of him. I make this statement all the more boldly because I have taken numerous occasions within recent years to make thorough investigation for myself, and in every case I found that he was leading a straight life.

Some time when you are not under such pressure, I wish that you could set a time when I could see you when we could go over the whole situation so far as the colored men in office are concerned with a good deal of deliberation. I shall be going North several times within the next few months and could stop either as I go or as I return for this purpose. There are several important points that cannot be covered in a brief conversation.[1]

I shall be writing you soon regarding Mr. Goodhue.[2] Yours truly,

[Booker T. Washington]

TLc   Con. 48   BTW Papers   DLC.

[1] Taft replied that he would meet with BTW but could not promise as much of his time as BTW might need. (Apr. 26, 1909, William Howard Taft Papers, DLC.)

[2] BTW reported Amos Goodhue of Gadsden, Ala., to be "a good fellow and that is about all," not an active Republican in Alabama. (BTW to Taft, May 3, 1909, Con. 48, BTW Papers, DLC.)

To George Eastman

Hotel Manhattan, New York. April 25, 1909

My dear Mr. Eastman: I want to thank you for the privilege of going through your works at Kodak Park. What I saw there was not only a revelation to me, but I got many new ideas which I can put into practice at Tuskegee. Everyone was most kind to me there.

Let me thank you in closing again for your very generous gift to our institution. You cannot realize what a load this lifts from my shoulders and how much additional good it will help us to accomplish. Yours very truly,

[Booker T. Washington]

TLc   Con. 390   BTW Papers   DLC.

From Charles H. Fearing[1]

Tuskegee Ala   Apl 29 1909

Mr. Oswald G. Villard telegraphs from New York as follows: ["]Is Melvin J. Chisum an honest reliable person asks me for loan."

Charles H. Fearing

HWSr   Con. 587   BTW Papers   DLC.

1 Charles H. Fearing was assistant secretary to the principal of Tuskegee Institute from 1908 until after BTW's death. He also served as associate editor of the *Tuskegee Student*.

To Hugh Mason Browne

New York. May 1, 1909

Dear Mr. Browne: Dr. Du Bois has really a very fine and sensible article in the May World's Work.[1] What would you think of having the Committee send it out? I do not know how Du Bois would take such a suggestion nor how the members of the Committee would take it. Du Bois is such a big dunce that one never knows how to take him, but I have an idea that he is learning a little sense but I am not sure of this. Yours very truly,

Booker T. Washington

TLS BTW Papers ATT.

1 W. E. B. Du Bois, "Georgia Negroes and Their Fifty Millions of Savings," *World's Work*, 18 (May 1909), 11550–54. Du Bois concluded that savings banks and ownership of land were keys to the economic emancipation of blacks.

To George Washington Carver

Hotel Manhattan, New York. May 2, 1909

My dear Mr. Carver: I have received your letter bearing upon the poultry yard, also your report of the analysis of the eggs. I confess that the report does not interest me over-much. What I want you to do is to devise some means by which you can get fowls. These reports which simply discuss matters pro and con do not help you in your getting of young fowls. I hope that you will buckle down to it and make a real earnest effort to have the poultry yard succeed. We have done everything that you have asked us to do. The poultry yard was built according to your directions, and I am sure we have bought everything in the way of eggs and fowls that you wanted; it only remains now for you to determine whether or not you can raise poultry.

93

I can see no reason why we cannot get some results from the geese and ducks. With the large number of geese and ducks on hand we ought to have two or three hundred young ones of each kind, but as it is we have almost nothing. Certainly we are not being troubled with the sore head, neither should there be any trouble about the eggs of the geese and ducks. I think what is most needed is for you to make an earnest effort to master the incubators so as to get some young fowls out of the eggs. Nobody in the South has such an excellent chance to show what can be done in raising poultry as you have right now at Tuskegee, and I hope that you can bring about results. The weather is unusually cool, and I am sure that you can with safety use the incubators up until the 20th or 25th of June.

You will remember that it was at your request that we stopped buying eggs from a distance.

A good many people have the idea that we are not able to put in practice what is taught in the class room in the agricultural teaching. Here is an excellent chance for you to show that you cannot only give instruction in the class room in poultry raising but you can actually get results in the poultry yard.

The poultry yard was moved from the old site because you said it was wholly unsuited for raising poultry, and this I agreed with, but certainly none of the excuses that existed in the old yard can apply to the present site.

I think if everybody will simply stop thinking and talking about difficulties and what prevents success and go to talking and working in the direction of getting chickens and at the same time be determined to get them regardless of difficulties that you will succeed. Yours truly,

[Booker T. Washington]

TLc Con. 589 BTW Papers DLC.

From Emmett Jay Scott

St Vincent: Cape Verde Islands: May 3, '09

My Dear Mr. Washington: I am pleased to report our safe arrival at this port. The trip out was pleasant in every way. The weather was not very rough, & except for three days of illness I came in feeling quite all right.

Capt. Wilson[1] of the *Chester* has been agreeable & in every [way] most kind & considerate of me. The officers *in the main* have also been agreeable. We have had our meals in the *Cabin mess* the Captain's sumptuous quarters & he only has been a *fellow diner*. So much for the newspaper sensations.[2] This place: St Vincent is of volcanic formation; & is one of the Cape Verde group. Some 10,000 colored people & about 250 to 300 English & Portug[u]ese live here. The place situated at the foot of the base of the mountain is rather pretty but the condition of the people is pitiable. I never saw in any city in America such hopeless conditions among the Negro people as I see here. They are poor: very poor: pitiably wretched with diseases which distort their limbs & their faces (in many cases) & have almost nothing upon which to live. Agriculture is practically impossible & it w'd take more than I saw Saturday to convince me they w'd care to work even if they c'd succeed at agriculture. The beggars are everywhere & they torture you with their appeals for money — for pennies, for anything. The women are a *modest* set & wash & iron & sell products in the quaint, picturesque market in the center of the town. These products are a variety of bean, some coarse tropical yams, fish & a few other things of a not altogether nutritious variety. I saw one poor dilapidated fellow going home joyfully from market with *one* coarse *yam* & *one* piece of dry fish! Think of that for a Sunday meal!! I shall of course talk more of this when I see you again.

We leave here tomorrow (Tuesday) for Liberia. The *Birmingham* came into port 2½ hours behind us & with leaky tubes. She will have to remain here till next Saturday & will be that late in joining us at Monrovia. We finish coaling today. I am very sorry that the squadron continues to diminish as we approach the *Black Republic*. We are going to (on my suggestion) take a week out of our 30 days (the last week) to visit Sierre Leone so as to compare conditions & arrive at some conclusions that may be recommended for the helping of the Liberians. The Captain has orders to report at the Canary Islands & at Madeira & so I am quite unable to accurately forecast just when I shall reach *New York*. Mail addressed to me: *U.S.S. Chester*, c/o *The Post Master, New York City* — up to and including June 5 (to be in New York June 5) will reach me & at regular American rates of postage. I almost wish I were back at Tuskegee now preparing for Commencement & relieving you as much as possible.

If I get to Sierre Leone in time I shall want to send a cable dispatch for Commencement Day.

I enclose *code* word & explanation of same.

Please keep it so that you may have the translation in case I am able to get off the dispatch. We are 3½ hours ahead of you in time here & shall be 5 hours ahead at Monrovia. I hope Mrs. Washington is well. Please remember me cordially to her & to Davidson.

I shall send cards to him & Booker. Yours sincerely

Emmett J. Scott

ALS   Con. 587   BTW Papers   DLC.

[1] Henry Braid Wilson (1861–1954) was a graduate of the U.S. Naval Academy in 1881. Wilson was a rear admiral during World War I and served as commander-in-chief of U.S. naval forces in France. After the war he was promoted to the rank of admiral and was commander of the Atlantic fleet. He was superintendent of the U.S. Naval Academy from 1921 to 1925.

[2] After New York reporters interviewed the southern officers of the U.S.S. *Birmingham* and reported their opposition to Scott's sharing their mess table, he was moved to the U.S.S. *Chester*, where he found conditions agreeable. Later in Liberian waters he traveled on the *Birmingham* without racial incident. (Harlan, "BTW and the White Man's Burden," 456.)

From George Washington Carver

Tuskegee Institute, Ala., May 4–1909

My dear Mr. Washington, Your letter received and read with great care. Your letter encourages me greatly. *I am determined to raise chickens regardless of difficulties, I mean just that.*

I only sent you the report for your information, and not as a complaint. I thought you would be glad, or rather that it was my duty to keep you posted in detail. I want you to know that I am not sitting down permitting such a condition to exist without trying to remedy it.

I fully appretiate the fact that we have a fine plant here for which I am extremely greatful. And without taking more of your time, will say in closing that you shall have chickens. Very truly

G. W. Carver

ALS Con. 589 BTW Papers DLC.

To William Howard Taft

Tuskegee Institute, Alabama   May 6th, 1909

Personal and Confidential

My dear Mr. President: In considering the matter of the new judge for the Northern District of Alabama, I hope you will bear in mind the interests of the Negro. The United States Courts have been, as it were, kind of "cities of refuge" for the colored people. I mean that in these courts they have been always sure of securing justice in cases that properly come under the jurisdiction of such courts by reason of the fact that the judges have been such broad and liberal men that the juries have represented a class of people who would see that a fair verdict was rendered.

Not only this, but in the United States Courts in the South Negroes have heretofore been placed on the grand jury and petit jury and in this way they have gotten recognition that they have not gotten in any other case. This matter, as small as it is, has gone to make them feel that they were citizens and has encouraged them not a little. With few exceptions, where narrow minded men have been made judges they have gradually used their influence in some way to keep Negroes off the juries and have made them feel that they had few rights in these courts.

Please do not take the time to answer this letter. Yours very truly,

Booker T. Washington

TLS William Howard Taft Papers DLC.

To Timothy Thomas Fortune

[Tuskegee, Ala.] May 11, 1909

Dear Mr. Fortune: Just before he left, Mr. Scott placed in my hands your letter of April 1st. I shall be glad to return the letters to which your letter refers. Before doing so, however, will you be kind enough to let me know where to send them, that is, whether to New York City, or to Red Bank.

I hope you are well and prospering. Yours very truly,

Booker T. Washington

TLpS Con. 45 BTW Papers DLC.

From Booker Taliaferro Washington, Jr.

Fisk University   Nashville, Tenn. May 13, 1909

My dear Father; I have received the sketch book on Abraham Lincoln, the box of writing paper and magazines, [for] all of which I thank you a great deal.

We are having lovely weather now. I think that it is about time that we should have some pretty weather as it has been very disagreeable so far.

To-morrow night is the annual glee club concert. I wish very much that you could be here at that time for I know you would enjoy hearing the kind of music that they sing.

This coming Sunday I go to a little town called Hendersonville Tenn. to make a speach.

In reading the "Student" I saw where you were one of the principal speakers at the forty-first anniversary celebration of the Hampton Institute.

I am making a double effort to bring my marks as high as will be possible for this last term. I am very tired now and feel like stopping school for the rest of the term. But whenever I have these tired feelings I always look at that little "motto" that you sent me, and get from it new vigor to continue. "The World Honors the Sticker, Never the Quitter."

Father I need twenty five dollars $25. Please send me this amount right away, as I need it badly. This is the last time that I shall ask you for any more money this year.

Hoping that you will send the money at once. I remain, Your devoted son,

Booker

ALS   Con. 588   BTW Papers   DLC.

To William Sidney Pittman

Tuskegee Institute, Ala., May 14, 1909

Please telegraph me at my expense how the baby[1] is today.

Booker T. Washington

TWpSr   Con. 588   BTW Papers   DLC.

1 William Sidney Pittman, Jr. (1908–67).

From Emmett Jay Scott

Monrovia, Liberia. May 14, 1909

My dear Dr. Washington: As you may know by now the Commission reached Monrovia last Saturday, May 8th. It occurs to me that you may be interested in some account of our reception and entertainment so far. For that reason I send you the following in which you may be interested.

May 8 — Arrived off Monrovia and anchored three miles off. Our boat fired a salute of thirteen guns and was answered by the fort with thirteen guns. Our Captain then sent an officer ashore to ask the American Minister, Dr. Ernest Lyon, when he could call on him; being a minister, Mr. Lyon has to be called on first, but as he wanted to get to work and see the Commission he waived his rights and came out at 12 o'clock to call on the Captain of the ship and upon the Commissioners. He brought with him Bishop I. B. Scott, the Secretary of Legation, Mr. Ellis,[1] and Edgar Allen Forbes,[2] a white man, who is here representing the World's Work. Bishop Scott and Mr. Lyon had dinner with the Commission and Capt Wilson on board the Chester and then we dressed in our frock coats (Prince Albert), silk hats &c., and came ashore. The Government sent the Launch for us all decorated with flags and colors of various kinds and the funny thing was the Launch had just been painted and we had a merry time with our finery on keeping out of the paint.

At last we landed and came through the Government Warehouse, where the band at once struck up the Star Spangled Banner and while we all uncovered — the natives and Liberians did the same thing. Then the Mayor and City Council were presented to us and made speeches of welcome. We replied through our Chairman.[3] I forgot to say our two army men had on white military suits with the *U.S.* &c. on the lapels (or collars rather) of their coats. We each had the escort of a Cabinet officer and as we ascended the hill we came at last to a huge arch made of artificial flowers and bunting and each one different — a pink one, a blue one, a green one and a yellow one. I replied to the welcome at the first arch, Dr. Sale at the second, Mr. Falkner at the third and the fourth was at the American Legation where we were to stop and where the great crowd had assembled. I spoke here as the Negro member of the Commission and then we went inside to be presented to the people. I forgot to say that we also had a military escort from the wharf all the way along. As each address was made by a lady representing a County of the Republic she and those holding the arch would come along with us holding it over our heads till the next one and the next one &c., till when we came to the Legation we had three over us and this made the fourth. The soldiers then marched and counter marched for us in front of the Legation and then after refreshments we went back to the ship for the night.

Sunday, May 9 — Dr. Sale and I came ashore, and also Major Ashburn[4] and Mr. Flower[5] and went to the Methodist Church. Bishop Scott preached the *sermon* and we then went to the Ship again and spent the day quietly reading &c.

May 10 — The whole Commission again rigged up in all the "Regimentals" of importance and came over to the office of the Secretary of State: who received us and then piloted us to the Executive Mansion to meet the President and his Cabinet. We spent an half hour here, were photographed, went to the American Legation, to call on the German Consul and then to the Ship again. It was quite warm and with these clothes on you may be quite sure it was not altogether so pleasant.

Tuesday, May 11 — We came ashore again to get our Headquarters in shape and to do some work of the *Commission:* and returned again to Ship. We found that it took entirely too much time coming and going and getting ready and so we have a fine house with large airy rooms — a room for each *Commissioner,* splendidly furnished and each has one of the arches in the room, in a corner over the large looking glass.

Wednesday, May 12 — We moved bag and baggage from the ship and as we had accepted an invitation from the President of the Republic, Mr. Barclay, to be the guests of honor at a reception in our honor we went to the Executive Mansion, again dressed in "Regimentals," and met the President, the Vice President, the Members of the Senate, of the House of Representatives, of the Supreme Court and the Superintendents of the various counties and then a number of very important men — Refreshments were served and all had a good time. Commander Wilson of the Chester in uniform and his officers in uniform and all of the foreign consuls were present. The persons who have decorations from the Republic all wore them and altogether we had a very pleasant time of it.

I enjoyed it all very much. The *American Minister*, Mr. Lyon, in all of these cases had charge of us and piloted us and introduced us. He is an "Old friend" of mine and we have got along famously. I think now I have given you a pretty good account of the preliminaries. We could not begin the work which brought us here till we had gone through with all of this and now we are hard at it and shall be till the time comes for us to end our work. Yours very truly,

Emmett J. Scott

I must not neglect to tell you that everyone asks for you & your failure to come is a great disappointment. Dossen & the others are here. The Legislature has been called in special session & they have appointed a *Commission* to confer with us — to prescribe us as far as they think they may. They play politics here always. I cabled you to have the secretary of navy cable permission for the Commander of the boat to bring the boy.[6] He cannot do so under the regulations without such permission. They also have another student whom they wish educated — to *work* his way — & that is why my cable mentioned 2 students. Everyone here is acquainted with your efforts in behalf of the *Republic.* We may be able to help these people — but it is all uphill & pulling at that. Many things here are pitiful — that is the only term I can *use.* I am keeping pretty full notes of everything.

I hope you are getting on well — & that you will remember me to Mrs W. I am perfectly well so far & the weather is *so far* no hotter than Washington or N Y in summer.

E J S

TLS Con. 587 BTW Papers DLC. Postscript in Scott's hand.

1 George Washington Ellis (1875–1919), a graduate of the University of Kansas (1893) and a former clerk in the U.S. Census Office, was secretary of the American legation in Liberia from 1902 to 1910. He wrote several books on West African culture.

2 Edgar Allen Forbes (b. 1872) was an editor of *World's Work* from 1906 to 1910.

3 Roland Post Falkner (1866–1940), an economist and statistician, was chairman of the U.S. commission to Liberia. Beginning in 1911 he was assistant director of the U.S. Census, and in 1913 he served on the U.S.-Panamanian joint land commission.

4 Percy Moreau Ashburn (1872–1940) was a major in the U.S. Army Medical Corps assigned to the Liberian commission in 1909. He was an expert on tropical diseases.

5 Frank Abial Flower (1854–1911), a Wisconsin statistician and editor, was an attaché to the Liberian commission.

6 Probably Charles Tedo Wardah, of Harper, Cape Palmas, Liberia, a junior in Phelps Hall in 1909–10.

From Emmett Jay Scott

Monrovia: Liberia   May 15, '09

Personal:

My Dear Mr. W: There is quite a nasty situation here at the American Legation. Bishop Scott & Dr. Lyon have both spoken to me of it, also Mr. Forbes, the *World's Work* man & others. Ellis, the present secretary is a very narrow & very little man, with little sense & no discretion. He constantly I hear goes out of the Legation to speak of the Legation business & to put Dr. Lyon in the hole. There are politicians & politicians here & he takes an active part in them altho' an American officer. He is from all accounts a strife breeder & more than that he seeks to embarras[s] every effort of the Minister so far as you are concerned. For instance: He made an outcry about your being put in charge of the Envoys last year & said *Du Bois* & the intellectuals were the proper people & that the mission w'd be a failure because you were in charge of it. *Then:* when the President & Congress at Lyon's request conferred the medal of the Order of African Redemption on you he again came out & said the Negroes of the U S w'd oppose it unless Du Bois also received *one*. Lyons then fought openly against this proposition & when the Envoys returned & said that they c'd not have succeeded without you — & when *Du Bois* jumped on the Envoys in the *Horizon* they saw what a fool Ellis is & refused Du Bois the medal, altho' it was given out by Ellis that *Du B* also received one. I read all of this in the papers last summer but did not know who it came from. We have on file *there* in the office a letter from *Ellis* telling of the Congress act to give you & Du Bois medals. You will find same, if you care to have it looked up. *Then* he makes copies of Legation stuff & keeps *Du B* supplied & everything that Dr Sale got from *Du B* on Liberia has Ellis name written on it — Lyon has the proof of this & has requested his removal. *Now* I have relied mainly on Bishop Scott for these facts as Mr Lyon is an interested party. You ought to know of it if his removal sh'd be contemplated. Mr. Lyon wishes W. F. *Walker,* a bright young fellow from Boston appointed secretary. He seems very competent, but Bishop Scott suggests that if *you* have a stronger man in mind that he ought to be sent *out*. It is the efficiency he has in mind. We ought to have a friend for this place & not *one* of the enemy. It pays $2000 a year. Senator Lodge is supporting *Walker*. I *know this!* No weak man ought to be selected. *Walker* is strong in many ways & *one* of our friends as you may know. He is from Alabama by way of *Boston*. Yours &c.

Emmett J. Scott

ALS Con. 587 BTW Papers DLC.

From James Jenkins Dossen

Monrovia, May 15th, 1909

My dear Doctor Washington: Since writing you last from Cape Palmas the American Commissioners have arrived in Monrovia. Their presence have aroused the deepest feelings of gratitude among our people; their reception was an unusual spectacle; the whole City literally turned out to greet and welcome them. At the entrance to the street leading from the landing stage they were met by the city authorities who gave them the freedom of the City. Under military escort they proceeded from thence to the United States Legation and made four stops en route at points where ladies bearing decorated arches representing the four counties of the Republic made appropriate addresses. It was a gala day, the people from all parts turning out to greet the American visitors. The only regret was the absence of "Booker" as our people young and old, are fondly calling you. Ladies had made new costumes to wear on your arrival. When I arrived on the scene and told them that you would not come their hearts sunk. But I assured them that it had become impossible for you to leave President Taft's side during the first months of his Administration, but that while you were absent in person your great heart was in the movement and that I felt that with you deeply interested in the movement, success was inevitable.

The members of the Commission have expressed themselves as being well pleased with the most cordial reception extended them as also with the general aspect of things. They have too been able to see for themselves the dirty game the British have been playing at out here and the false representations they have made about Liberia. With these facts before the Washington Government it may now see its way to give potential help to Liberia and thereby defeat the designs of England and France. One of our most urgent needs is *money* with which to pay off the English loans so as to enable us to get rid of English officials. We desire the Reforms in our Customs, Financial and other branches of Government to be carried out by *American* experts, but to do this we must first pay off the loans, by the provisions of which Englishmen have been brought into our administrations. Everybody in Liberia are in favour of Reforms; the Liberians are a patriotic people and are anxious to see their country move forward on improved lines; but Liberians are sufficiently intelligent to differentiate between genuine honest reforms introduced for the benefit of the people and country, and, those that may be introduced for sinister motives. Moreover we are persuaded that the difference[s] between British and Liberian political institutions are so pronounced as to render it impossible to work out smoothly British systems of Government in Liberia. I should like for you to write me as nearly as you can whether you think the United States Government would assist in some way the raising of a loan to liquidate our foreign and domestic liabilities including a sum sufficient to enable us to undertake such public works as are necessary to the development of our resources. I think five millions would be adequate for these purposes, and we should be willing to apothicate [*sic*] our Customs and internal revenue as a guarantee.

Another very important point which I sincerely hope that the United States Government will see its way clear to help in, is that of establishing civilized settlements on our frontiers and interior. Our civilized population is almost too sparse to govern the country and this accounts for the repeated outbreaks we have with the uncivilized population. The planting of new settlements and the increasing of the Americo-Liberian element would bring the country under more tangible control than punitive expeditions. You may not be an emigrationalist still I believe your knowledge of human nature will cause you to decide that no race has ever been found to dwell as a whole within its own domain, even when that domain is its natural habitat; the Negro race in the United States will furnish no exception to this general law; they will come to Liberia as soon as inducements offer and the way becomes possible: he is not an enemy to his race who will help to bring about this result in a sane and sound way, for the race in the States should have a field outside of that country, for the expansion of its energies and the investment of its money and brain capital. Fifty years hence the labour market of the United States may become so congested and flooded with cheap white labour as to produce the most acute labour problem for the race there and, when competition for bread winning becomes serious, it will intensify race hatred and lead to the most disastrous consequences. It is from this broad, statesman-like view of the question that leaders of the race should view the question of emigration to Liberia, with the view of securing what is already Liberia's and acquiring as much more as it is possible to acquire, so as to keep in tact an outlet and a future field for the American Negro. If we let Liberia slip from our grasp we will have committed one of the greatest blunders a race can commit and one which our children will weep over in future. I shall be very pleased to exchange views with you on this subject. I may mention that in a personal letter to Mr. Taft a few months ago I pointed out this as one of Liberia's greatest needs.

Mr. Scott informs me that you cabled him to bring the "Stoke's Student"; I am sending shortly another young man to be included in the number you promised me to take from Liberia.[1]

With very high consideration, I remain, Yours very faithfully,

James J Dossen

P.S. Do you suggest conferring the Liberian Order of African Redemption on ex-President Roosevelt and Ex-Secretary of State Root in recognition of their services to Liberia? Write me promptly your views on this point.

TLS Con. 394 BTW Papers DLC.

[1] In the school year 1909–10 and also in 1910–11 there were four Liberian students enrolled at Tuskegee.

To Mary Caroline Moore

[Tuskegee, Ala.] May 17, 1909

My dear Miss Moore: I thank you very much for your kind letter and invitation.[1]

It seems to me now possible that I might speak for you some-time during the month of November or December. If you will remind me of the matter a little later, I will try to make it more definite. You need not bother about any charge, etc.

I am sorry to say that Portia is having a very trying season just now on account of the serious sickness of her baby. He has been sick for three weeks — so very ill that we have been expecting every day to hear of his death. The baby may recover, but we have grave fears that he will not. We also have grave fears about Portia. She is undergoing such a trying strain and is in great danger of breaking down nervously. She has a beautiful home near Washington and is getting on well, except for this sickness of her baby.

Mrs. Washington asks to be remembered to you. Yours very truly,

Booker T. Washington

TLpS Con. 820 BTW Papers DLC.

[1] Mary C. Moore wrote BTW from Framingham, Mass., that the teachers of the town and normal school had formed an association for mutual improvement, and invited BTW to speak on industrial education. (May 12, 1909, Con. 820, BTW Papers, DLC.)

To Frederick Barrett Gordon[1]

[Tuskegee, Ala.] May 17, 1909

My dear Sir: I hope you will forgive the delay in answering your letter of April 21st.[2] I have been absent from my mail for sometime.

I have made a statement on several occasions that on the whole I find that the Colored people do better work out of doors than in doors. I think you will agree with me in this statement, but I do not mean to advise or to assert that under no circumstances is it wise to employ Colored people for inside work. It is a well known fact that they have done reasonably well in tobacco factories. It is, also, perhaps well known to you that there is a successful silk factory in Fayetteville N.C., which employs Colored labor altogether under a Colored Superintendent and it is said to be a successful concern.

I favor your plans. If for nothing else, I should like to see this whole matter of Negro labor in the cotton factory given a thorough trial, in order that many wrong impressions may be removed. As you perhaps know, the Negro has never had a fair trial as a cotton mill operater. I visited the mill in Charleston, which failed. This same mill had failed twice before when white labor was employed.

The difference there was that the mill owners had no control of the labor. The Colored people who worked in the mill lived in all parts of the city, in their own houses or in rented houses, and they worked, or not, as they pleased. Furthermore, when the time came to pick strawberries, many of the mill hands left the mill to pick berries.

I should strongly advise the colony system and that the mill be placed just as far as possible from any city or town, and the people who control the mill own the houses in which the Colored people are to live.

There is a Mr. Mebane[3] at Sprague,[4] N.C., who is a large and successful cotton manufacturer. He has told me over and over again that he would take stock in such a concern, if necessary.

I have read the pamphlet, which you sent to me, with the deepest interest and profit. If you have others to spare, I should like to have additional copies. I should strongly advise that in connection with the colony, churches, Y.M.C.A.'s, schools, etc. be encouraged. I really believe that it might be worth your while to make a visit to Buxton, Iowa, where there is a colony of some four or five thousand Colored people employed in coal mining. This to a large extent is a self governing colony, but it is a success. I think it would help the movement, if you could get a wide-awake Colored man to take the lead in the social organization and conduct of the work.

I certainly will watch with the greatest interest what you propose to do and if I can be of the slightest service in carrying out your plans, please do not hesitate to let me know. Yours very truly,

Booker T. Washington

TLpS Con. 391 BTW Papers DLC.

1 Frederick Barrett Gordon (b. 1857) was president of the Columbus Manufacturing Co., an executive of the Georgia Cotton Manufacturers' Association, and the Columbus Textile Manufacturers' Association. He also was twice president of the Columbus Chamber of Commerce and served on the city school and water boards.

2 Gordon suggested that blacks with industrial training be encouraged to enter cotton mills, and asked BTW's opinion prior to an attempt to raise capital for a mill employing black labor. (Con. 391, BTW Papers, DLC.)

3 B. Frank Mebane of Spray, N.C., was president of the Spray Water Power and Land Co., which owned cotton mills, warehouses, and other businesses in Spray and nearby towns. In 1904 he planned to undertake a black hotel to "let these negroes have a chance to show what efficiency they can render in service and cook-

ing." He also urged BTW to establish a black-owned and -operated cotton mill. (Mebane to BTW, May 23, June 14, 1904, Con. 869, BTW Papers, DLC.) He wrote BTW in 1909: "I am firmly convinced that justice will never be done the negro until he is given a proprietary interest in the cotton crop; when I say that, I mean in part that you cannot encourage him to be a producer of the staple and give him no interest in producing the cloth." (June 8, 1909, Con. 395, BTW Papers, DLC.)

4 Spray.

From Timothy Thomas Fortune

Maple Hall, Red Bank, N.J., May 17, 1909

Dear Mr Washington: Your letter of the 11th instant was received.

I will ship your letters, per express, tomorrow, to you. You may ship mine here, per express, if you care to.

I am very well, but am prospering not a bit, and have done no work since the close of the campaign. All doors, save those of the poor house, appear to be closed against me. And he who is down and out seems not to have any friends. I have filed application with the President and secretary of state for appointment as Minister Resident and Consul General to Liberia. Mr Lyon has been Minister more than ten years. We have had a long string of reverends as Ministers to Liberia, who have paid more attention to the Gospel needs of their denominations than to the commercial relations of the United States and Liberia and to the resources of Liberia and to the character and capabilities of the native people of Liberia. I would acquaint myself with these matters as well as encourage the Government to introduce and foster your idea of industrial education.

I enclose some letters on the subject, which please return.

I wish you could see your way clear to ask the President to give me this appointment, for old friendship's sake. I do not drink at all and have not for a long time. *My family and I are destitute*, and I have starved days in New York seeking work. Today I have but $2.00 in the world. I ask you to overlook any differences that may have come between us in the past two years, part of which time I suffered great nervous trouble, and to do me the favor and the service, in the interest of my family and myself, of asking the President to give me the appointment to Liberia. I shall not have heart again to bother you with a petition of mine.

With my kind regards, Yours very sincerely

T. Thos. Fortune

If you have endorsed someone else for the Liberian mission, can you not transfer it?

ALS   Con. 45   BTW Papers   DLC.

To Richard Carroll

[Tuskegee, Ala.] May 18, 1909

Dear Mr. Carroll: When I wrote you, a few days ago, I neglected to say that as I came South from Washington, I met Senator Tillman and Mrs. Tillman and had quite a talk with them. I will see them again sometime soon. I think we will become pretty good friends. Both of them spoke of you. Very truly yours,

Booker T. Washington

TLpS   Con. 389   BTW Papers   DLC.

From Timothy Thomas Fortune

Maple Hall, Red Bank, N.J., May 18, 1909

Dear Mr. Washington: I have pleasure in sending you today, per express, the personal letters concerning which I wrote you yesterday.

In separating myself from these letters I am constrained to say I have great sorrow at my heart, as they recall our intimate association for a period of twenty years, in which I strove always to promote and protect your name and interests without seeking unduly to promote my own. I rejoice that great success has come to you and your work, and I hope that you may have to the end friends as faithful and true as I strove to be. Your friend,

T. Thos. Fortune

ALS Con. 45 BTW Papers DLC.

To Timothy Thomas Fortune

[Tuskegee, Ala.] May 22, 1909

My dear Mr. Fortune: I am sending you by registered mail today, the letters referred to in your correspondence.

I do not think that you ought to have the feeling which you suggest in your last letter in parting from these letters. There is no earthly reason why our friendship should not continue, notwithstanding we have returned the letters purely for business reasons.

I have always valued your friendship and confidence and trust always to merit your friendship and confidence in the future.

When I am North I shall hope to see you when I can have a long talk. Yours very truly,

Booker T. Washington

TLpS Con. 45 BTW Papers DLC.

From William Sidney Pittman

Washington, D.C. May 24th, '09

My dear Mr. Washington: A copy of your letter to Dr. Francis was received this morning, and very highly appreciated. In this connection I might state that Dr. Curtis[1] paid us another call yesterday (Sunday), and on this trip he seems to have gotten a better and more hopeful opinion of the condition of our baby. The baby seems to have been slowly but gradually improving each day of the week past, and since Dr. Curtis makes only weekly trips, he was naturally surprised to see the difference in the condition of the baby between Sunday week ago and yesterday. To use his own words on this last trip he stated that although he was not quite out of danger yet, he was considerably improved. And this we are all glad to state to you. Dr. Jones[2] our resident physician is with us every day, and of course has never given up hope and in addition to this he has forced us all to be as cheerful and hopeful as he was. The trained nurse Miss Coats[3] who is with the baby every minute in the day and night and who has been with us over four weeks has also been a great help, and she too has always been hopeful.

All of these are merely details, but I write them feeling that they will be of interest to you and Mrs. Washington. The baby's appetite has gradually improved to its normal state and he has almost become physically normal from the effect. We have a good wet nurse in the house all the time with us, and the baby is fed all through the day. We all hope to see you soon and have you see the baby's condition as it contrasts with your last trip here. If he continues the Doctors think that three months more will make him on the safe side; and the summer months are in his favor. Yours very truly,

W. Sidney Pittman

TLS   Con. 588   BTW Papers   DLC.

[1] Austin Maurice Curtis, born in 1868, a graduate of Lincoln University and Northwestern University Medical School, practiced in Chicago from 1891 to 1898, when he became surgeon-in-chief of Freedmen's Hospital in Washington. In 1902 he became also professor of surgery at Howard University Medical School.

[2] Possibly William C. Jones, a black Washington physician.

[3] Nana E. Coates was a nurse affiliated with Freedmen's Hospital.

Last Will and Testament

[Tuskegee, Ala.] May 25th, 1909

IN THE NAME OF GOD, AMEN

I, BOOKER T. WASHINGTON, of the Town of Tuskegee, County of Macon, and State of Alabama, being of sound and disposing mind and memory, and considering the uncertainty of human life, do now make, publish and declare this to be my last WILL and TESTAMENT, hereby revoking all former Wills and codicils heretofore made by me:

FIRST: I direct that all my just debts and funeral expenses shall be first paid by my executrix hereinafter mentioned, as speedily as possible out of any available funds whatever belonging to my estate.

SECOND: From myself and from divers other sources, my beloved wife, MARGARET J. WASHINGTON, has already acquired a separate estate which I deem ample for her protection and support; and which it is my earnest request that she accept in lieu of all dower and all distributive share in my estate; and it is my further wish that she will not dissent from this Will, but fully approve and carry out all its provisions.

I give and devise to my said wife, Margaret J. Washington, my present residence house and lot, with all its appurtenances, in the Town of Tuskegee, across the street from the Tuskegee Normal and Industrial Institute, together with all the furniture, pictures, ornaments, books and bric-a-brac that may be contained in said residence at the time of my death; to have and use during the term of her life, and upon her death to go to my children, PORTIA WASHINGTON PITTMAN, BOOKER T., and ERNEST D. WASHINGTON, equally in fee simple.

THIRD: I give and bequeath to my son, BOOKER T. WASHINGTON, my gold watch and chain.

FOURTH: I give and bequeath to my sister, AMANDA, wife of Benjamin Johnson, of Malden, in the County of Kanawha, and State of West Virginia, Fifteen Hundred Dollars ($1,500.00)

FIFTH: I give and bequeath to my brother, JOHN WASHINGTON, Fifteen Hundred Dollars ($1,500.00)

SIXTH: I give and bequeath to my nephew, ALBERT JOHNSON, Four Hundred Dollars ($400.00)

SEVENTH: I give and bequeath to my faithful Private Secretary, EMMETT J. SCOTT, Four Hundred Dollars ($400.00)

EIGHTH: I give and bequeath to my adopted brother, JAMES B. WASHINGTON, Two Hundred Dollars ($200.00)

NINTH: I give and bequeath to my niece, LAURA MURRAY,[1] Fifteen Hundred Dollars ($1,500.00)

Tenth: I give and bequeath to my nephew, Thomas Murray, Jr., Five Hundred Dollars ($500.00)

Eleventh: I give and bequeath to my faithful agent, A. R. Stewart,[2] of Tuskegee, Alabama, Two Hundred Dollars ($200.00)

Twelfth: I give and bequeath to my said children, Portia Washington Pittman, Booker T. and Ernest D. Washington, share and share alike, the proceeds and royalties from the following publications or books of mine, to-wit: "Up from Slavery," "Work[ing] with the Hands," "Character Building," and "The Story of the Negro," published by Doubleday, Page & Co., New York; "The Future of the American Negro," published by Small, Maynard & Co., Boston, Mass.; "The Story of my Life and Work," published by J. S. Nichols & Co., Naperville, Ill.; and the proceeds and royalties which may accrue from any other books that I may hereafter write, publish or have published; and it is my further wish and desire that if any book be published on my life after my death, that the revenue derived from the same go to my said children equally.

Thirteenth: All the rest, residue, and remainder of my estate, of every kind, character and description, and wherever located that have not been specifically disposed of by this Will, I give and bequeath and devise to my said children, Portia Washington Pittman, Booker T. and Ernest D. Washington, share and share alike in fee simple; but to be divided and given to them as herein provided.

Fourteenth: I hereby constitute and appoint my said wife, Margaret J. Washington, the testamentary guardian of my son Ernest D. Washington, and I will and desire that she be not required to give any bond as such guardian. I also appoint and constitute my said wife, my sole executrix and trustee under this will, to carry out its provisions, and I also request, will, and desire that she be not required to give any bond either as such executrix or as such trustee; I having the utmost confidence in her and the full belief that she will do what is right and fair by my said children. My said wife as such executrix and trustee is hereby given as full power and authority as I could exercise, if living, to bargain, sell, convey, transfer or otherwise dispose of, or encumber, any part of, or all of, my property and estate from time to time, and distribute or divide the proceeds according to the terms of this will, or reinvest such proceeds or any part thereof, as she may deem best, and again from time to time, in like manner, bargain, sell, convey, transfer or otherwise dispose of, or encumber, such newly acquired property, and so on until she divides or distributes the same according to the provisions of this Will. She may make partial or total distribution, or division among and between my said three children, in money or in specific property, or partly in money and partly in property, and her estimate of values of property so divided and distributed shall be final and conclusive. She shall from time to time make such advancements to or for the support, maintenance and education of each of my said children as, in her judgment, is to the interest of such child; but shall not make final division and distribution between them until the youngest of my said three children arrives at the age of twenty-four years.

As it cannot be foreseen what, during the lifetime of my said wife, may become the condition of my said children, I express the wish and hope that my said wife make such provision for my said children out of her own income and estate, as she may at the time deem, in her good judgment, right and proper.

FIFTEENTH: In the event of the death of my said wife, before or after my death, or of her resignation, before the provisions of this Will are fully executed, I will that my brother, JOHN H. WASHINGTON, and my faithful and true friend WARREN LOGAN, of Tuskegee, Alabama, be and they hereby are, constituted the executors and trustees, under this Will, to carry out its provisions, and they shall be, as such executors and trustees, invested with all the powers and authority, including powers and duties requiring the exercise of judgment and discretion, which are herein given to my said wife, except that in making division or distribution among my said three children, they shall not divide or distribute in property at valuations fixed by themselves; but they may make division and distribution or advancements to said three children in property at valuations agreed on in writing by the three children.

IN WITNESS WHEREOF, and in conformity with the laws of the State of Alabama, I have hereunto subscribed my name to the foregoing three (3) sheets of typewritten paper, fastened together, my name being written in the lower left hand corner of each sheet, except this last one, for identification, and have hereunto sub-scribed my name in the presence of the three persons whose names are signed hereto as attesting witnesses, which said three persons as such witnesses have hereunto subscribed their names as such wit-nesses in my presence and in the presence of each other, on this the 25th day of May, 1909.

Booker T. Washington

ATTESTING WITNESSES:

Chas. H. Gibson

Wm H. Carter

Chas. H. Fearing

TDS   Office of Judge of Probate, Macon County, Ala.   A codicil was added June 13, 1911; see below, vol. 11.

1 Laura Murray (b. 1902), a niece of Margaret M. Washington, lived with BTW and his family beginning about 1907, after her mother's death. She sometimes took Washington as her last name. BTW later sent her to Spelman Seminary (later College) in Atlanta.

2 Alexander Robert Stewart, originally of Darien, Ga., a 1904 graduate of Tus-kegee, became BTW's personal agent in 1906, handling such business as the sale and distribution of BTW's books directly from Tuskegee Institute, collecting rents and mortgage payments on BTW's business and residential property in Tuskegee, and paying monthly allowances to BTW's children.

From Oswald Garrison Villard

New York   May 26, 1909

Dear Mr. Washington: I sincerely wish that you might be present at our approaching conference on the status of the American negro,[1] because I look for great results from it. We have an unusually fine list of speakers and the people who have promised to come, like Prof. Dewey,[2] Prof. Wilder,[3] Albert E. Pillsbury[4] of Boston, Judge Stafford[5] of the District of Columbia, Clarence Darrow[6] and others, are tried and fast friends of the colored race. There is not the slight-est intention of tying up this movement with either of the two factions in the negro race. It is not to be a Washington movement, or a Du Bois movement. The idea is that there shall grow out of it, first, an annual conference similar to the Indian conference and the Arbitration meeting which take place every year at Lake Mohonk, for the discussion by men of both races of the conditions of the colored people, politically, socially, industrially and educationally. Besides this, I hope there will grow out of it a permanent organization, a sort of steering committee of the race along lines which I have indicated to you in conversations in the past; an incorporated and endowed committee which shall have a press bureau, a bureau of study and investigation to let the country know exactly the facts about the progress of the colored race; a legal bureau to take up any case of crime against the negro; a political bureau to contend against political wrongs; an educational bureau to raise funds for distinctively negro institutions, etc., etc.

Now it is intended that this committee, when duly authorized and organized — perhaps a year hence at the second annual conference — shall absorb the association for the industrial improvement of the negroes in this city, and also, perhaps, the Constitutional League. It is intended that the organization shall be an aggressive one ready to fight hard for the rights of the colored people, to strike hard blows in and out of Congress, to take up precisely such wrongs as the Brownsville incident and fight them to a finish as did the Constitutional League in this matter.

Now, while I am not writing officially for the conference, I know that I express its feeling of friendliness for you and for the work you are doing, but as I explained to you in regard to the original call, the men who have gotten up this movement do not wish to embarrass you; they do not wish to seem to ignore you, or to leave you out, or to show any disrespect whatever. On the other hand, they do not wish to tie you up with what may prove to be a radical political movement. Hence, they have not felt like urging you very hard to join the new movement, but have wanted you to know that you would be welcome at the conference, or if you decided you could not attend, the conference would least of all misinterpret your absence. I do not know of any movement which bids fair to do so much for the colored people. So far as I, myself, am concerned, if it can be carried out as I, and others, am planning it, it will realize the greatest ambition of my life, and I shall expect to concentrate my interest upon it as strongly as possible, outside of my professional duties, and I feel that we can count on your sympathetic interest and help even if, because of educational affiliations, you do not desire to become closely allied with us. Of course, I feel more keenly the delicacy of your position in regard to all movements of this kind because I am one of your warm friends who is unhappy about your political activities and is worried by the danger of your being forced against your will into the untenable position of being the political clearinghouse for the colored race, a position no one can fill in the long run with success, or without causing the most intense hostility on the part of your colored fellow-citizens. I should take the same position if there were a German-American boss or an Italian boss, or a Frenchman through whom all appointments of French-Americans were made.

We are very happy to have your article, which has arrived, and shall print it on Saturday. Always sincerely yours

Oswald Garrison Villard

TLS Con. 261 BTW Papers DLC.

[1] See *Proceedings of the National Negro Conference, 1909.* Out of this conference grew the NAACP.

[2] John Dewey (1859–1952) briefly discussed recent scientific findings on heredity, environment, and mental ability.

[3] Burt Green Wilder (1841–1925), an expert on the brains of vertebrates, presented an address on "The Negro Brain."

[4] Pillsbury spoke on "Negro Disfranchisement as It Affects the White Man."

[5] Wendell Phillips Stafford (b. 1861), an associate justice of the Supreme Court of the District of Columbia (1904–31) and a poet, presided over one of the sessions.

[6] Clarence Seward Darrow (1857–1938), the famous defense lawyer, apparently did not attend the 1909 conference but was one of the main speakers at the 1910 conference.

To Oswald Garrison Villard

Tuskegee Institute, Alabama   May 28, 1909

Personal and Confidential.

My dear Mr. Villard: I thank you very much for your kind letter of May 26th and for the invitation to be present at the forthcoming conference. Now, I know you want me to be perfectly frank.

First, let me say, as my plans stand, it will be physically impossible for me to be present, but aside from that I do not believe that it would be best for me to be present at the first session at least, as I do not think it would help the conference. I fear that my presence might restrict freedom of discussion, and might, also, tend to make the conference go in directions which it would not like to go.

Secondly, I hardly feel that in the present conditions in the South, it would be best for the cause of education, in which you and I are both so deeply interested, for me to be present.

Now, I am sure that you will not misunderstand me when I make these statements. I am not afraid of doing anything which I think is right and should be done. I have always recognized, as I have stated to you more than once, that there is a work to be done which no one placed in my position can do, which no one living in the South perhaps can do. There is a work which those of us who live here in the South can do, which persons who do not live in the South cannot do. If we recognize fairly and squarely this, then, it seems to me that we have gone a long ways.

Third, I have always recognized the value of sane agitation and criticism, but not to the extent of having our race feel that we can depend upon this to cure all the evils surrounding us.

In the last analysis I am sure that both of us agree that it is through progressive, constructive work that we are to succeed rather than by depending too largely upon agitation or criticism.

I want to state, in conclusion, that in so far as I have followed the plans of the conference and noted the persons to be connected with it, you have made great progress in getting rid of an element of people who have always been a loadstone about the neck of such movements, and if this element is subdued, or kept quiet, or out of such meetings it will mean much in getting a good, strong following.

Please assure the members of the committee that I understand thoroughly their attitude toward me and their reasons for not insisting upon my presence, and that I have no feeling whatever, growing out of being left out.

I am writing hastily, just in the midst of our commencement exercises, and I may not make myself very clear. I shall try when I am in the North to see you, and go over matters more in detail with you. Yours truly,

Booker T. Washington

TLS   Oswald Garrison Villard Papers   MH.   A press copy is in Con. 48, BTW Papers, DLC.

From Emmett Jay Scott

Monrovia: 5/28/09

Personal:

My Dear Mr. Washington: We leave here tomorrow: ½ of the party (Mr. Falkner, Mr Finch[1] & Capt. Cloman[2]) start for the disputed boundary section where the British are pushing & the other ½ (Dr Sale, Maj. Ashburn, Mr. Flower & myself) start for Cape Palmas where Mr. Dossen lives & go up the Cavally River where the French aggressions are. We (last party) also stop at Grand Bassa[3] & go up the St. John River & also at Cape Mount & all of us meet at Sierre Leone (Freetown) & then go to the Canary Islands where the *Salem* is to meet us.

It has been an eventful trip. We have seen everybody & have quite closely looked into every disputed point. We have met the President, his Cabinet, a Commission from the Legislature — all the Foreign Consuls & all of the Trading Agents. We know more than we knew & yet it is all insufficient! Liberia *is* in a bad way — but fortunately it is worse from without than from *within*. It is fearful — the treatment they have had at the hands of the British & Harry Johnston is clearly the worst of the *lot!* His conduct & treatment of this people has been fearful in its consequences.

I do not yet know or see just what can be done & yet something *must be done!* The awful strictures of the British have not been justified — even as bad as conditions are. We are going thoroughly into everything & my concern now is — What & How can we say the *word* or *words* that sh'd be said. I know of no especial thing I can write you about. Your cable has come & I am to bring the boys with *me*. I am worrying about the Business League, but now I am in this thing & must go through with it. We ought to be home by July 1 to 5: that is NY City. Yours Faithfully

Emmett J. Scott

ALS Con. 587 BTW Papers DLC.

1 George Augustus Finch (1884–1957) was a clerk in the War Department (1905) and in the State Department (1906–11). In 1909 he was secretary to the Liberian commission. From 1911 to 1940 he was a secretary and assistant director of the international law division of the Carnegie Endowment for International Peace.

2 Sydney Amos Cloman (1867–1923), a West Point graduate and career army officer, was military attaché to the U.S. embassy in London from 1907 to 1911.

3 Later named Buchanan.

To Raymond DuPuy[1]

[Tuskegee, Ala.] May 29, 1909

My dear Sir: Since Mr. Clinton J. Calloway and Major Moton saw you regarding the trip over the Virginian Railroad, your friend and my friend, Mr. Rogers, has passed away. He was one of the dearest friends that I ever had, and I can never hope to have another one like him.

Unless I hear from you to the contrary, of course I shall take for granted that the previous plans are to be carried out so far as the trip over the road is concerned. Now that Mr. Rogers has passed away I have even more interest in having the thing done just as he would have it done, and I have telegraphed Major Moton to the effect that I will be ready to start on Sunday, June 20th, and remain on the road through the 25th if necessary. The details can be arranged through Major Moton. Yours truly,

Booker T. Washington

TLpS Con. 390 BTW Papers DLC.

1 Raymond DuPuy (1860–1933) was vice-president and general manager of the Virginian Railway. DuPuy arranged for BTW to use a special train and his personal coach "Dixie" during BTW's tour of Virginia. (R. R. Moton to BTW, May 18, 1909, Con. 46, BTW Papers, DLC.)

An Article in the New York *Evening Post*

New York, May 29, 1909

H. H. ROGERS AS
A CASH GIVER

HE ENJOYED HANDING OUT
THE CURRENCY

BOOKER T. WASHINGTON ON HIS GREAT
HELP TO SOUTHERN SCHOOLS — AT
LEAST SIXTY-FIVE WERE BEING
ANONYMOUSLY AIDED BY
THE FINANCIER WHEN
HE DIED

The more experience I have of the world, the more I am convinced that the only proper and the only safe way to judge any one is at first hand and by your actual experience. It seems to me that, outside of the immediate members of my family, I knew the late Henry H. Rogers during the last fifteen years as well as I could know any one. Of all the men that I have ever known, intimately, no matter what their station in life, Mr. Rogers always impressed me as being among the kindest and gentlest. That was the impression he made upon me the first time I ever met him, and during the fifteen years that I knew him that impression was deepened every time I met him.

I am sure that the members of his family will forgive me for telling, now that he has laid down his great work and gone to rest, some things about him which I feel that the public should know, but which he always forbade me to mention while he lived.

The first time I ever met Mr. Rogers was in this manner: About fifteen years ago, a large meeting was held in Madison Square Garden concert hall, to obtain funds for the Tuskegee Institute. Mr. Rogers attended the meeting, but came late, and as the auditorium was crowded he could not get a seat. He stood in the back part of the hall, however, and listened to the speaking.

The next morning I received a telegram from him asking me

to call at his office. When I entered he remarked that he had been present at the meeting the night previous and expected the "hat to be passed," but as that was not done he wanted to "chip in" something. Thereupon he handed me ten one-thousand-dollar bills for the Tuskegee Institute. In doing this he imposed only one condition, that the gift should be mentioned to no one. Later on, however, when I told him that I did not care to take so large a sum of money without some one knowing it, he consented that I tell one or two of our trustees about the source of the gift.

I cannot now recall the number of times that he has helped us, but in doing so he always insisted that his name be never used. He seemed to enjoy making gifts in currency.

An Uninformed Critic

Once, at least, I was compelled to disobey this injunction, and told about it. A well-known man from the North was visiting the Tuskegee Institute, and as he sat in my office something was said concerning Mr. Rogers. At once this individual began to denounce Mr. Rogers for his selfishness and stinginess. I did not make any reply for some moments, but at last I could not forbear telling him that the building in which we were then sitting was the gift of Mr. Rogers. He seemed to be taken off his feet with astonishment. He did not know Mr. Rogers, and the fact that a man so engrossed in business affairs should find time to interest himself in the fortunes of a negro school way off in Alabama was entirely out of keeping with the opinion he had formed of him.

As I grew to know Mr. Rogers better his interest in education in the South grew, and went beyond Tuskegee. He had assisted Tuskegee before this time, but he was anxious to see the work extended, and so at one time he gave me a considerable sum to be used in helping smaller industrial schools in the South. In this way he aided, I recall, about ten such schools in one year. None of these schools ever knew, however, the source of the gifts which they received.

About four years ago he asked me to lay out a scheme by which, through a period of years, he could systematically help a number of small rural schools in the South to obtain better schoolhouses, to prolong their school terms, and begin, to some extent, industrial training. I cannot go into details in regard to the progress of this work, except to say that when he died, all unknown to those who were receiving his aid, at least sixty-five small country schools were being helped by the money he contributed.

I think I have never seen him quite so happy as when I would make a report as to the results his gifts were getting in the way of better schools, or when I could show him a picture of one of the little new schoolhouses that he had helped the country people to erect.

In this connection I recall most vividly a trip which he invited me to take with him from New York to Fairhaven on his yacht, the Kanawha. During the course of the trip I had abundant opportunity to tell him more in detail than I had hitherto done about the good that his money was accomplishing for the uplift of the people in the South. It seemed to me that his face fairly radiated with happiness as, through the account I gave him, he was able to enter fully into the situation and realize the good that he had been able to do. All these gifts to these small schools were made on condition that the people who were aided should do something to help themselves. While the amount of money that Mr. Rogers gave was large, the sum which his gifts led the people to raise on their own account was still larger. In this way he made his gifts do the people a double service, since they not only had better schools, but they, at the same time, felt that they had obtained them to some extent as a result of their own efforts and sacrifices.

IN NEW YORK

I saw Mr. Rogers frequently when I was in New York. No matter how busy he was, or how much his name was being bandied about in public controversies, in which he was often misunderstood and often abused, he always had time and seemed glad to see me, and he always seemed very happy to take time to hear my report of the progress of the work he was aiding.

Only a few days before Mr. Rogers passed away, I had an extended interview with him in his office, when he arranged for me to make a trip over his new Virginia railway, for the purpose of studying the conditions of the colored people along the routes, and of devising some means by which he might assist them in their education and in the development of their agricultural life. It seemed to me that he was quite as much interested in the possibility of helping the people along the line of his railroad as he was in completing the road itself.

I remember asking Mr. Rogers once in what way he got the most enjoyment out of life. He replied that it was in hard work, in doing good, and getting caught at it. And yet one could not think of Mr. Rogers as being a slave to business. I remember that he remarked to me once that he pitied a man who had no resources outside the hard, daily routine and could find no relaxation except in business. He pitied the man, he once told me, who could not enjoy literature and the friendship of literary men.

OFFICE INCIDENTS

He seemed to get a great enjoyment out of doing the little unexpected things for people. For example, he had in his office three or four bright young colored men who served as messengers. He saw in some of my writings the following sentence: "I believe that any man's life will be filled with constant and unexpected encouragements, if he makes up his mind to do his level best each day — that is, tries to make each day as nearly as possible reach the high-water mark of pure, unselfish, and useful living." At once he made arrangements for this sentence to be put in an attractive form and given to the colored boys, so that it would be near them as they worked in his office day by day.

Another incident, which illustrates the kindness and gentleness of Mr. Rogers's disposition, happened in connection with his plan to which I have already referred of aiding a number of county schools to obtain better school buildings and prolong their school terms.

In order to stimulate the work of raising funds among the country people, we started a little county newspaper. In this paper, we printed, among other things, the names of all those who contributed anything toward the local community school fund. I remember the first time I showed him a copy of this little paper it contained an account of a school rally in which the farmers of one little community had gotten together and had raised, as I remember, something like one hundred dollars. He smiled as he began reading the account of this school rally, described in the true language of a country correspondent. It was interesting to watch the expression on his face as he read down the long column of figures, which showed how, out of their small earnings, every one seemed to have contributed something to support the little school. Before he had finished, the tears came to his eyes, and he seemed more deeply touched than I had ever seen him.

Such a man was Henry H. Rogers, as I have known him. He was one of the best and the greatest men I have ever met, and as it seems to me, one of the greatest men of his day and age, and he has left many lessons behind him which others can follow to their profit.

New York *Evening Post*, May 29, 1909, sec. 3:1.

From Charles William Anderson

New York   May 30—09

New York Sun today prints refusal of Seth Low   Thomas Wentworth Higginson[1]   Francis Lynde Stetson[2] to participate in negro conference   Higginson says negro suffrage was mistake   all feel that agitation of it just now is inexpedient   Higginson believes in Taft.

Charles W. Anderson

HWSr   Con. 43   BTW Papers   DLC.

[1] Thomas Wentworth Storrow Higginson (1823–1911), a Unitarian minister and abolitionist, was colonel of the first black regiment in the Union Army. After the war he wrote a number of books, including an account of his war experiences.

[2] Francis Lynde Stetson (1846–1920), a leading New York corporation lawyer, handled the negotiations leading to the formation of the U.S. Steel Corporation in 1901.

From Charles William Anderson

[New York City] Sunday May 30/09

Dear Doctor: I "wired" you this morning about the enclosed, which was clipped from the "Sun" of this A.M.

I am doing all I can to discredit this affair. I think I have succeeded in defeating the dinner project to Du Bois, by asking all of my friends and yours not to subscribe to it. They will either have to drop it, or give him a small private dinner.

I feel confident that a big public testimonial, such as was planned, cannot be pulled off.

Dr. Elbert[1] of Wilmington who is a candidate for the city Council, wants me to run over & speak for him next Thursday night. Am undecided. What sort of a man is he?

When will you be here? "Post" printed your Rogers article Saturday evening. Hastily,

Anderson

ALS Con. 43 BTW Papers DLC.

[1] Samuel George Elbert, an 1891 graduate of Howard University Medical School, practiced medicine in Wilmington, Del., where he ran for the city council on the Republican ticket in 1909. He lost the election, however, in a Democratic sweep of the city.

From Charles William Anderson

New York, May 31st—1909

Du Bois, Waldron, Walters, Sinclair, Max Barber, Wibecan, Dr Mossell[,] Bulkley, Milholland[,] Ida Wells, and entire cosmopolitan dinner crowd in Secret conference to-day. Public meeting to-night have had newspapers cover it   another secret session to-morrow. Think Villard is with them.

Chas. W. Anderson

TWSr Con. 43 BTW Papers DLC.

A Handbill Announcing Washington's Tour of Virginia

[ca. June 1, 1909]

NOTICE!

BOOKER T. WASHINGTON,

THE GREAT NEGRO EDUCATOR.

Will make a Tour of The Virginian Railway
in a Special Train

NORFOLK, VA., TO DEEPWATER, W. VA.

Stopping at the Following Stations to Deliver a
Series of Educational Addresses.

MONDAY, JUNE 21, 1909.	
Suffolk, Va.,	1.30 p m.

TUESDAY, JUNE 22, 1909.	
Burdette, Va.,	9.00 a.m.
Sebrell, Va.,	11.30 "
Jarratt, Va.,	12.30 p.m.
Purdy, Va.,	1.30 "

WEDNESDAY, JUNE 23, 1909.	
Alberta, Va.,	9.30 a.m.
Kenbridge, Va.,	10.30 "
Victoria, Va.,	1.00 p.m.
Meherrin, Va.,	2.00 "
Ward, Va.,	3.30 "

THURSDAY, JUNE 24, 1909.	
Phoenix, Va.,	9.00 a.m.
Brookneal, Va.,	11.00 "
Altavista, Va.,	2.00 p.m.
Salem, Va.,	8.00 "

FRIDAY, JUNE 25, 1909.	
Shelby, Va.,	Morning
Pembroke., Va.,	Afternoon
Pearisburg, Va.,	"
Princeton, W. Va.,	Night

SATURDAY, JUNE 26, 1909.	
Giatto, W. Va.,	12.00 noon
Slab Fork, W. Va.,	2.30 p.m.
Lester, W. Va.,	3.00 "
Page, W. Va.,	Night

SUNDAY, JUNE 27, 1909.	
Deepwater, W. Va.,	Morning

Don't Fail to Hear This Great Exponent of Negro Education.

From Robert Elijah Jones[1]

New Orleans   June the third, Nineteen hundred-nine

PERSONAL AND CONFIDENTIAL

Dear Doctor: I have your letter, under date of May the seventeenth, and must apologize for the delay in replying.

To answer your query concerning Mr. Walter L. Cohen, of this city, and at the same time recognize all the principles of justice involved, I must go somewhat into details, and hence the length of this letter.

I know nothing against Mr. Cohen's life and personal habits, except that he drinks and gambles and plays baseball on Sunday. I do not think that he denies this or attempts to conceal it. I do not know that we can say Mr. Cohen is allied with the forces that make for righteousness and moral uplift. While I do not mean to infer that his leadership is negative in this regard, it certainly is not positive. There are persons in this City who follow Mr. Cohen's political leadership, who feel at heart that a man who represents more in his ideals for the race would be more satisfactory as a leader. In talking with the Managing Editor of the Times-Democrat one night, we Colored people were upbraided for keeping Cohen to the front. Now this statement, of course, must be taken with a degree of allowance. This Editor may or may not have had reason for saying what he did concerning Mr. Cohen, and it is likely enough that any colored man who is as active, politically, as Mr. Cohen is, would be objected to by a certain set of whites.

Now, my personal attitude toward Mr. Cohen is this: I greatly admire, along with others, his courage and force as a political leader. I believe the organization which he represents as its leader deserves to live because it is righteous. Of course, I am opposed to Lilly-Whitism. I am, therefore, in favor of the Republicani[sm] for which Mr. Cohen stands, and he is beyond doubt the leader, and is recognized by the City and State Press and the public in general as the leader of the faction known as the Black and Tans. In this capacity Mr. Cohen has had whatever support I could give him, and I have supported him openly, and without any apology, whatever. He is shrewd and capable. In his official position, as Registrar of the Land Office, I have heard no criticism, whatever, of his administration. On the other hand it is understood that he has done good work, and I should unhesitatingly say that he deserves reappointment.

He is a fine man to meet; congenial, big hearted and princely in many of his ways.

Now, Mr. Washington, I have written you thus because of the nature of your letter asking for a personal and confidential reply. It is a hard thing to give a just estimate of a man when so many things are involved. Mr. Cohen is a Catholic; I am a Protestant, and he looks at life from a very different standpoint than myself. Things Protestants might think should not adhere in a leader would pass unnoticed by Catholics in general. I have never made such a statement as this before concerning Mr. Cohen in public or in private. On the other hand I have felt called upon to say whatever I could, in justice to conscience and a sense of right, to aid him in his political plans.

With very best wishes, I am, Yours truly,

Robert E. Jones

TLS   Con. 44   BTW Papers   DLC.   A copy is in Con. 392, BTW Papers, DLC.

1 Robert Elijah Jones, born in Greensboro, N.C., in 1872, was a Methodist Episcopal clergyman and, beginning in 1904, editor of the *Southwestern Christian Advocate*. He served as president of the black YMCAs in New Orleans, and was a trustee of Bennett College and Gammon Theological Seminary. Jones was also an officer of the National Negro Press Association and the NNBL.

To Walter L. Cohen

New York. June 4, 1909

Personal

My dear Mr. Cohen: I telegraphed you today as follows: "Saw our friend yesterday. Your case seems to be held up because waiting for decision to be reached regarding consolidating land offices and where they will be located. Am writing."

I had a talk with the Secretary of the Interior,[1] also with the President. The only matter that now seems to be holding up your case is that of the consolidation of the offices. It seems that there are three land offices in Louisiana. The work has been so reduced that the Secretary says according to the law he is compelled to arrange to have only one office. Since there are no public lands near New Orleans he says the proper thing to do is to locate one office at either Lacooque[2] — I am not sure what the name is — or Alexandria. As to just who the officials will be has not been determined, but I have impressed upon him and the President the importance of having you kept somewhere in the service and they seemed to be impressed with this view of the case. I have tried to get them to see the importance of locating the office at New Orleans and in this am not sure that I have succeeded as they are not sure that they can under the law properly do so. The point that was holding up your case at the time I wrote you before I think I have gotten rid of. There is no need of my mentioning it in this letter, but I will tell you about it when I see you, but I do not think this point need trouble you. I think everything is straightened out except the matter of turning the three offices into one and the decision as to just who will occupy the positions in this office. Of course, that involves a matter of much importance to you. I told them I did not know whether you would feel like going to either one of the two points, but that would have to be a matter which you yourself could determine when the point is finally reached. My own feeling is that they are not going to make any move in the direction of consolidation or change within the near future. I think they are going to delay it just as long as possible.

In the meantime I advise that at any time you are going North before the President leaves on his vacation that you drop in and talk with him. There is nothing like keeping in close touch with him and presenting your own side of the case. You can do it better than anybody else. A personal talk is worth a good many letters. Yours very truly,

[Booker T. Washington]

TLc Con. 44 BTW Papers DLC.

[1] Richard Achilles Ballinger (1858–1922), Secretary of the Interior from 1909 to 1911.

[2] No such name could be found. The two places considered for the land office were Natchitoches and Alexandria. (See BTW to Taft, June 18, 1909, below.)

From Emmett Jay Scott

On Board "The Birmingham" Sunday June 6, 1909

My Dear Mr. Washington: We completed the Liberian mission at Cape Palmas where Mr. Dossen lives on Friday evening & left there for Monrovia again where we stopped long enough to put Mr Lyon, the American Minister ashore, & came up to Cape Mount the furthest north of the Liberian ports & left there last night for Sierre Leone (Freetown) where we shall be early tomorrow, Monday morning.

I think I have explained to you that we spent three weeks in the Capital — Monrovia — developing such facts as we could & then our party divided: Mr. Falkner, Mr. Finch & Capt. Cloman, the military attache left at the same hour we did for Freetown going from there to the Kawe Lahun[1] District where the disputes with the British are acute. We went South to Grand Bassa (the most important commercial center[)] & to Cape Palmas & from Cape Palmas overland to the mouth of the Cavally River & up the Cavally River: which is the point of dispute with the French. It is wise that these trips were arranged. They gave us a better opportunity to see the Country than we had had & the people a chance to testify as to their interest in the coming of the American Commission. At Grand Bassa we went overland to all of the surrounding towns as we did at Cape Palmas & at both of these places very elaborate & popular receptions & public exercises were held. Dr Sale & I spoke several times at each of these several towns. Everywhere people asked of you & expressed their disappointment that you did not come. You are as well known among these Liberians — natives & others — almost as in the States & it w'd have been a great treat for these people to have seen you & to have heard you. At Sierre Leone we join the members who went to Kawe Lahun & on Tuesday evening start north again. We are to meet the British Governor of Sierre Leone & at the request of the British Government discuss with him the several disputes between Liberia & Gt. Britain. The Chester has gone ahead to coal at Dakar & we carry the whole party & meet off Dakar about 150 or 200 miles & transfer a part of the Commission to the Chester (as we started out from New York) & proceed in that way to the Canary Islands, to the Madeira Islands & to *New*

York. At present it seems we shall not be in NY till July 2, 3 or 4 & maybe the 5th or 6th. The party will disband for a week or 10 days & then meet again to compile the report.

The whole party has kept well. I have been sick only twice & that from constipation only & partially from over doing it in the matter of the 30 mile overland trip from Cape Palmas to the Cavally River. We had ideal weather all the time — so far as rainfall is concerned, but of course it has been hot to the point of exhaustion. We have had to conserve strength all along the line. It has surprised everyone out here in the matter of rainfall. Never, say the people, have they ever seen so little rainfall at this season of the year.

Liberia has the richest possible possibilities if its resources can be developed. You, I feel sure, will never regret the time, money & strength you have expended to serve the little Republic. The official classes give you full credit for the Commission & your name has been toasted with Mr Tafts & Mr Barclays at every reception given us. Yours very sincerely

Emmett J. Scott

ALS   Con. 587   BTW Papers   DLC.

1 Kawilahun, a village in the northern coastal district of Liberia.

To Henry Huddleston Rogers, Jr.[1]

Hotel Manhattan, New York. June 7, 1909

Dear Mr. Rogers: Two matters I omitted to mention to you this morning in my conversation.

First, I hope very much that you will write me the letter which you said you had in mind to write today, as I should like to have it for the sake of associating it with your father.

Second, for a number of years your father has been in the habit of giving to our institution a certain sum of money each month. I think he began by sending us $100 each month, then he increased to $150, and finally $250 a month. So far as I now remember, there was never any definite understanding by him as to how long he meant to continue making this monthly gift to the school itself, but

I have an idea that he meant, judging by some things he said, that he meant to give it for a year, although, as I have stated, there was nothing definitely stated or promised. Perhaps Miss Harrison may know a little more about it.

Of course in writing I am not suggesting that you or any member of the family continue this gift, but I thought I ought to mention it.

I am very glad indeed that you are going to see to it that the $500 per month for the helping of the small schools in the South is to be continued to the end of the time that Mr. Rogers planned for it. This is rendering a service which you can hardly appreciate, and at some time in the future I hope to let you and the members of your family see something of the fine results which have been accomplished through these gifts.

[Booker T. Washington]

TLcf Con. 397 BTW Papers DLC.

1 Henry Huddleston Rogers, Jr. (1879–1935), took over his father's business interests.

To William Passmore Pickett[1]

[Tuskegee, Ala.] June 14, 1909

Dear Sir: I have received your kind letter of June 3d,[2] also a copy of your book. While I have not as yet had time to read the book through, I have hurriedly glanced through a few pages. I shall try to read it carefully in the future.

In glancing the book through I find some mistakes that it seems to me very unfortunate for anybody to make who is putting a book intending to be of a serious character before the public. For example, in referring to the Jeanes Fund Board and the work of this board you speak as follows:

["]To any one familiar with Southern views upon the subject of the education of the Negro, the difficulties confronting these trustees appear formidable. In the first place no Southern white man of social standing, no public official or leader of thought can afford to jeopardize his standing among his people by in any degree associating himself with Negro men upon a board of this character. To sit in conference with members of the African race, on terms of equality, is a thing not for a moment to be contemplated.

["]Further, upon the well established principle that in every character of enterprise those controlling the financial resources are in a position to dictate the conditions under which the funds are to be expended, it is clear that the Northern theorists with their Negro coadjutors can never hope to agree with the local authorities in Southern communities as to the methods to be employed or the ends to which the interest of the fund is to be applied. . . . Against this spirit, which, as we have seen in a preceding chapter dominates the South, the $60,000 income of the Jeanes fund will have about as much effect as the circulation of an anti-slavery pamphlet had in Mississippi in the years preceding the Civil War.["]

If this statement is an illustration of the correctness of any large proportion of the other statements in the book, I very much fear that it will count for little in any serious consideration of the race problem. You make the emphatic statement that no Southern white man of social standing, political leader, or any public official or leader of thought could afford to be a member of this board or to sit in council with members of the African race.

Permit me to state that we had no trouble whatever in getting an acceptance from every Southern white man who was asked to accept a position as member of the Jeanes Fund Board. Aside from this, we had at least a dozen letters from various parts of the South written by white people themselves urging that their white friends be put upon this board. I do not recall how many meetings we have had since the board was organized, but at every one the Southern members have been present and have sat around the same table with Northern white men without the least sign of friction. At the present time the President of the United States is a member of the board, and he has already invited us to hold our next annual meeting in the White House.

You say that no white man of social standing can afford to be a member of this board. At present the Southern members are Chancellor David C. Barrow[3] of the University of Georgia, Dr. Samuel C. Mitchell,[4] president of the University of South Carolina, Mr. Belton H. Gilreath, a large and successful coal operator in Alabama, Dr. James H. Dillard, who up to the time of his election as a member of our board was Dean of Tulane University in New Orleans. Permit me to add that Dr. Dillard is not only the president of the board, but at our solicitation he gave up his official connection with Tulane University and is now devoting all of his time to work for the board in connection with the distribution of this fund.

I would add further that we have had not the slightest difficulty in finding counties where the local school authorities were ready to cooperate in every way possible with us in the expenditure of this money: in fact, if we had ten times as much we would have no trouble in finding Southern white men who hold official positions who stand ready to cooperate with us in the expenditure.

Attached you will find all the names of the members of our board, with those who are colored and those who are white indicated, as well as the section of the country in which they live. I think you will find that these men represent the very highest social elements in our Southern country, that is, I know of none who stand higher socially.

For over twenty years we have had upon the trustee board of the Tuskegee Normal and Industrial Institute about an equal number of Northern white men, Southern white men, and Negroes. The Southern white men on the board include bankers, newspaper editors, planters, etc., Southern white men of the very highest business and social standing. And during all these twenty years there has never been the slightest friction in our board. Sometimes we meet in New York and sometimes in the South; in either case there has been not the slightest difficulty on account of social differences in the board.

Let me add further, there came the enclosed letter from Dr. Dillard, the president of the Jeanes Board. This is a letter from a county superintendent in Virginia with whom Dr. Dillard is cooperating.

I wish very much that before you begin circulating such a book that you would have gotten hold of somebody who lives in the South and knows conditions by actually facing the facts in this section of the country. I do not in any case overlook the difficulties nor the elements of injustice and wrong that often crop out in the situation, but I think in all cases it is right that we be very sure of sticking to the truth, but in your case I fear somebody has seriously misled you. Yours very truly,

Booker T. Washington

Of course I realize how unjust it is to pick out a few sentences for adverse criticism in a book in which perhaps there is much that ought to be commended, and in writing you as I do about that which I think you are mistaken in I do not wish to seem narrow and ungrateful.

B. T. W.

TLpS Con. 397 BTW Papers DLC.

[1] William Passmore Pickett (b. 1855) was a graduate of Cornell University (1878). He was a deputy collector of internal revenue from 1880 to 1884, and later practiced law in New York City. In his book *The Negro Problem: Abraham Lincoln's Solution* (1909), Pickett argued that blacks could never be assimilated into American society and that colonization of American blacks in Liberia, Haiti, or the Panama Canal Zone was the only solution to the race problem.

[2] Pickett's letter pointed out that he had praised BTW's efforts in his book and asked BTW for his opinion of the work. (Con. 397, BTW Papers, DLC.)

[3] David Crenshaw Barrow, Jr. (1852–1929), a racial moderate, was chancellor of the University of Georgia from 1906 until 1925, after many years as professor of mathematics.

[4] Samuel Chiles Mitchell (1864–1948), born in Coffeeville, Miss., was a Ph.D. in history at the University of Chicago (1889). He was professor of history at Richmond College (1895–1908), president of the University of South Carolina (1908–13), and president of Delaware College beginning in 1914. Mitchell was active in the Conference for Education in the South and became a member of the Southern Education Board. His liberal views on race brought an abrupt end to his presidency at the University of South Carolina. The economic historian Broadus Mitchell and the liberal publicist George Sinclair Mitchell were his sons.

To Helen Van Wyck Lockman

Brooklyn, N.Y. June 16, 1909

My dear Mrs. Lockman: Enclosed please find check for $500 dollars. I had already anticipated your letter by a few hours and had directed that the check be made out.

We are sorry to be detained from Huntington so long. I am planning at present to reach there on the 28th. Mrs. Washington,

I fear, will not reach there until a few days later, as she is anxious to remain here until our son, Booker, Jr., returns from college and gets settled here for the summer. Both Laura and Tom,[1] however, remind us every day that they want to go to Huntington. We shall certainly hope to see you and Mr. Lockman, as well as the other members of the family at Huntington this summer, if you do not go to Europe.

If the size of this check does not comply with my promise let me know and I will pay the whole or make it larger. Yours very truly,

Booker T. Washington

TLpS Con. 393 BTW Papers DLC.

[1] Laura Murray and Thomas J. Murray, niece and nephew of Margaret M. Washington.

To William Howard Taft

[Tuskegee, Ala.] June 18, 1909

My dear Mr. President: Your kind letter of June 14th, regarding R. L. Smith being dropped from Marshal Houston's office, in Paris, Texas, has been received, and I appreciate thoroughly all that you and the Attorney General say regarding this case.

Of course, it is natural and right that the Attorney General should consider the matter from the standpoint of his department, but I am sure that you will agree with me that it is sometimes necessary to take the large view rather than the departmental view wherever it can be done with no injustice or unfairness.

The Attorney General, perhaps, misunderstood me on one point. I did not state that there was no colored man holding a position in any Marshal's office in the United States, but I did state that R. L. Smith, so far as I knew, was the only colored man in the whole state of Texas, who held any federal office of any importance. This, I think, I am correct in.

In order that you may be kept fully informed as to just what changes have taken place or [are] likely to take place, in reference to Negroes holding federal positions, I enclose to you a memorandum on that subject. Of course, I realize, I think, what you are trying to do and how you are trying to do it, and I am in full sympathy with you. I believe that in your own time and in your own manner you will do whatever is necessary to let the colored people see that you are not inclined to decrease materially the number of Negroes holding office throughout the country.

If the Land Office in Louisiana is moved away from New Orleans to Natchitoches, or to Alexandria, this will mean that both colored men, that is Mr. Cohen and the Negro Registrar of the Land Office, who are holding office will have to go out, as I do not think they could hold office in any of the small towns in Louisiana outside of New Orleans. If they have to go, it will mean that every Negro holding a federal office in Louisiana will be out, since after the first of July, Cohen and the Negro Registrar will be the only two.

The colored people throughout the country watch very closely these little changes, and they are becoming not a little stirred up, and it is for this reason that I call these matters to your attention, from time to time. Wherever I get an opportunity of speaking to the individual colored people or to them in a body, I have said to them that in your own way and in your own time you would see that the best thing is done in the interest of the colored people, whether this is in the direction of appointing them to office or in some other direction, and that you were their friend and would stand by them.

If, in your own way you could find some position in the state of Texas which Smith can be appointed to, it would help much. I happen to know that ever since he has been in office, he has spent more than half of his salary each year in helping forward the education of our people in that state. Yours truly,

Booker T. Washington

[*Enclosure*]

Memorandum for President Taft

1. Negroes who have Disappeared from Office, since March 4th Last for one reason or another.

Dr. W. D. Crum, Collector of Port, Charleston, S.C. — Resigned.
Mr. R. L. Smith, position in Marshal Houston's office, Paris, Texas — Asked to resign.

Mr. John Deveaux, Collector of Port, Savannah, Ga. — Died.

2. Negroes who will go out of Office July 1st, unless something is done before that time.

Col. James Lewis, Surveyor General of the Land Office, New Orleans, La. — Position abolished.
Mr. William H. Lewis, Assistant District Attorney, Boston.
Mr. S. Laing Williams, Assistant District Attorney, Chicago.

3. Negroes who are likely to go out of Office in Louisiana if Land Office is moved from New Orleans.

Walter L. Cohen, Receiver of Public Money and Negro Registrar.

4. Negroes who are likely to go out of Office sometime in the near future.

Dr. J. E. Wilson,[1] Postmaster, Florance, N.C.[2] — On account of being refused confirmation before Mr. Taft took office.

TLpS Con. 48 BTW Papers DLC. The enclosure was also a press copy. BTW may have personally carried the letter and memorandum to Washington, D.C., since the letter is docketed: "Mr. Washington took letter with him."

[1] Joshua E. Wilson.
[2] Florence, S.C.

From William Howard Taft

[Washington, D.C.] June 24, 1909

My dear Dr. Washington: I have your letter of June 18th and have read it with a great deal of interest. The matter of appointments and filling places is a most difficult one to carry out, for the reason that the places are so few and vacancies come so rarely that it is difficult to shape a plan of action; but I intend nevertheless to carry out the ideas I have already explained to you, and I hope that circumstances will so adjust themselves that I can demonstrate it. Very sincerely yours,

Wm H Taft

TLpS William Howard Taft Papers DLC.

From William Henry Lewis

Boston   July 2, 1909

Dear Mr. Washington: I cannot tell you how much I appreciate your kindness in calling me up over the phone this morning, in fact, I have been "down in the mouth" for several days. When the letter to the District Attorney, copy of which is enclosed, was brought to my attention I felt very much as Lincoln said the boy did, who stubbed his toe "hurt too badly to laugh and too big to cry." Since last March in view of promises made and the support of earnest friends I had hoped for something different, perhaps for too much.

You will see by the letter that the Attorney General asked that I be retained as Assistant in the office of the District Attorney here at my present salary "assuming that you will have enough work in your office to keep him employed."[1] In the first place there is not enough work there as there are three assistants in the office at present. Before my first appointment in that office there were only two. Mr. French[2] himself while kindly disposed toward me, and as you probably saw from his letter endorsing me for Assistant Attorney General is willing to help in any way, frankly said he was somewhat annoyed by the request. He appreciates my feelings in the matter and says I ought to have been given something better. As I said to you over the wire, the appointment is purely a political one and an unnecessary one. However, Mr. French is willing to do whatever I suggest about it. I have not yet seen his letter to the Attorney General.[3] From my point of view, the appointment is a retrograde one although it carries the same salary. It takes me back to the Federal Building where I am not my own boss and *I feel absolutely certain that if it is a permanent* one when it becomes known will necessarily provoke criticism.

I cannot explain the result except upon the one theory, which you know. (race) The Attorney General stated to Mr. Searle that he never saw a finer endorsement of anyone. As I said in my letter, I cannot afford to remain longer in the Federal service unless there is some chance for promotion. If I could get a chance in Washington in the Department of Justice, I feel certain that I could "make good," and put race prejudice to flight in that department. I regret that under the circumstances I must consent to this arrangement for the time being. If I were a single man it would of course be easier. I trust that you will not feel that I am wanting in appreciation for what you have done or in any degree lacking in gratitude, but I have simply expressed my honest feelings in the matter, whether warranted, justified, wise or unwise.

Please write me at an early date and let me know what you think about it. Believe me, Faithfully yours,

William H Lewis

TLS   Con. 393   BTW Papers   DLC.

[1] A copy of George W. Wickersham to Asa P. French, June 26, 1909, is attached to this letter in Con. 393, BTW Papers, DLC.

[2] Asa Palmer French (1860–1935) was a district attorney in Massachusetts from 1901 to 1914. He was a graduate of Yale and of the law school of Boston University. In 1917–18 he was a delegate to the Massachusetts constitutional convention.

[3] Lewis obtained a copy of French's letter to Attorney General Wickersham before mailing his letter to BTW and enclosed a copy. French said: "I am particularly glad to have Mr. Lewis come back to the general work of the office, in accordance with your suggestion." He added, however, that Lewis's return to the office "will intensify the intolerable inconvenience resulting from our cramped and insufficient accommodations, which were the subject of my recent earnest appeal to you." (July 1, 1909, Con. 393, BTW Papers, DLC.)

To Samuel Laing Williams

Huntington, L.I., N.Y. July 3, 1909

My dear Mr. Williams: After returning from my Virginia trip, I am just finding time to reply to your kind letter bearing upon the conference at which Mr. Manning of Alabama was present. Really I do not believe you need give any serious attention to him, although I thank both you and Mrs. Williams for what you said in the conference. Manning is one of those fellows who will take care of himself very soon. I mean he very soon disgusts everybody. He is one of these unprincipled fellows with whom one cannot afford to get on intimate terms. He scarcely knows a fellow before he is after his pocket book, that is, wants them to give him money or borrow money. He disgusts everybody in that way. I guarantee to say that if he is in Chicago that he has already disgusted the white people with whom he has come in contact by trying to get money from them. I do not know what it is he has against me, except he cannot use me to carry out his selfish purposes. He is a fellow that nobody has any confidence in who knows him. He has no influence with anybody that I know of in Alabama. Yours very truly,

[Booker T. Washington]

TLc   Con. 48   BTW Papers   DLC.

An Address by William Taylor Burwell Williams[1] on Washington's Tour of Virginia

[Hampton, Va.] July 4, 1909

With Dr. Washington Through Virginia

It has been my good fortune to accompany Dr. Booker T. Washington on two trips this year. I went with him through South Carolina in March, and a few days ago I spent a week with him on his tour through Virginia and West Virginia. Both of these trips were full of interest. Indeed it is an interesting experience just to be with Dr. Washington, to see him at close range under normal conditions and to study him as a most effective speaker before ever varying audiences, and to learn something of the spirit that underlies his work.

In South Carolina we went to a number of the larger cities of the state, and were confined to no particular section. On the recent Virginia and West Virginia trip we passed through but few cities and were limited to the Virginian Railroad. We saw fewer colored men in Virginia who own farms of five hundred or a thousand acres than we did in South Carolina. There were, however, more colored landowners in Virginia, and the average value of their lands per acre is higher than that in South Carolina. In Virginia, too, the colored farmers grow more diversified crops, especially outside of the tidewater section.

The trip was made over the Virginian Railroad, recently built by the late Mr. Henry H. Rogers. For a new road it is the best I have ever ridden over. From the mountains of West Virginia to the sea its grades are exceptionally easy. It was built to enable one engine to haul a hundred loaded cars. We passed a coal train of ninety-three loaded cars and four empties. This train carried into Norfolk something over six thousand nine hundred tons of coal. The road extends from Norfolk, Va., to Deepwater, W.Va., and passes through southside Virginia, a portion of the state which is south of the James River. It pierces the heart of the black belt of the state, opens up regions not hitherto easily accessible, and touches counties in the two states in which at least two hundred twenty-five thousand colored people live. It was fitting then that Dr. Washington should make a trip through this section.

Dr. Washington was invited to South Carolina by colored men, and all the arrangements for the trip were made and carried out by them. He was invited to make the trip through Virginia by Mr. Henry H. Rogers shortly before he died. A special train was placed at his disposal. Again and again Dr. Washington stated to his audiences that he was making the trip at the suggestion of Mr. Rogers, who had asked him to study the condition of the colored people, say whatever he could to help improve those conditions, and to encourage and cement the friendly relations existing between the white and colored people. It was pleasing to notice the many evidences of good feeling between the races. The colored people own one-twenty-fourth of the land of the state and it was especially gratifying to find so many prosperous Negroes in these formerly isolated districts, and to see the development they are making in education, in farming, in manners, dress, and in home-making.

The first meeting of the trip was held at Newport News. There several thousand colored mechanics and laborers are employed in the shipyards of the Newport News Shipbuilding and Dry Dock Company. It was the first time Dr. Washington had ever spoken at Newport News. The arrangements were in the hands of an efficient colored committee that was also ably and materially assisted by the white citizens who turned out in large numbers to hear the address and completely filled the lower floor of the local theatre. The mayor of the city introduced Dr. Washington and classed him among the great sons whom Virginia had produced. Here, as everywhere on the trip, the white people were among the most enthusiastic listeners to Dr. Washington and many remained to shake hands with him. Later in the afternoon Dr. Washington and his party were given a banquet by the colored citizens.

The next meeting was held at Suffolk. It proved to be the largest and in many respects the best of the meetings of the trip. Doubtless the largest audience that ever assembled in Suffolk came to hear Dr. Washington. Over six thousand persons from all over the country were there. Every officer of the county and every member of the city council was present. Here white and colored men worked together to make this an important day for Suffolk. The party was driven over the city in automobiles, the mayor riding with Dr. Washington in the finest automobile in the city, lent by its owner for this purpose. Introductory addresses were made by both white and colored citizens.

The outlook for a good meeting at Norfolk was not encouraging. Norfolk is probably the most conservative of Virginian cities, especially in its relations to the colored people. We were pleasantly surprised, however, for the floor of the Granby Theatre was crowded to its utmost with the best white people of Norfolk. The best colored people were present in overflowing numbers. At the Norfolk meeting Major Robert R. Moton, of Hampton Institute, presided. Dr. L. T. Royster, acting chairman of the board of trustees of the public schools, introduced Dr. Washington to the large and enthusiastic audience.

Never before in the history of the city, have so many of the best people of both races come together for any purpose whatever. Dr. Washington commands, as almost no other man in the South, an audience of all the people, and thus he has an opportunity to speak to assembled white and black people of the affairs that concern them in common. During the South Carolina trip an interesting comparison suggested itself. President Eliot, of Harvard, was then making a tour of the South. He spoke to the best white people — the educated classes. Dr. Washington spoke to the colored people and also to the leading progressive element.

After leaving Norfolk we came to no more large towns till we reached Roanoke. We stopped at way stations and little towns and Dr. Washington usually spoke from the rear platform of the railroad car. Crowds were invariably waiting to hear this distinguished Negro. Often they had come from twenty to thirty miles. At Kenbridge, a new thriving little town, we left the car and held the meeting in a large tobacco warehouse where several thousand persons had assembled. Among them were at least two hundred white ladies and gentlemen. Our party were driven from the railroad station through the town. One of the wealthiest young white men took Dr. Washington in his buggy. The mayor presided at the meeting. Kenbridge is in a fine farming section. Nowhere on the trip did the colored people present greater evidences of successful industry, thrift, and comfort than at Kenbridge. They were orderly and both men and women were well dressed. The latter wore the finest collection of really pretty hats that we saw anywhere. Colored men operate a very good store in the town, and in the neighborhood they own and work a number of fine farms. Mr. John B. Pierce,[2] a Hampton graduate in charge of demonstration farm work under Dr. Seaman A. Knapp and the United States Department of Agriculture, has been engaged in this neighborhood.

The next large meeting was at the St. Paul Normal and Industrial Institute at Lawrenceville, Brunswick County, in which ten thousand Negroes live. More than two thousand of them came to hear Dr. Washington. Many white people were also present. With the exception of Hampton, St. Paul is the largest industrial school in the state. Its community is well acquainted with the teachings of Dr. Washington, and it accorded him an unusually appreciative welcome. We spent the night there and held a second meeting in the evening. Other members of the party, as well as Dr. Washington, spoke. A white man whose wife was not with him in the afternoon when Dr. Washington first spoke sent her to hear him in the evening.

The next meeting of special importance was at the court house in Charlotte County. The supervisors of the county offered the use of the old court house, made famous by Patrick Henry and John Randolph, of Roanoke, but it proved entirely too small for the crowd. A large hall owned by a colored society had to be used. Here in the country, just as at Newport News and Norfolk, white ladies and gentlemen formed a large and interested part of the audience. Here, too, we spent a night. When we had driven back to our train next morning over five miles of one of the roughest roads in Virginia, we found a landslide just ahead of us and were delayed for the greater part of the day. We had to break an engagement at Stone Mountain, where a son of the man who had owned Booker Washington as a slave had especially requested that we stop. The gentleman himself, however, waited until late in the night to shake hands with Dr. Washington and to spend a few minutes with him. That night we spent at Salem, where we found one hundred fifty colored men employed in a tannery and a colored man as the master mechanic of this and other tanneries. He has been with the company eighteen years.

About thirty miles from Salem among the mountains of Montgomery County is Christiansburg Institute which is in the charge of a graduate of Tuskegee.[3] Here we stopped after a drive of four or five miles across the mountains behind some of the finest horses we had seen. No pains had been spared to make this meeting successful. The white people were no less enthusiastic over it than the colored people themselves. A great many of them found a place in the audience, and a number of the more distinguished ones were on the platform. Among the latter were ex-Governor Tyler[4] and the Honorable John R. Johnson, who introduced Dr. Washington. Many of the stores of Cambria and Christiansburg were closed so that the merchants and clerks might hear the address. The local paper said there were more white than colored people present. In his preliminary remarks the principal of Christiansburg Institute said to Dr. Washington: "You are to-day in a country where there has never been a lynching, where the jail is empty and the schoolhouse is full. During my thirteen years of residence in this community, I have never known a serious altercation between a white man and a black man. You might be interested to know that nine out of every ten colored men living in this community own their homes. There are less than a thousand colored people here, yet there are six grocery stores operated by colored men. This is made possible by the interest and assistance of our white friends. * * * You are speaking to a people interested in the development of the Negro race and especially in the work you are doing at Tuskegee." When Dr. Washington began to speak he commented upon the evidences of industry, thrift, intelligence, and refinement that were apparent every where in this community. Throughout this section of southwest Virginia splendid farms with good crops of wheat, corn, grass, besides horses and cattle, were to be seen on every hand. Our farmer, Mr. George Davis,[5] spent all his time looking at these crops. He declared that he had never seen so much wheat before in his life.

We spent a night at Page, West Virginia, in the midst of coal mines and coke furnaces, and had a fine meeting there with the colored miners. We made a short stop at Deepwater, the end of the Virginian Railroad, and then went for our last meeting to Montgomery. Here Dr. Washington was at home, for it was in this vicinity that he spent his young manhood. The town solicitor presided at this meeting and presented the Secretary of State of West Virginia,[6] who came as Governor Glasscock's[7] special representative to introduce Dr. Washington. Among other things he said: "You went from us a West Virginia boy; you return to us a citizen of the world." Dr. Washington paid a glowing tribute to West Virginia. Referring to her treatment of the Negro, he said: "If all the states had treated the Negro as fairly as West Virginia in the matter of schools, education, and the franchise, there would be no Negro question." He rejoiced that West Virginia had had the wisdom so to treat the colored people that all her citizens might be helpful to one another.

Throughout the trip Dr. Washington spoke to the colored people frankly of the simple, practical, fundamental affairs of life. He constantly told them of the duty and the possibilities for improving their condition. And he always won their interest and sympathy, as well as that of the white people.

In fact this trip through Virginia was no small test of the regard in which Dr. Washington is held by both white and black people. It is very apparent that both are becoming increasingly appreciative of his efforts. The amount of good the trip will do it is difficult to estimate.

Southern Workman, 38 (Aug. 1909), 452–57. Address delivered at Cleveland Hall Chapel, Hampton Institute, July 4, 1909.

1 William Taylor Burwell Williams (1866–1941) was born at Stonebridge, Va. After graduating from Hampton Institute in 1888 he attended Phillips Academy, Andover, Mass. (1889–93), and Harvard, where he received an A.B. degree in 1897. For five years he was principal of an Indianapolis elementary school. From 1902 to 1904 he was a field agent of the Southern Education Board. While serving as field director of Hampton Institute from 1902 to 1919 he also did field work for the General Education Board, the John F. Slater Fund, and the Anna T. Jeanes Foundation. He aided Robert R. Moton of Hampton in founding the Negro Organization

Society of Virginia. In 1919 he joined the faculty of Tuskegee Institute, where he was dean of the college (1927–36) and vice-president from 1936 to 1941.

[2] John B. Pierce, after graduation from Hampton Institute, was supervisor of gardening at Whittier School at Hampton about 1904. He moved to Wellville, Va., where he was an agricultural demonstration agent. In 1910 he spoke on the improvement of rural schools and of country life at the Hampton Farmers' Conference.

[3] Edgar Allen Long.

[4] James Hoge Tyler (1846–1925), a farmer and politician of an old Virginia family, was lieutenant governor of Virginia in 1889 and governor from 1897 to 1902.

[5] George Jordan Davis.

[6] Stuart Felix Reed (1866–1935) was secretary of state of West Virginia from 1909 to 1917. He served as a Republican in the U.S. House of Representatives from 1917 to 1925.

[7] William Ellsworth Glasscock (1862–1925), Republican governor of West Virginia from 1909 to 1913.

From Calvin E. Henike[1]

Bluefield, W.Va. July 5th, 1909

Dear Sir: It is with much pleasure that I now undertake to fulfill the promise made you at Giatto, W.Va. and during the conference between yourself and N. & W. Ry. employees to write you upon the subject of railways being forced to agree with organized labor to discontinue the employment of colored men in train service.[2] I know that the officials are perfectly satisfied with our service. They were handicapped by the labor unions taking the matter before them at the beginning of the year 1907 when the financial conditions of the road was not in a good shape and was threatened with a strike if they disagreed. The company not caring to enter into a strike of course agreed.

To my belief if there is no law one should be enacted to prevent such trusts as the labor trust to even demand such unreasonable measures of any corporation employing laborers. And the matter should be left entirely to them to employ any color or nationality they deem proper. Inter-State Commerce it seems to me could interfere when such demands are made as such tie ups means the delay to the mails and perishable freight. As I stated to you in your travels you might some times come in contact with some members of our board of directors who might be shown that colored labor is much cheaper and safer to handle trains. As you may know, the whites of the country do not want us to hold high positions on railroads neither in the Federal Government or other places. Now if we are not allowed to do common every-day railroading such as the white man did not want until just here lately, the question is to be answered by those who have the work to do what may we expect of the Negro. He is here with them, and it will be left to them whether they make him a desirable citizen or a thief and hobo. Cut him out of honorable employment and he will be obliged to steal. After you have had a good chance to talk these matters over with the unprejudiced capitalist[s] of our country I would be glad to hear from you as to what steps you think would best be taken. And do you think the Virginian will share their jobs with us.

I am, dear Sir, Yours truly,

C. E. Henike

P.S. You will no doubt have a letter from Mr. N. M. Martin, our secretary, Y.M.C.A., asking that you pass this way sometime in the near future. Hope you can answer favorable.

TLSr Copy   Con. 391   BTW Papers   DLC.

1 Calvin E. Henike was a brakeman, according to the Bluefield, W.Va., city directories. His stationery listed him as Master Trainman of the Bluefield local of the Railway Trainmen of America.

2 Henike sent BTW a four-page handwritten article, "The Norfolk and Western Railroad and the Negro," in which he argued that white unions needed to be checked in their efforts to exclude blacks from railway jobs. For more than forty years blacks were hired as brakemen, Henike stated, because it was a hard and dangerous occupation that white men avoided. But "many changes have taken place. The White man thinks and says it is his job and the Negro must get down and out." Henike pointed out that white railway unions were threatening railroad officials with strikes if blacks continued to be hired as brakemen or firemen. (Undated manuscript, Con. 391, BTW Papers, DLC.)

To Calvin E. Henike

Huntington, L.I., N.Y. July 7, 1909

My dear Sir: I am in receipt of your communication and thank you for writing me. Permit me to say that just as soon as I return to Tuskegee, which will be within a few days, I shall take up the whole matter and give it attention.[1] In the meantime let me express the great delight which I experienced in meeting your committee.

It seems to me that the decision in reference to the Georgia firemen ought to help your case immensely. While of course the Georgia decision on its face seems to be in the interest of the colored firemen, on the other hand it will have to be borne in mind that it places the colored firemen exactly on equality with the white firemen with reference to the kind of service rendered and if a weakness can be found in their service, they will be placed at a great disadvantage. Yours very truly,

[Booker T. Washington]

TLc Con. 391 BTW Papers DLC.

[1] BTW further replied to Henike on July 30, 1909, offering to speak to some of the higher officers of the Norfolk and Western Railway in the fall on the subject of black employment, and suggested that Henike make a personal call on Vice-President Raymond DuPuy of the Virginian Railway. BTW said: "I am all the more willing to do this for the reason that Mr. Rogers before he died asked me to suggest to him anything at any time which he could do to advance the interests of the colored people." (Con. 591, BTW Papers, DLC.) See also his letter to Raymond DuPuy, Sept. 29, 1909, below.

From Charles William Anderson

New York, N.Y., July 12, 1909

(Personal)

My dear Doctor: I wrote a strong letter to Mr. Loeb, which he in turn forwarded to the President (according to agreement between us) in which I have advised that some action be taken at once with respect to those fellows who are abusing the President and the President's friends, and at the same time, drawing salary from the administration. I urged that Murray, the Washington correspondent of the Boston Guardian, be dismissed at once, and if this course be impossible, that he be demoted and given some employment sufficiently arduous to keep him from having spare time enough to write these scurrilous articles. I called attention to the fact that these men were keeping track of all of the colored men whose terms of office are expiring, and whose places are not being filled by other colored men, and in this way are creating a great deal of opposition to the administration. I attached the outside page of the "Guardian" to my letter as an exhibit, and marked the several violent references to the President, contained in it. Loeb concurred with me, and joined in my recommendation that Murray be relieved at once. He is the head devil, for he is on the scene at Washington, and can keep the Boston fellow supplied with the very latest information. If "our friend" will only have nerve enough to fire this scoundrel, there will be an immediate cessation of hostilities all along the line. If he does not, he can prepare for jagged forks of lightening from all the little fellows under the administration, during his entire term of office. Hence, you see I have put the matter squarely up to him, the responsibilities for the future will therefore be his. Yours truly,

Charles W. Anderson

TLS   Con. 43   BTW Papers   DLC.

To James Hardy Dillard

Huntington, L.I., N.Y. July 30, 1909

My dear Mr. Dillard: I am very glad to see the interview concerning the removal of the Southern University. This is in the right direction. I had already seen one of the leading colored men of Louisiana who had told me about the interview. What you said met with his hearty approval.

Just as soon as I return to Tuskegee I shall take up seriously the matter of recommending a man for the work in Lowndes County. I think, however, before anything definite is done it would be well for you to go into the county and have an interview with the county superintendent. I do not know what kind of a fellow he is. Conditions in Lowndes County generally are about as bad as they are in any county in the South, but there may be a good superintendent there. I think it would help the work along much faster if what is done could have his approval, though I do not favor keeping the people in ignorance simply because one man may object to their being made intelligent. There are some very wealthy and strong white planters in Lowndes County with whom I am personally acquainted and who take interest in our work at Tuskegee. It might be well to reach the superintendent through some of these men.

I shall be glad to hear from you after you have seen Mr. Caldwell.[1] What you say concerning your interview with Superintendent Harris[2] is very satisfactory and interesting.

At the Lake George meeting I think that something strong ought to be said in favor of Negro education in the South. As a matter of fact, much of the advance in the way of white education in recent years has been made at the expense of Negro education, that is, money has been actually taken from the Negro schools to advance the education of the white people. I do not want to see the education of the white people slip back a single inch, but I do think it possible for the education of both races to go forward at the same time. Yours very truly,

[Booker T. Washington]

TLc   Con. 44   BTW Papers   DLC.

[1] B. C. Caldwell, originally from Illinois, took a leading part in the Louisiana educational campaigns of the 1890s, as a faculty member of the Louisiana Chautauqua, a summer training institute for teachers, and as president of the Louisiana State Normal School at Natchitoches from 1896 to 1908. A close co-worker with J. H. Dillard, he became about 1910 a field agent of the Slater and Jeanes funds, serving until his retirement in 1931.

[2] Thomas H. Harris (1869–1942), after about ten years of teaching experience, became Louisiana state superintendent of schools in 1908 by appointment of the governor, and served until 1940. His annual reports frequently urged improvement of black schools, including more and better-trained teachers.

From Charles William Anderson

New York   Aug 7. 09

Dear Doctor: Governor,[1] who is here, tells me that he wrote you some days ago advising you that the white papers of the country had treated him handsomely, and that it was left to one or two little colored papers to oppose him. I told him that I had heard that the Southern papers had "roasted" him. He is boasting about his treatment by the white papers, and seems to think that he could have been confirmed by the Senate for a cabinet position. When you answer him, you must say something to correct this impression, or he will feel that he is immensely popular, and the mention of his name for a small place, was due to your timidity in his behalf, and not to his general reputation. Jim Lewis of New Orleans, wrote him that the daily papers of that city spoke handsomely of him. This has swelled his head, I fear. I am taking some of the swelling out, but you must complete the job.

I secured the printing of those Concurrent resolutions for The Age. The Secretary of State of this state is my friend, and sent them in at my request. They ought to net the paper $300 or $400. I see Moore is booming Ransom and Chief Lee[2] in his paper. These are two of the men who helped to shut our folks out of the soldier affair. Why didn't Moore show up the graft? Suppose "we" had done such a thing. What would the Guardian have said? It is very difficult to work with such fellows. Yours truly,

Anderson

ALS Con. 43 BTW Papers DLC.

[1] P.B.S. Pinchback.

[2] Edward E. ("Chief") Lee, a Virginia-born hotel bellman, was for fifteen years the leader of the United Colored Democracy, founded in 1898 to unite the black Tammany Democrats in New York City. Though illiterate, he wielded power by securing city jobs for blacks. A favorite of Mayor Richard Croker, he was asked to resign in 1902 by Croker's successor, but he returned to control of the black Tammany faction in 1907. In 1910 he was appointed deputy sheriff. Two years later, however, his opponents ousted Lee from the organization.

To Jesse Edward Moorland

Huntington, L.I., N.Y. August 11, 1909

My dear Mr. Moorland: Your letter has been received. It is impossible, of course, for me to visit Arundel.[1] I am simply overwhelmed with responsibilities and work.

In regard to the employment of Dr. Du Bois. I have had a conference with the president of the University, and he understands my position thoroughly. Personally I have no feeling in the matter one way or the other. I have told Dr. Thirkield I should agree to whatever was for the best interests of the University. I should be surprised, however, if a man of Dr. Du Bois' importance can be secured at the small salary which the University is able to pay.

I shall talk with you further when I see you. I understand there is to be a meeting of the board on the 21st of September and I hope to be present.

I very much hope your health is improving. Yours very truly,

Booker T. Washington

TLS Jesse Edward Moorland Collection DHU. A press copy is in Con. 395, BTW Papers, DLC.

1 Arundel-on-the-Bay, on the western shore of Chesapeake Bay near Annapolis, was a summer resort where a number of leading black Washingtonians owned cottages. In 1922 it was incorporated as Highland Beach.

To Hilary Abner Herbert

Huntington, L.I., N.Y. August 12, 1909

My dear Sir: It has been my purpose for sometime to write to thank you for the wise, generous and brave decision reached by you in determining the protests against the employment of black men on the Georgia Railroad.[1] The Negro people everywhere feel under the greatest obligation to you for the position taken by you and Chancellor Barrow[2] at that time. I think that I can say that every one of them with whom I have talked feels that this decision rendered by Southern men will be as far-reaching in effect as any single thing in helping forward the progress of the Negro people. Yours truly,

Booker T. Washington

TLS Hilary Abner Herbert Papers NcU. A carbon copy is in Con. 391, BTW Papers, DLC.

1 In May of 1909 white firemen of the Georgia Railroad struck against the employment and upgrading of black firemen who were non-union. Herbert was one of the three arbitrators who on June 26, 1909, found against the union and in favor of employment and equal pay for black firemen. (For a detailed account of the strike see Matthews, "The Georgia 'Race Strike' of 1909.")

2 BTW wrote the same letter to another of the arbitrators, David C. Barrow, on the same date. (Con. 387, BTW Papers, DLC.) Barrow replied: "I am afraid that we have done a vain thing, but I tried to give justice. It was sworn in the case that no

railroad in a northern state with the single exception of a short line in Ohio would use negro firemen. In the light of this statement, I imagine that the powerful labor organizations of the country will ultimately prevail in excluding negroes from this line of work." (Aug. 17, 1909, Con. 388, BTW Papers, DLC.)

To Wilbur Patterson Thirkield

Huntington, L.I., N.Y. August 15, 1909

My dear President Thirkield: Although I tried at several places, I could not get the book which we discussed.

As to the employment of Dr. Du Bois at Howard, I repeat in substance what I said to you. Personally, I do not believe that he will be of any value to the institution. On the other hand, my fear is that he would be a hindrance. Then, too, I question whether a man of his importance can be secured for the small wage which Howard University is able to pay.

Now that I have stated my personal feeling in the matter, I wish you to feel perfectly satisfied if you as President of the University nominate Dr. Du Bois to the position I shall support you with my vote. On the other hand, if you feel that he ought not to enter the service of the University, I shall stand by you. In a word, I feel that you as President of the University know more than anybody else what it needs, and it seems to me that this is a matter in which you will have to largely if not wholly decide for yourself. That would certainly be the attitude I would take if Tuskegee were placed in a similar position. In the conduct of any large organization I believe that the only way for success to be attained is to support the man at the head. In the last analysis he bears the burden and should have the credit or censure for success or failure. In this case I feel all the more hesitation in expressing my views for reasons you well understand, but as a trustee of the institution I cannot shirk any duty however unpleasant it may be.

Let me repeat, that I shall be willing to follow your guidance in the matter.

All that I am trying to say can be summed up in this: If you as President of the University decide that you want him, I think the trustees will follow you in carrying out that wish, but, on the other hand, if you decide you do not want him, I think the trustees will support you. Yours very truly,

[Booker T. Washington]

TLc Con. 45 BTW Papers DLC. A copy is in Con. 48, BTW Papers, DLC.

To Charles William Anderson

Louisville, Ky. August 20, 1909

Personal and Confidential

My dear Mr. Anderson: We are having a fine meeting, by far the best we have ever had; the largest in attendance and largest in sanity and enthusiasm.

It is almost pathetic, however, to note the deep feeling of disappointment and sadness expressed by practically every man who comes here concerning the supposed attitude of President Taft. Last night in my annual address to an audience of some three thousand people in the theatre, gathered from all parts of the country, I referred to President Taft in as complimentary and strong terms as I could. You would be surprised to know that there was not a single handclap or a single move anywhere in the audience that indicated approval of my remarks.

I shall hope to see you within a few days. Yours very truly,

[Booker T. Washington]

TLc Con. 43 BTW Papers DLC.

To William Goodell Frost

Huntington, L.I., N.Y. August 26, 1909

My dear President Frost: Mr. W. Sidney Pittman, of Washington, as perhaps you know, is the architect for the new buildings being erected by the State of Kentucky at the State Normal School at

Frankfort. I think you will find by inquiry of the state officials that Mr. Pittman has done very satisfactory work at Frankfort. He has had large and wide experience in planning and erecting buildings. He has drawn the plans for some of the most substantial and costly buildings at Tuskegee. As you perhaps know, he drew the plans for the Negro Building at the Jamestown Exposition, and this building was widely commented upon as being one of the best on the grounds.

Mr. Pittman is the husband of my daughter Portia. While I should not like to have this weigh anything in his favor, I do ask that if he can perform as good service as anybody else in connection with the erection of your new buildings at the Lincoln Institute, that you give him a chance and I believe he will give you satisfaction. Aside from this, I think it would be a good idea to have it known that a colored man had drawn the plans. It would help in many ways.

Mr. Pittman has an excellent letter of endorsement from the Superintendent of Education in Kentucky.

Mr. Pittman's Washington address is, 494 Louisiana Ave. N.W., Washington, D.C. Yours truly,

Booker T. Washington

TLS KyBB.

To Oswald Garrison Villard

Huntington, L.I., N.Y. August 28, 1909

Personal

My dear Mr. Villard: There appeared not long ago in the Evening Post a review of Mr. Murphy's new book, "The Basis of Ascendency," which I cannot think received your personal attention. The review, as I remember it, dealt mainly with the literary form of the book and criticised that adversely.

If you have not done so, I very much hope that at your earliest opportunity you will read for yourself this book. In my opinion and in the opinion of a great many others who have read it, it is by far the strongest, most philosophic and bravest word that has been spoken yet by any Southern man concerning conditions in the South.[1] I believe you will come to this conclusion yourself after you have read the book if you have not already done so. I shall be very glad to hear from you after you have read it, and if another and different word can be spoken in the Evening Post concerning it, I am sure it will help. Yours very truly,

Booker T. Washington

TLS   Oswald Garrison Villard Papers   MH.

[1] BTW's favorable response to *The Basis of Ascendancy* was presented in more detail and with lengthy quotations in his review article, "The Negro and the 'Solid' South," *Independent*, 67 (Nov. 25, 1909), 1195–99. He said the book's significance was "not so much the fact that it condemns and discredits the policy which would deny to the negro the opportunity to advance along the lines in which he has the capacity to do so, but because it shows the futility of it, and outlines a policy which is based upon mutual good will, and gives to both races an opportunity to share in the upbuilding of the new South" (p. 1195). BTW glossed over Murphy's assumption of white superiority, however, and seemed to acquiesce in Murphy's principal concern that whites justify their dominance by their benevolence. The article was reprinted in pamphlet form by the Committee of Twelve for the Advancement of the Negro Race.

From Edgar Gardner Murphy

New Haven, Conn. Sept. 3–09

My dear Mr. Washington: I thank you for your suggestion to Mr. Villard: it was most thoughtful and generous of you.

But I wrote at once to tell him that deeply as I valued his own personal friendship (he expressed to me his great mortification at the "review") I had no favors to ask of the Evening Post or the Nation. "The Present South" has taken its place in American letters in spite of their sneers; the Basis of Ascendancy will do the same. They simply hate the South, and anything they might say would probaby do quite as much harm as good. My intense indignation is due not to their fault-finding (I have stood *that* from many quarters all my life) but to the gratuitous personal aspersions of their opening sentences. I want nothing to do with that sort of journalism, and if they comment further on the book they must do so in justice to the *cause* and to *themselves*.

The many beautiful letters I am receiving from the strong men of both sections give me confidence in its ultimate future: I only hope it can become well enough *known* for it to be fairly considered by our more intelligent public, North and South. For your own interest in it I thank you cordially. Faithfully Yours,

Edgar Gardner Murphy

ALS Con. 47 BTW Papers DLC.

To John R. Francis

[Tuskegee, Ala.] September 4, 1909

Personal

My dear Dr. Francis: Replying to your letter of recent date I would state that according to my present schedule it will be impossible for me to reach Washington before the night of the 20th or the morning of the 21st. All my plans are usually mapped out months ahead even to the very hour, and the change of a day means much. I am to speak at points in Ohio up until the very last hour that will enable me to reach Washington in time for the trustee meeting. I shall do my best to get there on the night of the 20th or the morning of the 21st when we can have our conference.

So far as Dr. Du Bois is concerned, I think it is not treating Dr. Thirkield with unfairness to send you a copy of a letter which I wrote him on the subject. This letter expresses my own feeling frankly and fully. Of course, I should not like for any one aside from yourself and Dr. Moorland to see this letter, because it would be unfair to President Thirkield to write him on the subject then pass the letter around generally to be seen by others. I very much prefer to have you return the Thirkield letter to me after you and Dr. Moorland have read it.

I am sorry that I could not get to Arundel, but as I have already stated, I am simply swamped with responsibilities and duties in many directions.

I always enjoy being at your house, and I hope to look in upon you and Mrs. Francis at least for a few minutes when I am there in September. Yours very truly,

Booker T. Washington

TLpS   Con. 45   BTW Papers   DLC.

An Article in *Outlook*

Sept. 11, 1909

THE NEGRO'S LIFE IN SLAVERY

Some years ago one of the frequent subjects of discussion among the white people and the colored people was the question, Who was responsible for slavery in America? Some people said the English Government was the guilty party, because England would not let the colonies abolish the slave trade when they wanted to. Others said the New England colonies were just as deep in the mire as England or the Southern States, because for many years a very large share of the trade was carried on in New England ships.

As a matter of fact, there were, as near as I have been able to learn, three parties who were directly responsible for the slavery of the Negro in the United States.

First of all, there was the Negro himself. It should not be forgotten that it was the African who, for the most part, carried on the slave raids by means of which his fellow-African was captured and brought down to the coast for sale. When, some months ago, the Liberian embassy visited the United States, Vice-President Dossen explained to me that one reason why Liberia had made no more progress during the eighty-six years of its existence was the fact that for many years the little State had been engaged in a life-and-death struggle with native slave-traders, who had been accustomed for centuries to ship their slaves from Liberian ports and were unwilling to give up the practice. It was only after the slave trade had entirely ceased, he said, that Liberia had begun to exercise an influence upon the masses of the native peoples within its jurisdiction.

The second party to slavery was the slave-trader, who at first, as a rule, was an Englishman or a Northern white man. During the

Colonial period, for instance, Newport, Rhode Island, was the principal headquarters of the slave trade in this country. At one time Rhode Island had one hundred and fifty vessels engaged in the traffic. Down to 1860 Northern capital was very largely invested in the slave trade, and New York was the port from which most of the American slave smugglers fitted out.

Finally, there was the Southern white man, who owned and worked the bulk of the slaves, and was responsible for what we now ordinarily understand as the slave system. It would be just as much a mistake, however, to assume that the South was ever solidly in favor of slavery as it is to assume that the North was always solidly against it. Thousands of persons in the Southern States were opposed to slavery, and numbers of them, like James G. Birney, of Alabama, took their slaves North in order to free them, and afterward became leaders in the anti-slavery struggle.

As with every other human thing, there is more than one side to slavery, and more than one way of looking at it. For instance, as defined in the slave laws in what was known as the Slave Code, slavery was pretty much the same at all times all over the South. The regulations imposed upon master and upon slave were, in several particulars, different for the different States. On the whole, however, as a legal institution, slavery was the same everywhere.

On the other hand, actual conditions were not only different in every part of the country, but they were likely to be different on every separate plantation. Every plantation was, to a certain extent, a little kingdom by itself, and life there was what the people who were bound together in the plantation community made it. The law and the custom of the neighborhood regulated, to a certain extent, the treatment which the master gave his slave. For instance, in the part of Virginia where I lived both white people and colored people looked with contempt upon the man who had the reputation of not giving his slaves enough to eat. If a slave went to an adjoining plantation for something to eat, the reputation of his master was damned in that community. On the whole, however, each plantation was a little independent state, and one master was very little disposed to interfere with the affairs of another.

The account that one gets of slavery from the laws that were passed for the government of slaves shows that institution on its worst side. No harsher judgment was ever passed on slavery, so far as I know, than that which will be found in the decision of a justice of the Supreme Court of North Carolina in summing up the law in a case in which the relations of master and slave were defined.

The case I refer to, which was tried in 1829, was one in which the master, who was the defendant, was indicted for beating his slave. The decision which acquitted him affirmed the master's right to inflict any kind of punishment upon his slave short of death. The grounds upon which this judgment was based were that in the whole history of slavery there had been no such prosecution of a master for punishing a slave, and, in the words of the decision, "against this general opinion in the community the court could not hold."

It was a mistake, the decision continued, to say that the relations of the master and slave were like those of a parent and child. The object of the parent in training his son was to render him fit to live the life of a free man, and, as a means to that end, he gave him moral and intellectual instruction. In the case of the slave it was different. There could be no sense in addressing moral considerations to a slave. Chief Justice Ruffin,[1] of North Carolina, summed up his opinion upon this point in these words:

> The end is the profit of the master, his security, and the public safety; the subject, one doomed in his own person and his posterity to live without knowledge and without the capacity to make anything his own, and to toil that another may reap the fruits. What moral consideration shall be addressed to such a being to convince him, what it is impossible but that the most stupid must feel and know can never be true — that he is thus to labor upon a principle of natural duty, or for the sake of his own personal happiness? Such services can only be expected from one who has no will of his own, who surrenders his will in implicit obedience to that of another. Such obedience is the consequence only of uncontrolled authority over the body. There is nothing else which can operate to produce the effect. The power of the master must be absolute to render the submission of the slave perfect.

In making this decision Justice Ruffin did not attempt to justify the rule he had laid down on moral grounds. "As a principle of right," he said, "every person in his retirement must repudiate it. But in the actual condition of things it must be so; there is no remedy. This discipline belongs to the state of slavery. It constitutes the curse of slavery both to the bond and free portion of our population."[2]

This decision brings out into plain view an idea that was always somewhere at the bottom of slavery — the idea, namely, that one man's evil is another man's good. The history of slavery, if it proves anything, proves that just the opposite is true; namely, that evil breeds evil, just as disease breeds disease, and that a wrong committed upon one portion of a community will, in the long run, surely react upon the other portion of that community.

There was a very great difference between the life of the slave on the small plantations in the uplands and upon the big plantations along the coasts. To illustrate, the plantation upon which I was born, in Franklin County, Virginia, had, as I remember, only six slaves. My master and his sons all worked together side by side with his slaves. In this way we all grew up together, very much like members of one big family. There was no overseer, and we got to know our master and he to know us. The big plantations along the coasts were usually carried on under the direction of an overseer. The master and his family were away for a large part of the year. Personal relations between them could hardly be said to exist.

John C. Calhoun, South Carolina's greatest statesman, was brought up on a plantation not very different from the one upon which I was raised. One of his biographers relates how Patrick Calhoun, John C. Calhoun's father, returning from his legislative duties in Charleston, brought home on horseback behind him a young African freshly imported in some English or New England vessel. The children in the neighborhood, and, no doubt, some of the older people, had never before seen a black man. He was the first one brought into that part of the country. Patrick Calhoun gave him the name of Adam. Some time later he got for him a wife. One of the children of the black man, Adam, was named Swaney. He grew up on the plantation with John C. Calhoun, and was for many years his playmate.

The conditions of the Negro slave were harder on some of the big plantations in the far South than they were elsewhere. That region was peopled by an enterprising class of persons, of whom many came from Virginia, bringing their slaves with them. The soil was rich, the planters were making money fast, the country was rough and unsettled, and there was undoubtedly a disposition to treat the slaves as mere factors in the production of corn, cotton, and sugar.

And yet there were plantations in this region where the relations between master and slave seem to have been as happy as one could ask or expect under the circumstances. On some of the large estates in Alabama and Mississippi which were far removed from the influence of the city, and sometimes in the midst of the wilderness, master and slaves frequently lived together under conditions that were genuinely patriarchal. But on such plantations there was, as a rule, no overseer.

As an example of the large plantations on which the relations between master and slave were normal and happy I might mention those of the former President of the Confederacy, Jefferson Davis, and his brother Joseph Davis, in Warren County, Mississippi.

The history of the Davis family and of the way in which their plantations, the "Hurricane" and "Brierfield," came into existence is typical. The ancestors of the President of the Confederacy came originally from Wales. They settled first in Georgia, emigrated thence to Kentucky, and finally settled in the rich lands of Mississippi. In 1818 Joseph Davis, who was at that time a lawyer in Vicksburg, attracted by the rich bottom-lands along the Mississippi, took his father's slaves and went down the river, thirty-six miles below Vicksburg, to the place which is now called "Davis's Bend." There he began clearing the land and preparing it for cultivation.

At that time there were no steamboats on the Mississippi River, and the country was so wild that people traveled through the lonely forests mostly on horseback. In the course of a few years Mr. Davis, with the aid of his slaves, succeeded in building up a plantation of about five thousand acres, and became, before his death, a very wealthy man. One day he went down to Natchez and purchased in the market there a young negro who afterward became known as Ben Montgomery. This young man had been sold South from North Carolina, and because, perhaps, he had heard, as most of the slaves had, of the hard treatment that was to be expected on the big, lonesome plantations, had made up his mind to remain in the city. The first thing he did, therefore, when Mr. Davis brought him home, was to run away. Mr. Davis succeeded in getting hold of him again, brought him back to the plantation, and then, as Isaiah, Benjamin Montgomery's son, has told me, Mr. Davis "came to an understanding" with his young slave.

Just what that understanding was no one seems now to know

exactly, but in any case, as a result of it, Benjamin Montgomery received a pretty fair education, sufficient, at any rate, to enable him in after years, when he came to have entire charge, as he soon did, of Mr. Davis's plantation, to survey the line of the levee which was erected to protect the plantation from the waters of the Mississippi, to draw out plans, and to compute the size of buildings, a number of which were erected at different times under his direction.

Mrs. Jefferson Davis, in her memoir of her husband, referring to Benjamin Montgomery, and to the manner in which Joseph Davis conducted his plantation, says:

A maxim of Joseph E. Davis was, "The less people are governed, the more submissive they will be to control." This idea he carried out with his family and with his slaves. He instituted trial by jury of their peers, and taught them the legal form of holding it. His only share in the jurisdiction was the pardoning power. When his slave could do better for himself than by daily labor, he was at liberty to do so, giving either in money or other equivalent the worth of ordinary field service. One of his slaves kept a variety shop, and on many occasions the family bought of him at his own prices. He shipped, and indeed sometimes purchased, the fruit crops of the Davis families, and also of other people in "The Bend," and in one instance credited one of us with $2,000 on his account. The bills were presented by him with promptitude and paid, as were those of others on an independent footing, without delay. He many times borrowed from his master, but was equally as exact in his dealings with his creditors. His sons, Thornton and Isaiah, first learned to work, and then were carefully taught by their father to read, write, and cipher, and now Ben Montgomery's sons are both responsible men of property; one is in business in Vicksburg, and the other is a thriving farmer in the West.

Some years after the settlement on the bottom-lands at Davis's Bend had been made, Mr. Jefferson Davis joined his brother and lived for several years upon an adjoining plantation. The two brothers had much the same ideas about the management of their slaves. Both of them took personal supervision of their estates, and Jefferson Davis, like his brother, had a colored man to whom he refers as his "friend and servant, James Pemberton," who, until he died, seems to have had practically the whole charge of the Brierfield plantation, in the same way that Benjamin Montgomery had charge of the Hurricane. After the war both of these plantations were sold for the sum of $300,000 to Benjamin Montgomery and his sons, who conducted them for a number of years, until, as a result of floods and the low price of cotton, they were compelled to give them up.

As illustrating the kindly relations and good will which continued to exist between the ex-President of the Confederacy, Jefferson Davis, and his former slaves, both during the years that they lived together on the plantation and afterward, Mrs. Davis has printed several letters written to her by them after Mr. Davis's death.

From all that I have been able to learn, the early slaves, and by these I mean the first generation which were brought to America fresh from Africa, seem to have remained more or less alien in customs and sympathy to their white masters. This was more particularly the case on the large plantations along the Carolina coast, where the slaves came very little in contact with their masters, and remained to a very large degree and for a considerable time merely an African colony on American soil.

But the later generations, those who knew Africa only by tradition, were different. Each succeeding generation of the Creole Negroes — to use the expression in its original meaning — managed to pick up more and more, as it had the opportunity, the language, the ideas, the habits, the crafts, and the religious conceptions of the white man, until the life of the black man was wholly absorbed into that of the plantation upon which he lived.

The Negro in exile from his native land neither pined away nor grew bitter. On the contrary, as soon as he was able to adjust himself to the conditions of his new life, his naturally cheerful and affectionate disposition began to assert itself. Gradually the natural human sympathies of the African began to take root in the soil of the New World, and then, growing up spontaneously, to twine about the life of the white man, by whose side the black man now found himself. The slave soon learned to love the children of his master, and they loved him in return. The quaint humor of the Negro slave helped him to turn many a hard corner. It helped to excuse his mistakes, and, by turning a reproof into a jest, to soften the resentment of his master for his faults.

Quaint and homely tales that were told around the fireside made the Negro cabin a place of romantic interest to the master's children. The simple, natural joy of the Negro in little things converted every change in the dull routine of his life into an event. Hog-killing time was an annual festival, and the corn-shucking was a joyous event which the whites and blacks, each in their respective ways, took part in and enjoyed. These corn-shucking bees, or whatever they may be called, took place during the last of November or the first half of December. They were a sort of a prelude to the festivities of the Christmas season. Usually they were held upon one of the larger and wealthier plantations.

After all the corn had been gathered, thousands of bushels, sometimes, it would be piled up in the shape of a mound, often to the height of fifty or sixty feet. Invitations would be sent around by the master himself to the neighboring planters, inviting their slaves on a certain night to attend. In response to these invitations as many as one or two hundred men, women, and children would come together.

When all were assembled around the pile of corn, some one individual, who had already gained a reputation as a leader in singing, would climb on top of the mound and begin at once, in clear, loud tones, a solo — a song of the corn-shucking season — a kind of singing which, I am sorry to say, has very largely passed from memory and practice. After leading off in this way, in clear, distinct tones, the chorus at the base of the mound would join in, some hundred voices strong. The words, which were largely improvised, were very simple and suited to the occasion, and more often than not they had the flavor of the camp-meeting rather than of any more secular proceeding. Such singing I have never heard on any other occasion. There was something wild and weird about that music, such as I suspect will never again be heard in America.

One of these songs, as I remember, ran about as follows:

I

Massa's niggers am slick and fat,
Oh! Oh! Oh!
Shine just like a new beaver hat,
Oh! Oh! Oh!

REFRAIN

Turn out here and shuck dis corn,
Oh! Oh! Oh!
Biggest pile o' corn seen since I was born,
Oh! Oh! Oh!

II

Jones's niggers am lean an' po';

168

Oh! Oh! Oh!
Don't know whether dey get 'nough to eat
　or no,
Oh! Oh! Oh!
REFRAIN
Turn out here and shuck dis corn,
Oh! Oh! Oh!
Biggest pile o' corn seen since I was born,
Oh! Oh! Oh!

Little by little the slave songs, the quaint stories, sayings, and anecdotes of the slave's life, began to give their quality to the life of the plantation. Half the homely charm of Southern life was made by the presence of a Negro. The homes that had no Negro servants were dreary by contrast, and that was not due to the fact that, ordinarily, the man who had slaves was rich and the man who had no slaves was poor.

The four great crops of the South — tobacco, rice, sugar, and cotton — were all raised by slave labor. In the early days it was thought that no labor except that of the Negro was suited to cultivate these great staples of Southern industry, and that opinion prevails pretty widely still. But it was not merely his quality as a laborer that made the Negro seem so necessary to the white man in the South; it was also these other qualities to which I have referred — his cheerfulness and sympathy, his humor and his fidelity. No one can honestly say that there was anything in the nature of the institution of slavery that would develop these qualities in a people who did not possess them. On the contrary, what we know about slavery elsewhere leads us to believe that the system would have developed qualities quite different, so that I think I am justified in saying that most of the things that made slavery tolerable, both to the white man and to the black man, were due to the native qualities of the African.

Southern writers, looking back and seeking to reproduce the genial warmth and gracious charm of that old ante-bellum Southern life, have not failed to do full justice to the part that the Negro played in it. The late Joel Chandler Harris, for instance, has given us in the character of "Uncle Remus" the type of the Negro storyteller who delights and instructs the young children of the "big house" with his quaint animal stories that have been handed down to the Negro by his African ancestors. The "Br'er Rabbit" stories of Uncle Remus are now a lasting element in the literature, not only of the South, but of America, and they are recognized as the peculiar contribution of the American Negro slave to the folk-lore stories of the world.

In my own State of Virginia Mr. Thomas Nelson Page has given us, in "Uncle Billy" and "Uncle Sam," two typical characters worthy of study by those who wish to understand the human side of the Negro slave on the aristocratic plantations of that State. In Mr. Page's story "Meh Lady" Uncle Billy was guide, philosopher, and friend to his mistress and her daughter in the trying times of war and in their days of poverty. He hid their silver, refused to give information to the Union soldiers, prayed the last prayer with his dying mistress, comforted her lonely daughter, and at last gave her away in marriage.

In the story of "Marse Chan" Mr. Page lets Uncle Sam, the slave bodyguard, tell in the following language what happened to his young master during the Civil War on the field of battle:

Marse Chan he calls me, an' he sez, "Sam, we'se goin' to win in dis battle, an' den we'll go home an' git married; an' I'm going home wid a star on my collar." An' den he sez, "Ef I'm wounded, kyah me, yo' hear?" An' I sez, "Yes, Marse Chan." Well, jes' den dey blowed boots an' saddles an' we mounted — an' dey said, "Charge 'em," an' my King ef ever yo' see bullets fly, dey did dat day. . . . We wen' down de slope, I 'long wid de res', an' up de hill right to de cannons, an' de fire wuz so strong dyah our lines sort o' broke an' stop; an' de cun'l was kilt, an' I b'lieve dey wuz jes' 'bout to break all to pieces wen Marse Chan rid up an' cotch holt de flag and hollers, "Follow me." . . . Yo' ain' never heah thunder. Fust thing I knowed de Roan roll head over heels an' flung me up 'gainst de bank like yo' chuck a nubbin over 'g'inst de foot o' de corn pile.   An' dat what kep me from being kilt, I 'spects. When I look 'roun' de Roan was lying dyah stone dead. 'Twan' mo'n a minit, de sorrel come gallupin' back wid his mane flying and de rein hangin' down on one side to his knee. I jumped up an' run over de bank an' dyah, wid a whole lot ob dead mens and some not dead yit, on de one side o' de guns, wid de flag still in he han' an' a bullet right thru' he body, lay Marse Chan. I tu'n 'im over an' call 'im, "Marse Chan," but 'twan' no use. He wuz done gone home. I pick him up in my arms wid de flag still in he han' an' toted 'im back jes' like I did dat day when he wuz a baby an' ole master gin 'im to me in my arms, an' say he could trus' me, an' tell me to tek keer on 'im long as he lived. I kyah'd 'im way off de battlefiel' out de way o' de balls an' I laid 'im down under a big tree till I could git somebody to ketch de sorrel for me. He was kotched arter a while, an' I hed some money, so I got some pine plank an' made a coffin dat evenin' an' wrap Marse Chan's body up in de flag an' put 'im in de coffin, but I didn't nail de top on strong, 'cause I knowed de old missus wan' to see 'im; an' I got a' ambulance an' set out fo' home dat night. We reached dyah de nex' evenin' arter travelin' all dat night an' all nex' day.

In the Palace of Fine Arts, in St. Louis, during the Exposition of 1904, there was a picture which made a deep impression on every Southern white man and black man who saw it who knew enough of the old life to understand what it meant. The Rev. A. B. Curry,[3] of Memphis, Tennessee, referring to this picture in a sermon in his home city on November 27, 1904, said:

When I was in the Palace of Fine Arts, in St. Louis, this summer, I saw a picture before which I stood and wept. In the distance was a battle scene; the dust of trampling men and horses, the smoke of cannon and rifles filled the air; broken carriages and dead and dying men strewed the ground. In the foreground was the figure of a stalwart Negro man, bearing in his strong arms the form of a fair-haired Anglo-Saxon youth. It was the devoted body-servant of a young Southerner, bearing the dead body of his young master from the field of carnage, not to pause or rest till he had delivered it to those whose love for it only surpassed his own; and underneath the picture were these words — "Faithful Unto Death"; and there are men before me who have seen the spirit of that picture on more than one field of battle.

The slaves in Virginia and the border States were, as a rule, far superior, or at least they considered themselves so, to the slaves of the lower South. Even in freedom this feeling of superiority remains. Furthermore, the mansion house-servants, of whom Mr. Page writes, having had an opportunity to share to a large extent the daily life of their masters, were very proud of their superior position and advantages, and had little contact with the field-hands. It is, perhaps, not generally understood that in slavery days lines were drawn among the slaves just as they were among the white people. The servants owned by a rich and aristocratic family considered that the servants of "a poor white man," one who was not able to own more than half a dozen slaves, were not in the same social class with themselves. And yet the life of these more despised slaves had its vicissitudes, its obscure heroisms, and its tragedies just like the rest of the world. In fact, it was from the plantation hands, as a rule, that the most precious records of slave life came — the plantation hymns. The field-hands sang these songs and they expressed their lives.

I have frequently met and talked with old men of my race who have grown up in slavery. It is difficult for these old men to express all that they feel. Occasionally, however, they will utter some quaint, humorous turn of expression in which there is a serious thought underneath.

One old farmer who owns a thousand acres of land not far from Tuskegee said: "We's jes' so ign't out heah, we don' see no diff'rence 'twe'n freedom an' slav'ry, 'cept den we's workin' fer some one else, and now we's workin' fer oursel's."

Some time ago an old colored man who has lived for a number of years near the Tuskegee Institute, in talking about his experience since freedom, remarked that the greatest difference he had found between slavery and freedom was that in the days of slavery his master had to think for him, but since he had been free he had to think and plan for himself.

At another time out in Kansas I met an old colored woman who had left her home in Tennessee directly after the war and settled with a large number of other colored people in what is called "Tennessee Town," now a suburb of Topeka, Kansas. In talking with her about her experiences in freedom and in slavery, I asked her if she did not sometimes feel as if she would not like to go back to the old days and live as she had lived on the plantation.

"Sometimes," she replied, "I feel as I'd like to go back and see my old massa and missus" — she hesitated a moment and then added, "but they sold my baby down South."

Aside from the slave songs very little has come down to us from slavery days that shows how slavery looked to the masses of the people.

There are a considerable number of slave narratives written by fugitive slaves with the assistance of abolitionist friends; but, as these were composed for the most part under the excitement of the anti-slavery agitation, they show things, as a rule, somewhat out of proportion. There is one of these stories, however, that gives a picture of the changing fortunes and vicissitudes of slave life which makes it especially interesting. I refer to the story of Charity Bower, who was born in 1779, near Edenton, North Carolina, and lived to a considerable age after she obtained her freedom. She described her master as very kind to his slaves. He used to whip them sometimes with a hickory switch, she said, but never let his overseer do so. Continuing, she said:

My mother nursed all his children. She was reckoned a very good ser-vant, and our mistress made it a point to give one of my mother's children to each one of her own. I fell to the lot of Elizabeth, the second daughter. Oh, my mistress was a kind woman. She was all the same as a mother to poor Charity. If Charity wanted to learn to spin, she let her learn; if Charity wanted to learn to knit, she let her learn; if Charity wanted to learn to weave, she let her learn. I had a wedding when I was married, for mistress didn't like to have her people take up with one another without any minister to marry them. . . . My husband was a nice, good man, and mistress knew we set stores by one another. Her children promised they never would separate me from my husband and children. Indeed, they used to tell me they would never sell me at all, and I am sure they meant what they said. But my young master got into trouble. He used to come home and sit leaning his head on his hands by the hour together, without speak-ing to anybody. I see something was the matter, and begged him to tell me what made him look so worried. He told me he owed seventeen hun-dred dollars that he could not pay, and he was afraid he should have to go to prison. I begged him to sell me and my children, rather than go to jail. I see the tears come into his eyes. "I don't know, Charity," he said; "I'll see what can be done. One thing you may feel easy about; I will never separate you from your husband and children, let what will come."

Two or three days after he come to me, and says he: "Charity, how should you like to be sold to Mr. Kinmore?" I told him I would rather be sold to him than to anybody else, because my husband belonged to him. Mr. Kinmore agreed to buy us, and so I and my children went there to live.

Shortly after this her new master died, and her new mistress was not as kind to her as he had been. Thereupon she set to work to buy the freedom of her children.

"Sixteen children I've had, first and last," she said, "and twelve I've nursed for my mistress. From the time my first baby was born I always set my heart upon buying freedom for some of my children. I thought it was more consequence to them than to me, for I was old and used to being a slave."

In order to save up money enough for this purpose she set up a little oyster board just outside her cabin, which adjoined the open road. When any one came along who wanted a few oysters and crackers, she would leave her washing and wait upon them. In this way she saved up two hundred dollars, but for some reason or another she never succeeded in getting her mistress's consent to buy one of the children. It was not always easy for a master to emancipate his slaves in those days, even if he wanted to do so. On the contrary, as she says, "one after another — one after another — she sold 'em from me."

It was to a "thin, peaked-looking man who used to come and buy of me," she says, that she finally owed her freedom. "Sometimes," she continued, "he would say, 'Aunt Charity, you must fix me up a nice little mess, for I am poorly to-day.' I always made something good for him; and if he didn't happen to have any change, I always trusted him."

It was this man, a Negro "speculator," according to her story, who finally purchased her with her five children, and, giving her the youngest child, set her free.

"Well," she ended, "after that I concluded I'd come to the free States. Here I am takin' in washing; my daughter is smart at her needle, and we get a very comfortable living."

There was much in slavery besides its hardships and its cruelties; much that was tender, human, and beautiful. The heroic efforts that many of the slaves made to buy their own and their children's freedom deserve to be honored equally with the devotion that they frequently showed in the service of their masters. And, after all, considering the qualities which the Negro slave developed under trying conditions, it does not seem to me that there is any real reason why any one who wishes him well should despair of the future of the Negro either in this country or elsewhere.

Outlook, 93 (Sept. 11, 1909), 71–78.

[1] Thomas Ruffin (1787–1870).

[2] The footnote in the original article read: " 'Slavery in the State of North Carolina,' by John Spencer Bassett."

[3] Albert Bruce Curry (1852–1939), a Presbyterian minister in Memphis from 1903 to 1931.

To Jacob Henry Schiff

[Tuskegee, Ala.] September 18, 1909

My dear Mr. Schiff: Referring to the use of the Three Thousand Dollars ($3,000) to the credit of the Southern Education Fund, I would make the following suggestions:

$1,000 — to the Tuskegee Normal and Industrial Institute, according to your own previous decision.

250 — to the Hampton Normal and Agricultural Institute, about which you already know.

100 — to Atlanta University, about which you already know.

100 — to the Fort Valley Normal and Industrial Institute, Fort Valley, Ga., about which you already know.

100 — to the Snow Hill Normal and Industrial Institute, W. J. Edwards, Principal. This institution, located in the "Black Belt" of Alabama was started through the joint effort of the former owner, a white planter, and a colored man, one of our graduates, of the family of this young white man. For years Mr. R. O. Simpson, the white man, and Mr. W. J. Edwards, the colored man, have worked together, and the result is they have a school plant now worth $125,000 with 27 teachers and 400 students. Their annual expenses are about $25,000. They are sending out good men and women as teachers and industrial workers.

100 — to the Utica Normal and Industrial Institute, W. H. Holtzclaw, Principal, Utica, Miss. This institution I visited a year ago and found it doing good work. It was started by William H. Holtzclaw, one of our graduates and is about the same size of the Snow Hill School, and doing the same kind of work for the same kind of people.

100 — to the St. Paul School, located at Lawrenceville, Va., Archdeacon J. S. Russell, Principal. You have an application for help from Rev. S. H. Bishop of this school. I had the privilege of visiting Lawrenceville a few months ago, and found them doing fine work. The St. Paul School is an outgrowth of the Hampton Institute. It has about 47 teachers and about 500 students, and has the good will and confidence of both white and colored people.

100 — to the Hungerford Normal and Industrial Institute, at Eatonville, Fla., R. C. Calhoun,[1] Principal. This is a school about the same size as that of the Snow Hill School in Alabama, except that it is located in a strictly colored community. The town of Eatonville is one of the few incorporated Negro towns. It has been governed by Negroes from the first. The Hungerford School has been visited by several of our teachers and several prominent white people from the North, and all report that it is doing good work.

100 — to the Farmers' Improvement Society, Agricultural College, located at Ladonia, Tex., R. L. Smith, President. This is a unique school in that it has confined itself wholly to training in agriculture. Mr. R. L. Smith, the head of it, for a number of years, supported the school almost wholly out of his personal salary. Now, it is being supported much more generously by colored people in Texas, and by white people in different parts of the country.

100 — to Fisk University, Dean H. H. Wright,[2] President. This, in my opinion, is the best school, giving strictly college education for our people anywhere in the country. It is doing a high grade of college work. Many of the graduates are teachers here at Tuskegee. The property is valued at about $450,000. They have about 43 professors and teachers and about 600 students.

100 — to the Voorhees Normal and Industrial Institute, located at Denmark, S.C., G. B. Miller, President. This institution has almost the same history as the Snow Hill School, except that it was started through the joint efforts of a colored woman, Miss Wright,[3] and a rich white planter in that neighborhood. Miss Wright died a few years ago but the work is going on in an encouraging way. I, also, visited this school a few months ago.

In making these recommendations I have kept in mind the following points:

1. To recommend institutions that are located in territory where their work is most needed. I have not, however, in any case, recommended any institution that is doing strictly local work.

2. To keep on the list the institutions which you have already been helping and know about.

3. You will note that this leaves unappropriated $850. I would suggest that this remain intact until later in the year, as there are applications which may be made to you, and because I may find out something more about other schools. I thought you might like to reserve something that might be used in case of special emergency or in case of other schools making applications, which you might like to help.

Yours very truly,

Booker T. Washington

TLpSr Con. 47 BTW Papers DLC. Signed in Emmett J. Scott's hand.

1 Russell Climuel Calhoun (ca. 1869–1910) was an 1896 graduate in carpentry at Tuskegee Institute. He and his wife, a Tuskegee graduate, founded the Robert Hungerford Normal and Industrial School in 1897.

2 Herbert Hornell Wright was professor of mathematics and vocal music at Fisk University beginning in 1882, and became dean of the university in 1907.

3 Elizabeth Evelyn Wright Menafee.

To Raymond DuPuy

[Tuskegee, Ala.] September 29, 1909

Dear Mr. DuPuy: There are two or three very intelligent colored men, who live in Bluefield, West Virginia, and who stand high in the railroad service, that want to have a personal interview with you. These men met me when I went over the Virginia Railroad in June and I told them that later, I should ask you, if possible, to grant them an interview. They will state their own case more plainly than I can do it.

I was surprised, and I think you will be, at the keen intelligence, and solid character of these men. Whether anything comes of the interview or not aside from meeting them, I think it will be worth while.

They will be writing you a letter soon, asking you for a date, and I hope that you can grant the audience.[1] Yours very truly,

Booker T. Washington

TLpS Con. 891 BTW Papers DLC.

1 BTW sent a copy of this letter to C. E. Henike, of the Railway Trainmen of America, on the same date and offered to write a similar one to Norfolk and Western officials. (Con. 391, BTW Papers, DLC.)

An Article in *The Independent*

Sept. 30, 1909

ACHIEVEMENTS OF NEGROES

The fact that a colored man, Matt Henson, accompanied Commander Robert E. Peary practically to the North Pole on his recent expedition has caused a great deal of comment and discussion. This discussion leads me to remark that the people of America, I fear, do not realize to what an extent negroes have taken part in nearly every important event connected with the history and development of this country.

Negroes accompanied the first Spanish explorers and discoverers of America across the Isthmus of Panama with Balboa, and assisted in constructing the first ship that was launched on the Pacific. They were with Cortez in Mexico in 1522.

A negro by the name of Little Stephen was the first discoverer of the country of the Zunis, what is now called New Mexico.

Negroes were with De Soto in 1540, and the first stranger who settled in the State of Alabama was one of the negroes who accompanied De Soto on his march thru that State.

A negro accompanied William Clark, of Lewis and Clark's expedition, which, in 1804, explored the sources of the Missouri River and gained for the United States the vast and rich extent of land known as the Oregon country.

Negroes were among the first adventurers to look for gold in California, and when John C. Frémont, in 1848, made his desperate and disastrous attempt to find a pathway across the Rocky Mountains, he was accompanied by a negro named Saunders.

Negroes have taken part, so far as I can learn, in all the wars that have been fought on American soil. They fought at Bunker Hill, in the Revolutionary War. In the War of 1812 James Forten, a negro sailmaker of Philadelphia, raised a regiment of negro soldiers to defend the city from the intended attack of the British soldiers. Negroes were in the famous battle on Lake Erie under Perry. They fought on both sides in the Civil War. In the Spanish-American War negroes not only did their full part at El Caney and San Juan Hill, but after these battles were over, they took up the more difficult and more dangerous labor of working in the hospitals in the malaria-haunted camp at Siboney.

Independent, 67 (Sept. 30, 1909), 731–32.

Extracts from an Address
at the Howard University Medical School

Washington, D.C., October 4, 1909

I am glad to be permitted, on invitation of your Faculty, to speak at the opening session of the Howard University Medical School. The growth of the Negro doctor indicates the progress of the Negro race. A little more than a score of years ago, there were only 500 Negro doctors in the whole country. At the present time, there are 3,500 doctors, most of them located in the Southern states. Practically all of these, of course, have been educated since the close of the Civil War.

When we are inclined to grow discouraged regarding the present and future, we should make a comparison. No one who lived fifty or sixty years ago would have dared dream that at this time there should be over 3 thousand intelligent and successful Negroes engaged in one of the most exclusive and highest professions in the world.

I have referred to the fact that there are 3500 Negro doctors at the present time. Let me also call your attention to the fact that this is only about half the number that there should be. In the case of the white race, there is one doctor to every six hundred people. Even if the number of Negro doctors is increased to 3,500, we will only have one Negro doctor to every 7000 Negroes in America. I am not indicating or advocating that the color line should be drawn in the practice of medicine. That is, I do not mean to say that the Negro doctor alone should practice among Negro people, but I do think any fair and just person will agree with me that we ought to have a fair proportion of Negro doctors to practice among Negro patients. We need, in a word, 4000 additional Negro doctors. It devolves upon Howard University and two or three other medical schools for our race to largely prepare these doctors.

In that respect, then, Howard University has a serious responsibility resting upon it, as well as a great opportunity. Wherever I have gone in my travels, I have met graduates of the Medical Department of Howard University, and with very few exceptions, I have found them succeeding, having the confidence and good will of the Colored people. Further, I have found them, in most cases, on easy and on good terms with their professional brethren of the white race. The doctor, as a rule, is a gentleman and it is not a difficult matter for two gentlemen, no matter how they differ in color, to get on well with each other.

The great and successful doctor in the future is not going to be the one who devotes himself to curing aches and pains, but one who will devote himself to keeping the human family well. The work of the doctor in the future is going to be that of preservation; preserving the body, rather than repairing the body. This idea involves a more unselfish disposition to be cultivated on the part of the doctor.

In my own community at the Tuskegee Institute, where we have a population including students, teachers and other families of about three thousand people, at the present time only 9 are in doors on account of sickness. We have this high record because we have a doctor who devotes himself to keeping people well, and curing them after they have gotten sick.

One of the most important functions for the leaders of the Negro race to consider at the present time is the preservation of the health of our race, especially in large cities in congested districts. The work of the Negro doctor in preserving the health of the Negro, however, is not unimportant in establishing our race. It is equally important from the standpoint of the white race.

There are ten million Negroes in this country. In many sections of our country, especially in the South, these people are equal in numbers to the white people and in not a few sections, they out-number the whites.

It is just as important to the health and prosperity of the white race that the Negro have a sound, well, clean body as it is to the Negro race itself. Ten million weak and diseased bodied people cannot live in the midst of other people without the one race affecting the health of the other.

There are some directions in which no color line can be drawn. Disease draws no color line; filth draws no color line. If a Negro, by reason of his ignorance of the laws of health, carries about in his body the germs of consumption, of smallpox or of the disease known as the hook-worm, these germs will spread from his body to that of the white people by whose side he lives. Negro women prepare and serve the food of the white people. Negro women launder the clothes of the white people; Negro women nurse the babies of the white people. In a word, Negroes touch the white man at almost every vital point in his life. If the Negro is ignorant as to the laws of health, she can convey disease to the white man's family through her unclean hands, or unwashed body, or the most deadly germs can be taken to the house of the white man by reason of the filth of the cabin in which the white man's clothes are laundered.

It is the mission, in a large part, then, of the Negro doctor to teach the gospel of health to our people and in this much needed work, institutions like the medical school of Howard University should have the support and confidence of all people of this country regardless of race or color; and especially is it important that Southern people realize what Howard is doing for the whole South in helping to preserve the health of the Negro.

All this leads me to say that the medical school of Howard University ought to be enlarged, better equipped and more generously supported. I believe the time has come when all the people are seeing the value of the Negro doctor so clearly that Howard University will not be long in wanting for the money with which to have here one of the largest and best equipped medical schools in the whole country.

TM BTW Papers ATT. Numbers were added to the text by hand. Less complete extracts appeared in the Washington *Star*, Oct. 4, 1909, 2.

To George Augustus Gates

Parker House, Boston, Mass. Oct. 7, 1909

My dear Dr. Gates: I was sorry not to see you the other evening before I left New York, but I was detained at dinner longer than I had expected.

I had talks with Mr. Cravath and Dr. Buttrick, and everything so far as I know seems to be going smoothly and satisfactorily.

I shall be in New York, according to my present plan, at the Hotel Manhattan a part of the day October 15th, and can see you if anything turns up.

If you take the position of President of Fisk, and later on you feel that I can be of real service as a trustee, I shall be willing to think favorably in that direction. I do not think well to act, however, in the matter now. Serving as a trustee of Fisk will not take so much of my time as in the case of the other institutions for the reason that I am already pretty well acquainted with the Fisk plant and also with the methods and policy of the institution, and I take for granted that a large part of the meetings will be held in New York. As I stated to you in my verbal conversation, in case you take the position, in my humble way I will stand back of you and support you in every way possible, and Dr. Frissell I am sure will do the same thing. Both of us feel that there ought to be at least one strong central institution in the South for the higher education of the Negro, and that all things considered, Fisk is by far the best institution to be strengthened and supported in a way as to make it serve this purpose. Yours very truly,

Booker T. Washington

TLS Original in possession of the editors, courtesy of Donald S. Gates. A carbon copy is in the BTW Papers, ATT.

From Calvin E. Henike

Bluefield, W.Va., Oct 7th 1909

My Dear Sir   I am in receipt of yours of Sept 29th and was very proud of The Letter of Introduction to Mr Dupuy. Also The Copy you Had sent him. I am also Writing him today asking for an Interview. Should we succeed in get[t]ing to see him I will Write you the Results.

Now in Regards to What favor you may be able to do for us with The Norfolk and Western People, is that about 2 years Since the Brotherhood of Railroad Trainmen, a White Labor Organization after many years of failure succeeded in get[t]ing an agreement with the Company, That they would [not?] Employ any more non-promotable men this applies to only Colored men notwithstanding the fact that Colored men make Better Trainmen that [than] White men. One Reason why they do is that a Colored man is Submissive and Obedient to his Conductor. I am sure Our Record as Trainmen are far above that of the White man Both in accidents and Deportment. But I am quite sure that It was not their desire at that time. I think it was to prevent a Strike. I Dont know just what Steps can be taken to Breake up this, Unless we can appeal to their Sympathy Since nearly all avenues of Industry are already Closed against us. In one Explaination They Claim the Young Colored man was not up to Standard. If this were true There would not Be over five hundred old men now in The Service. To my opinion this matter can only Be handled Through Some member of the Board Influencing the President and General Manager. Showing them that in the Long Run When the Road will only have a Solid White Force Their Demands will be much Greater than they are now and upon a Refusuial There will be a Strike then as in all Cases Colored men will be called in. This will make it Very Dangerous. But where a mixed Force is Employed not [no] such things happenes. Trust in your dealings with them you will Refrain from using my name as There might be some hidden Danger For me. As I am Being Watched By the Labor Organization Having Already accomplished many favors from the Company they do not approve of. Further I want to say any Extra Expenses you may be put to Will Be Paid upon Receipt of notice. Trust you will be able to do some good along this Line And If you Should fail we feel sure no one else can do more. I Shall be glad to furnish any further Information you may need And will be glad to hear from you after you have made an attempt. I Am   Yours Very Truly

C E. Henike

ALS   Con. 893   BTW Papers   DLC.

To James Griswold Merrill

Parker House, Boston. Oct. 8, 1909

My dear Dr. Merrill: Your letter of October 2d has just reached me.[1] While in New York a few days ago Dr. Frissell and I had a conference with Mr. Cravath, with Dr. Gates, and still later I had a conference with Dr. Buttrick. Everything now seems to be shaping itself in the direction of electing Dr. Gates. On the whole, I think he is the best man. I think he has outgrown the tendency towards socialism. I confess that the more I talk with him the more I feel that he is the man, so does Mr. Cravath.

I hope you and family are well. Yours very truly,

[Booker T. Washington]

TLc   BTW Papers   ATT.

1 Merrill, retiring president of Fisk University, had written that he had been informed that George A. Gates was "useless as a money getter" and "weak in respect of the matter of being carried away with socialism." He believed, however, that if Gates was favored by Carnegie and the General Education Board, he would be "an excellent figure head." (Merrill to BTW, Oct. 2, 1909, BTW Papers, ATT.)

To William Howard Taft

[Tuskegee, Ala.] Oct. 21, 1909

My dear President Taft: I have asked our mutual friend, Mr. Jos. O. Thompson, to hand you this note.

In the year 1913 the Negro race will have been free in this country fifty years. I have been asked by the National Negro Business League and other prominent organizations and individuals among our race to initiate a movement looking toward the celebration of this event by some kind of an exposition in which the material, educational, moral and religious growth of the Negro will be shown.

If the matter is taken up, I not only have in mind emphasizing the points named, but especially getting the Southern white people to take an interest in it and getting the two races to take an interest and part in the exposition since the progress that the colored people have made has been made in the South in the midst of the Southern white people and largely through their guidance and assistance.

My especial point in writing you just now is to suggest that you not commit yourself in any direction on this subject until I can have an opportunity of seeing you in person, which I shall try to do sometime after you have gotten back to Washington and have gotten some of your hard work off of your hands. Yours very truly,

Booker T. Washington

TLpS BTW Papers ATT.

To Charles W. Carpenter[1]

Tuskegee Institute, Alabama   October 22, 1909

My dear Carpenter: I have just received your letter and am glad to hear from you. I am sorry that you did not find conditions favorable at Mound Bayou.

I am not sure how we stand financially. Will you be kind enough to let me know what your understanding is of the conditions. If I owe you anything, I will be glad to settle it.

Now, one other point, I am sorry to hear you say that you are planning to go into the railway mail service. In my opinion, you are making a mistake. Persons who go into the United States mail service seldom ever grow much, they become mere machines, and in the end have little money and little initiative. You have ability to lead and originate. You will become a mere machine in the mail service, and will accomplish little good though you may get a comparatively large salary for a while.

I think it will be much wiser for you to stick to your original plan of starting a truck garden somewhere. A truck garden in Macon County would pay. In fact, it would pay almost anywhere.

You must not be too ambitious to get money too quickly, you had better lay a good foundation. Yours very truly,

Booker T. Washington

TLS MiU-H. A press copy is in Con. 890, BTW Papers, DLC.

1 Charles W. Carpenter (1886–1971), born in Stanford, Ky., entered Tuskegee Institute night school in 1904. During the summer of 1908 he worked at BTW's summer house on Long Island. Graduating in 1909 as valedictorian, he studied theology at Wilberforce and at Garrett Biblical Institute. He was an active Baptist minister for fifty-four years, serving at churches in several cities in Illinois, Indiana, Michigan, and Canada. For thirty-six years after 1929 he was pastor of a church in Ann Arbor, Mich.

To Olivia Egleston Phelps Stokes

[Tuskegee, Ala.] October 27, 1909

My dear Miss Stokes: I wrote you a few days ago that I was waiting to have a conference with the American Minister to Liberia and also with Bishop Scott before making definite recommendations regarding answering your letter of August 19th more fully.

Minister Ernest Lyon has been spending a good part of the week here with us. Bishop I. B. Scott came over on the same ship with the Minister and both are very much interested in anything, of course, that concerns the development of Liberia.

After considering the whole matter very carefully, we recommend the following: that the three Liberian students who are now here be kept here during a period of two years or more, if possible; that two additional students be sent, these to be selected by the American Minister and Bishop Scott. They are to be the sons of chiefs from the Liberian hinterland, the idea being to get some of the best blood in Africa. We feel that if we can get hold of and properly educate these five, that they can return, together with some other American students from here, if possible, and establish later on an industrial school that would mean something. We feel that to start an industrial school at present might not be a successful thing, taking for the reason that they would not have proper backing in the way of teachers, who understand the method and policies to be pursued at an industrial school thoroughly enough to make it a success. In a word, we feel that the five students returned there from here thoroughly indoctrinated with the idea of industrial education would itself prove such a power that it would give the school an impetus which would make it go.

Our Treasurer has made out a memorandum which shows exactly how we stand with reference to the three Liberian students who are already here; what it would cost to maintain them here for a year and also what it would cost to bring the two sons of chiefs here and maintain them each year. The statement rendered by our Treasurer shows how we have used the money which you gave us some time ago.

We should be very glad to carry out your wishes, however, in any way that we possibly can. Yours very truly,

Booker T. Washington

TLpS Con. 47 BTW Papers DLC.

To Samuel Sidney McClure

Tuskegee Institute, Alabama   Oct. 29, 1909

Dear Sir: I have read with interest your letter of September 30th, and have considered the article in McClure's Magazine to which you referred.[1] It is hard for me to believe that Europe is in such imminent danger as your article suggested. But were it so, I do not believe the world's peace can be permanently maintained at the present time by force. Do not understand by what I have said that I do not appreciate the enormous importance to the world of peace, but it seems to me that that peace can only be maintained at the present time by organizing those particular interests in the world, that are dependent upon the world's peace for their success. Very truly yours,

Booker T. Washington

TLS Lilly Library InU. A press copy is in Con. 896, BTW Papers, DLC.

[1] An article in *McClure's Magazine* for October 1909 by the London correspondent of the New York *Sun* predicted a probable war between Germany and England in the near future. To prevent this, McClure proposed that the United States organize an alliance against Germany, through which the United States would become "the dominating nation of the world." (McClure to BTW, Sept. 30, 1909, Con. 896, BTW Papers, DLC.)

Emmett Jay Scott to Frederick Randolph Moore

[Tuskegee, Ala.] Nov. 1, 1909

Confidential

Dear Fred: Judge Gibbs has telegraphed us as follows: "Registered 'Banquet Speech' Age Oct. 20. Money order. Wrote 24th. No re-

plies. Hear you are principal stock holder. Will they answer why[?]"
I have replied to him as follows:

"Dr. Washington not here and in no way responsible in matter to
which you refer. Regret unpleasantness. Am writing."

You will notice I have refused to quote the Doctor as being a
stock holder. It certainly shows, however, that something in the
office is pretty loose and I am sure that you will want to get it
straightened up right away. It would be too bad for the old man
to be entering suits on the ground that it receives money from him
without giving value received. Yours very truly,

Emmett J. Scott

TLpS Con. 46 BTW Papers DLC. A note at the top and bottom of the
letter in Scott's hand reads: *"He does not know I am writing you.* That Vernon publication is unwise! It puts all of our friends under cloud."

To John Robert E. Lee

Denver, Colo. November 2, 1909

Dear Mr. Lee: I am satisfied that there is a great deal of waste of
time in Tuskegee growing out of our present methods of teaching
rhetoric, etc. It means little to spend a lot of time teaching definitions, including figures of speech and what not, such as the average
text book on rhetoric is full of before the student has actually
learned to express himself or write in a simple, direct way. It is
just the same as having a man spend months learning the definitions of carpentry before he undertakes to do real carpentry work.

Hereafter, I wish you would have the teachers place stress upon
having the students write in simple language descriptions of what
is going on about Tuskegee, about their own observations, their
travels, etc. Above all things, what our students want to learn is
how to write, and no amount of talk or committing of terms or
what not to memory will accomplish this. After they have actually
learned to write good, simple, direct English, then time can be
spent if necessary learning rhetorical definitions, etc. Yours truly,

[Booker T. Washington]

TLc Con. 393 BTW Papers DLC.

From Thomas Jesse Jones[1]

Washington   November 3, 1909

Dear Dr. Washington: Through the cooperation of Director Durand of the Census Bureau and Dr. Frissell, it has been made possible for me to spend a few weeks in the Census Bureau. The purpose of my work in the Bureau is to do all within my power to make the census of the Negro as accurate as possible.

The accuracy of the census depends, first of all, upon the interest and intelligence of the supervisors and enumerators and, secondly, upon the cooperation and intelligence of the people who are to reply. The Director plans to use both of these elements in his effort to have the enumeration of the Negro race correct.

The first task is to enlist the interest of the colored people in the census and to instruct them in the questions to be asked. In this work no person can do as much as you and no institution can surpass Tuskegee in giving instruction to the masses of the colored people.

The director is eager that a vigorous educational campaign in census questions shall be carried on among the colored people. The farm schedule is particularly difficult as the crop returns desired are those for 1909, while the property holdings are those for April 15–1910. You can readily understand how many errors could be made on this point alone and how great the need of education will be when the census is taken.

The present plan is to call for the cooperation of the private and public schools, churches through their state and district organizations, possibly insurance companies and fraternal lodges, newspapers and all other agencies which influence the colored people.

I desire your cooperation and advice in my part of the work. If you have any suggestions to offer that will add to the efficiency of the Negro Census, they will be greatly appreciated. Later I hope to call upon you and your institution for definite aid. I am sincerely yours,

Thomas Jesse Jones

TLS Con. 392 BTW Papers DLC.

1 Thomas Jesse Jones (1873–1950), a Welsh immigrant to the United States, was a Ph.D. in sociology at Columbia University, where he was strongly influenced by

the "consciousness of kind" racial theories of Franklin H. Giddings. From 1902 to 1909 he was director of research at Hampton Institute. He was a statistician in the U.S. Census Bureau (1909–12) and a specialist in education in the U.S. Bureau of Education, 1912–19. The result of his statistical study was a two-volume work, *Negro Education: A Study of the Private and Higher Schools for Colored People in the United States* (1917). In 1920–21 Jones toured black Africa as chairman of an educational commission sponsored by the Phelps-Stokes Fund. He used his African tour to encourage African leaders to study the Hampton-Tuskegee philosophy of industrial education. He was director of education of the Phelps-Stokes Fund from 1913 until his death. (King, *Pan-Africanism and Education.*)

To Frank Abial Flower

[Tuskegee, Ala.][1] November 4, 1909

My dear Sir: I have been discussing with Minister Lyon and with Mr. Scott educational matters in Liberia.

It will cost an immense sum of money for an industrial school, modeled after Tuskegee, to be located in Liberia. This institution has decided to educate, beginning this year, five boys from Liberia. Three of these boys are already here and two are soon to come.

Personally, I feel that such a school would have immense opportunity for usefulness.

I hope to be of whatever assistance I can to the Liberian people in working out their problems. Yours very truly,

Booker T. Washington

TLpSr Con. 892 BTW Papers DLC.

[1] BTW was traveling between Denver, Colo., and New York City at the time of this letter. It was written at Tuskegee and signed for BTW by Emmett J. Scott.

From Emmett Jay Scott

Tuskegee Institute, Alabama November 6, 1909

My dear Mr. Washington: Mr. J. O. Thompson was down to see me a day or two ago. He came by to make personal report in the

Negro Exposition matter. I will try to tell the story as he related it to me.

First of all: at Birmingham he sat opposite the President at the banquet, but had no opportunity for personal talk with him until just as the President was leaving the city, when he asked him at the depot how far he was going down the road with him. This was an invitation which Mr. Thompson embraced and so he rode from Birmingham to Opelika with the President, appearing with him on the platform at each of the places where he spoke. The President gave him the privilege of presenting your letter and of pointing out to him the advantages of such an Exposition. The President said that he was not only in favor of holding such an Exposition, but that he would make it up in just such a way as you would desire and would make such references to it as would give you full and complete credit for the idea, etc.

Mr. Thompson said that he spoke to him quite at length and among other things said to him that he thought he ought to be doing something for the Colored people. He states that the President thumped the desk and said that he meant to keep all of his promises with regard to the Colored people, that he did not feel so far he had done his duty by them, but that he meant to carry out in letter and spirit what he had to say in his inaugural address.

Mr. Thompson, unfortunately, I think, although I did not say so to him, suggested to the President that he ought to try to bring you and Mr. Hitchcock together; nevertheless he states that the President said that he would do that. He went further and stated that every time he brought up anything in his Cabinet about the Colored people, one Cabinet officer tried to shift to another the responsibility of providing for a Colored man, but that from now on he meant to put it up to them so strongly that they would not be able to get out of it.

Taken as a whole, I think the interview was most satisfactory and I am very glad to send you this information.

I hope that the whole situation may eventuate to the satisfaction of all concerned. Yours truly,

Emmett J. Scott

TLS Con. 898 BTW Papers DLC.

To Wright W. Campbell[1]

New York. November 8, 1909

Dear Sir: Some months ago you mentioned your desire to have Mr. Carnegie give the money for a library for the white people in Tuskegee. Mr. Carnegie is now at home, and I think this might be a good time to take the matter up with him if you desire. As I remember the conversation, you wanted to find out whether he would not make an exception and not require the town to agree to give ten per cent for the maintenance of the library, but a smaller per cent.

Of course I am anxious that my name not be used in connection with this matter, but I want to help in any way that I can. Yours truly,

[Booker T. Washington]

TLc   Con. 389   BTW Papers   DLC.

1 Wright W. Campbell of Tuskegee, son of the first chairman of the board of trustees of Tuskegee Institute, George W. Campbell, was himself vice-president of the trustees in 1910.

To Clinton Joseph Calloway

New York. November 8, 1909

Dear Mr. Calloway: Sometime after I return to Tuskegee, I want to spend a portion of a Sunday in making a trip among the colored people on Zion Hill and among them on the Baptist side. I wonder if you could not take hold of the matter with the teachers in the Children's House and the Washington Public School and start a campaign of painting and whitewashing and general improvement among the people in these two communities, something similar to the one which has been going on in the county. I think a trip among these people will accomplish a great deal of good. I sometimes fear that in our ambition to improve the people in the country that we neglect those right at home. I hope you will take up the matter with Mrs. Jones[1] and Mr. Welch[2] at once. I shall be willing to give some money to encourage whitewashing where it is necessary if you think wise.

I am very anxious for the grounds around the schoolhouse at Chehaw to present a model appearance. More people see the Chehaw school than any other school, but there is nothing on the outside to indicate that it is different from any other public school. I wish very much that we might have a first class flower garden in front of the schoolhouse, and a vegetable garden around the schoolhouse. Yours truly,

[Booker T. Washington]

TLc Con. 389 BTW Papers DLC.

1 Laura Terrell Jones, principal and teacher of the first grade in the Tuskegee Institute Children's House. She was a sister of Robert H. Terrell.

2 W. M. Welch, principal of the black Washington Public School in Tuskegee, Ala.

To Robert Curtis Ogden

Hotel Manhattan, New York. Nov. 9, 1909

My dear Mr. Ogden: I am writing to thank you and the Finance Committee most heartily for your generous contribution toward the expenses of my Tennessee trip. I believe that good results will follow.

I am glad to know that you are well and able to do so much fine, good work. I shall hope to see you soon. Yours very truly,

[Booker T. Washington]

TLc Con. 396 BTW Papers DLC.

To James Carroll Napier

New York. Nov. 12, 1909

My dear Mr. Napier: Regarding my visit to Nashville; as you know, I have spoken to the colored people there a good many times. What

I am especially anxious to accomplish when I speak in the Auditorium is to get before a large and representative class of Nashville white men and white women. Of course, I shall expect the colored people to be present also, but the colored people know my views pretty well. I hope you can get hold of the white institutions of learning in a way to secure the attendance of both the professors and students.

I am very anxious that you incur no personal expense on account of this trip. If you will keep me informed of what you need, I shall try to see that it is supplied. Yours very truly,

[Booker T. Washington]

TLc Con. 396 BTW Papers DLC.

To Albert B. Lovett[1]

New York. Nov. 12, 1909

My dear Mr. Lovett: I am writing you about a matter which I want you to keep entirely to yourself, not telling even Booker about what I have asked you to do.

I have just asked Mr. Stewart to ship you 125 of my pictures. It is my wish that you paste on the bottom of each picture the printed slip which I will send you by tomorrow's mail. After you have done this, or had it done, I wish you to see to it that these pictures are hung up in the windows of restaurants, barber shops, stores, in the parts of Nashville where the colored people live in large numbers. I am very anxious that they be put not only where the more prosperous and successful colored people live, but in the districts where the ordinary and poorer classes of colored people live, as they are the class I am very anxious to speak to.

Enclosed I send you ten dollars which I wish you to use in paying the expenses of having this work done. You can hire some men to do it if you think it wise, but you will have to follow them up closely day by day to see that they actually hang the pictures, otherwise they will be tempted to throw them away and not carry out your directions.

I do not wish you to tell anyone who told you to have these pictures put up or make any explanation to any one about it, but simply have the work done.

If the money which I send you does not cover the full expense let me know and I will reimburse you when I see you.

I hope that you are getting on well in your studies and that you like the new president. Yours truly,

[Booker T. Washington]

TLc   Con. 393   BTW Papers   DLC.

1 Albert B. Lovett of Macon, Miss., graduated from Fisk University in 1912 and became a teacher in Chicago.

To George Washington Carver

[New York City] November 12, 1909

Dear Mr. Carver: I am very anxious to have you get out a simple, short pamphlet that can be used as a text book by the teachers in Macon County on the subject of growing cotton. It should be put in simple, direct form so that any teacher or boy or girl could understand it. It should embrace something of the history of cotton, the manner of cultivating it, the manner of harvesting, ginning, and working it up into cloth. It should also describe the different grades of cotton, the manner of classifying cotton for sale, and something about the usual price of cotton.

There ought to be suggestions in the book that would lead the teacher to keep exhibits of the best cotton constantly in the school room.

Cotton is what the masses of the people in that county and many others in Alabama depend upon for their living, and it ought to have a prominent place in every school.

I hope you can begin the preparation of the manuscript right away. Yours truly,

[Booker T. Washington]

TLc   Con. 389   BTW Papers   DLC.

To Andrew Carnegie

[New York City] November 13, 1909

Dear Mr. Carnegie: Mr. Bertram suggests that I write you my opinion concerning the Atlanta Baptist College and its work. This institution is applying to you for $20,000 for a new building on condition that the institution raise an additional $20,000.

This is one of the oldest and best established colleges for our people in the South. It is doing real college work and sending out men of the highest type of usefulness. We have several employed as teachers at Tuskegee, and I know what they are accomplishing in useful directions all through the South. Besides, this institution has the confidence and good will of the leading white people in Atlanta. Several of the leading white people are on its board of trustees.

Professor John Hope, the president is a man of the highest and cleanest character.

I feel that if you can see your way clear to help this school, you will be doing a good thing.

I hope you will not become scared at the word "Baptist," as it does not mean much in this case. It simply means the interest of the Baptist in the education of the colored people of the South.

I am planning to see you Monday. Yours truly,

[Booker T. Washington]

TLc Copy   Con. 389   BTW Papers   DLC.

From Paul Drennan Cravath

New York. November 13, 1909

My Dear Dr. Washington: The trustees of Fisk, at a meeting held yesterday, unanimously and with great pleasure, elected you a trustee. The trustees will probably not hold a meeting for several weeks, and an effort will be made to arrange for a date which will insure the presence of as many of the trustees as possible.

Dr. Gates is still at Nashville. I am writing him of your intended trip to Tennessee, and will be very glad if you will send him, as soon as you conveniently can, the probable dates of your visit in Nashville.[1] Very sincerely yours,

Paul D. Cravath

TLS Con. 389 BTW Papers DLC.

[1] BTW agreed to serve as a trustee, promised to attend the next meeting, and said he would doubtless see Gates in Nashville next Sunday. (BTW to Cravath, Nov. 16, 1909, Con. 389, BTW Papers, DLC.)

Emmett Jay Scott to Frederick Randolph Moore

[Tuskegee, Ala.] November 13, 1909

Dear Mr. Moore: The agreement reached with regard to capital stock of The Age was as follows:

Peterson stock *reduced* is to amount to $6,375.

The Doctor's stock *reduced* is to amount to $9,375. You are to give a note for the $2,700 and such additional sums as may be put into the plant in cash to the Doctor. This note is to bear interest at 5%. You will note I am counting in the $500. which he gave you while here, but am not mentioning sums as he may furnish after that date. Please let me have a record of these additional sums. Yours very truly,

E. J. Scott

TLpS Con. 46 BTW Papers DLC. A copy for BTW is in Con. 898, BTW Papers, DLC.

To Robert A. Franks

Hotel Manhattan, New York. Nov. 15, 1909

Dear Mr. Franks: Confirming our conversation this afternoon at Mr. Carnegie's house, I am writing to say that for the past two or three years Mr. Carnegie has been giving the Committee of Twelve $2700.00 per year to be used in distributing literature showing the progress of the colored people throughout the country, especially in the South.

Mr. Carnegie very kindly said this afternoon that he would continue this donation for another twelve months. The payments can be made as heretofore if this is convenient for you. Yours truly,

[Booker T. Washington]

TLc Con. 391 BTW Papers DLC.

From James Hardy Dillard

[New York City] November 15, 1909

Dear Sir: It may be remembered that at the last meeting of the Board[1] Mr. Taft very cordially extended an invitation to us to hold our December meeting in the White House. I have just received from Mr. Taft a notice, saying that the President would be very glad to meet with us in his office on Thursday, December 16, at one o'clock.

Kindly inform me at your earliest possible convenience whether you would be able to attend a meeting at this time. Please address me at 2 Rector Street, New York.[2] Yours very truly,

James H. Dillard

Dear Dr. Washington: Under the circumstances I thought I had better send out these notices at once.

J. H. D.

TLS Con. 390 BTW Papers DLC. Postscript in Dillard's hand.

[1] The Jeanes Fund.
[2] The office of George Foster Peabody, treasurer of the Anna T. Jeanes Foundation.

To Albert B. Lovett

New York. November 16, 1909

Dear Mr. Lovett: By this mail I am sending you 300 small circulars. I wish you to hire some boys and have these circulars given out at the colored churches Sunday morning as the people come out from the church services. Be sure that it is closely and carefully attended to. Be sure that you get reliable boys.

Enclosed I send you $3 to cover all or a portion of this.

I am very anxious that you say nothing to Booker about any of this work, because I do not wish his mind disturbed. He becomes very nervous and worked up over such matters. Yours truly,

[Booker T. Washington]

TLc   Con. 393   BTW Papers   DLC.

To John Hope

New York. Nov. 16, 1909

My dear President Hope: I called you up yesterday afternoon, but they said at Bishop Walters' that you were out and would not return until this morning. I left word for you to call me up this morning, but as I have not heard from you I take for granted that you have left the city.

I was at Mr. Carnegie's house yesterday afternoon at five o'clock, but the fact was Mr. Bertram, I found, had not had time to take up any business matters with him. He had been out playing golf all day, and when he returned after five o'clock he was surrounded by so many people it was impossible for Mr. Bertram to get at him in any satisfactory way for business. I think this matter will have to wait for a seasonable time for Mr. Bertram to put it before Mr. Carnegie. Mr. Bertram seems deeply interested, and that is always a favorable sign. My own belief is that the effort is going to succeed, though you may have to wait a little while for a decision. Yours very truly,

[Booker T. Washington]

TLc   Con. 391   BTW Papers   DLC.

Accounts of Washington's Tour of Tennessee

[Nov. 18–Dec. 10, 1909]

DR. WASHINGTON ON TOUR

NEGRO LEADER IS WELCOMED ON EDUCATIONAL
PILGRIMAGE

ON FIRST DAY OF HIS SOUTHERN TRIP TUSKEGEE EDUCATOR
SPEAKS TO THREE LARGE AUDIENCES IN MOUNTAINS OF
EASTERN TENNESSEE AND IS ENTHUSIASTICALLY RECEIVED
BY BOTH RACES

[Special Correspondence of The New York Evening Post: Issue of
Nov. 22, '09]

Knoxville, Tenn., November 18. — Booker T. Washington ended
the first day of his "educational pilgrimage" with an address at
Greenville last night. He spoke to more than 6,000 people yesterday, about equally divided between Negroes and whites, at three
different places, stretched out over some hundred miles in the
eastern Tennessee mountains. A remarkable degree of interest has
been manifested in the meetings by both races. On all sides the
opinion was expressed that the progress of the Tuskegee educator
would be memorable as marking the beginning of a new era in
co-operative relations between the races in this part of the South.

Bristol was an appropriate place in which to begin. It lies at an
altitude of 1,800 feet on the border line between two states, and
has been called the "eastern gate" of Tennessee. Half of its population of 22,000 live in Tennessee, and half in Virginia. The state
line runs along the main street, and the Tennessee part of the city
is a prohibition town by state law. As a result, on the Virginia side
of the main street almost every other building is a saloon. But that
does not mean that Bristol is a wide-open place; on the contrary,
it has the reputation of being one of the best-ordered municipal-
ities of its size in the South.

It is an educational centre of considerable importance, too, being
the seat of four institutions of learning, Virginian Southwest Institute, a Baptist academy for women; King's College, a Presbyterian
college for men; Sullins College, a Methodist college for girls, and

Bristol Normal Institute, a Negro school for both sexes, under Presbyterian auspices. It is by no means, either in appearance or the character of its population, a typical Southern town. But there are some 5,000 progressive Negroes living there, and, as the event showed, they were eager to welcome the leader of their race.

Dr. Washington and his party, which included I. B. Scott, missionary bishop of Africa, arrived in Bristol in a driving flurry of snow yesterday morning. There were several hundred people — white and black — at the railway station to meet him, and irrespective of race, they vied with each other in their efforts to get a look at him. A committee of the local branch of the Negro Business League, which Dr. Washington organized, surrounded him and escorted him through a cheering crowd to carriages, in which the party were driven away for a tour of the city.

Crowds to Hear Address

Dr. Washington's address was delivered at 11 o'clock in the opera house. The main street was decorated with flags, and most of the principal shops were closed. The white population had indeed joined with their black neighbors in making the day a virtual holiday. The crowd that blocked the street was so great that a lane had to be opened to admit the party. More than 5,000 people gathered in the theatre, occupying every available seat, crowding the wings and galleries, and standing in a solid mass in aisles and about the doors.

Color lines, of course, were pretty faithfully observed, both on the stage and off. On the white side of the gallery were marshalled a hundred girls, from Sullins College, in mortarboards and blue uniforms. On the stage were seated city officers, judges, college presidents, and business men. Robert E. Clay,[1] who presided, is a young Negro leader in eastern Tennessee, president of the local Business League, and a temperance lecturer of a good deal of power. Once he was a bootblack in Bristol; then he became a barber; now he is proprietor also of a coal yard and a grocery store. He has lectured at Winona Assembly; he still keeps his barber shop, and practices the doctrine of work of Booker Washington.

Judge J. H. Price, the son of a slaveholder and one of the Democratic leaders of Western Virginia, introduced Dr. Washington as "one of the Old Dominion's most distinguished sons."

"I don't know what he is going to talk about," he said, "but I am willing to endorse anything he says, before he says it."

PLAIN SPEAKING APPLAUDED

Dr. Washington spoke for more than an hour. He handled without gloves matters that Northern people think must be spoken of only with the greatest caution south of Mason and Dixon's line. Some statements at first seemed almost to take the breath away from his hearers, but it was not long before they paid tribute to his sincerity and fearless plain speaking by hearty applause. Speaking to both races he told them they might just as well make up their minds to stay where they were, and work out the problem.

"The white men in the South cannot get along without the Negro," he told them, "any more than the Negro can get along without them. Each would be lonely without the other."

Turning to his own race he urged them to cultivate reliability. "You have as a race the tendency to be constantly on the move. Get over that tendency. Cultivate a reputation for reliability. Be dependable. Pick out the place you want to live in and make up your minds to stay there and rear your families there. Buy your homes and become taxpayers instead of rent-payers. Start a bank account. Support the institutions of your city. Make yourselves valued and respected members of the community. Whatever work or business you engage in put your best efforts into it. Don't be satisfied with doing anything half-well."

These were only a few of the counsels he gave them. The meeting closed with the singing of plantation songs, in which the audience joined. As they filed out of the hall, one heard only words of praise. If anything the white men were more outspoken than the Negroes.

"Yo' cayn't tell me," drawled one tall and stately man who might well have borne the title "colonel" if he didn't actually — "yo' cayn't tell me that man ain't inspired. Why he's inspired just as surely as Moses was sir; yes, sir, Moses."

"Yo' are right, sir," returned his companion, "God did cert'nly raise him up to lead his people out of darkness."

"I don't believe you can calculate the amount of good this speech will do," said Dr. S. R. Preston, himself an educator of note. "He didn't utter a sentiment that every white man cannot endorse fully.

Racial conditions here in Bristol are unusually good anyway, but this meeting cannot fail to better them. It will set both black and white to thinking, and it will surely inspire both to ponder how they may live up to the standard that Dr. Washington has set before them. He is a great man and a true leader of men."

IMPROMPTU RECEPTION IN TRAIN

From the hall Dr. Washington was driven back to his special train, where he held an impromptu reception. Five hundred men, women and children, black and white, filed through the car to shake his hand and thank him for coming to Bristol. It was a proud day long to be remembered for some of these little children when he patted them on the head and told them to grow up to be good men and women.

One of those who came was a clergyman, the Rev. A. H. Burroughs,[2] who is known as the "marrying clergyman" of Bristol, because in the past twenty years he has united more than 3,000 couples. When he told Dr. Washington that he was one of the Burroughs family of Franklin County, Va., the Negro leader turned to his friends and exclaimed: "Why, Dr. Burroughs and I belong to the same family. I was born on the Burroughs plantation over in Franklin County."

Dr. Burroughs stayed to see the train draw out.

"What changes time does bring," he said over and over. "Just to think of it. That great man once belonged to our family. I'm proud of him, sir — mighty proud of him."

From Bristol the train proceeded to Johnson City, one of the new manufacturing cities of East Tennessee. Ten years ago it was a village. Today, it is a bustling, though somewhat "spread out" city of 12,000 with steel mills, tanneries, a Carnegie Library, and a fine $75,000 Federal building in process of construction — a tribute to the influence of Congressman Brownlow,[3] the East Tennessee Republican boss, with the Appropriations Committee in the House of Representatives.

ANOTHER CROWD GREETS LEADER

Here, too, was a great crowd at the railway station, and as Dr. Washington appeared on the car steps the band from the National Soldier's Home, which is situated here, struck up a welcoming tune.

Johnson City has its "Hippodrome," a large rink-like hall a few blocks from the station, and to this place the crowd went. Here as in Bristol, business had practically been suspended; schools, both black and white, had been let out early, and the children, marshalled by their teachers, marched to the Hippodrome in a body. Between 2,500 and 2,800 persons crowded into the barn-like structure, filling it to the doors. More than half were white.

Mayor Burbage introduced the speaker, who was received enthusiastically. After the speech hundreds accompanied Dr. Washington to his train, shook his hand, and cheered long and vigorously till the train drew out.

Greenville, the next stop on the route, was reached about 5:30. This town is proud of having given the country a President, and visitors are always directed to a little street, just off Main Street, where a dilapidated, weather-beaten little shop bears a cracked signboard on which is barely decipherable the legend, "A. Johnson, Tailor." President Johnson was buried here on a hill overlooking the town. Greenville is a city of perhaps 5,000 inhabitants. Its chief industry is centered about tobacco.

It was dark when the special train reached Greenville, but there were a hundred men and women at the station to welcome it. Dr. Washington's party was driven in 'buses to Greenville College, a Negro school located a half mile out of town. The moon was shimmering through a thick haze, which was settling down over the hills, and the college bell clanged a welcome. Dinner was served in the commons room of the college, after which all were driven back to town, where the meeting took place in a crowded hall. At 10:30 the special left for Knoxville, and the first day of the Tennessee pilgrimage was over.

PILGRIMAGE OF EDUCATION

DR. WASHINGTON ENDS SECOND DAY IN CHATTANOOGA

WELCOME THROUGHOUT EASTERN TENNESSEE FOR NEGRO EDUCATOR, WHICH HAS DONE MORE TO BETTER RELATIONS OF THE RACES, AND TO AID THEIR FRIENDLY CO-OPERATION

[Special Correspondence of The N.Y. Evening Post: Issue of Nov. 24, '09]

Chattanooga, November 20. — Chattanooga outdid itself last night in entertaining two distinguished Americans. One was W. W. Finley,[4] president of the Southern Railway, here attending the celebration of the opening of the new union terminal station; the other was Booker T. Washington, who ended in this place the second day of his educational pilgrimage through Tennessee.

President Finley spoke to a hundred leading business men at a banquet at the Hotel Patten. Dr. Washington spoke to more than six thousand men, women and children of both races at the auditorium. Both made pleas for industrial co-operation, but they approached the subject in somewhat different manner. Whatever things President Finley specifically accomplished in his address, it is clear that Dr. Washington's talk will increase the spirit of cooperation existing between whites and Negroes in Chattanooga.

It was at Knoxville, Tennessee's pioneer capital, that the second day's speaking began. The special train arrived during the night, and was run onto a side track near the depot. Before the sun had broken through the morning haze, a committee of the Negro Business League appeared and escorted the party to Knoxville College, a Presbyterian institution for Negroes, in the suburbs. Here breakfast was served, after which Dr. Washington spoke to the students in the college chapel. It was then time to return to the city, and, headed by an escort of Negro policemen, of whom Knoxville has a number, and accompanied by a Negro band, the start was made.

There were twenty carriages in line, draped with bunting. Houses and places of business were decorated with flags, and at least ten thousand people crowded the streets in the business portion of the city to see the Negro leader pass. White and black alike cheered heartily. Exercises were held in Market Hall, where 3,000 people awaited him. The Negro schools had been dismissed in honor of his coming, and from the older pupils a large chorus had been organized, which greeted him as he entered.

BENEFICIAL EFFECTS OF TOUR

John M. Brooks,[5] the Mayor of Knoxville, presided, and introduced Dr. Washington. The greatest interest was shown by the audience, which was about evenly divided between the races. Many of the most prominent white business men of the city were seated on the platform.

A president of one of the largest banks voiced the sentiment of the white population when he declared:

"The so-called 'race problem' has never been a very serious one here in Knoxville, where, we are proud to say, the Negro population has always been honest and industrious. But Dr. Washington has helped us, I am sure, to keep on in the way we have been going. I am sure that if he carries the same message of hope and inspiration throughout Tennessee, from Bristol to Memphis, that the time will come, and come soon, when the relations of the races will be as favorable in every section as they are here among us."

FEATURES ALONG ROUTE

Leaving Knoxville at noon a stop was made at Clinton, where Dr. Washington spoke to a crowd of several hundred from the rear platform of his train. The last long stop before reaching Chattanooga was made at Harriman at 2:30 o'clock. This is a town established eight years ago by the late E. H. Harriman,[6] who built here a steel rolling mill and other manufactures. Once it had 5,000, but it is considerably smaller now.

Harriman was a prohibition place long before Tennessee became a "dry" state. It was one of the terms its founder imposed on those who settled there. They say, however, that it is easier to get anything you want to drink now since prohibition has come.

Harriman turned out in force to see and hear. The Washington party was escorted to the hall by an old ex-slave on a prancing white horse, resplendent in a sombrero with a cockade, a black velvet coat, a green sash, and a sword. The audience, largely made up of working men, a majority of them white, was responsive and interested.

With the Chattanooga speech Dr. Washington ended his tour through east Tennessee, making in all nine addresses. It has been an ovation. If the rest, as seems likely, arouses enthusiasm in the same degree, this tour will probably mark an epoch in the educational history of the state.

A MESSAGE FOR THE RACES

Dr. Washington's Tour as Seen in Middle Tennessee

NEGRO EDUCATOR SPEAKS TO LARGE AUDIENCES IN SOUTH PITTSBURG, WINCHESTER, DECHERD, COLUMBIA AND PULASKI — DIFFERENT CONDITIONS FROM THOSE MET IN EASTERN COUNTIES

[Special Correspondence of The N.Y. Evening Post: Issue of Nov. 26, '09]

Pulaski, Tenn., November 21. — Booker T. Washington addressed an open-air audience of 3,000 at "the park" here today, completing his tour of the southern counties of Middle Tennessee. Within the last day and a half since leaving Chattanooga he has spoken to some 10,000 people at six different points. At every place he has been welcomed by the leading white citizens, who have shown as great a desire to honor the Negro educator as the Negroes themselves.

In the counties just traversed the problem has been in some respects different from that met in the beginning. Bristol, Johnson City, Knoxville and Chattanooga were prosperous manufacturing towns, in which commercial and industrial classes predominated. There are many Northerners in those East Tennessee cities, and to some extent, it may be said, they have transplanted the Northern idea of the public school in their new homes. At any rate, Negroes there enjoy practically the same educational advantages as the whites. The communities feel the responsibility toward the one as strongly as toward the other.

With the first meeting yesterday, at South Pittsburg, down on the Alabama border, the conditions changed. The special train has now been running through the edge of the cotton belt, where both races have for generations tilled the soil. There has been progress of course, but, for the most part, only on the surface; underneath, conditions are still largely those of the "old South." Negroes compose the great bulk of the working population; employers of labor are planters and sons of planters of the days before the war. When these facts are taken into consideration, the tour of Booker Washington through this region must be esteemed a double success, for the interest shown by these old landed proprietors has been whole-souled and sincere.

"He brings a message to both races, suh," said a representative Southerner at Columbia, a man who has served his state in various capacities for a generation.

TYPICAL SOUTHERN TOWN

South Pittsburg, the first stop yesterday morning, is a manufacturing center on the edge of the iron ore hill region, but the audience was made up largely of white men who had come in from the country. The mill hands were busy. Two stops were made in the afternoon, at Winchester and Fayetteville, and at both Dr. Washington spoke to typical country audiences in the county court houses. In all these towns, which are county-seats, the court house stands in a large square, about which stores, shops and hotels are grouped — there are no longer any saloons in Tennessee.

As is always the case in agricultural communities, when the crops are in and work is slack, the square is the congregating place of hundreds of loungers on the lookout for anything for amusement or entertainment. Doubtless it was in this light that many of those who gathered to hear Booker Washington at Winchester and Fayetteville looked upon his coming.

At Winchester the Washington party was driven to the court house, followed by a great crowd of Negroes. As they passed into and about the square hundreds of lanky, scrawny, roughly dressed white men appeared as if by magic from every side and sauntered leisurely across to the court house. White and black together crowded up the narrow stairs and filled the worn, wooden benches that had been whittled away by inches. It was a dark, ill-kept room that they entered. The only decorations on the walls were little signs which read: "Gentlemen will please not spit on the walls." The stains which decorated the floor demonstrated how well this injunction was observed.

NEGROES ARE LAND HOLDERS

Judge Floyd Estill,[7] a fine type of the old-time Southern lawyer of ante-bellum days, presided. He lauded the Negroes of Winchester as "the best Negroes in the whole state of Tennessee," recalled to the audience the love and reverence in which certain old "elders" and "uncles" had been held; told how their descendants were all land-holders today — there are not a dozen Negroes paying rent in all Winchester, according to the report — and closed by introducing Dr. Washington as "one of the most distinguished citizens and truest men that has ever spoken from this platform."

It was an instructive thing to watch the faces of those lanky countrymen as Dr. Washington made his point with telling effect. They had possibly never heard anyone talk quite so plainly about these matters he discussed so freely. His stories illustrative of the failings and foibles of the two races were received with shouts.

But there was not one word of resentment or criticism. If any men with hair-trigger feelings on the race question were there they were either converted or pretended to be. And there were almost as many whites as blacks in the crowd that trooped to the station to bid the visitor good-bye.

At Decherd and Columbia

Before reaching Fayetteville, Dr. Washington talked to a crowd at Decherd from the rear platform. At Fayetteville the scene enacted at Winchester was repeated. The same sort of an audience listened in the same attentive way, and expressed similar sentiments in regard to the speaker and his mission.

Columbia was reached about seven o'clock. At least a thousand Negroes had gathered at the station, and they literally stormed the train and carried the guest away by force. Accompanied by a procession carrying flaring torches, and by 'bus loads of school children, the party was conveyed to a lodge hall, where a school exhibition had been arranged. From here they went to the Opera House, where Dr. Washington addressed an audience of 3,000. The white part of the audience was as typical as could be gathered together in the South. It included all the best known citizens, professional men, merchants and farmers.

Columbia a "Difficult" Place

Columbia was in some respects the most "difficult" place that had been visited. "Carmack's town," they call it, for here lived the late Senator Carmack[8] who was shot by the Coopers, father and son, in the streets of Nashville a year or so ago. Two things were noticeable in this Columbia audience. No Negroes were allowed on the ground floor of the opera house, and no white man took part in the exercises. Apart from these two things, however, there were no differences in the reception accorded Dr. Washington here and at other places, and the widely expressed opinion of the white men who listened to him was that Columbia would feel as a result the impetus toward the solution of the problem as it concerns its own welfare.

Dr. Washington and his party came on to Pulaski this morning. Here one of the most remarkable welcomes of the tour awaited him. More than a thousand Negroes, dressed in their Sunday-go-to-meetin' clothes, surrounded the station. The white folks at the hour of arrival were mostly in church, but the Negro church population had turned out in force and a procession was formed at the depot.

Pulaski is the centre of a big farming community. When Dr. Washington and his party started for the park in carriages, more than a hundred and fifty Negroes in vehicles of all sorts, fell into line behind, and every one of them owned his own horse and wagon. There were several floats, on which school children rode, and a calvalcade of fifty mounted Negroes preceded. The procession circled about the court house square, in which stands the statue of Sam Davis,[9] the Confederate spy.

From the crowded square the party went to the park where Dr. Washington spoke in the open. Half of the audience consisted of white people, who had come thither from their churches by hundreds. Round after round of applause greeted him from beginning to end of the speech. When it was over the audience poured back to the town.

WHERE NEGROES SUCCEED

WELCOME OF RACE IN NASHVILLE FOR DR. WASHINGTON

TUSKEGEE EDUCATOR CARRIES MESSAGE OF INDUS-
TRIAL WORK AND RESPONSIBILITY TO TENNES-

SEE CAPITAL, WHERE NEGROES ARE LARGE
PROPERTY OWNERS AND ON THE BEST OF TERMS.

———————

[Special Correspondence of The New York Evening Post: Issue of Nov. 27, '09]

Nashville, Tenn., November 22. — Booker T. Washington carried his educational campaign into the capital of Tennessee last night, and spoke to one of the largest audiences that ever gathered under roof in Nashville. Seventy-five hundred men and women of both races crowded the auditorium to the doors, and more than a thousand who arrived too late to get inside stood long in the street, hoping to get an opportunity to hear the advocate of Negro industrial education.

Nashville presents a noteworthy example of what education has done for the Negro. Nowhere in the South is the average of intelligence and literacy among them higher than here. There are three Negro educational institutions, Fisk University, Walden University, and Roger Williams University. With Walden is connected Meharry Medical College, the pioneer Negro medical school, which has turned out about one-half of all the Negroes who practice medicine today.

This has all tended to make the Negro population stable, law-abiding, and industrious. They are respected by the white inhabitants, and racial friction is rare. Property and commercial interests of the Nashville Negroes are large, and rapidly increasing. A half-dozen individuals possess property ranging in value between $100,-000 and $500,000. Many of the Negro residences are well up to the average of dwellings in the best white residence districts. The total of all the taxable property held by Negroes has a value of several millions. They have two banks, a hospital, and several publishing houses, one of which, the National Baptist Publishing Board, is one of the most extensive in all the South.

These are the people and these the conditions that assured for Dr. Washington a remarkable demonstration from his own race. But the white people who know and are proud of the progress of their black neighbors contributed to it in almost as great a degree. R. L. Jones,[10] state superintendent of public instruction, and Hilary Howse,[11] Mayor of Nashville, extended the welcome of state and city, and occupied seats on the platform with other representative citizens of Nashville. Dr. Washington repeated the appeal for justice on the part of the whites, industry and reliability on the part of the Negroes, and co-operation on the part of both, that he has made throughout. He said in part:

ONLY THE WORST IS KNOWN

"We of both races in the South have suffered much by reason of the fact that the worst that occurs in the South is spread readily to all parts of the world, while the best things are seldom heard outside of the community in which they take place. If one Negro burns down a house, the news is spread broadcast. If a dozen Negroes build houses, it is never known outside their own town, if even there. If a single white man assists in lynching a Negro, all the world knows it. If fifty white men join in assisting a Negro to get an education or establish himself in some business in the community, no one ever hears of it.

"In the matter of labor our race has an advantage which I fear it does not rightly appreciate. In Europe and the large cities of our own North many people walk the streets in a vain search for work. In our case no Negro who wishes to find work need go without it. In fact, instead of the black man having to seek labor, labor seeks him. The only difficulty is that it sometimes has to run pretty hard to catch him.

"In the punishment of crimes of omission and commission the law draws no color line. Since it draws no line at the finishing end, the Negro should have an equal chance with people of other races in the preparing end of life. If the Negro fails to pay his taxes, if he steals, fights, or kills, he is punished just as the white man is.

EQUAL CHANCE IN PREPARATION

"I am sure that every white man in Tennessee will agree with me that if this is true, the Negro should have the same chance of preparing himself for life, so that he may understand the law and know how to obey it. This can only be brought about by proper methods of education — I mean education of the head, heart, and hand, that education which will teach every member of our race the dignity of labor and at the same time will teach every member some trade or occupation by which a living can be made.

"Wherever I have gone in Tennessee or any other state I have found the Negro very much what the white man is. This fact imposes upon the white men of the South a tremendous responsibility — the responsibility of setting such an example to the Negro as will help him to a higher and more useful life. If I find in any community the white people ignorant, lawless, and immoral, the Negro will be found leading the same sort of life; if I find an intelligent, law-abiding, and cultured class of white people, the Negro is certain to be also intelligent, law-abiding, and cultured.

"There are hundreds of white men in Nashville who would trust their families, their wives and daughters, and every dollar they possess in the hands of certain Negroes, and feel perfectly sure that their trust would not be betrayed. As I travel through Tennessee and get into individual communities I find that in ninety-nine cases out of one hundred the relations between the individual Negro and the individual white man are all that could be desired. This individual relation between the races is a basis for the settlement of whatever problems remain."

NEGROES URGED TO FARM

DR. WASHINGTON THINKS THEIR SUCCESS LIES IN COUNTRY

IN TOBACCO BELT OF KENTUCKY AND TENNESSEE, TUSKEGEE HEAD ON EDUCATIONAL PILGRIMAGE REPEATS APPEAL FOR RURAL LIFE AND ACQUISITION OF LAND AS BEST FOR RACE.

[Special Correspondence of The New York Evening Post, Issue of Nov. 29, '09]

Brownsville, Tenn., November 23. — Yesterday noon Booker T. Washington entered the tobacco belt, and the seven meetings he addressed in as many different towns in Tennessee and Kentucky were fully as responsive to his appeal for just and sensible solution of the problems confronting the two races in the South as any of those in the East Tennessee mountains, in the cotton belt, or at Nashville.

As Dr. Washington takes pains to point out, the problem in one section of the South is not the same as that in another section. It is different in every state and often in every county. In East Tennessee, where the proportion of Negroes to whites is small, and where the influence of the inheritance of strong Union spirit of war times is evident, the problem differs from that in the Southern tier of counties, where the Negro population constitutes 50 per cent. of the whole, or in Nashville, where the high average of education and the complexities of urban life have had their bearing.

In particular is it true that the race problem in the city differs from that in the country and rural towns. Dr. Washington is the special advocate of country life for the Negro; he believes that in tilling the soil his greatest success and greatest hope for race advancement lie. And this he emphasized to the assemblies, largely rural, which he has addressed since leaving Nashville.

That this appeal to his people to stay in the country, acquire land of their own, work it, and bring up their children in the freer and purer atmosphere of the rural districts, will have its effect, the enthusiasm and unanimity of the audiences leave no room for doubt. The inadequate school facilities for Negroes in the country is the chief argument against their remaining on the farms. The burden of maintaining country schools must lie primarily on the white population. The Negro farmer can do something, but he must have the support of his white neighbors.

PLEA OF PRESSING IMPORTANCE

It is just here that Dr. Washington's plea is of the most pressing importance. The general acknowledgement, by the leading white men who spoke at the meetings, that these conditions must be improved, and the many personal expressions of determination to help better them, argue well for the future. If the next few years show an advance along these lines, it will be largely traceable to Dr. Washington's efforts, and one of the prime objects of his tour will have been achieved.

Springfield, Tenn., was the first stop out of Nashville yesterday. Springfield is a tobacco town of about 3,000 inhabitants, but at least a thousand Negro and white farmers came from the outlying districts to hear the address, some of them travelling as far as fifteen miles. Business in the town was practically suspended and every shop and store on the main street, whether belonging to a white or Negro proprietor, was decorated for the occasion. A thousand people met the train at the depot, and, led by the band and a cavalcade of mounted Negroes decorated with broad red scarfs and yellow rosettes, a procession of a hundred or more gayly bedecked carts and wagons, proceeded to the hall where the speaking took place. In this almost half the population of the town crowded.

The Mayor,[12] who delivered the address of welcome, declared that the coming of Mr. Washington marked a new era in the history of both races in the South, and that the monument he had erected in the hearts of all the people, black and white, would long outlast mere monuments of brass or stone.

"We've been so busy raisin' tobacco down here," commented a prominent white man afterwards, "that we ain't given enough thought to raisin' educated young folks. I guess we're all beginnin' to see the point now, and Washington done a lot of good by droppin' off here."

First Entrance into Kentucky

From Springfield, Dr. Washington's train proceeded north across the Kentucky border. Just over the line he addressed several hundred people at the railway station at Guthrie, where a thirty-minute stop was made. These people, too, were largely farmers and farm hands.

Hopkinsville, Ky., where the evening meeting took place, presented a more complex problem. It is one of the greatest tobacco markets in the world, a busy well built town of 16,000 inhabitants. Here was the most serious night-rider disturbance last year, when a band of masked men rode into the city and practically took possession of the place while they burned tobacco ware-houses and shot down all who opposed them.

Kentucky Negroes are in a class by themselves. They are clannish to a great degree. They remember that before the war they were largely of the house-servant class, and they are apt to take advice slowly. There has never been any difficulty about their voting, either.

"Any man who knows a log cabin when he sees it can vote," is the way they put it. The log cabin is the Republican emblem in Kentucky, and this county has only gone democratic once since the war; that was last year. All this made it seem probable that the Negroes at least would hesitate about accepting Dr. Washington's strictures as applicable to themselves.

This was not the case, however. The audience of three thousand five hundred that heard him was, perhaps, the most demonstrative in its expression of approval that he has yet addressed. Negroes in the audience were not all townspeople, as at Springfield several hundred had driven in from the country with their own teams to hear him. The railroads had taken the opportunity to advertise the affair, and ran several excursions into Hopkinsville from near-by towns. One of these was from a coal-mining town, where the chief proprietor had been interested enough to give a day off to all of his employees who wanted to make the trip.

SUCCESSFUL MEETING AT CLARKSVILLE

From Hopkinsville the train ran back into Tennessee, where this morning one of the most successful meetings of the trip took place at Clarksville, another big tobacco centre. On the stage, taking part in the exercises, were some of the most prominent white men in northern Tennessee. Matthew Sprague, one of the prosperous men in the tobacco trade, in his capacity as president of the Chamber of Commerce, delivered the address of welcome.

T. J. Ford, state Senator and lawyer of state-wide reputation, introduced the speaker, emphasizing his coming as an opportunity which both races should embrace to unite in renewed determination to solve their joint problem for themselves. It was a Southern problem, he said, for Southern men to solve, and he for one, was ready to join hands with Dr. Washington to accomplish it.

Dr. Washington's plea for sobriety and morality was made directly and specifically. The response was hearty and immediate. Again he repeated his adjuration to his race to settle down, be peaceable, and become landholders. Again he made his appeal to the whites for an opportunity to make these things possible. He was cheered several times, and when the meeting adjourned hundreds crowded forward to shake hands with him, and other hundreds followed, cheering, to the train.

Exhibition of School Children

An incident of the stop here was a specially arranged exhibition on the part of the Negro school children, which was arranged and conducted personally by the white superintendent of schools.

While the procession of some hundred carriages, a battalion of school children, and two bands were passing through the cheering throngs on the main street to the hall, one of the Clarksville shop-keepers, standing in the door of his place of business, commented thus:

"Say, I guess those fellows do love that man. They're always a-copyin' some one. Seems to me, if they want to do some copyin' that'll do good, they ought to copy him. If they all did that, I 'spose there wouldn't be any race problem. I ain't been much of a nigger lover, but I do believe in givin' them a chance."

From Clarksville the train passed southward. At Paris, Dr. Washington spoke to a large crowd at the station. At Big Sandy, where, it is said, no Negro is allowed to remain after sunset, a curious crowd congregated, and members of the Washington party descended, "just to say they'd been there." At Humboldt, one of the growing towns of western Tennessee, a stop of an hour was made, and Dr. Washington talked in a church, where people stood up in the windows and peered in from points of vantage on adjacent telegraph poles. At Brownsville the last address of the day was made this evening to a crowd of farmers and cotton-pickers. There are many small Negro farmers hereabouts, who applauded the speaker's laudation of country life. Tomorrow the day will be spent in Memphis.

NEGRO PROBLEM IN CITIES

Dr. Washington Warns Race in Memphis Address

TUSKEGEE EDUCATOR URGES NEGROES TO BETTER CONDITIONS BY THEIR OWN EFFORTS AND SHOULDER BURDEN OF REFORM IN TENNESSEE RIVER COMMUNITY IN TALK AT CHURCH'S PARK

[Special Correspondence of The New York Evening Post: Issue of Nov. 30, '09]

Memphis, Tennessee, November 25th. — Booker T. Washington

talked sharply to the Negroes of this city in his address last night, at Church's Park. In words driven home with telling force he admonished them to clean house, urged them to set about driving out the lazy and vicious from their midst, to be vigilant and energetic in their efforts to bring about and maintain order and morality, and to suppress disorder, lawlessness, and crime.

He made it clear that, irrespective of the attitude or deportment of the white people in Memphis, conditions demanded that the Negroes take this burden of reform upon themselves. Only by drastic action could they be relieved of responsibility for serious results which might follow a continuance of existing conditions. He "put it up to" the educated business and professional men of his race, asserting that their acquiescence in present conditions made all the heavier their responsibility for their black brothers.

This was plain speaking, or more, bold speaking. But Memphis is in need of that sort of thing. With one exception it has probably a larger Negro population than any city in the country. For years — generations, indeed — it has had the unenviable notoriety of being a "wide-open" town. And its doors have never been quite so wide open as today, when it flaunts defiance of the new state-wide prohibition law, when its barrooms run day and night and all day Sunday without license, when its gambling joints and disorderly houses are kept with window shades flung up.

Geographically, this city lies near the junction of three states; Tennessee, Mississippi, and Arkansas, whose vicious and criminal classes, of both races, make it the centre of their operations. Here, too, in great numbers congregate the idle and lazy from whom the criminals are recruited. There is no reason, it is said, why any man in Memphis should be out of work for a day, yet there are thousands of idle blacks and whites loitering along the streets and quays. Competent observers declare that here exists, in a greater degree even than at Atlanta, all the elements which generate racial friction.

Dr. Washington's Warning

Dr. Washington's warning to the Negroes, therefore, to stop carrying weapons, to keep sober, to cease from the petty bickerings to which they as a race are given, and finally to unite with the better element of the white population in preservation of order and administration of justice, was well considered and well timed. That there is reason to believe his advice will be heeded, expression of opinion by Negro leaders who are determined to begin before it is too late the work of regeneration leaves no room for doubt.

Dr. Washington reached Memphis, the westernmost point of his educational pilgrimage, yesterday morning. His party was taken in carriages and automobiles to the several Negro schools and colleges, the medical school and hospital, and through the Negro residence sections of the city. The members were given opportunity to see the Negro at work and in idleness. In the afternoon, there was a banquet, and in the evening five thousand people gathered at Church's Park to hear Dr. Washington speak. The address of welcome was delivered by Judge J. M. Steen of the Circuit Court, who said in part:

"We believe that as the patriarchs of old were inspired by God to lead their people out of darkness into light, to guide them on the right road to right living and success, so he who is to speak to us tonight is inspired to lead his race to higher, better things.

"But his message is not for you alone. It is not alone for this city or this state. By helping you he helps us; by helping you he helps every man, woman and child in all this broad land of ours. God in His infinite wisdom has placed two races here side by side to work out their destinies. But He has so interwoven these destinies that we must rise or fall together. Whatever goes into the lives of the black people to make them honest law-abiding men of character, those same things go to make the white people honest and law-abiding and upright. If it takes industry, sobriety and morality to make me a man, in just the same degree those elements must enter your lives to make you men."

Local Conditions in Memphis

Dr. Washington's address as far as it dealt with local conditions, follows[:]

"The leaders among our people to whom I am speaking tonight, chiefly ministers, teachers, lawyers, doctors, and business men, should make it a part of their duty to reform the criminal loafers, or have them move on to some other part of the world. If these characters are not reached and changed, they will tear down and disgrace our entire race in this city. Loafing brings together the worst elements of whites, and the worst elements of blacks. Nothing hurts our race more than for one to go through a city and find whole corners and sometimes blocks occupied by a set of loafing men and women who seem to have little or no purpose in life.

"There is a law in this city and state to the effect that it is illegal to sell whiskey or strong drink. That law should be upheld and supported by the best element of our race whether we believe in the wisdom of the law or not. The white man who breaks the law to sell whiskey to a Negro today will be tempted to break the law when he wants to lynch a Negro tomorrow.

"It is the duty of the leaders to whom I talk tonight to do their part in seeing that in every community the footpads, the pocket-book-snatchers, the pistol-toters, those inclined to murder, are reformed or gotten rid of. One of the worst sources of danger grows out of carrying concealed weapons. I have lived in the heart of the South practically all of my life. I travel constantly in every section of the South, meet all classes and conditions of the people, and I have never yet found it necessary to carry a pistol upon my body or even keep one in my house.

"There is another evil that is likely to show itself among the masses, and it should be guarded against among our leaders. I do not know how it is in Memphis, but I know in many large cities the Negro is yielding too largely to the temptation to sell his vote for a price. No matter if it is said that white people of the same class do the same thing, that does not justify the Negro in trading away his vote. The Negro, so far as the franchise is concerned, is on trial, and, if in a city like this, the Negro vote becomes purchasable, the next step will be an effort to take that vote from him.

NEGROES SHOULD HELP THEMSELVES

"Now, I don't care how high any colored man or woman is in Memphis, how much education, culture, or wealth they may have, they should concern themselves with the condition that I have described. They should concern themselves with the condition of the lowest characters, the most unfortunate in the city. Either we must pull them up or they will pull us down. Besides, where there is a large loafing, vicious element among both races in any community, this more largely than anything else furnishes the fuel out of which mobs and lynchings grow.

"We must not permit it to be said in any part of the country that we are inclined to shield black criminals because they are members of our race. We should have the reputation for being just as much interested in bringing the criminals to justice as anybody else in the community, and when such criminals are brought before the courts, those charged with the administration and execution of the law should see to it that in every case the Negro receives justice and protection. One cannot, however, expect the Negro race to be active in discovering those charged with crime unless one feels that the individual in every case is going to be protected in his life, and receive absolute justice before the courts.

"I wish too that there might be a reform in all of the larger centres of Negro population that would prevent our people from taking petty cases before the courts. During the course of the year thousands of dollars are absolutely thrown away in petty squabbles, before the courts, that might be settled by the minister or by some mutual friend or might be settled within the family. The spectacle of a lot of women and girls constantly appearing before the police courts and other courts is hurtful to our race.

"While I have spoken plainly on all these points, I beg of all of you to understand that nothing but a love for my race has prompted me to do so, and I feel that if these suggestions are heeded our people will make even greater progress in the city of Memphis than in the past. In speaking as I do, I do not overlook the fact that here in Memphis there are thousands of earnest, successful, hardworking men and women who are a credit to any race. There are hundreds of well-to-do business men, professional men whose success we are all proud of. It is because I want to increase this class that I am in your city, and have discussed this subject so fully and frankly."

THE SOUTH'S OWN PROBLEM

BOOKER T. WASHINGTON'S WORDS
TAKEN TO HEART

EDUCATOR'S RACE MESSAGE ON TENNESSEE TOUR IMPRESSED WHITES AND NEGROES ALIKE — REALIZATION OF NECESSITY OF CO-OPERATION ONE OF THE FRUITS OF THE NOTABLE JOURNEY

[Special Correspondence of The N.Y. Evening Post: Issue of Dec. 2, '09]

Jackson, Tenn., November 25. — Booker T. Washington, the Tuskegee educator, brought to a close here with a speech at Royal Street Park an eight days' tour through Tennessee that promises to be long remembered as an event of immeasurable benefit, not only to the Negroes of this state, but throughout the whole South. In twenty-two cities and towns lying between Bristol, on the Virginia line, in the northeast corner of the state, and Memphis, on the Mississippi River, in the southwest corner, he has talked to upward of fifty thousand persons, probably twenty thousand of whom were white. A third as many more, it is estimated, have tried to hear him and have been turned away at the doors.

He has talked to men and women of all sorts and conditions, and he has seemed to have a direct and specific message for each and every one.

To the miners and manufacturers of the East, to the cotton planters and cotton pickers of the South and West, and to the tobacco planters and workers of the northern and central counties, he has appealed; and, while he has deftly adopted his pleas to the existing condition in each district he has visited, his message has been substantially the same for all. To all he has declared that, whatever race problem there was in the South today was a problem for Southern men, black and white, to settle between them, and he has urged harmonious co-operation in education, and industry as a means to that end.

The list of places in which he has spoken is as follows: Bristol, Johnson City, Greenville, Knoxville, Chattanooga, South Pittsburg, Winchester, Decherd, Fayetteville, Columbia, Pulaski, Nashville, Springfield, Guthrie (Kentucky), Hopkinsville (Kentucky), Clarksville, Paris, Humboldt, Brownsville, Memphis, Jackson and Milan.

Certain it is that this state-wide tour will leave its impress on the white people of Tennessee, as well as on the black. They have flocked to hear Dr. Washington by the thousand, and nine out of every ten white men who have heard him have gone away convinced that his solution of the problem is the true one. It is not too much to say that these men will take the earliest opportunity to put into practice, or to assist the Negroes in putting into practice, the gospel that this leader of his race is preaching.

Southern Newspapers Aiding

Another significant sign of the importance in which this tour has been held in the community is the way it has been treated in the local newspapers, which by their full reporting of Dr. Washington's speeches have greatly widened the scope of his influence. Nothing like this has ever occurred before in the South.

Knoxville, Chattanooga, Nashville and Memphis papers have devoted columns to the meetings, and to what the speakers have had to say. This, it may be pointed out, is but one more example of the way in which the great newspapers of the South are assisting in bringing about better relations between the races in their localities.

Only a few years ago the newspapers were looked upon as the chief obstacles to a solution of the problem. It was to newspaper agitation that the Atlanta riots were chiefly attributed. Today these newspapers are adopting practical methods of solution. They are systematically suppressing or minimizing the news of Negro crime and lawlessness, as well as of all race troubles, and are emphasizing the educational and commercial activities of the race.

In another respect the tour has demonstrated the progress that has recently been made toward a betterment of racial conditions and relations in the South. At every point visited, the leading white men of the community, professional and business men, have shown their interest and sympathy in Dr. Washington's efforts by appearing on the platform with him and taking part in the meetings. There have been meetings in the South where prominent white men from the North who have gone South to assist the cause of Negro education have participated in this public manner, but this tour developed an interest of another sort.

Tribute from Old Confederates

It was the Southern white men, the old ex-slave-holders, and sons of slave-holders, men who had fought in the Confederate armies, and had grown up among the Negroes, who paid this tribute to

Washington and his work. And the lasting effect of such an example as they set, or of the words of interest and hope they uttered, cannot be too strongly emphasized.

How one Southerner felt the responsibility of his own race to the Negro was well set forth by Judge Bond[13] at Brownsville, in these words, uttered with much feeling, after he had heard Dr. Washington speak:

"I was born and reared here in the South, and have associated all my life with Negroes, and I feel that I owe a debt to the Negro that I can never repay. During the war the Southern white man left his home, his wife, and his children to the care of the Negro, and I have yet to hear of an instance where that trust was betrayed.

"Ever since I have sworn that I shall be grateful to the colored people and never be unfair to that race. The white man who does not admit that he owes a duty to the Negro in the sight of God is not a man; he is not a man if he does not at all times and in all circumstances acquit himself of that duty. If there was ever a people in this country who owed a debt to another people, it is the Southern white man to the Southern Negro. The white man who lives north of the Ohio River owes him a debt too, but his debt is as nothing compared with ours.["]

Wherever he has spoken Dr. Washington has urged his race to settle down where they are and make up their minds to become useful and respected members of the community. He has urged them to remember that because they are black they are no less Southerners than their white neighbors in feeling, training, and character. He has pointed out to them that the solution of the so-called "race problem" can be accomplished only by the Southern Negroes working in co-operation and harmony with the white people among whom they have grown up.

Hope in Mutual Understanding

He laid stress on the point that the Southern white man understands the Southern Negro better than any other white man, just as the Southern Negro understands the Southern white man better than he does any other sort of white man. In this mutual understanding lies the greatest hope for a successful solution.

He has told them that the question before them is not one of social equality — the Negro does not want or expect that, he declares. But he does want and expect equality before the law, and equality of opportunity to earn a living. That means, he told them, an equal chance with the white people for an education which shall enable them to become productive members of the community. This point he emphasized in the rural districts, where the school facilities were poor.

He has exhorted them to become taxpayers instead of rent-payers, to start bank accounts, and to see that their children learn some useful trade or profession. Achieve a reputation for reliability, orderliness, dependability, he told them. He warned them too, while today they constituted the bulk of the working population of the Southern States, there was no guarantee that this situation would last always, and that if they did not keep abreast of the times they would be forced out of employment by the Italian and the Pole.

Everywhere he emphasized the necessity for the improvement of sanitary conditions. The Negro benefit and benevolent organizations were all right, he told them, but he remarked that it was more important to make sure of a good place to live in this life than an expensive and elaborate burial after death. "One bathtub is worth ten coffins," was the way he put it.

All along the line of his tour he has expressed the belief that the Negro's greatest chance for success lay in the country, where his opportunity to become a landholder was greater and his temptations were less. But to those who must remain in the city he has urged attention to the promotion of orderliness, industry, and sobriety. He has warned them bluntly that unless they eliminate the vicious, and idle Negro from their communities the responsibility for any race friction that may follow can with justice be laid at their own doors.

Nor has he feared to touch on the dangerous question of politics.

"The Negro acts with his white neighbor in every walk of life," he declared in effect; "but when election day comes along he goes in the opposite direction. When he learns that the white man whose lead he follows, whose advice he seeks every day in the year except one, may be just as good a leader or adviser on that day as any other, another long step toward the co-operation of the races will be taken."

This has been the burden of Booker Washington's plea from

the Great Smoky Mountains to the Mississippi and the response has been everywhere so immediate, so hearty, so sincere, that it can have no other meaning than that the South is at last thoroughly awake to the necessity of solving its own race problem for itself.

PRINCIPAL WASHINGTON'S CAMPAIGN

[Dr. R. E. Park, in The Springfield (Mass.) Republican]

Memphis, Tenn., November 24, 1909. — At noon November 18 a party of colored men, headed by Booker T. Washington, started by special train from Bristol, Tenn., on an eight days' campaign through the state in the interest of Negro education and of racial peace. The party was made up, for the most part, of colored business and professional men from different parts of Tennessee, members of the local Negro business leagues in the towns and cities through which the party passed. At different points along the route the party was joined by other noted colored men, from other and more distant parts of the country, who are interested in the plans and purposes for which this expedition was undertaken. Among these were: William H. Lewis, assistant United States district attorney of Boston; John E. Bush, receiver of public moneys of Little Rock, Ark.; Bishop I. B. Scott of Monrovia, Liberia, who is in charge of the missions of the Methodist Episcopal Church of the West Coast of Africa, and Major R. R. Moton, Hampton Institute, Virginia. The party was in charge of J. C. Napier of Nashville, who was the last colored man to represent the colored people of the city in the Nashville city council and who is now cashier of the One Cent Savings Bank, the older of the two Negro banks in that city.

Among the other members of the party were bankers and business men, teachers and preachers, all of them men who have worked their way up to positions and influence among the colored people in their communities. Their presence was a guarantee that the statements made by Mr. Washington who was their spokesman, represented the sentiment of the most influential of the Negro people of the state. The plan of the journey and arrangement of local committees provided that the party should visit 20 or 30 towns between Bristol, which is [on] the northeast line between Virginia and Tennessee, and Memphis, which is in the southwest corner of the state. The eastern, middle and western portions of Tennessee, of which Knoxville, Nashville and Memphis are respectively the centers of population, are widely different in their industries, in their history and in the character of their people. The journey to these different cities and intervening points gave Mr. Washington and his party an opportunity to see the masses of the Negro people and to note their condition in all the varied circumstances which Southern life presents.

In the eastern part of Tennessee they saw for the most part, a mining population in which the whites largely outnumbered the Negroes. In Central Tennessee, in the region north of Nashville, they found a large population at work in the coal mines and in the tobacco fields. In the region around Memphis, they saw a Negro population which is composed of people who come from the cotton plantations. Memphis probably has, at the present time, the largest Negro population in the United States, and Shelby County, in which Memphis is situated, probably has the most concentrated Negro population in the United States. In each of the principal cities visited the party found a little group of prosperous Negro business men. In Chattanooga for example, two of the best drug stores in the city are conducted by colored men. A colored man also owns the handsome three-story brick building adjoining the municipal auditorium where Mr. Washington spoke Friday night, November 20, to an audience of 6,000 persons.

Nashville probably has the most prosperous and the most intelligent community of colored people of any city in the South. There are not less than six Negro business men in that city who are estimated to be worth at least $100,000. Nashville has also two Negro banks, and is the home of the National Baptist Publishing company, which prints most of the literature for the million and a half colored Baptists in the United States. This concern publishes nine periodicals, and does an annual yearly business of more than $200,000.

Memphis has in it R. R. Church, who is said to pay taxes on $220,000 worth of property, the wealthiest Negro in the state. Mr. Church owns, among other things, an amusement park in the center of the city, which contains the auditorium in which Mr. Washington spoke during his visit to the city. The colored people of Memphis also have one bank, a hospital and two colleges, one of them a medical school, and all of them supported entirely by the contributions of the Negro people in this vicinity.

The colored people seem to be doing particularly well in the country districts. One of the places visited by the party was the city of Hopkinsville, Ky., which is just over the edge of Tennessee, and the center of the Burley tobacco region. Hopkinsville was the scene a few months ago of one of the famous exploits of the Kentucky night riders. The colored tobacco farmers in this region are doing particularly well, and one of them, Tom Wright of Cerulian Springs, is said to have taken the prize regularly for a number of years for the best sample of dark tobacco produced in Christian County. Near this city, also, is the famous St. Bernard mining company's properties, where 3,600 colored and 2,000 white miners are employed. The head of this company, J. B. Atkinson, is recognized as a friend of the colored people. For example, his private secretary, bank boss in one of his mines, that is to say, the man that has charge of all the operations below ground, and a number of other men occupying responsible positions are Negroes. Mr. Atkinson employs three Negro electricians who were educated at Armour Institute, Chicago, at his expense. One of the wealthiest citizens of Hopkinsville was Peter Postelle,[14] a colored man who died a few years ago worth $300,000.

At the meeting in Chattanooga, Mr. Washington was introduced by L. H. Coleman, a distinguished attorney of Chattanooga, who varied the usual formulas of introduction by relating to the audience facts to show to what extent the colored people have improved in Chattanooga in the 10 years since Mr. Washington had spoken in that city before. Among other illustrations of this progress, he mentioned the fact that no less than 100 telephones are used by the colored people of that city in their homes and places of business. In conclusion he said: "Our colored citizens are too busy to meddle with politics, though they have two representatives in the city legislature."

Although colored people vote in Tennessee, they do not seem to be represented in the city or state governments outside of Chattanooga. Nashville, however, has a company of Negro firemen who have been in service in that city for more than 30 years. Knoxville has four colored policemen, and in Clarksville it is said that all the letter carriers in the city are colored.

Among professional men, Negro doctors, dentists and pharmacists seem to have been unusually successful in Tennessee. There are about 200 Negro physicians in Tennessee, of whom about 165 or 170 have graduated from the Meharry medical school at Nashville. Nashville has 30 colored physicians, four colored dentists and four colored drug stores. Memphis has something over 30 physicians, and maintains a flourishing local colored medical society, which is doing considerable service in the effort to improve the sanitary conditions of those parts of the city in which the majority of the Negro population live. Everywhere throughout the state the visit of Mr. Washington and his party created the most profound interest, both among colored and white people. Nowhere was it possible to obtain an auditorium large enough to hold the immense crowds that thronged to hear him speak, not even in the Ryman auditorium in Nashville which holds 8,000 people.

Some of Mr. Washington's utterances indicate the tenor of his argument and speeches. "A large part of our race troubles in the South," he said, "are in the newspapers. When a man is running for office he will say most anything. Frequently I have found that the persons who talk the loudest in public against the Negro are in private, when at home, his best friends. Negro business men whom I have met in every part of the South have confessed to me that they owe a large part of their success to the advice and assistance they have received from Southern white men. It would be impossible for us to have gained as much property and made as much progress as we have in the South if there was not a very large proportion of the population who was interested in our success. Every Negro in the South has a white friend, and every white man has a Negro friend. Many honest Southerners are still unconvinced that the Negro is able to profit by education. It is the business of the people of my race to convince these men by the results of our education that every time a Negro boy or girl is educated he becomes a better and more useful citizen. Negro schools in the South should seek to interest Southern men in the work they are doing. They should have a larger number of Southern trustees than they do at present. More than that, when it comes to voting, the colored people must learn to stand by the white people who are their friends. It frequently happens that a colored man will follow the advice of some Southern white friend in all the practical matters of life until it comes to election day; then they part company."

Mr. Washington's practical suggestion was that the friendly personal relations, existing between the races in the South, to which he referred again and again in the course of his speeches, should constitute the basis for the solution of the race problem. The purpose for his journey through the state, he said, was to arouse the colored and white people to a larger and deeper sense of the fact that in all the fundamental things of life the interests of the two races were one.

BOOKER WASHINGTON'S GREATEST SERVICE

[Editorial: New York Evening Post, Dec. 2, '09]

The remarkable success of Booker T. Washington's latest speaking tour in the South emphasizes again his great usefulness to the whole country. In this role as an interpreter of one race to another, pleading for harmony, mutual respect, and justice, he is performing a patriotic service which it would be hard to overestimate. One of the foremost white educators now at work in the South, exclaimed on hearing of the details of Mr. Washington's recent trip through Tennessee: "Now I believe there is going to be a revolution in the South in favor of the Negro." Of the fifty thousand persons, who, according to the estimate of the special correspondent of this newspaper with Mr. Washington, attended his meetings, nearly half were white; and in every case he was received with an enthusiasm which would have turned the head of any less balanced and sagacious leader.

Lest we be accused of exaggeration, we would remind our readers that Judge Floyd Estill, at Winchester, Tennessee, introduced Washington the Negro, once a homeless and destitute wanderer as "a fine type of the true Southern gentleman"; that Judge J. H. Price, another typical Southerner of high position, classed Booker Washington with the first president, with Thomas Jefferson, Madison, and Monroe, Lee, and other Virginia worthies, as among that state's most distinguished sons; and that Judge J. M. Steen of the Circuit Court introduced Mr. Washington with these words:

"We believe that as the patriarchs of old were inspired by God to lead their people out of darkness into light, to guide them on the right road to right living and success, so he who is to speak to us tonight is inspired to lead his race to higher, better things. But his message is not for you alone. It is not alone for this city or this state. By helping you he helps us; by helping you he helps every man, woman and child in all this broad land of ours." All of this is enough to make any man accustomed to the ravings of the ordinary Southern office-seeker, or firebrand lecturer * * * [15] rub his eyes and ask whether a revolution is not actually at hand. Yet these compliments to Mr. Washington and his work were received with the heartiest approval by the earnest white thousands present who have become convinced of his unselfishness and wisdom.

Still this turning to Mr. Washington by such men of prominence ought not to surprise us. It is just the better self of the South coming to the front. Men like the judges we have quoted have come to see that if the races are to live in peace and comfort, the Negroes who are progressing, who are laboring in Mr. Washington's spirit, must be sustained and upheld. More and more, too, men of standing are bound to recognize the obligation the South owes to the Negro. Speaking at Brownsville in Mr. Washington's presence, Judge John R. Bond of the Tennessee Circuit Court said: "I was born and reared here in the South, and have associated all of my life with Negroes. I feel that as a Southern white man I owe a debt to the Negro I can never repay." His gratitude was specially for the way in which the Negroes protected and cared for the white women and children who were left at home during the war. But there is even a higher and more sacred obligation than that — the duty of caring for a backward race because it is backward, and of helping it onward and upward. The man who would injure a defective or crippled child must be an utter outcast from society; the time will come when all nations will take a similar attitude toward those human beings who are handicapped, particularly if, as in the case of our Negro, their plight is largely no fault of their own.

To this quiet but ever-present appeal the true Southern gentleman is bound to respond because he has a heart, because essentially he believes in fair play, and because he is an American. Further proof of this lies in the space given to Mr. Washington's trips in South Carolina, in Virginia, in Mississippi, and now in Tennessee, by the newspapers of those sections. The Tennessee press has yielded to Mr. Washington its first pages and reported his speeches in full, even where the proceedings called for four or more columns. At Charleston, last winter, the prominent editors joined the Mayor in welcoming the colored orator; in Tennessee the editors have sat upon his platforms. More than that, the Memphis Commercial-Appeal has recently honored itself and its profession by instructing its correspondents to bear down as lightly as possible upon Negro crime and to say as much as possible about Negro strivings for betterment. The Nashville Banner is another journal that is doing its best to be just to the Negro and trying not to lay undue stress upon the crimes of the rascals who unfortunately disgrace their race — just as there are plenty of white men who do the devil's work. The Columbia State has also long battled for fair play; recently it has incurred unfair criticism for denouncing the unjust punishment of a Negro because he was a Negro.

To come back to Mr. Washington, the greatest service he can render today is plainly not at Tuskegee, and not at the White House conferring as to appointments, but on the stump in the South. His bearing and popularity enable white men to speak out freely where it would sometimes be difficult to do so if the Negro endorsed were less well known. Public opinion is far more dreaded in the South than in the North; it takes vastly more courage there to break the bonds of custom and habit than anywhere else in this country, for social ostracism is more quickly brought to bear. Let him who doubts this read Walter Page's new novel, "The Southerner." The reason why the educator we have quoted sees a revolution coming is because Southern men everywhere are beginning to break away from the conventions, even the terrorism, which have kept them silent heretofore. At any rate, Mr. Washington is today both a great intrepreter and an inspired apostle. This must be recognized, whether one agrees with him in all his views or not. It is fifty years today since the death of John Brown; who could have thought in 1859 that a colored man in 1909 would have so won the gratitude and esteem of the nation?

A NOTABLE SPEECH

[Dr. R. E. Park, in The Boston Transcript, December 10, '09]
One of the most interesting incidents of Booker T. Washington's recent educational campaign through the state of Tennessee to

which reference was made in The Transcript a few days ago, was the hearty response it called forth from the white people. The addresses of welcome made by prominent white men at different cities not only showed sincere interest in the success of the enterprise Mr. Washington had undertaken, but several of them were in other respects unusual.

The most impressive speech by a white man during the eight days that Mr. Washington and party were on the road was made, however, by John R. Bond, judge of the Circuit Court of Brownsville, Tenn. This speech, which was taken practically in full by one of the members of the party, was in some respects remarkable. It is especially interesting just now, in view of the subject of Mr. Washington's address at the New Old South Church next Sunday, as showing the disposition of many of the better Southern white people toward the Negro. Judge Bond said:

"I was born and reared here in the South and have been associated all my life with Negroes. I feel that as a Southern white man I owe a debt to the Negro that I can never pay, that no Southern white man can ever pay. During the War, the Southern white man left his home, his wife and his children to be taken care of by the Negroes, and I have yet to hear of a single instance where that trust was betrayed or where they proved unfaithful, and ever since that time I have sworn by the Most Divine that I shall ever be grateful to the colored people as long as I shall live, and that I shall never be unfair to that race. I have always since thought that a white man is not a man who does not admit that he owes a duty in the sight of God to the colored people of this country; he is not a man if he is not willing at all times and under all circumstances to do all he can to acquit himself of that duty. If there was ever a people in this country who owed a debt to any people, it is the Southern white man to the Southern colored man. The white man who lives on the other side of the Ohio River owes him a debt too, but by my honest conviction in the sight of God his obligation is nothing compared to that of the Southern white man to the colored people, and I have often wondered what will be the judgment on the Southern white man and his children and his grandchildren in failing to discharge his duty toward the old Negro, his children and his grandchildren for their many years' faithful and true service.

"My mother died at my birth. Now I am growing old. An old

black mammy, who, thank God, is living today, took me in her arms and nursed me and cared for me and loved me until I grew strong and to manhood, and there has never been a day since that she has not been willing to do the same for my wife and children, even in spite of her years.

"I remember some time ago very well, when I was sitting in a darkened room nursing my youngest child, who was confined with the dreaded disease, smallpox, my wife in a most distressing manner appeared at the head of the stairs (we had been separated because of our little girl's condition and we were kept from the rest of the family up stairs). My wife called down to me and informed me that she feared another of our children had fallen victim to the smallpox. We were in a predicament, you may easily see. It was necessary to at once remove the child from the rest, but there still remained a doubt as to her being a victim, so we could not bring her into the room in which we were and it was also necessary that she be taken out of the room in which she was. She must be kept in a separate room and neither was it safe for her mother or myself to be in the room in which she would be taken. She must remain in this room all night without care or attention from either, but just about that time the old black mammy, this same black mammy who nursed and cared for me, appeared. Black mammy was heard from. 'Smallpox or no smallpox, that child cannot stay in that room by herself tonight or no other night, even if she takes the smallpox and dies tomorrow'; and she did go into that room and stayed in that room until morning, and was willing to stay there as long as it was necessary. God bless her old soul!

"I am glad to see Mr. Washington here and to have him speak to us. He is a credit to his race, and would be a credit to any race. I wish we had many more men like him all over this country.

"Mr. Washington, I pray to God that the Spirit may ever guide you in your purpose to lift up your people and that you may inspire all Southern white men as well as Southern colored men to lift up and elevate your race."

The paradox of Southern life, from the point of view of a Northerner who does not understand the local conditions, is that while Southern people frequently seem opposed to Negroes in the mass, the personal relations between the races are on the whole kindly. These friendly personal relations between individual colored men and individual white men, Mr. Washington insists, must be made the basis for the final reconstruction of the Southern States.

THE SIGNIFICANCE OF THE TOUR

[Editorial: Boston Transcript, December 10, '09]

Anyone who has fears that the race problem at the South is unsolvable can find no better strengthener of his hope and courage than the address of Judge Bond of the Circuit Court of Brownsville, Tenn., which appears in another column. Born and reared in the South, and in constant association with Negroes, his attitude toward them is one of respect and gratitude, instead of scorn and criticism. He places the emphasis upon their best traits, and not on their worst, and those traits are strong and numerous enough to deserve all the help that the white people of both the South and North can give for their more complete development.

The address of Booker T. Washington yesterday at the meeting held in the interest of the Robert Gould Shaw House, a social settlement for our colored population, is a confirmation from another point of view of the attitude taken by Judge Bond. "Wherever I have traveled," he said, "every Negro has a white friend and every white a Negro friend." That is, the personal relation is closer and more friendly between the races at the South than at the North. He advanced the opinion that to get up a real war, it would only be necessary to attempt to take the Negroes away from the South. This bodes ill for the colonization schemes of Bishop Turner and all others who have been urging a hegira of the colored race to Africa.

The ties of good will and mutual helpfulness between Southern whites and blacks are steadily growing stronger. The lynching barbarities still continue, and too severe criticism cannot be passed upon them, but they are not the sole basis upon which the situation is to be judged. Their shocking sensationalism obtrudes itself upon public attention, to the partial obscuration of those influences steadily and constantly at work cementing friendship between the two races. The leaven of the enlightened civilization and humanity is stronger in the long run than the forces of barbarity. The world's history has proven them so, and this instance will be no exception.

Judge Bond does not stand alone in his feelings and opinions on this question. There are thousands who share them and are ready to give their aid and sympathy in every way possible to this devoted leader of his people, struggling upward toward the plane of good citizenship.

PD Con. 821 BTW Papers DLC. Pamphlet reprinted from articles in the New York *Evening Post*, Springfield *Republican*, and Boston *Transcript*.

¹ Robert E. Clay, barber of Bristol, Tenn., was a member of the NNBL and a speaker at its 1916 convention. He was active in the Tennessee prohibition movement. In 1919 he helped to found the People's Cooperative League of Tennessee and became its executive secretary. For a time he was state agent of the Rosenwald Foundation. During the 1920s he toured the state in behalf of the Tennessee Agricultural and Industrial State School at Nashville.

² Ambrose Hammet Burroughs, a grandson of BTW's former owner, James Burroughs.

³ Walter Preston Brownlow (1851–1910), a Republican politician of Jonesboro, was the nephew of U.S. Senator William Gannaway Brownlow. He served as Jonesboro postmaster and as doorkeeper of the U.S. House of Representatives. He was a member of Congress from 1897 to 1910.

⁴ William Wilson Finley (1853–1913) was vice-president (1895–1906) and president (1906–13) of the Southern Railway.

⁵ John M. Brooks, born in 1840, a Confederate veteran, was an insurance broker and prominent Democrat in Knoxville, Tenn. He was elected mayor of the city in 1908.

⁶ Edward Henry Harriman (1848–1909), a Wall Street capitalist, was president of the Union Pacific and president or director of many other railroads.

⁷ Floyd Estill, born in 1858, was a prominent lawyer and farmer of Winchester and an active Democrat. He was circuit court judge from 1897 to 1902.

⁸ Edward Ward Carmack (1858–1908) was editor of newspapers in Nashville and Memphis. He served in the U.S. House of Representatives (1897–1901) and U.S. Senate (1901–7) as a Democrat. He was assassinated at Nashville on Nov. 9, 1908.

⁹ Sam Davis (1842–63), a Confederate spy born in Smyrna, Tenn., was shot after his capture and refusal to give information about his fellow spies.

¹⁰ Robert Lee Jones, born at Sparta, Tenn., in 1867, was state superintendent of public instruction from 1907 to 1911, when he became president of Middle Tennessee State Normal School at Murfreesboro.

¹¹ Hilary Ewing Howse, a businessman born in 1866, was mayor of Nashville from 1909 to 1913.

¹² According to the Nashville *American*, Nov. 23, 1909, 3, BTW was introduced at Springfield by Col. W. W. Pepper, a prominent Springfield lawyer.

¹³ John R. Bond, born in 1849, the son of a planter and banker in Haywood County, received a law degree from the University of Michigan in 1870 and returned home to practice. He was state attorney general from 1896 to 1900, when he was appointed to the state circuit court, retiring in 1910.

¹⁴ Peter Postelle (or Postel), an ex-slave, was a successful merchant and real estate owner.

¹⁵ The pamphlet version omits the words "of the Tillman order." (New York *Evening Post*, Dec. 2, 1909, 8.)

To William Howard Taft

[Chattanooga, Tenn.] Nov. 19, 1909

Personal

My dear Mr. President: I am very glad that you are planning to take up the matter of the report of the American Commission to Liberia at an early date. I feel quite sure that its publication will accomplish great good in calling attention to the interest of this administration in helping the little Negro Republic. There is very general interest throughout the country among the colored people and many of the white people as well, in the report which this Commission has made. This Liberian report and your interest in the National Negro Exposition project will afford opportunity for letting the colored people appreciate the interest your administration has in those matters which are of interest to them. Yours very truly,

Booker T. Washington

TLS William Howard Taft Papers DLC. A carbon is in BTW Papers, ATT.

To Whom It May Concern

[On tour in Tennessee] Nov. 20, 1909

To whom it may concern: This is to state that from this date and until further notice the endorsement which I have hitherto given to the East Tennessee Normal and Industrial Institute, Harriman Tenn. and its principal, John W. Ovletrea, is withdrawn. I am withdrawing my endorsement for the reason that by recent personal inspection I have found that the school is not what it represents itself to be. There are pratily [practically] no industries being taught, there are very few students, in fact there is scarcely enough there in the way of a school to warrant the name of school.

An additional reason for my withdrawal of endorsement grows out of the fact that I find that the principal, Mr. Ovletrea, does not have a good reputation for moral and sensible living in the community of Harriman and parts of Tennessee.

The school has a valuable plant, and my hope is that it will be speedily reorganized so that the people for whom the school exists can really be benefited. I believe it is possible to so reorganize and overhaul the school both in its officers and work so as to make it of real service.

[Booker T. Washington]

TLd Con. 593 BTW Papers DLC. Two penciled insertions in BTW's hand. On stationery of Tuskegee Institute.

From Emmett Jay Scott

Montgomery, Ala. Dec. 2/09

Dear Mr. W. I have telegraphed you the Underwood attitude. He was very kind in listening to me & I certainly went after him as earnestly as I could, but he is afraid — that was very plain. He spoke of being the 2d leader on the democratic side & said that if politics sh'd be played for or against the measure[1] he w'd have to be free & that he c'd not promise in advance to introduce the bill till he had talked with his colleagues & that it w'd take him 4 or 5 days to decide as to their attitude. I told him it is advisable to have the bill introduced the first day following the President's message & he said under all the circumstances he c'd not do that.

I told him that you had mentioned his name to President Taft. He said that was kind but in 1915 he may have to fight for an exposition for Birmingham & wants to keep his powder dry. He promises earnest support when measure is introduced but that is as far as he w'd go. Mr Thompson went with me to see him. I got there at 1 pm & Underwood left at 3. I had to go to the Depot to see him. I am sorry of the outcome. I know of no other man to introduce the bill. I hope some good republican may be found.

Emmett J. Scott

ALS Con. 898 BTW Papers DLC.

[1] A bill to seek appropriations for a Negro exposition to be held in 1913 on the fiftieth anniversary of emancipation.

To George Woodward Wickersham

[Boston, Mass.] December 3, 1909

Personal and Confidential

My dear Attorney General Wickersham: You are doubtless aware of the fact that Mr. Robert H. Terrell, a colored man, is at present one of the Municipal Judges in the District of Columbia, and that his time expires on December 31st when he comes up for reappointment.

Mr. Terrell is one of the very highest type of colored men in the country. He is a graduate of Harvard University, has practiced law in the District of Columbia and has held the position which he now holds for a period of three or four years.

Enclosed I send you at his request letters written by lawyers in Washington who have practiced before his court, in which they give their opinion of him. Mr. Terrell has the happy faculty of making friends with all people of both races with whom he comes in contact. I very much hope that you can see your way clear to decide to reappoint him to his present position.

I call your attention to the further fact that many of the lawyers in Washington who have signed Judge Terrell's endorsement are not only Democrats but are Southern men.[1] Yours truly,

[Booker T. Washington]

TLc   Con. 901   BTW Papers   DLC.

[1] Wickersham replied that Terrell in a visit to his office had made a favorable impression, but he enclosed a copy of a complaint against Terrell, saying: "If the facts are as stated in that complaint, he ought not to be reappointed." The complaint was that Terrell, as a director of the bankrupt Capitol Savings Bank, had made no effort to repay depositors, including "poor washer women and laboring men of his race." (Dec. 9, 1909, Con. 901, BTW Papers, DLC, enclosing without signature a copy of a letter dated Dec. 1, 1909.)

From James Carroll Napier

Nashville, Tenn. Dec. 3rd, 1909

Dear Mr. Washington: I am constantly stopped as I pass through the streets and public buildings of Nashville by persons who wish

[to] talk about your tour through Tennessee and to commend in the most flattering terms all that you said and did. The colored people and the white alike unite in declaring it a great occasion. Judge John W. Judd,[1] one of the most noted and prominent members of the Tennessee Bar, and a professor in the Law Department of Vanderbilt University meeting me on the street this morning said, "I have for a long time been reading Mr. Washington's speeches. I have kept close watch of all he said on his recent tour through Tennessee. He seems simply to be a wonderful man. The effect of his tour through this State will be far reaching and will work an incalculable amount of good among all the people. Napier, come to my office at the Vanderbilt Law School next Tuesday morning. I want to talk at length with you about these matters." I shall try to go and hear what he has to say. You have all the people thinking and talking and have done great good. Very truly yours,

J. C. Napier

ALS   Con. 396   BTW Papers   DLC.

[1] John Walters Judd, born in 1839, after many years as an attorney and federal judge in Tennessee and Utah, practiced law in Nashville (1899–1907) and became professor of law at Vanderbilt University in 1907.

From Robert Curtis Ogden

New York   December 3, 1909

My dear Doctor: I have read with very great interest the story of your recent educational campaign in Tennessee and with most especial approval the leading editorial in last night's issue of the Evening Post.[1] As your campaigns progress through the various Southern states I think they rise constantly in influence and power. In Tennessee especially I think I notice what I have believed in and hoped for these many years, namely that the best South is gaining courage to speak publicly in a pronounced fashion upon the race question. I think you know my views on this subject as I believe I have expressed them to you quite frequently.

When you were last at my house, we were in some anxiety concerning Mrs. Ogden. I regret to inform you that through many vicissitudes her case has grown worse until now she is in an absolutely hopeless condition. Yours very sincerely,

Robert C Ogden

TLS Con. 735 BTW Papers DLC.

[1] The editorial, entitled "Booker Washington's Greatest Service," appeared in the New York *Evening Post*, Dec. 2, 1909, 8. It was reprinted in *The Nation*, 89 (Dec. 9, 1909), 560–61, and in a pamphlet. See Accounts of Washington's Tour of Tennessee, Nov. 18–Dec. 10, 1909, above.

To Sarah Newlin

Parker House, Boston, Dec. 4, 1909

My dear Miss Newlin: I have your kind letter of November 14 which I regret has not been answered earlier. Soon after your letter came, I began a trip lasting eight days through the state of Tennessee. During this time I spoke to 26 audiences, about equally divided between colored and white. I have never felt more encouraged regarding the future of our people and their relations toward the Southern white people than at the present time as a result of this trip.

I am very glad that you are pleased with my articles. The Outlook articles with additional ones have now been put into book form. The name of the book is "The Story of the Negro." I hope that you will read it.

I think it wise for you to continue to help Edwards, Holtzclaw and Cornelia Bowen. They are all doing good work, and the same is true of N. E. Henry. The only reason that the other schools are not helped by the Jeanes Fund is owing to the fact that they are too large. Miss Jeanes was very emphatic in her deed of gift to the trustees that she wanted the money used to help only the very small schools located in the country districts.

There is a school located some distance in the country from

Nashville, Tenn., which deserves help. It is in reality a reform school. A colored man, one of the finest characters that I met on my trip in Tennessee, has taken a number of small boys who have been sentenced for various crimes or misdemeanors and is trying to educate them. The man is doing it very largely at his own expense, and if you would care to help him I could put you in direct correspondence with him.

I thank you very much for your suggestion regarding the Southern Letter and the use of post cards. I shall try to put them into practice.

I suppose you know that we are to have a public meeting in Philadelphia in the interest of Tuskegee on February 10. Yours truly,

[Booker T. Washington]

TLc   Con. 396   BTW Papers   DLC.

From Frederick Randolph Moore

New York. December 7, 1909

My dear Dr. Washington: I am planning on and after January 1, 1910, to change the name of The Age to The New York Negro Age. I believe that this change will be helpful to us as a race, and make us stand out stronger before the people. It will mean in my opinion, greater respect for us from the whites, when they see that we are proud of our racial identifications, and we insist on it always being capitalized. I would like very much to have your opinion for publication on this change.[1] With kind regards. Yours very truly,

Fred. R. Moore

TLS   Con. 395   BTW Papers   DLC.

[1] Moore also wrote to E. J. Scott on Dec. 20, 1909, asking for an expression from him. "There is much diversity of opinion," Moore wrote, "on the name we should be known by. Some want Colored, others Afro-American, and some Negro." Moore said the word *Negro*, when capitalized, "is stronger and comes nearer giving us a recognized standing before the people of the world than any other name." (Con. 46, BTW Papers, DLC.)

A Memorandum on the New York *Age*

[ca. Dec. 7, 1909]

Decisions Reached with Regard to the New York *Age*

1st — Proceed at once to reduce the capital stock to $25,000.

2d — B. T. W. is to have credit for the $2,200. now carried on books of New York Age as "Fred R. Moore Special." The New York Age Publishing Company is to give Mr. Moore notes for $2,200. with interest at 5% and this note is to be transferred to B. T. W.

3d — Mr. Moore is to be given $500.00 worth of stock in exchange for the machinery he owns at present used in The New York Age office. The $500.00 he owes The New York Age Publishing Company is to be cancelled over against the $500.00 which is owed him for type, which he has turned over to The New York Age Publishing Company. A note for $1,000, which B. T. W. held to his order drawn by Fred R. Moore, is to be cancelled. The Colored American Magazine is to be discontinued in sixty days, if a sale cannot be effected.

4th — Mr. Moore is at once to notify Mr. Peterson as to the present condition of affairs and as to the likelihood of the $40. now appropriated per month being withdrawn.

5th — Mr. Moore is to include the "machinery" of the office, that is, he is to gear his office up so as to make it an effective instrument for service.

6th — Mr. Moore is to proceed at once to have photographs taken of the building or the part of the building where The Age is to go. He is to have a proper sign made and this sign is to appear in the photograph.

7th — Mr. Washington is to have credit for all the money he has paid to Mr. Smith, Auditor, and his father; that is, this is to be entered as a proper charge against the New York Age Publishing Company. In return therefor, B. T. W. is to receive stock for same. When the paper moves to its new quarters, the name is to be changed to that of The New York Negro Age and an editorial is to be written calling attention to this change in the name of the paper.

8th — Mr. Scott is to work out a scheme whereby subscriptions along the line of The Outlook suggestion can be secured; that is the paper is to be sent three months for 25 cents and the 20,000 names in hand are to be circularized.

TMc Con. 261 BTW Papers DLC. Docketed: "Copy for Mr. Moore."

From Jacob Godfrey Schmidlapp[1]

Cincinnati, Ohio, December 7, 1909

My Dear Mr. Washington; I thank you very much for copy of your last production. As far as I have gone into it I am sure it will be both interesting and enjoyable. I have already noticed your experience in one of the most interesting cases of your race, and that is the ability of those of pure blood as compared to those of mixed blood.

My son tells me that while he was a student at Cornell, his impression was that Professor Willcox's examination into this subject was different from yours. According to his statistics, however, only fifteen to twenty percent of negroes were of mixed blood, and this may account for the prize scholars being of equal number, the pure blood having so much larger number to draw from. My son also said that Professor Willcox felt very much discouraged on account of the greater criminality among the negroes, stating that it was increasing with alarming rapidity. I need not go into details, as no doubt you are familiar with the statistics of one as prominent as Professor Willcox.

However, it may interest you to learn of a recent experience in our city. A Mrs. McCall, who died during the present year, left her whole estate for the purpose of establishing and operating an industrial school for the colored. She selected twelve trustees, six from either race. I doubt if she had a personal acquaintance with more than two or three of the total number, the selection being made upon the reputation of the men, and it happened that not one of the negroes was of pure blood. Indeed, by appearance the mixture was very strongly in favor of the white race. One of the trustees, Mr. DeHart, a school teacher, since died. The vacancy was to be filled by his colleagues, and, strangely, it did not occur to

244

them to select one of pure blood until it was suggested by me, and we then found a very desirable member.

I used to live in Tennessee, and while there had correspondence with Mr. Montgomery, of Ursino Landing, Miss., to whom you refer. Indeed, I have often made the statement that among all the letters we received in my business, his were the best. I understood from Mr. Jefferson Davis that he came from his family of slaves, and that he attributed his superior intelligence to his forefathers who happened to be from the central part of Africa, instead of from the coast, where most of the slaves had been drawn from.

I have been hoping for some years to have the pleasure of meeting you sometime on your visits to the North. Wishing you continued success in your great work, I remain, Very truly yours,

Schmidlapp

TLSr Copy   Con. 739   BTW Papers   DLC. Docketed: "letter A sent him." After Schmidlapp's second letter on Jan. 3, 1910, however, BTW personally replied. See BTW to Jacob Godfrey Schmidlapp, Jan. 12, 1910, below.

1 Jacob Godfrey Schmidlapp (1849–1919) was the founder of the Union Savings Bank and Trust Company of Cincinnati, serving as president (1890–1907) and chairman of the board (1907–19). He had begun his business career in Memphis during the Reconstruction era in the cigar and liquor trade. He was a supporter of the Cincinnati Conservatory of Music, the Cincinnati Art School, and the Cincinnati Art Museum, and was active in the peace movement, being a director of the Carnegie Peace Fund and treasurer of the American Society for the Judicial Settlement of International Disputes. A few months before BTW's death in 1915, Schmidlapp arranged for the black educator to meet Henry Ford.

From Emmett Jay Scott

Washington, D.C. December 9, '09

My Dear Mr. Washington: I went at once this morning to see Mr. Busby.[1] He was very cordial to me and spoke quite freely about the matter in question.[2]

I will try to relate his suggestions. He thinks that the introduction of a bill simply makes it one of some 30 or 40 thousand others introduced at a single session. He thinks it not inadvisable for me to see Mr. Gillette[3] and Mr Taylor[4] & especially mentioned also

Mr. Brownlow of Tennessee. He thinks an individual bill will have but little or no show, while if we can get a member of the Appropriations Committee to tack on a provision to the *Sundry Civil Bill* it will stand a better show of getting through, especially if influences are put to work to wean the influences of members of the Congress. He points out however that even here it will be subject to a point of order. Mr Taylor & Mr Gillette were so busy this morning that I could not arrange for an interview, but Mr Taylor wants Mr Tyler & me to come to his house tonight & we shall go over the whole matter in detail. Mr Busby says the Sundry Civil Bill cannot pass till about next June & you want to get action on the President's recommendation as early as possible.

I shall exhaust every resource to get the matter started & shall advise you fully. If I can get it started by Saturday I will plan to leave here Sunday morning. Have telegraphed you today & shall wire you again as soon as I get a line on the proper procedure after conferring tonight with Mr Taylor. A long fight seems ahead to get action on which to proceed toward the development of plans. Yours very truly,

Emmett J. Scott

ALS   Con. 900   BTW Papers   DLC.

¹ L. White Busbey (b. 1852), a journalist and Republican publicist, was secretary to the speaker of the U.S. House of Representatives from 1905 to 1911.

² The introduction of a bill to get appropriations for a Negro exposition to be held in 1913 on the fiftieth anniversary of emancipation.

³ Presumably Frederick Huntington Gillett (1851–1935), Republican congressman from Massachusetts (1893–1925) and U.S. senator (1925–31).

⁴ Edward Livingston Taylor (1869–1938), Republican congressman from Ohio (1905–13). A resident of Columbus, he probably knew R. W. Tyler, formerly a reporter for the Columbus *Ohio State Journal*.

From Emmett Jay Scott

Washington, D.C. Dec. 10, '09

My Dear Mr. W: I have just wired you that the Bill is in process of incubation. Mr Taylor last night agreed to go over the whole matter with Cong. Rodenberg[1] Chairman of the Com. on Expositions &c: to which Com. was referred the part of the message referring to the National Negro Semi-Centennial Celebration. This morning he saw Rodenberg & he (R.) agreed enthusiastically that the matter deserved to go through & they are to meet this afternoon to draft it & it will be introduced when Congress convenes again on Tuesday by Rodenberg or Taylor. By courtesy R——— is the one who ought to do it as it will go to his Committee, but he has told Taylor he ought to do it &c &c. I find the latter strong, enthusiastic & willing to push all possible.

Both of them may want to go on the Commission also & if they do it will mean a great deal for the success of the movement. I am promised a copy (carbon) of the bill tomorrow & when it is introduced as many *printed* copies as we may wish. I have some publicity plans to get it well sent out throughout the country & especially to all of our newspapers.

I expressed some fears in my letter as to whether we are likely to get quick action or not. Mr Taylor tells me that when bills are passed (or considered) the amounts they carry are grouped together for the Appropriation Bills & passed at end of the session in a lump &c. If that sh'd be so the amount to be appropriated w'd not be available till next June & the President c'd not appoint till that time. In that case the appropriation is more of a hindrance than a help. You will have opportunity to talk that feature over with the President when you come on next week. He ought to find a method to facilitate the matter so that work may be undertaken. I ought also to tell you that Rodenberg comes from East St Louis, Ill (across the river from St Louis) & has a large Negro element in his district.

Will send you draft as soon as I can get it from Mr Taylor. They promise to draw it themselves (preserving the sense of the draft you sent me) but putting it in form — such as yours is not. Yours very truly,

Emmett J. Scott

Mr Tyler has greatly aided me.

ALS Con. 898 BTW Papers DLC.

[1] William August Rodenberg (1865–1937), an Illinois Republican, served in Congress 1903–13 and 1915–23.

To George Woodward Wickersham

Parker House, Boston, December 12, 1909

My dear Attorney General Wickersham: Your letter with enclosure regarding Judge Terrell has been received, and I thank you for writing me.

When Judge Terrell was appointed to his present position, my understanding is that the whole matter of the charges against him was looked into by the Judiciary Committee of the Senate before he was confirmed and that the Senate Committee held him blameless. This has been my understanding of the case all along. I shall be very much surprised and greatly pained if Judge Terrell cannot make a satisfactory explanation to you about the serious charges which have been brought against him. I am glad that you have sent him a copy of the charges, and shall be anxious to know what answer he makes.

Sometime when in Washington I shall drop in to see you if I may. My address from now on will be Tuskegee Institute, Alabama. Yours very truly,

[Booker T. Washington]

TLc   Con. 901   BTW Papers   DLC.

James A. Cobb to Emmett Jay Scott

Washington, D.C. Dec. 21, 1909

Dear Emmett: I have already mailed to you today the last two copies of the Horizon. Saw Kelly Miller and he says Prof Du Bois has made himself impossible so far as the University is concerned, by his last but veiled attack upon the Dr. None of our friends have been re-appointed, if so, they have not been notified, however, we have no further fear so far as the Judge[1] is concerned; Baker's[2] case looks very bright and we have every reason to believe that he will come thru all right.

When the Dr. was here he hammered the Judge's case right thru, he saw both the Pres. and the Atty General and had the Atty Gen to make a definite promis[e] in the case. Judge says that Dr. Washington is the greatest man in the world excepting none.

You ought to have been at the banquet, it was rough house from beginning to end. Chase introduce[d] Horner[3] in what he thought a facetious way, but H. took it otherwise and denounced Chase in the most scathing language. Chase replied and Armond Scott jumped on Pres. Thirkield, tho he was not present.

Shall look out for the presents as per your request.

A merry Xmas and a happy New Year to the whole family. Sincerely,

Jim

Read the Star of this date and tell me what you think of Cook![4]

Jim

ALS BTW Papers ATT.

[1] Robert Heberton Terrell.
[2] D. W. Baker.
[3] Probably Richard R. Horner, a black member of the District of Columbia school board.
[4] An article on the rejection by the University of Copenhagen of Dr. Frederick W. Cook's claim to have reached the North Pole before the Peary expedition did so. (Washington *Star*, Dec. 21, 1909, 1.)

To Andrew Carnegie

[Tuskegee, Ala.] December 22, 1909

My dear Mr. Carnegie: Your letter of December 10th,[1] which I found when I reached home from the meeting of the Jeanes Fund Board at Washington, is a very precious one to me. Each word is priceless to me. I prize your opinion more than you can ever know.

I did not know that you were following my trip through Tennessee so closely. When I see you, I must tell you more in detail about the results of this trip. Everywhere I went a most hearty reception was extended, not only by thousands of Colored people, but the best white people throughout Tennessee were equally enthusiastic. I am sure that the more I can get into the South, talk face to face to black people and white people, the sooner all of our difficulties are going to be cleared away.

Let me repeat that I owe the opportunity of doing this precious work to your great generosity and bigness of soul.

I shall hope to see you sometime during the month of January.

Mrs. Washington begs to be remembered to you. Yours very truly,

Booker T. Washington

TLpS Con. 44 BTW Papers DLC.

1 Carnegie called BTW's tour of Tennessee a "triumphal march." "You are beginning to enjoy the fruits of your labors," he wrote, and added: "Posterity is to do you full justice—more and more as time rolls on." (Con. 43, BTW Papers, DLC.)

To Jesse Edward Moorland

[Tuskegee, Ala.] Dec. 22, 1909

Dear Dr. Moorland: I thank you very much for the information which your letter contains, and I shall try to treat it in a manner to accomplish, so far as I am able to do so, the results which you have in mind.[1]

You can say to our friends there that it is not my disposition or intention to do anything in a selfish manner, but to recognize the influence and work of all racial organizations. There are several men in various states, including Professor Wright, who deserve recognition, and such recognition I am sure will be accorded them. Just now, however, in the initial stages of the program it is difficult to advise that certain positions be given to certain individuals.[2] We are not to that stage yet but, as I have stated, I believe in the end Professor Wright and others will be satisfied if all of us can work together for a common end.

In writing to Dr. Brown,[3] I said to him the following:

"I think I might say to you very confidentially that I have gone over this whole matter carefully with the President of the United States, and he is determined to see the matter through. He is more interested, in my opinion, in this exposition than in almost any other one event in connection with what is to take place during his administration. He means to make it an epoch in his career as President. He has told me in the most frank manner that he is going to see that the bill goes through Congress in the form that

Taylor and Rodenberg have introduced it, and will stand by the matter as outlined in his message from beginning to end. Since we have the influence and active backing of the President of the United States in this matter, all of us should come together and work together toward a common end, and I believe that all, including Professor Wright, will be willing to do this." Yours very truly,

Booker T. Washington

I confess that I am greatly troubled about your Y.M.C.A. building. Have you gotten any money toward it? Would not a whirlwind campaign among white and colored people in Washington be in a measure successful? The longer the building stands unfinished, the harder it will be to get money to complete it. I am ashamed that I myself have not been able to be of more real service in getting money for the completion of the building.

B. T. W.

TLpS   BTW Papers   ATT.

[1] Moorland wrote to BTW on Dec. 17, 1909, that a group of Washington ministers had met to discuss the question of whether to support the movement for a semicentennial of the Emancipation Proclamation. He reported that some favored the leadership of R. R. Wright rather than the NNBL, and expressed the hope that a divisive struggle for control could be avoided. (Con. 395, BTW Papers, DLC.)

[2] In an earlier draft BTW wrote: "When I see you, I can tell you privately and confidentially about matters that will open your eyes. It is almost discouraging and often disgusting when one finds out how much dishonesty and deceit there is, in the action of prominent men of our race." (Dec. 21, 1909, Con. 395, BTW Papers, DLC.)

[3] Rev. Sterling N. Brown (b. 1857) was chairman of a committee of Washington ministers considering the question of support of the emancipation celebration. A graduate of Fisk (1885) and Oberlin Theological Seminary, he was pastor of the Plymouth Congregational Church, Washington, D.C. (1889–97), Park Temple (1897–1901), and a merger of these two congregations, Lincoln Temple, beginning in 1901. He served for three years on the District of Columbia Board of Education.

To Robert Heberton Terrell

Tuskegee Institute, Alabama   December 22, 1909

Very confidential.

My dear Judge Terrell: I am writing to ask a favor of you.

I very much fear that our opponents have "stolen a march" on us that may be serious in its consequences, unless we act quickly and effectively. It seems rather evident that they have gotten Senator Jones[1] to introduce a bill into the Senate providing for a Commission. Our bill, as you know, was introduced into the House. If Jones' bill passes, it will give them a tremendous advantage, as the man that passes the bill usually has the "say-so" regarding the personnel of Commissions, etc. I had hoped that the bill introduced by Jones was the same bill introduced in the Senate by Rodenberg and Taylor, but I fear it is not. I think it is a bill inspired by our opponents.

Will you be kind enough to have a personal interview with Jones just as soon as possible and "feel him out." Gradually and tactfully you can let him know who the other people are and how shallow and weak their claims are. If we can gradually bring him around to the point where he will let his bill die and substitute for it the Taylor-Rodenberg bill, that will be the thing, which we want, or perhaps he will agree to amend his bill so as to make it the same as the other bill. In a word, we must get hold of Jones and not let the other side capture him. If we do not, we will be in a bad fix. As soon as you have seen Jones and have gotten an impression of his attitude, please telegraph me so that I will know how to act. Yours very truly,

Booker T. Washington

TLS   Con. 1   Robert Heberton Terrell Papers   DLC.

[1] Wesley Livsey Jones (1863–1932), Republican congressman (1899–1909) and U.S. senator (1909–32) from Washington.

To Ulysses Grant Mason

[Tuskegee, Ala.] December 23, 1909

Personal

Dear Dr. Mason: You do not know what great pleasure it gives me to read your article in The Age Herald of Sunday, December 12th. This is a magnificent piece of work; conscientiously, bravely, and wisely done, and I am sure it will accomplish good.

Would it help the matter to have this article put in pamphlet form? How would it do to print say, five hundred (500) copies, and put a copy in the hands of every prominent white man and woman in the city of Birmingham? If you think the putting of it in pamphlet form will accomplish good, I should be willing to be responsible for the work. I should like to know, however, your opinion regarding it, just as soon as possible.

Do not stop, keep pegging away, is all I ask the colored people to do. In the various groups, get somebody to see one prominent white man and somebody another, and bring things to bear upon them in having the school conditions changed.

I have just had a talk with Judge Lindsey,[1] of Colorado, and he told me something of the long years of hard trying work he had, even with the white people of Denver, to get them to organize a Juvenile Court. If he had to work as long and hard with white people as he did to get results, you must not become discouraged if you have to work long and hard to bring the white people around to give the Negroes proper educational facilities. Yours very truly,

Booker T. Washington

TLpS Con. 395 BTW Papers DLC.

[1] Benjamin Barr Lindsey (1865–1943), judge of the juvenile court of Denver, Colo. (1900–1927) and of the superior court of California (1934–43), was a reformer and authority on juvenile delinquency and correction. He wrote, with Wainwright Evans, *Companionate Marriage* (1927). BTW had met him on a trip to Denver in the fall of 1909. Lindsey regretfully declined an invitation to speak in behalf of Tuskegee at Carnegie Hall, but may have changed his mind. (BTW to Lindsey, Dec. 7, and Lindsey to BTW, Dec. 13, 1909, Con. 393, BTW Papers, DLC.)

From Seth Low

New York   December 23rd, 1909

Confidential.

My dear Dr. Washington; At a meeting of the Investment Committee held on Tuesday, the 21st, I took the liberty of suggesting that I thought you ought to take a good vacation, if possible, during the summer. Such speaking campaigns as you have conducted last year and this, through different sections of the South, seem to me as important work as you have ever done, not only for your own race but for the country as a whole. I know very well, however, that that sort of thing is very exhausting; and I want you, if you can, to arrange your plans so that you may get some of the rest and refreshment of mind and body which will enable you to keep up that sort of service for more years. I am happy to report that the Committee was unanimously in sympathy with this suggestion, and I am writing to you now to say that I have at command the sum of One thousand dollars, made up by a number of your friends, for the purpose of enabling you to go to Europe next summer, or to any other place where you think you can get real rest. We do not want to send you away in order that you may do work elsewhere. Our purpose is to secure for one who has legitimately earned it, the sort of let-up which is so necessary now and then to keep one's powers at their best. I am writing to you at this early day, so that you may have plenty of time to plan for your absence, if you think you can go. Please write to me frankly just how you feel, and what you would like to do. Yours sincerely,

Seth Low

TLS Con. 50 BTW Papers DLC.

From Joel Elias Spingarn[1]

New York Dec. 24, 1909

My dear Mr. Washington In reply to your letter of the 21st, I am enclosing my cheque for $25 as a contribution to Tuskegee.

I hope you will not judge my interest in your work by the size of my cheque. There is no cause which interests me more deeply than the welfare of the American negro; and I am proud to help in this cause on all occasions and in any possible way. Sincerely yours

J. E. Spingarn

ALS Con. 736 BTW Papers DLC.

1 Joel Elias Spingarn (1875–1939) was professor of literature at Columbia University (1899–1911) and a distinguished scholar. One of the founders of the NAACP,

he was its board chairman (1914–19, 1932–34), treasurer (1919–30), and president (1930–38). Although he was firmly committed to the NAACP strategy and its goal of civil and political equality for blacks, Spingarn supported BTW's educational program through small donations to Tuskegee beginning in 1908. (Spingarn to BTW, Nov. 28, 1908, Con. 732, BTW Papers, DLC.) Spingarn worked closely with W. E. B. Du Bois within the NAACP without breaking with BTW. (For a different portrayal of Spingarn as sharply critical of BTW, see Ross, *J. E. Spingarn*, 29–31.) In 1916, after BTW's death, Spingarn convened the first Amenia Conference at his country estate to effect a reconciliation between the Du Bois and Washington factions.

From Kelly Miller

Washington, D.C. Dec. 27, 1909

My Dear Dr. Washington, I beg to acknowledge receipt of your favor bearing upon the proposed semi-centennial celebration of our emancipation. I regard your attitude toward Prof. Wright as being very generous and feel that if understood by him it would be entirely satisfactory to his friends. I should be glad to inform Prof. Wright of your attitude with reference to him if you have no objection to my doing so.

Permit me to touch upon an entirely different matter. You doubtless have seen by reports in the public press that there is a spirit of unrest and rebellion among the student body of this institution. I can assure you with fullest inside knowledge that no such spirit exists.

President Thirkield in a number of eloquent appeals urged the singing of plantation melodies as an important part of the University's musical repertoire. A considerable number of our students do not feel that it is becoming this Institution devoted to the higher aims and ideals of the race to emphasize these melodies as a part of the mission of Howard University. The spirit of the opposing ones is in every sense as loyal to the authority and discipline as those who are quiescent in the proposition. The New York Sun came out in an editorial on December 21 headed "A Just Rebellion."[1] To this editorial I made reply in the issue of December 24.[2]

It must be borne in mind that unlike Fisk University, Hampton

255

and Tuskegee, Howard University has no sentimental tradition based upon the plantation melodies. We have never made a feature of singing them. Our student body comes largely from the North and West where these melodies are not generally appreciated because probably, their spirit and meaning is not fully understood. My personal attitude toward these melodies is set forth in Race Adjustment in the chapter entitled "Artistic Gifts of the Negro Race." At the same time I recognize that Howard University is no singing school and at best music can be made only a secondary feature. To urge the singing of these melodies at this time would unnecessarily divide our student body[,] Faculty, Alumni and Trustee Board. There are numerous and strong opponents in all of these bodies. I have urged President Thirkield in the interest of internal harmony and good will to drop the proposition entirely for the present at least. I fail to see the wisdom of arousing a bitter a[nd] long drawn out controversy when no corresponding good is to be accomplished whichever set may triumph.

I have ventured to present this matter to you knowing that as a Trustee of the University, you are interested in all our activities. Yours truly,

Kelly Miller

TLS BTW Papers ATT.

[1] The editorial reported that Howard University students were rebelling against President W. P. Thirkield's insistence that they sing old plantation songs to entertain guests. The students objected that the songs were a vestige of slavery, but the editorial contended that the students were missing the main point, that the songs were not conceived by slaves or even in the South, but were written by northern whites "in a maudlin vein to touch the sympathies of Northern audiences, and there is no imaginable reason why the educated colored youth of our time should treat them with respect . . . these trivial melodies did not originate with them; do not speak for them and should not be imposed upon them by pedagogues, however admirable otherwise." (New York *Sun*, Dec. 21, 1909, 8.)

[2] In his reply, entitled "The Spirit of Howard University," Kelly Miller said that the editorial was "absolutely misleading" in even suggesting that there was a spirit of rebellion at Howard. He added: "The question of a musical repertoire is merely a matter of taste and appreciation, and has little or no bearing upon the serious workings or spirit of the university. Your ingenious theory as to the origin of the 'Plantation Melodies' is indeed interesting as an intellectual curiosity, but with us the question is not considered as a serious or essential university function." (New York *Sun*, Dec. 24, 1909, 6.)

To Lawrence Fraser Abbott

[Tuskegee, Ala.] December 31, 1909

Personal.

My dear Dr. Abbott: In your own way, I am wondering if through The Outlook at sometime you could not call attention to the great wrong being done the colored people in a state like South Carolina, for example, in the distribution of the public school fund. I send you an extract from The Daily Mail, a white paper published in Anderson, S.C., which gives the facts. You will note that in [one] county, Bamberg, the white children receive $18.50 annually for their education and the Negroes in the same county receive 89 cents. Yours truly,

Booker T. Washington

TLpS   Con. 888   BTW Papers   DLC.

An Article in *Good Health*

Dec. 1909

WORK AND HEALTH

Among the many methods which have been suggested from time to time, by which an individual may get and keep health and strength, there is one, which, it seems to me, has not been sufficiently emphasized. My own experience is that one of the best means for preserving the mind and body in sound and healthful condition is some definite form of labor.

As a rule, I think it will be found that the people who are constantly sick in body, just as the people who are sick in mind and weak in morals, are the people who have little or nothing to do.

I never remember of seeing a professional tramp or loafer who seemed to me to be in thoroughly good condition physically, and I have noticed that among the wealthier classes of people those who are constantly complaining, who break down nervously and have to be constantly traveling about from one place to another in search of health, are usually people who have nothing to absorb their thought and attention; in short, they have no work.

I never knew or heard of a case of neurasthenia among people who worked with their hands, and particularly not among those who worked in the open air.

I do not overlook the fact that under the new and complex conditions of modern life there have sprung up kinds of labor that are specially dangerous to human life. It is the duty of the public and of the government to perceive these dangers and improve these conditions. But aside from improvements and safeguards the man who works has in himself a means of overcoming these dangers and difficulties; men who labor show a marvelous ability to adapt themselves to new conditions, to make themselves strong enough to resist these adverse conditions and overcome them. The very effort that is put forth to do a piece of work gives the strength and vigor to withstand hardships and resist diseases.

There is one kind of disease, if I may refer to it in that way, which rarely attacks the man who works, no matter whether his labor is with the head or with the hand. The disease I refer to is pessimism. So long as a man has something to do which absorbs all his thought and attention, he remains hopeful and, as a whole, contented. If he sees evils, no matter how great they seem, he is pretty likely to be reasonably happy if he finds he is overcoming them, no matter how slowly.

It is when the laboring man goes on a strike or gets out of a job that he becomes dangerous to himself and to society.

In my opinion there is nothing that is so certain to make a man or woman healthy in body, in mind, and in spirit, as to find somewhere in the world a kind of work that he or she can do, something by which to make himself or herself useful to the people around.

The ordinary daily tasks are, under normal conditions, the great source of contentment and happiness, and as such are symptoms of sound minds and healthy bodies. The best insurance against disease and death is a good job, one that taxes all the individual's strength of body, mind, and purpose.

A great task is an inspiration, and the man or woman who has the good fortune to be connected with some part of the world's work has, in my opinion, found the secret, not only to health but to happiness as well.

Good Health, 44 (Dec. 1909), 936–37. Reprinted in *Tuskegee Student*, 21 (Dec. 18, 1909), 1.

To Clinton Joseph Calloway

[Tuskegee, Ala.] Jan. 3, 1910

Mr. C. J. Calloway: In making the plan for the remaining 8 or 9 months for the administration of the two funds,[1] I wish you to keep these two points in view.

1. Before we get through we want to place a good schoolhouse in each school district in the county. I do not mean by this that we are to build the schoolhouse outright, but in every case we must get as much help from the people as possible. Unless they take an interest in trying to do something in the direction of erecting a schoolhouse the effect will be largely lost. This means of course that you will have to concentrate efforts in the direction of stimulating the people to self-help.

2. In the case of all the schools that you are helping and in the case of the schools you are to help, you must gradually work on a policy that will make these schools self-supporting either through what the colored people themselves provide or what they get from public funds. They must not get the idea that these two funds are to carry them for any length of time.

I want to concentrate a good part of the Rogers fund in advertising in a thorough, vigorous manner the advantages of this county for residence. We must get in new blood into every part of the county. As to the details of the method of doing this, I want you to see me in my office as soon as possible.

Booker T. Washington

TLpS Con. 601 BTW Papers DLC.

[1] Jeanes Fund and Rogers Fund.

To Jacob Godfrey Schmidlapp

[Tuskegee, Ala.] January 12, 1910

My dear Mr. Schmidlapp: I thank you very much for your letter of January 3d,[1] also, for yours of December 7th, which I did not have the privilege of answering in person.

We thank you for your subscription of One Hundred Dollars toward the Repair Fund. This will help us much.

I am very much interested in what you say concerning your son's impression of Prof. Willcox of Cornell University. I would state, that while Prof. Willcox and I are good friends, his brother being one of our Trustees, we do not agree for the most part on many matters touching the Negro, in fact, I think Prof. Willcox rather takes a hopeless view. On several occasions, he has strongly stated that the Negro would disappear as a race by death within a few years. Notwithstanding Prof. Willcox's prediction, the race continues to increase in numbers. In some way, I think Prof. Willcox got started sometime ago on a false scent and has been following it ever since.

I am deeply interested in the institution to which you refer to be started in Cincinnati to improve the condition of the Negroes there. I might say to you in confidence that I have studied the condition of our people pretty thoroughly throughout the country and there are few, if any, centers where in my opinion the Negro is worse off than he is in Cincinnati. Cincinnati, in a large sense, is the dumping ground for a class of Negroes who desire to get out of the South, but have not the money or the energy to go further than the Ohio River. Consequently they stop in Cincinnati and the average white man living in Cincinnati, I think, is likely to get a false idea of the race, if he takes the Cincinnati Negro as a fair type.

I wish very much that you could come to Tuskegee and spend some days with us in studying our work here. I think you would find many things to interest you.

I am going to fulfill my promise within the near future to stop in Cincinnati for an hour or so and have a conversation with you.

If I can help in the way of advice in the starting of the new school there, please let me know. Yours very truly,

Booker T. Washington

TLpS Con. 739 BTW Papers DLC.

¹ Schmidlapp enclosed a copy of his letter of Dec. 7, 1909, declining to aid Tuskegee's building fund but sending $100 for the repair fund. (Con. 737, BTW Papers, DLC.)

From Emmett Jay Scott

N Y [City] Jan. 12/1910

Dear Mr. Washington: I have written you that the speakers for the N Y meeting are to be: Dr. J. H. Finley, Dr. Dillard & yourself with Mr Schieffelin calling the meeting to order and Mr Low presiding.¹

In addition, the Hampton singers are to appear & we are to have the Moving Pictures — a pretty full program I think you will agree. I saw the pictures this a.m. with Dr. Park, Miss Pusey² and Miss Parmei — & all of us agree that they are likely to be a pleasing feature. I cut out the slides & told him to use only the Moving Pictures. *As a whole*, they are very good & yet only the outside work can be shown — none of the girls industries & none of the mechanical industries except in the case of masons & carpenters on new heating plant. The farm pictures are very good. I think quite frankly that it is needed to have a word said about some features of the moving pictures — the others all agree with me. Just who ought to do this is a problem. The pictures will take 25 minutes only at the outside & with this cost & also the cost of a man from Tuskegee will make it quite considerable. Mr. Broome³ will give full rehearsal the morning of Jan 24 with anyone we may select. I am to meet at Armstrong rooms tomorrow (Thursday) to finally decide upon detailed arrangement &c. Mr Schieffelin after I had spent 6 or 7 hours trying to reach him simply left to me a decision as to all the matters regarding the program. Mr. Low secured Mr. Finley.

Mr Howard (Sunday Editor N Y Tribune, whom I met three years ago) was visited by me yesterday & he agreed to use in Sunday's Tribune a special article bearing upon the Moving Picture & other features &c.[4] Dr. Park prepared it. I think it will prove effective. He remembered his former promise to help Tuskegee in any way possible. I have seen Mr Anderson. I think it unfortunate that he sh'd want you to handle such matters as he had in mind in the way he desired & in my conference with him I told him I thought it w'd not be very dignified for you to do so — & after some talk he agreed with me — & it is now off.

I will see Mr Shepard[5] if I can tomorrow. I shall not go to Trenton till I hear from Senator McVeagh.[6] If he & Gov. Wilson[7] accept, with yourself, it will be necessary only to have one other — Mr. Shepard. Secretary McVeagh is to let me know by letter I hope tomorrow.

I have Mr Fearing's letter telling me of your selection of himself for the place at Monrovia. I will help all I can as I go through Washington if I have to stop. I will write Mr. Finch anyway & ask him to push Mr. Fearing. I hope he can be landed. Enclosed clippings may enlist your interest. Please telegraph me your wishes — as to when I sh'd leave here for Tuskegee & as to your further desires. I ought to be able to leave Friday night, or Saturday night at latest. Yours truly

Emmett J. Scott

Senator Jones[8] told me in Washington that nothing had been done to advance the Exposition matter. He will call his Com. together whenever you can be present. He says he has not polled the Com — & does not know how it stands. He says that the fate of the measure depends on what you & others do to arouse interest in it & to force its passage — not very reassuring, I think.

E. J. S.

ALS   Con. 596   BTW Papers   DLC.

[1] A meeting in Carnegie Hall, New York City, on Jan. 24, 1910, for the first showing of a motion picture on Tuskegee Institute. (New York *Tribune,* Jan. 16, 1910, pt. V, 8; New York *Age,* Jan. 27, 1910, 1, 2, 5.)

[2] Possibly Elizabeth H. Pusey, proprietor of a novelty shop in New York City.

[3] George W. Broome, of Medford, Mass., was general manager of the Broome Exhibition Co., a black enterprise in Boston making and distributing films about

black education and economic life. Tuskegee was the subject of one of his motion pictures.

[4] The movie conveyed, more clearly than words could, the size and varied activities of Tuskegee Institute; in one scene it showed the whole body of 1,600 students in motion, marching into the chapel.

[5] Edward Morse Shepard.

[6] Franklin MacVeagh (1837–1934), a Chicago wholesale grocer, was U.S. Secretary of the Treasury (1909–13).

[7] Woodrow Wilson, governor of New Jersey.

[8] Wesley Livsey Jones.

From Nelson Edward Henry

China, Ala., Jan. 13, 1910

Dear Principal   I received your letter expressing your disapproval of the name of my school.[1] I must say that it was not by any means my intention to mislead. I meant to convey the idea that we teach some industries along with books, and also that its mission is to help all the people regardless of denominations.

The name has been sent to you and all of my trustees for a number of years on my reports. As I heard no complaints from any one, I took for granted that it was all right. It is the object of the school to lay an English foundation and have the boys learn some lessons in carpentry, shoe repairing and farming. The girls are being taught sewing and cooking. Our students are licensed to teach in this state. Our plan is to have the students complete a trade at Tuskegee. My work here is precisely what you have advocated all these years, only on a small scale. This place is possibly too far off your road for you to visit us but quite a number of the teachers from Tuskegee have been here. Wishing your continued approval of my work, I am yours for education

N. E. Henry

ALS Con. 425 BTW Papers DLC.

[1] The Colored Union Literary and Industrial School.

To George Augustus Gates

[Tuskegee, Ala.] Jan. 15, 1910

Dear President Gates: I saw so many things at Fisk during my visit there that were both satisfactory and encouraging that I hesitate to mention anything in the way of adverse criticism. Three points, however, dwell constantly in my mind.

1st. The condition of the boys outhouses. At any reasonable cost or effort, the condition of the boys outhouses ought to be speedily improved. It would be hard to find an out closet that is in worse condition than that. The location is most unfortunate, and besides it is not kept clean and in good repair. I am sure that no boy ever goes to the closet and comes away with any added respect for the University. I am also sure that no boy goes there unless he is absolutely forced to do so. When this is true it does not add to the health of the students. The closets used by the boys at night in Livingston Hall are not what they should be by a good deal. It seems to me that much attention ought to be given to them.

2d. With one or two exceptions, the basements of the buildings into which we went were not clean and orderly, neither were they clean on the inside nor on the immediate outside.

3d. As soon as the trustees can see their way clear to do it, some arrangement, however simple, ou[gh]t to be made so that the students can bathe. This refers to both men and women. I am sure that you will agree with me that at the present stage of civilization bathing facilities is no longer considered a luxury but a necessity, especially where large numbers of people congregate.

I realize fully that it is much easier to make suggestions and criticisms than it is to provide the money with which to change conditions, and I shall not be satisfied until I do my part in trying to help provide the money, but I am especially anxious about the boys' toilet room because no amount of poverty will excuse filth and disorder, and I feel sure that if some of the supporters of the University were to see the boys' closet that they would be tempted to withdraw their sympathy and perhaps their money.

Please remember me kindly to Mrs. Gates. Yours very truly,

Booker T. Washington

TLpS Con. 907 BTW Papers DLC.

To Charles Allmond Wickersham

[Tuskegee, Ala.] January 17, 1910

Personal and Confidential.

Dear Sir: I do not believe that you know to what extent the colored end of the coach is taken up by the newsboy.

I came from Atlanta with my wife and several other persons on Train No. 35, last Thursday morning, and I had an opportunity to see that the colored coach is used almost as a store.

1st — By actual count there were in the coach — 4 willow baskets, two of large size; there was one trunk; 4 cases of cocoa cola; 1 satchel, and a half barrel of cocoa cola. Besides a half dozen seats were taken up by these wares, and two windows were wholly occupied with candy, nuts, etc., laid out as one would use the window in a store to exhibit his goods.

2nd — Of course, all this not only resulted in a lot of room being taken that rightly belongs to the colored passengers, but this constant trading kept the floor filled with trash of all kinds, and the worst of this consists in the fact that since the colored coach is made the headquarters for trading, that naturally brings constantly into the coach white men from all parts of the train.

3rd — These white men come into the coach to buy cigars, cigarettes, etc. In nine cases out of ten, I observed, after they buy their cigars they light them in the presence of the colored women, and while each man may not remain very long to smoke, when one considers that there is a constant stream of white men coming into the car to buy cigars and light them, it results in turning the colored coach largely into a smoking car. They not only come to get tobacco but to drink cocoa cola.

I am wondering, that since the colored people only have this part of the coach, if it would not be just as well to let the newsboy keep his wares in the smoking car rather than in the colored end of the car.

I am sure that you will be inclined to take whatever action is proper in this case. I prefer, of course, that you not use my name in connection with this information. Yours truly,

Booker T. Washington

TLSr Copy   Con. 414   BTW Papers   DLC.

Seth Low to Andrew Carnegie

[New York City] January 29th, 1910

Dear Mr. Carnegie; You will remember that I spoke to you about the fund of a thousand dollars that I am raising to enable Booker Washington to take a vacation next summer. I am happy to say that he is making his plans to be absent from the middle of August to the first of October, so that I am now getting the money together which I promised him. I have myself given $100., and have secured a like amount from four other gentlemen. I am hoping from what you said to me that you will be glad to send me $500. to make up the full sum that is needed.

I gave your message to the President the other day, and he was glad to know that you approved of his position in regard to the regulation of interstate commerce and Federal incorporation.

With kind regards, Yours sincerely,

[Seth Low]

TLc   Seth Low Papers   NNC.

From Charles Banks

Mound Bayou, Miss. 2/1/10

Dear Mr. Washington: Touching the displacement of Negro office holders in this State, I am writing to advise that it has just been brought to my attention that the National Committeeman for this State and the Post Master General's referee[1] has recommended a white man and Democrat to take the place of Thos. I. Keys, a Negro post master at Ocean Springs, Jackson County, Mississippi. Mr. Keys has served under every Republican President since Harrison, and now, at this late day, it seems advisable to the "Gods" to turn him out for a white man and democrat. While the recommendation has been made, the appointment has not yet been made, and it may be that some speedy work can save him. I will write you later giving the information you asked for, touching the number of offices lost by our people in Mississippi since this administration began. Vardaman and Percy had a word battle in Jackson yesterday. I send you a clipping from the Commercial Appeal of this date, in which Mr. Percy mentions your name in a connection that is, no doubt, pleasant to you.[2] Look after Keys matter at once, if practicable. Yours truly,

Chas. Banks

TLS Con. 49 BTW Papers DLC. Addressed to BTW in New York City.

[1] Lonzo B. Moseley (b. 1852), a former planter, merchant, and U.S. marshal, was a member of the Republican National Committee from Mississippi beginning in 1904.

[2] On Oct. 6, 1908, while BTW was speaking before a packed house in Jackson, Miss., the Jim Crow gallery collapsed, injuring a number of persons including some whites. (See Reports of Pinkerton Detective F. E. Miller, Oct. 3–12, 1908, above, vol. 9.) According to Senator LeRoy Percy, James K. Vardaman wrote in his newspaper after the incident: "I am glad that no one was killed or seriously wounded, but especially the negroes. The white people who attended were out of place and a few scratches and bruises, lost hats and torn coat tails, and being sat upon by a few rancid negro women were no more than they deserved. I am opposed to white folks and negroes associating even on such occasions as this. The negro can't stand it, and I am in favor of protecting the negro in his racial rights." (Memphis *Commercial Appeal*, Feb. 1, 1910, 2.) Shortly after the 1908 incident BTW had written Francis Jackson Garrison: "Since I left the state, Vardaman has come out in a savage attack, through his paper, on the white people who attended my meetings. This is just what I wanted. This attack on the white people has resulted in a division of white public sentiment; and, of course, in proportion as we can get such a division, why, things will be more hopeful in the future." (Oct. 21, 1908, above, vol. 9.)

From John Henry Washington

Tuskegee Institute, Alabama   February 2d, 1910

Dear Brother: I am enclosing to you a list of persons who have not paid their poll tax, which Mr. William V. Chambliss asked me to hand you. Your brother,

J. H. Washington

[*Enclosure*]

LIST OF PARTIES IN TUSKEGEE WHO HAVE NOT PAID POLL TAX

W. T. Adams, owes from 1901 to date
J. L. Adams owes from 1901 to date

W. P. Frazier, owes from 1901 to date
M. D. Garner owes for 1907, 1908 & 1909
J. C. Greene owes from 1901 to date
Wm. Gregory owes from 1901 to date
Wiley J. Harris owes for 1901, 1902, 1903, 04, 1908 and 1909
J. T. McMillan owes for 1904 and 1906
W. A. Richardson owes for 1902 and 1904
J. B. Ramsey owes for 1902
Bell C. Stevens owes from 1901 to date
J. B. Washington owes from 1903 to date

TLS and Enclosure   Con. 597   BTW Papers   DLC.

To Emmett Jay Scott

New York. February 3, 1910

Dear Mr. Scott: In your own way I wish you would take measures to find out *at once the names* of colored people in each state who have been dropped out of important positions since Mr. Taft became President.[1] As far as you can I hope you will push this matter forward rapidly. It might be well, in order to be sure of our ground, to write two or three different persons in each state. Yours truly,

Booker T. Washington

TLS   Con. 596   BTW Papers   DLC.

[1] See A Memorandum Prepared by Emmett Jay Scott, Mar. 4, 1910, below.

From Charles Banks

Mound Bayou, Miss. February 5, 1910

Dear Dr. Washington: I beg to confirm telegram of this date, "Ocean Springs party in my office now. Additional facts will follow in letter to-day." I have gone over the whole situation with Mr. Keys. It seems that the National Committeeman, and referee, Mr.

L. B. Moseley sent for him to come to his office at Jackson, and there informed him, Mr. Keys, that he desired very much to recommend him, but that it was the President's policy to not appoint any negroes in the south, and advised Keys to go home and arrange his affairs for getting out. To this, Keys objected, stating that there was no friction there, that he had served twelve years satisfactorily and felt that he should be retained, and filed his application with some good endorsements, including that of the Mayor, whose signature is now on the petition submitted. I hand you herewith acknowledgement of the 1st Asst. Postmaster General of the receipt of the papers. Aside from those interested in getting the office themselves, and one or two radicals who are against every move we make upwards, up to the present, there is no uprising or fight on Mr. Keys, and he is now peaceably in possession of the office, and were it not for the cue that the National Committeeman has given, stating that the President did not want to appoint a Negro, everything would have gone on, and Mr. Keys reappointment accepted as a matter of course. So far as the Party (Republican) is concerned he is endorsed by the County and District Committees. He also has the names of two white ministers on his petition, Rev. Peter de Grunder and Rev. Holmes. Under the circumstances, it seems to me to be grossly unfair to allow the referee in this state to use the President's name in forcing our people out of offices they have held for years without any trouble. The fact is, there is more of this wolf cry raised by Republicans, who want offices, and to get us out of the way than by anybody else. Very truly yours,

Chas Banks

TLS Con. 53 BTW Papers DLC.

To Charles Dewey Hilles[1]

[Tuskegee, Ala.] February 9, 1910

Personal and Confidential.
Dear Mr. Hilles: You will remember stating that you thought the time had come for Banks to make a test case in Mississippi. I conveyed to him your suggestion, and he has written me as per the

enclosed letter. I enclose, also, a copy of the letter he has written to Mr. Vorys.[2]

It seems to me that now, if ever, is the time for Mr. Vorys to be of help to the man who lined up with him at a time when Moseley was absolutely obstructing the situation in Mississippi and while you may never believe it, it is due more to Banks than to anyone else that we were able to get out of Mississippi a Taft delegation. This will not appeal to the President, of course, but it ought to appeal to those who were in charge of his interests.

Will you kindly handle this as you think wise?

Personally, however, I do not wish to become embroiled in the matter as I think that Banks' letter to Mr. Vorys gives you all the opportunity you wish to proceed upon.

With kindest regards and sincere regrets that we must trouble you so much, I am   Yours truly,

[Booker T. Washington]

TLp   Con. 50   BTW Papers   DLC.

[1] Charles Dewey Hilles (1867–1949) was assistant secretary of the treasury from 1904 to 1911 and secretary to President Taft from Apr. 4, 1911, to Mar. 4, 1913. From 1912 to 1916 he was chairman of the Republican National Committee, and a member until 1938.

[2] Charles Banks to A. I. Vorys, Feb. 8, 1910, Con. 55, BTW Papers, DLC.

To Charles William Anderson

[Tuskegee, Ala.] February 19, 1910

My dear Mr. Anderson: There is a serious disposition to remove our friend, Dancy.[1] While, of course, you and I both know about his faults, on the whole I believe you will agree with me that his loyalty and strength in certain directions compensate for a great deal of weakness; especially in view of the fact that if Dancy goes out we are not sure of getting even as good a man in his place, and for this reason I am writing to say that I hope you will agree with me that we ought to do everything we can to retain him in his place as long as possible or, at least, unless we are sure that some

equally good man is going to replace him, which I very much doubt.
Yours very truly,

Booker T. Washington

TLSr Copy   Con. 49   BTW Papers   DLC.

1 James A. Cobb wrote Emmett J. Scott from Washington, D.C.: "Everything here
is going to the demnation bow-wows—so Dancy thinks. The President has practically
asked for his resignation, to be specific, he sent for him and told him that so much
pressure was being brought to bare on him for the place that very likely he would
have to make a change." (Feb. 18, 1910, Con. 403, BTW Papers, DLC.)

To William Howard Taft

[Tuskegee, Ala.] February 19, 1910

My dear Mr. President: I very much hope that you will not consider seriously the matter of removing John C. Dancy any time in
the near future from his present position. I very much doubt
whether you can get in the position a colored man anywhere in the
country who will be of more service in the way of influence and
activity than Dancy. He has back of him the solid support of the
A.M.E. Zion Church which has a stronghold in all parts of the
country. The Bishops are some of the strongest and most influential
men in the country.

When a certain element of the colored people were doing all
that they could to defeat your nomination and later on to prevent
your election, through Mr. Dancy's assistance together with what
service I could render in that same direction, the whole A.M.E.
Zion Church with all of its Bishops, with one exception, came
around solidly to your support both in the direction of securing
the nomination and in securing your election.

Mr. Dancy was among the first to come out boldly in favor of
your nomination. He did not shirk and wait until he saw which way
the "tide was turning" before he announced himself in favor of
your nomination; and I am sure that Mr. Hitchcock will tell you
that during the campaign no Negro rendered better and more constant service than did Mr. Dancy. Aside from his church connection

271

Mr. Dancy is a public speaker and writer of great ability and popularity, and stands high among the masses of our people.

All things considered, I doubt whether you could fill his place with a colored man that has such national influence as is true of Mr. Dancy. Yours very truly,

Booker T. Washington

TLSr Copy   Con. 49   BTW Papers   DLC.

To Charles Dewey Hilles

[Tuskegee, Ala.] Feb. 21, 1910

Personal and Confidential

My dear Mr. Hilles: I understand that the President is considering very seriously the matter of removing John C. Dancy, the Recorder of Deeds for the District of Columbia.

I very much hope that you can see your way clear to use your influence with the President to prevent this. I have already written directly to the President on the subject, but of course knowing how crowded he is with so many important matters, I fear he may be compelled to overlook my letter. To my knowledge there are about fifty colored men in various parts of the country applying for Mr. Dancy's job. Of course if either one of the fifty is appointed the other 49 will be mad at the President, so from that point of view nothing will be gained; but aside from that I know the colored people and the influence which they exert pretty well throughout the country, and I do not know of a single colored man applying for this position who has anything like the influence that Mr. Dancy has among all classes of colored people North and South. He is a man who knows how to mix among the common masses and make himself at home with them, and he is thoroughly popular with the masses of the colored people. Aside from this, you yourself of course know something as to the work some of us had to do to bring the colored people to the position where they would support Mr. Taft, especially in the midst of the Brownsville excitement. Mr. Dancy was one of the colored men on whom I relied to take off his coat and work without hesitation for Mr. Taft when other colored people were either on the fence or opposing him.

I very much hope for all these reasons and more that the President will see his way clear to not remove Mr. Dancy or at least to defer taking up the matter for quite a while.

Please let me hear from you. Yours very truly,

Booker T. Washington

TLpS   Con. 55   BTW Papers   DLC.

From William Howard Taft

The White House   Washington   February 22, 1910

My dear Dr. Washington: The truth is that Mr. Dancy has not made a satisfactory Recorder of Deeds, from all that I can learn. I am inclined to put Henry Lincoln Johnson, of Atlanta, in the place. Johnson was a very efficient man in the convention, and seems to be one of the ablest colored men of the country.[1] Sincerely yours,

Wm H Taft

TLS   Con. 55   BTW Papers   DLC.

[1] Ralph W. Tyler wrote Emmett J. Scott two days later: "When I learned that the President wanted no interference with his plan, and especially from the Doctor (and this in confidence) I was sick, sore, and disgusted and was ready to step out and join the insurgents." (Feb. 24, 1910, Con. 413, BTW Papers, DLC.)

To Charles William Anderson

[Tuskegee, Ala.] February 24, 1910

Personal

My dear Mr. Anderson: I have recently had a letter from our Big Chief in Washington in which he states that he is inclined to remove Dancy and put Johnson of Atlanta in his place. Whether or not he will finally carry out this plan I do not know, but I think you will agree with me that this administration has been more successful in turning people out than it has been in putting them in. Dancy of course is making a hard fight. I do not know whether he knows who is going to take his place or not. The impression prevails around Atlanta that the general scheme is to turn Rucker out as soon as Johnson goes in, that is in case he goes in. The Big Chief gives me as his reason for being inclined to change Dancy is that he has not made in his opinion, a very efficient official. Yours truly,

Booker T. Washington

TLpS Con. 49 BTW Papers DLC.

From John Campbell Dancy

Washington, D.C. Mch. 1—1910

Confidential.

My dear Dr. Washington: I have not been in the best humor for writing, hence my failure to let you hear from me sooner, except to wire my undoing.

This whole thing was done so suddenly and unexpectedly that I hadn't time for scarcely anything. And yet I got in some of the strongest sort of endorsements from all parts of the country. Your endorsement I will prize during my natural life as more valuable than any I ever filed, and I have filed them from the strongest men in this country.

I talked with the President full three-quarters of an hour. He conversed freely and pointedly and seemed thoroughly in sympathy with me. He finally said that he would take the matter under advisement further, and would inform me when he would take it up again. In the meantime he read nearly every endorsement I carried with me and commented on their strength.

I went away feeling I had won a signal victory, when to my great surprise and amazement the next morning there was a note on my desk stating that I would please call again, that the pressure was so great he could not withstand it, whereupon I tendered my resignation at once to be effective May 1st 1910.[1] He had told me in the meantime that Henry Lincoln Johnson was the man being pressed for the place and I knew at once that it was Mr. Hitchcock back of it — *our friend Hitchcock.* I have no doubt that he (Hitchcock) followed me the day of the lengthy interview, and insisted that the appointment be made at once. I was meeting pressure with pressure and so something had to be done. All my Bishops, Chas. W. Anderson, my Congressman, Congressmen from other states, leading men of our race in all parts of the country were writing, telegraphing and seeing him, and so he put an end to it all by hurrying me up and getting my resignation, — appointed my successor.

I was terribly sore at the time, but am recovering in great shape now, and am feeling quite comfortably. Any time I can serve you command me. I am always your friend. Very sincerely

Jno. C. Dancy

ALS   Con. 905   BTW Papers   DLC.

[1] According to R. W. Tyler, Dancy did two things that hastened his removal. He asked the President who his rival was, and when told it was H. L. Johnson, began to criticize Johnson. "It never pays to knock your adversary when you are pleading for your own place," Tyler commented. Second, Dancy showed the Secretary of the Treasury a "private and confidential" letter from H. A. Rucker reciting charges of immorality and criminality against Johnson, an indiscretion that precipitated the demand for his resignation. (Tyler to E. J. Scott, Feb. 26, 1910, Con. 413, BTW Papers, DLC.)

A Memorandum Prepared by Emmett Jay Scott[1]

[Tuskegee, Ala.] March 4, 1910

Changes affecting Colored people since
Mr. Taft's Inauguration

SOUTH CAROLINA: Dr. W. D. Crum held position as Collector of Customs. His place filled by appointment of a white man. The following Negroes have also been removed, namely: J. E. Wilson, Postmaster, Florence, S.C. Julius Durant,

Postmaster Paxville, S. C. (Fourth Class Office) J. A. Briar, Revenue Inspector, Greenville, S.C. R. E. Williams, Deputy Collector, Newberry, S. C.

All of these have been succeeded by white men.

LOUISIANA:

Col. James Lewis, Surveyor of the Land Office was dropped because of place being abolished, leaving only one Colored man now holding Presidential appointment in Louisiana.

Clipping from the Times-Democrat, New Orleans, La., from Washington, gives an account of an effort to consolidate the land offices at New Orleans and Natchitoches at Alexandria, La. If the office is carried to Alexandria, it will result in the only colored man now holding Presidential office in Louisiana being forced out of service, as he could not hold the office at Alexandria.

GEORGIA:

Col. J. H. Deveaux, Collector of Customs at Savannah, died summer of 1909. Place filled by an appointment of a white man.

ARKANSAS:

Deputy Internal Revenue Collector J. H. Donohue resigned under pressure or otherwise not known; place filled by the appointment of a white man.

A great many of the Negro fourth class postmasters have been displaced and white men put in their places; reason given they are following out the policy of the President.

TEXAS:

R. L. Smith, Deputy U.S. Marshal, dropped. M. M. Rogers and N. Q. Henderson, Deputy Internal Revenue Collectors, both forced out.

The postal clerks of Texas complain that they are being given considerable annoyance and trouble on the ground that the President is of the opinion that these places should be held by white men.

MISSISSIPPI: While none have been removed, it is well to note what is on foot. Because of unpleasantness which has come about, largely by reason of parties feeling that the administration would "weed out" the Negroes anyway, E. E. Perkins, Postmaster at Edwards resigned, and his successor is a white man and Democrat.

Thos. I. Keys, Ocean Springs, and L. J. Piernas at Bay St. Louis, each Negro postmasters, have been notified by the National Committeeman and referee that they need not apply for reappointment because the President has decided to give their places to white men. Keys term was up last December and Piernas was up in June.

DISTRICT OF COLUMBIA: M. M. Holland,[2] Chief of the Division, has been succeeded by a white man.

VIRGINIA: S. A. Morse, Postmaster, Denbigh, Va. and Albert Christian, postmaster, Yorktown, Va., have been both removed under circumstances closely approaching sharp practice. Some of the most influential citizens, white and black, of Virginia have protested against both of these removals.

TMc Con. 411 BTW Papers DLC.

[1] Information supplied by the following correspondents: Henry A. Rucker, J. C. Gilmer, W. T. Andrews, William D. Crum, M. M. Lewey, John E. Bush, James C.

Napier, Robert L. Smith, Robert R. Moton, George W. Clinton, Charles Banks, and Robert E. Jones.

2 In 1909 M. M. Holland was chief auditor in the Post Office Department.

To Anna Norwood Hallowell Davis[1]

[Tuskegee, Ala.] March 14, 1910

Personal and Confidential.

My dear Mrs. Davis: Replying further to your letter of some days ago, in which you make inquiry as to the immigration of Italian labor in the South, I would say that Italian labor has been introduced to some extent into Louisiana and Arkansas and into some parts of Mississippi. Reports as to its success are conflicting. I think the Italian is undoubtedly a better laborer than the average Negro farmhand, but he is more difficult to manage. He is an alien; he does not desire to settle in the country, as a rule, and remains only long enough to make enough money to return to Italy. The effect upon the Negro farm laborer is, I believe, on the whole good. The competition is stimulating to him, but I am doubtful about the ultimate effect upon social conditions.

I am sending you under separate cover today two copies of an illustrated report. We are also placing your name on The Southern Letter list so that you may receive this paper regularly hereafter. I am also sending you the last two issues of this paper. Yours very truly,

Booker T. Washington

TLpSr Con. 739 BTW Papers DLC. Signed in Emmett Jay Scott's hand.

1 Anna Norwood Hallowell Davis, originally from Medford, Mass., was the wife of New York lawyer and Republican Horace A. Davis.

To James Jenkins Dossen

[Tuskegee, Ala.] March 16, 1910

My dear Mr. Dossen: I have your kind letter of February 16th.[1] You are wholly mistaken in the assumption that I have not written you because of the intervention of someone whom you refer to as "a certain gentleman anxious that everything appertaining to America should pass through his hands."[2]

The truth of the matter is, the whole Liberian situation has moved rather slowly. In November, Dr. Lyon, Mr. Scott and I called upon the President and the Secretary of State urging that they take up the Liberian question at once. The Department, however, have just been able to get to it and Dr. Lyon is being held in America so that he may receive definite instructions before departing.

I am happy to say that I believe that matters are going to work out in an entirely satisfactory way.

Upon the same occasion as referred to above, Minister Lyon and I called upon the Secretary of the Navy and urged him to send from time to time a Government war vessel to the Liberian coast. He promised to take the matter under advisement and to do what he could in the matter. I have seen in the newspapers a report of troubles at present brewing between the natives and the Government. I hope that by this time the Government has the situation well in hand.

With kindest regards, I am: Yours very truly,

[Booker T. Washington]

TLp   Con. 905   BTW Papers   DLC.

[1] J. J. Dossen to BTW, Feb. 16, 1910, Con. 404, BTW Papers, DLC.
[2] Possibly President Arthur Barclay or Isaiah B. Scott. On May 12, 1910, I. B. Scott wrote BTW: "Dossen is wild to be president be careful what you write him. He is making capital out of everything." (Con. 412, BTW Papers, DLC.)

From Alain LeRoy Locke[1]

On board the R.M.S. "Mauretania." March 16th [1910]

My dear Sir, I should be forwarding your letter of introduction from Dr Parkin of the Rhodes Trust and from my friend and fellow-student Mr. Isaka Seme, did I not prefer to go upon the assumption that you will require none of any young man, seriously contemplating race work who asks your counsel.

I am returning to America after two and a half years absence to get into practical touch with race affairs, and with the express purpose of meeting certain of our representative men. I am hoping you will be disposed and able to grant me a personal interview, and will undertake to present myself at your convenience and appointment, should you happen to be in New York, Philadelphia or Washington anytime between now and April 16th. My vacation is so short that I could hardly undertake to visit Tuskegee, at this time, though I would attempt to should it prove impossible to meet you elsewhere: which fact I hope you will take as a guarantee of my serious purpose, and of my sense of indebtedness should you be so kind as to grant my request. Believe me, Sincerely yours

Alain LeRoy Locke

ALS   Con. 912   BTW Papers   DLC.

1 Alain LeRoy Locke (1886–1954) was one of the outstanding black scholars of his time, with a particular interest in the study of black artistic achievement. After an undergraduate education at Harvard he became the first black American Rhodes Scholar at Oxford (1907–10). He also studied for a year at the University of Berlin and in 1918 received a Harvard Ph.D. in philosophy. With BTW's support he joined the Howard University faculty in 1912. In 1925 he edited *The New Negro*, a collection of essays on the movement also known as the Harlem Renaissance. He wrote a number of books and essays on black art and culture, and helped to introduce African art to Americans. At Howard, where he spent most of his academic career, he was at the forefront of the effort to introduce general education, dramatic arts, and philosophy courses.

To James Jenkins Dossen

[New York City] March 17, 1910

My dear Vice President Dossen: Replying further to yours of February 16th I would state that there must be some mistake regarding our correspondence. In looking over my files I find that I have written you twice since I have received a letter from you. I very much fear that some of my correspondence has fallen by the wayside.

I shall do all I can in regard to the war vessels, but it seems to me even more fundamental to get matters hurried up so that the Liberian government can get substantial support in the way of clearing off its financial difficulties; that, it seems to me, is at the bottom of nearly all other troubles.

Now what I suggest is this. Will you be kind enough to write me a letter in some detail stating just why it is necessary to have the recommendations of the American Commission carried out as far as possible just as early as possible. This information will enable me to bring pressure to bear upon the State Department and President Taft in a way to hurry matters up.

You must not become impatient over delays, although I know they are very embarrassing. You must bear in mind that a change in the Washington government always means that everything is thrown back and delayed, and that you must also bear in mind that some Secretaries of State do not move as fast as others, although I am convinced that Mr. Knox is just as much interested in your problem as was true of Mr. Root.

I sent you sometime ago an extract from President Taft's message to Congress bearing upon Liberia. Did you get it?

Mr. Lyon is being detained in this country waiting for further instructions, that is, waiting until something definite is decided upon in regard to financial and other matters.

Let me know whether I can serve you. Yours very truly,

[Booker T. Washington]

TLc   Con. 905   BTW Papers   DLC.

To George Augustus Gates

Hotel Manhattan, New York. March 18, 1910

My dear Dr. Gates: When I saw you I meant to mention one matter to you which attracted my attention when I was at Fisk.

I noticed in the recitations which I visited that the students did not rise when they recited. This seemed to me rather awkward and unusual and did not indicate proper respect for the teacher. Besides, it seems to me that unless a student rises on his feet that there is not the importance attached to a recitation that there should be, and to one who has been accustomed to seeing students rise in all

281

classes of institutions it strikes one, as I have stated, as a little unbecoming not to have a student rise when he is called upon by the
teacher.

Do not mention my name in connection with this suggestion.
Yours very truly,

[Booker T. Washington]

TLc   Con. 906   BTW Papers   DLC.

To Samuel H. A. Ammon[1]

[Tuskegee, Ala.] March 22, 1910

My dear Sir: I have been deeply interested in reading your letter
and the newspaper clipping describing the political situation in
Oklahoma. I have heard with great regret, the turn that things
have taken in your state, and if any word that I could utter would
serve in any way to improve conditions, you may be sure I would
be glad to speak it. I have never excused the wrongs or injustices to
which members of our race have been subjected. What I have urged
upon our people everywhere, is that in face of injustice and discrimination, they should have patience and not lose hope.

I have said to white people and to colored people that a wrong
or injustice in one part of the community always reacts in the end
upon the other part of that community. It is the interest of the
whole community, white as well as black, that the Negro should
have justice and, in the long run, the interest of the whole community is bound to control.

As a matter of fact, we have friends in both parties and in both
sections of the country. We should not overlook the fact that some
of the best friends we have are in the South and that men who have
helped us as individuals, and have protected our lives, have frequently belonged to a class who opposed us in political matters.

On the other hand, the people in the North who are disposed to
give us the widest liberty in the matter of voting, frequently deny
to us the more fundamental rights of labor.

I am not saying this to discourage any wise or practical effort you or your friends may choose to make to better your condition by means of political parties or in any other way. We must get out of the idea that our salvation depends upon the success or failure of one political party or one political measure or another.

In the end it will be found as I have frequently said, that our success as a race rests, not upon a law, not with a party, but with ourselves. If there is hope for us anywhere, it is within ourselves.

I do think, however, that in political as well as other matters we ought to have some more definite plan of action than merely yelling when we are hurt.

My faith in the future is based on my confidence in the race. Yours truly,

Booker T. Washington

TLpS Con. 902 BTW Papers DLC. A typed draft dated Mar. 10, 1910, also is in Con. 902.

[1] Samuel H. A. Ammon was listed as a barber in the 1908 city directory of Oklahoma City, Okla.

To Robert Russa Moton

[Tuskegee, Ala.] March 24, 1910

Dear Major Moton: I presume you have seen my Independent article on Fisk University.[1] I notice that the editor in an editorial note puts me in rather an awkward position, that is, in the position of defending higher education. I meant to do no such thing. I meant to tell a simple story of the work that Fisk is doing. This matter of defending and explaining these so-called higher institutions makes me tired. The sooner these institutions can learn that they are simply making a contribution to the general education of the people, the better it is going to be for all concerned. Yours very truly,

Booker T. Washington

TLpS Con. 51 BTW Papers DLC.

[1] See An Article in *The Independent*, Mar. 24, 1910, below.

To Frederick Randolph Moore

[Tuskegee, Ala.] March 24, 1910

Dear Mr. Moore: On February 28th I wrote you a letter reading as follows:

"You will remember when I was last in New York that I said to you that it was impossible to go on as we are in the conduct of The Age. There must be a reduction in expenses, or an increase in income. At present, the paper is going in debt about at the rate of $100.00 per month. This of course can only mean one thing, that the paper will be swamped within a few years. We must stop. We must make a change. Please let me know what definite recommendations you have to make. We have no right to take property that belongs to stockholders and deliberately run it into debt with our eyes open month after month."

It is most important that I have an immediate answer to that letter. I expected to have had such an answer when I reached Tuskegee. Yours truly,

Booker T. Washington

TLpS Con. 607 BTW Papers DLC.

An Article in *The Independent*[1]

Mar. 24, 1910

A UNIVERSITY EDUCATION FOR NEGROES

Fisk University, located in Nashville, Tenn., was founded by the American Missionary Association in 1866, and it is under its fostering care that it has done its work up to the present time. It began in an abandoned army barracks, took its name from Gen. Clinton B. Fisk, who was at that time stationed at Nashville, and its first permanent buildings were erected on the site of Fort Gillam.

Coming thus on the heels of the war, it was one of the first tangible fruits, so far as the negro is concerned, of emancipation.

Those were wonderful days, directly after the war! Suddenly, as if at the sound of a trumpet, a whole race that had been slumbering for centuries in barbarism awoke and started off one morning to school.

It was a sight to stir the heart and, moved by a generous enthusiasm, hundreds of young men and a still larger number of young women, came from the North to help the newly enfranchised race on its road to freedom. It was under these conditions, and by men and women of this type, that Fisk University was founded and, in sending out year after year since that time, into all parts of the South, young colored men and women who were inspired with the enthusiasm and high purpose of those early teachers, this school has performed a service to the negro race and the South greater than can be measured in definite terms.

A few years ago there was not a school for negroes in the South so well known as Fisk University. It gained its fame thru the singing, by its students, of the old slave songs which the young freedmen had learned in the laps of their slave mothers. The Jubilee Singers, in the course of a seven years' campaign, made Fisk University known all over the world and brought back $150,000 to the school to help erect its first permanent buildings. If Fisk had done nothing else or more, its work in gathering and popularizing these folksongs of the race has entitled it to be remembered with gratitude by the negro people and the world.

Thruout the South, and in other parts of the country as well, the colored people cherish a feeling of love and even reverence for Fisk University that is not generally understood by the rest of the world. It is a great advantage to a school to have gained that sort of a reputation among the people for whom it exists.

Fisk has, in this respect, an additional advantage. From time to time, as I have gone to Nashville, I have been careful to note how highly the work of this school is esteemed by the white people in Nashville and thruout that part of the State. I have never heard a white person in Nashville speak in any manner except in the most friendly way of Fisk University. As between the Southern white people in Nashville and Fisk University, there is little or no race feeling and their relations do not, as is sometimes the case elsewhere, constitute a special problem that has to be considered and solved. I have been at Fisk on public occasions when I have seen every inch of space in the auditorium crowded by the best white people in Nashville. This fact needs to be considered in estimating the value and usefulness of this school.

Mrs. Washington and I recently spent two days in Nashville, during which time we had an opportunity to go thru every department of the college in company with the new president, Dr. George A. Gates. I confess that I was surprised that any institution, with so little means, could do so much work and such good work, and care for so large a body of students, as is the case here.

Fisk University, because of the work it has already done and because of the high place that it holds in the hearts of the colored people, is in a position where, if its work could be enlarged and perfected, it could and should be of vastly greater service in the future than it has been in the past. The fact is, however, that it has reached a point where it is clear to any one versed in educational matters that the school must have more money or it must go backward instead of forward.

From the first, Fisk University has been most fortunate in the type of its instructors. The late president, Dr. E. M. Cravath, was a high example of what I mean. More than to any one other single individual, Fisk University is indebted to Dr. E. M. Cravath for the character of work done and for the atmosphere which surrounds the university. The son of Dr. Cravath, Mr. Paul D. Cravath, of New York, one of the most eminent lawyers in the country, is a trustee of Fisk and has been deeply interested in keeping the university up to the standard of usefulness which it reached when his father lived. Following President Cravath the standard of the university was maintained under the late Dr. James G. Merrill.

The new president, Dr. George A. Gates, whose formal inauguration will take place Thursday, March 31, altho he had been at the institution but a short time, had already, when I made my visit there, gotten a firm grip upon his work and had found a strong place in the hearts of both faculty and students as well as the citizens of Nashville. In this respect the university seems to have held its own.

The faculty is divided between white and colored professors. The white people are now, as they have always been, men and women of an exceptionally high character and purpose, who are in the work not for dollars and cents, but for the good that they can accomplish. The colored professors for the most part are graduates of Fisk University.

It was a pleasure for me, during the two days that we spent at the school, to mingle freely among the students. They are a fine lot. Nothing bumptious or foolish about them. They seem to have but one object in view, that of preparing themselves for service to their race. In looking over the list of the Fisk graduates, I find that considerably more than half of them have gone out into different parts of the South as teachers. Some of the strongest men who are leaders in education, religious work and in the professions are graduates of Fisk University. In my recent trips thru Southern States, I have been surprised as well as gratified at the large number of Fisk men and women whom I have met, and almost without exception I have found that they are leading useful and honorable lives. For a number of years, we have had from twelve to fifteen Fisk men and women at Tuskegee, in different departments. For example, Mr. Clinton J. Calloway, who has been so largely responsible for the organization and upbuilding of the rural schools thruout Macon and other counties in Alabama adjoining Tuskegee, is a Fisk graduate.

It should be remembered that the responsibilities, as well as the opportunities, of the colored teacher are greater than are those of the white teacher who is engaged in the same kind of work. For example, in Alabama, and I hope it will soon be so everywhere thruout the South, a teacher who goes out into the rural districts is generally expected, in places where school exists for only three or four months, to extend the term to six or eight months. In order to do this it is necessary, of course, to devise some form or method of voluntary taxation. Frequently the raising of this money is the most important work a teacher has to do, because upon these voluntary contributions, not merely the character, but the very existence of the school depends.

On the other hand, a teacher may go into a community where there is no school building or where the building that has been used is so worn and old that it is no longer fit for use, and a good many of the country schools are in that condition. In such a case, the teacher is likely to be called upon to raise money and erect a new building or repair the old one.

In many parts of the South in the country districts, the burden of erecting and maintaining the school system, so far as it touches the negro, is thrown largely upon the negro teacher. Not only this, but to a very large extent the success of negro education in the South depends upon the character of the individual teacher and the spirit in which he or she undertakes the work. If the teacher has learned to bring education so into touch with the life of the community that the people, both black and white, can be made to feel and see the effects of it in their daily life, then education will become popular in that community, and white people, as well as the colored people, will be glad to support it. Altho conditions are somewhat different in the cities the negro teacher there — to a much larger extent than the white teacher — has the responsibility of showing, by the results of his teaching, the value of the kind of education that he is giving his pupils.

I mention these things in order to emphasize the fact that when his responsibilities are the same or greater, the negro teacher or the negro doctor ought to have just as sound, just as complete and just as thoro an education as the white man who performs the same work or shares the same responsibilities.

It sometimes seems to me that we spend too much time in the discussion of the relative value of higher education and lower education for the negro. As a matter of fact, it does not make so much difference whether education is high or low, professional or common, but it does make a great deal of difference whether the education the negro receives is real or merely a sham. If we are to have negro doctors, then I think every one will agree they should be good doctors. If we are to have negro teachers, ministers, bankers and business men, they should be just as efficient and just as moral as those of any other race.

For this, if for no other reason, we must keep up the standard in our schools. We must not draw the color line in the negro colleges as we will do if we voluntarily accept a low standard or less complete preparation in negro colleges than is required in the schools of any other race.

This is a matter, let me add, that touches the white man just as closely as it does the negro. We are all bound together in a system of relations; we cannot tear asunder if we would. Disease draws no color line. If a contagious disease breaks out in the part of the city inhabited by black people, it is pretty sure to reach, sooner or later, the part of the city inhabited by white people. The negro doctor, in looking after the health of the individual negro, to a certain extent is looking after the health of the whole community. Morality draws no color line. If one portion of the community is living in helpless ignorance and degradation, every other portion of the community will sooner or later be infected with these conditions. For this reason, it is important that the negro teacher and negro preacher should be properly trained.

It is just as true in business and in all the economic relations of life, as it is in the matter of disease that the success and prosperity of one part of the community is dependent upon the success and the prosperity of every other part. If one part of the community performs its work and fulfils its obligations in a slipshod, careless way, the whole community will feel the effects. For this reason, it is important to every one that we should have in every Southern community well-trained, enterprising, thrifty and honest negro business men who will serve as examples to the other members of their race.

In all these respects Fisk has been, to a certain extent, a model for the other colored schools in the South. For its efforts to maintain its standards under peculiar disadvantages Fisk deserves especial credit. As indicating what those disadvantages are, let me make a comparison.

Thirty years ago, the University of Chicago was, like Fisk, a comparatively small and unimportant school. Without pretending to any definite knowledge of the facts, I believe I am safe in saying that Chicago University was not, at that time, much ahead of Fisk either in the character of its work, in the number of its students or in the extent of its influence upon the communities. That was the day of small colleges. I do not believe there was a university in the country that had much over a thousand students.

How do the two institutions compare today?

According to the report of the Commissioner of Education for 1908, Fisk had 516 students, while Chicago had 5,617, which is but 2,882 less than the number of students in the twenty negro colleges reported by the United States Commissioner of Education. The total annual income of Fisk in that same year was $24,590. The value of its scientific apparatus, library and buildings was estimated at $419,000, of which $400,000 was buildings. The total annual income of Chicago University in 1908 was $1,772,015. The value of its scientific apparatus, library and buildings, exclusive of its endowment, was estimated at $10,320,036.

In order to show just what this means, let me make a further comparison. While the income of Chicago University in 1908 was $1,772,015, the total annual income of the twenty negro colleges mentioned in report of the Commissioner of Education was $804,663. In other words, the annual income of a single school in the North was more than twice as large as that of all the negro colleges in the United States.

Fisk University has an endowment at the present time of but $60,000. The total endowment of the twenty negro colleges reported by the Commissioner of Education in 1908 was only $1,383,726. In that same year, $1,468,129 was added to the endowment fund of Chicago University, while the total endowment of that school was $14,000,000.

I have mentioned Chicago University because it is a convenient illustration of the rapid development of the larger educational institutions in the North, not only with respect to the size of the plant employed, but in respect to the character of the teaching and the influence of these schools upon the community. But Chicago University is by no means exceptional. There are at least fifteen larger institutions of learning which expend more money every year for current expenses than is expended for all purposes by negro colleges in the South. Several of these large institutions expend annually twice, and one of them, Harvard University, nearly three times as much, as all the negro colleges in the United States.

In addition to the fifteen larger universities to which I have referred, there are at least seventeen other and smaller institutions, among them technical schools and agricultural colleges, which spend nearly or quite as much as any ten negro colleges south of Washington, D.C. One of these schools to which I refer is an agricultural and mechanical college for white students in the State of Mississippi.

In the matter of endowment, Chicago University is not exceptional. The University of Pennsylvania, for example, has an endowment of $12,000,000. The endowment of Harvard University amounts now to over $20,000,000; that of Columbia is $23,000,000, and Leland Stanford has an endowment of $24,000,000.

In making these comparisons I do not intend to reflect in any way upon the work of the colored colleges. From all I can learn, most of them are doing the best they can. In pointing out the difficulties under which these schools labor, my purpose is to make the world understand their needs.

I would not take a single dollar from any of the institutions in the North to which I have referred. They are doing a good work and need even more money, but I am using their names simply for comparison.

In all the discussion which is taking place as to the effect of one kind or another of education in solving the negro problem, we should bear in mind that education of no kind has been tried on a sufficiently large scale or with a sufficient consideration of what are the actual needs of negro people to show what education for the masses of the people will do. There are ten millions of negroes in the United States today. Why not have somewhere — in the South — at least one large, thoroly equipped university where the actual needs of the negro people could be studied and where such of them as desire to be teachers, doctors or ministers of the gospel could be thoroly equipped for their work?

Independent, 68 (Mar. 24, 1910), 613–18.

1 An editorial note introducing the article commented on the timeliness of the piece, since George A. Gates was scheduled to be inaugurated as president of Fisk University on March 31. The editors stated that BTW's defense of higher education for blacks "shows how mistaken is the idea that he is concerned only in the industrial training which will fit the race to support themselves in a humble station of life."

From Seth Low

New York   March 25th, 1910

Personal

My dear Dr. Washington; Referring to my letter of the 23rd,[1] in regard to the discrepancy between the rate of pay and the number of hours of work upon the Farm, I am writing to say that I fully appreciate that the re-adjustment suggested in the relation of hours paid for to hours of work done, may be very far-reaching in its effects, and that it may be necessary for you to consider every aspect of the question before you make any move at all. If it be a necessary condition of farm work in connection with the school work, that can of course be pointed out; and, so far as it goes, it will explain why a school farm cannot help being costly. I am hoping, however, that you will find a way to make the hired men, at any rate, give a full day's work for a full day's pay, so that full value may be gotten out of the teams. It is absurd to have the farm teams and all the farming apparatus used for only two-thirds of the day.

I perceive, also, that, if the rate of pay to be credited to students is cut down, one effect of it may be to show that the students do not entirely pay their way through the Institute. It is worth consideration, however, whether it is not better to show a loss, at this point, than to make the cost of the farm artificially greater than it is; for I cannot escape the feeling that if agriculture is to be commended to the Southern negro, Tuskegee has got to make it clear that its own farm can be conducted at a profit. You perceive, of course, that my suggestion does not imply that either the hired labor or the student labor should receive less per hour of work than they now receive; but simply that they should be credited with seven hours of work, which is all they give, instead of receiving full pay or full credit for a ten hour day. Yours, very truly,

Seth Low

TLS   Con. 50   BTW Papers   DLC.

1 Con. 50, BTW Papers, DLC.

Extracts from an Address before
the Alabama Colored State Teachers Association

Birmingham, Ala. March 25th [1910]

I wish to congratulate the Negro teachers of Alabama upon having present here in the city of Birmingham at this annual meeting the largest number of teachers of the children of our race that has ever been gathered in one meeting in our state. I question whether there is any other state in the South that has an organization of this character that is so largely composed of teachers who are so much interested in their work, and who are so determined to see to it that everything in their power is done to further the education of the Negro boys and girls of Alabama.

The Negroes of Alabama have some special reasons for gratitude. In our state the relations between the black people and white people are friendly. It is very seldom that we have racial conflicts and racial outbreaks of the character that so often disgrace the [and?] hurt both races in our country. In Alabama both black people and white people understand each other and are determined to live together in peace and in friendship. It is often said that the Southern white man understands the Negro better than anybody else. While I will not question or dispute this statement, I wish to add also that the Southern Negro understands the Southern white man better than anybody else. Despite what sensational newspapers may say, and despite what political demagogues may express, when one goes into the local communities of Alabama he finds that the relations existing between the individual Negro and the individual white man are closer than they are in any other portion of America or in any other part of the world outside of America that I have seen. When we get into the local community we will find that every Negro has his white friend and every white man has his Negro friend. When the Negro gets into trouble he usually goes straight to his white friend and usually gets what he wants. Wherever in Alabama you find the Negro working at a trade, owning a store, conducting a drug establishment or a bank, you will find an individual Southern white man or a group of Southern white men who are ready to encourage, guide and assist these colored people in their business enterprises.

I believe the time has come when more interest is going to be taken in the education of the Negro boy and girl throughout Alabama than has ever been done in the past. All that is necessary for us to do is to prove to the school officials and to the white people in the community where our schools exist that Negro education benefits the Negro child, makes him of more service to his own race, of more service to the white people by whom he is surrounded. When we shall have once done that, hundreds of thousands of dollars will be poured out for the education of our children both in the city, town and country districts.

.   .   .   .

Too much time is wasted in discussing the difference between higher and lower education. The highest education is that which best fits the boy or girl to live successfully in the environment in which his life is thrown. The lowest education is that which fails to fit the individual to live successfully in the community where his life is thrown. The object of all education, no matter by what name it is called, should be to fit the individual to articulate what he has learned in the school room into the active, every-day life of the community in which he lives. We must get rid as speedily as possible of the old idea that education is something strange, something sublime, something that should be classed among the supernatural things of life. Everywhere we must impress the idea that education should be just as common and just as necessary as the use of water, the use of farm products, the use of animals. The Negro is not the only part of the human race that still looks upon education as something strange and far off and likes to clothe it and surround it in an atmosphere of mystery. The average medical doctor, for example, still clings to the practice of writing his prescription in Latin; instead of placing upon the prescription to the drug store so much "water" he likes to say "Aqua." Instead of asking on his prescription for so many ounces of straight whiskey, he likes to say so many ounces of "spiritus frumenti." The wording of the prescription in this way keeps the doctor's work and profession surrounded in mystery, and incidentally he can charge more for writing a prescription in Latin than he can in expressing his desire in plain English, but that practice in the light of civilization will soon pass away.

If your school is located in a farming district, see to it that there is a vital connection between what is taught in the school room and the life that the people live who surround your school house. There is nothing more dismal and disappointing than to see standing up in some old field one lonely isolated building in a farming community. In most cases so far as anything done on the inside of the school house is concerned that is connected with the life of the people, the school building might as well be located fifty miles away from the immediate community. There should be around the country school house vines, there should be surrounding it a flower garden, a vegetable garden. There should be used plenty of white-wash and plenty of paint. Wherever possible the boys and girls should not only be instructed in the book, but they should be instructed how to care for poultry, pigs and cows. Their lessons in mathematics, in composition, in what not, should be largely based upon the production of farm products which in most cases can be seen within a few yards of the school house. How dismal is the experience which many of us often have on visiting a school teacher in a farming community, and have placed upon the table for dinner canned tomatoes perhaps brought from Baltimore, or canned turkey or salt meat brought from Chicago, when bushels of luscious fresh tomatoes could be produced within a few yards of the school house, when plenty of fowls of every character could be raised in the farming community.

· · · · ·

The kingdom of Holland teaches us all a great lesson in the direction of articulating school life into actual life. A few years ago Holland was faced with the problem of finding an industry by which its people could live. The leaders of life in Holland found that they could make it a great dairy producing country. The result is that dairying was taught to the smallest child in the public school, in the high school, in the college, in the university. To-day Holland not only supplies all of its own dairy products but ships millions of dollars worth of these products to other European countries.

We want to see to it that education is made to concern itself with the common, ordinary things of life and not with the extraordinary things of life.

I will guarantee to say that the average Negro child in Alabama hears more about the city of Peking in China, or the desert of Sahara in Africa than that child does about the kind of pigs or the kind of cows, or the kind of vegetables that will best grow in the community where that child is. I have seen many Negro girls who have learned in the school how to locate successfully on an artificial globe, the city of Calcutta, or the Congo Free State, but who could not locate for the life of them on an actual dinner table the proper place of the meat and vegetables, or the proper place for the carving knife and fork.

Every family in Alabama has meals prepared and served three

times a day. The average individual in Alabama buys a pair of shoes about three times in a year. When one goes to the store to buy shoes, he is waited upon by an individual who is clean, educated, cultured. That individual puts a piece of leather on the outside of the feet three times a year. I claim that throughout Alabama, the time has come when we should convince the people that it is just as important that the person who prepares and serves food three times a day to go on the inside of the stomach should be just as clean, just as well educated, just as skilled as the person who puts a piece of leather on the outside of the feet three times a year.

I am sure that it will pay ¾ of the teachers who are here gathered to dismiss their school for a week after their return home, so far as the old style of teaching is concerned, and let teachers and pupils occupy themselves in cleaning and beautifying the inside of the schoolroom, in whitewashing or painting the outside of the schoolroom, in putting the palings on the broken down fence, in putting new hinges on the gate, in cleaning up all the trash and rubbish around the schoolhouse, in planting some flowers and vines and vegetables near the schoolhouse. It will pay them to occupy a week in putting in the old broken window panes, in making the desks and tables in the schoolroom attractive and decent, in teaching the boys and girls how to keep themselves clean, to clean their teeth, to properly patch and darn their clothing.

This is real education. We must get rid once and for all of the old idea that the boy or girl can only get education within the four walls of the stilted schoolhouse. Education can be gotten anywhere at any time regardless of one's surroundings.

Education should fit one, as I have stated, to live successfully in the environments in which he is placed. In our case, the Negro child in the South is surrounded by another race of a different color with a different history. We are not exceptional in that respect. There is scarcely any portion of the world that is occupied wholly by one single race. Where two races different in language, different in color, different in antecedents dwell together, it is mighty important that each child be taught that he must be liberal, broad, generous, sympathetic in relation to the other race. Nothing would more quickly dam and fetter and injure for all time the Negro child than for him to grow up with a spirit of racial hatred in Alabama. Teach him on every occasion that love is better than hatred, that sympathy and goodwill are better than selfishness and ill-will. Teach the Negro child that the nine millions of black people in our Southland are getting on better in proportion to their numbers than any nine millions of black people in any part of the world who are surrounded by so large a number of white people. There is no other man with a white face, who is more patient, more long suffering and more interested in the elevation of the Negro than is true of the white man in Alabama.

Just in proportion as we can convince the white man in Alabama that our education is going to mean something, is going to make us more useful to our race, to his race, on the farm, in the kitchen, in the dining room, in the school room, in the professions, and everywhere that minute plenty of money will be forthcoming for our education.

Much improvement has been made, in public school education of our race in Alabama, still greater improvement can be made, and I think will be made in the near future. The Negro child cannot fit himself properly for the duties of life when he is in school only four months out of the twelve months, and has spent upon him for his education, as is true in this state at the present time about $1.78 per child. The Negro child cannot learn as much off of $1.78 as the white child can out of $15.84, and those who think that the Negro child can get as much education out of $1.78 as the white child can out of $15.84 pay too high a compliment to the natural intelligence and the natural ability of the Negro child.

What we want to do throughout Alabama in reference to our education is to do just what Dr. U. G. Mason has done in the City of Birmingham, get hold of the best white people, the business men, and the officials, and take them to the Negro schoolhouses; let them see the poor facilities that the Negro teachers have to work with in many cases, and when they once become convinced that we are in earnest about improving the condition of our race, and when they once see for themselves the poor facilities by which the Negro teacher is surrounded, especially in the rural districts, the white school officials will take more interest in the education of the Negro race.

We must not content ourselves with talking about what the white man does not do for us, but we must talk to him about the ways in which he can help make the schools in Alabama better.

The Negro woman or the Negro girl who works for most of the white families of Alabama cooks their food and serves their food; the Negro woman or the Negro girl nurses the white man's children; she launders his clothes; she cleans his bedroom, and his sitting room, and his parlor. It is just as much to the interest of the white race, then, that the Negro girl or the Negro woman who comes in touch with the white race every day in these vital points should be clean, should be skillful, and should be highly moral as it is to the interest of the Negro race that she should be properly educated in these directions.

For all time, black and white people are going to live in Alabama together, and we are setting an example to the world showing how the two races in one state can live together, separate in their social relations, and one in all that concerns their mutual and highest welfare.

TM   Con. 607   BTW Papers   DLC.

A Sunday Evening Talk

[Tuskegee, Ala.] March 27, 1910

THE RESURRECTION SEASON

This is the season of the year when the thought of the world, especially the Christian part of the world, is concerned mainly with matters relating to the resurrection. This is not only true in relation to the resurrection of the spiritual and bodily life of Christ, but it is also true in relation to the new life — the resurrection of all kinds of life with reference to vegetable life, life that relates to food of all kinds, berries, shrubbery, flowers, fowls — life of every character.

The thing to which I wish to direct your especial attention for a few moments this evening is this: that God has put into the world everything to be of value to man, to promote his happiness, to serve his purpose, and if we do not make what God has put here of the highest service to us, it will be largely our fault and the fault mainly is our failure, in most respects, to take a practical, direct view of life: in a word, in our failure to connect that which God has put here for our every-day life.

There is a serious gap, a serious lack, in most cases, between what God has put here and the use that we make of it and, it seems to me that if a school of this character, or of any character has direct practical value to the life of the people for whom it exists, one of the functions of that school should be to teach people in a direct, plain, practical manner how to take everything God has put here in this world and make it of the very highest service to the people to whom that school ministers.

One of the objects of surrounding us with vegetables, with grain, berries, flowers and everything with which we are made happy at this season of the year is to help us to make our bodies better fitted for the uses of life, to make our bodies stronger, to make them more healthful. It is a surprising fact that in parts of the country where nature has been most lavish, where nature has poured out most that should be of service to man, there you will find people making the very least service of what nature has provided for them right at their very doors. This shows itself in a number of forms. One has but to travel through certain sections of the South where nature is most lavish in providing a rich soil, in providing opportunities and conditions for all kinds of growth, almost even without the touch of man, when he will be, in most cases, horrified and surprised at the conditions of people's bodies. If you will travel through certain sections of Alabama today, if you will travel through certain sections of the mountainous sections of Tennessee, you will find where nature has been most rich, the people have taken the least advantage of the opportunities which nature has provided. This is very largely true, because for too long a time we have not made the connection between education and the common, ordinary things by which people are supposed to live, because for too long a time we have failed to make any direct, vital connection between vegetable life and the life that sustains our body.

Wherever you find that people have not made that connection, you will find bad looking bodies. When I say "bad looking" I mean ugly looking bodies, ugly looking men and ugly looking women. You will not only find, where people have failed to make this connection, bad looking bodies, ugly looking bodies, but you will find, in most cases, weak bodies. Travel through many of the sections not very far from us, many of the sections to which I have referred, and you will find ugly bodies, bad looking bodies and weak bodies — people who are not able to work many hours in the day because of the weaknesses of their bodies. You will find this showing itself in wrinkled faces, in people growing old, or seeming to be old when they ought to seem, so far as the appearance of their faces and bodies are concerned, to be just beginning life.

Many of you know people at your own homes, people in your own communities, people in your own counties, who have ugly weak bodies, wrinkled faces, almost deplorable in their looks — simply because in our schools, public schools, high schools, industrial schools, colleges, universities — everywhere — people have failed to make the connection between plant life and real life, between plant life and bodily life. You have sometimes, perhaps, gone into the very communities where educational institutions exist, which should above all things teach this connection, emphasize this connection and there you found the poorest looking bodies, the weakest looking bodies, and faces with the most wrinkles in them.

Not only this, but because the people have failed to make this connection between plant life and the life of man, you will find diseased bodies. You can trace a very large proportion of the sickness which exists among our people and among other people right back to the fact that their bodies are not sustained day by day with plenty of good, tempting, well-cooked food — in a word, these people are hungry. When you have a weak body, it invites all kinds of diseases.

Go among the average people of our race in the South and you seldom find anybody who is well. Ask a person how he is and he will answer, "just tolerable," or he will tell you that he has a pain, or an ache, or rheumatism — something always wrong. Very seldom you will find anybody who can look you squarely in the face and say: "I am well." In nine cases out of ten, you will find the body lacks the sustaining power of good, nourishing food day by day.

We have an example of this in what is called the hook-worm which we have been discussing a good deal in recent years in connection with life here in the South. The hook-worm simply means that people have not had enough to eat. Wherever you find people who have the hook-worm, they have not had good enough food to eat day by day. If we could teach these people by some process how to utilize the food by which they are surrounded, how to utilize plant life, how to cook their food well, how to serve it well, how to make it palatable, the hook-worm would keep out of their bodies. This condition, this failure to make connection between plant life and man life not only results in ugly, weak, diseased bodies; but a weak body, as you already know, means a weak mind — a mind that is not able to hold what it should hold; and a weak mind results in bad morals.

There is no person who so readily yields to the temptation of losing his temper as the person who has not had enough to eat. Show me the person who never is able to control his temper, who is always blue, who is always taking a gloomy, dark view of life, ready to bite and scratch and snap at every one who talks to him, in nine cases out of ten, the trouble is his body lacks the sustaining power of good fresh food three times a day, and this condition not only results in bad temper, but often results in crime. It results in the kind of crime which people commit when they lose the power of self-control; it leads to the jail, to the penitentiary; it leads them to the point where instead of being moral, upright, law-abiding citizens, they become a burden upon the community in which they live.

When I go to church and hear people preach for hours on all kinds of subjects, especially in country districts, where the soil is fitted for growing all kinds of vegetables, all kinds of fowls, all kinds of useful shrubbery, how very much I wish the minister would take a few hours and teach the people how to fill their bodies with some of the beautiful things with which nature has surrounded them.

This leads me to suggest that as you go out from here — and you can only do it as you prepare yourselves here for this kind of service — I want you to make a study. Now you think I mean you have got to get a book and sit down and bury yourself in it for two or three hours when I say I want you to make a study, but I mean after you leave here, in the first place, find out what will grow in the community where you will reside. Study the soil; find out what the soil will produce. I do not care what you are going to be in life, whether you are going to be school teachers, whether you are going to be business men, or professional men, this applies to all of you — in the first place, make a study of the soil, make a study of the climatic conditions around you; find out what will grow in that soil. Then after you have found out what will grow in that soil and after you have found out the methods of growing it, make a careful investigation, a careful study as to the best methods of preparing the food products of that community. When I say "preparing food products," I mean — to put it in plain language, in a more direct way — I simply mean make a study of the best methods of cooking that food. You know what I mean when I say "cooking." Sometimes girls get so mixed up on this subject of Domestic Economy that they forget all about cooking. I am talking about cooking, not about Domestic Economy.

The word "cooking" as it relates to food involves a great deal; in the first place, it involves a study of the composition of the body; what the body needs at this season of the year; what it will need during the summer months; what it will need during the fall and during the winter. Study the body until you find out that the body in the spring of the year needs a change of food; needs plenty of good, fresh vegetables — and I think you will agree with me that our Boarding Department is trying to give us plenty of good, fresh vegetables, not only for dinner, but for breakfast.

When I say make a study of the preparation of food, I mean for you to study it until you can make the most ordinary food, the most ordinary dish tempting for people to eat. You can take an ordinary garden product, an ordinary vegetable of any kind, and by surrounding it with proper delicacies, by studying it you can make a very tempting, delicious meal out of what would otherwise have proven almost distasteful.

In studying this up-keep of the body, every girl who is the head of a family and every man who has any connection with a family should not only feel it a part of his duty to encourage the proper preparation of food in connection with that family, but they should see to it that there is a regular time for eating that food. One of the discouraging features in connection with the average home consists in the fact that people do not have any regular time to eat. You know that. In your homes, when you go back, first of all, insist upon it that there shall be a certain hour for the preparing of the food and for partaking of it.

To do that does not require wealth. It does require system. Many of our bodies, the bodies of our people, and the bodies of other people are weak and not able to perform their proper functions, not able to perform their proper duties in life, and not only because they do not get good food, but because of the irregularity in the time of taking that food. All this leads, as I said a minute ago, to ugly bodies, to weak bodies, to diseased bodies, to weak minds, to bad morals.

People should see to it that in every home the conditions to which I have referred not only exist, but that a certain ceremony, a certain importance, be attached to partaking of the food. See to it, in the first place, that there is a time, thoroughly understood by father and by mother, thoroughly understood by each member of the family, when each meal is to be served. Then the head of the family should see to it that the food is not only prepared in the most tempting way, but that it is served in the most attractive and beautiful way. See to it that plenty of time is given to the preparation of the table, to the cleanliness of the cloth, to the decoration of the table, and above all things, give attention to the place where the food is to be taken.

In most cases, as you know, the place where the food is taken, in too many families, is the most dismal, the most gloomy place in the whole home, and people want to get out of it just as soon as possible. See to it that when you build your own home, when you have any control over a home, any influence in a home, that the dining room is the most beautiful, the most convenient, the most tempting room in the whole home.

I have spoken to you tonight in this direct, plain, frank manner because as I have said, all that God has surrounded us with will mean nothing — the vegetables, the grain, the shrubbery, and the flowers — all of it will perish and go to waste and we will be no better off for it, unless we make a connection between what God has put here, between that which is resurrected this Easter season, and our every-day life, unless we in some way realize fully that all these things are put here for us and that our bodies will be made stronger and more beautiful and our lives will be lifted up and be made more serviceable by reason of it all.

Tuskegee Student, 22 (Apr. 2, 1910) 1, 2. Stenographically reported.

From Charles William Anderson

New York, N.Y., March 28, 1910

(Personal)

Dear Doctor: Replying to your favor of the 25th instant, I beg to say that I have noticed that the Washington American has made a great feature of what it chooses to regard as the Age's assault on Mr. Hitchcock. I felt confident that this would be done, and I am equally confident that certain persons have told the Postmaster General that the article was either inspired by you, or had your approval. I also believe that there are those who will connect me with it, as Mr. Peterson is at present a deputy in my office, and Moore was formerly one. It is ever thus when you set a wood chopper to painting pictures. If the majority of the stockholders of the Age would secure the services of an editor with, at least, a thimble full of brains, and give Moore charge of the advertising and business work, with strict instructions not to interfere with the editorial policy of the paper, I think some good would be accomplished. As it is, the paper is neither, fish, flesh nor good smoked herring, and is as devoid of a sound policy as a billiard ball is of hair. About the only news it ever prints is some complimentary twaddle about the United Colored Democracy and Chief Lee, and yet, it poses as a republican paper. If it ever secures any more assistance from the Republican party in this State, under present management, it will have to secure it over my dead body. I am not in the habit of fattening democratic papers, and if I were I could find enough friendly journals among the white democratic papers to use up everything I could throw in their way. Moore has established a policy of not saying anything about any man he does not like, and as he does not like anybody but himself, and possibly Chief Lee, he has nobody to write about — the two of them would not make one good man. I think Scott could do the cause more service by coming here and turning this paper upsidedown than he did by going to Liberia, although this last service was a great one.

Hoping you are very well, I remain, Yours truly,

Charles W. Anderson

TLS Con. 49 BTW Papers DLC.

To James Samuel Stemons[1]

[Tuskegee, Ala.] March 29, 1910

My dear Mr. Stemons: I thought I ought to write you a little more frankly and fully[2] concerning my opinion as to accomplishing the object which you have in mind.

I do not believe that any public abstract discussion of the question would answer the purpose to the extent you think it would and I fear might result in harm, rather than good.

In the first place, I do not think the impression ought to be given to the world that the Negro cannot find work. True, in a few spots here and there, where perhaps two or three persons of our race live, they have difficulty in finding work, but in the South and in most other parts of the country, where the large numbers of our people live, they have no trouble in finding work. In the South, the Negro can get three times as much work to do as he can perform. Here is where the millions live.

I sometimes fear that in a city like Philadelphia, one becomes deceived by reason of the fact that he hears about and sees the fellow who is out of a job, but does not hear about or see the fellow who has a regular job, hence one is likely to get the idea that more of the Colored people are out of work than actually are. The man who has work goes on steadily performing it day by day without making any noise, without making any complaint and thus is likely to be overlooked, while the fellow who has not work exhibits himself.

Second: I do not believe in going about matters in a negative way, when an affirmative way would answer the purpose better. For example, if instead of having a number of people come together to advertise the fact that the Negro cannot get work, suppose you have people come together in Philadelphia who are employing the Negro, who have made a success in some line of business by giving the Negro labor. Have these people describe how valuable the Negro is as a laborer from their own experience, also have colored people come and tell their experiences who are employed. This would give an affirmative atmosphere to your meeting which would be of value and would be to other people, who now fear to employ the Negro. The minute you advertise to the world that the Negro is ostracized in labor, people are going to ostracize him more than they are at present.

In connection with such a meeting, if possible, I should also have a physical exhibition of the products of Negro labor.

In all cases, my experience teaches me that it is better to attack a problem from an affirmative direction than from a negative, critical one.

I should be glad to hear from you after you have had time to read these suggestions. Yours very truly,

Booker T. Washington

TLpS Con. 912 BTW Papers DLC.

[1] James Samuel Stemons (1870–1959), born in Clarksville, Tenn., was editor of the Philadelphia *Courant* in 1906. In 1907 he became editor of *The Pilot*, another black weekly in Philadelphia. He opposed political and civil rights agitation and favored instead efforts to improve black employment and promote economic advancement.

[2] A letter to Stemons dated March 28, 1910, signed for BTW in E. J. Scott's hand, agreed with Stemons that exclusion of blacks from the building trades and other established industries was a serious problem, and urged Stemons to secure the support of the Armstrong Association of Philadelphia and the Committee for Improving Industrial Conditions of Negroes in New York City. (Con. 912, BTW Papers, DLC.) It is clear that in this case Scott misread BTW's views. Stemons wrote back that the letters of March 28 and 29 were so conflicting that he did not know how to reply to either. Stemons criticized BTW for his complacency and failure to face the seriousness of the black labor problem. He declared the Armstrong Association's efforts inadequate to cope with the employment problems of 100,000 blacks in Philadelphia, the city having found intermittent employment for only 300 blacks. (Apr. 7, 1910, Con. 912, BTW Papers, DLC.)

To James A. Cobb

Tuskegee Institute, Alabama   April 1, 1910

Personal and Confidential.

My dear Mr. Cobb: I meant to have written you several days ago to say that I wrote to the Attorney General in the way you suggested and I hope some good will result.

I think it is exceedingly important at this time that the true friends of President Taft not permit him to be deceived concerning the present state of mind of the colored people of the country. In all of my conversation with the President and in all of my correspondence with him, I have always been perfectly frank and I have found that he appreciates frankness and has always thanked me for my information, in fact, the President himself knows that there is unrest and dissatisfaction.

In reply to the last letter I wrote him calling attention to the unrest and dissatisfaction, he said that he did not blame the colored people for being dissatisfied up to the present point in his administration, so far as his treatment of them was concerned, but in the end he felt sure the results would satisfy them.

Unless one is perfectly frank with the President, he may go on feeling that the Negroes are satisfied, when they are not and when the time comes to expect their support, he will be disappointed, hence it is disloyalty for any person to deal in a manner that is not frank with the President. The class of colored men to be benefited more than any other element by dealing frankly with the President just now are the men who hold Federal office in Washington and elsewhere.

If the Republicans feel that they can carry Ohio next fall, no matter how the Negroes are treated in the country, they will pay no attention to them, but if they feel they need their support and good will, they will not only keep the present men in office, but will seek to put more in.

I have the highest respect for President Taft. Certainly to me he has been most kind and considerate and I always feel that I can exhibit my gratitude to him for his kindness and confidence in no better way than by telling him always a straight story.

Persons holding Federal position ought always to be thankful to somebody on the outside who does let the President know frankly how conditions are, because of course the President discounts anything an office holder may say to him in favor of his administration, and at the same time, an office holder cannot criticise an administration adversely, hence the importance of those who are not obligated to the President in the way of office holding keeping the President informed in a frank, friendly manner of the exact situation.

I always take pleasure in telling President Taft when the colored people are pleased as a class and I am equally frank with him in telling him when they are not. I pursued the same course with President Roosevelt and both President Roosevelt and President Taft have always exhibited the greatest degree of gratitude to me for my actions. Yours very truly,

Booker T. Washington

TLS James A. Cobb Papers DHU. A press copy is in Con. 904, BTW Papers, DLC.

An Editorial in the New York *Evening Post*

New York, April 1, 1910

Mr. Washington in Politics

The old issue as to what attitude the colored people should take towards their political disabilities is recalled anew by a recent speech in this city of Dr. W. E. B. Du Bois of Atlanta University and a letter from him to the Boston *Transcript*. Few people are yet aware, we believe, of the extent of the cleavage between him and his followers and those negroes led by Booker T. Washington, or of the bitterness that has developed. Dr. Du Bois's attitude is one of resentment toward wrong, of steadfast opposition to disfranchisement, and to the withdrawal of civil and political rights guaranteed by the Constitution of the United States. He believes that agitation and protest are necessary not only to recover lost ground, but to prevent the loss of more. He will not sit silent in the presence of wrong. He will not refrain from denouncing oppression any more than the German Poles will refrain from opposing their Prussian over-lords, or Russians of the type of Madame Breshkovsky[1] and Nicholas Tchaikovsky[2] will abandon their advocacy of freedom for Russia. With this attitude the *Evening Post* has frequently sympathized. It counsels no man to wear a padlock when his rights as a citizen are endangered.

Dr. Washington, on the other hand, subordinates everything else to the uplifting of the negro industrially and economically. His success at Tuskegee needs no affirmation, North or South. His inestimable usefulness as an interpreter of one race to the other in the South we dwelt upon at length after his recent extraordinary trip through Tennessee. To be industrious, sober, honest, and to acquire property, this is his doctrine for the colored man. He lets discussion of political rights severely alone — an attitude which is justified by most people as the right one for the head of an institution located in the South in the midst of deep racial prejudices. There is much to be said for all college heads keeping bravely aloof from political entanglements. Dr. Washington counsels his people to submit to disfranchisement. Hence he is welcome in the South wherever he goes. He arouses no prejudices; his industrial doctrine fits in well with the controlling Southern opinion that the negro should aspire to be nothing more than a hewer-of-wood and a drawer-of-water, and so he reaches the ears and broadens the minds and softens the hearts of thousands who would not listen to a word from Dr. Du Bois. Moreover, Dr. Washington is heartily supported in the North by all conservatives — those who believe that the South should be allowed to work out the problem unmolested by criticism or agitation, and are convinced that time will heal all present sores and wounds.

Now, as we have intimated, this is a defensible attitude for the principal of a school to take. It commends itself particularly to those who believe in compromises for the sake of peace and living pleasantly with their neighbors. If Dr. Washington were to keep silent altogether and immerse himself exclusively in his work at Tuskegee, no colored man would, we think, object to his silence. It is his advice to his people to submit to government and taxation without representation that has hurt, and the fact that he has at the same time assumed or been forced into the place of political boss of his race. The two positions are hopelessly inconsistent. As Dr. Du Bois puts it in his letter to the *Transcript:*

> Mr. Washington has for the last eight years allowed himself to be made the sole referee for all political action concerning 10,000,000 Americans. Few appointments of negroes to office have been made without his consent, and others' political policies have been deferred to him. Now, if Mr. Washington was consulted solely because of his knowledge of men and wide acquaintanceship, there would be less ground of criticism. But whatever the purpose, it has been inevitable that only those negroes should be

put in political control of black men who agree with Mr. Washington's policy of non-resistance, giving up of agitation, and acquiescence in semi-serfdom.

And he properly asserts his right as a free man to protest against the establishment of any political boss of a section of the population, white or black, Christian or Jew, Italian or German.

There is high authority for Dr. Du Bois' position. The late Carl Schurz once warned Mr. Washington that if he heard of the head of Tuskegee going into politics he would know that the waning of Mr. Washington's influence had begun. But the White House has insisted on making use of Dr. Washington's rare knowledge of Southern conditions. It is hard, if not impossible, to resist requests for advice or counsel from this source. Dr. Washington naturally has the deepest interest in seeing that fit colored men only are appointed to office. Could he refuse to answer if Mr. Roosevelt asked him whether John Smith or Thomas Brown would represent his race better in an internal revenue office or as an assistant United States District Attorney? If we are correctly informed, the reason for Dr. Washington's withdrawal from the Liberian Commission to which Mr. Roosevelt appointed him a year ago was Mr. Taft's insistence that he stay within reach. At least, this was current gossip in Washington at the time, and instead, Mr. Washington's secretary went to Liberia. Moreover, Mr. Washington is such a national figure that everyone turns to him for advice on matters relating to the colored people. It is not as if there were three or four men of equal rank in the public estimation.

In other words, we have here the usual conflict between the uncompromising and those who believe in progress one step at a time, with the least friction possible. Time will fight on the negro's side, in any event, and the accumulation of wealth and the possession of land, together with the increased national respect which follows material success — all these will lend power to the negro, when the time comes for the issue of political equality to be joined by all concerned. We are frank to say that if we were of the colored race we should feel that that time had come now; that every moment's failure to protest by those who can against present discriminations means the tightening of chains that must some day be broken if this is to be a republic in more than name. Eternal vigilance is the price of liberty for the negro as well as for the white man, and Dr. Du Bois is merely living up to the highest traditions of American life when he fights for the rights of his own people to a voice in their government. We must say frankly, too, that we wish tomorrow might be the day that will free Dr. Washington from his embarrassing position as political dictator. Then he would begin to win back in some measure the regard of the most intellectual portion of the colored people, of which he is now largely deprived.

New York *Evening Post*, Apr. 1, 1910, 8.

[1] Catherine Breshkovsky (1844–1934), the Russian revolutionist.
[2] Nikolai Vasilievich Chaikovski (1850–1926).

To John Clarence Wright

[Tuskegee, Ala.] April 5, 1910

Mr. Wright: I am very glad to have had the opportunity of reading the essays which you have sent to me. On the whole I think they are good and they show improvement in the method of teaching. The only adverse criticism that I venture is this: There are too many big words in some of them. The sentences are too long and involved. Nothing is stronger in the teaching of English than to teach the students to use the smallest words possible, and the shortest and most simple sentences. Let them use the same kind of language in writing that they do in talking. For example, I find this sentence in one of the compositions: "The pressed steel wheel has arrived and at the psychological moment when the users of timber have begun to realize that the products of forests have been wastefully misused and that they are face to face with an irreparable timber shortage." I know of no student who uses this kind of language in general conversation. There are other sentences running through the compositions that are equally faulty in this direction.

Booker T. Washington

TLpS Con. 597 BTW Papers DLC.

From George Augustus Gates

Nashville, Tenn., Apr. 5, 1910

My dear Dr. Washington: Your letter of April 2nd begins with the words, "fulfilling my promise." Well, my dear friend, you have made me many promises but I am unaware that you had promised to do the magnificent thing which you are now doing.

If you will excuse me for saying it I want to express to you my conviction that I have never met, in my fifty-nine years of life, a man who has shown by every move he makes and word he speaks or writes or dictates a more generous spirit than you are showing in this matter. I think it exceeds anything I have ever known. It is a beautiful lesson to us all in Christian magnanimity.

One other thing I want to say, that is, that in all the times I have heard you speak I never heard you do so with more directness and efficiency than in connection with our inauguration ceremonies. Every word told. I think you used that Gilreath incident superbly. I have written Mr. Gilreath about it.

Now in regard to this communication. Let me write quite fully that you may see my mind and plan. This Living Endowment scheme upon which we have hit seems to be taking with the alumni with fine enthusiasm. Nearly everybody (and they are now about forty, making about $350, that is interest at 5% on about $7000) adds to the letter a hearty and generous approval of the plan. Some of the words are so strong that we can use them in the next circular we put out, to stir up the alumni who have not yet responded.

Now my thought is enlarging itself to take in not only the alumni but friends. Room was left for this in the first circular we sent out for we deliberately stated there that it was for friends of the University as well as for the alumni. That we must enlarge and emphasize. I have been talking with Dean Wright this morning about it and he seems to be agreed on the plan. Now the explicit point to which this letter is addressed in writing you is this; how far and in what way may we best use your name?

For us to send out a letter to the special friends of yours without some such introduction would be a round-about tedious process. Indeed it might seem to these people, your special friends, to be ungenerous, as if by some hook or crook I had obtained the individual names and was attempting to get in ahead of Tuskegee somehow. Now let me suggest that we try to cover this point:

First; I will address each one, stating your position in just the way you want it stated either in my own language or, far better if you are willing to do it, such language as you will dictate and send to me to use.

Second; that will show your extraordinary generosity of spirit toward a sister institution.

Third; we can state the facts;

a   Your interest in Fisk University because Mrs. Washington graduated there.

b   Your son is a student here.

c   Your interest in the higher education of picked spirits among the Negro people, as is abundantly manifested by your taking a place on our Board of Trustees.

Fourth; it will show to our friends in the North that two institutions at least are able to work hand in hand in the utmost harmony and generosity. This point will be of value to the more thoughtful givers. It will particularly appeal to Dr. Buttrick and such men who you know are always talking about institutions getting together and working in harmony.

Fifth; and not least, this way of doing it will, in my opinion and I think you will agree with me, redound quite as much to the advantage of Tuskegee as to the good of Fisk. In other words, I have confidence in the great fine principles on which the universe exists to such an extent that I believe such an attitude of really astounding generosity on your part will return to you in double handfuls.

Sixth; Instead of duplicating your methods shall I not join this general plan with the Living Endowment scheme as we are working it for our own alumni, so that the relation will be just enough different between prospective donors to Fisk on the one hand and the donors to Tuskegee on the other, not to confuse the two in their minds or methods and thus one work against the other?

Now if this plan meets your approval will you kindly write me your thought concerning it at once in order that no time may be lost in pushing the good work along. Of course I should want the privilege of saying in what I send something to this effect: my respect for and loyalty to Tuskegee must not be less than your interest in Fisk. No gift to Fisk must be taken away from anything that goes to Tuskegee.

I am off for Little Rock tonight but expect to return at once at the end of the week to Nashville.

We are all feeling here that we had a great day on the 31st. No small part of its virtue and success is due to you, Dr. Washington, for your insistence and enthusiasm in pushing it and working for it, and the part you took in it. Sincerely yours,

George A. Gates

TLS   Con. 929   BTW Papers   DLC.

To Charles William Anderson

[Tuskegee, Ala.] April 7, 1910

My dear Mr. Anderson: All three of your letters have been received, and I have read them with care.

I am sorry about the estrangement between yourself and Mr. Moore, but in dealing with the matter I must be frank with you. I have no control over Mr. Moore except in a friendly manner. My own view is that it would be wiser for you to talk directly to Mr. Moore; see him and have a good, frank, personal talk, and settle if possible your personal differences.

Wherever there is a matter of principle involved I never hesitate to make a choice between friends, but in this case for the life of me I cannot understand nor have I ever known what the trouble is between you and Mr. Moore. Aside from this, it is a dangerous proceeding for one living at a distance to permit himself to be drawn into local and personal quarrels unless there is some great vital principle involved.

I understand fully all of Mr. Moore's weak points, but at the same time my actions with Mr. Moore must be based upon my experience with him. With all of his weaknesses he had always been loyal and true to me. I would treat you in the same way. No matter what anyone might say about you to the contrary, no one could make me waver in my friendship toward you so long as my dealings with you personally had convinced me that you had been loyal and true to me as you have been.

In all Mr. Moore's conversations with me he has never spoken of you except in terms of respect and praise. As to others to whom he may have spoken I do not know, but except in the case of the unfortunate and regrettable remarks made in my presence by both of you at the Business League dinner at Mr. Thomas'[1] house, I have never heard him speak of you except in terms of the highest respect.

Now, in this case as in others, I must be guided by my own experience with Mr. Moore.

While writing, if you will permit it, I think I ought to make one other suggestion. I am quite sure, and many of your best friends take the same position, that you do not help but rather hurt yourself by permitting yourself to be drawn to such an extent into personal and local bickerings. They consume your time, your strength, and your thought which otherwise could be devoted to higher ends. You occupy a high, exalted position; a higher one and more difficult, and in my opinion honorable one than any member of our race; and it does not help you to yield to the temptation of being drawn into these little personal quarrels and squabbles. I think it would be far better for you to take higher grounds, and act as the leader and the counselor, and the guide of the little fellows rather than to get down in the same plane with them. When ever you do that they are going to treat you as they treat each other.

For example, I could not be frank and friendly with you unless I stated that at the Thomas dinner, the words which you and Mr. Moore used toward each other, and the manner in which you referred to the address which I delivered in Carnegie Hall were very unfortunate, and it pained me seriously the next day when several people from a distance, who were at the dinner and heard the remarks, expressed themselves as being disappointed in you. They, of course, had heard of you as holding a high, government position, and they never dreamed that they would hear such a personal controversy between you and another person, who is beneath you, at a dinner at a private house.

You could easily imagine my embarrassment when I was referred to in the presence of the Executive Committee of the Business League as "slobbering over Major Moton" referred to by yourself.

I beg of you as among your best friends to think over this and consider it seriously; whether it is worth while, or whether anything of real value comes out of it, for you to give so much of your time and your strength to listening to these personal bickerings, and getting down on the plane where you permit yourself to be in the same class with the most ordinary person in New York. If you will take the high grounds which I have stated you will be looked up to by all classes as a guide, as a counselor, and will be for all time the true leader of the people in Greater New York.

A person in Bible thought if not in Bible language cannot get down among the swine without being injured by the swine.

Unless there is some difference resting upon such serious grounds that I do not understand, I believe that in a talk of thirty minutes you and Mr. Moore could settle all of your differences, and that he could help you, and you can help him, and you can rid yourself of all the little fetters, burdens, and troubles that now unnerve and I fear weaken your life.

There is no man in the United States, who in my opinion, could have such a potent and at the same time helpful influence in helping Mr. Moore make his paper strong, and to guide it wisely than yourself, if you enter into sympathetic and friendly relations with him. I believe that he would gladly be guided by your advice and your wishes, and that you could, in a word, govern the policy of the paper in so far as you desire.

These are the words of one of the truest and best friends that I believe you can ever hope to have, and they are spoken with nothing but the purest and most unselfish motives.[2] Yours very truly,

Booker T. Washington

TLpS Con. 49 BTW Papers DLC.

[1] James C. Thomas, born in Harrisburg, Tex., in 1863, worked his way to New York on a steamer and found employment as a hotel steward. After graduation in 1897 from the Philadelphia Training School for Embalmers he founded in the Tenderloin district a prosperous undertaking business, which later became the largest mortuary in Harlem. He also invested in real estate and was the first president of the Afro-American Realty Co. In 1911 he was a co-founder with Bert Williams and the lawyer J. Frank Wheaton of the Equity Congress, a group that met every Sunday at Thomas's establishment to discuss and deal with community issues. The organization succeeded in obtaining a black national guard regiment in New York, financed suits against restrictive covenants, and encouraged patronage of black businesses. Out of the Congress grew the United Civic League for a "civic, industrial, political, and educational campaign" among blacks in New York City, and through

the League's influence Thomas's son was elected an alderman in 1917. (Lewinson, *Black Politics in New York City*, 54–57, 63; Scheiner, *Negro Mecca*, 79; Osofsky, *Harlem*, 96–97.)

[2] Anderson promised to do his best to follow BTW's advice, but reiterated that he could not help being annoyed "when an associate in a good cause is found working hand and glove with the enemies of that cause." (Anderson to BTW, Apr. 9, 1910, Con. 49, BTW Papers, DLC.)

To Henry Cabot Lodge

[New York City] April 10, 1910

Dear Sir: President Taft, whom I saw a few days ago, asked me to speak to you concerning Liberia. I very much hope that you can see your way clear to favor some of the suggestions which Secretary Knox has put before the Foreign Affairs Committee of the Senate in regard to Liberia. If something is not done to help Liberia, it will be in a worse condition than it was before the American Commission visited that country. I have gone over the matter pretty fully with both the President and the Secretary of State, and they are deeply interested. The colored people in every part of this country are also deeply interested in saving and helping Liberia.

I called to see you at your residence, but you were not in. I shall be glad to talk to you further regarding the matter sometime when I am passing through Washington if it will be convenient to you. Yours truly,

[Booker T. Washington]

TLc   Con. 411   BTW Papers   DLC.

To James Jenkins Dossen

New York City. April 10, 1910

My dear Vice President Dossen: I have just been to Washington where I had an interview with President Taft and also with Secretary Knox on the subject of Liberia. Both are deeply interested. A few night ago Secretary Knox had the whole Foreign Affairs Committee at his house at dinner where the Liberian situation was discussed fully. Later he went before the Foreign Affairs Committee of the Senate. In both cases he made a strong appeal for Liberia. Yesterday when in Washington, I saw both President Taft and Secretary Knox, and they told me about their plans for helping Liberia, and asked me to keep in close touch with them and to keep them reminded about the importance of doing something during the present session of Congress. I do not care to go into details as to methods, but am sure if the plans of the President and Secretary can be matured that much good will result.

I hope you are keeping informed as to conditions and what can be done on this side. Two points I urged upon the Secretary and the President. One was that the United States stand as the next friend to Liberia. The second was that the United States lend its assistance to the matter of straightening out financial affairs. To both of these points both the Secretary and the President gave their unmodified approval, but of course both of them are dependent upon the action of the Senate Committee on Foreign Affairs. Yours very truly,

[Booker T. Washington]

TLc   Con. 404   BTW Papers   DLC.

To George Augustus Gates

Easton, Pa. April 12th, 1910

My dear Dr. Gates: I had to leave Tuskegee very soon after receiving your letter of April 5th, hence the delay in replying to it. I thank you for your kind and generous words. I am always glad that you feel that what I said at the inauguration accomplished some good.

If I understand your letter fully I would state that I do not think it well to confuse or mix the two plans, that is, I think it best to appeal to the alumni and their special friends to help in the matter of the living endowment, but I do not think it wise to make such an appeal to the people whose names I sent you. I find that most people in the North who are interested in Tuskegee rather shrink from doing anything that seems to bind them beyond the making of an annual donation, that is, they do not feel like being committed beyond a period of twelve months. I think the idea of the living endowment has an element in it that will appeal to the alumni and their friends in the South especially. Of course an appeal for this endowment would interest certain kinds of people in the North who might be your personal friends, but I do not think it would pay to make such an appeal general.

Now in regard to sending with the appeals to Northern people any words from me, I would state that I think a general statement expressing my faith in and interest in Fisk University that might be printed or sent in any form that you please would answer every purpose. I do not think it well to do anything that would give the impression that the names have been gotten from me. Any college president has the right, and most of them practice it, to gather names in any way that he can; this it seems to me is legitimate business, and I do not see why the president of Fisk should not do as others are doing.

Enclosed I send you a statement which you can use in any form you think wise. If it does not answer your purpose let me know and I will modify it.

I have refrained in this statement from saying anything about my son for two reasons. First, because mentioning both Mrs. Washington and my son may make it appear that I am a special pleader for Fisk and this would weaken my statement. Second, I do not think that such a statement in case he were to get hold of it, and he most likely would, would help the boy. I want Booker to feel that he has to go through Fisk on his merits and not because I am his father or especially interested in Fisk.

I shall be glad to hear from you fully and freely as to your progress and as to your plans.

I fear this statement is too long. If you agree with me, cross out anything you see fit, and if it does not suit you, do not hesitate to send it back and I will redictate it. Yours very truly,

[Booker T. Washington]

[*Enclosure*]
To the Friends and Well Wishers of Fisk University:

This is to state that I have recently accepted a position on the trustee board of Fisk University located in Nashville, Tenn. I have accepted this position because I believe in the work that Fisk University is doing for the Negro race. I have frequently visited the institution and know something of its fine spirit and of the far-reaching results of its work for the Negro race. Mrs. Washington is a graduate of Fisk University, and for this reason and others, both of us feel that we owe more to Fisk University than we can ever repay.

During a long period of years Fisk has gone on quietly rendering fine service in the training of some of the best men and women to be found anywhere in the South at work for our race.

Fisk University has now reached the point, however, where it must have larger support. Every time I visit the institution I am surprised to note how such fine work can be done on such slender income. Much is needed in the way of strengthening the physical plant, and much is needed to enable the trustees to meet the annual current expenses. I am exceedingly anxious just now that the friends of Fisk University and Negro education should encourage the new president Dr. George A. Gates, by generous and immediate financial support.

TLc and Enclosure   Con. 906   BTW Papers   DLC.

From Helen Van Wyck Lockman

Huntington [N.Y.] Apr. 14/10

My dear Dr. Washington   If you wish me to arrange for the telephone for you I shall be very glad to do so.

The rate is $69.00 for the year or season. I am going to try to get it for less if possible. However if you do not object I should like to use the difference for *"grease."* As you know my enemies have done every thing to shatter the strength of my telephone connection as they think it will make my remote place worthless. My sister is going to have one so that it will make the Telephone Co. more anxious to stand by us. I feel that we are quite safe for the present as they have not been successful in buying the piece over which I have a temporary right of way.

The country is very beautiful now, and we are quite busy getting things in order for the summer. Kindly return cheque if you wish me to arrange. Cordially yours

Helen Van Wyck Lockman

ALS Con. 408 BTW Papers DLC.

To James Jenkins Dossen

[New York City] April 19, 1910

My dear Vice President Dossen: Enclosed I send you a copy of a letter which I have just received from Senator Lodge.[1] Of course this must be treated in a very confidential way. Please tear it up after you have read it. I do not [want] to give encouragement to this plan without your approval. What about it?

I had a long conference with both the President and the Secretary of State last week. Both are doing all they can to push forward Liberian interests. Yours very truly,

[Booker T. Washington]

TLc Con. 404 BTW Papers DLC.

1 Lodge stated that he would be glad to discuss Liberia with BTW. "The proper way," Lodge wrote, "it seems to me, for the United States to act is to use our good offices with France and England, and Germany also, to bring about an arrangement which shall settle the boundaries, arrange for their debt and give them proper persons to train their forces." (Lodge to BTW, Apr. 12, 1910, copy enclosed in BTW to Taft, Apr. 21, 1910, William Howard Taft Papers, DLC.)

To Daniel Merriman[1]

Hotel Manhattan, New York. April 25, 1910

Personal

My dear Dr. Merriman: I meant several days ago to have sent you a line to thank you for your article which appeared in the Springfield Republican. Mr. Bowles,[2] the editor, very kindly told me confidentially who wrote it. This article expresses the real condition.

I do not know why it is that Dr. Du Bois and Atlanta University take the attitude that they do. I never abuse Dr. Du Bois, never refer to him in public except in some complimentary manner. Wherever I speak, in nine cases out of ten I refer in a complimentary way to Atlanta University. In my recent book, "The Story of the Negro," I refer many times to Dr. Du Bois.

The most unusual and indelicate part of the whole proceedings it seems to me is that a representative of one institution should go before the public and criticise a sister institution, but notwithstanding any attitude that Dr. Du Bois may pursue in the future, and no matter what he may say or do, I shall not be taken off my feet. I will not grow bitter, but will go on with my work hoping at some time that he and Atlanta University may see the better way of doing things.

I shall hope to talk the whole matter over with you and at length sometime when I see you.

I suppose you know that Dr. Du Bois and two of his friends publish a monthly magazine. This publication is almost filled every month with either insinuations or bitter criticisms either against Tuskegee Institute or against myself. What his object is for all this I cannot understand. Certainly no good purpose so far [as] I can see is being accomplished. Yours very truly,

[Booker T. Washington]

TLc Con. 409 BTW Papers DLC.

[1] Daniel Merriman (1838–1912), a Congregational clergyman and writer, was minister of the Central Church of Worcester, Mass., from 1878 to 1901, and emeritus pastor from 1901 to 1912, residing in Boston.

[2] Samuel Bowles IV (1851–1915), editor of the Springfield (Mass.) *Republican* from 1875 until his death. His newspaper was an early supporter of Tuskegee Institute, and his daughter Ruth married William H. Baldwin, Jr., who became chairman of the Tuskegee board of trustees.

To Robert Heberton Terrell

New York City. April 27, 1910

Personal and Confidential

Dear Judge Terrell: I suppose you have seen the printed program of the meeting to be held here sometime in May under the auspices of the opposition crowd.[1]

Not a few of your friends here are nonplussed as to why Mrs. Terrell's name appears among the members of the executive committee and as one of the speakers on the program. This kind of thing is really embarrassing. I think it but just to your friends to let us know where you are at. This organization, as was true last year, is likely to engage in wholesale abuse of the President of the United States as well as other friends of ours. Whenever your name comes up for confirmation, your friends unhesitatingly go to the front. To have Mrs. Terrell's name appear on a program where the opposition is in charge naturally makes it harder for your friends to help you when the time comes, but makes it embarrassing from every point of view. Of course I am not seeking to control anybody's action, but I simply want to know where we stand. You can easily see that for your friends to be called upon to go to the White House or to see the Attorney General in your behalf one day and the next day a tirade appears abusing the President at a meeting where Mrs. Terrell is a member of the executive committee and one of the principal speakers becomes really embarrassing for us. Yours truly,

[Booker T. Washington]

TLc Con. 913 BTW Papers DLC.

[1] The second annual meeting of the National Negro Committee (NAACP), May 12–14, 1910.

To Ray Stannard Baker

[Tuskegee, Ala.] May 3, 1910

Personal

Dear Mr. Baker: Replying to yours of April 29th I would state that the sentence quoted in your letter is true so far as local requirements are concerned. As you already suggest, there are several counties in the South where they make it a habit not to register colored people, but I am glad to say that these counties so far as Alabama is concerned are the exception rather than the rule.

Sometime, perhaps, you might bring out the point that it is largely the fault of colored people themselves that they do not vote. In most cases where there is some foresight to be exercised or some money to be paid in the form of taxes in advance, the colored people cut themselves off. You would be surprised, for example, in a state like Georgia where there has been no law prohibiting the colored people from voting until recently, to see how few colored people vote. I think you will find, for example, that Dr. Du Bois of Atlanta, who tries to lead in the matter of agitation in the matter of the franchise, has never voted in Atlanta or attempted to register, and I do not believe he votes anywhere in America. His case illustrates many others. Here at Tuskegee for example, there is practically no trouble in any colored man registering and voting. Notwithstanding this is true, I find it the most difficult task to get our teachers, especially those who are graduates of colleges, to pay their taxes and vote. If you were to go into a city like Atlanta and make an individual canvass, you would be surprised at the large number of educated colored people who have never attempted to register or vote. Yours very truly,

Booker T. Washington

TLpS   Con. 902   BTW Papers   DLC.

From James Jenkins Dossen

Harper, Cape Palmas, [Liberia] May 3rd, 1910

My Dear Doctor. Since writing a week ago things have assumed a more satisfactory aspect with regard to the suppression of the native revolts. At Grand Bassa where a pretty formidable rising among the Kroos was going on, our forces have captured a number of their villages and have matters fairly well in hand. At Cape Palmas, where the rising is more pronounced and wide-spread, we have had to delay active operations pending the arrival of arms and ammunition, which as I wrote in my last will be here about the 5th inst. After their arrival, and if reinforcements are hurried forward, we shall at once start active operations. The Greboes are armed with the most modern rifles; such as the "Mauser," the "1888 Carbines," the "Lee Mitford" the Martini Henry etc. and are using the "Dum dum" and steel bullets. It is a disgrace to the civilization and honesty of Europe that they should have armed our natives with such arms in the face of the Brussels Act which Europe inaugurated as a means of disarming the native African and thereby destroying his amenities for warfare. But it is but another demonstration of the unjustness of the *role* pursued by the colonies of Europe in West Africa toward Liberia. What is positively a violation of that very solemn international Compact and is made the subject of stringent protest when attempted to be practiced in their spheres, is carried out with impunity when it comes to Liberia. Our natives go to the coast to English, French, and German colonies for service; it is at these points they are supplied with rifles and ammunition which they oftener than not, succeed in smuggling into the country. Quite recently two rifles were seized by the Customs authorities at Harper bearing the stamp of the Southern Nigerian (British) government. Just how it was possible for rifles of the Nigerian force to be gotten out of the service without the knowledge of some of the officials is a puzzle to us.

I am inclosing for your perusal and information a copy of the minutes of the Council held in 1876, when Commander Semmes of the Alaska gave his *"Moral Support"* to the Government of Liberia in the settlement of the rebellion of the Greboes. There is also a letter there from Commander Schley. It is most painful to me that Commander Fletcher of the Birmingham, instead of pursuing the course followed on that occasion (which might well be taken as a precedent) should desire to play the *role* of an *arbiter* and to have proposed to convene a council in which the disloyal faction of our uncivilized natives should be as fully represented and have the same status as the established government; (*vide* his proposal for an Arbitration Commission April 17th) and, in which the Government would have been powerless to inflict such punishment as in its opinion would be exemplary and proper. It should cause no wonder that we did not agree to such a course; and, our reasons for not doing so, were set forth in a dispatch to the Commander with all the clearness and logic, and at the same time, in such a friendly and respectful manner which to us appeared necessary. The Commander, however, appears to have become displeased because his proposals were not acceptable, and from that time forward has shown a stronger desire to afford support to the insurgents than to the Government of Liberia. In support of this view I might state that in the face of our gunboat lying off their towns to prevent intercourse with vessels in port which had been effectually enforced since February, the insurgents, relying upon the support which they now feel they have by the presence of the Birmingham, are repeatedly going on board of her, and, their canoes have been discovered returning to the shore heavily loaded with what appeared, at a distance, to have been provisions. The Commander has been several times to their towns and has sought information from them and it seems given credence to all they have told them; while on the other hand he has studiously avoided the Liberians and made no effort, even in a private way, to acquaint himself with our side of the question and with real conditions. It is most natural then that our people should feel the strongest remonstrance against such conduct on the part of a representative of the American nation, with whom, at least in these premises, there exists most positive and friendly compact. As I have already stated, it is very painful to me that an officer of the make-up of Commander Fletcher should have been intrusted with the responsible task of inaugurating this new policy of Naval support for my country, a policy which I have long advocated and in which I feel the deepest solicitude. But in this regard you have perhaps been as zealous as myself, and, it is chiefly with the view that no erroneous impression which may have been imparted through the reports of the Commander be permitted to find lodgement on the minds of the Naval department that I am writing you so fully and in detail with the hope that you will lose no time in calling on the officials of that department and give them such light on the subject as I have tried in this letter to supply you with.

Grandcess and Sassatown — points on the Kroo coast that were giving trouble at the time the American Commission was here are now peaceful and loyal. I am not sure that I wrote you before how, after about 18 months hard effort, I finally succeeded in getting

the Sassatown Kroos to submit to our laws and we have now established a port there.

The present rebellion of the Cape Palmas Greboes must be put
down with a firm hand. The Grebo tribe have had more consideration, civil or otherwise, than any of our tribes, and yet they are
the most rebellious. Previous revolts have been settled after much
loss of means and lives, without inflicting any adequate punishment. I believe it is now felt by all that that policy has been productive of no good but that on the contrary our desire to conciliate
has been misconstrued into weakness. It is the purpose of Government at this time to inflict such punishment as will not only un-
deceive that tribe but teach a good lesson to other tribes.

We are anxiously waiting to get some tidings from the States on
financial matters. If we are to be saved from bankruptcy and consequently denationalism the recommendations of the American
Commission should be speedily and effectually executed. After
raising the hopes and expectations of our people to look forward
to some help from that quarter I am afraid to allow the whole thing
to come to naught would throw our people in a state of despond
from which they may not easily recover.

I hope to hear from you soon that matters have been practically
settled and in a favorable way.

By the way! will you please let me know how far you have been
able to give shape to my suggestion last year for the establishment
of an Industrial School (or a second Tuskegee in Liberia). I have
read something about such a movement in the press but have not
had a hearing from you about it recently.

Remember me tenderly to Mrs. Washington and to my other
Tuskegee friends especially Mr. Scott whom I shall write shortly.

Wishing you every success. Yours Sincerely,

James J Dossen

P.S. I have recently seen an "ads." of your new book; I congratulate
you on this further effort in behalf of your race every where. My
library will be incomplete without a set. I send under another
cover some reports. The mining report is exceedingly interesting.
Before I left Monrovia last month the Liberia Development Company, a British concern, were working both gold and diamonds on

the St. Paul. Please see that the mining report reach quarters that it will interest and accomplish the greatest good. Sincerely Yours:

James J Dossen

TLS Con. 404 BTW Papers DLC. On stationery of the "Office of Special Commissioners to settle Grebo Rising in Maryland County."

An Invitation to a Picnic

[Tuskegee, Ala., ca. May 4, 1910]

Principal Booker T. Washington
cordially invites you to attend an
Old-Fashioned Fishing Picnic
and "Shore Dinner"

Friday, May 6, 1910

On the Banks of the Uphapee
(Near Chehaw, Ala.)

Vehicles to convey the party
    will leave Institute grounds
    at 1 o'clock p.m. from
    Horse Barn.

PD Con. 599 BTW Papers DLC. Docketing indicates that Ernest T. Attwell sent a sample copy to BTW on May 4.

To William Howard Taft

Tuskegee Institute, Alabama   May 6, 1910

My dear Mr. President: I do not know what you may have in mind with reference to promotion of Mr. William H. Lewis, of Boston. I have been informed that there is a strong possibility of a vacancy in the office of the Surveyor of the Port of Boston by reason of the nomination of Jeremiah J. McCarthy, the present incumbent, to be Fire Commissioner of the city of Boston. I have thought it would do no harm to call that fact to your attention.

With the feeling that you still strongly desire to do something for him, I am prompted to call your attention to the situation at present.[1] Yours very truly,

Booker T. Washington

TLS   William Howard Taft Papers   DLC.

[1] Taft forwarded BTW's letter to the two Massachusetts senators with a favorable recommendation. (Taft to William Murray Crane, May 9, 1910, William Howard Taft Papers, DLC.)

From Oswald Garrison Villard

New York   May 11, 1910

Dear Mr. Washington: I am very much gratified and honored by your invitation to speak before the National Negro Business League on August 17th, 18th and 19th. Are you really sure, however, that you want me? I am becoming more radical, you know, as time goes on, and my natural instinct would be, if I were speaking of the Business League and its aims, to call attention to the higher and more important things before the colored man, and to beg him not to let slip the more precious privileges by concentrating his attention entirely on the important matter of making himself a solid and substantial citizen.

With kind regards, Sincerely yours,

Oswald Garrison Villard

TLS   Con. 411   BTW Papers   DLC.

Extracts from Helen M. Chesnutt[1]
to Charles Waddell Chesnutt and Family

[Tuskegee, Ala.] May 15, 1910

This is about the only time I shall have to write today, so I have gotten up early to do it. Have I written anything about social affairs since last Sunday?

There is always a great deal going on here, and one can keep very much occupied, but Mrs. Washington told people when I came that I was down here for my health, and besides the usual affairs which have almost used me up, people haven't given many extra things.

The big annual military hop took place last night in the dining hall. The school is a military school and the student officers are permitted to have this ball once a year. All the teachers attend and it is the greatest social event of the year. The dining hall is huge — large enough to seat 1600 students, so you see that we were not crowded.

Mrs. Lettie Nolan Calloway is also visiting Mrs. Washington and we three went over about half-past eight. . . .

I danced a great deal and enjoyed myself immensely, although at first, I felt terribly stiff. Not being accustomed to much social life, I found it rather hard to be hurled into the midst of a real ball. During a dance one of the men said to me, "Miss Chesnutt, are you having the kind of visit that you enjoy? We understand that you are down here to rest and that you want a very quiet time, so we haven't had as lively a time as we otherwise would have given you."

I responded, "A quiet time! If you call this kind of visit quiet, I should certainly hate to be involved in a lively one. I am nearly dead now."

He thought I was joking, but I told him, though Tuskegee might seem tame to him, it was absolutely hilarious to me.

Even dull as Cleveland is, I have actually been homesick this week. It is quite cold here, and I think that has affected me. . . .

I must tell you about seeing Halley's comet. Thursday night I determined to see it. I shall have to make a little introduction first. The Washington home is guarded every night from five o'clock until five in the morning. They don't bother to lock doors and windows, but have guards who patrol the grounds and thus protect the place. I sleep on the first floor, windows up, and often the guard stalks by my window in the middle of the night.

Well, Thursday night I awoke at 2:30. Dead silence and inky blackness. I got up and put on some clothes and went to the parlor windows to see the comet. No comet visible. Then I opened the front door and tiptoed out, way out to the end of the porch to see what could be seen. I was scared to death all this time. Just as I got to the port-cochère, a great big guard loomed up in front of me. Well, he was scared and so was I. However, he told me that the comet wasn't visible yet, but that when it appeared, he would call me. I walked him around to the other porch and showed him my windows and at 3:30 he appeared with a lantern and called me and we went way down to the end of the grounds where it could be seen beautifully. It certainly was an awe-inspiring experience to see it spreading out all over the sky. . . .

I must stop now and begin to get dressed. We have some distinguished guests for breakfast this morning, and I am going to get ready for church before breakfast. Love to all of you.

Helen M. Chesnutt, *Charles Waddell Chesnutt: Pioneer of the Color Line* (Chapel Hill: University of North Carolina Press, 1952), 236–37.

1 A daughter of Charles Waddell Chesnutt.

Emmett Jay Scott to Hightower T. Kealing

New York. May 16th, 1910

Personal

Dear Mr. Kealing: I happen to be in New York, but shall be returning home in the next day or two.

Your friends and the Niagara Movement are trying to resuscitate that moribund organization by the formation of a new organization to be called the National Negro Conference which is now holding a meeting here in New York City. Your name I learn, has been proposed as a member of the Executive Committee. I hope I may have the privilege of talking to you before you accept of this proffered place.

With kindest regards to Mrs. Kealing and the children, I am, Sincerely yours,

[Emmett J. Scott]

TLc Con. 407 BTW Papers DLC.

To William Howard Taft

Tuskegee Institute, Alabama   May 21, 1910

My dear Mr. President: Let me thank you for commuting the sentence of Lieut. David J. Gilmer.[1] This will be pleasant news to his friends and relatives.

I am also taking the liberty of making your action known to the colored people through the colored newspapers. Yours truly,

Booker T. Washington

TLS   William Howard Taft Papers   DLC.

[1] David Jarvis Gilmer (b. 1872) was court-martialed in the Philippines in January 1910 for conduct unbecoming an officer. Gilmer was charged with lying about his abilities while on practice marches. He was sentenced to be dismissed from the service, but Brigadier General Tasker Howard Bliss, assistant to the chief of staff in the Philippines, recommended a lighter sentence of reduction of twenty-five files in rank. President Taft further lightened the penalty to reduction of fifteen files in rank. After the court-martial Gilmer took the examination for promotion from lieutenant to captain for the third time. He failed the examination and was honorably discharged, the usual army procedure. Gilmer tried to be reinstated on the ground that he was a victim of racial discrimination and personal prejudice, charging that his commanding officer hated him and had persecuted him while on maneuvers. A 1912 investigation failed to turn up important new witnesses, and the reinstatement effort failed.

To George Augustus Gates

[Tuskegee, Ala.] May 21, 1910

Dear Dr. Gates: Replying to that portion of your letter which refers to your inaugural address, I would state that I do not agree with your general idea as employed in this passage regarding industrial education. However, you in this respect are not different from a majority of the educators who have not had direct experience in industrial education. Most people who have not had such experience fail entirely to see and recognize the purely educational value of hand training. Unless this element is recognized there is no basis for argument. As I have stated, in this matter you are not different from the majority of educators.

Much, too, in education, depends upon the ends sought. This is an element that ought always to be recognized. For example, while you say in effect that it requires a certain number of years for a graduate of Hampton or Tuskegee to prepare to enter Fisk or complete the course at Fisk, one might reply that it would require at least two or three years for a graduate of Annapolis to complete the course at West Point. It would require two or three years for a graduate of West Point to complete the course at Annapolis. It would require certainly several years of study for a graduate of the Institute of Technology in Boston to complete the course at Harvard and vice versa. But because of the fact that several years would be required in the case of an Annapolis graduate to complete the course at West Point no one would, I think, argue that the Annapolis man has not received any education. I hope you see my point. I shall try to make it plainer when I see you. Yours very truly,

Booker T. Washington

TLpS Con. 51 BTW Papers DLC.

To Ray Stannard Baker

[Tuskegee, Ala.] May 24, 1910

My dear Mr. Baker: Your letter of May 13th[1] has been received. I note what you say regarding the effect of your address on the Negro Conference. I am not surprised at the kind of reception that it was given. I happen to know the individuals who compose this conference. Nothing that has real sense in it would be received with any degree of enthusiasm. What they want is nonsense.

I would have some sympathy with this organization if I did not know that a majority, not all, of the white men who are leading in the matter are not sincere, and that a majority of the colored people in it are not sincere. I know the individuals. I have tried to work with them. I have found them in most cases either without sincerity or without stability. For the most part the white people who are in this organization are deceived as to the character of the colored people in it. There are few colored men in this organization of any real standing in their own communities.

And then it is sinful in the highest degree for any set of white men to lend their influence of deceiving the colored people into the idea that they can get what they ought to have in the way of right treatment by merely making demands, passing resolutions and cursing somebody. No individual in America realizes more keenly than I do the injustices put upon our race, but at the same time I realize fully that we cannot change conditions by merely demanding that they should be changed.

Of course this organization with a certain element of our people holds out a great temptation. If a child is sick and you offer it candy in one hand and castor oil in the other, the child is more likely to ask for the candy than the castor oil, though the one may result in making him more sick and the other in curing his body; but the masses of the colored people are not deceived and are making real progress.

I shall send in the Bert Williams[2] article soon. Yours very truly,

Booker T. Washington

TLpS Con. 402 BTW Papers DLC.

[1] Baker had written after attending the annual NAACP conference: "I delivered my address last night at the Negro Conference here, and I am afraid it did not meet with the approval of most of the radicals there. The more I see of this whole matter, the more I feel sure that you are on the right track—that it is only by patient development and growth that the evils can be met." (May 13, 1910, Con. 402, BTW Papers, DLC.)

[2] Egbert Austin Williams (1875?–1922) was the partner of George Walker in vaudeville (1895–1903) and musical comedy (1903–9). For a number of years beginning in 1909 he was the leading comedian in the Ziegfeld Follies. See An Article in the *American Magazine*, September 1910, below.

Hightower T. Kealing to Emmett Jay Scott

Ladonia, Texas, May 27 1910

Dear Mr. Scott: Yours from N.Y. reached me here. I am glad to be put in guard, otherwise I might not have suspected the Trojan horse. I have so far had no intimation of the intention of the gentlemen to add my name to the Ex. Com. of the new organization. I showed your letter to Mr Smith, to which I was sure you would not object.

I wish I could see you for a general talk, but unfortunately before you reach Texas for June 19th, I shall be out of the State.

You may rest assured, however, that I shall not be led into any movement animated by the spirit of bitterness and complaint. Sincerely,

H. T. Kealing

ALS Con. 407 BTW Papers DLC.

To Oswald Garrison Villard

Tuskegee Institute, Alabama   May 30, 1910

Dear Mr. Villard: I am sorry not to have had time to reply to yours of May 20th earlier, but I have been away from home a good part of the time since your letter was received.

When I wrote you inviting you to deliver an address before the National Negro Business League on August 17th, 18th or 19th, I meant exactly what I said, and shall be very glad to have you deliver an address, and I am sure the members of our League will listen with satisfaction to anything you may say. Of course we should be glad to have you, in so far as it would answer your purpose, throw the drift of your remarks in keeping with the object and character of the meeting. I think this is the usual course, but if you do not care to do this, we shall be very glad to have you say anything that is in your heart to say. We should like to hear you not only for your own sake, but for the sake of your grandfather whose memory none of us wants to let fade, no matter how much we may differ on minor questions. Yours very truly,

Booker T. Washington

TLS Oswald Garrison Villard Papers MH. A press copy is in Con. 411, BTW Papers, DLC; an earlier draft, dated May 24, 1910, is in BTW Papers, ATT.

To Ernest Lyon

[Tuskegee, Ala.] June 11, 1910

Confidential:

My dear Mr. Minister: Of course, you are advised by now of Dr. W. D. Crum's appointment and confirmation as Minister Resident to Liberia.

You have also received my letter, advising as to the fact that a change was being contemplated.

All that could be done in the way of staying your removal was done, but when the Department got to the place where it would simply state that it could not ignore some of the charges that had been brought against you, I was put in the position of not being able to do anything, especially, when I could not learn what the charges were.

I do not know how soon Dr. Crum will be arranging to take the place, but I felt that I should let you know that I kept in touch with the situation, and that I did not hesitate to do what I could.

When you return to America, I shall want to see and talk with you. Yours truly

Booker T. Washington

P.S. I enclose herewith copy of the telegram which came to me from the President in response to one which I sent to him regarding the matter of the proposed change.

B.T.W.

TLpS Con. 411 BTW Papers DLC.

To Charles William Anderson

[Tuskegee, Ala.] June 13, 1910

Confidential.

My dear Mr. Anderson: Yours of June 9th has been received. Your remark regarding the Atlanta man I am sorry to say is only too correct. The whole thing is to be kept quiet for the present. Just what our friend means by such procedure I cannot understand.

Vernon, it is understood, is to remain for the present.

After I saw that they were determined to remove Lyon I asked the President to put Crum in the place, and he complied with my request. Of course, Crum is far from an ideal man, but as things are going I am quite sure they would have put a worse man than he is in the place, and besides it is known, however, that Crum is our friend.

The card has been received, and I am most grateful to you for it. I am planning to reach New York Friday, and shall see you as soon thereafter as possible.

Enclosed I send copy of a telegram which I have received from our friend in Washington relating to the Lyon case. Yours very truly,

B.T.W.

TLpI Con. 49 BTW Papers DLC.

To William Demosthenes Crum

[Tuskegee, Ala.] June 13, 1910

(Personal and Confidential).

My dear Dr. Crum: When you go to Monrovia, I very much hope that you will bear in mind that Bishop I. B. Scott, whom you will find there, is one of our warmest and best friends. He has been of the greatest service to us here, and to your friends and our friends.

There are certain cliques in Monrovia that will likely try to alienate you from the Bishop. But I have known him for twenty years, and during all this time he has proven a staunch, sincere friend, that you can depend on in season and out of season. Yours truly,

Booker T. Washington

TLpS Con. 904 BTW Papers DLC.

From John Andrew Kenney

Tuskegee Institute, Ala. June 13, 1910

Mr. B. T. Washington: We graduated *four* nurses this year and *four* last year, and *one* year before last. Recognizing the great demand for nurses and the fact that we have such a large school here, this is not a third of what we should do. We should graduate a class of ten or fifteen each year. Tuskegee has the opportunity of being a center for nurse training, medical and surgical treatment for a large district in the Southland. I know of no other place south of Washington, with the possible exception of Nashville, which has such an opportunity. We should grasp this opportunity *NOW*. Of course we can do much with what we have here. I think you will agree that we have done much.

Compare our condition now, with what it was eight years ago. At that time it was akin to an insult with most of our families and teachers to suggest that they go to the Hospital for treatment. Now there is scarcely a teacher or a member of a family who will not enter the Hospital with pleasure, if their conditions demand it. *Then* people were afraid to visit our Hospital. *Now* we are delighted daily by visitors.

Up to that time the largest operation done in our operating room, was the removal of the remains of a girl's hand crushed in the Laundry. Since that time we have done 201 operations with 7 deaths; and, in the past twenty-two months ——[1] operations without a single death. Ten days ago we removed a tumor from a patient's neck, grown from the wind pipe and deeper structures, lifting it from beside the great blood vessels of the neck; the patient talking and even laughing all through the operation — about two hours. Yesterday the patient went to Church, nearly well.

Recently one boy brained another with a piece of 2 x 4 scantling. His skull was broken in two places, both on the side of the head and at the base. The victim was unconscious for hours. Looked as though he would die, and give us the embarrassment before the world, of one of our students having killed another; and would have done so had we not taken a button of bone from his skull in another place and lifted the several fragments of bone from the brain.

I think it right that I mention these things to you that you may know that we are developing this work, and that it is compelled to add to the already great fame of Tuskegee.

At this writing we have three convalescing operative patients; one from Kowaliga Alabama; one from Savannah, Georgia, and one from Denmark, S.C. All paying the stipulated charges. We can do more. We should do more. We must do more, even with what we have. But nothing would place our work on a firmer basis, give us a greater incentive, and be a greater drawing card for patients and a high class of nurses than a thoroughly modern, and perfectly equipped, up-to-date, brick, Hospital.

In our reports and publications the present Hospital building does not do us any credit at all. I have tried to show you that we are making an effort to be up-to-date in our work, but our building is just eight years behind the school.

I have an idea that you have embarrassment in presenting the cause of a new Hospital, but this should not stand in the way. The present building was designed for a school and community with 1,000 or 1,200 people, with the old Torbert Cottage, batallion ground cabins, the old pavillion, Porter Hall, Wayside Inn, Annex, Willow Cottage, and other little wooden structures; kerosine oil lamps, open wells, stove & fire place heating, which have now given way to those imposing, gigantic, hard brick and concrete structures, with 2,200 or 2,300 people, Bank and Post Office, Artesian System, electricity and steam heat; surely it is time that the Hospital and Nurse Training Department should be accorded its due dignified position.

What should be done with the present building? One of our real needs in [this] connection is a nurses home. The present building will fit in there nicely. I assure you I appreciate what you have done for us, and this gives me the spirit to urge upon you our further needs. I suggest a two story building with basement and to cost, roughly speaking, not less than $50,000.00, with its equipment. Very truly yours,

J. A. Kenney

TLS Con. 601 BTW Papers DLC.

1 Kenney wrote BTW later the same day that he had failed to insert the figure 101 as the number of operations without a death in the past twenty-two months. (Con. 601, BTW Papers, DLC.)

From Wallace Buttrick

New York June 18, 1910

Dear Dr. Washington: Your letter of June 15 was received this morning. Some time ago, I think on your suggestion, I began inquiries regarding public high schools for negroes in the Southern States. Many facts have been gathered and one of these days we shall be in position to know something about it.

Our Board does not employ and control any field agents. The professors of secondary education in the Southern States are not under our control or direction. All of our work is done through existing institutions. I feel confident that this policy will not be changed. If the Board should decide to do something to promote high schools among the colored people the question would arise as to the particular institution of higher learning that could undertake the supervision of such work. The state universities exercise such supervision in the case of high schools for the white people. I will be glad to talk this over with you when next we meet. Cordially yours,

Wallace Buttrick

TLS Con. 49 BTW Papers DLC.

To Emmett Jay Scott

New York. June 20, 1910

Dear Mr. Scott: Enclosed I send you a clipping from the New York Sun which shows that Secretary Knox in his recent address before the University of Pennsylvania referred at length to Liberia and said in effect that the State Department had decided to carry out practically all the recommendations made by the Commission.[1] This certainly is high praise and ought to cause each member of the Commission to feel greatly satisfied. Yours very truly,

Booker T. Washington

TLS Con. 489 BTW Papers DLC.

1 In his commencement address at the University of Pennsylvania, a review of current U.S. foreign policy, Knox said that "the Department of State is now engaged in working out the details of a plan in harmony with the commission's recommendations which will give Liberia a new start on the path to national stability and individual progress, so that she may be in a position to accomplish the purpose of her original American founders." (New York *Sun*, June 16, 1910, 5.)

From Robert Heberton Terrell

Washington, D.C. June 20, 1910

My dear Doctor Washington, In reply to your telegram I beg to say that we are on the alert for the bill of which you spoke. I saw Tyler and Cobb yesterday and today about the matter and we shall take it up as soon as it passes the House. I hope that it will pass both bodies this session. Tyler has just told me that he wrote to the Congressman in charge of the bill urging its immediate passage.

My own matter went through the Executive Committee of the Board of Trustees of Howard University after a hard fight against me by Grimke, Waring and the anti-Booker Washington element. Grimke and Waring, who dislike me personally, made a lot of charges against me which it was impossible for them to substantiate and which were false, and Dr. Sinclair, Prof. Richards, Prof. Tunnell[1] and Prof. Hart asserted that Dr. Thirkield was trying to interfere with the radicalism of the law school by appointing a man like myself, representing what they chose to call the B. W. element. There again they brought out the bank case in a new phase. Doctor Francis championed my cause and made a splendid fight for me. Moorland and Purvis supported me.

I seem to be a shining mark for these folks around Washington. I should think they would let me alone for awhile. They are bent on making me fight for everything I get.

With best wishes, I am, Yours Sincerely,

Robert H Terrell

ALS Con. 408 BTW Papers DLC.

1 William Victor Tunnell was a member of the Howard University faculty (1891–1928) and a trustee of the institution.

From Ray Stannard Baker

East Lansing Mich   June 20 1910

Dear Mr. Washington: I had your letter of the 24th some time ago; and I have waited to answer it until I could enclose a copy of my Cooper Union address. I wish you would read it, and make any suggestions or criticisms, for I intend to have it published where it will reach as many thinking people as possible. Particularly, on page 8, I make a rather sweeping generalization as to the legal aspect of Negro Suffrage. Am I right in that? I think possibly my view of the subject is over-optimistic, but I'd rather err on that side than on the other.

I had hoped for a good deal from the conference; but fear it will not be effective. They have asked me to serve on the committee, but I have refused, thinking it better not to appear to support a cause with which I find myself in disagreement at so many points. Sincerely yours,

Ray Stannard Baker

ALS   Con. 402   BTW Papers   DLC.

From William Taylor Burwell Williams

Hampton Institute, Virginia   June 20, 1910

Personal

My dear Dr. Washington: Your letter including letter to Dr. Buttrick regarding colored high schools in the South is at hand. This is a very timely move for you to make, in so far as the need for such training is concerned. I hope it may be equally timely in getting results. Without such schools there is little hope of getting a sufficiently large number of well prepared teachers for the elementary schools. Our private schools of good grade cannot begin to supply the demands, especially now that so many other opportunities are being made for the better educated young colored man or woman to earn a living by means of his superior training.

In regard to your last suggestion that a white man would probably have more influence in securing support for colored high schools, you are, of course, doubtless in the right. Nevertheless a question comes to my mind regarding such suggestions on the part of colored men. Might not some disadvantage arise, if leading colored men regularly suggest white men for the more commanding positions in Negro education? Should we get these high schools at public expense and under the direction of a Southern white man, would it not be quite natural that he would look to white men to man these schools? He would be better acquainted with white men of the right stage of development intellectually than he would be with colored men of the same type, besides it is an easy assumption that there are no colored men, or very few, fitted for such work. And more than this, there are several very suggestive examples of white men at the head of colored public high schools, viz. in Richmond and Lynchburg, Va. An effort was also made to get a colored principal for the new industrial school now building in Charleston; but a white man instead was, or is to be, appointed.

With the developing of a new grade of education at public expense it would not be at all difficult to create a class idea, and to establish the precedent that such public money should go only to white teachers. The salaries would probably be sufficiently large to attract white men to brave what little ostracism might follow from work among Negroes. Little or none, however seems to attach where white men want the jobs. "The jingling of the guinea helps the hurt that Honor feels."

Then again, Dr. Washington, if white men are pushed forward for the better positions in Negro education, what inducement is there for the younger Negro men to prepare themselves for the advanced work? And if not with some hope at least of getting some of the better things why prepare at all? I think the need of well educated, capable, colored men in our public schools will [be] greater in the future even than in the past. Yours truly,

W. T. B. Williams

TLS Con. 414 BTW Papers DLC.

343

To Robert Heberton Terrell

Huntington, N.Y. June 22, 1910

My dear Judge Terrell: I see that our exposition bill failed. That is not a serious matter, however. The great thing was to have made the fight. The Democrats evidently feared that the Republicans would get an advantage in the fall elections by passing this bill, and the Democrats were shrewd enough to see their chance to put the Republicans in the hole. I think that was all there was to it. One of my congressmen from Alabama who is a friend of mine, aside from politics, indicated to me sometime ago that the matter might become a party measure and in that case notwithstanding he personally favored the bill he might have to vote against it. Just what he predicted has happened.

In regard to the Law School matter. I hope you will remind me another year several weeks before the election is to take place as I would like to have a hand in the matter. I am surprised that Dr. Waring should oppose you. I have tried to be a good friend of his for many years. If possible we will try to arrange it next year for the election to come up at a time when I am sure to be present. Yours very truly,

[Booker T. Washington]

TLc Con. 413 BTW Papers DLC.

From Thomas Jesse Jones

Washington June 24, 1910

Dear Dr. Washington: Major Moton has conveyed to me your invitation to travel with you through the State of Maryland. I thank you very much for this invitation. It will give me great pleasure to avail myself of this opportunity. I suppose that I will be informed of the time and place of meeting you.

Some pressure has been brought to bear upon the Census Bureau to use the word Colored for Negro in the census volume to be issued. I would like very much to have your opinion as to the relative merits of these two words. I am not at all sure that we could substitute Colored for Negro, even if we desired, but if it is the wise thing to do I want to bring it up before the Director with your advice one way or another. I sympathize with those who feel that there is a certain stigma connected with the term Negro. On the other hand, it is exceedingly difficult to distinguish the colored people of Negro origin from colored people of other origin when only the term Colored is used.

My attention has been called to the fact that the New York Age has been criticising the double system of enumeration. I fully understand that a number of colored people are out of sympathy with this system. It is not an ideal system from my point of view, but I regard it as the best under the circumstances. I favor the system at present, not only because it has enabled us to obtain the facts more accurately than we could have if it were all in the hands of the white people, but also because I hope that its successful execution may lead to a system of employing colored constabulary in southern states for the care of colored people. I am not sure that you approve of this scheme of having a colored constabulary, and would like very much to discuss it with you some time.

With very kind regards, I am, Sincerely yours,

Thomas Jesse Jones

TLS Con. 407 BTW Papers DLC.

To William Taylor Burwell Williams

Huntington, N.Y. June 26th, 1910

My dear Mr. Williams: I am writing very hastily. In regard to the suggestion in my letter to Dr. Buttrick of employing white men to push forward the interests of Negro high schools, I had in mind the fact that I thought the Board might take more kindly to this suggestion than it would otherwise, that is to say, I had the idea that it would be better to have these high schools although they were engineered by white people than not to have them at all. My main point was to get the schools. I will talk to you further about it in detail, however, when I see you, and will explain my position more fully. Of course I agree with you that the best thing is to have the schools superintended by colored men if that can be brought about. Yours very truly,

[Booker T. Washington]

TLc   Con. 414   BTW Papers   DLC.

To the Editor of the Washington *Post*

[Huntington, N.Y.] June 27th, 1910

Editor Washington Post: I read with interest a few days ago your editorial on the "Southern Labor Famine."[1] While what I am going to suggest may not reach the foundation of the difficulty, I think that what I am going to say will help in a slight degree.

There is in the South a tremendous amount of unused labor. This is especially true in the towns and large cities.

A few Sundays ago I made a trip in company with a number of our teachers and others, extending through 40 miles of Macon County, the county in which I live. During this 40 mile trip we visited six or seven Negro schools. I speak especially just now of two communities where large white planters live on their farms right in the midst of the colored people. During this trip we visited a community known as Fort Hull where Mr. Morgan S. Russell, a Southern white man, is a large planter. In this community there is a neat, comfortable schoolhouse for the Negro children. The house is neatly painted inside and outside, and everything is attractive and comfortable about it. There is a good teacher, and the school is in session eight or nine months every year. Near the schoolhouse there is a church house which is painted and attractive and comfortable and convenient on the inside. During our visit, notwithstanding it was Sunday, an exhibition was made in the church of the vegetables and other farm crops grown by the colored people in their gardens and on their farms. There were also many exhibits of the sewing and cooking including canned vegetables, berries and what not. There were on exhibit specimens of the work done by the children in arithmetic, reading and writing, as well as exhibits of what the children had grown on their little school farm or garden. Our party was met at the outskirts of this little community by a delegation mounted on mules, and as we entered the community itself, fireworks were set off. Our party was treated to a barbecued dinner that would have done credit to any community.

Referring again to the exhibit in the church, it was so large and so complete that one would have thought he was visiting a county fair. Right in the midst of it all, and deeply interested in it all was Mr. Morgan S. Russell himself with his son and clerks and helpers. He sat upon the platform, he spoke to the people, he welcomed our party, he was as proud in showing to our party the evidences of progress of the colored people in that community as any father could have been.

On Mr. Russell's plantation we saw at least 50 houses in which his tenants live. Each house was neatly whitewashed or painted. There was a garden and many flowers. Each house contained from two to three rooms.

Toward the close of our visit I asked Mr. Russell what difficulty, if any, he experienced in getting labor for his own farm. He replied at once that he not only experienced no difficulty, but this year he had to refuse people who applied to him for permission to work on his farm because he was overstocked.

A few days before the trip referred to, with a company of our teachers from the Tuskegee Institute I spent a half day on a plantation consisting of some 12,000 or 13,000 acres some eight miles from the Tuskegee Institute, owned by Mr. W. W. Thompson, brother of the late Congressman Charles W. Thompson. Here I found practically the same conditions as I have described existing on Mr. Russell's plantation. Mr. Thompson lives in the community near his farm. There was a good schoolhouse, a good church on his farm, practically every house was whitewashed and contained from two to three rooms. He encourages his tenants to have their gardens, their chickens, pigs and what not. The school is in session from seven to eight months with a good teacher. Mr. Thompson, as was true of Mr. Russell, takes a personal interest in each Negro family.

During the trip of 40 miles through the county, we found another white family who offers an annual prize to the colored woman who keeps her house the cleanest, another prize to the family who has the best looking front yard, another prize to the

Negro child who makes the best record in public school, another prize to the farmer who raises the most cotton and corn on an acre of land.

I asked Mr. Thompson the same question that I asked Mr. Russell regarding labor, and Mr. Thompson replied at once that he had more labor every year than he could use.

The explanation for this is that the white people in the South do not realize that they cannot get the best class of labor and keep that labor on their farms contented and happy unless they have a good public school with a good teacher, a good schoolhouse and a school term lasting from seven to eight or nine months. Planters cannot keep the best class of colored labor either unless they take some pains to furnish them decent houses in which to live. The best class of Negro laborers will not remain on a farm contentedly in a little one room, uncomfortable cabin. A close investigation would reveal the fact that a large proportion of the colored people who have left the farms and moved to the towns and cities have done so because they cannot get decent houses to live in or because they are not provided with public school facilities for their children. I believe that close investigation would show further that wherever a planter provides good houses, a good school, and encourages the people to have a good minister, a good church, that that planter never lacks for labor.

[Booker T. Washington]

TLc Con. 411 BTW Papers DLC. The letter appeared in the Washington *Post*, July 3, 1910, 7.

1 The editorial stated that southern black laborers were not as efficient as northern black laborers or black laborers from the Caribbean who were working on the Panama Canal. The *Post* suggested that the South needed the kind of efficiency demonstrated by the workers in Panama. (Washington *Post*, June 22, 1910, 6.)

A Tribute to Mark Twain
in the *North American Review*

June 1910

It was my privilege to know the late Samuel L. Clemens for a number of years. The first time I met him was at his home in Hart-ford. Later I met him several times at his home in New York City and at the Lotos Club. It may be I became attached to Mr. Clemens all the more strongly because both of us were born in the South. He had the Southern temperament, and most that he has written has the flavor of the South in it. His interest in the negro race is perhaps expressed best in one of his most delightful stories, "Huckleberry Finn." In this story, which contains many pictures of Southern life as it was fifty or sixty years ago, there is a poor, ignorant negro boy who accompanies the heroes of the story, Huckleberry Finn and Tom Sawyer, on a long journey down the Mississippi on a raft.

It is possible the ordinary reader of this story has been so absorbed in the adventures of the two white boys that he did not think much about the part that "Jim" — which was, as I remember, the name of the colored boy — played in all these adventures. I do not believe any one can read this story closely, however, without becoming aware of the deep sympathy of the author in "Jim." In fact, before one gets through with the book, one cannot fail to observe that in some way or other the author, without making any comment and without going out of his way, has somehow succeeded in making his readers feel a genuine respect for "Jim," in spite of the ignorance he displays. I cannot help feeling that in this character Mark Twain has, perhaps unconsciously, exhibited his sympathy and interest in the masses of the negro people.

My contact with him showed that Mr. Clemens had a kind and generous heart. I think I have never known him to be so stirred up on any one question as he was on that of the cruel treatment of the natives in the Congo Free State. In his letter to Leopold, the late King of the Belgians, in his own inimitable way he did a service in calling to the attention of the world the cruelties practised upon the black natives of the Congo that had far-reaching results. I saw him several times in connection with his efforts to bring about reforms in the Congo Free State, and he never seemed to tire of talking on the subject and planning for better conditions.

As a literary man he was rare and unique, and I believe that his success in literature rests largely upon the fact that he came from among the common people. Practically all that he wrote had an interest for the commonest man and woman. In a word, he succeeded in literature as few men in any age have succeeded, because he stuck close to nature and to the common people, and in doing so he disregarded in a large degree many of the ordinary rules of rhetoric which often serve merely to cramp and make writers unnatural and uninteresting.

Few, if any, persons born in the South have shown in their achievements what it is possible for one individual to accomplish to the extent that Mr. Clemens has. Surrounded in his early childhood by few opportunities for culture or conditions that tended to give him high ideals, he continued to grow in popular estimation and to exert a wholesome influence upon the public to the day of his death.

The late Mr. H. H. Rogers, who was, perhaps, closer to Mr. Clemens than any one else, said to me at one time that Mr. Clemens often seemed irritated because people were not disposed to take him seriously; because people generally take most that he said and wrote as a mere jest. It was this fact to which he referred, I have no doubt, when at a public meeting in the interest of Tuskegee at Carnegie Hall a few years ago, he referred to himself in a humorous vein as a moralist, saying that all his life he had been going about trying to correct the morals of the people about him. As an illustration of the deep earnestness of his nature, I may mention the fact that Mr. Rogers told me that at one time Mr. Clemens was seriously planning to write a life of Christ, and that his friends had hard work to persuade him not to do it for fear that such a life might prove a failure or would be misunderstood.

As to Mark Twain's successor, he can have none. No more can such a man as Mark Twain have a successor than could Phillips Brooks or Henry Ward Beecher. Other men may do equally interesting work in a different manner, but Mark Twain, in my opinion, will always stand out as an unique personality, the results of whose work and influence will be more and more manifest as the years pass by.

North American Review, 191 (June 1910), 828–30.

From Helen M. Chesnutt

Cleveland. July 1—1910

Dear Mr. Washington: Since my return to Cleveland we have been in the greatest trouble, as you have doubtless heard, and now that Father seems to be recovering, and our minds are relieved from such great anxiety, I wish to express to you my appreciation of that most delightful and beneficial visit at Tuskegee.

The month that I spent there will always be one of my happiest recollections — every moment of it was full of interest and enjoyment. It was a wonderful experience to have had and I heartily thank you and Mrs. Washington for so graciously taking me into your family life as well as into the activities of the school.

My brother[1] seems to have the same view of Tuskegee that I have, and I trust that he will prove satisfactory in every way. I feel in a way responsible for his being there and want him to do well. With many thanks to all of you for your many kindnesses, I am Sincerely yours,

Helen M. Chesnutt

ALS Con. 403 BTW Papers DLC.

[1] Edwin J. Chesnutt was a stenographer in the principal's office from 1910 to 1912.

To Thomas Jesse Jones

Huntington, N.Y. July 2d, 1910

My dear Dr. Jones: Replying to a portion of your letter I would say that, on the whole, I am inclined to agree with you that if you can substitute the word "colored" for Negro in the Census reports it would be more agreeable to a majority of the colored people. I find that they take more kindly on the whole to that term than to any other. I have discussed this matter with Major Moton.[1]

I am thoroughly in favor of a colored constabulary. It now looks as if colored policemen will be appointed sometime soon in Charlotte, N.C.

I noted at the time what the Age said in criticism of the method of taking the Census. In many matters the Age follows my advice. In others it does not. There have been certain parties who for a number of months have tried to make it appear that I own the Age. The fact is, I do not own a single penny's worth in it, neither do I own a single penny's worth in any other Negro paper. At the time the editorial appeared I told Mr. Moore I thought he was hitting the administration too hard, but he seemed not to think so.

I shall be glad to talk with you further when I see you. Yours very truly,

[Booker T. Washington]

TLc Con. 407 BTW Papers DLC.

1 Jones replied: "I shall take this matter up with the Director as soon as he returns and try to make any change which is possible." (July 5, 1910, Con. 407, BTW Papers, DLC.)

To Ray Stannard Baker

[Tuskegee, Ala.] July 7, 1910

My dear Mr. Baker: On my return to Tuskegee I find your letter of some days ago. I have read particularly the paragraph to which you call my attention on page 8. I think, as you say, that the statements are rather sweeping but I am at the same time myself convinced that they are correct. Legally, as you say, the Negro as a Negro is not cut off from the ballot, but of course we all know all too well the practical application of the various discriminatory enactments. I think, however, we can well afford to take a position on the platform that if the ballot is to be restricted that the restriction should apply equally to white and black citizens alike. The grandfather device is to my mind a wholly unfair one and it has a place in several of the state constitutions. To this extent then, the grandfather law as a device has not been defeated by the vote of the people or by the decision of the courts. Perhaps if the matter is ever carried up properly this latter action may be taken up, but for the present this has not been done.

I return herewith your manuscript. Yours very truly,

Booker T. Washington

The more I observe conditions in the South, the more I am con-vinced that we are inclined to lay too much stress upon the physical act of voting. I hold that the colored man who has the most polit-ical influence in his community — I mean in the broadest sense — is the one with property, education, and high character, and he ex-erts that political influence whether he is a registered voter or not.

I think you will find by close examination that in most, if not all, of the states the grandfather clause only has a limited life. It has already disappeared in several of the states.

TLpS Con. 402 BTW Papers DLC.

A Review of *The Story of the Negro* in *The Nation*

July 9, 1910

In his "Story of the Negro," Dr. Booker T. Washington has brought out in book form papers contributed to a magazine, as well as much interesting material which he has given to the public at one time or another in his platform addresses. This is no attempt at a scientific, historical relation of that remarkable rise of the American negro in the forty years since emancipation which so eminent a Southerner as Henry Watterson[1] has declared to be with-out parallel in the world's history. Instead, we have an easily flow-ing, loose-jointed, but readable narrative, bristling with interesting anecdotes and incidents in men's lives and interspersed with useful statistics on nearly all the phases of the negro's life and labor in this country.

As was to be expected, Dr. Washington all but ignores the ques-tion of disfranchisement and other political issues. Those of his race who would find in these volumes any outspoken denunci-ations of injustice or race discrimination, or indeed any stirring note of leadership, must look elsewhere. Dr. Washington is not an agitator. His happy optimism, his cheerful confidence that by building upon the foundation of industry and social usefulness the negro will eventually come into his own, find here ready expression. Truly, no one can contemplate the achievements of the negro since emancipation without certain confidence that, however discouraging the problem may be at times, however disheartening the present reaction, North as well as South, against the negro, in the years to come the negroes are bound to make greater and greater contributions to the industrial and intellectual progress of the nation. No other conclusion is possible after reading Dr. Washington's pages. We wish his work might find the widest circulation, despite certain defects of style and construction, for it presents in an attractive form facts which everybody ought to know. Particularly is this true of the introductory part of the first volume in which the author sets forth something of the past and present conditions in Africa. One of the fundamental difficulties of the negro problem is the cock-sureness with which many persons assert that all African negroes are, and have been, on the lowest level of intelligence and civilization; that there never was any civilization or progress among them. Few know that according to undoubted scientific authority the average primitive negro community in the darkest continent is "a model of thrift and industry." Unfortunately, Dr. Washington often weakens his presentation of such important facts by interjecting rather irrelevant observations on some phase of the Southern problem of to-day. The book bears, too, marks of hasty construction. There are numerous errors of typography and editing. Thus in volume one, page 25, Major R. R. Moton becomes Moten; on page 217 it is James A. Smith; on the next page the same person becomes Samuel A. Smith. On page 266 we learn that a church was built in 1972; on page 323 Gov. Andrew becomes Gov. Andrews. In volume two Brig.-Gen. A. S. Daggett appears as A. D. Daggett, etc., etc. Careful revision would have avoided much repetition and rendered the argument more effective.

The Nation, 91 (July 7, 1910), 16.

1 Henry Watterson (1840–1921), editor of the Louisville *Courier-Journal* from 1868 to 1918.

To Charles William Anderson

[Tuskegee, Ala.] July 11, 1910

Personal

Dear Mr. Anderson: I see that our friend, Du Bois, has finally decided to locate in New York.

In order to counteract such evil tendencies as may ensue, I strongly urge that you pursue the policy of getting one representative of every strong organization in your club. To bring about this result, it may be necessary for you to broaden your club somewhat. I think your club should become in a large degree the "clearing house" for Negro organizations in New York City. That is you ought to have in it one representative from every organization, in that way you could easily control the whole situation.

I should like to talk this matter over with you more at length. Yours very truly,

Booker T. Washington

TLpS   Con. 49   BTW Papers   DLC.

From Robert Curtis Ogden

Kennebunkport, Maine   July 15th 1910

Dear Mr Washington, I have allowed yours of the 7th inst from Tuskegee to remain a day or two awaiting reply.

There is very little material upon which to base such an article as you propose for the Metropolitan Magazine. My business activities covered a period of about 56 years with very moderate material results but with a decided executive success with the Wanamaker business in New York. In business administration I have always been something of an idealist, believing in strict justice toward both capital and labor and endeavoring to so guide my action as to be perfectly fair to both sides. Labor has a right to organise — in spite of its many mistakes of administration, just as capital exercises the same right. The "open shop" is demanded by human rights. A good bargain is good to both buyer and seller — and I may add, in large affairs, to the public also. Success for one gained by pulling down another is not success in any true sense. Money that is made by *compelling* another to lose is dishonestly obtained. In brief these are some of my business notions. In administration I acted with decision upon them and I believe, gained the affectionate respect of my subordinates.

In other affairs I have been somewhat active.

In religious association Presbyterian — of the broader type, only destruction of traditional faith when it can thereby be made constructive.

In educational matters I have been Armstrong's follower and so the great privilege of my life has been to help Hampton and all it stands for to both races. I have seen every class graduate at Hampton, save only two, the one in which you graduated and the Class of 1907. In the first instance the cause was illness in my family in the second personal illness. I have worked with and for the "Conference for Education in the South" and the Southern Education Board. They are both valuable and influential and the Board especially has done its work quietly and without ostentation. My position has never been fully understood in these affairs and cannot be fully and publicly explained without leading to more misunderstanding. Both have for their objects the public education of all the people. My address at Little Rock last spring has some information that may be useful. I will have a copy sent to you in the Report of the Thirteenth Conf.

My principle has been to hold and conserve all influence possible to the end that intelligence may spread and the whole community may have an uplift in Democracy. My action under this principle has been very conservative and may have made me misunderstood. But I never explain. If my course has any importance I simply stand on the record and say nothing.

At present I am President of the Hampton Board, of the Board of Directors of the Union Theological Seminary of New York, member of the Sage Foundation Board, President Conference for Education in the South and of the Southern Education Board. Of these last two details could be given indefinitely. Also a member of the General Education Board and of the Presbyterian Board of Home Missions.

If I have in any small way been useful it has been principally through the Educational Boards. Yours Very Sincerely

Robert C Ogden

ALS Con. 51 BTW Papers DLC.

To E. H. Paul[1]

Huntington, N.Y. July 28, 1910

My dear Sir: Replying to yours of June 16th, enclosed I send you a list of schools which I recommend that Mr. Schiff help during the present year. I have not made many changes.

I have taken time to answer your letter in order that I might inform myself definitely upon the value of the work being done by each institution.

In three cases I have asked Mr. Schiff to give an extra $50 for this year. In the case of the school at Utica they have recently had a storm that blew down several of their buildings. In the case of the school at Ladonia, Texas, under Mr. R. L. Smith, they have recently had some extraordinary expenses, and as the school is doing good work I recommend that he should be given $50 additional this year.

You will recall that there was some $80 or more unexpended on last year's account. This will leave, as I understand it, a total unexpended balance of something over $100. Yours truly,

[Booker T. Washington]

TLc Con. 411 BTW Papers DLC.

[1] Private secretary of Jacob H. Schiff.

To James Bryce

Huntington, N.Y. July 29, 1910

My dear Ambassador Bryce: I have read the chapter on "Further Reflections on the Negro Problem" carefully and on the whole

I consider it very, very good and just. There are one or two points which I wish to call to your attention.

On page 6 I have marked two paragraphs wherein I think you overstate the matter of the strained relation between the races. For example, in the second paragraph there is the unmodified sentence, "Everywhere there is friction between the races." This I do not think is true. If you lived in the South and had daily contact with the people as I do, I think you would agree with me that that is putting the matter entirely too strong. The trouble is, the people on the outside hear of the communities where there is racial friction, they rarely hear of the communities where everything works as smoothly as clockwork. In nine-tenths of the communities in the South there is little or no friction. I see a good many cases frequently where colored and white people sit down to eat together in the South.[1]

On page 10 I think you overstate the matter a little concerning the disposition of the mulattoes and quadroons to look down on the pure blacks. Among individuals there is somewhat of that disposition but it does not take any organized shape and I question whether any light colored person in the North or anywhere else would permit it to be known if he could prevent it that he did not care for dark colored people. I have [heard] a good deal about friction between light colored people and dark colored people, but I have not come into contact with it in any way to make me believe that there is to any degree such a separation.[2]

On page 14, so far as the South is concerned, I think you overstate the matter of difficulties attendant on competition in the labor market. In the South the one question is to get labor, and there is little friction between white and black labor. In the South at present labor is seeking the man to such an extent that people do not find time to discriminate much as between whether a laborer is a black man or a white man. This applies to skilled labor and common labor. White men and black men work in the South together on the same brick wall, often work at the same carpenter's bench.[3]

If you have not done so, I wonder if at some point you might not like to call attention to the opportunity surrounding the Negro in the South in the business or commercial world. In this aspect the Negro has an opportunity in the South that is not afforded him in like degree in any part of the country or perhaps in the world. The Negro can borrow money at the white bank just as easily as the white man. If the Negro owns a bank it is patronized by white people. The same is true of drygoods stores, grocery stores and all kinds of commercial business. In the matter of commerce little thought is taken of the color of the skin.[4]

Let me repeat, however, that the chapter on the whole I consider very, very good and fair and I think will accomplish good.

If I can serve you further please let me know. Yours very truly,

[Booker T. Washington]

TLc Con. 402 BTW Papers DLC.

[1] Bryce modified this sentence in his 1915 revision to say: "In all States, though happily not in all parts of any State, there is friction between the races." (*American Commonwealth*, 2:549.)

[2] Bryce in his 1915 revision wrote: "In some cities, especially in the North, mulattoes and quadroons are said to have formerly looked down on the pure blacks, and sought to create an exclusive society of their own. But that racial consciousness to which I have already referred has been drawing all sections of the African race together, disposing the lighter coloured, since they can get no nearer to the whites, to identify themselves with the mass of those who belong to their own stock." (*American Commonwealth*, 2:536.)

[3] Bryce wrote in his 1915 revision that in the North racial friction existed "chiefly between the labouring class." He added: "In the Southern States the friction is perhaps less marked, and is least when one element, whether black or white, is in a large majority, less also in the rural districts than in the cities, where the negro work-people are supposed to be less submissive, where the proportion of bad characters among them is largest, and where the white working men are most rude and suspicious, the jealousy of labour competition being added to the jealousy of colour." (*American Commonwealth*, 2:549–50.)

[4] Bryce in his 1915 revision, after a recital of the economic and social discrimination blacks faced in the northern cities, concluded: "So the negro is after all better off in the South and on the land than anywhere else; and in the South, where the need for labourers is great and he is not generally discriminated against in business matters, a wider door is open to him both in town and country." (*American Commonwealth*, 2:552.)

To Charles Dyer Norton[1]

Huntington, N.Y. July 30, 1910

Confidential

Dear Mr. Norton: Before proceeding to fulfill my promise in the other matters that we talked about, I am writing you regarding a case that I thought the President might like to act upon at once.

Walter L. Cohen, of New Orleans, who holds the position either of Receiver of Public Money or Register of the Land Office in New Orleans, has never been reappointed. His time expired over a year ago. Two colored men have disappeared from Presidential offices in New Orleans since the present administration came in. This, together with the failure to reappoint Cohen has served to add to the bitterness throughout the country. Since Cohen is already holding the office, and in my opinion would have no trouble in being confirmed when the Senate meets, I believe it would be a fine stroke just now for the President to reappoint him at once. The element of colored people that are opposed to President Taft under Bishop Walters and others, hold a meeting in Atlantic City August 4th. Aside from throwing a damper on this meeting, Cohen's appointment just now would help the situation in Ohio as he is well known in that state. If the President decides to reappoint him, will you be kind enough to send me a telegram even before it is given out officially so that I can get the matter in the colored press next week in order for it to have its effect on the Atlantic City meeting. Yours truly,

[Booker T. Washington]

TLc Con. 411 BTW Papers DLC.

1 Charles Dyer Norton (1871–1922), who had been a Chicago life insurance executive (1895–1909) and assistant secretary of the treasury (1909–10), was President Taft's secretary in 1910–11. He moved to New York as vice-president of the First National Bank of New York, and was a director of a number of corporations.

To William Howard Taft

Huntington, N.Y. August 3d, 1910

My dear Mr. President: This is just a little note to remind you of your kind suggestion about speaking to Mr. Frick[1] concerning the needs of our institution at Tuskegee.

If it will not embarrass you in any way to mention it, I think he might become interested in enlarging our endowment. It is now a million and a half dollars and ought to be four millions.

There are several very much needed buildings also, and then there is the matter of our annual current expenses which is always with us.

I am taking up several of the matters with Mr. Norton which we discussed the other evening.

Let me say it was a great pleasure and satisfaction to be able to spend so much time with you Friday night, and what pleased me most was to see that you are not becoming disturbed or permitting yourself to be unnecessarily wrought up or nervous over what some elements are saying and trying to do. It is a real satisfaction to see that adverse criticism neither sours nor disturbs you. I am sure you will win, and that magnificently. Yours truly,

[Booker T. Washington]

TLc Con. 411 BTW Papers DLC.

[1] Henry Clay Frick (1849–1919), coke and steel manufacturer, was one of the founders of the U.S. Steel Corporation in 1901.

To Joseph Oswalt Thompson

Huntington, N.Y. August 3d, 1910

My dear Mr. Thompson: I thank you for yours of July 26th. I note carefully what you say. I feel quite sure that you are going to poll a large vote and that good will be accomplished through your nomination. My one fear is that you will over-exert yourself and in this way get a setback. I hope you will be very, very careful to preserve your strength.

You and Albert will be interested to know that I was sent for a few days ago by the President's secretary and went to Beverly Friday night where I had a two hours' conference with President Taft and his new secretary. They asked me to state frankly what the mood of the colored people is and what the cause of their dissatisfaction is, and I spoke right out from the shoulder. I feared a little that I was too frank and outspoken. I did not hesitate to call names of people who were at the bottom of the cause of the trouble. Both of them were deeply interested and promised to take matters up and I think there is going to be a turn around of policy. The new secretary is a gem. He is the kind of man that Mr. Taft ought to have had from the beginning. I am to go to Beverly again soon. I am engaged just now pretty strenuously in trying to help them straighten matters out and get the colored people into a different mood. Yours very truly,

[Booker T. Washington]

TLc Con. 413 BTW Papers DLC.

From Oswald Garrison Villard

Winter Harbor, Maine, August 4, 1910

My dear Mr. Washington, I do not know if your attention has been called to the Pink Franklin case.[1] I enclose copy of a letter just received, from Ex-Attorney General Bonaparte who takes the same view as Mr. Pillsbury, that Franklin has been sacrificed to the stupidity and conceit of his colored counsel. In any event, an innocent man who shot in self-defence, will be done to death unless prompt measures are taken.

We are endeavoring to circulate a petition through our organization. I am wondering if we could not get the President to take an interest in the case. A word from Mr. Roosevelt would help, of course. You yourself may have certain lines of action among white and colored people which could be quickly put into effect and might at least cause the commutation of the sentence. If you care to see it and have not already done so, you can obtain a copy of Mr. Bonaparte's brief on the Pink Franklin case from my office. Do help to save this victim of race prejudice! Very truly yours,

Oswald Garrison Villard

Mr. Miller[2] writes contrary to B's opinion that we should petition.

TLS Con. 411 BTW Papers DLC. Last sentence and postscript in Villard's hand.

[1] The Pink Franklin case was the first significant legal effort undertaken by the National Association for the Advancement of Colored People, and the only one in

which BTW and the NAACP cooperated. A warrant had been issued for Franklin, an illiterate farmhand, under a South Carolina peonage statute already declared unconstitutional by the state supreme court. Two law officers entered Franklin's bedroom while he, his wife, and his son were sleeping. In the shooting affray that ensued, all but the son were injured, and one of the policemen later died. The Franklins narrowly escaped a lynching, but were arrested for murder. Two black lawyers defended them; Mrs. Franklin was acquitted, but Franklin was sentenced to be executed. When the state supreme court upheld the verdict and Franklin's lawyers prepared to request a writ of error from the U.S. Supreme Court, the Constitution League asked former Attorney General Charles J. Bonaparte to argue the case, but Franklin's lawyers, eager for the publicity of a Supreme Court trial, refused to relinquish control.

When the U.S. Supreme Court upheld the lower courts, O. G. Villard asked BTW to help the NAACP persuade President Taft to use his good offices to secure a commutation of the sentence. BTW advised the employment of a white South Carolina lawyer to argue the case before Governor Martin Frederick Ansel, but Villard replied that the NAACP had insufficient funds. Washington then suggested that the NAACP ask Rev. Richard Carroll, an influential conservative black leader in Columbia, to intercede with the governor, and BTW's friend R. C. Ogden also prodded the governor to act. Franklin's lawyers wanted to begin an appeal procedure that would carry the case over into the governorship of the extreme racist Cole L. Blease, but the NAACP officers persuaded them to allow Governor Ansel to make the decision. He commuted the death sentence to life imprisonment. (Kellogg, *NAACP*, 57–60.)

[2] Possibly Kelly Miller, a member of the general committee of the NAACP in 1910.

To Oswald Garrison Villard

Huntington, N.Y. August 7th, 1910

My dear Mr. Villard: You may recall that there has been considerable talk from time to time in the South about securing Italians to take the place of the Negro as a cotton farmer. You may also recall that Mr. Alfred Holt Stone in his book and in all of his lectures on the subject has laid considerable emphasis upon what the Italians have done on a certain farm in Arkansas in replacing the Negro.[1]

Because of all that Mr. Stone has said, I thought perhaps you could make some use of the enclosed marked article from the Daily Graphic of Pine Bluff, Ark., which shows that Mr. John M. Gracie,[2] the man who employed the Italians to which Mr. Stone refers, has gotten rid of the Italians and replaced them by Negro labor. Yours very truly,

[Booker T. Washington]

TLc   Con. 411   BTW Papers   DLC.

1 Stone maintained that Italian immigrants would provide a better source of labor for southern agriculture than black Americans because the Italians were more intelligent, did not require white supervision, and provided better crop yields than their black counterparts. (Stone, *Studies in the American Race Problem,* 172–97.)

2 John M. Gracie, born in New Gascony, Ark., owned and operated three large cotton plantations in New Gascony, Rob Roy, and Hannaberry, Ark., totaling more than 50,000 acres.

To Oswald Garrison Villard

Huntington, N.Y. August 9, 1910

My dear Mr Villard: Answering your letter regarding the Pink Franklin case, I would state that in my opinion I do not believe anybody outside of South Carolina can be of much service. I would suggest one of two courses.

First, if the money is available, to employ one of the strongest white lawyers in the state of South Carolina that can be gotten to take the matter up with the Governor.[1]

Or failing in this, I would suggest, secondly, that Rev. Richard Carroll, of Columbia, S.C., be asked to undertake to secure what is desired from the Governor. Richard Carroll is a man who has many qualities that neither you nor I would admire, but at the same time there is no discounting the fact that he has tremendous influence with the white people of South Carolina. Papers like the Columbia State stand by him and believe in him thoroughly. I believe that if Carroll could be gotten to undertake the case that he would have even greater influence than a lawyer. It might be necessary to let him have forty or fifty dollars to pay for traveling expenses in connection with working up interest in the case. When I was in South Carolina last I was surprised to see how he had the help and influence of mayors and state officials. If you think well of the latter course you can either write directly to Carroll yourself, or I shall be glad to do so if you think it wise.

We are looking forward with interest to seeing you on the 18th. Yours very truly,

[Booker T. Washington]

TLc   Con. 411   BTW Papers   DLC.

[1] Martin Frederick Ansel, governor of South Carolina from 1909 to 1911.

From Robert Heberton Terrell

Washington, D.C., Aug. 10/10

My dear Doctor Washington: I have just returned from Ohio where I spoke about ten days ago on the occasion of the Emancipation celebration in Cleveland. I found a condition out there among the colored voters that was simply startling. Never before have I met a situation that approached it. I visited several cities and talked with the leading colored men and I found all of them and their friends bitter in their expressions and their attitude against the national administration. Those who did not talk were ominously silent. The President's Inaugural Address and the manner in which the colored office holders have been ousted came in for the harshest kind of criticism. The colored voters in Ohio, in their present temper, are likely to desert the Republican party in large numbers this fall, some few by voting the Democratic ticket and many by staying away from the polls. If the President will do something for the Ohio colored voters by giving them some official recognition the speakers who go into that state to talk will be able to get a fair hearing, otherwise they will be helpless before the opposition.

What I found in the Ohio cities I also found in Detroit. The colored men are mad and disgruntled and take no interest in the coming elections, unless that interest be hostile to the Republican party. They say that Republican victory means the endorsement of the national administration's attitude to the Negro and they will not help achieve it.

I made the argument that the President is the friend of our race and he was a much misunderstood man, and that his subordinates had taken advantage of his Inaugural utterance to do things that he never intended should be done. I am frank to confess that I did not make a very deep impression.

When you get a chance to talk to the leaders you had better consider this situation.

I hope the Business League will have its biggest meeting this year. If I can get away I shall come over for a day. Very truly yours,

Robert H. Terrell

TLS Con. 411 BTW Papers DLC.

From Oswald Garrison Villard

Winter Harbor, Me. Aug 12, 1910

Dear Mr. Washington, Many, many thanks for your prompt reply. Please do everything you can thru Carroll for this unfortunate man. We have no money to hire a prominent white lawyer. Hastily yours,

Oswald Garrison Villard

ALS Con. 51 BTW Papers DLC.

From Andrew Carnegie

Skibo Castle, Dornoch, Sutherland. [Scotland] Aug 13th 1910

Dear Mr Washington   Glad you are to get a holiday. Let us know a day or two before you come here & you will be met at Bonarbridge Station. Bring your friend along. Highland welcome awaits you. Yours Ever

Andrew Carnegie

ALS Con. 52 BTW Papers DLC.

To Alexander Robert Stewart

New York City. August 17, 1910

Dear Mr. Stewart: My son Booker is going to buy a small farm and try to put it under cultivation before he starts back to Fisk. I wish you would assist him in every way you can. I take it for granted that some of the mules on my farm will be idle during the next few weeks, and if he wishes to use any one of the mules please let him do so. Yours truly,

[Booker T. Washington]

TLc Con. 412 BTW Papers DLC.

To Emmett Jay Scott

R.M.S. "Carmania." August 22nd 1910

Dear Mr Scott, In connection with the North Carolina trip, I want to arrange, if possible, so that I can be present one or two days at least while the Montgomery Fair and the Tuskegee white Fair are going on — You will have to use your judgment in this matter, of course it may not be possible to make such an arrangement.

As soon as I return I want to send you quite a number of letters to prominent people of our race with the idea of making up a purse for the relief of Mr Fortune. I think there are not a few who would like to make a small cash contribution. Perhaps during my absence you could draft the form of such a letter.

One other thing; I wish you would send me to London three copies of the Columbian Magazine[1] for September, as I fear I cannot get them in London. I wish also that you would take up the matter of having several newspaper correspondents accompany us on the North Carolina trip. Perhaps Mr Villard might like to send a man under the same conditions that he did in Tennessee. I think it would be a good plan to get the Minister in Boston,[2] if he is not abroad, to accompany us. I want to have, if possible, 2 or 3 good influential papers represented. Mr Gilman is the man that I have in mind for Boston.

I hope that matters are going well at the School and that you and your family are well. I am having a very splendid voyage, but want to get back as soon as possible. Yours truly,

Booker T. Washington

I am very anxious that the Boston Transcript be represented.

B. T. W.

TLS Con. 596 BTW Papers DLC. Postscript in BTW's hand.

[1] Edward Marshall, "Booker T. Washington: The World's Most Extraordinary Negro," *The Columbian*, 2 (Sept. 1910), 1845–57. The illustrated article, replete with anecdotes and incidents from BTW's life, told of his remarkable rise from slavery to world prominence.

[2] The only Bostonian on BTW's North Carolina tour was the lawyer William H. Lewis.

An Item in the *Tuskegee Student*

Tuskegee, Alabama, August 27, 1910

Principal Washington sailed from New York on August the 20th for Europe, where he hopes to secure a well needed rest. During his stay on the continent, he plans to visit England, Scotland, Denmark, Germany, Austria, Romania, Bulgaria, the Turkish Empire, and Italy. It will be his purpose while visiting these points to gain information regarding agricultural and labor conditions, especially in the Turkish Empire and lower Italy. He will be joined in Europe by Dr. R. E. Park of Boston and will remain away until late in the fall.

Tuskegee Student, 22 (Aug. 27, 1910), 2.

A Notebook of Washington's Tour of Europe

[Aug. 28–Oct. 7, 1910]

Burns work only
an example — many
others.

Negroes in South
outter edges of
cities. No

light. Little government.
No parks, little
to make life
attractive. Less
crime if surroundings
were more
sanitary. Drink
in these improved
places reduced 50%

Price of wages.
America & help
Europe.

Market cheapest
things — second handed.
Good schools.

Sunday market
Cheapest things at
Smallest Price.
Wanamakers Negro

Oneness of Language.
  ″   ″ religion
 ″ climate.
Oneness of Race.

Women in fields.

A[u]stro-Hungarians
separated Negro can act.

No talk on trains.
Negro would know every one.

Austro-Hungarians
like Negro
love pleasure.

Renters are
protected by
law — Scotch
crofter — not
so with Negro.

Farm wages
in Austria
$15 to $20 per
year for men —
women $10 to
$15 per year &
keep.

Race competit[i]on.

In Bohemia
Factory — men earn
$2.00 to 2.50 per week.
Women $1.00 to $1.50
per week.

Industrial & technical
education in
Bohemia.

Wife is
purchased in
Austro-Hungary.

Religious hatred.
Different dress.
Mohamedans —
7000 Emigrated.

Permission to speak.

Women.

Women, carrying bricks,
  ″   ″   water
  ″   making mortar.
  ″   unloading coal.
Women get 14 cts in
factories.
Have to return some
to boss, boss
returns to owner.
Working people now
have more than

369

two rooms, order &
cleanliness.

Separate Schools,
   officer to
   hear speech.

Low wages in city
   due to people leaving
   country.

Women in
   Brick yard.

Soldiers 2 cts a day

Bohemian

Wooden shoes,
   Cows, chickens
   Women 10 & 15 cts
   men 15 & 22 cts
   Board selves,
   1 Room,
   Brick yard.

Rich Jew — Dairy
   Negro & world Tongue,
   ″   ″ One Religion.

Women in Brick-yard.

3 sepa[ra]tions in Schools.

Children at
   work on farms.

Wooden Shoes.

20 Languages

Can not judge looks of houses.
Bad farm conditions
   drives people to city.
   3 classes of
   Waiting rooms.

No money consideration
   when Negroes marry.

One woman filling
   wagon in Vien[n]a and two
   men by her side.

Women working as section
   hands. Sickness &
   Consumption among women.

Jewish Dairy farm —
   calves, rake, feed,
   manure.

Children not enough
   to eat in Austria.

White Women in Sewer.
   What colored woman does.
   Not public works.
White men standing
white women as bosses.

Food eaten by poor in Europe.

Food of Negro South.

Drinking in Europe of working
   classes as compared with
   Negro.

Naples.

milking cows
   Bakery —
   Shoemakers.
   Man barefooted behind mule
   to wagon.
   Few windows.
   Letter Writers.
   Advancing — old fashion
   methods on farm.

Italians & Negro cooks.
   6 & 8 in Room.

Candles burning.
One Room No windows.
Sick boy.

Followed by 50 beggars.
  Filth, disorder.
  Picking lice from head.
  Poultry yard in bed room.
  Black smith shop in bed room.
  Donkeys & cattle.
  One quarter of a mile of
    Poverty
  Everybody begging.
  One room 3 x 8 ft one
    family —
  & Shoemaker in front part.
  No sunshine enters.
  Compared to N. O. Atlanta &
  N. Y.
  Negro seldom begs.
  Gambling
  Wet, dirt floor,
  Sick babies,
  goats & sheep.
  $2 & $3 a month for 1 Room.
  Lottery tickets.

Crowded with children.
  Good natured like Negro.

Milking cows on street
  Naples is 51% illiterate
  Secret criminal societies not
  know[n] to Negro — Southern
  Italy full of them.
  Lottery under control of
  Government adds to misery.

Meat rarely gotten except on
  feast days
  maj. R.R. uniting[?].

7 per cent of Population voters.
  Property, educational
  qualifications for voting.
  16% in England
  Superstitious,
  Church life a mere form.
  Crawling in dust.

Sicily
Robbers pray to saints.
Emigration to America has
  helped native workman.
  meat 2 a month.

School

Stealing farm truck, Lemons

Goats in house.
5000 in machinery 3 acres.

Negro & stealing crops.

Fences.
  over 50% ignorant

12 Per month.
  & No board
  Bread & Raw tomatoes for
    dinner.

Sicily

50% charge to farmers.
  Yet send no [*illegible word*]
  Size 2 to 10 acres.

Guns —

to 3 A.M.
  stealing.
  Brigandery & Mafia.

Absentee ownership
  miserable hovels for houses.
  Old fashioned water wells.

Leaving the luxury &
beauty Palermo
Poor Parched land.
Farmers live in village for
protection away from farms.

5000 to 15,000 acres.
12 bushels of wheat ⅓ or
half for rent.

Crime in rural districts of
Cicily.
murder, theft
brigandage, &
destruction of crops,
cutting of animals
miserable hovels to live in.

Dr. Park & Italian Grammar.

Sulphur mines.
Two mines.
Good nature,
No tips.
Dinner Bread & celery or
onion.

Protect women.

Drinking water five miles.
Coal 5 miles.
Improvement as compared
with
old times.
Hospital

Naples being cleaned.
Man from W.Va.
Hell & brim stone.

Down, down, down, into mine,
man from W.Va.
All will stop all work to be

kind to you.
Type writing machine.

Catania.
whole family working for
17 cts. a day.

Girl weeping over new shoes.

Responsibility for Church
& State for Present condition.

Baby in hammock.

Control of water power.

Cemetery
Wine 2 cts quart
Gambling
Cactus fruit for food.
Classes that emig[r]ate
to America.

20,000 in park.

25 guards to tax produce
from country.

Guards to keep people from
getting salt water.

Negro encour[ag]ed to produce,
they not.

Poverty in C[atania]

Beef Hoof

Child labor
boys 6 & 7 at brick yard
Industry of people.
Treading grapes,
18 & 40 cts per day for
11 hours.
For dinner bread & peppers.
Meat once a year.

Ground down by land lords.
School or nursery in Catania.
Users of wine
treading song, —
Everybody works
Children & mandolin.
Children & trade.
Horse, buggy & Chickens, in
one room.
No windows.
Cooking in St.
10 in one room.
Houses built in lava beds.
Cooking in street
Child 7 years decorating bed.
No toilet arrangements use
streets.
Duty on fish
People crushed
man had to leave 6 fish
Fish sell for 6 cts — 2 cts duty
Boy 7 building boats.
Woman cooking beef tripe.
More skills than Negro.

Boy 8 decorating carriage
   Absence of drink in Catania.
   Mafia stories &c.

Fiume
Man with gun in Sicily.
   Poor farms within an hour of
   Rome.
   Between Naples & Rome.
   Man with hoe must be
      reached.
   Discussing farming
   Little education in country
   Voting
   Type writing machine

De[s]cribe in detail houses
   and farms near Rome.

Starvation in England.
   England drink and other
      nations.
   Others may be poorer but
      not so much drink.
   Describe farms in extreme
      lower
   Italy also immigrants.

Hungary
   Experiences & observations in
   "strike" Fiume
   What the government is
      doing to
   help Hungarian Farmers

Raising seed potatoes for free
   distribution.
   Corn seed distributed at cost
      price.
   82 model tobacco farms.
   Lends machinery.
   Cattle for breeding.
   Grape growing and wine
      making
   schools
   One year gave away
   100,000 fruit trees.
   950,000 apple seedlings
   391,000 pear   "
   163,000 plums
   81,000 cherries,
   92,000 Peach trees,
   Papers & magazines
   Local fruit shows.
   Cooperative Fruit Shows
   People taught to grow, pack
   and market.

Money lent farmers to build houses.
School for poultry farmers.
School for bee keeping, given away 77,000,000 mulberry trees.
Stal[l]ions loaned to farmers.
Farm land held in tracts of 1,000 to 40,000 acres.
100 market people in Budapest.
sleep on side walk.

Harvesters
Work from 2 A.M. till 10 P.M.
Sleep in fields.
Paid percentage of crop — not money.
Farm "strikes"
Soldiers make them work.
Boot[?] hands $10 per month without board.
Farmers in *mud houses*.
German children taught to forget Hungarian language learned in school.

Ignorance of Slaves [Slavs] — must
always be Shoemaker
Circular printed in 6 languages
in Budapest.

Slaves [Slavs] oppressed in courts &c
by Hungarians.

Separate racial colleges.

Austria — women R.R.

Bare feet in the field.

Farm strikes in Hungary & the South.

Hung[a]ry improving land, trees & horses, but not the man furthest down.

I wanted to study the methods employed in Europe of getting the man up who is "farthest down.["] Negro farmer is using more up to date machinery than white farmer in Europe — is less conservative. Negro farmer in the South has 50% more comforts than European farmer.

Cracow, Austria.
visits to Salt mines.

Farmer — One Room
Dirt floor, bed
brick oven, pig and
sewing machines.

Whole family in one room, and in next room cow, pigs, geese & chickens, smell.

10 women & girls threshing rye and man sitting down — Women do most of the work.

New lang[u]age every time change trains.

Upper classes of whites know little about actual

life of peasants
around Crowcow —
like whites about Negro.
Negro in South more flexible
than farmers near Crowcow.

Women walk the 10 miles to
and from market to sell
products in market. Get
up and 2 A.M. walk back
home and do days work.
Met woman who owns one
cow walks 6 miles to
market to sell the milk.

Farm village near Crowcow.
Filth, cows, pigs and
chickens, in house.
Dirt floors
Solemn people,
cheap gaudy pictures
American sewing machin[e]s
in houses. Best house
in town. Women without
shoes in fields — women
and girls every where
at work.

Russian Village

Smiling & hat off.
Dirt and ignorance of farmers.

6 men eating out of one bowl
in a farm house — in Russian
village.

Sleeping on straw bed in
cottage near Crowcow.

Kosciusko & Negro.

Polanders, a hardy vig[o]rous
race.

Peasants are primitive in
civilization,
must see civilization
from their point of view —
would get ahead of Negro
in South.

Hill village.
Bar Room.
Priest & people.

Peasant cottage,
one room, dirt floor,
straw bed, cow, chickens and
a horse all in one room.
Filth and seeming misery.
Not always poverty but
primitive conditions.
In actual house keeping
Negro a head of them, as
to comforts, conveniences
and necessities of life.
Saw purposely the *worst*.
Best people in Crowcow to
see inside of poor houses.
Saving, frugille race,
but poor. High taxes.

No schools teaching poor how
to live as in South.
Women & men work stone
quarries, Cement work.
Women rolling stones
bushing [pushing?] carts,
Coal mines.

No fire & Negro warmed by
heat from cows & Pine Knots.
Outside of houses deceptive.
600 to $1000 per acre for
common land

375

$10 to 20 South.

All farm work after most
primitive fashion
Frails [Flails] & best farmer

No books or papers seen in
farm houses of poor in
Poland.

Grinding taxation

Negro & Sunday.

Jew can not curl hair in Russia.

Every Pole in Russian Poland
must have one Russian
clerk in store.

Seldom locked Hotel door in
Sicily.

Copenhagen

King & Queen[1] —
Dr. Eagan,[2] Had read up
from Slavery.
Looks of children.
People bought
Wine jugs at Catania.

De[s]cribe two schools.

Change in looks of children.
Happy Prosperous
Spoke to 1500 people.
Intelligence of farmers —
men & women —
Denmark has improved —
land & man.
Books, papers, &c. in farm
houses. Speaking to country
people. Like trip through
Macon County.
Farm School.
Ag. High Schools.
Describe in detail Program of
study &c.
Wives & husbands knew me
as well as my own Race.
American flags.
Denmark is saving people
before they go to Devil
rather than before [after?].

Apple slow[?].

Denmark has begun at bottom
rather than at top.

Can't get work in
Liverpool.
3 days work.

AD   Con. 607   BTW Papers   DLC.   A 4x6–inch ruled pocket notebook.

1 Frederick VIII (1843–1912), King of Denmark from 1906 to 1912, and Queen
Louise (1851–1926).

2 Maurice Francis Egan (1852–1924), a former English professor at Notre Dame
and Catholic University, was U.S. minister to Denmark from 1907 to 1918.

A News Item in the London *Standard*

[London, Aug. 29, 1910]

FAMOUS NEGRO LEADER

MR. BOOKER WASHINGTON'S VISIT TO LONDON

Mr. Booker Washington, the famous American negro leader, arrived in London yesterday, the object of his visit being to inspect the social and industrial conditions of the working classes in England and some of the Continental countries. Mr. Washington has had an extraordinary career. Born a slave some 60 years ago, he has come to be the leading representative of the American negroes. He has been honoured by Harvard University, and was received by Mr. Roosevelt during the latter's Presidency, an occurrence which led to considerable controversy.

Accompanied by Dr. Parke and the Rev. J. Harris, hon. secretary of the Anti-Slavery and Aborigines Protection Society, Mr. Washington yesterday visited the famous Jewish market in Middlesex-street, formerly known as Petticoat-lane, where he entered into conversation with many of the tradesmen, and inspected stalls, shops, a publichouse, and a lodging-house. From Middlesex-street he drove through Bethnal Green on the way to Waltham Abbey, where he was entertained at lunch by Sir Thomas Fowell Buxton.[1]

"I hope," said Mr. Washington yesterday, "to see a little of London and to spend a few days with Mr. Carnegie at Skibo Castle. I shall also see something of your agricultural, mining, and industrial life. When I leave England I am going to visit some of the other great European cities, including Berlin, to compare the position of the people there with that of the Southern negro. I hope to include Denmark and the Balkan regions, and also visit South Italy and other agricultural regions of Southern Europe, whence come the bulk of our immigrants."

ADVANCE OF THE NEGRO RACE

Discussing the general condition of the coloured race in America, Mr. Washington said: "There is progress, both moral and material, to report in the condition of the negro, and there is also an improvement in the relations between the two races. People in Europe always hear the worst. You do not hear of progress as quickly as you do of lynchings. If coloured people build a college or found a bank it is not noticed. But solid proof of the advance of the negro is to be found in the fact that 45 years ago only 2 percent. of the coloured population could read or write, whereas now the percentage is 57. In the only two States where separate taxation returns are made for the two races, Georgia last year showed an increase of 40,000, and Virginia an increase, 52,000 acres of taxable property owned by negroes. Statistics enable one to estimate the increase in the wealth of the negro at nearly 3,000,-000 a year, and their total wealth at about 120,000,000.

"The racial bar is fast disappearing in business in the South, where negro shops, banks, and factories are patronised by both races. There is practically no social mingling of the two races, but the laws regarding the segregation of the negro on the railways, for instance, are being less stringently applied, and some few negroes travel in the Pullman cars nowadays. Of course, the great distinction in the treatment of the two races is in the field of politics. The franchise is restricted in all States by property qualifications, and the demand that the voter shall know how to read or write. There is, however, a growing disposition in the South, to permit the educated negro and the property owning negro to exercise the franchise."

Referring to the race problem in South Africa, Mr. Washington said that Earl Grey once asked him to travel through the country and report on the best means of improving the native population.[2] It appeared to him that the question would have to be handled in the same way as it had been in the United States of America — namely, by education. In America education had taught the negro a number of wants which he had up till then never experienced. To satisfy these wants he laboured. This must be done in South Africa, where the negro problem could not be taken in hand properly until the native had been taught needs which went beyond the primitive appetite of man.

"In the Tuskegee Institute there are at the present time," said Mr. Washington, "a number of South African negroes, who are being trained with a view to the education of their fellows in South Africa."

London *Standard*, Aug. 29, 1910, 4. A similar interview in the London *Morning Post*, Aug. 29, 1910, was reprinted in *Tuskegee Student*, 22 (Sept. 17, 1910), 1–2.

[1] Thomas Fowell Buxton (1837–1915), governor of South Australia from 1895 to 1898, was active in the antislavery movement and forest conservation. He was the grandson of the antislavery crusader Thomas Fowell Buxton (1786–1845).

[2] For a brief account of this invitation, see above, 7:181–82.

An Interview in the London *Daily Chronicle*

[London, England] August 29, 1910

FUTURE OF THE
BLACK RACES

DR. BOOKER WASHINGTON
ON NEGRO PROGRESS

S. AFRICA PROBLEMS

Twenty years ago an unreasoning Tory critic wrote, after the manner of his kind, about the colour problem in the United States:

"It is coming to this in America that, in the interests of the black himself, some form of slavery, to the State if not to the individual, must be re-established."

When a representative of "The Daily Chronicle" asked Dr. Booker T. Washington, who arrived in London yesterday, his opinion about this old pronouncement, he laughed joyously.

"Never," he said. "Slavery in America is absolutely dead, and cannot be revived either to the State or the individual."

Mr. Washington was born into slavery, and is now one of the most respected men in the States, the President of Tuskegee College in Southern Virginia, and a man who has spent his life in a great endeavour to elevate his race. He has come to Europe to study the industrial conditions in some of the big towns and amongst the agricultural population.

He began by paying a visit to Whitechapel yesterday morning. Accompanied by Dr. Park, an American authority on the coloured races, and Mr. J. Harris, secretary of the Anti-Slavery and Aborigines Protection Society, he motored to Petticoat-lane, and walked through that famous, if somewhat noisy and malodorous thoroughfare, afterwards making a tour of other streets. There, it is interesting to note, he was much impressed with the cheapness of the meat and vegetables on sale — much cheaper, he said, than in America.

Of the present condition and future of his own race he spoke hopefully.

"All the worst things," he said, "are recorded, but hardly any of the best things. If there is a lynching all the world knows about it next day, but if the coloured people build a college, establish a bank, or a store, or erect houses for themselves, nothing is known about it except in the community. Forty-five years ago, when the race was freed, 2 per cent. could read and write, and it was then illegal to educate the negro. To-day 57 per cent. can read and write, and many have, of course, attained a good education.

"As to material progress, take two of the States where the taxable property is separated according to race — Georgia and Virginia. Last year the coloured people in Virginia owned 52,000 acres of taxable land, and in Georgia 40,000 to 50,000. The statistics also showed that the coloured people owned over 300,000 farms and more than 400,000 homes.

WEALTH OF THE BLACK RACE

"Basing the rate of increase of taxable property upon the accurate records of these two States, I think it is safe to say that the property of that class owned by the race is increasing about 12,-000,000 dols. a year, so that, at a very conservative estimate, the taxable property of the negro race is placed at about 600,000,000 dols."

But it is not only in material matters that the coloured people are making progress.

"In the Southern States of America," said Mr. Washington, "the negro has a better chance than in almost any country in the world for his labour. That leads one step further. There is in the South practically no prejudice between the two races. In politics there is still friction, for the negro vote is restricted by many devices; but in business the negro has his store, his real-estate agency, his factory, his bank."

Mr. Washington could not see his way to discuss any theories as to how the Southern negro might work out his own political salvation, and when asked what he thought about the colour problem in South Africa frankly admitted that he did not know enough about the conditions to express an opinion.

"It is very hard to generalise," he said, "and impossible to do so upon insufficient data. But there is one thing I have no hesitation in saying, and that is that the same policy ought to be pursued towards the negro in South Africa as is being pursued in our Southern States. The negro there has his weaknesses, and sometimes his vices, but you will find that, as a rule, he works. You hear a great deal about the lazy ones, but not about the workers, although nine-tenths of them are hard-working men. They work because their needs have increased by contact with the white men. The negro wants the same thing as the white man. Instead of stopping when he has enough money to buy a 'chew' of tobacco, he works five or six days in the week. The negro in South Africa is not going to improve his position as a labourer until his wants increase, and that will come only with education in the broad sense of the term. No man works unless he has an incentive."

Returning to the position of the negro in the Southern States, Mr. Washington admitted that, strictly speaking, there was no social intermingling between the races and there was no marrying between them. But the relationship of individual white men and families to negroes retains something of its old protecting spirit.

BLACK AND WHITE FRIENDSHIPS

"At many of the meetings I address," he said, "the white people are present in almost as large numbers as the blacks, and although they know that I am there to advocate the education of the negro race, they, in many cases, pay the expenses of the meeting. There is hardly a white man who has not a negro friend, or a negro who has not a white friend, and it is a real, genuine friendship that exists between them. In the case of families whose ancestors once owned slaves, the descendants of these slaves find the old family takes a great interest in them, and frequently educates the children, or looks after them in other ways. The white man, in these circumstances, will help the negro if he is in trouble or, perhaps, give him assistance in his business."

It was interesting to learn from Mr. Washington's lips that on the part of the descendants of the men and women who survived the horrors of the "middle passage," there is a sentimental feeling towards Africa as their Fatherland.

"Is there," he was asked, "any 'Back to Africa' movement amongst the American negroes comparable to the Zionist movement amongst the Jews?"

"Well," replied Mr. Washington, laughing, "I think it is with the African pretty much as it is with the Jews, there is a good deal of talk about it, but nothing is done, there is certainly no sign of any exodus to Liberia."

Mr. Washington leaves for the Continent in a day or two, after a flying visit to Mr. Carnegie at Skibo Castle, and will see something of France, Germany, Denmark, and Italy before returning to London in October.

London *Daily Chronicle*, Aug. 29, 1910, 3.

To Emmett Jay Scott

Skibo Castle, Dornoch Sutherland. [Scotland] Sept 2, 1910

Dear Mr. Scott: I have just gone carefully over the Proof of the 2nd chapter of "my experiences." I see nothing to change in it. I think Mr. Page wrote me that he thought some expressions ought to be modified. I wish you would take the matter up with him at once. I will agree on any changes that you and he makes. It will be too late for me to see the proof again.

It is perfectly fine here. I played golf with Mr. Carnegie yesterday.

I am sending you a great deal of stuff from English papers, much of it I thought you would have republished in colored and white papers. Be sure to advertise the N.C. trip well. I am simply swamped by letters and reporters and visitors. You might advertise pretty widely the fact that I am to speak before the National Liberal Club Oct. 6. I really think that it is going to be an important occasion. Yours Sincerely,

Booker T. Washington

Later since writing the above I have made all the changes in Chapter 2 and have sent it direct to Mr. Page.

ALS   Con. 54   BTW Papers   DLC.

From James Bryce

Kings House   Jamaica   Sept 7/10

Dear President Washington   Thank you very much for your letter and its observations on my chapter. I have turned them to account; & am glad that you think the view I have presented is generally correct.

This would have been written sooner, but I heard you had gone to Europe. I am myself on my way to South America, & write this in Jamaica, where we have stopped for a day. Things are going pretty well in the island, and the relations of the races seem quite satisfactory. You will, I hope, some time visit it and other parts of the British West Indies. I know you have at Tuskegee many students coming thence. You would have a welcome from every body.

As respects the use of the capital N in negro, the difficulty is that if we [are] always to write the word we would also have always to write White; & this would be unusual: besides the capital letter seems proper to denote a particular nation or nationality — Pole, Turk, Chinese, whereas the negroes are of many races. Even the Bantu race includes many races, such as Ba Suto Matabili, Betshuana, &c. However where ever I found that the capital N could with least appearance of breach of regular usage be employed, I have done so.

I hope you are having a pleasant & profitable time in Europe. Had I known you were going, I would have introduced you to some friends who would have been specially interested in Tuskegee. Yours very truly

James Bryce

ALS Con. 402 BTW Papers DLC. A typed copy is in Con. 903, BTW Papers, DLC.

To Lawrence Fraser Abbott

Vienna, September 10th 1910

Dear Mr. Abbott, I am now in Austria. I have got some very interesting matter. I cannot however carry out the plan which I first had in mind. My first plan was to send in letters from the various points that I did visit here. This I found impracticable because if I did this there would be a lot of repetitions. I wanted to write a letter on the conditions of the women in the countries I visit. Of course to carry out this plan, I should have had to see the women in all the countries.

I want to devote another letter to the conditions of the poor farmers, but I want to say all that I have to say on the subject in one letter. Thus you see I shall have to complete the trip before completing the articles. I am however writing out my impressions fully at each point that I visit. It now appears to me that I can gather enough material to make 5 or 6 interesting articles.

I start for Italy next week. A lot of my time has been taken by newspapers and public men in London, I was simply swarmed by the newspapers and I think the same will be true in Berlin when I get there. Yours truly

[Booker T. Washington]

TLc Con. 50 BTW Papers DLC.

Charles Dyer Norton to Emmett Jay Scott

Beverly, Mass., Sept. 15, 1910

My dear Mr. Scott: I am very desirous of seeing you when you come north in October. I am interested in the attitude in the negro newspapers. The President's position in his Inaugural Address was, as I understand it, approved of before it was uttered. It represents his convictions, and it appeals to me as the one fair and strong position for him to take. It does not bar negroes from office in the South. It sets for them a higher standard perhaps of fitness for public office, but that is something that the race in my judgment should welcome, and will, just as white men should welcome it. I think matters are so shaping themselves that before very long some appointments will be made which will speak for themselves. Before they are made, however, I should like to see you personally, and perhaps one or two of the leading publicists of your race, and have a discussion of this matter on its merits. The Press must not be held to too strict accountability, probably, but the attitude is very unfair.

By the way, if you find yourself in a position to point out to me any place in the South where a colored man could be appointed, and still have the appointment harmonize with the President's position in his Inaugural Address, I wish you would be sure to let me know. Sincerely yours,

Charles D. Norton

TLSr Copy   Con. 55   BTW Papers   DLC.

Oswald Garrison Villard to Charles Dyer Norton

New York   September 20, 1910

Dear Mr. Norton: I am in receipt of your letter of September 14th asking me for the names of three or four editors or public men of the negro race whose opinions carry the most weight with their fellows, and who are not merely of the job-hunting kind. I take pleasure in enclosing herewith a list of names of some admirable men whose opinions could be taken with profit, since they are distinctly not of the office seeking kind, but men who are successful in professional or business life.

Before, however, submitting these names to you, permit me to call your attention to certain phases of the situation among the colored people which may, perhaps, be of service to you in elucidating some of the problems before you. You are, I think, generally aware that the colored people in the United States are split into two parts, or factions, one headed by Booker Washington and the other by Dr. Du Bois, who has reached a greater intellectual height than perhaps any other colored man. Because Dr. Du Bois, and rightly in my judgment, insists upon fighting for the rights guaranteed to the colored people by the 13th, 14th and 15th Amendments to the Constitution, he has been set down in some places as aspiring for "social equality," and as being wholly antagonistic to Booker Washington. The two schools have represented, also, in the public mind the question of higher education and manual training, though Dr. Du Bois has repeatedly endorsed the work of such schools as Tuskegee, and Dr. Washington has similarly urged the absolute necessity of more institutions of the higher kind like Atlanta, as has Mr. Taft recently, I believe. So far as Mr. Washington's position is concerned, I can assure you that the opposition to him among his own people increases steadily. The great majority of the men who have risen above the ranks consider him a traitor to the race. You would be surprised at their vehemence, but you must know about it because one reason for the opposition to Mr. Washington is that he has become, not by his own volition, but through the friendship of Mr. Taft and Mr. Roosevelt, the office broker for the race, a position into which, as I have told Mr. Washington frankly, no man ought to allow himself to be forced, however gratifying it may be, or how little he may have sought the honor. Of course, the negro office holders, like McKinlay, W. H. Lewis, and others, and many of the negro editors, are entirely on Mr. Washington's side. If you consult only with them you will please only them, and you will correspondingly offend the other faction. I am, therefore, submitting names of both sides, marking the Washington men individually. Of the others I know each and every one personally, with the exception of Mr. Carter,[1] and I know that you can thoroughly rely upon them, and if they are free to speak their minds frankly to you they will confirm everything that I have written. I am also enclosing herewith a statement[2] drawn up for me by a very able colored man in whom I am much interested, which gives in answer to my question, the exact reasons for a good deal of the bitterness against Mr. Taft among those who are not mere office seekers, and do not measure the advance of the negro race by the number of offices it holds. Very truly yours,

Oswald Garrison Villard

[*Enclosure*]

W. J. Carter, Attorney at Law, Harrisburg, Pa.
Dr. C. E. Bentley, Dentist, 100 State Street, Chicago, Ills.
Dr. O. M. Waller, 762 Herkimer Street, Brooklyn, N.Y.
Dr. W. L. Bulkley, Principal Public Schools, New York.
Mr. C. W. Chesnutt, Author, Cleveland, Ohio.
Mr. John Hope, President Atlanta Baptist College, Atlanta, Ga.
Mr. L. M. Hershaw, War Department, 1460 T Street, Washington, D.C.
Dr. W. E. B. Du Bois, 20 Vesey Street, New York City.

Washington men

Bishop Alexander Walters, New York City.
Kelly Miller, Howard University, Washington, D.C.
Charles W. Anderson, Collector of Internal Revenue, Washington.[3]
M. C. B. Mason, Freedmen's Aid Society, Cincinnati, Ohio.
Mr. Hunton[4] of the International Y.M.C.A. Committee.

TLS   William Howard Taft Papers   DLC.

[1] William Justin Carter, born in Virginia in 1866, was a graduate of Howard University Law School (1892) and a successful corporation lawyer in Harrisburg. In 1910 he was a member of the Committee of 100 of the NAACP.

[2] The statement was not found with the letter.

[3] Actually New York City.

[4] William Alphaeus Hunton (b. 1865), born and educated in Canada, became the first black secretary for YMCA work in the United States beginning in 1888. In 1891 he became secretary of the Colored Men's Department of the YMCA's international committee.

To Frederick Randolph Moore

Budapest, [Hungary] Sept 24, 1910

My dear Mr Moore: Please telegraph Mr. Scott (collect) to bring all mail when he comes North to speak at Worcester[1] and to remain North till I reach home.

Am well, but want to get home. No place like U.S. Lots of Negros storming over here. Yours Sincerely,

Booker T. Washington

ALS Con. 607 BTW Papers DLC. Written on stationery of the Grand Hotel Hungaria.

1 Emmett J. Scott delivered the principal address before a conference of college presidents and professors on Africa and the Near East held at Clark University in Worcester, Mass., in early October 1910. He spoke in defense of the Liberian government and the progress the country had made, concluding that Liberia was worth saving and that the United States should aid the struggling republic in its boundary disputes and financial difficulties. Scott was entertained at the home of Clark University's president, G. Stanley Hall. (New York *Age*, Oct. 13, 1910, 1.)

An Article in the *American Magazine*

Sept. 1910

Bert Williams

When I go to the theatre, which is not often, I generally go to hear the colored comedian, Bert Williams. I go to hear him, however, as often as I have opportunity, and I am seldom in the same city with him that I do not find myself, if I happen to have an hour of leisure, drifting in the direction of the theatre in which he is playing.

If I were a dramatic critic I suppose I might give some sound logical reasons for liking Bert Williams's style and methods. But I am not a critic, and vaudeville performances, as a rule, strike me as tiresome. There is so much that seems to me strained and artificial and lacking in the flavor of ordinary wholesome human nature. But Bert Williams's humor strikes me as the real thing. There is nothing second-hand or second-rate about it. His fun seems to flow spontaneously and without effort, as if it came from some deep natural source in the man himself. Besides, there is a quality and flavor about Williams's humor which indicates that it is the natural expression of a thoughtful and observing mind.

I have noticed him standing about in a barber shop or among a crowd of ordinary colored people, the quietest man in the whole gathering. All the time, however, he was studying and observing, enjoying the characters that he saw around him and getting material for some of those quaint songs and stories in which he reproduces the natural humor and philosophy of the Negro people.

As I have said, if I were a dramatic critic I might give some sound reasons for liking Bert Williams, but I suppose the best reason I can give for liking his quaint songs and humorous sayings is that he puts into this form some of the quality and philosophy of the Negro race. In fact, it seems to me that Bert Williams has done for one side of the Negro life and character just what the old plantation Negroes did for another — given expression and put into a form which everyone can understand and appreciate something of the inner life and peculiar genius, if I may say so, of the Negro.

There is occasionally, as there is, I suppose, in all real humor, a touch of real pathos, as for instance in his quaint little song in which he explains "Why Adam Sinned":

"Adam neber had no Mammy
For to take him on her knee,
And tell him what was right, and show him
Things he'd ought to see.
I know, down in my heart,
He'd a let dat apple be;
But Adam neber had no dear old Mammy.

"Adam neber had no childhood,
Playin' 'round de cabin do'.
He neber had no pickaninny life.
He started in a great big grown-up man, and what is mo' —
He neber had no right kind ob a wife."

Bert Williams was born at New Providence, Nassau, in the British Bahama Islands, and is now thirty-five years of age. His grandfather was a white man, the Danish and Spanish Consul for the Bahama Islands, who married a quadroon. His grandfather, who owned a number of small ships, made considerable money during the Civil War, which he lost later in investments in the United

States. When he was two years old, Frederick Williams, Mr. Williams's father, came to New York. Here he learned the trade of papier-maché maker, and this brought him into connection with the New York theatres. Thus Bert Williams got his first acquaintance with the theatre when he was a boy.

From New York his father moved to Riverside, California, and Bert Williams, later graduating at the Riverside High School, went to San Francisco, with the idea of preparing there for college. His purpose was to be a civil engineer. He was for a time bell boy at the Hollenbeck Hotel in Los Angeles and went to school at night.

At this time, Williams says, he was "a great almanac man." He was the young man who always read, remembered and related the latest jokes, and he was always popular at the entertainments that the colored people were accustomed to give at the churches and elsewhere.

One day a colored man named Lew Johnson, who kept a barber shop in San Francisco, asked Bert Williams if he did not want to join a little company that he intended to take up along the coast to play the lumber camps, between San Francisco and Eureka, and then come back by way of the mining camps at the western edge of the mountains. That was the way Bert Williams gained his entrance to the stage. After his return from this trip he went to work in a vaudeville theatre, in San Francisco. It wasn't a very high-class theatre, but it was a great school for him, and Mr. Williams says he learned his profession there.

Starting in this humble way, as a member of a little mountebank minstrel show, Mr. Williams has gone on quietly, modestly gaining the goodwill of the public and the respect of his associates, until he now has a secure and established position in public favor.

Perhaps I ought to mention one incident in that career. In 1903, when the Williams and Walker Company were playing at the Shaftesbury Theatre in London, England, Mr. Williams was invited to attend a lawn party at Buckingham palace to entertain the guests at a birthday party of the present Prince of Wales, grandson of the late King Edward VII. There he succeeded in making himself a great favorite with the little prince, and princes, who were anxious, expecially, that he should teach them all his dances.

Let me add, in conclusion, that during all the years I have known Bert Williams I have never heard him whine or cry about his color, or about any racial discrimination. He has gone right on, in season and out of season, doing his job, perfecting himself in his work, till he has reached the top round in his specialty.

A few years ago, George Walker, his partner, lost his health and for a number of years has been unable to do any work on the stage. The finer side of Mr. Williams's life is shown by the fact that during all Mr. Walker's illness Mr. Williams has contributed regularly toward his support and has left nothing undone to make Mr. Walker comfortable and happy.

Bert Williams is a tremendous asset of the Negro race. He is an asset because he has succeeded in actually doing something, and, because he has succeeded, the fact of his success helps the Negro many times more than he could help the Negro by merely contenting himself to whine and complain about racial difficulties and racial discriminations. The fact is that the American people are ready to honor and to reward any man who does something that is worth while, no matter whether he is black or white, and Bert Williams's career is simply another illustration of that fact.

American Magazine, 70 (Sept. 1910), 600–604.

A News Item in the New York *Evening Post*

Copenhagen, October 3 [1910]

BOOKER WASHINGTON HONORED

RECEIVED BY DANISH KING — TO DINE WITH ROYAL FAMILY

King Frederick[1] received Booker T. Washington and conversed at length with him on the subject of the colored race to-day. The King asked Mr. Washington for a copy of one of his publications.

Afterward, as the guest of prominent Danes, Mr. Washington motored to Roskilde, the old-time capital, where he visited a school and had luncheon. To-night he will dine at the palace, meeting the members of the royal family, including Queen Alexandra, the widow of King Edward.[2]

New York *Evening Post,* Oct. 3, 1910, 1.

[1] Frederick VIII (1843–1912), King of Denmark from 1906 to 1912.
[2] Edward VII (1841–1910), King of England from 1901 to 1910.

From Pinckney Benton Stewart Pinchback

Washington, D.C., Oct. 4, 1910

My dear Doctor: I am sure you will be pleased to know your unceasing efforts to secure me Government employment fructified at last. Early this morning a communication from the Treasury Dept. notified me of my appointment for ninety days as an assistant agent of the Revenue Service, at ten dollars per day. It was signed by Mr. Hilles, Asst. Sec. Treas. Later in the day I called upon Mr. Hilles and thanked him for his good offices in my behalf, and assured him that you would be highly pleased to learn of my appointment. I took the liberty to show him your letter to me, written in mid-ocean, and he seemed greatly pleased with it. I remarked to him, after he had read your letter, that I did not take your tip to call upon him frequently, because I knew he was a very busy man, and I felt assured he would do his best for me since you had requested it. In the course of our conversation he said my appointment would have been made two weeks earlier if it had not been for a hitch in the Napier case. The President desired to keep his promise to make Napier's appointment the first act. He could not get the consent of Senator Curtis[1] until last Saturday for the displacement of Vernon. Vernon goes out Feb. 1, 1911, and Napier will take his place. This will be a death blow to the antis. The political pot is boiling, which you will note by the prints.

Mrs. Pinchback is slowly improving, and I have hopes of her full recovery. She had a close call.

I see by the papers that you are having a royal time over there

— dining with kings and princes and royal families. I wonder what old Ben Tillman thinks of this?

Mr. Scott passed through the city yesterday and was the first person to inform me of my appointment. Mr. Hilles showed him a telegram from the President saying, "Go ahead with the Pinchback appointment."

My heart goes out to you in grateful thanks for the great service you have rendered me.

With assurances of highest esteem, I am   Your obedient servant and friend,

Pinchback

HLSr Con. 911 BTW Papers DLC.

1 Charles Curtis (1860–1936), Republican senator from W. T. Vernon's home state of Kansas (1907–13, 1915–29) and Vice-President of the United States from 1929 to 1933.

Maurice Francis Egan to Philander Chase Knox

American Legation, Copenhagen   October 5, 1910

Sir: I have the honor to report that Mr. Booker Washington, well known as the founder of the Tuskegee College, arrived on October 2nd and left on the night of October 3rd. His visit had been announced many times in the local papers. The Master of Ceremonies at the Court informed me that Their Majesties[1] desired to see him. I replied that he was a very modest and self-effacing man and that a formal presentation by the American Minister might annoy him. It was then arranged that he should meet His Majesty informally at ten o'clock on Monday, I sending the carriage for him. His Majesty invited him to dine with the Royal Family (not including the Empress Dowager of Russia or Queen Alexandra, who are here) at Charlottenlund. I was not included in the invitation to Mr. Washington, as I did not present him. This was done by the Marshal of the Court. Mr. Washington seems to be a sensible and reasonable man; he served a good purpose in showing Their Majesties, and (in his lecture) the Danish public, that, if the Danish

Antilles were acquired by the United States, immediate lynching of the negroes there would not necessarily follow.

I have the honor to be, Sir, Your obedient servant,

Maurice Francis Egan,
American Minister

TLS   State Department Decimal File, 1910–29   Box 317   RG59   DNA.

¹ King Frederick and Queen Louise.

Extract from the Minutes
of the Tuskegee Institute Executive Council

[Tuskegee, Ala.] Oct. 6, 1910

Mrs. B. T. Washington's request to be allowed to organize a class for the purpose of teaching at Dorothy Hall manicuring, facial massage, hair dressing and kindred work is approved without expense to the school in regard to teachers' salary.

HM   Con. 1009   BTW Papers   DLC.

A Circular Letter by John Elmer Milholland

Kensington, London, W. October 6th, 1910

Tuskegee and the American Negro

DR. BOOKER T. WASHINGTON'S INDUSTRIAL EDUCATION PROPAGANDA
Dispassionately Reviewed in the Light of Actualities
by an AMERICAN CITIZEN

Rev., Dear Sir, I must decline your Society's kind invitation to the Luncheon in honour of my fellow countryman, Dr. Booker T. Washington. I do so with regret. Dr. Washington, like myself, is a Citizen of the United States. He is also a friend of many years. Our relations have been cordial. More than once he has been my guest. The Sunday following his famous Luncheon at the White House with President Roosevelt, when the consequent excitement — that exhibition of barbarism — was at its height, I gave a dinner in his honour at the leading hotel of New York. Not less than $50,000 was realised for his school on that occasion. At the time I also held his view on the Tuskegee propaganda.

From this you can perhaps infer that if your Luncheon involved merely the personal equation, I would gladly come, but it involves a great deal more, as you and your friends will all see within a short time, and because it does, I deem it proper, out of regard for the host of the occasion, the noble organisation which you represent, that I should set forth briefly the reasons that compel me to decline an invitation from a Society that all good people delight to honour.

Dr. Washington and his institution at Tuskegee practically stand for the industrial education or material progress of the American Negro, and for that alone.

I do not. Neither do I stand for the industrial education of the Jews, the Irish, the Dutch, or any other race. It would be just as rational to say that the men of Kent or Surrey shall all be wheel-wrights, every Welshman an electrician, every Scotchman a gardener, or that the young women of Yorkshire, even when qualified to go in for the Mathematical Tripos at Cambridge, shall all become Red Cross Nurses, as to lay down one course of study and development for 10,000,000 American citizens whose skins are coloured, but who differ from one another in brain and body just as much as the people of other nations.

More than a hundred years ago, when Slavery flourished in the United States, North and South, Alexander Hamilton, one of the greatest Statesmen, keenest observers, and among the most logical reasoners ever produced in America, declared, after exhaustive examination, that the Negro's "natural faculties are every bit as good as ours." A century's experience confirms this view, for even that ancient lie about certain "fundamental differences in the brain structure," has been so completely demolished in the cold processes of scientific demonstration, notably by Professor Wilder, of Cornell, the French, German and other savants, that we shall be troubled less with it in the future consideration of this subject. There are Negroes, and possibly the majority of them, as in the case of the Whites, who may or may not be fit for higher education; but to say that the hundreds of thousands who unquestionably are shall be denied the cultivation of their faculties is an outrage upon the individual and a crime against humanity.

Again, Dr. Washington stands for the inadequate education of his Race, and tacitly accepts the shameful violation of the Constitutional rights of the Afro-American. About 3,000 students of both sexes attend Tuskegee and his theory seems to be that by a gradual multiplication of his School throughout the country the entire field will be covered in time. It certainly will require a very long time even to supply industrial education, but, as I heard him declare — and in doing so strikingly illustrated Sir Harry Johnston's remark that none were more callous to the Negro's sufferings than the Negro himself — in the Manhattan Hotel, New York, that "a hundred years would be required to qualify his people for citizenship." I suppose he feels more reconciled to this deliberate procedure than are the overwhelming majority of American Citizens, whose representatives in Congress more than forty years ago wrote into our Constitution that fitness for Citizenship was no longer to be conditioned upon "race, colour or previous conditions of servitude." I stand upon the Constitution, which was amended in the Negro's interest when, as an illiterate race, they had just emerged from slavery, whereas now more than fifty per cent. of them can read and write.

The authorities estimate that more than four million children, about equally divided between white and coloured, are growing up in the United States to-day without an opportunity to acquire even the rudiments of an education. It is part of slavery's aftermath, as Mr. Archer realised in his recent journeyings through the South.[1] Deplorable under any circumstances, it is doubly so in this instance because it is absolutely unnecessary. The United States, spending tens of millions for a new Navy and hundreds of millions for a Panama Canal, is abundantly able to provide for the educational needs of every boy and girl beneath the flag. It is able, and the great mass of our people are willing to do so. They were willing to do so twenty years ago, when that practical, comprehensive scheme of legislation known as the Blair Education Bill, put forth as an adequate expression of the popular desire, was passed again and again by the Senate, and only beaten finally by one of the most discreditable combinations of political selfishness, foolish leadership, misguided philanthropists and religious bigotry ever evidenced at Washington. Had it passed, this Bill would have eliminated illiteracy completely from every Southern State, and given the Negro, as well as the white child, not only a primary education, but an enlightened environment, within which lynching, mob law, and colour prejudice would gradually have become impossible.

Those who were responsible for the Bill's defeat — and Dr. Washington has some knowledge on this point — boasted that ample school facilities would be provided by the various States, supplemented with private philanthropy. The prediction has not been fulfilled. In one State, at least, the annual provision for popular education does not amount to a dollar a year, *per capita*, and all the private enterprises, the Peabody Fund, Slater Fund, Mr. Carnegie's and Mr. Rockefeller's large donations, Hampton, Fisk, Nashville, Howard and Tuskegee, all rolled together, are but a drop in the bucket, and fail to do more than ripple the surface of this sea of ignorance.

Not in their inadequacy, however, lies the gravest objection to these attempts to substitute spasmodic philanthropic enterprise for a stern, imperious Government duty. The argument rests upon deeper foundations. If popular education is, according to Burke, the bulwark of any nation, what sort of statecraft is it that would have this tower of strength dependent upon the humanitarian impulse of rich men and women, or the mendicancy of Dr. Washington and others like him? Education is not to be sought or bestowed as a charity; it is nothing if not an inherent right of every American child, sanctioned by the overwhelming majority of American tax payers, whose will has been thwarted by misguided people in magnifying the importance of their individual efforts to the detriment of the masses, and whose experiments, after a fair trial, extending over a quarter of a century, as a solution of the Race problem, have been dismal failures. Such individual institutions as Tuskegee have grown and prospered, but the social and political condition of the Negro in the South has become steadily worse, until to women like Mrs. Terrell and men like Dr. Du Bois it is to-day simply intolerable. The Armenian, under the old Turkish *régime*, was only at times more desperate, for when the mob's passion is aroused a Negro's life is regarded with less concern than that of a dog.

Please understand that I do not deplore Tuskegee's prosperity. I rejoice that thanks to Mr. Carnegie and others, Dr. Washington has been able to collect such large sums of money. He would be successful in any calling. A shrewder, a more adroit man would be difficult to find in Dixie. He has the genius of persuasion and diplomacy. What I object to is his endeavour to make people here believe an untruth, as he has done to an alarming extent in America, namely, that his scheme of industrial education is a panacea, when he should know perfectly well that it is nothing of the kind. Industrial education was had by the Negro in Slavery. They were the mechanics and artisans of the South, as well as the tillers of the soil, and whatever may be said on behalf of the system, it surely will not be admitted by sane, thinking people that a man must acquire a trade at the price of his individual or political manhood. That is the crux of the situation.

It has become fashionable among shallow thinkers and crude generalisers to say that the great Statesmen of the Civil War, Sumner, Stevens, Fessenden, Wade, Conkling, Blaine, and Shellabarger, with the aroused Nation behind them, were mistaken in granting the Negro the right of suffrage. Nothing could be further from the truth, and all the lying in connection with the so-called "Carpet Bag" period cannot make it otherwise. The Negro has proved his right to Citizenship. He has been right on every great question since the War. He has voted intelligently and with keen discrimination; he left his imprint on the South by the wisest legislative measures in its history; among others, the existing system of Public Schools, and when the History of the Reconstruction period becomes something more than an accepted lie, the true story of Negro domination of the South will cause such a revision of opinion as to humiliate his traducers and confound his adversaries.

Some years ago I published a pamphlet setting forth in detail the history of the Negro vote in our national elections since the close of the Civil War, thereby demonstrating that the Negro had voted in the Republic's interest on every important issue, thus vindicating his judgment at the polls. That pamphlet has been circulated widely, but not a single statement in it has ever been challenged. In other words, the Negroes have proved themselves as worthy of citizenship as any other element of our population, and yet, notwithstanding this, they are to-day without a single representative in Congress, the Courts, the Cabinet, or practically in any of the State Legislatures, something that cannot be said of any other body of American citizens. The German Americans are no more numerous, but you find few Municipal or State governments in which they are not represented in accordance with their numerical strength in the electorate; their spokesmen are conspicuous in the halls of national legislation. The same is true of the Swedes, the Hungarians, the Italians, and, of course, conspicuously true of the Irish. The Indians have a United States Senator. The Jews are represented even in the Cabinet, and no sensible man thinks it should be otherwise. The Negro is excluded, not because of any personal unfitness (his representatives were always among the ablest in Congress), but for no other reason than that of his colour and Race. He is a victim of shameless class legislation, of force, fraud, intimidation and murder. No fair-minded man familiar with the way in which the disfranchising of the coloured voter was brought about in the Southern States has any question whatever as to the wholesale fraudulent character of the entire procedure. It was contrary to the spirit, contrary to the letter of the Constitution. It is in clear violation of the solemn pledges of the seceding States when they were re-admitted to the Union. It is an outrage on our American citizenship, a disgrace to Republican Government, an affront to advancing civilization.

To sum up, Dr. Washington stands for private, spasmodic schemes of education based upon private charity; condones the disfranchisement of the Negro, in fact if not in form, negatively if not positively; deems it unwise to denounce lynching or peonage, or protest against the numberless shameless outrages perpetrated upon his Race throughout the country. He thinks he can do more by overlooking them and by persuading everybody else he can to overlook them also. He has been tolerably successful up to the present time, but he has reached the limit. His staunchest upholders in America, such, for example, as *The Evening Post* of New York, which was foolishly led to oppose the Blair Education Bill years ago, has at last become aroused to the absurdity of the Tuskegee proposition as the salvation of the Negro, typifying in this

399

the beclouded brain clearing and long dormant conscience awakening of the Nation.

The lynching habit has grown in America until the average during the past few months has reached one a day, or about double that which has prevailed during the last twenty years. Sixty men were massacred in Texas in July without any Government investigation or inquiry, and yet Dr. Washington comes over here and blandly assures the British public that the Races are dwelling together more amicably than in the past. He is utterly mistaken, and in refutation of what he says, I offer you this unchallenged statement made in the United States Senate by one of the most widely-known of that body, a Southerner of Southerners, Senator Tillman, of North Carolina, who in a speech delivered before the Senate openly declared:

> Race hatred grows day by day. There is no man who is honest, going through the South and conversing with the White People and Blacks, but will return and tell you this is true. Then I say to you of the North who are the rulers of the land, who can change this or do something to relieve conditions, what are you going to do about it? Are you going to sit quiet? If nothing else will cause you to think, I notify you, what you already know, that there are a billion dollars or more of Northern capital invested in the South in railroads, in mines, in forests, in farm lands, and self interest, which fact, if nothing else — ought to make you set about hunting some remedy for this terrible situation. As it is the South is helpless. We can do nothing. We are one-third of the population. You are two-thirds. Every year your members are being added to by a million immigrants in the North, who stay there, while none go to us. The million who came in last year represent five Congressmen. Those who came in year before last represent five more Congressmen. There is no danger of political power ever drifting away from the North. Therefore we say to you it is your duty to do something. It is your duty to move. It is your duty to begin the discussion. For the time being the South is occupying an attitude of waiting. It is occupying an attitude of constant friction, race riot, butchery, murder of Whites by Blacks and Blacks by Whites, the inevitable, irrepressible conflict.

Thanking you again for your kind invitation, wishing your Society all prosperity, and your Guest health of body and a clearer vision, I beg to remain, Yours sincerely,

JOHN E. MILHOLLAND

PLSr Con. 410 BTW Papers DLC. Addressed to John Hobbis Harris, secretary of the Anti-Slavery and Aborigines Protection Society.

1 William Archer (1856–1924), the British theater critic and playwright, was a prolific writer on many topics, including several travel accounts. In 1910 he pub-

lished *Through Afro-America: An English Reading of the Race Problem.* (See An Excerpt from a Book by William Archer, 1910, below.)

A News Item in the London *Times*

London, October 7, 1910

THE PROBLEMS OF RACE

LUNCHEON TO MR. BOOKER WASHINGTON

The Anti-Slavery and Aborigines Protection Society entertained Mr. Booker T. Washington at luncheon yesterday at the Whitehall Rooms. Sir Thomas Fowell Buxton (president of the society) occupied the chair, and among those supporting him were the Archbishop of the West Indies, the Bishop of Hereford, the Bishop of Exeter, Archdeacon Potter, the Postmaster-General, Lord and Lady Courtney, Sir Colin and Lady Scott-Moncrieff, Sir Richard and Lady Stapley, Sir John Kennaway, Sir Arthur and Lady Conan Doyle, Sir Albert and Lady Spicer, Sir H. H. Johnston, Lady Scott, Mr. Valentine Chirol, Mr. Stephen Collins, M.P., Mr. Fisher Unwin, Mr. Cobden Fisher Unwin, Mr. Sherwell, M.P., Mr. Whitehouse, M.P., Sir Percy and Lady Bunting, Mr. Alden, M.P., Mr. A. H. Scott, M.P., Mr. J. R. MacDonald, M.P., Mr. and Mrs. W. T. Stead, Mr. and Mrs. E. D. Morel, Miss Octavia Hill, Sir J. Glover, Sir H. Cotton, and Mr. J. Cadbury.

Many expressions of regret for enforced absence had been received by the secretary (the Rev. J. H. Harris). Mr. Balfour wrote from Whittingehame stating that his engagements would make it impossible for him to be in London. The following letter was sent by the Archbishop of Canterbury:

"It is a great disappointment to me that paramount engagements far away from London render it impossible for me to be present at the gathering which is to give greeting and God-speed to Mr. Booker Washington. I have for some years had the pleasure of Mr. Booker Washington's acquaintance, and I share with all those who know the facts the appreciation of the services he has rendered and is rendering to the solution of one of the gravest and most perplexing problems of our time. He is a man who, in every sense, deserves well of his contemporaries, and I believe that, when hereafter the story is written of Christian people's endeavour in our day to atone for and to amend the racial wrongdoings of the past, Mr. Booker Washington's name will stand in the very forefront of those for whom the world will give thanks."

The Prime Minister wrote from 10, Downing-street:

"I much regret that my engagements do not allow me to accept your invitation to be present at the luncheon which it is proposed to give in honour of Mr. Booker Washington. I feel sure, however, that he will be welcomed with a cordiality which his persistent and successful labours in the cause of the education of the American negro deserve, especially at the hands of Englishmen, whose difficulties in many parts of the Empire have been helped towards a solution by the results of his work."

A REPRESENTATIVE WELCOME

The health of the guest was submitted in speeches by the Chairman, the Bishop of Exeter, Mr. Herbert Samuel, Dr. R. F. Horton, Sir H. H. Johnston, and Sir A. Conan Doyle.

Mr. Herbert Samuel said the letter which had been read from the Prime Minister expressed the cordial sympathy and appreciation with which the British Government regarded the work of their guest, a work which was as successful in its result as it was lofty in its aim. The problem with which Mr. Booker Washington had been dealing was not merely a domestic problem of the United States of America. It was one that faced all Empires and countries in which there was a mixing or a juxtaposition of races of widely divergent types. Nowhere would Mr. Washington find a more real sense of moral obligation to the coloured races of the world than he would find in England. Nowhere, for that reason, would he find plished for others, but also because he was the symbol of the rehis own work more fully appreciated. (Cheers.) They welcomed Mr. Washington not only in recognition of what he had accomgeneration of the race to which he belonged and because he was in his own person a message of hope to the negro populations of the world. (Cheers.)

Sir H. H. Johnston, speaking of his own visit to Tuskegee, said he could find no fault whatever with its principles and teaching. One of the best things that was being done by the institution was to give the negro a good conceit of himself while saving him from becoming conceited. It was to men of Mr. Washington's composite character that the African and new African in America would look as leaders rather than to the pure white man who, in spite of the best intentions, might not be able always to be so completely in sympathy with the black.

THE WORK AT TUSKEGEE INSTITUTE

Mr. Booker Washington said that in legal form the negro race throughout the world had freedom, but they must all realize that freedom, in its deepest and widest meaning, could never be a bequest; it must be a conquest. In America his race both enjoyed advantages and suffered from disadvantages. Among the former it might be said that the negro was the only race that went there by reason of the fact that it had a pressing invitation to do so. (Laughter.) Some people suggested that they should go back, but in so far as he could discern their intentions they were planning to remain in the United States, and he believed that in that country there was wisdom, patience, forbearance, Christianity, and patriotism enough to enable each race to live side by side, working out its destiny with justice to the other. They possessed the advantage, too, that, as races were counted in this age, the negro in America was a new race, and they stood in the position of being ready and anxious to bend themselves in any direction that offered the best course for their uplifting. The Tuskegee Institute was started in a little shanty with one teacher and 30 students. To-day it had between 1,600 and 1,700 men and women students, who came from 36 States in the Union and 22 foreign countries, and 176 instructors and helpers. It stood on 3,000 acres, and with four exceptions its 96 buildings were almost wholly constructed by the labour of the students. The property was valued at about $1,000,-000, and there was not one dollar of mortgage upon it. The annual expense of carrying on the work of the Institute was $256,000. While the Institute thoroughly believed in University and professional education for a large number of the negro race, it also believed that in their present stage of civilization it was important to emphasize hand training. When the negro was freed he felt that labour with the hand was past, and students came to him in disgust when they found they had to put up their own buildings. His answer to them was that the object of the Institute was not to work the negro, but to teach the negro how to work. There was a vast difference between being worked and working. (Cheers.) The greatest single achievement at Tuskegee was to be found in the change that had come over the millions of his race in regard to the subject of labour, for there was no hope for any race until it had learned that all forms of labour were dignified and all forms of idleness a disgrace. (Cheers.) If he had learned anything during his visit here it was the importance of teaching the negro race, before it was too late, to love the soil. From the Tuskegee Institute alone 6,000 men and women had been sent out who would be found at work in all parts of the Southern States, and in demand by whites as well as blacks for the supervision of farms, industrial establishments, and schools. Tuskegee was criticized for paying too much attention to the material things of life. They believed thoroughly in the ethical and more important side of life, but it was difficult to make a good Christian of a hungry man. His race was responding magnificently to the efforts which had been made on their behalf, and tremendous progress had been made. (Cheers.)

In the evening Mr. Booker Washington delivered a lecture at the National Liberal Club on "The Economic Progress of the Negro in America."

London *Times*, Oct. 7, 1910, 4.

A News Item in the Manchester *Guardian*

[Manchester, England, Oct. 8, 1910]

NEGRO DISABILITIES

DR. BOOKER WASHINGTON'S LAST SPEECH IN ENGLAND

Dr. Booker Washington, who sails for America to-day, addressed his final meeting in this country in Liverpool last night. He described the policy of lynching human beings for crime as a disgrace to any civilised nation, and said the habit, if persisted in, would damn any Christian nation. Much depended on the attitude the British nation would assume towards the weaker of the darker races under its flag. No man could inflict wrong upon another without being more injured himself than the man he was wronging. The negro knew he was down, and wanted to get up, and we could always help a race when it appreciated the fact that it was down. It was comparatively easy to overcome the weaknesses of the negro race, but along with its spiritual and moral growth must go economical growth, as the foundation for its human life. If a negro burned down a house everyone heard of it, but if ten negroes built a house we never heard anything of it; if one white man killed a negro everyone knew of it, but if ten white men helped and encouraged a negro every day no one heard of it.

Manchester *Guardian*, Oct. 8, 1910, 10.

To Benjamin Jefferson Davis

Boston, Mass. October 16, 1910

Personal
Dear Mr. Davis: Mr. Scott has called my attention to your communication or communications to him during my absence regarding the New York Age.[1] Of course, ordinarily you would understand that one does not care to discuss his personal business with any one covering his investments in regard to property. I, however, do not mind stating to you in answer to your questions that I do not directly or indirectly own a single dollar's worth of stock or property value in any manner, shape or form in the New York Age. When I spoke to you in New York I thought I made myself plain. I said to you at the time that I had no control over Mr. Moore nor any property interest or financial interest in The Age, but I had taken the liberty of urging Mr. Moore to keep away from personal attacks and criticisms. The fact that Mr. Moore disregarded my advice and made the publication to which you refer is evidence within itself it seems to me that I had no control over the paper. From the first I have pursued the policy of not having any financial interest in any Negro publication for the reason that

I knew that such financial investment would bring upon me criticism of the kind which I did not care to have. I do not, however, want to leave the impression that I am not on friendly terms with Mr. Moore just as I am on friendly terms with scores of other colored editors throughout the country and sometimes he is kind enough to regard my wishes and advice and sometimes not, just as is the case with others. Yours truly,

[Booker T. Washington]

TLc Con. 905 BTW Papers DLC.

1 Davis asked Scott repeatedly whether BTW owned stock in the New York *Age*. Scott replied in BTW's absence that it was an improper question: "Dr. Washington has not a dollar's worth of interest in The Age, and I certainly have no money at all for newspaper ownership. I should feel quite outraged with myself if I should sit down to categorically catechize you as to whether you owned stock in various corporations of one kind and another." (Davis to Scott, Oct. 8, 1910, and Scott to Davis, Oct. 13, 1910, Con. 905, BTW Papers, DLC.)

Extracts from an Address
before the American Missionary Association

Tremont Temple, Boston   October 19 [1910]

The two months which I have recently spent in Europe in observing the condition and the progress of the people who are farthest down, convince me that the Negro in America is by no means the race that is farthest down. The special work of the American Missionary Association for a long period of years has been in dealing with that class of American people who are considered most backward, but the task before this Association in uplifting the millions of Negroes of this country has many more hopeful elements in it than I found in Southern Europe in relation to the uplift of backward classes in that country.

Before I go further, let me add that I owe a personal debt of gratitude to the American Missionary Association for what I have been privileged to do in America. Out from the American Missionary Association grew the Hampton Institute, so that in a large degree Tuskegee is the granddaughter of this Association. In no less degree do the ten millions of Negroes in America realize that they owe a lasting debt of gratitude to this potent and helpful organization.

.   .   .   .

During the last forty years you have had before you a double problem: one of uplifting the Negro, the other of so helping the Negro to articulate his life into that of the Southern white man by whose side he lives that there will be peace, harmony and friendship existing between the two races.

When we consider all that has taken place in the past, when we consider the tremendous amount of territory covered by these two races and the immense population to be reached, I consider that you have been most successful in mastering this task, and I need not occupy your time in stating in detail how my race has responded to your efforts to help it. I need not state here in detail how it has responded in buying land, in building houses, in establishing stores, banks and other business enterprises; how it has responded in building schools, industrial institutions, colleges and universities; how it has responded in erecting churches and spreading the gospel of high and righteous living.

As compared with other races in Europe, in dealing with my race the American Missionary Association has this advantage — it is dealing with a race whose future is before it rather than behind it, with a race whose eyes are toward the rising sun, not toward the setting sun. This Association has the advantage, too, of dealing with a race while it is in the process of being moulded into a higher civilization. Just now my race is in a pliable condition, unwedded to anything in the past, willing and anxious to take advantage of the very ripest and best things in education and in Christian civilization.

.   .   .   .

It is most important that this and similar organizations appreciate the advantage which is before it in saving the race before it gets into the ditch. In my observation of conditions in the older countries of Europe I found that in many cases millions of dollars are being spent to help people up who are down, who have lost out as it were, who are wallowing in the ditch. This organization has the chance to keep a race from getting into the ditch. It is so much easier and so much more satisfactory to keep a man from getting in the ditch than it is to help him after he has gotten there.

Among the methods to be used in preventing the Negro from getting further down is that of using our influence to induce the Negro to buy land, to become the owner of a piece of soil especially in the Southland while land is cheap and plentiful; and then in the second place all of our influence should be used to keep the Negro for the most part in the rural districts out of contact with the temptations and the complications of large and complex city life until the race can get that experience and that strength which will enable it to withstand these temptations.

In the Southern part of Europe I found that where agricultural education has been neglected, where it was impossible for the poor man to buy land, that he had gone into the city and had become a burden and a menace to the civilization of many of the cities of Southern Europe; that mistake should not be made in dealing with our race.

Your work, however, is not done. Much is yet to be accomplished in the South. The American Missionary Association for years to come will need the hearty and generous support of churches and individuals throughout the country. There is still a large class of people throughout America, and they are not confined to the South, who contend that it is necessary to educate the people of every other race — to educate the German boy, the Irish boy, the Italian boy, but they say by implication at least that the Negro is naturally born into the world with so much intelligence that he is an exception to all the rest of the races in that he does not need any education.

Your work will not be completed while it is true of any part of our country that human beings are lynched, are burned at the stake, or are murdered by the mob without trial by jury. Your work will not be completed until in every portion of America it is thoroughly understood that any man, black or white, charged with crime shall be given a legal, fair and just hearing before a proper tribunal. Your work will not be completed until it is thoroughly understood that the law, both state and national, in its making and in its execution, shall be applied without equivocation to all people without regard to race or color.

Your work will not be completed until people everywhere realize that neither state nor national law makes any difference between the black man and white man in punishing crime — that the Negro finds that if he steals, if he commits murder, he is tried before the same judges, before the same court, under the same law under which the white man is tried; and that since it is true in the punishing end no color line is drawn, it should be equally true that no line should be drawn in preparing the individual to know the law and to respect and keep the law. It is unjust and unmerciful to keep the Negro in ignorance and then expect him to know what the law is and to have that degree of self-control that will enable him to keep the law while the white man is made highly intelligent and the Negro remains in ignorance.

As to the methods pursued in educating the Negro, there is a pressing demand that some organization or institution take the leadership in the matter of systematizing Negro education, of seeing that every phase of the work is so organized and systematized that there will be no waste. In too large a degree too much money is being spent in certain portions of the South in a hap-hazard, hit or miss fashion without any certain aim in view. In my opinion the time has come when there should be such organization and such system in connection with the education of the Negro that there shall be no duplication and that every effort shall be made toward a certain purpose. This idea of systematizing and properly organizing Negro education upon a national basis should extend from the kindergarten through the university, and in proportion as that plan is perfected, larger sums of money will be commanded from business men and others for the support of this work. What we want in the South in connection with Negro education is more organized team work, even though such organized team work cuts through denominational lines.

·   ·   ·   ·

Another advantage. You are not calling upon the public to give money to buy clothing or food or shelter for the millions of Negroes in America. Since the days of Reconstruction the Negro has supported himself in food, clothing, and shelter. Unlike many groups of people in other parts of the world, the Negro is not a beggar so far as his personal needs are concerned. The only call that we have made upon the public has been for aid in securing education and moral and religious development, the same kind of call that all races and nations have a right to make upon the public.

In view of the pressing demands that pour in upon the officers of the American Missionary Association from every quarter of the South, I urge the American public with all the emphasis that I can command to see to it that the work of this Association is supported, enlarged and made permanent. I know of few organizations in America that have more thoroughly proven the right to exist, or their right to be supported by the public.

The men and the women whom you have sent out from such institutions as Fisk, Talladega, and a score of others are reflecting the highest credit upon our race, and but for the self-control and wise leadership of the men sent out from these institutions it would have been impossible for us to have maintained during all these years peace and good will to such a large extent between black men and white men in our Southern States. When the history of the South shall have been written, no class of people will be entitled to a larger degree of credit for the progress of the South than is true of the educated Negroes whom this Association and other organizations have been putting into every corner of the South during the last forty years.

TM   Con. 824   BTW Papers   DLC.

An Account of Washington's Reception
in New England

Boston, Mass., Oct. 20 [1910]

HONOR TO WASHINGTON

BOOKER T. WASHINGTON IN
NEW ENGLAND

ROYAL RECEPTIONS TENDERED HIM

Fresh from his European experiences Booker T. Washington came to Boston Saturday night from New York, where the night before he had been banqueted at a dinner in honor of his return by leading Negroes from New York City and State, Massachusetts, Pennsylvania, Delaware and the District of Columbia at famous Kahil's, 18 Park Place, New York.

He has spoken at a series of meetings here and in the vicinity which have tested the capacity of the assembly rooms wherever he has appeared. Beginning Sunday morning, October 16, at 11 o'clock, he spoke in the aristocratic First Parish Church of Brookline. He was whisked in an automobile at the close of the meeting to Brockton, where he also spoke at the morning service at the Porter Congregational Church. In the afternoon at 4:30 o'clock, having made the trip by automobile, he appeared at a meeting held in the Eliot Congregational Church at Newton, and wound up the day with a meeting at night at the Congregational Tabernacle at Salem.

All of these meetings were held in the interest of Tuskegee Institute, and were attended by crowds so large that in each case hundreds of people were turned away, being unable to gain admittance to the churches.

The indefatigable Tuskegean not content with these efforts in behalf of his famous institution, filled engagements in its behalf on Monday night, October 17, at the Central Congregational Church, Fall River, Mass.; and at famous Bradford Academy for Girls, Bradford, Mass., and at the First Baptist Church, Haverhill, Tuesday evening, October 18.

The meeting at Fall River was presided over by Congressman Green,[1] who made a particularly interesting and eloquent address in introducing Dr. Washington to his friends and constituents.

At Bradford Academy, one of the most important and most exclusive girls' schools in New England, the young women assembled in the yard, and on Dr. Washington's arrival gave their college yell in his honor and followed him with cheers and the waving of handkerchiefs into the hall. Dr. Washington's daughter, Mrs. Portia M. Pittman, is an alumna of this institution.

Returning to Boston Tuesday evening, Dr. Washington found at the depot an automobile which had been provided by the United Committee of Colored Elks, which conveyed him to Paine Memorial Hall on Appleton street, where a reception and band concert were being held by the Elks. Some seven or eight hundred ladies and gentlemen were present. They welcomed the Negro leader with cheers, hand-clapping, the waving of handkerchiefs, etc., and gave every evidence of sincere pleasure in being able to entertain him as a guest of the occasion. A detachment of Company L of the Sixth Massachusetts Regiment met him and his party at the door, and acting as an escort of honor, conducted him to the platform, where he was received by Stewart E. Hoyt,[2] Grand Esteemed Loyal Knight, and introduced to the audience in glowing terms of welcome. Negro Boston, as represented by these seven or eight hundred ladies and gentlemen, was certainly responsive to the occasion, and drowned with their applause again and again the eloquent words of appreciation which fell from the lips of the recently returned traveler.

On Wednesday evening at huge Tremont Temple the monster meeting of the week was addressed by Dr. Washington. It was the closing meeting of the series being held under the auspices of the Congregational Church. Dr. Washington's address before the American Missionary Association drew thousands of people. The streets were choked with Boston's leading people, white and black, for an hour before the meeting, and even then only those who sought admission were able to do so. It was a typical Boston audience, with many delegates from all parts of the country, that came to its feet in the most enthusiastic and spontaneous welcome of the session. It was only after repeated efforts that quiet could be secured so that the orator could proceed.

The demonstrations of good will and the huge audiences that everywhere have greeted Dr. Washington on this the first visit of his fall campaign in Boston and vicinity is eloquent testimony to the hold the man has on the community; there is no indication of any lack of continued interest in the man and his work. His has been the dominant personality, honored and welcomed wherever he has appeared during this week of triumphs.

Washington *Bee*, Oct. 29, 1910, 1.

1 William Stedman Greene (1841–1924), Republican congressman from the Fall River district of Massachusetts from 1898 until his death.

2 Stewart E. Hoyt was a clerk in the Boston city tax collector's office for many years after 1906.

Extracts from a Sunday Evening Talk

[Tuskegee, Ala.] October 23, 1910

Principal Washington spoke in the Chapel, last Sunday evening, to an audience that literally overflowed the seating capacity of the audience-chamber. It was his first appearance in the Chapel since the close of the school term, last May. The large student body, teachers, many persons from the town of Tuskegee, as well as families and others from the Greenwood community, were present to listen to his first Sunday evening talk of the year. Principal Washington spoke somewhat at length, detailing many interesting instances in connection with his recent European trip. Because of his contract, however, with the Outlook Magazine of New York City, in which at least six articles describing the trip are to appear, it is not possible for us to reprint entire what he had to say, Sunday evening. Among the other statements, however, the following may be quoted:

Some time later in the year, after I have fulfilled a promise which I made to a publication in New York, I hope to tell you more in detail something about the things I have tried to observe and tried to learn during the time I spent in various countries in Europe.

One of the things which surprised me most and impressed upon me our responsibility as a school is the fact that everywhere we went — I refer to Dr. Park and myself — we found that people knew about this school. We found in parts of Europe, where we might think they would never hear of a school like this, that they were more intimately acquainted with our methods and with some of our results and are watching us more keenly and closely than you can realize.

I think we were never more surprised than when we went into the kingdom of Denmark to see how intelligent the people were concerning the history of the Tuskegee Institute and concerning the methods of education which we are employing here and you would find, as we found, if you were to go there, that they not only know about our methods, but in a very large degree, especially in farming, are putting these methods into practice, and in many cases, I think, have perfected them and have gone far ahead of us.

We spent a good deal of time in traveling through Denmark in an automobile away from the railroads and in the rural districts, and we were constantly reminded during these trips of the trips that we make from time to time through Macon County. The people assembled in the same way at the little schoolhouse. They had up their flags and had a dinner prepared, and they had their agricultural exhibits, their sewing exhibits, their industrial exhibits of every character, so that one would have thought it was a repetition of some of the trips we have made through Macon County. And you would have been surprised, as I have said, to see how intelligent the ordinary farming class of people are concerning what Tuskegee is doing and what we are trying to stand for.

That brings to us, as I have said, a great responsibility. The fact that so many people, in so many parts of the world are watching keenly our methods, our efforts, watching for the results that come from such work as this, brings to us a tremendous responsibility.

I hope to speak more in detail, as I have said, before the year closes concerning Denmark. But there were other parts of Europe visited by us, England, Scotland, some portion of Holland, some portion of Germany and Austria Hungary, Poland, Russia, Sicily, and Italy, proper, but in none of these other countries, possibly with the exception of Germany and Holland, will you find any such conditions as the intelligence in methods of living that we observed in Denmark.

I was constantly impressed with one or two fundamental things in connection with our life here in the South, in connection with the life of our people throughout the country in reference especially to the advantages, some of the advantages at least that we enjoy in this country, which we do not always, I fear, appreciate.

No one can go into these countries of Europe, especially into the smaller countries, without being impressed, first of all, with the tremendous advantage which we, as a race of people, enjoy in being permitted to understand and to speak a great world language — one language — a language that the civilized world respects and that the civilized world is learning more and more every year. We, as a race of people, have that privilege in a larger degree than any poorer class of people that we found in any portion of

Europe. We have the advantage through the medium of this great world language to come into contact daily with the best thought, with the best literature, with all that is best and most uplifting in civilization. It is a great privilege for us to be permitted to think through and talk through the medium of a language which places us every day in the year in contact with the very ripest and best there is in civilization. I know of no race, at least we found no race in the relative stage of civilization anywhere in Europe, which has that privilege to a larger degree than is true of our race in America. We do not realize what a tremendous handicap many of those people labor under, because of the fact that their language, their contact with each other is confined to a language that is, in many cases, spoken in a very small territory.

For example, if you will study the history of Austria, you will find that it is divided up into seventeen different peoples. We speak about race problems here, but we do not know anything about race problems. There are seventeen peoples in Austria alone and each race has its own language and each race contends that it is the superior race. All the other sixteen races are inferior and each one is contending that the other sixteen must learn its language and sometimes they won't speak to other persons unless they talk to them in their own language. So that you see they have some problems as well as we in this country.

I remember seeing in Budapest, Hungary, a printed circular advertising a public meeting. In order that all the people residing in Budapest might understand the purpose and object of this meeting, it was printed in six different languages. Think of that! Think of the advantage we have in coming into contact with each other, knowing each other, and speaking to each other in a language all of us can understand. Then think of their disadvantages, their awkwardness in communicating with each other, when in order to get hold of the general public, they have to do so through the medium of six languages.

I remember an experience which Dr. Park and I had in Russia. We got over the border line and we wanted to get some information concerning conditions in Russia. I wanted to talk to some of the Russian officials, and in order to do so, I had to talk to Dr. Park in English. He found a man who could talk German and spoke to him in German, then this German spoke to the people there in Russian, and then it all had to be translated back through this German and through Dr. Park to me.

You get some idea of the tremendous handicap of many of those people. In Austria, for example, they have seventeen different racial groups. If you will go still further, and get in among these races, you will find they have two or three different dialects which they speak, so that sometimes the people of one race, living across the river, perhaps, cannot understand the people of the same race, who live on the other side of the river. It is impossible, under such circumstances, for them to print a newspaper that contains the news of the world. It is impossible for them to print books that contain the best literature of the world, because groups of people who speak these various languages are not large enough to sustain great newspapers or to sustain great printing presses. They are handicapped in a number of ways which I have not time to explain, so one of the things for which you and I should be most grateful is that we are brought into contact day by day and are permitted to use a great language — the English language.

Tuskegee Student, 22 (Oct. 29, 1910) 1, 4. Stenographically reported.

To Robert Russa Moton

Tuskegee Institute, Alabama   October 24, 1910

Personal and Confidential.

Dear Major Moton: The enclosed is a circular which John E. Milholland had printed and distributed in London while I was there.

I am wondering in view of Mr. Villard's protests and explanations to you as we came from Bar Harbor to the effect that their movement is not in opposition to me, if you would not like to send Mr. Villard this circular and call his attention to the fact that in spite of his protests Mr. Milholland, who is the writer of this circular, is one of the main movers in company with Mr. Villard and is the principal backer of the Du Bois movement; and in view of this circular the advantage would be rather to make anybody believe that the movement has not for its principal object the discouragement of the fundamentals of Hampton and Tuskegee and everything that we stand for.

It might be well also for you to ask Mr. Villard if Mr. Milholland is authorized to make a statement to the effect that "The Evening Post" is against me.

I think if you could couch the substance of what I have stated in a letter to Mr. Villard it would put him to thinking a little and stir matters up in an interesting way.

Of course the circular had no effect whatever as people in London readily saw that the man had some personal end to gain and besides Milholland is as well known in London as an unbalanced agitator as he is in this country. Yours very truly,

[Booker T. Washington]

TLc   Con. 51   BTW Papers   DLC.

To Robert Ezra Park

[Tuskegee, Ala.] October 24, 1910

First article received and very good. Do not fail to keep them light, and in natural, easy, conversational style. Outlook people very much afraid we will make them heavy and scientific.

Booker T. Washington

TWpSr   Con. 51   BTW Papers   DLC.

Emmett Jay Scott to Charles Banks

[Tuskegee, Ala.] Oct. 24, 1910

Confidential

Dear Mr. Banks: Just a word to say that [I] went over with the President at Beverly the announced policy of weeding out Negroes in all of the Southern States. I spoke to him quite frankly as to what

417

was going on in his name by these various Southern referees. He seemed very indignant, indeed. I was kind enough to say to him that we all quite appreciated his own position in the matter, but these so-called spokesmen were creating situations and conditions without his knowledge and consent. He agreed with my statement of the matter and said that he meant to look into the whole matter most keenly and wherever injustice had been done to rectify it. We must accept the President's statement in the matter, and I hope that you will write Mr. Norton frankly whenever it occurs to you that some injustice should be called to his attention. Yours very truly,

Emmett J. Scott

TLpS   Con. 49   BTW Papers   DLC.

To George A. Myers

[Tuskegee, Ala.] October 25, 1910

Personal:

My dear Mr. Myers: I have just gotten home and got somewhat settled, and I am taking advantage of the first opportunity that I have had at my command since reaching home to write you a line.

I hope that you and family are well and that you and all our good friends in Cleveland are happy and prosperous. Cleveland sent a strong and fine looking body of men to the National League in New York, and personally I was very sorry we could not accept the invitation to go to Cleveland for our next meeting, but this invitation will pave the way I am sure for some future meeting in Cleveland.

By the way, I see by the papers that my enemies are trying to plant themselves in Cleveland. They are making a herculean effort just now to try to down me. Just why they are putting forth this extra effort in the expenditure of money and time I am not quite able to understand, neither can I understand why there is a class of white people who have heretofore taken no interest in the elevation of the Negro, have all at once sprung up and proclaimed themselves the undying friends of the Negro. I, however, am rather onto their game and scheme and do not become frightened. The people in the long run can be trusted. I see, too, somewhat to my surprise, that they seem to have gotten hold of Mr. Chesnutt and gotten him into their camp to represent the colored people of Cleveland.

Please remember me kindly to your family and our friends. Yours very truly,

Booker T. Washington

TLpS Con. 909 BTW Papers DLC.

To Maurice Francis Egan

[Tuskegee, Ala.] October 26, 1910

My dear Dr. Egan: After stopping for several days in New York and Boston to deliver addresses I have at last reached Tuskegee where I find matters in good shape and where a hearty welcome awaited me.

The very first letter that I am writing to anyone in Europe is to you, and I want to let you know how very grateful I am to you for your many kindnesses to me while I was in Denmark. I wish to assure you that I appreciate it all from the bottom of my heart. I can see more clearly than I did at first what a delicate task you had to perform and how well you did it.

Of course, the matter of my being entertained by the King and Queen has been spread widely into every corner of the United States, and so far I have not seen a single word of adverse criticism. In fact, the whole press as well as the general public has received the news with the utmost satisfaction.

Here in the South the Southern white people seem to be about as proud of the recognition as anybody else.

All through the dispatches, however, I cannot fail to note the influence of your strong hand in the shaping of the wording of the dispatches which, of course, had a great deal to do with the impression which has been spread abroad. I am sure that nothing but good has come of the event.

I shall always remember you with deep gratitude. I hope that I may know when you are in this country, so I may call to see you.

I am going to send the King and Queen a copy of "Up From Slavery" within a few days.

Would it be out of place for me to ask both the King and Queen, or either of them, for their photographs?[1] I should not like to make the request unless it were perfectly proper. Yours truly,

Booker T. Washington

TLpS Con. 905 BTW Papers DLC.

[1] In February 1911, BTW received autographed photographs of King Frederick and Queen Louise. (*Tuskegee Student*, 23 [Feb. 11, 1911], 2.)

To Frederick Randolph Moore

[Tuskegee, Ala.] October 26, 1910

Personal and Confidential

My dear Mr. Moore: I think I ought to say to you in the most friendly and frank way that not a few of your friends entertain a feeling and a fear that The Age is receiving financial support from the Democratic party in New York. I very much hope that there is not the slightest foundation for this feeling. Nothing could more permanently injure you or The Age than for you to receive support from that source. While you might get a few dollars in the immediate present, in the end both you and the paper would be damaged to such an extent that you would not recover from it. As I have already stated, I very much hope that you will soon get to the place, if you are not there now, where you will not have to ask or receive financial aid from any political party, but certainly your influence and the influence of the paper would be permanently crippled were you to receive one cent from the Democratic party. Yours very truly,

Booker T. Washington

TLpS Con. 607 BTW Papers DLC.

To Charles William Anderson

[Tuskegee, Ala.] October 26, 1910

Personal and Confidential

My dear Mr. Anderson: Your kind letter has just been received. I cannot answer it fully just now, but I will in a few days. For the present I am enclosing copy of a letter which I have just written Mr. Moore. Please do not permit any one to know I have sent you a copy of this letter.

You have no idea how much people talk and gossip around New York. This reminds me that I ought to let you know that some little fellow[1] in New York, a graduate of Harvard who was formerly employed on The Age, is rather active in stating to his friends and therefore to the public, that you and he have a certain understanding as to certain items of news which he is to send to the Boston Guardian.

One other thing. Nothing could hurt our cause worse just now than for any newspaper or any individual to get the idea that we could be moved to take certain action or refrain from taking certain action by reason of a threat to go over to a certain person if this or that is not done. In all of my experience I find that the man who expects to move you in this or that direction by a threat sooner or later will betray you, and I very much hope that our friends in New York will let it thoroughly be understood that we cannot be moved to do this or that thing by reason of a threat that somebody makes to go over to Du Bois or anybody else. Yours very truly,

Booker T. Washington

In writing Moore as I have, I wish it thoroughly understood that I do not own or control, directly or indirectly, a single dollar in the New York Age property notwithstanding frequent statements to the contrary.

B. T. W.

TLpS Con. 49 BTW Papers DLC.

[1] This was Aubrey Bowser, soon to be T. Thomas Fortune's son-in-law. See Anderson's reply, Oct. 29, 1910, below.

An Open Letter
to the People of Great Britain and Europe
by William Edward Burghardt Du Bois and Others[1]

Headquarters National Negro Committee,
20 Vesey St., New York, U.S.A. October 26, 1910

To the People of Great Britain and Europe: The undersigned Negro-Americans have heard, with great regret, the recent attempt to assure England and Europe that their condition in America is satisfactory. They sincerely wish that such were the case, but it becomes their plain duty to say that if Mr. Booker T. Washington, or any other person, is giving the impression abroad that the Negro problem in America is in process of satisfactory solution, he is giving an impression which is not true. We say this without personal bitterness toward Mr. Washington. He is a distinguished American and has a perfect right to his opinions. But we are compelled to point out that Mr. Washington's large financial responsibilities have made him dependent on the rich charitable public and that, for this reason, he has for years been compelled to tell, not the whole truth, but that part of it which certain powerful interests in America wish to appear as the whole truth. In flat contradiction, however, to the pleasant pictures thus pointed out, let us not forget that the consensus of opinion among eminent European scholars who know the race problem in America, from De Tocqueville down to Von Halle, De Laveleye, Archer and Johnston, is that it forms the gravest of American problems. We black men who live and suffer under present conditions, and who have no reason, and refuse to accept reasons, for silence, can substantiate this unanimous testimony. Our people were emancipated in a whirl of passion, and then left naked to the mercies of their enraged and impoverished ex-masters. As our sole means of defence we were given the ballot, and we used it so as to secure the real fruits of the war. Without it we would have returned to slavery; with it we struggled toward freedom. No sooner, however, had we rid ourselves of nearly two-thirds of our illiteracy, and accumulated $600,000,000 worth of property in a generation, than this ballot, which had become increasingly necessary to the defence of our civil and property rights, was taken from us by force and fraud. Today in eight states where the bulk of the Negroes live, black men of property and university training can be, and usually are, by law denied the ballot, while the most ignorant white man votes. This attempt to put the personal and property rights of the best of the blacks at the absolute political mercy of the worst of the whites is spreading each day. Along with this has gone a systematic attempt to curtail the education of the black race. Under a widely advertised system of "universal" education, not one black boy in three today has in the United States a chance to learn to read and write. The proportion of school funds due to black children are often spent on whites, and the burden on private charity to support education, which is a public duty, has become almost intolerable. In every walk of life we meet discrimination based solely on race and color, but continually and persistently misrepresented to the world as the natural difference due to condition. We are, for instance, usually forced to live in the worst quarters, and our consequent death-rate is noted as a race trait, and reason for further discrimination. When we seek to buy property in better quarters we are sometimes in danger of mob violence, or, as now in Baltimore, of actual legislation to prevent. We are forced to take lower wages for equal work, and our standard of living is then criticised. Fully half the labor unions refuse us admittance, and then claim that as "scabs" we lower the price of labor. A persistent caste proscription seeks to force us and confine us to menial occupations where the conditions of work are worst. Our women in the South are without protection in law and custom, and are then derided as lewd. A widespread system of deliberate public insult is customary, which makes it difficult, if not impossible, to secure decent accommodation in hotels, railway trains, restaurants and theatres, and even in the Christian Church we are in most cases given to understand that we are unwelcome unless segregated. Worse than all this is the wilful miscarriage of justice in the courts. Not only have 3,500 black men been lynched publicly by mobs in the last twenty-five years without semblance or pretense of trial, but regularly every day throughout the South the machinery of the courts is used, not to prevent crime and correct the wayward among Negroes, but to wreak public dislike and vengeance, and to raise public funds. This dealing in crime as a means of public revenue is a system well-nigh universal in the South, and while its glaring brutality through private lease has been checked, the underlying principle is still unchanged. Everywhere in the United States the old democratic doctrine of recognising fitness wherever it occurs is losing ground before a reactionary policy of denying preferment in political or industrial life to competent men if they have a trace of Negro blood, and of using the weapons of public insult and humiliation to keep such men down. It is today a universal demand in the South that on all occasions social courtesies shall be denied any person of known Negro descent, even to the extent of refusing to apply the titles of "Mr.," "Mrs.," and "Miss." Against this dominant tendency strong and brave Americans, white and black are fighting, but they need, and need sadly, the moral support of England and of Europe in this crusade for the recognition of manhood, despite adventitious differences of race, and it is like a blow in the face to have one, who himself suffers daily insult and humiliation in America, give the impression that all is well. It is one thing to be optimistic, self-forgetful and forgiving, but it is quite a different thing, consciously or unconsciously, to misrepresent the truth.

(Signed)

J. MAX BARBER, Editor of The Voice of the Negro;[2] C. E. BENTLEY, formerly Chairman of Dental Clinics, St. Louis Exposition; W. JUSTIN CARTER, Barrister, Harrisburg, Pa.; S. L. CORROTHERS, Pastor A.M.E. Zion Church, Washington, D.C.; GEORGE W. CRAWFORD,[3] Barrister, formerly Clerk of Court, New Haven, Ct.; JAMES R. L. DIGGS,[4] President of Virginia Seminary and College, [Lynchburg] Va.; W. E. BURGHARDT DU BOIS, Author of "Souls of Black Folk," etc., Fellow of the American Association for the Advancement of Science, Member of International Law Society and Secretary of the National Afro-American Committee; ARCHIBALD H. GRIMKE, late U.S. Consul to San Domingo; N. B. MARSHALL, Barrister, Counsel in the Brownsville Soldiers Court Martial; FREDRICK L. McGHEE, Barrister, St. Paul, Minn.; G. W. MITCHELL,[5] Barrister, Philadelphia; CLEMENT G. MORGAN, Barrister, formerly Alderman of Cambridge, Mass.; EDWARD H. MORRIS, Grand Master, G. U. O.

of O. F., in America; N. F. MOSSELL, Medical Director of Douglass Hospital, Philadelphia, Pa.; JAMES L. NEILL,[6] Recording Secretary of the National Independent League; WILLIAM PICKENS, Professor of Latin, Talladega College, Ala.; WILLIAM A. SINCLAIR, Author of "The Aftermath of Slavery," and Field Secretary of the Constitution League; HARRY C. SMITH, Editor of The Cleveland Gazette, for six years Member of the Legislature of Ohio; B. S. SMITH, Barrister, formerly Assistant States Attorney of Kansas; WILLIAM MONROE TROTTER, Editor of The Boston Guardian; J. MILTON WALDRON, Pastor of Shiloh Baptist Church, Washington, D.C.; OWEN M. WALLER, Physician, Brooklyn, New York; ALEXANDER WALTERS, Bishop of the A.M.E. Zion Church.

Cleveland *Gazette*, Nov. 12, 1910, 2. The newspaper ran a photograph of W. E. B. Du Bois with the article.

[1] Du Bois claimed authorship of the document in *Dusk of Dawn*, 229. BTW believed that John E. Milholland was the instigator of the protest. (See BTW to Travers Buxton, Nov. 19, 1910, below.) He also noted the words "Headquarters, National Negro Committee," and charged that the signers had tried to create the impression that the NAACP was a sponsor of the document. Villard, however, was convinced that the heading was the result of a stenographer's neglect to erase the words from the old stationery Du Bois used to draft the document. Details of the controversy are in Rudwick, *W. E. B. Du Bois*, 134–37.

[2] Former editor. The magazine was defunct after 1907.

[3] George Williamson Crawford (b. 1877), a graduate of Tuskegee Institute (1900), received a law degree from Yale (1903) and was admitted to the Connecticut bar. After serving for four years as a clerk in the New Haven probate court, he began a law practice. Crawford was a member of the NAACP's Committee of 100 and served on the first board of directors.

[4] James Robert Lincoln Diggs (b. 1866) had a considerable academic background that included study at Wayland Seminary, Bucknell University (A.B. 1902), Cornell, and Illinois Wesleyan University (Ph.D. 1906). He was one of only a few blacks to receive a Ph.D. from an American university. After several academic posts in Virginia and Kentucky he became president of Virginia Seminary (1908–11), dean of the college at Selma University (1911–14), and president of Clayton-Williams University in Baltimore after 1914. Diggs also was pastor of Trinity Baptist Church in Baltimore beginning in 1915. He was a member of the NAACP.

[5] George Washington Mitchell, born near Chatham, Va., in 1865, graduated from Howard University Law School in 1896 and established a law practice, largely with white clients, in Philadelphia. He was active in establishing the Keystone Aid Society, the Banneker Building and Loan Association, and other black institutions in Philadelphia.

[6] James Lincoln Neill, a graduate of Fisk University and Howard University Law School, practiced law in Washington, D.C.

To William Howard Taft

Tuskegee, Ala., Oct. 27, 1910

I want to thank you most heartily for deciding to appoint Wm. H. Lewis to such an important position.[1] It will do good in many directions. I shall use this to the very best advantage.

Booker T. Washington

TWSr   William Howard Taft Papers   DLC.

[1] In early 1911 Taft officially nominated Lewis to the position of assistant attorney general, the highest appointive post held by a black American until that time. Although Lewis assumed the office in March 1911, he was not confirmed by the Senate until June 14, 1911.

To George Ruffin Bridgeforth

[Tuskegee, Ala.] October 27, 1910

Mr. Bridgeforth: While in Denmark, I found that the people there have a plan by which wives actually live in the farm schools for two weeks each year. Then the wives go home and the husbands live in the schools for the same length of time and in each case receive practical training in farming and how to live.

I am wondering if it would be possible and practicable to put in operation some such plan regarding Macon County.

Please think the matter over and let me have your opinion.

Booker T. Washington

TLpS   Con. 598   BTW Papers   DLC.

To King Frederick of Denmark

[Tuskegee, Ala.] October 27, 1910

Your Majesty: By this mail I am taking the liberty of sending you according to promise, a copy of my book "Up From Slavery," which I hope you and the Queen will be gracious enough to accept with my compliments.

While writing, permit me to thank both of you again and again for your great kindness to me while I was in Denmark. I assure you that I shall always feel deeply indebted to both of you. Your humble servant,

Booker T. Washington

HLpS   Con. 905   BTW Papers   DLC.

An Item in the *Tuskegee Student*

Tuskegee, Alabama, October 29, 1910

"AT HOME"

The return of Principal Washington to the Institute last Friday night, October 21, was signalized by rather unique and interesting incidents. Along the road from Chehaw, many of the colored people built bonfires, and as his carriage passed skyrockets and Roman candles were sent up. Arriving at the Institute grounds the entire student body of nearly 1,500 students, the 180 teachers, and the people of the Tuskegee Institute community were gathered along the line. The Institute Band headed the procession and with lighted pine torches the whole body proceeded to the home of the Principal. Eager young men had taken the horses out of the carriage at the barn and substituted a long rope drawing it themselves. Arriving at his home, Mr. Washington spoke in appreciation of the welcome which had been extended him and said that though he had visited many places during his European trip he had found no place that he loved more than Tuskegee nor any people, white or black, that he loved more than those of Macon County. The demonstrations of welcome were kept up until 11 o'clock, the Institute Band playing, "Hail to the Chief," "Home, Sweet Home" and "Auld Lang Syne." The rich, mellow voices of the whole body singing "The Tuskegee Song" were well worth hearing. During his absence in Europe, he not only visited the important capitals of Europe but also went into the agricultural

427

and mining regions of England, Scotland, Denmark, Austria-Hungary, Sicily, Italy proper and Poland. His experiences are to be detailed at length in a series of articles to appear in the "Outlook," New York City, to be entitled, "The Man Farthest Down."

On Saturday evening, October 22nd, the annual dinner in honor of the members of the Executive Council and their wives was given at "The Oaks" by Principal and Mrs. Washington. The occasion was timed for Principal Washington's return after his extended European tour and was an occasion of very great pleasure to all present. The dinner was scheduled to begin at 7:30 o'clock, and it was not until 10:45 that the party arose from the tables which had been set in the long dining room of the Principal's home.

Those present in addition to the hosts, were Mr. Logan, Treasurer, and Mrs. Logan; Mr. J. H. Washington, General Superintendent of Industries, and Mrs. Washington; Mr. Taylor, Director Mechanical Industries; Mr. Scott, Secretary to Principal, and Mrs. Scott; Mr. Carver, Director Agricultural Instruction and Experiment Station; Major Ramsey, Commandant, and Mrs. Ramsey; Mr. Attwell, Business Agent, and Mrs. Attwell; Mr. Lee, Director Academic Department, and Mrs. Lee; Mr. Gibson, Resident Auditor, and Mrs. Gibson; Mr. Bridgeforth, Director Department of Agricultural Industries, and Mrs. Bridgeforth; Mr. Palmer, Registrar, and Mrs. Palmer; Dr. Kenney, Resident Physician, and Mrs. Kenney; Miss Porter, Dean Woman's Department; John W. Whittaker, Chaplain, and Mrs. Whittaker; Rev. A. F. Owens, Dean Phelps Hall Bible Training School, and Mrs. Owens; Mr. C. J. Calloway, Head Extension Department, and Mrs. Calloway; Mr. Williston, Head Department of Buildings and Grounds, and Mrs. Williston. Others invited and present were, Mr. and Mrs. Roberts,[1] Mr. and Mrs. Fearing, Mr. and Mrs. Woodard,[2] Mrs. Laura T. Jones, Miss Caroline C. Smith, and Dr. George C. Hall of Chicago.

The menu was prepared by the young women of the school and served also by them, and was:

MENU

Blue Points

Sauce

Brown Bread Sandwiches

Consomme   Cheese Straws

Olives   Cheese   Radishes

Swedish Timbales   Mushrooms
Broiled Halibut   Tartar Sauce
Bread Sticks   Cole Slaw
Brown Hashed Potatoes
Orange Sherbet
Birds on Toast   Jelly
Green Peas   Rolls   Candied Potatoes
Tomato Salad
Ice Cream   Lady Fingers   Bon Bons
Wafers   Cheese
Black Coffee

This dinner in honor of the Executive Council was the first social event of the Tuskegee Institute season.

———

A reception given in honor of his return from Europe was tendered Principal Washington by the faculty of the Tuskegee Normal and Industrial Institute in Tompkins Hall Monday evening, October 24, 1910. Mr. and Mrs. Washington were assisted in receiving by a party of ladies: Mrs. Logan, Mrs. J. H. Washington, Mrs. H. E. Thomas, Mrs. Ramsey and Mrs. Scott.

A musical program of surpassing excellence was rendered as follows:

1. Sextette
   (from) "Lucia di Lammermoor" — Donizetti
                                          — Orchestra
2. Vocal Solo
   "Carissima," Capt. N. Clark Smith
   (Old Spanish)
3. Religioso
   "Angels' Serenade" — Braga
                                          — Orchestra
4. Recitation
   Selected — Mr. Charles Winter Wood
5. Anvil Chorus
   (from) "Il Trovatore" — Verdi
                                          — Orchestra
6. Vocal Solo
   Selected — Miss M. P. Winter[3]

7. Intermezzo
   (from) "Cavalleria Rusticana" — Mascagni
                                        — Orchestra
8. Saxophone Solo — Orchestra Accomp.
   "Serenade" — Schubert — Capt. N. Clark Smith

At the conclusion of the musical program Principal Washington was requested to say a few words, and spoke for fifteen or twenty minutes most interestingly of some of his European experiences, particularly those in Scotland and Denmark. It was one of those intimate family talks and was greatly appreciated by all who were privileged to listen to the more intimate discussion of some of the things with which Mr. Washington came in contact while visiting about in various parts of Europe.

The menu served by Captain Snyder[4] and his aides was as follows:

MENU
Bouillon in Cups
Deviled Crabs
Creamed Peas in Timbales
Punch
Chicken Loaf   Lattice Potatoes
Finger Rolls
Olives   Pickles
Fruit Salad in Apple Cups, Cheese Straws
Saltines
Ice Cream   Cakes
Cheese   Crackers
Coffee

The committee in charge of the arrangements was composed of Mr. Attwell, chairman, Major Ramsey, Miss C. C. Smith, Mr. Williston, Mrs. Landers, Mr. Lee, Mr. Taylor, Mr. H. E. Thomas, Mr. Wood, Mr. Ammons.[5]

The souvenir card for the occasion was a splendid example of the printers' art. It was composed of some six sheets tied with the Tuskegee Institute colors, old gold and crimson, and bore as a frontispiece a recent picture of the Principal with the words that follow thereunder: "No man who has the privilege of rendering service to his fellows ever makes a sacrifice," from speech at banquet at Hotel Metropole, London, October 4, 1910.

The committee in charge of the arrangements had decorated the Teachers' Dining Room most beautifully. Vari-colored lights on a dark cloth background intertwined with vines were wound around the high pillared columns. Flowers and ferns were banked in various corners of the room and in the windows, rugs and reception chairs suitably arranged conspired to transform the room into a veritable "thing of beauty."

The Principal expressed himself as being deeply touched by the many evidences of cordiality which teachers and students alike have bestowed upon him since his return to the Institute.

Tuskegee Student, 22 (October 29, 1910) 1, 2.

[1] Ezra C. Roberts taught mathematics at Tuskegee from 1906 until after BTW's death. In 1910 he became assistant to the director of the academic department.

[2] Dudley W. Woodard taught mathematics at Tuskegee from 1907 to 1914.

[3] Miranda P. Winter, teacher of instrumental music at Tuskegee from 1908 to 1911.

[4] Edward L. Snyder, steward of the boarding department at Tuskegee from 1909 to 1912.

[5] Captain Benjamin E. Ammons was assistant commandant at Tuskegee from 1910 until after BTW's death.

From Charles William Anderson

New York, N.Y., October 29, 1910

(Personal)

My dear Doctor: Referring further to the New York correspondent of the Boston paper, I beg to say that his opposition to Moore and seeming friendliness to me, is due entirely and exclusively to his belief that Moore is in some way responsible for Fortune's downfall, and that I have been his friend, financially, on several occasions. I do not think there is any just reason for him to feel as he does toward Moore, but I am told that he does feel that way. He has evidently taken his inspiration from Fortune, with regard to us both. I presume I have loaned — given — Fortune One hundred and fifty dollars, in various amounts. I have done so because it is always difficult for me to refrain from helping any fellow who is down and out. I advanced money on two or three occasions to W. H. "Windy" Butler, who was my bitterest and meanest enemy in this city, after he had become bankrupt in pocket, and in health. I fight my foes with all the strength in me, but when evil times come, and poverty comes, and distress and misery come, somehow or other, I cannot refrain from going down in my pocket, if there is anything in it to give them. In Fortune's case, he seemed to be so surprised that I should help him out, in view of the fact that when he was on top, he did not try to help me, and has told it both in Gath and Askalon. Among others to whom this information was given, was Bowser, who is keeping company with Fortune's daughter. I presume brother Fortune has emptied the vials of his wrath on Moore. You know they were close friends in the old days, and when one friend succeeds and the other fails, it is always easy for the unfortunate one to convince himself that the other fellow has succeeded at his expense. Whatever the reason, Tim seems to feel kindly toward me and bitter toward Moore, and Bowser is reflecting this in the twaddle he is writing. It is not that he loves me very much, as it is that he hates Moore. I hope you will believe me when I say, that I do not think I would recognize this man if he came into my office today, although I have met him on two occasions. I have never had ten minutes' talk with him; never had any communication with him, telephonic or epistolary, in my life. Whatever he has said about me, has been said to hurt the other fellow and without the least hint from me, and without my knowledge and consent. One thing you can always rest assured of in me, and that is, no matter how much I may oppose a man on "my side of the fence," I will never allow my opposition to him to drive me into association, open or secret, with the enemy. I have always pursued this course, even in politics. I may fight a man or a group of men in politics, with all my might, but I never allow my opposition to them to drive me into the ranks of the enemy, or into the camp of the politically unclean, because they happen to be with the forces of cleanliness and right. I try to stand for the right and for the clean side of issues, even if in doing so I am compelled to stand by the side of my bitterest foe. Those who think me capable of secretly conspiring with the correspondent of that infamous Boston sheet, because I happen, temporarily, to feel that Mr. Moore is not acting altogether fair with me, little know me, and wholly misappreciate my character. My experience is, the man who suspects such conduct in another, is usually the man who is capable of it himself. As for me, with all my faults, I do my fighting out in the open. My friends always know where I stand. I am never on but one side at the time. I am never pro-Roosevelt in New York and anti-Roosevelt in Brooklyn. I never fight for a cause and then secretly try to destroy one of my allies in the battle, even if that ally is distasteful to me. My worst enemies here have never accused me of any such conduct, and I do not think there are twenty men, of any party or race in this city who would believe it of me. God knows there is enough that they can say against me without charging me with duplicity, but I suppose I ought not to complain, for somehow or other notwithstanding what they say against me, I managed to have won out in every contest in which I have engaged for a long period of time, and I have had to stand alone oftener than any man of my race north of Mason and Dixon's line, when the real fight came up. I have generally had lots of approval after the victory was won; but little aid during the battle. I have nearly always been on the side which the colored people hereabouts opposed, and most of them have been on the side which would have ruined me, had it won, and I do not think I could have retained the strong friends that have helped me so long, if I had been capable of the duplicity of which I have been charged. I am sure you do not believe it. It is not like me to strike from behind.

Hoping you are very well, I remain, Faithfully yours,

C. W. A.

TLI   Con. 49   BTW Papers   DLC.

From George A. Myers

Cleveland, October 31, 1910

Dear Dr. Washington: I thank you for your favor of the 26th and the good expressions therein.

Please accept the congratulations of Mrs. Myers and myself upon your safe return and the honors bestowed upon you while abroad.

I received an invitation to the New York Banquet, but it arrived too late for me to attend or even to send my contribution.

I carefully note what you say relative to the Cleveland contingent that attended the Business League and their invitation for the League to meet in Cleveland. You did well not to accept and do not contemplate coming to Cleveland until the matter shall have been thoroughly canvassed. Cleveland as you know is a hard town to work, because we have no wealthy citizens who stand in the spot light as the champion of the brother or his cause and no colored ones who will spend a dollar for anything to further the interest of the race. Every effort put forth by the Cleveland Association of Colored Men I have had to finance and in order to be successful, have been compelled to appeal to a few charitable or philanthropic white friends.

To the matter upon which you wrote I have to say "Let not your heart be troubled." Your friend Mr. Chesnutt came to me with his proposition for a meeting, I told him it would be impossible for him to have a meeting in Cleveland if it was known that this Association, of which he was a part was antagonistic to Dr. Washington. He declared it was not and pointed to the fact that Mr. and Mrs. Villard were introduced by you and spoke to the Business League upon your invitation and gave me to understand while they labored along other lines they were in perfect accord with you. I sent him to Wm. R. Green,[1] President of the Cleveland Association of Colored Men and told Mr. Green to give him a meeting. Mr. Chesnutt came in to say that he was at loss to entertain Mr. and Mrs. Walling[2] — particularly so as they desired a mixed meeting and wanted to get in touch with the white people of the community who were friendly to the brother. He further said that he would have a few gentlemen meet Mr. Walling at his office. He invited the whole membership of the Cleveland Association of Colored Men to his residence to meet Mr. and Mrs. Walling. It being Saturday night neither Mrs. Myers nor myself attended. I received full particulars the next day.

After an informal discussion of the brother, John P. Green suggested Mr. Chesnutt for a chairman that their discussion might be more orderly. Mr. Walling, Green, Chesnutt and Martin[3] spoke. Mr. Eubanks[4] informs me their talk was very Anti-Washington, so much so that he, Eubanks, declined to talk to avoid argument.

At the church next day I heard Dr. Thwing and Mrs. Walling speak. I left before Mr. Walling spoke and the impromptu remarks by John P. Green and Alex. Martin. I am told however, with the exception of Green there was no reference to you or your work.

I have gone into detail, first that you might know the sincerity of some who to your face profess friendship and are ever in evidence when you come this way. Second that you might see the full extent of the Anti-sentiment in this community.

Concluding I reiterate "Let not your heart be troubled." As the small boy said to the one begging — "There aint going to be no core." There will be no more meetings. I graciously complimented Mr. Chesnutt in assenting to this one, but compliment was not appreciated.

The recognition of Cottrill[5] is giving eminent satisfaction. I trust the President will find something for him in event of the Hawaiian Proposition failing to carry.

With best wishes, I am, Very truly yours,

George A. Myers

TLS Con. 909 BTW Papers DLC.

[1] William R. Green (b. 1873), the son of the prominent Ohio politician John Paterson Green, was a law partner in Cleveland of his father and brother Theodore. As members of Cleveland's black elite, William and his brother Theodore played prominent roles in Cleveland politics, but William was more conservative than his brother and avoided an activist role in the local chapter of the NAACP. (Gerber, *Black Ohio*, 411; see also Kusmer, *A Ghetto Takes Shape*.)

[2] William English Walling (1877–1936) married in 1906 a fellow socialist and writer, Anna Strunsky (1879–1964). He was one of the founders of the NAACP, the Women's Trade Union League, and what became the League for Industrial Democracy.

[3] Alexander H. Martin (1873–1962), a black lawyer, practiced in Cleveland for sixty-five years.

[4] Henry T. Eubanks (b. 1853) moved to Cleveland in 1881 and worked as a waiter. He eventually became a successful barber and was the first black man to become a vice-president of the Ohio League of Republican Clubs. He won election to the state legislature and served from 1904 to 1906 and from 1908 to 1910.

[5] Charles A. Cottrill (b. 1863), of Toledo, Ohio, was a longtime holder of various patronage positions beginning in the 1880s. BTW urged Taft to appoint him to a federal office, and in 1910 Cottrill was considered for the post of collector of

internal revenue for Hawaii. On Sept. 6, 1910, Ralph Waldo Tyler wrote to Emmett J. Scott: "The Cottrill matter has gone by the boards. The president balked on sending a colored man to Hawaii." (Con. 413, BTW Papers, DLC.) Cottrill, however, was eventually appointed to the Hawaiian position and served from 1912 to 1915, when the Wilson administration removed him from office. Cottrill remained in Hawaii after his office expired and became a permanent resident.

From Thomas Jordan Jarvis[1]

Greenville, N.C. Nov. 2nd 1910

Dear Sir. I have learned with great pleasure of your visit to Eastern North Carolina and of your addresses to our colored people and I very much regret that circumstances and conditions are such that we cannot have you visit Greenville.

The colored people are a part of the citizenship of the State, and a very important part, and I heartily welcome and endorse every movement and influence to make them better citizens. I believe the teachings contained in your address will be helpful to those who hear and heed them and I wish it were possible for you to visit more of our people and speak to more of them.

Prof. C. M. Epps, the Principle of our Colored Graded School is likewise doing a good work but his sphere of activity is, of course, very limited as compared with yours. He goes to hear you and will deliver you this letter with my high regards and best wishes in your great work to lift up and improve the condition of a race of people who have a place a destiny and a duty in this Southland of ours. I have no doubt Prof. Epps will be benifi[t]ed and better prepared for his work by hearing you and I am glad that he [is] going to meet you.

With high regard and good wishes I am   Very truly yours,

Thos. J. Jarvis

ALS Con. 907 BTW Papers DLC.

1 Thomas Jordan Jarvis (1836–1915), a former governor of North Carolina, served briefly in the U.S. Senate in 1894–95, and then resumed his law practice in Greenville, N.C.

From Portia Marshall Washington Pittman

[Washington, D.C.] Nov. 3, 1910

My dear father: I thank you with all my heart, for the assistance rendered me and my family. We appreciate it beyond words. You have no idea how much it was needed. My poor husband is under such tremendous obligations just now — I trust we can pull through. I am so worried and nervous I don't know what to do. I pray each night for work to come for the sake of these little folks of ours.

That trip was such a grand one papa. You must be a happy man to cause the people to worship you so for the good you do. I wish my life could be so full of service as yours is. It is certainly a grand thing to be like that and I am so proud of you — and Mr. Pittman almost worships you. Lots of love, Your daughter

Portia

ALS Con. 911 BTW Papers DLC.

To Horace W. Carpentier[1]

Wilmington, N.C. Nov. [4], 1910

My dear General Carpentier: I thank you so very much for your kind letter relating to my return from Europe.[2] I had a very interesting trip. I am glad that you see the point which has been impressed upon me more and more since I returned, and that is that my trip through Europe has had a reflex influence in this country which has been most helpful. Curiously enough, I find that the Southern white people are just as proud of the fact that attention was shown me by royalty in Europe as was true of any other class of people.

I am writing from North Carolina. I have just finished making a tour through this state in company with about twenty prominent colored men from North Carolina and elsewhere. I have been speaking on an average of from four to five times a day, and these meetings have been composed of thousands of colored people and large numbers of the best white people throughout the state. I am overcome with surprise at the large numbers of white people, both men and women, who attend these meetings. It is an educational campaign. In these meetings I am making one appeal to the colored people to do their duty in the way of making themselves industrious, thrifty, and to improve along intellectual and moral lines as well; and then I am appealing to the white people to spend more money in the education of the colored people and see to it that they are protected in the courts in all their civil rights. The response on the part of the white people has been most enthusiastic and encouraging.

I really wish that the Tuskegee Institute was to such an extent relieved from financial needs that I could spend a larger part of each year in doing this kind of work.

I shall hope to see you if you are in New York sometime during the winter. Yours very truly,

Booker T. Washington

TLpS Con. 903 BTW Papers DLC.

1 Horace W. Carpentier, active in the New York Society for the Prevention of Cruelty to Animals, apparently had a residence in New York City and another in Galway, N.Y., where this letter was sent. In 1903 he gave $3,000 to Tuskegee Institute. (Carpentier to BTW, May 29, 1903, Con. 252, BTW Papers, DLC.)

2 Carpentier had written: "Your work has become international; and the future is yours." (Oct. 27, 1910, Con. 903, BTW Papers, DLC.)

From Emmett Jay Scott

New York   Nov 5, 1910

Dear Mr. Washington: The Washington trip I have telegraphed you about.

Mr. Slater[1] says he cannot make the trip till after January 15 & before March 1 at any time agreeable & acceptable to you. He is most anxious to make it & says he will talk with you about it all *Dec 12* when you visit Washington for the Jeanes meeting. He took notes of everything as to trains. I said to him (when he inquired as to a hotel) that I felt sure you w'd want him to stay with you & this pleased him *much*. He mentioned his friendship for Mr H. C. Perkins[2] who told him that "one of the most delightful incidents of his life was an Evening spent at your home with you & Mrs Washington." He will have a man with him & will want us if possible to have a wheel chair that he can use. He was most agreeable.

Mr Wickersham was out of town. His secretary was not very talkative; so I went to the White House. After remaining in the halls waiting for an hour & a half I was admitted to Mr. Norton's presence. He is simply happy over the way the thing[3] has been received by the colored people & also the white people. He had on his desk a pile of letters from colored men (some 50 apparently) all catalogued with the names & occupations of each man on a list pinned to the letters. He made me promise not to discuss the matter except with you. He says a place has been found for the other man at a salary of same size ($5000) & that the Attorney General had to say that "there is no vacancy" to save the man's face. Also the man's backer is still standing by him but the change will be made.

He says the man is out now canvassing in the district of his backer & that it would be impolitic to make the change now. It will be done after the return from Panama. I urged that Lewis be put to work before Congress meets & he made note of it & said he w'd try to have it done for he could appreciate the importance of such appointment; having him at work. I told Mr Norton that no upheaval would follow & that it would all be in Lewis' favor.

He told me that *Grief* will reign among our folks in the South soon however, as it is probable that no Negroes will be holding places soon; as the President is going to carry out pretty fully his program as to holding office in the South. I told him we c'd not agree with me [him?] as to the program, but that [it] is better to have something to offset the feeling of the colored people in the way of these Northern appointments, as formerly we had *not* even them for an "argument." Cohen is pretty sure to go. I asked him directly if this is not what he meant & he said he could not tell, but that all the papers w'd be taken on the Panama trip to be studied fully. He had me write out fully what I had to say regarding New

Orleans being a place for a Decent Negro appointment. I referred to Kennedy & Lewis & made as strong a case as I could. I shall write again for him to have another letter before Wednesday.

Cottrell will hardly be appointed to Hawaii but probably to some other place. The Governor & all the leading officials have protested against an "interloper" coming in; *not* on grounds of color, & besides Cottrell has told him (Norton) he hopes he can find a place in the *U S* as he does not want to go Hawaii; so that is the status for the present.

You have halted the *Winton* case in *N.C.*[4] He says that the President & PM General agree that you have made a good case; that this place w'd come under the present program: having Indorsement of business interests &c: but the Inspector has reported the man has tuberculosis, so probably they will get rid of him anyway.

He went out of his way to assure me that Hitchcock is with *you* on this case! I told him I so understood.

I showed Chase your telegram. He is well pleased, but is trying now to get his son in Johnson's office & says he will appoint the boy "*If* the President will write him a letter suggesting that it be done." I ridiculed that but Chase will probably ask you to have the President write such a letter. I did not discuss my interview with Norton with Terrell, Cobb, or Tyler: altho' they were all anxious to know what I was doing there. I forgot to say that I got Norton to agree that the Lewis appointment be made approximately about Thanksgiving Day. I told him for all concerned a definite time sh'd be named & he then said that approximately Thanksgiving w'd be the time.

I got around pretty well & hope what I have been able to do & find out is satisfactory. Yours Truly,

Emmett J. Scott

See "Bee" & "Age."

ALS   Con. 597   BTW Papers   DLC.

[1] William Albert Slater (b. 1857), a cotton manufacturer and the son of John F. Slater, was president of the John F. Slater Fund beginning in 1909.

[2] Possibly Henry Cleveland Perkins, a broker and mining engineer in Washington, D.C.. who was a trustee of George Washington University from 1910 to 1921.

[3] The removal of William T. Vernon and the appointment of James C. Napier as register of the treasury.

[4] BTW wrote to Charles D. Norton, Nov. 21, 1910, that J. B. Catus, black postmaster at Winton, N.C., did not have tuberculosis as reported. BTW had received

a favorable report of his examination for tuberculosis by the president of the county medical society. (Con. 55, BTW Papers, DLC.)

An Address at the Macon County Fair

[Tuskegee, Ala., Nov. 5, 1910]

Mr. Hare,[1] friends and citizens of Macon County: During the past eight days I have been travelling through the state of North Carolina and have been making, or trying to make, on an average of about six speeches a day and I have very little voice left, but as I went through North Carolina and saw the progress the people are making, going to many fairs of this character, I could not help but wonder and wish that the time might come when in Macon County we should have something of the same character. So I am glad to come here and see what is being done in opening this first Macon County Fair. Surely if this is the beginning, the good Lord only knows what the end may be, if you can start so successfully as you have.

I have been surprised, as I have gone through these various exhibits to see to what an extent you have a real, genuine, old-fashioned agricultural county fair. That, it seems to me, is the only kind of fair that means anything, that enables the people to see what they can get out of their own soil right about their doors.

Mr. Hare has very kindly referred to the fact that I have spent some time across the water. I have. I spent nearly 3 months in Europe. I went into a good many countries; I saw a great many different kinds of people; I was in a great many different kinds of climate, on a good many different kinds of soil and after having that experience, I come back to Macon County saying to you with all the earnestness I can that I love Macon County better than any spot in the world I have ever seen. I love these people, white and black, better than any people I have ever seen; I love the town of Tuskegee better than any town I have visited. I like a community where when you meet people on the street you know who each one is. He calls you by your name and you know his name. That is real life, where one is surrounded by friends, by neighbors who understand us and know us and I would not exchange my residence

441

in Tuskegee or in Macon County for any spot on earth that I have ever seen.

Now I wish to speak especially to the colored farmers at this point. We have advantages here in this county that we do not always, I fear, consider. The average man gets so into the habit of talking about his troubles and disadvantages, that he sometimes fails to give attention to his advantages. It does not pay a man, it does not pay a race to advertise its troubles too much. It certainly does not pay a business man to advertise his troubles too much. Suppose some of these bankers Mr. Campbell or Mr. Drakeford should go about the streets, beginning on Monday morning and talk about the hard times their banks are having, saying collections are poor, that they have few depositors and the few depositors they have in their banks are taking their money out every day and they do not know how long they can keep their doors open. It does not pay a race to advertise its troubles. We have advantages here that we have never thought properly about; advantages in the fundamental things of life. In the first place, we have an advantage in the natural resources. The soil in Macon County does not draw any color line, does it? The black man can get as much out of the soil here as the white man. We have the chances that the average man has and we must think about these chances right near our door rather than the grievances. Here in Macon County, the colored farmer has the same chance to buy land as the white man; they will not only sell you land, but will actually lend you the money to pay for it at the same time. Do you know any other class of working people who have any such chance as that?

When I was in Europe recently, I found that the land there is held in tracts ranging from 2,000 to 40,000 acres in size. A poor man cannot touch it and when he does here and there get a chance to buy a few acres, he has to pay from $800. to $1,000. for it. They can only get one to three acres and they call one to three acres a farm. How different are the conditions around here, where any colored man can buy land at a cheap rate, almost given to him, in some cases. Certainly, if it is not given to him, there are many cases where he can go on the land and live until he has paid for the land.

Around here we have one of the most genial and beautiful climates in the world — a climate where there is health, a climate that is suited to our conditions, suited to our nature. There is something about the soil here that is suited to our race; something about the climate that suits the temperament of our race; in fact, I always feel happy when I am in a county where colored people and mules live.

Then again, we are surrounded by a class of white people whom we understand and who understand us. I know of no class of working people anywhere in the world, who get so near to the best class[,] the aristocratic class of white people as is true of the colored people in the South. In Sicily, for example, where I spent a lot of time, the average working man there, the average farmer does not come in contact with the aristocratic class of people in the way the Negro does here. They know very little about each other, and I find in studying the condition of my race, that we make the greatest progress not when we are living by ourselves, but when living by the side of the best white people of this country. I have seen that illustrated all this week in North Carolina. As I went through that state, when I saw a Negro doing the best, having the most property, succeeding the most, getting education, he was living right in the midst or near a high type of Christian white people.

Here, my friends, we have that chance all through Macon County. The white man has something that he can give us in the way of example in the way of encouragement. We have something we can give him and I repeat that my race is best off, makes the highest degree of progress when it is living by the side and in the midst of the highest type of white people, so for all these reasons we should thank God that our lot is cast here in a county like this.

In addition to these advantages, we have the advantage of being able to find plenty of work. Why I was in Liverpool recently, before that in London, where I saw thousands of people walking the streets night and day. I saw thousands of men and women sleeping on the side walks every night, or sleeping out in the open parks under the trees. Why, because they could not find work. Whenever there was one job of work to be done, there were 6 to 8 men or women looking for that job. Here in Macon County, the average black man does not have to look long for work; instead of having to seek a job, the job seeks him. Some of you spend more time in running from the job than you do in seeking it. How different is our condition as compared with the class of working people in other parts of the world where they starve, in many cases, because they cannot find work. Here you can get plenty of work every day in the year and you can get work at a wage that is three or four and even ten times as high as many working people get for their labor in Southern Europe. Over and over again during the past summer I found strong, able bodied men working on the farms, working in the sulphur mines, working in the coal mines, and in the grape fields, when they only get 12 and 14 and 15 cents per day and were glad to get work at that price. How different here where we get from 4 to 5 and 6 and even 8 times as much money for our work as those figures indicate.

We sometimes complain about our dwellings, about our surroundings. Sometimes it is pretty bad; it is growing better in Macon County every year. Better houses are being built for you. Improvements are being made in that respect, but let me tell you something of what I have seen. Among working people, farming people, recently in Europe — and these were not colored people, they were white people — I have seen people by the thousands living in one room, on a dirt floor, no board floors, simply the dirt, and I have seen them living in one room, where they had no bed, nothing but some raw straw. In the same room, I have seen time and time again in Southern Europe, besides the man and his wife, sometimes 5 or 6 children, and the cow, the calf, the pig, chickens, all there together. My friends, think of your lot in Macon County as compared with the lot of those people living under those circumstances. Why there is not a Negro farmer in Macon County that lives under such circumstances.

Then, as a matter of fact, the food you have is a great advantage here over these people. You eat all kinds of good food here, fresh food. Stay here in the country; do not go to Montgomery, or Birmingham. Some of you have tried it in Montgomery. I can pick out in this audience any one who has tried it in these large cities — lean, weak, hungry looking individuals. You know how it was up there. Sometime you got breakfast and sometime you did not and when you do get it, it consists of a little cheese and crackers. Here in Macon County you can get up Sunday mornings and have fresh food, fresh chicken, fresh pork, fresh vegetables, fresh eggs, fresh buttermilk, fresh butter, opossum in November and December. You can live like a King in a country like this. Why then leave the country and go to any city when you have these chances here right about your door every day in the year in Macon County. I took great pains when in Europe to go to the farms and the mines when the people were eating their dinners and I saw case after case where men worked hard on the farm or in the mine and then when 12 o'clock came, what did they have for their dinners? Just some black bread and onions. That was all. Think of that compared to what you eat in Macon County. If some of you cannot get meat every day you go crazy. Why my friends, the working class of people over there, in many cases, only get meat at the most three times a year and then on some holiday or at Christmastime. I have seen whole families living there day by day upon the fruit of the cactus, the cheapest fruit that can be produced.

In Macon County, be it said to the credit of the liberal white people and to the credit of the School Board of Education in the country districts, you have good schools, better schools, longer school term, than any county in the South that I know of, so far as the country schools are concerned. Then you have every advantage, every inducement, so far as I can see, to help you to raise your children so that they will love the country and remain, and let us help to make this county the most beautiful county of the South. Let us stand by these good liberal white people in their endeavor to do everything to make Macon County a model for all other counties.

In too large a degree the money that comes into Macon County stays here for a little while in the hands of the bankers, then it goes to Chicago, to New York and everywhere under the sun to be used in paying for things that you can produce right here in Macon County. I am going to give you a little illustration. Everyone of these things here on this table I have bought from the stores in Tuskegee. That is where our money goes. We get money for cotton, but where does it go? It does not stay here in Macon County. We send it away to buy something that we can produce. The first thing I take up here, and I bought it in a store here, is a cabbage. It was raised in Virginia, in a climate like this, a soil like this. We are sending up there to Virginia and telling those people to raise some cabbage for us and we have to pay the freight from Virginia on these cabbage. I find here blackberries. We even buy blackberries. There is not a county in the world that has more blackberries in it than Macon County. Every bush has blackberries on it. Why you cannot turn around for blackberries in the South, but we let the blackberries go to waste and then we get a little cotton money and as soon as we get it, we send that money away to Baltimore. That can came from Baltimore. Instead of canning our own blackberries in Macon County, we took the little money we got from our cotton and sent it up to the people in Baltimore. We said to them: gather these blackberries, can them, and we said we will pay you for the tin, we will pay the freight on these blackberries back into Macon County. Do you wonder why we grow poor when we send a large part of our earnings away?

Do you know of any soil that will produce better tomatoes than we have in Macon County? There are stores here selling tomatoes in Tuskegee. Where did we send to get them? New York. Too aristocratic to eat Macon County tomatoes. Sell a bale of cotton, take a part of the money and send it to New York and tell them to send some of their tomatoes down here. Tell the farmers there we will pay them for growing them, for canning them and we will pay the freight to Macon County. Tomatoes from Rome, N.Y. Do you know an acre of land in Macon County that won't grow tomatoes? Here we are sending to Rome, N.Y. for strawberries. Corn and tomatoes come from Virginia; asparagus from California. My friends, every one of these things I bought in your stores in Tuskegee. Every single thing I bought before I left in your stores. String beans from Indianapolis, Ind. You evidently don't care for Macon County string beans. They are even sending us onions from Florida.

I am glad to see, my friends, that this Macon County Fair will be the means of regeneration of this county. We are going to produce these things ourselves. That is the value of a Fair like this. There is no county in the world that will produce better sweet potatoes than Macon County. I am glad to see such fine potatoes here, but some merchant sent down in Geneva County to get canned sweet potatoes. Taking your money from your cotton and paying those people in Geneva County for things you can raise right at your door every year. Spinach from Ohio; canned corn from Tennessee; pork and beans from Indianapolis; even sent to Indianapolis for hominy; peaches from Georgia; celery from Michigan; canned beef from Chicago; pickled cucumbers from Detroit.

Let this Macon County Fair teach us all this lesson and I believe it is going to teach us this lesson, we of both races, that we are going to stop spending our money for things not produced in this county, that we are going to turn over a new leaf, instead of throwing away the winter, we are going to work all the winter. We are not going to send somewhere else for vegetables we can raise ourselves. We are going to raise pigs and chickens. We are going to have our own milk and butter and our own geese and we are going to have our own vegetables and with it, we are going to raise the best cotton in the world and we are going to have the finest county in the state of Alabama. We have the best white people and best black people in the world and next year we are going to have the best fair in Alabama. Goodbye and God bless you.

TM   Con. 980   BTW Papers   DLC.

1 Charles W. Hare introduced BTW as "a home booster" and "one of the best farmers and stock raisers of Macon County." The fair was organized by J. H. Drakeford, president, and Ernest W. Thompson, general manager.

To Robert Ezra Park

[Tuskegee, Ala.] November 8, 1910

Dear Dr. Park: I have received the second chapter and it is quite interesting, however, I think we will make a mistake if we fail to describe with considerable detail what occurred in the police courts in London, also, the horrible sights one witnesses around the bar rooms at night, where women and children get whiskey. Yours very truly,

Booker T. Washington

TLpS   Con. 54   BTW Papers   DLC.

From Charles Lee Coon

Wilson, N.C. November 8, 1910

My dear Sir: I write to express my personal appreciation of your visit and its effects here in Wilson. You had a good audience representing all classes of our white and colored population. Numbers of the best white people in town have told me that your address was the very best ever made here. Many of them say you must come back. Some want to get a warehouse so that everybody can hear you.

The negro school here is stronger in the affections of the colored people, and white people are prouder of it, than before you came. I was delighted that we had a school building in which you could speak. The negro school will get better each year. It is not doing near all it ought to do, but we are moving forward. There will be a slight opposition from now on. I am more than ever convinced that white people will believe in and stand for the education of the Negro children, if the matter is put to them in the right shape. Our Negro school has more colored than white opposition. In fact, the last white man in town who counts *one* was converted by you! I rejoice over this sinner's making his peace with me! I want you to tell me frankly whether you think I ought to accept an invitation to speak in New York, at the meeting of some organization to which Mr. Oswald Garrison Villard belongs. He urged me last April or May to come to New York to speak, but I was afraid of it then. He said he would repeat the invitation later. I do not know very much about this organization and what it stands for. I am, however, not so much interested in that as I am in whether my going would in any way make me less useful here in the South, in my work for both races. Of course, I feel like I ought to do what I may be able to do to help along the work of the education of everybody. Still I do not think I ought to mix up with any body which will make my work harder or less effective. I usually say what I think should be said, down here, but I hesitate about saying it in New York and may be under circumstances which will cause bitter comment. Please tell me what you think, and I'll appreciate it.

Remember, you are to come back to Wilson before long. Very truly yours,

Charles L. Coon

I have just read November World's Work. We have a few *intellectuals* here who can't make a living!

TLS   Con. 823   BTW Papers   DLC.   Postscript in Coon's hand.

To Walter Hines Page

[Tuskegee, Ala.] Nov. 9th., 1910

My dear Mr. Page: Please forgive me for failing to reply to your letters of October 28 and November 3. When I reached home I simply found myself deluged with correspondence, and I am just now beginning to get my head a little above the water.

Thank you very much for your congratulations regarding my European trip. I had a very interesting time from beginning to end. I am going to cover some of my European experiences in one of the chapters for the World's Work, especially my experience with the king and queen in Denmark. One thing that overwhelmed me with surprise all through my European trip was the knowledge that people had of our methods and work at Tuskegee.

I am a very poor business man, but I have the feeling that if my book, "Up From Slavery," had a good, live, wide-awake publisher in London it would have had an immense sale during my visit to England, as the newspapers were full constantly of matter regarding Tuskegee and myself. The same was true at every point I touched in Europe.

Now, regarding the pay for my articles. I leave this absolutely to you. Whatever you send will be acceptable.

I shall return the chapter on My Experience in Politics very soon.

There are many matters I want to talk over with you. There is something curious about our good Southern friends. While they made a great howl about my dining with President Roosevelt, you will be surprised at the number of Southern people who have told me that they were glad that I dined with the king and queen of Denmark.

I have just completed a seven days' tour of the state of North Carolina during which time I addressed on an average five and six meetings daily. I was simply overwhelmed with surprise at the cordial reception I received at the hands of both white and colored people. In two cases the leading white people were so anxious to have me visit their county that they paid the expenses of a special train. In these two cases I had not originally planned to go into these counties. At Wilmington the opera house, the largest in the city, was simply packed with white and colored people. The man[1] who led the Wilmington mob was on the platform, and at the close of my address he got up and said he was a convert to Negro education. There were many more equally interesting incidents. Wherever we went the leading white men and women placed their automobiles and carriages at our disposal, and in several cases the luncheon or dinner was served by the servants of white people. In one case, at Winston-Salem, the richest white lady[2] in the city loaned her dishes and table ware to the colored family where our party was entertained, but I want to talk this and many matters over with you.

I shall be in New York during the latter part of November. Yours very truly,

Booker T. Washington

TLpS Con. 49 BTW Papers DLC.

[1] George Rountree. See BTW to Rountree, Nov. 11, 1910, Con. 823, BTW Papers, DLC.

[2] Mary Katherine Smith married the tobacco tycoon Richard Joshua Reynolds in 1905. She supervised the construction of their country estate, Reynolda. Robert R. Moton wrote of the Winston-Salem incident: "Mrs. Reynolds, one of the wealthiest ladies of the place, telephoned Dr. Jones, with whom we were staying, offering to loan Mrs. Jones her silverware, china, and anything else she needed. Further, she sent down in her carriage her two colored butlers to assist the hostess by serving the breakfast." ("The Washington Party in North Carolina," 647.)

To Charles William Anderson

[Tuskegee, Ala.] November 9, 1910

Personal and Confidential

My dear Mr. Anderson: My tour through North Carolina occupied, all told, eight days, hence I am fearfully behind with my correspondence.

Well, the fight is all over. I have not seen the daily papers as yet as we live in the country, but from what I gather through the telephone and telegraph operators at Tuskegee, it seems that our forces have been defeated all along the line with few exceptions. In the end it will do good and teach a great lesson.

It is too bad, it seems to me, that our friend, T. R., came back home just at the time to let a large part of the blame for this disaster fall upon him, and it is very regrettable that he has seemed to act and speak in a manner to enable his enemies to place all the responsibility upon him, when the whole responsibility was on somebody else, but he always comes out on top in the end. I should not be surprised if the seeming present defeat did not make him a strong candidate for 1912.

I have telegraphed you regarding The Canadian Club. I think it is a fine thing for you to accept.

I thank you for the other matters which you have discussed at length in your letters. I have read them with deep interest.

Of course, I had no thought myself that you had any connection with the Harvard man,[1] but thought it well to let you know how he was talking and acting. It seems that he was in Moore's employment at one time and Moore turned him out, and this, I presume, had something to do with his feeling toward Moore.

I am very glad that you helped Mr. Bennett[2] in the way that you did, and am also glad to note the generous manner in which you helped Mr. Moore. You see I did not fall into the trap to write a letter which could be read in favor of Mr. Bennett.

I am very glad to read what you say about the promotion of Mr. Josephs[3] and Mr. Loeb's fine attitude in this and all other matters that concern our interests.

According to my present plans I shall not be in New York before the last week in November; in the meantime I shall be glad to hear from you.

It looks now as if Lewis will go into office December 1st.

Do you ever eat possum? If so, I should like to send you and Mrs. Anderson a genuine old-fashioned, Southern possum. Yours very truly,

Booker T. Washington

TLpS Con. 49 BTW Papers DLC.

[1] Aubrey Bowser.

[2] William M. Bennett (b. 1869), a lawyer with the firm of McElheny and Bennett, was a Republican member of the New York state legislature from 1908 to 1910. He

was elected to the New York state senate as a Republican-Progressive for one term beginning in 1915. In 1917 he was the unsuccessful Republican nominee for mayor of New York City.

During the 1910 political campaign black supporters of Bennett, led by Gilchrist Stewart, sought a letter of endorsement from BTW. Charles W. Anderson squelched the idea, but explained to Bennett that BTW was doing all in his power to support Bennett's campaign. Anderson wrote BTW: "We are doing all in our power to help Mr. Bennett, without, in any way, exposing you to criticism hereafter. I am sure this is just what you would have us do." (Nov. 4, 1910, Con. 49, BTW Papers, DLC.)

3 James S. Josephs, a black man appointed inspector of customs through Anderson's influence. (Charles W. Anderson to BTW, Nov. 4, 1910, Con. 49, BTW Papers, DLC.)

To Monroe Nathan Work[1]

[Tuskegee, Ala.] November 9th, 1910

Mr. Work: Sometime before the meeting of the Alabama Legislature in January I think it is, I want to address an open letter to the members urging them not to repeal the temperance law. I want to base my appeal upon the good that has resulted to the Negroes from this law, and the harm that will come by its repeal. I want to back up this appeal by definite facts as to the improvement of the Negro and also as to the lessening of crime, especially rape. I should also like to get definite facts regarding the decrease of crime in the large cities of Alabama since the temperance law went into effect. I would like to make a comparison between the old conditions and the new conditions. Of course, we might use Macon county as one example.

B. T. W.

TLpI Con. 604 BTW Papers DLC.

1 Monroe Nathan Work (1866–1945), head of Tuskegee Institute's division of research and records beginning in 1908, was a graduate of Chicago Theological Seminary (1898) and the University of Chicago (Ph.B. 1902, M.A. 1903). He was the founder and editor for many years of the *Negro Year Book*, first published in 1912. In 1928 he edited and compiled *Bibliography of the Negro in Africa and America*.

To Thomas Jordan Jarvis

[Tuskegee, Ala.] Nov. 10th, 1910

Dear Sir: I received your letter of November 2d while I was in the state of North Carolina. It has been very seldom that I have received a letter from any human being that has ever given me more pleasure and satisfaction than your letter. I thank you from the bottom of my heart for it. The world little knows how much my race owes to the cultured, high-class type of white people in the South for the progress that we have made in the South.

If I ever come to the state again I shall certainly go to Greenville.

I was surprised, too, at the high type of colored people who came to Washington [N.C.] from Greenville to attend our meeting. I have always noticed that wherever the colored people are treated fairly and have a good example set before them by the white people that they are of a high class, useful and law-abiding.

I found Professor Epps to be a sensible, strong man, and I am very glad that he is doing such good work in your community.

I thank you again and again for your letter. Yours very truly,

Booker T. Washington

TLpS   Con. 907   BTW Papers   DLC.

To James Carroll Napier

[Tuskegee, Ala.] November 10, 1910

Confidential. Planning to reach Nashville Saturday morning three fifteen o'clock from Montgomery. Wish to spend day with Booker and to see no one. Thank you in advance for your hospitality. Please make no mention of my intended presence in your city.

Booker T. Washington

TWpSr   Con. 910   BTW Papers   DLC.

To Charles Lee Coon

[Tuskegee, Ala.] November 11, 1910

Personal and Confidential.

My dear Sir: Thank you very much for your letter of November 8th. It has been a long time since I have had a letter from anyone which has given me so much encouragement and satisfaction as is true of your letter.

I am glad that you feel that my visit to Wilson accomplished some good. If I ever go to North Carolina again and am anywhere near you, I shall go to Wilson.

Now regarding the New York meeting: To speak frankly, I do not believe that you could accomplish any good by going there, and further, I believe that your fine influence in the South would be crippled by so doing. Mr. Villard, in my opinion, is a well-meaning, unselfish man, but he does not understand people. He has gathered about him a class of colored people, who have not succeeded, who are bitter and resentful and who, without exception, I think, live in the North. The white people who are with him, for the most part, with few exceptions, are dreamers and otherwise impractical people, who do not understand our conditions in the South. So far as you, yourself, are concerned, I am sure you would take care of yourself, so far as your own words are concerned, but you would necessarily, I think, become entangled with the general sentiment that would go out from this meeting. No one on earth knows what these people are likely to do, or likely to say at one of these meetings.

I always speak more strongly in the South when speaking to the Southern white people concerning their duties toward the Negro than I do in the North. It is one thing to speak to a people and another thing to speak about them. I think we can accomplish more good by speaking to the Southern white people than by speaking about them.

Your own influence is so unique and fine in North Carolina that I often think of you and all of us are proud of you and are most grateful to you for what you are doing. Yours very truly,

Booker T. Washington

TLpS   Con. 823   BTW Papers   DLC.

An Account of Washington's North Carolina Tour
by William Henry Lewis

Boston, November 12, 1910

WITH BOOKER WASHINGTON

William H. Lewis on One of the Negro Leader's Typical Trips South

Dr. Booker T. Washington of Tuskegee Institute, fresh from his triumphs abroad, where he had been dined by the king and queen of Denmark and had received marked attention from other notable personages, with little more than a week's rest, plunged at once into his life's work in the South — that of improving the condition of his own race and bringing about more friendly relations between the two races. The tour through North Carolina, which he has just finished, is the sixth in order of the visits he has made to the different Southern States, having heretofore visited Arkansas, Oklahoma, Tennessee, Mississippi and South Carolina.

The tour of North Carolina began at Charlotte on Oct. 29 and ended at Wilmington on Nov. 4, occupying little more than a week, during which time thirteen cities and towns were visited, and stops made at five or six others, where speeches were made from the rear end of the train. The party was conducted by Rt. Rev. Bishop George W. Clinton of the A.M.E. Zion Church of North Carolina, assisted by Mr. John Merrick,[1] president of the North Carolina Mutual and Provident Association, a life insurance society, with assets of over $100,000, and also president of the Mechanics and Farmers Bank at Durham, a prosperous Negro institution; also by Mr. C. C. Spaulding,[2] an enterprising and surprising young man, who is engaged in various business activities and is vice president and general manager of the insurance company referred to. The party included Mr. Emmett J. Scott, the private secretary to Dr. Washington and former Commissioner to Liberia, and other officials from the institute, among whom was Mr. John Washington, a brother of Dr. Washington, an ardent co-worker of his and a most lovable man. The party included also President W. T. McCrorey[3] of Biddle University, a Presbyterian institution at Charlotte; Mr. E. H. Clement, editor of the Star of

455

Zion; Professor J. B. Dudley, president of the Agricultural and Mechanical College at Greensboro; Dr. J. E. Shepard, president of the National Chautauqua and Religious Training School at Durham; Professor Charles H. Moore,[4] national organizer of the National Negro Business League, the first colored graduate of Amherst College, the class of 1878; Major R. R. Moton of Hampton; W. T. B. Williams, agent of the Slater fund; Messrs. Slatter,[5] King[6] and Thompson,[7] newspaper correspondents, and other well-known business and professional men in their communities, some twenty or more in number. During the tour Dr. Washington must have reached nearly 100,000 people. Wherever the train stopped or even "hesitated," as the old man said, crowds had gathered to greet and to get a glimpse of this distinguished citizen of the South. At points where the stops were made, the whole colored population seemed to have turned out. Brass bands, carriages, motor cars, to take the party to their place of meeting, were on hand. Men, women and children crowded round the carriage, all eager to grasp his hand. "God bless you," was the cry and the fervent prayer of many an old granny who came to see the first man of her race. He was their friend and their champion, and they were correspondingly proud of him and happy to see and to be with him and to hear what he had to say.

WINNING THE ESTEEM OF BOTH RACES

I do not recall any occasion in this country where a mere private citizen who has not held high public office has been received with greater general acclaim, by both white and colored citizens, because of his services to his fellows, than was Dr. Washington upon his trip through the Old North State. The attitude of his white fellow citizens was hardly less noticeable than that of the blacks. Everywhere he was introduced by the mayor or some leading citizen of the town. Prominent citizens occupied the platform and in some instances his audiences were more than half white. Those who came out of curiosity, or came with doubts or misgivings, went away with praise upon their lips and giving hearty expressions of good will and approval and support, and absolutely sure that Dr. Washington was pointing the true and the only way.

One could not follow Dr. Washington upon such a trip without becoming thoroughly convinced of his sincerity, his simplicity, his unselfishness, his desire to serve not only his own race, but his country. His oratory was of the popular type, powerful, pleasing, convincing, making new converts of every soul he reached. His language was simple, straightforward, direct. His points were made clear by convincing logic or illustrated by one of his inimitable stories. The dominant qualities of his oratory were his humor and logic; there was little pathos and less poesy, evidencing the intensely human and practical side of the man — the courageous worker rather than the theorist, the bewailer and the dreamer.

The object of the tour through North Carolina and other Southern States, as expressed by Dr. Washington, was to see the actual conditions of the colored people and find out how best to elevate them and to "better cement the relationship between the white man and the Negro." That, he said, was the only object. How well he succeeded, the future alone can tell. The immediate results, however, were gratifying indeed, and most promising, judged by the expressions of leading white and colored citizens.

Economic Progress the Safety of Negroes

The first stop of the Washington party was at Charlotte, the largest city of the State in point of population. Three thousand or more people, white and black, crowded into the largest auditorium of the city to listen to the great leader. He was introduced by Mr. T. W. Hawkins, whom Mr. Sanders, a colored citizen and lawyer, characterized as the greatest mayor in the United States. For two hours Mr. Washington appealed to the blacks to lay the foundations of progress and civilization by improving their economic conditions; to the whites for sympathy, for a fair chance and for justice. While he handled the subject, charged with a high explosive, nobody seemed to get nervous or the least bit uneasy. A reception was given in the home of Bishop Clinton, who is as handsome, scholarly, cultured and well-balanced a black man as one could wish to see. The party visited Biddle University, one of the first schools in the South for the higher education of the Negro; and also the A.M.E. Zion Publishing Company, with its large and extensive plant.

The next stop was at Concord, where the usual crowd met the distinguished visitor. Doctor Washington here addressed the students of Scotia Seminary, numbering 265 pupils, and went from

457

there to the Opera House, where he was introduced by Mayor Wagner, who welcomed him as "one of the ablest and most distinguished educators of the South." The mayor said of him: "By sheer force of manhood and strength of character he has risen from humble conditions, overcoming obstacles and almost insurmountable limitations of environment, until today he is recognized not only in this country but the world over as one of the men who has accomplished great things for his day and generation. At the head of one of the great institutions of learning of the South, he has used his influence toward bringing about better social and industrial conditions for his people; and he is a man whom the South does honor and is delighted to honor because he is a great factor in solving the problems that confront it. When the final day of reckoning is come, no greater laurels shall rest upon any man than upon him who has spent his life in the service of his fellow-man."

The party was welcomed at Salisbury by ex-Mayor Boyden,[8] who, after Mr. Washington had spoken, declared: "I am glad to be here and hear Dr. Washington, and I know that both whites and Negroes profited by what he said. The principles inculcated by Dr. Washington will not only help the Negro people in working out their part of the problem, but will help the white people also." The mayor spoke touchingly of the faithfulness of the Negroes during the war and adjured his audience to give them fair play. Here, in addition to a speech at the Opera House, an address was made at Livingstone College, founded by the lamented, gifted, talented and eloquent Jesse [Joseph] C. Price.

Mr. Washington was given an enthusiastic reception and ovation at High Point. Winston-Salem was reached Sunday morning, the 30th, where an immense concourse of people was waiting to receive the party. They were entertained at the Slater Normal and Industrial Institute. In introducing Dr. Washington to an audience of two thousand or more in the Elks' Auditorium, Mayor Eaton[9] declared that he, Mr. Washington, possessed in the most wonderful degree the qualifications of common sense, sound character and diligence. He said: "He has had the sense to select the right field for his labors, and with untiring diligence has set in action his wonderful creed." The party was also breakfasted at the home of Dr. J. W. Jones. One of the richest white ladies[10] in the town sent her silver and linen and two servants to assist in entertaining the large party.

THE GOSPEL OF TOLERATION ON BOTH SIDES

The prosperous and thriving city of Greensboro was the scene of a most remarkable demonstration. Three thousand people, white and colored, gathered in the railway station to catch a glimpse of the distinguished visitor. So great was the crush that a committee of the Chamber of Commerce that went to meet him missed him, and the party found it difficult to get their carriages. The white churches held an early service so that everybody could go to hear Mr. Washington. An audience of four thousand people heard the address upon that occasion. The speaker was introduced by the Hon. E. J. Justice, ex-Speaker of the House of Representatives of the State. He said: "Long ago he (Dr. Washington) saw the position the Negro race ought to occupy, and must occupy in America if they would reach that destiny that had been planned by our Creator. He saw before others did the necessity for the Negro men and women and sought to prepare the Negro men and women for usefulness and tried to bring the races into closer relations rather than to widen the breach between them. His one aim has been to have the races in the South work together in peace and harmony."

While at Greensboro the party visited the Agricultural and Mechanical College, an industrial school for colored youth, supported by the State; also Bennett College, an A.M.E. Zion institution presided over by Dr. S. A. Peeler;[11] and the Emanuel Lutheran College, supported by the Lutheran denomination, with white teachers, a strong body of earnest and enthusiastic young men. Mr. Washington made a short address in all three institutions, appropriate, helpful, practical and to the point.

Monday morning, the 31st, found the party at Reidsville, a small, flourishing country town. The school children turned out with flags and supported by the brass band made things lively enough. They lined the pathway to the hall and pelted him and strewed his pathway with flowers. One could not help thinking of the thorny path this man had trod to his present place of usefulness and honorable service to his race and to his country. Three prominent white citizens came to the hall where the party was breakfasted to welcome Dr. Washington in the name of the City Government. The mayor introduced the speaker to an audience of about 3000 in an old tobacco warehouse. In this and a few other North Carolina towns and cities the colored children have a school term of nine months. The Negro vote there is only 150, but the mayor was elected by nine votes, so that the Negro vote, though small, holds the balance of power. More than 1000 people followed the party to the depot to see Mr. Washington off for Durham where the party arrived at nightfall. Durham is perhaps the richest city in the State, being the home of the Dukes and the American Tobacco Company. The colored people are well off here, living in and owning beautiful and even luxurious homes. Negro business enterprises are many here — three Negro insurance companies; one bank; two drug stores; one shoe store; one dry goods store; one millinery store; one iron foundry; one textile mill; twenty-five groceries; a mattress factory; two tailoring establishments; and one of the largest brick manufacturing plants in the country. The Negroes own about $125,000 worth of business property upon the principal streets. This was the only place where Dr. Washington spoke in a colored church and was introduced by one of his own race, Dr. J. E. Shepard, a brilliant young man of rare intellectual gifts who is conducting here a Chautauqua and Bible Training School for his race. But, as usual, the audience was about half white. Here Dr. Washington also addressed the Bible Training School and the graded school, presided over by Professor Pearson.[12] The public school term in this town is ten months. Mr. Washington showed his versatility by being able to entertain and instruct little ones between six and twelve years of age.

En route to Wilson, the train stopped at Selma for ten minutes, where a brief speech was made from the rear platform to crowds of two hundred or three hundred people. At Wilson he spoke in the assembly room of a large school for colored children. The audience was more than half white. Prominent citizens occupied the platform. Ex-Congressman Woodard[13] introduced Dr. Washington. After he had completed his address, Professor Charles L. Coon, superintendent of schools, asserted, with figures to back it up, that the Negroes are not only paying their proportion of the school tax, but in some instances educating white children. Professor Coon made a strong address, commending the efforts of Dr. Washington and said that he would be ashamed to call himself a man if he opposed the education of any human being because of his color.

Everywhere Cordiality for the Negro Leader

Rocky Mount was a Southern town to delight the eye. Everything is up-to-date — water, sewerage, electric lighting, new buildings, and so forth. In twenty years the railways have worked a miracle here. The population is about 12,000, half white and half black. A uniformed brass band met the party at the station, and many carriages. There was a parade through the city and a banquet at mid-day. These banquets had been steady things all through the trip, usually at night after the speaking at the one-night stands. One of the party said at one of the numerous banquets that we had been eating our way through North Carolina, digging our graves with our teeth. Here we found our largest audience, of six thousand people, gathered in a cotton warehouse. The schools were closed and some of the business houses as well. Dr. Washington was in his happiest vein and for two hours moved that vast audience first to laughter and then to sober, serious things. Mr. Thomas Battle,[14] president of the Bank of Rocky Mount and former mayor, made an extended address in introducing Mr. Washington. He said in part: "It gives me pleasure, at the request of our City Government, to introduce to you the eminent citizen who is with us today. He is a man to be proud of. We who have watched him and read his speeches and his writings feel that he is best fitted to settle the greatest question of our time, on the proper solution of which depends the welfare of our entire Southland."

Rear end speeches were made to crowds at Tarboro and Parmelee. Washington, N.C., was the next stop. The venerable rector of the white Episcopal Church, ex-superintendent of schools, introduced Mr. Washington to a crowd overflowing the Opera House. When he had finished speaking he was presented with flowers and with a gold-decorated fountain pen. Mayor Wooten of the neighboring town of Greenfield [Greenville] sent a cordial letter of greeting to Dr. Washington at this place. The former governor and ex-United States Senator Jarvis also sent a letter, in which he said: "The colored people are a part of the citizenship of the State, and a very important part, and I heartily welcome and indorse any movement and influence to make them better citizens. I believe the teachings contained in your address will be helpful to those who hear them."

New Bern was no exception to the rest of the towns and cities. Here automobiles and carriages and the inevitable and inexorable brass band were in evidence. The opera house was thrown open. Ex-Mayor Bryan introduced Mr. Washington to an audience including the Board of Education, the Board of County Commissioners and other leading citizens.

A DELICATE SITUATION HAPPILY MET

Wilmington was the last stop. We had traversed the State almost from the mountains to the sea. There was considerable anxiety as to how Dr. Washington and his party would be received here, owing to the riot of ten years ago, in which a number of Negroes and whites were killed. However, three thousand people jammed the approaches to the railway station. The police had to be called in to hold the people in check, so that the party could reach the carriages in waiting. The best auditorium in the city, the beautiful and spacious Academy of Music, was thrown open. The whites occupied one side of the orchestra and one tier of boxes; the colored people the other side and boxes and both galleries. The available standing room was fringed on one side with the whites and on the other side with the blacks. The stage was beautifully decorated with potted plants. Leading white citizens sat cheek by jowl with leading colored citizens. Dr. Washington was introduced by Mayor McRae in a few fitting words.

After Dr. Washington had spoken for nearly an hour and a half several leading white citizens arose and made generous acknowledgement of the fact that they came in some doubt of the value of such a meeting, but could ever after be counted as warm friends of Dr. Washington, his programme of education and of friendship between the races. Dr. Washington referred to the fact that his last visit to Wilmington was in 1898, just before the riot, and that the problem had changed somewhat; that they were having a political campaign with the Negro left out. The subject was a delicate one and the situation rather tense, but, as usual, the speaker got away with it by one of his inimitable stories. He said the situation reminded him of an old colored man down in Alabama who had a pig and sold it to a white man for three dollars. The pig came back, and he sold it to a second white man for three dollars. The first white man, going back to the old colored man to look for his pig, found the second man coming out with his pig, and said to him: "That is my pig; I paid Uncle Jim three dollars for it." The second man said: "It is my pig; I paid Uncle Jim three dollars for it." So they decided to go back to Uncle Jim and put it up to him. So in a few moments they met him and the first man said: "Uncle Jim, didn't I pay you three dollars for this pig?" "You certainly did, boss." The second white man said: "Uncle Jim, didn't I pay you three dollars for this pig?" "Yes, boss, you gave me three dollars, too." "Well, Uncle Jim, whose pig is it?" Whereupon the old man said: "Fo' de Lord, can't you white folk settle your own troubles without bothering a poor colored man?"

The sentiment created here for fair play and equal opportunity is bound to work good for both races. There were many instances which showed that Dr. Washington was winning the South for his race. The leading citizens, men and women, not only crowded the platform to shake his hand; they came to the car and asked to meet him. A fine looking, prosperous business man came into the car one day, shook hands with Mr. Washington, thanked him for what he was doing, and said he was glad that the king and queen had dined him. At another time there came along a farmer lad, lithe of limb, cleanly but poorly clad, took off his old slouch hat, exposing a shock of red hair, and warmly grasped Dr. Washington's hand.

The meetings were of the most unique character. After prayer and perhaps a solo by some local talent or a classical selection by the choir, Major R. R. Moton would lead the audience in singing some of the Negro melodies — "Climbing Jacob's Ladder," "In Bright Mansions Above," "Swing Low, Sweet Chariot," adjuring the audience that singing these old songs was one thing the colored people could beat the white folks doing, and that they should not be ashamed to sing these melodies, the folk songs of their race, which keep in memory the strivings of the fathers. Then there came an introduction of the speaker by some of the leading white citizens and of the mayor of the town.

THE GIST OF WASHINGTON'S MESSAGE TO HIS PEOPLE

What was the message that Dr. Washington carried to these people? It would be impossible within the scope of this article to give his speeches in full, and yet it is equally impossible to give any adequate idea of it without doing so. The speaker called attention to the fact that nine million of the ten million of the Negroes in this country must permanently reside in the South, and showed that the extinction and expatriation of the Negro were impossible. The white man, he said, came here a few years before the Negro, got lonesome and sent for him, paid his passage for him, a thing which had not been done for any other class of immigrants, and it would be discourteous and impolite for the Negro to leave. The Negro didn't want to go, and the white man didn't want him to go, and that about settled the question. He referred to his recent trip abroad in these words: "I have studied the condition of the black race in most parts of the world, and I am frank to say that I know no portion of the civilized or uncivilized world where there are so many white people residing by the side of so many black where the relations are so satisfactory and friendly as they are between the two races right here in our Southern States. This statement I make despite the fact that I know there is often wrong, oppression and injustice practised upon the Negroes, and that there is much to be done before conditions will be entirely satisfactory. But we are on the road to progress and while we are making progress there is always encouragement." He said that recently he had been in a country where there were seventeen different races residing, speaking seventeen different languages, each race thinking itself superior to all the rest. They had seventeen race problems there. In this country the problem was very simple because there was only one race thinking itself superior to the other. The Negro should emphasize his advantages, said the speaker, and not his disadvantages.

Nowhere in the world does the Negro have so large a monopoly of the labor market as he does in the South. In the cities of the Old World, London and Liverpool, Dr. Washington said he had seen people sleeping in the parks and upon the sidewalks and other out of the way places, men and women, looking for work and finding none. The Negro could buy land in the South, and sometimes the white man would sell him the land and lend him the money to pay for it. In the old countries the land was held by the old families in large estates and could not be obtained by the poor man except in small acreages and at a very high price. He said that in order to make progress the Negro must settle down in one place and get hold of the soil. To hold the labor market he must learn to put brains, dignity and skill into every occupation. The educated colored man must learn that it is no disgrace to work with his hands. He advised the colored people to get bank accounts, get something that the white man wants.

The necessity for getting money was illustrated by one of his stories, of the old colored man at the ferry. A white man came along and said to him, "Uncle, lend me three cents to get across the river." The colored man looked at him and said: "Look here, boss, you look like a white man and I suppose you is, but I ain't going to lend you no three cents today. Let me tell you another thing, boss: the man that ain't got no money is just as well off on one side of the river as on the other." The race, he said that had no money was just as well off on one side of the river as on the other. He spoke of the emotional side of the Negro; that sometimes he sang about being washed in the blood of the Lamb; but he particularly was a great deal more interested in seeing that every Negro had a nice bath tub so that he could be washed in good, clean, pure water down here; that the best preparation for heaven was decent, clean living down here; that he was not so much interested in getting people into heaven as getting heaven into people. He was not so much troubled about keeping people out of hell as keeping hell out of people. It was hell getting into people down here that made most of the trouble. He advised the Negroes to draw the line between the moral and the immoral, so that the people would understand that they were not all alike; to get rid of the idle, shiftless and disorderly. The speaker would talk to the blacks for a while, and then he would talk to the whites, and then talk to the whites over the heads of the blacks. The whites admitted that what was said to the blacks was good for them as well, because his advice to his own people was so wholesome that it contained the fundamentals of life and civilization.

It was interesting to note how Dr. Washington, right in the heart of the South, dealt with the things considered so vital by race leaders in the North. He would say to the colored people: "Stay in the country. If you come into the cities there are a lot of little problems, vexing problems, you must consider; which end of the street cars you can ride in, which side of the street you can walk on and where you can get a glass of soda water. Stay in the country where all the seats are free, where all the roads are yours, and there is plenty of good spring water. The soil draws no color line; it yields the same crops to the skilled black hands that it does to the white. There is as much rain for the poor Negro's crop as there is for the white man's, and the sun, if it discriminates at all, is in the Negro's favor."

As to Lynching

On the subject of lynching, he said that he had the hardest time in the world to convince the people abroad that the average Southern white man didn't get up in the morning and go out and lynch two or three Negroes before breakfast in order to get up an appetite. He said: "Our white friends can help again by preventing the influx of our people to the cities in large numbers by seeing to it that the people are just as well protected in their lives and property in the country as in the cities. When the Negro feels that he is likely to be lynched or likely to be made to suffer for any kind of crime, here again he is tempted to move into the city, where he can receive police protection." Again: "The rule of the mob, the lynching bee, is widely heralded, while the quiet work of educating, of civilizing, of property getting, of schoolhouses built, of churches built, that is going on day by day, is seldom heard of. The white men who kill Negroes are heard of outside the United States; the white men in every community who will help the Negroes to get an education, to get property, to build churches, are seldom heard of." Here was no denunciation or abuse, but the argument was just as effective.

At Washington, N.C., he said, with tremendous emphasis, at the close of his magnificent address: "We would not thrust ourselves socially upon anybody. What we want is justice in the courts, education and a fair chance." He argued strongly against the use of the Negro as a political issue. He said that he found that the Negro was abused occasionally by some man for the purpose of getting some office; that when a man wanted an office he would say anything about anybody; and when he inquired about that particular man, how he treated the colored people in the community, he was one of their best friends.

A Strong Plea for Equal Education

The plea for education was one of the strongest ever heard anywhere. Without pretending to quote accurately, he said that in some of the rural districts the Negro children had only three months' schooling, while the other race had six or more months. Some people thought the Negro had really more sense than he had. He was willing to admit that Negroes couldn't learn as much in three months as a white boy could in six; that was too high a compliment. While the Negro boy is handicapped in his training at the beginning, yet there was no discrimination made when the black boy was accused of crime. He was tried by the same law, the same courts, the same juries and judged by the same standards of ethics and morality as the educated white boy was. There was no discrimination made in the punishing line, and there ought not to be any in the education line. He said: "If I were a white man sitting upon a jury and called upon to decide the guilt or innocence of a Negro accused of a crime, I would lay my hand on my heart and ask myself upon my conscience and before my Maker, whether I had given that black boy a fair chance to know right and wrong, to curb and restrain his passions and desires, to know the law and to obey it." Between the individual white man, he said, and the black man there was the strongest tie of friendship. Each Negro had a white man picked out upon whom he relied and upon whom he could call. Each white man had a Negro upon whom he could rely, with whom he would trust his dearest possessions, and each would lay down his life for the other. He said that the worst enemy of the Negro is the man who unnecessarily stirs up racial strife, and the worst enemy of the white man is an individual who unnecessarily stirs up the feelings of bitterness and hatred between the races. He said that last year, while in some city abroad where the language was strange, the people were strange, and he couldn't eat the food, he heard there was a Southern man from Mississippi in that city, and the Southern man heard of him, and they got together and they were like two long-lost brothers.

The important thing that Mr. Washington emphasized was the making of progress; not to worry about details. He illustrated his point with the story of the old-time colored preacher who was travelling with him and his party in South Carolina, who wanted to get a carriage to take him to the depot. The first hackman he struck was a white man, and he told the fellow to take him to the depot. "I am sorry, Uncle," he said, "but I can't drive Negroes in my hack." The colored man said: "That is all right, boss. We will settle this right here. You take the back seat and do the riding, and I will take the front seat and do the driving." So in a few minutes they were both at the depot; the white man got his quarter and the colored man got his train. What Mr. Washington wanted to show was that both races are going to the depot. He said: "I believe in talking to the whites frankly in the South and not abusing them in the North," and his frankness and sincerity carried conviction to the hearts of his hearers.

The better day is dawning for the Negro in the South. In North Carolina alone he owns nearly $50,000,000 worth of property and there are 3000 Negroes who can be registered if they wish to be. The reduced vote is still swaying the destination of the State. Ex-Mayor Battle of Rocky Mount said that in the ten years of his official life the Negroes always stood with him for the best government, and he never paid a cent to a single man. Mr. Washington is different from the old leaders; he does not talk about the past or the glories of the future to come, but lives right close to the hour and now; he lives right down among the masses of the people and is trying with heart and soul to help them here and now.

This article cannot be closed better than by quoting once more from one of his speeches: "If we learn to be frank with each other, to trust each other and cultivate love and toleration instead of hatred we will teach the world a lesson, how two races different in color can live together in peace and harmony and in friendship."

Boston *Transcript*, Nov. 12, 1910, pt. 3, p. 4.

1 John Merrick (1859–1919), the son of a slave mother and a white father, became the most successful barber in Durham, N.C. In 1883 he launched a fraternal insurance agency, the Royal Knights of King David, the forerunner of the North Carolina Mutual and Provident Association, founded in 1898. Merrick also developed a real estate company and a bank. Merrick served as president of his insurance company until his death. (See Weare, *Black Business in the New South*.)

2 Charles Clinton Spaulding (1874–1952) operated a successful black grocery business in Durham when he joined with John Merrick and Aaron McDuffie Moore to form the North Carolina Mutual and Provident Association, which in 1919 changed

its name to North Carolina Mutual Life Insurance Co. Spaulding became general manager and expanded the sales force and added a newspaper, *The North Carolina Mutual*, to espouse the ideology of racial economic solidarity. He was also a partner of John Merrick in a land company and a textile mill. In 1923 he became president of North Carolina Mutual, and in 1931 he was the first black man appointed to the Slater Fund board.

3 Actually Henry Lawrence McCrorey (b. 1863), president of Biddle University beginning in 1907. McCrorey later served as president of the black chamber of commerce in Charlotte, N.C.

4 Charles Henry Moore (1853–1952) was professor of English at North Carolina A & M College in Greensboro (now North Carolina A & T State University) from 1894 to 1907. He later served as a national organizer for the NNBL, was president of the Greensboro Negro Hospital Association, and in 1917 was named supervisor of building for the Rosenwald Fund schools in North Carolina.

5 Horace D. Slatter, a general press correspondent from Hopkinsville, Ky.

6 George H. King, a reporter for the Greensboro *Daily Industrial News*.

7 Richard W. Thompson.

8 Archibald Henderson Boyden.

9 Oscar Benjamin Eaton.

10 Mrs. R. J. Reynolds.

11 Silas Abraham Peeler (1864–1948), born in Cleveland County, N.C., was educated at Bennett Seminary, Clark University in Atlanta (A.B. 1893), and Gammon Theological Seminary (B.D. 1895). He was president of Bennett Seminary (1905–13) and thereafter served as pastor of a number of North Carolina churches of the Methodist Episcopal denomination.

12 William Gaston Pearson, born in 1859, graduated from Shaw University and Cornell University. He was principal of a black graded school and later a high school in Durham. He also invested in many black business enterprises in Durham and owned twenty-two tenement houses. He was the co-founder with John Merrick of the Royal Knights of King David and of the North Carolina Mutual Life Insurance Co.

13 Frederick Augustus Woodard (1854–1915) was a Democratic representative from North Carolina (1893–97) and a lawyer in Wilson, N.C.

14 Thomas Hall Battle (b. 1860) was mayor of Rocky Mount, N.C., from 1886 to 1896.

From William Holcombe Thomas

Montgomery, Ala. [ca. Nov. 13, 1910]

Dear Dr   I thank you for your kindness. We have done it gladly. It[1] has cost much; of which Dr Abbott furnished $100.00 Ray Stannard Baker $150.00 and Mr Peabody $50.00. I should like them [to] know about it.

I am now liable on two bonds $750.00 on the 1st appeal & $250.00 on second appeal, *in event we loose to cover the expenses of the state of Alabama in defending the statute.* I hope we will win & not take the risk of procedure by the State. They may not seek to recover on them. I am   Yours Truly

William H Thomas

ALS   Con. 913   BTW Papers   DLC.

[1] Appeal of the Alonzo Bailey case.

To Monroe Nathan Work

[Tuskegee, Ala.] November 15, 1910

Mr. Work: Whenever you can conveniently do so, I want you to go to Durham, North Carolina and get up a full memorandum for me to use in an article for either "The Independent" or some monthly magazine. Judging by what I observed during the few hours I was there recently, I think the colored people in Durham, in proportion to the size of the city, are making more progress than is true of them in any part of the United States.

My idea is to have you get data including figures, etc., as well as general information showing the progress that the colored people are making in the tobacco factories, in all lines of business and, of course, bringing in the progress they are making in school and church work, but the business and industrial sides I want emphasized most.

You will note that there is some little division, I fear, between the prominent colored people, for example, there are two insurance companies in different buildings and I think there is some feeling between them. You must give both of them a fair show. I advise, however, that you put yourself in the hands of Messrs. Merrick and Spaulding, as they are fine fellows and you can be perfectly frank with them.

I want you to get pictures of both inside and outside of the buildings and also of the individuals employed in these buildings.

Whether or not it would be cheaper and more satisfactory for you to take Mr. Robinson[1] from here to make the pictures, you will have to decide.

I think you can get matter there which will enable me to prepare a very interesting and helpful article.

If you think you can go, I will take the liberty of writing Messrs. Merrick and Spaulding about your coming.

Booker T. Washington

P.S. I ought to add that I wish you to plan your memorandum upon the work of the Local Business League of Durham, that is the only way I can make a connection between Tuskegee and Durham, and the only justification I can find for having you go to Durham and do this work. You might begin with the statement, if you can justify it, that a large part of this progress in Durham grows out of the work of the Local Negro Business League.

Booker T. Washington

TLpS Con. 604 BTW Papers DLC.

[1] Charles D. Robinson, official photographer of Tuskegee Institute.

To William Pickens

[Tuskegee, Ala.] Nov. 15th, 1910

Personal

My dear Sir: I see that you have signed a protest against a speech which I was supposed to have delivered in England bearing upon the condition of the colored people in the South.

I wonder if you would mind sending me a copy of anything that I actually said in London to which you object. I shall be careful to return whatever you may be kind enough to send me. Yours truly,

Booker T. Washington

TLpS Con. 911 BTW Papers DLC.

Robert Russa Moton to Oswald Garrison Villard

[Hampton, Va.] Nov. 15, 1910

My dear Mr. Villard: In view of the conversation which we had on the steamer, while returning from Bar Harbor last summer, regarding the National Association for the Advancement of Colored People, in which you assured me that the movement did not have for its object the attacking of Hampton, Tuskegee, or Dr. Washington, I am taking the liberty to enclose you herewith a printed circular[1] which I got from Dr. Washington. This circular was circulated in London while Dr. Washington was there. In view of the fact that Mr. Milholland was one of the promoters of the movement and is at present an important officer in the Association, it would be difficult, in the light of this circular, to persuade any one to believe that the Association was not trying to tear down what Hampton and Tuskegee stand for. While the Association is not mentioned in the circular, a person so prominent in its development must influence its policies. Just what authority he has for stating that the Evening Post has at last become aroused to the absurdity of the Tuskegee proposition, etc., you, of course, know better than I.

I am informed also that in an address, recently delivered in Washington, Dr. Du Bois devoted much time to an attack on Dr. Washington. I understand also that in a recent meeting in Chicago, much of the time was taken up with a discussion of the faults and failings of Dr. Washington. All of this leads me to doubt whether you yourself are entirely acquainted with the workings of the organization. It does look as if the effort is along the same old lines of trying to tear down what many of us have been trying to do. Of course I shall be glad to know that I am mistaken in my impressions.

A number of us, when we heard of the new organization, felt hopeful that it was going to accomplish a great good in working along needed lines, without antagonizing those forces that are trying to accomplish the same results through different methods. I was strengthened in this after our talk last summer. I had hoped also to have had a talk with Dr. Du Bois.

What I would like to see is the uniting of the forces that are working towards the same end, and I still think there is patience enough and christianity enough to bring it about.

You will forgive me for being frank. I shall be glad to have you equally as frank with me.

I am sending a copy of this letter to Dr. Du Bois. Yours very truly,

[R. R. Moton]

TLc   Con. 51   BTW Papers   DLC.

1 See A Circular Letter by John Elmer Milholland, Oct. 6, 1910, above.

To George Augustus Gates

[Tuskegee, Ala.] November 17, 1910

Dear Dr. Gates: I am going to make some suggestions to you which may or may not have anything of value in them.

I have had a pretty wide experience in dealing with the graduates of our colored colleges in the South, and while in most cases their training is satisfactory in one respect, I note a great weakness in the ability of the student to write English.

I think there are few of our colored colleges that lay enough stress upon English. In observing the catalogues of most of the colored colleges, and also in observing their actual work in the class room, I find in most cases a good deal of time taken up having the student study about authors who have written good English, and in studying what noted authors have written, but very little time is given to the matter of having the student himself actually write. In many cases where the student does do some writing, it is in preparation of his commencement oration.

Then too, in too many cases, when the student writes English, he covers abstract subjects rather than concrete subjects. Of course, I am sure you will agree with me that it is necessary to have the student learn to write upon abstract subjects, but I think too much stress is put upon the abstract, and too little upon the concrete.

For example, when I was in Nashville on Saturday, I spent a good deal of time in going through the capitol grounds and I found much that interested me and much that I had never known about before. I wondered how many of the men who are in the various colleges in Nashville had ever written a description of these capitol grounds, buildings, etc.

Do not take the time to answer this letter. I am merely thinking aloud on this subject. Yours truly,

Booker T. Washington

TLpS   Con. 906   BTW Papers   DLC.

To Emmett Jay Scott

Tuskegee Institute, Alabama   November 17, 1910

Mr. Scott: I wish you to be considering the following matter: You might take it up with Dr. Park and others.

My recent European experience convinces me that I can make a trip through Europe to great advantage. I believe that a trip, properly planned and organized, can be made to pay the expenses of myself and those who accompany me, and aside from that, can be made to accomplish great good in its reflex influence upon the colored people of this country and the attitude of the white people toward the colored people in America.

In order, however, to accomplish the desired result, I am thoroughly convinced that it will be well to have Dr. Park go three months ahead and study the field thoroughly and map out plans thoroughly. In addition to Dr. Park, I should want yourself and a stenographer to go. With this organizing I am sure we could do effective work and get good results. It is absolute nonsense for a person whose name is known to go to Europe without having plenty of facilities to take care of the immense correspondence that floods one.

1st — It would be my plan to visit all of the important European capitals.

2d — To include large and important cities, whether they are capitals or not;

3d — To go to the principal universities, or university towns in the principal parts of Europe.

I should want to carry out this plan sometime within the next two years, if not earlier. As to the time, I believe if the scheme is well mapped out, that I ought to cover the ground within six weeks. As to the time of year best suited for the trip, I think Dr. Park's idea will be pretty valuable.

A very high toned and reliable lecture bureau man in London is anxious to undertake the planning of the trip, not on the usual lecture bureau basis, but on some other basis, but whether or not it will be necessary to have anybody undertake the planning, except Dr. Park, I am uncertain.

I should not want, except under very exceptional circumstances, any charge made at the door, but in a perfectly dignified way enough money could be taken in to cover expenses.

Booker T. Washington

TLS Con. 51 BTW Papers DLC.

To the Editor of the St. Louis *Post Dispatch*

[Tuskegee, Ala.] November 18, 1910

Replying to your telegram, I would say that in this enlightened age of advanced civilization and generosity, it is hard for me to understand how Mr. Samuel Gompers or any other American citizen, can advocate that any class of people not be given every opportunity to make themselves of the highest degree of usefulness, whether in trades unions or out of trades unions. The motto of enlightened people everywhere now is, "All men up and no man down" and I do not believe that the working men of America, who actually work with their hands, will endorse a doctrine that would shut the Negro out from the opportunity of earning his daily living.

I myself have been a coal miner and was a member, for a number of years, of the Knights of Labor. I always found the white man, with whom I worked, to be generous, broad and sympathetic. I do not believe that the masses of white working men today wish to take any attitude that would keep the Negro down, because no man, whatever his color, can be down without, in some degree, pulling some other man down.

Of ten million Negroes in [the] United States, nine millions live in Southern states and happily and fortunately, no matter what other people may advocate or do, the average native Southern white man prefers in the matter of labor to give the Negro a square deal. It will be many years, if the time ever comes, when through the medium of trades unions or any other organization the Negro in the South can be displaced either as a skilled laborer, or as a common laborer.

While in Alabama there are comparatively few trades unions, still in the large centers of industry, the white man and the Negro have unions that work in harmony with each other, there seems to be little or no disposition on the part of the white working men of Alabama to shut the Negro out.

In 1905, the Chicago Labor Union issued the following statement:

"The trades-union movement knows no race or color. Its aims are the bettering of the conditions of the wage-earner, whatever his color or creed. In this spirit we appeal to the colored workman to join us in our work. Come into our trades unions, give us your assistance, and in return receive our support, so that race hatred may be forever buried and the workers of the country united in a solid phalanx to demand what we are justly entitled to — a fair share of the fruits of our industry." This, in my opinion, represents the enlightened and progressive public sentiment of the American working man.

I have recently been in Russia, where the Jews are oppressed by being shut out from many industrial occupations. This oppression has awakened the sympathy of the world and protests against the treatment of the Jews, in regard to labor, are constantly being made in this country. Under the circumstances, I cannot believe that any large proportion of Americans would be willing to agree that the Negroes of America should be treated as the Jews are being treated in Russia. Is not Mr. Gompers of German Jewish extraction? When Mr. Gompers first arrived in America, he was an ardent advocate of the abolition of Negro slavery, an institution which compelled a man to work without pay. I am sure that Mr. Gompers would find it hard to explain why he now advocates a policy that would prevent the Negro from working for pay, when he is ready and anxious to do so.

It is pathetic, I repeat, in this enlightened age to know that there is any man who advocates a policy of shutting some other human being out and of trying to keep him down in the matter of labor.

Booker T. Washington

TWpSr   Con. 911   BTW Papers   DLC.

From George H. Bodeker

Birmingham, Ala., Nov. 18, 1910

Sir: Yours of November 16th received, and in reply beg to advise you that it would be impossible for me to give you the exact figures of crimes committed by the colored people, however, I wish to say that the Prohibition Law as I see it has not benefited the white people or the negroes, as Prohibition is a farce wherever it has been tried. I do not see any difference relative to crimes committed by either race. Respectfully,

Geo. H. Bodeker
Chief of Police

TLS   Con. 402   BTW Papers   DLC.

From William Pickens

Talladega, Ala. 11/18/10

My dear Dr. Washington: Yours of the 15th is at hand, to which I may give a more specific reply within a few days.

I will say now that I saw the written protest, of which you speak, and in letter it is not exactly the thing which I signed. To those who first called my attention to an *impression* which was getting abroad in Europe, I put the same question, almost word for word, which you put to me. My attention was then called to the *impres-*

sion rather than to the words that caused it, and against the impression that the condition of the Negro in America is satisfactory, or has been for the last ten years progressing toward a satisfactory solution, against that impression I am willing to give my word, from whatever quarter the impression comes, or from whatever words.

I suggested modifications in the protest, modifications which would tend to show that it was not the sense of the signers that Dr. Washington intended to give the impression above-mentioned. And I see that altho the words were later modified, my suggestion was not fully adopted.

I have maintained that the white press make the words of Dr. Washington a *pretext* for their own attitude towards the Negro.

I believe in the ultimate welfare of the American Negro, but not much in the drift of the last ten years or more. I object to the opposite impression. The impression is just as bad, whether intended or not, but I stated clearly to the protest-maker that to Dr. Washington's specific words on this special occasion I saw little to object to, that I was no enemy of his and not disposed to be over-critical. You know the advantage which the press takes of our words.

I shall look up carefully the words that were quoted to me in print, and write you a brief word concerning them. Very cordially yours,

Wm Pickens

TLS Con. 911 BTW Papers DLC. On Pickens's stationery as district grand secretary of the Odd Fellows.

To Travers Buxton[1]

[Tuskegee, Ala.] Nov. 19, 1910

Personal

My dear Mr. Buxton: Thank you for your kind letter of November 8th. I very much hope that your committee will pay no attention whatever to the circular letter which has been gotten out and printed in one or two of the London papers. I understand perfectly well the origin of this circular letter; the whole thing was engineered by Mr. John E. Milholland, the same man who got up the circular when I was in London. The colored people who signed the letter at Mr. Milholland's instigation amount to very little in their influence in this country; in fact, most of them are of a class of colored people who are ashamed of the race to which they belong and are angry because they are not white people. In the majority of cases they have made failures in life and this has soured them against the world. I do not blame them, I pity them. I am glad, however, that we do not have a large class of colored people in America that would come under the description I have given.

It seems, on reading the circular, that the main reason for protest is because I have represented the Negro as making progress in this country, and they claim he is making no progress. At the bottom of the circular letter are signed the names of one or two editors of newspapers and magazines, two or three lawyers, one bishop, and one professor of Latin. Now it seems to me that a country which could produce such men within 45 years after the freedom of a race is a country where colored people are making some progress at least.

The designation[s] which Mr. Milholland gave the signers to this circular are deceptive or fictitious. For example, one man was signed as editor of The Voice, a magazine. This magazine has been dead for six years. Another man was signed as field agent for the Constitutional League with a membership of 15,000 ministers, and representing a large majority of the Negro race. The fact is, the Constitutional League was started some seven or eight years ago by Mr. Milholland, and has been completely dead for many months. I do not believe that one could find in the whole United States one active, live Constitutional League. It is pitiful to see a man like Mr. Milholland dissipating his strength and time in an effort of this kind.

Nothing would please Mr. Milholland more than publicity and controversy, and this so far as I am concerned he will not have.

I want to thank again and again your committee for its great kindness to me. Yours very truly,

Booker T. Washington

TLpS Con. 903 BTW Papers DLC.

1 Travers Buxton (d. 1945), a descendant of Thomas Fowell Buxton (1786–1845),

pioneer British antislavery leader, was honorary secretary and later vice-president of the Anti-Slavery and Aborigines Protection Society. He also led in the international movement for reform of the Congo Free State.

From George Washington Carver

Tuskegee Institute, Ala., Nov. 19—1910

Mr. B. T. Washington, I have read, thought and pondered very carefully over your scheme for the reorganization of the Agricultural department.

As this seems the best thing to do I beg of you to carry it out; but I cannot be honest with you and true to the cause for which I have given nearly 15 years of the best of my life; So therefore I tender to you my resignation to take effect as soon as my work can be put in order and the Dept. inventoried over.

Trusting the work will grow and prosper as never befor[e]. I shall always be greatful to you for past favors. I am   Yours truly,

Geo. W. Carver

ALS Con. 596 BTW Papers DLC.

William Edward Burghardt Du Bois
to Robert Russa Moton

[New York City] November 21, 1910

My Dear Mr. Moton: Enclosed is my address delivered at Washington. Will you kindly look it over and mark those passages to which you object?

The circular issued by Mr. Milholland in London was on his own personal responsibility. On the other hand, the one which I wrote for London is enclosed. It was not, however, an official publication of the Committee.

I may say with regard to Mr. Washington or you or President

Taft or anybody else that whenever they do things which are, in my opinion, hurtful to the Negro race I propose to criticize them. I am going to make that criticism open and courteous, but it is going to be criticism and good plain criticism. I hope I may never be in a position where it will not be possible for me to do this. On the other hand, this committee is not organized to attack or tear down, it is perfectly sympathetic with all uplift work, whether at Hampton or Tuskegee or Atlanta or Fisk, and the thing that I cannot understand about a good man like you is that your eagerness to keep Mr. Washington, for instance, from well-merited criticism is greater than your eagerness to help the Negro race. I see no reason why you should not be an active member of our organization and I hope some time you will be. Very sincerely yours,

W. E. B. Du Bois

TLSr Copy   Con. 54   BTW Papers   DLC.

John Hope to Robert Russa Moton

Atlanta, Georgia, November 21, 1910

My Dear Major Moton: Your letter of November 17th as well as enclosure of copy of your letter to Mr. Villard has been received and read with a great deal of interest. I believe that I am more hopeful than you as to the possible closing of the chasm between those two gentlemen, Doctors Washington and Du Bois. Each thinks that he has good grounds for opposition to the other; but I do think that they could be made to see and feel that they could and ought to work together for the good of our people. I think with you, that public utterance will do little good towards bringing the men together. I rather fear that even such friendly correspondence as you are carrying on just now will do little good. I do think, however, that a conversation between these two men would be helpful and that is what I would like to get them to consent to. Neither one of them need say of what the conversation consisted if he did not want to. The misfortune of that famous meeting in New York several years ago was that Mr. Washington and Mr. Du Bois were talking before other people and not to each other. It would be better if that convention had never occurred. If some of us could have these two gentlemen meet and then leave them to talk out their ideas for five or six hours in the freest possible way, they would know each other better and probably all of us would be better off. This, I believe, is possible and if this can not be brought to pass, I see no way of having any co-operation between Messrs Du Bois and Washington. As I have said to you, the fact that both of them are doing good service apart is not sufficient argument for their not coming together. I am sure that both can do a better work if they are more in harmony. Young Negroes especially are being greatly injured, in their point of view and in progress by the fact that these two men seem to be at such cross purposes. If I can be of any assistance I shall be very glad to render it.

With kind regards to you and my friends at Hampton, I am, Sincerely yours,

John Hope

TLSr Copy   Con. 54   BTW Papers   DLC.

To John L. Staples[1]

Tuskegee Institute, Alabama   November 23, 1910

Dear Sir: I am greatly interested in the question of the reduction of crime among the people of my race in the state of Alabama.

Knowing that you have exceptional facilities for observing the criminals of my race, I write to you to get some information concerning them. What in your opinion are the chief causes of Negro crime? What effect does strong drink have in making the Negro a criminal? Since the Prohibition Law has gone into effect has there been any decrease in the number of crimes committed by the Negroes in your County especially rape, murder and other serious offenses? I enclose stamped envelope for reply.

Thanking you in advance for any information you may see fit to give concerning the above,[2] I remain, Sincerely yours,

Booker T. Washington

TLS BTW Papers ATT.

[1] Sheriff of Jackson County, Scottsboro, Ala.

[2] Staples's undated reply at the bottom of BTW's letter said: "Crimes of all nature have decreased materially in this section since the prohibition law has gone into effect. . . . I am of the opinion that whiskey is the chief cause of the majority of crimes committed by negroes in this County."

To Clark Howell

[Tuskegee, Ala.] November 23, 1910

Personal.

Dear Sir: I have read with care both your kind letter and the letter of Rev. R. D. Stinson,[1] which you so kindly send.

I appreciate, of course, your motives and deep interest in this matter, but I cannot feel at present anything would be gained by my making a statement, coming out in print, regarding the men who have signed this circular.

As Dr. Stinson says, these men are well known and they represent the same old gang that has been trying to oppose me and stir up race hatred during the last twelve or fifteen years. You will notice, that with but few exceptions, these men live in the North and know little about the South and have little interest in the masses of the colored people. In most cases, they are men with no influence with our race, simply because they have proved themselves to be absolute failures. They have a grievance and they think everybody else has a grievance; because they have failed, they think the whole race has failed. If I were to write a letter calling attention to their circular, I think it would be just what they would want. They crave notoriety and they like to feel that they are stirring somebody up and I do not believe it well to accommodate them in this regard.

Their special point of grievance against me just now seems to be that I told the people of Europe that the Negro in America was succeeding, that he had friends in the South, as well as friends in the North. I also told the people wherever I spoke in Europe that there is no spot in the world where there are so many black people and white people living side by side, where the relations, all things considered, are friendly and helpful as they are in our Southern states.

I came back from Europe feeling more strongly than I ever did that the South is the best place in the world for the American Negro. He is making more progress, has more friends and has a better opening than is true in any other part of the world and I am glad to say to you that more and more the entire colored race is agreeing with this point of view.

Permit me also to add that your own editorials and news items, within recent months bearing upon the duty of the white people to help the Negro, has had much influence in bringing about better racial conditions.

I think it is too bad that an institution like Atlanta University has permitted Dr. Du Bois to go on from year to year stirring up racial strife in the heart of the South. While Du Bois, as I understand it, has left Atlanta for New York, he is to come back to Atlanta in the spring and summer and conduct some kind of racial conference.

I very much hope that you will at some time visit Tuskegee. Both white and colored people in this section will give you a hearty welcome. We have the best white people in our County of any county in the South.

I also want to thank you for standing by our mutual friend, Dr. Stinson in the way you have. He is a man who sees conditions clearly and is not afraid to speak out. Yours very truly,

Booker T. Washington

TLpS Con. 907 BTW Papers DLC.

1 Richard D. Stinson, a presiding elder of the A.M.E. Church in Atlanta, began teaching at Morris Brown College in 1904, and later became the school's financial agent. In 1910 he was voted out of office by the Morris Brown trustees in a dispute over industrial education. Stinson wanted to enlarge the industrial department at Morris Brown. About 1914 he founded the Atlanta Normal and Industrial Institute, and served as its principal until 1927.

To William Alexander MacCorkle

[Tuskegee, Ala.] November 23, 1910

Personal and Confidential.

My dear Governor MacCorkle: Your kind letter has been received.[1]

I am very glad to hear of your election to the State Legislature.

I am very sorry to hear, however, that the question [of] disfranchisement of the colored people is likely to come up, b[ut] I feel now that in your hands and in the hands of other libera[l] white people in West Virginia, that no injustice will be impos[ed] upon the colored people, as has been in several states.

I am a Republican and at all times desire to see the success of that party in State and national affairs, but I am n[ot] a narrow Republican, in fact, the first vote I ever cast was for the late Senator John E. Kenna,[2] a Democrat.

If I wanted to try to get something done which would solidify th[e] colored vote against the Democrats, I should advocate the passin[g] [of] a bill by the Legislature of West Virginia restricting the franch[ise] as has been done in some other Southern states.

I have just received a letter from Mr. Charles W. Anderson, the colored leader in New York, and one sentence reads like this: "I have never in all my experience seen so many Negroes wearing Democratic badges as was true during the past election." Throughout the country the Colored people divided their vote, in many cases, about equally between the two parties, but no one thing would go further in my opinion in the direction of driving them back to the Republican party than for West Virginia to pass such a law as some are thinking of passing.

My observation, extending through most of the Southern states, convinces me in this direction: if a simple, straightforward poll tax requirement is enacted into the law, it will answer every purpose in keeping out ignorant and shiftless and undesirable voters. If a law is passed requiring a poll tax to be paid as a requisite for voting, and the time of this payment is set a long way in advance of the election itself — I mean long enough to prevent anyone from running the risk of paying poll taxes for individuals — I repeat it would answer every requirement and there would be no chance for the colored people, or anybody else, to feel they have been wrongly treated. Here in Alabama no one acquainted with the working of the new constitution can fail to see that a very large number of white people have been disfranchised through the operations of the new law; but in West Virginia, in my opinion, is an unusually industrious and progressive and liberal class of colored people and I for one would very much dislike to see the feeling of race hatred inculcated in a state that has been so long free from it — but I did not start out to write so long a letter.

By this mail, I send you a lot of printed matter bearing on the subject, some of which I think will be of value to you. Yours very truly,

Booker T. Washington

TLpS Con. 909 BTW Papers DLC.

[1] MacCorkle, who had just been elected to the West Virginia state senate, wrote BTW requesting information on black disfranchisement, since it was likely to be an issue in the next session of the legislature. (Nov. 14, 1910, Con. 909, BTW Papers, DLC.)

[2] John Edward Kenna (1848–93) was a congressman from West Virginia (1877–83) and U.S. senator (1883–93).

To George Ruffin Bridgeforth

[Tuskegee, Ala.] Nov. 23, 1910

Mr. Bridgeforth: The following change has taken place and is to go into effect at once in regard to Prof. Carver:

1. A Department of Research — Consulting Chemist, with Prof. Carver as the Director of this department, work to embrace the following:

1. Experiment Station.
2. Bulletin publications.
3. Bacteriological Work.
4. Analysis of

> Water,
> Milk,
> Food stuffs for human and stock,
> Paints, oils, etc.

5. Special lecturing on agriculture and domestic science.

6. Poultry yard.

7. Museum.

2. That a first class laboratory be fitted up for Prof. Carver so as to enable him to carry out whatever investigations he may wish to undertake along the lines mentioned above.

3. That this department be an entirely independent department subject only to the Principal as is true of every department of the institution.

He may teach agricultural classes if he desires.

Booker T. Washington

TLpS   Con. 598   BTW Papers   DLC.

Oswald Garrison Villard to Robert Russa Moton

New York. November 23, 1910

Dear Major Moton: I beg to acknowledge receipt of your letter of November 15th. The National Association for the Advancement of Colored People cannot be held responsible for the individual opinions or actions of its members. Whatever Mr. Milholland's personal opinions the fact remains that the Association is in no wise endeavoring to injure what Hampton or Tuskegee stand for. Of course, Mr. Milholland has no warrant or authority whatever for stating that the Evening Post has "At last become aroused to the absurdity of the Tuskegee proposition." At the same time, if you have read what the Evening Post has had to say about Dr. Washington during the last two years you must be aware that there is a strong similarity between Mr. Milholland's views and our own, at least to this extent: We, too, believe that Dr. Washington's political activities are most hurtful to the negro race and to his own influence, so much so, that if they are persisted in they must deprive him to a considerable extent of the high position he now holds. We have pointed out that Dr. Washington is popular in the South because he says to the Southerners what they want to hear; because they believe that he is with them in thinking that the sole destiny of the negro race is to act as hewers of wood and drawers of water. I find myself more and more opposed to Dr. Washington's entire philosophy of compromise and expediency and of saying nothing about the unquestioned wrongs of the race, politically and socially. I could justify that, if Dr. Washington confined himself absolutely to his educational duties and assumed neither to speak for his race to the nation nor to be the political broker for his people. But as long as he assumes to be the spokesman for the race I cannot but feel that his London utterances gave a totally wrong picture of the situation in America. Had I been in London, while I should not have been as extreme or as violent as Mr. Milholland, I should have unquestionably sought the opportunity to protest that in my opinion as a grandson of Garrison, this continual crying that all is well with us is nothing short of a real betrayal of the race. But while I hold these views, I am, of course, no more opposed to Tuskegee or to Hampton than I am to Manassas, for which I am, to my cost in the way of strength, time and labor, responsible; any more than I am opposed to Harvard or Atlanta University. I am devoted to all kinds of education and so is the Evening Post. That will, I think, answer your question on that point.

As to Dr. Du Bois, he has sent you his speech and you can judge for yourself how far he has gone. I reiterate my statement to you that so far as I have succeeded in moulding it or putting spirit into it, the National Association is not anti-Washington or pro-Du Bois, but is just what its title makes it. If, however, Dr. Washington should go further and do something which in the opinion of that Association called for emphatic protest as being inimical to the welfare of the race, I could not, of course, personally undertake to prevent the Executive Committee from making a public reply to Dr. Washington. At the same time, I have never failed in every meeting of the Committee in which Dr. Washington's name has come up to express my hope that some day we shall have him standing on our platform and speaking for us at one of our annual conferences. We ought to have his support in every way, even though it should appear to him that we are his critics along certain lines, so great is the service we can render to the race.

You must yourself be aware how the race has progressed under Dr. Washington's leadership, in many ways, but race prejudices and discrimination have progressed still faster, and he, himself has done almost nothing to stop them. You must also be aware that the great majority of the highly educated members of the race find themselves more and more in opposition to him. That this is a highly regrettable condition of affairs I have repeatedly stated publicly, but, as I have said before, my criticisms of Booker Washington do not prevent my helping both Tuskegee and Hampton to the extent of my ability. You will remember that I raised about $157,000 for Tuskegee as the Baldwin Memorial Fund, which is now a part of Dr. Washington's endowment. I stand ready to help him again whenever the occasion offers, and have given him the support of the news and editorial columns of the Evening Post without stint, and I am, as you know, always ready to help Hampton, too.

Finally, you may rest assured that although the policy of the Association may not commend itself to you, there is not the slightest effort, and never will be an effort, to "tear down" anything that has been built up for the colored man. Our only desire is to build up in this and every other direction, but that does not mean that we shall be tongue-tied, like Dr. Washington, on the fundamental problems of negro citizenship, or that we shall even bear the appearance of acquiescing in monstrous injustice to the black man. Very truly yours,

Oswald Garrison Villard

TLSr Copy   Con. 409   BTW Papers   DLC.

From William Pickens

Talladega, Ala. 11/24/10

My dear Dr. Washington: I promised to write you again when I should have looked up the matter you asked about.

I am still convinced that the impression which was created, with perhaps innocence on your part, was not altogether true.

I am by no means assuming the position of instructor in this letter. Far from it! I am simply saying what must be said in order to answer the question you ask. As to instruction, I am the pupil.

The London Morning Post had a long interview, in which they pretend to have gotten the impression from Dr. Washington that the reports of mob violence are greatly exaggerated, and that it is wrong to suppose that the American Negro is suffering. That is on the whole a most misleading and damaging statement: the only thing that is usually exaggerated about a lynching, is the crime of the lynched Negro. In some cases the lynching deviltry may be exaggerated, but I risk the assertion that the worst picture of lynching that any man's pen ever described, was not quite as bad as the worst lynchings that we have had. Why, from the very fact that the white men manage the press and news, it becomes an impossible construction of human nature to say that the side against the Negro would not be exaggerated and the side for the white man palliated. And that the black folks of America do not suffer wrong, and great wrong, is an absolute error.

People who live outside of America would be easily misled by such impressions.

The Paris edition of the New York Herald reports Dr. Washington as saying that the franchise in the Southern States is restricted to property qualifications and the ability to read and write. That statement is so absolutely wrong and erroneous, that I do not believe that Dr. Washington said so, but the paper, as papers sometimes do, gave it as a quotation. The plain, unvarnished truth is that our franchise is restricted in the main to white people, regardless of any other consideration. We understand that here in America, and the opposite statement could be made with much less misconstruction here than abroad.

It will not be well for us to alienate the sympathy of the outside world, and to have our protests against real wrong understood as the exaggerated complaints of children.

I may be wrong in all this. I am a learner. I may change, if I learn better. I know that I am no enemy of Dr. Washington, as a man, a citizen, and a fellow-worker for a common race. I am not sympathetic with the loud and inconsiderate opposition that is directed against him. I do not love Caesar less, but I certainly do love the welfare of my people more. Very cordially yours,

Wm Pickens

I can give you quoted matter from the newspapers, if you desire it.

Wm P.

TLS Con. 911 BTW Papers DLC.

To Olivia Egleston Phelps Stokes

[Tuskegee, Ala.] November 25, 1910

My dear Miss Stokes: I have not written you lately regarding the Liberian matter. I have a reason for the delay. I do not know, however, whether you will agree with me as to the wisdom of the delay, but I thought I would not put the question before you for a number of months.

The American Government has been trying to re-adjust the financial affairs of Liberia, and to re-adjust boundary disputes as between Liberian and certain European Governments so as to give Liberia a chance for stable government and for permanent life. Involved in this plan is a loan to Liberia of about a million and a half dollars on the part of American and European bankers. This means that an American official would be put in charge of the collection of the revenue which is to repay this loan, and it also involves the expenditure of a certain amount of money in improving roads and school facilities of the Liberian Government. The whole thing is being carefully worked out.

It has seemed to me that in view of all this, it would be wise to delay any attempt to establish an industrial school until matters have matured, and especially until some strong and wise people from the United States are on the grounds.

I am glad to say to you that it looks now as if the whole matter of the loan and the other matters, and re-adjustments needed will be consummated within a short while. When all this is done, I think then we can see our way clear to make the right move in the direction of establishing a first-class industrial school.

As I said in the beginning, I do not know whether you will agree with me or not regarding this delay.

491

Dr. Falkner, one of the American Commissioners to Liberia, is the leading spirit just now in connection with the re-adjustment we have mentioned and he will be in Liberia for some time. I think when matters are ripe, he will be of the greatest help to us in giving advice as to what to do and not to do.

I should be very glad to have your opinion, however, concerning the wisdom of any further delay.

Of course, it is not possible for us to go very far or do very much until we know more definitely what money is in sight and can be depended upon for the development and maintenance of the school. Yours very truly,

Booker T. Washington

TLpS   Con. 51   BTW Papers   DLC.

To Charles Dyer Norton

[Tuskegee, Ala.] November 25, 1910

Personal.

My dear Mr. Norton: Mr. Scott has spoken to me of his interview with you at the White House, November 5th, and of your confidential statement that there would "probably be grief below the line," because of the President's intention to further pursue his Southern policy with regard to Negro office holders in the South.

He also advised me that it was your statement that the President while on the Panama [trip] would study the situation at New Orleans with regard to the consolidation of the United States la[nd] offices.

He has also advised me of your inquiry of him during the summer as to whether there is any city in the South where the President can carry out his Southern policy without fomenting strife.

I do not believe that there is any place in the South better than New Orleans. For many years in the past, and until recently, in the distribution of patronage at New Orleans, as a rule, a white man has been appointed Collector of Customs, a colored man Naval Officer; a white man Receiver of Public Monies, and a black man Registrar of the Land office, etc., etc. This condition obtained from the inauguration of President Grant (during Republican administrations) up to the inauguration of President Roosevelt. During a part of President Roosevelt's term a colored man was Naval Officer. He died in office.

I understand that the term of the present Naval Officer at New Orleans has expired, or is about to expire. It occurs to me to suggest, in case the land offices are consolidated and removed from New Orleans, that you might care to ask the President to consider the suggestion of a colored man for the Naval Office vacancy. Yours very truly,

Booker T. Washington

TLpS   Con. 55   BTW Papers   DLC.

From the Postgraduate Girls of Tuskegee Institute

[Tuskegee, Ala.] November 25, 1910

Dear Mr. Washington: Thanksgiving evening the post graduate girls were invited over to Mrs. J. R. E. Lee's home. Some of the post graduate young men asked Miss Porter if the young women could attend, and she refused on the ground that she did not have a chaperone for them, and that the Council had decided that the post graduates could not have any dancing this term.

Since we could not go over to Mrs. Lee's, and we did not wish to go to the students' social, we spent the evening in walking around on the grounds with young men. We went to our rooms at the ringing of the first retiring bell (9:30).

Miss Porter came to our rooms and reprimanded us in a severe manner for spending the evening in such a way. She told us we were not to go around on the grounds either day or night without first coming to her office and getting permission. She said our territory was not beyond the Library or White Hall.

Mr. Washington, we do not find any pleasure in being post graduates at Tuskegee. We do not feel at home at all. We feel that we should at least be given the privilege of being with young men on Sunday evenings without permission. As it is, we are not supposed to be with them on any evening without *permission* and if we wish to see them, we must come to the students' sitting room after work hours. After working all day, we feel that we should have some recreation out of our rooms some of the evenings.

It is not our desire to ignore Miss Porter nor the rules governing the post graduates, but she seems to think that it is our intention to do so. It seems to be impossible to convince her otherwise. We consider it our duty to do the right thing at all times, and feel that we are capable of doing so.

Mr. Washington, we hope you will consider this matter. Sincerely and thankfully yours,

POST GRADUATE GIRLS

TLSr Copy   Con. 600   BTW Papers   DLC.

From Helen Van Wyck Lockman

West Neck [N.Y.] Nov. 29—1910

My dear Dr. Washington: There has been such a change in the prices of real estate since the opening of the Tunnel, that I feel that the time has come for me to get a larger price for the Homestead, if I rent it at all. The East Neck cottages are renting from $900.00 for a small one, up to $2000.00. One no larger than this and nothing to compare with it for location is rented for $1750.00 a year on a three years lease. As you have been such a good tenant I do not wish to put mine on the market without notifying you, but as people are already looking for next summer, I want to feel privileged to show it.

From the newspaper I judge that you had a delightful tour abroad.

With kindest regards to you and Mrs Washington I am   Sincerely yours

Helen Van Wyck Lockman

ALS   Con. 428   BTW Papers   DLC.

From Charles William Anderson

New York, N.Y., November 30, 1910

(Personal)

My dear Doctor: James W. Johnson is very anxious to be transferred from his post at Corinto, Nicaragua, to some place where the climate is not so severe — preferably a post in Southern Europe. Mr. Griscom[1] is working to that end with the State Department. Will you not use your good offices to bring about an early transfer for Johnson? He has made a splendid record there, and having been five years in the hot climate of the tropics, is, in my judgment, entitled to a change. His post was recently inspected by the Consular Inspector, and he was given a fine recommendation. Mr. Dawson,[2] who was recently sent to Nicaragua on a special diplomatic mission, told Johnson that he was highly regarded by the Department, and ought to be transferred, and advised him to "talk pretty to Mr. Carr."[3] Mr. Carr, as you know, is the head of the Consular Bureau at Washington.

There are two colored men now in France — Jackson at La Rochelle and Hunt at St. Etienne. They have both been there quite a while, and as neither of them are as well equipped as Johnson, it seems to me that one of them might take a little of the tropics for a while. Hunt is, as you know, the son-in-law of Judge Gibbs and the brother-in-law of Napoleon Marshall. Hence, it appears that he has not influence enough with the members of his own family to prevent them from working against an administration which has given him the choicest berth held by any colored man in the Consular service. If nothing better can be done for Johnson, it seems to me he ought to change posts with Hunt.

Corinto is a town of six or seven hundred people, all of whom (but five or six) are a cross between digger-Indian and dog, with not a drug-store, or any other of the institutions of modern civilization. The houses with the exception of five or six, are all thatched huts, and the climate simply intolerable. When you recall that he has taken a young bride, who is quite frail, to this hot and unsanitary hole, you will readily see that St. Lawrence, on his gridiron, was not in a much more uncomfortable situation than Johnson. Please do all in your power to get him away from there at once. He is not only my warm friend, but a man of such splendid scholastic attainments and gentlemanly deportment, that I shall never rest until he is given a suitable post. I hope you will take up his case at once and push it with your accustomed vigor, for in so doing you will be obeying the scriptural injunction to lend a helping hand when a neighbor's ass falls in a ditch. Yours truly,

Charles W. Anderson

TLS   Con. 49   BTW Papers   DLC.

1 Lloyd Carpenter Griscom (1872–1959), a lawyer, newspaperman, and diplomat, served in a number of diplomatic posts including minister to Japan from 1902 to 1906, ambassador to Brazil from 1906 to 1907, and ambassador to Italy from 1907 to 1909. In 1910 he became a member of a New York law firm and county chairman of the Republican party and was largely responsible for the dispensing of patronage in New York City.

2 Probably Claude Ivan Dawson (b. 1877) of the consular service. In 1910–12 he was consul at Puerto Cortes, Honduras, about 150 miles from Corinto.

3 Wilbur John Carr (b. 1870), a lawyer, was chief of the consular bureau in the State Department beginning in 1902. In 1909 he was appointed director of the consular service.

To Thomas Jesse Jones

Hotel Manhattan, New York. Dec. 2d, 1910

My dear Dr. Jones: Thank you for your kind note of November 26th. I am answering it briefly.

I do not know where the clipping came from that you sent me regarding the Jews and Russia. What I did say or attempted to say was this, that in Russian Poland there is a law which prevents the Jew from curling his hair. I do not think this law applies to the whole of Russia. As you know, Poland is divided up into three parts; a part belonging to Austria, a part belonging to Germany, and another part belonging to Russia. I am quite sure that a close examination into the matter will show that I am right so far as Russian Poland is concerned. You know, perhaps, that in the Jewish centers such as Cracow the Jews almost without exception wear their hair long and curl it on each side. I shall be glad to hear what the outcome of your further investigation into the Russian matter is.

I thank you also for writing me regarding Professor Carver and Secretary Wilson. Professor Carver's case is rather a sad one. Professor Carver is a fine instructor, but he has absolutely no ability to do practical farm work, nor has he any ability in the direction of organizing and carrying forward the organization of classes. His strong forte is in inspiring and instructing young men after they are secured and placed before him in a class. He also has very unusual ability in the direction of original research. All that I have been trying to do at Tuskegee is to have Professor Carver realize what his forte is and to get him to concentrate upon that which he can do and to leave aside that which he cannot do. For example, when Professor Carver first came to Tuskegee, we put him in charge of the practical operations of the farm, but within a few months we found everything was going to pieces, and if it had remained in his hands we would have had no farm at Tuskegee today. We gave him charge of our practical work, but gradually we had to take it nearly all from him and encourage him to concentrate upon that which he can do.

I would state — and I wish you would tell this same thing to Secretary Wilson if you choose that I spent nearly a week before leaving Tuskegee in consultation with Professor Carver and all of our leading teachers there with a view of trying to get Professor Carver's work so arranged that he could do the work for which he is best suited, and I am glad to say that before I left Professor Carver readily accepted my view and has already begun work under the reorganized plan, and I am sure he will be happier and much more successful than he has been before. I am glad to say that there are the most pleasant relations between him and the other teachers in the Agricultural Department. Professor Carver has not an enemy so far as I know, at Tuskegee. All the old teachers realize his strong points and his weak points, and all are deeply interested in helping him. I do not believe that there will be any trouble in regard to him in the future, as I think he is now so fixed that he can do his best work. You will be glad to know that we are fitting up a large laboratory for him so that a good deal of his time can be given in the direction of original research, and then he will have all the opportunity to teach what he desires. No one can listen to a recitation conducted by him, or listen to a lecture delivered by him to a popular audience without becoming inspired, but when Professor Carver attempts to go further and put his teaching into practice on the farm, there he is weak. I think the kindest thing is to recognize one's weakness as well as his strength and place him in a position, as I have said, where he can do his best work. Yours very truly,

[Booker T. Washington]

TLc   Con. 907   BTW Papers   DLC.

From Robert Russa Moton

Hampton, Va., Dec. 2, 1910

My dear Dr. Washington: I am enclosing you herewith copies of letters received from Mr. Villard,[1] Dr. Du Bois,[2] and Professor Hope[3] of Atlanta College. I have not acknowledged them yet but will. I must frankly confess that I doubt whether we can do anything with these people. I have Dr. Du Bois' Washington address which I have not finished reading yet. The circular which you sent me was written, of course, by Dr. Du Bois himself and the contention of Mr. Villard and Dr. Du Bois that the Committee is not responsible for the actions of its members is all moonshine. Yours very truly,

R. R. Moton

TLS   Con. 51   BTW Papers   DLC.

[1] Oswald Garrison Villard to Moton, Nov. 28, 1910, above.
[2] W. E. B. Du Bois to Moton, Nov. 21, 1910, above.
[3] John Hope to Moton, Nov. 21, 1910, above.

An Open Letter on Negro Public Schools

Tuskegee Institute, Alabama, December 5, 1910

NEGRO PUBLIC SCHOOLS

Through the medium of your valued newspaper I desire to say a word to the colored people regarding the importance of good public schools. It has been some months since I have had anything to say on this important subject. I wish to repeat that which I have tried to emphasize from time to time, that there are few, if any subjects, which are of more vital and far-reaching importance to the masses of our race in the South at the present time than that of building up a good public school system.

Only a very small percent. of our people can ever go to a large boarding school, or any kind of college, or industrial school for their education. The masses must depend upon the public school in their neighborhood for whatever education they get. If the public school is a failure the masses grow up in ignorance, and so I am making this direct appeal to every minister, teacher and business man and woman throughout the South to take a personal and deep interest in the condition of the Negro public schools.

First of all, we should bear in mind that we are American citizens and that we should have our rightful share of the public school fund. Where we are not getting our just share of the public school fund, a direct appeal should be made to the public school authorities for a more just distribution of the public school funds. This kind of appeal should be repeated again and again until we do receive our just share. We should not give up or stand still, in cases where the public school authorities are not willing or unable to give more money. It will be no excuse to the future generation of children, if they grow up in ignorance, to tell them that they might have been educated, if the public school authorities had done their duty.

In travelling through the South, I have observed that wherever a good public schoolhouse is provided, in most cases, the result is, that that community will have a good teacher and a school term of respectable length.

I advise then, that every community set to work to secure either through the public fund or from private gifts in that community a good public school building. In many cases, where people are not able to give money toward the erection of a good schoolhouse, they can give the use of their teams to haul lumber, or they can give material, or give without charge so many days' work each week, but in some way, every community that is now without a comfortable schoolhouse should set to work to secure one.

In many cases, the schoolhouses in which the children are taught are not fit for pigs to live in. The roofs leak, the floors are full of holes, there is no stove, and in many cases, the benches and other furniture are so rude and worthless that it is impossible for teacher and children to stay in such houses without being in continual misery.

A schoolhouse is not completed until it has been either painted or whitewashed on the inside or outside; neither is a schoolhouse complete until it has been ceiled or plastered on the inside, and every schoolhouse should be thoroughly furnished with good seats; a teacher's desk, with good blackboards, etc., before it should be considered completed. It is almost as cheap to build a good school-house as it is to build a poor one.

If every community will organize and come together, with the direct object of providing a good schoolhouse, I am safe in saying I believe that before the present school year passes, a large number of communities will have good, first-class schoolhouses. I also advise that an architectural plan be drawn, whenever possible, for these schoolhouses. In many cases, a good deal of money is practically thrown away in the erection of a building, because no plans have been drawn. Aside from the building being almost useless, when a plan is not drawn, it does not usually present a good appearance.

I shall hope to hear, as a result of this letter, that a larger number of communities throughout the South have erected school-houses.

One other thing: My travels through the South convince me that the public schools for our race are often crippled and weakened by reason of the fact that denominational jealousies and rivalry enter into the public school system. It should be understood in every community that the public school must be separated wholly from church influences. In some communities, the public school system is weakened because the Baptist element want a Baptist teacher, the African Methodist element want an African Methodist teacher, and the Zion Methodists want a Zion Methodist teacher. This kind of contention and jealousy is all nonsense and results only in weakening the public schools. In some communities, the people are now trying to support three little weak schools, with three different teachers, representing so many church denominations, when the people in the community should have one, good strong public school, regardless of denomination. In some cases there are three little public schools lasting only three months in the year, when, if the people were united, they might have one good public school lasting seven or eight months in the year. In public school education, there is not Baptist Arithmetic, or Methodist Arithmetic, or anything of the kind. What the people want are good, sensible, moral, upright, Christian teachers, regardless of the church to which they belong.

There are other matters in connection with the public schools of the South, to which I shall hope to call attention soon through another letter.

Booker T. Washington

Tuskegee Student, 22 (Dec. 17, 1910), 1, 3, 4.

To Emmett Jay Scott

New York, Dec. 8 [1910]

E. J. Scott: Received telegram from Mr. Hare and other parties in Alabama asking me to meet them in Washington in the interest of the pardon of someone. I suspect this refers to the recent peonage cases. Please explain privately to Mr. Hare would be very dangerous just now when I am under fire from certain parties in my race to interfere in this matter. I must consider the feeling of my race as well as that of others.

B. T. W.

TWIr Con. 906 BTW Papers DLC.

To Emmett Jay Scott

New York   Dec 8 [1910]

Mr E J Scott   Dubois & crowd getting number of letters published in New York and other daily papers[1] think these letter[s] prepared by Dubois and signed by weak pliable colored men   as usual our friends are silent   think good plan for you to have three or four good strong letters sent the Sun — World & Times signed by three or four different people not office holders re[pre]senting different parts of the country   letters should be short & pointed Substance of letters might be prepared by you.[2]

B T W

HWIr   Con. 597   BTW Papers   DLC.

[1] The New York *World* commented editorially on the appeal by Du Bois and others, saying complacently: "It is a world in which, after all, men are judged not so much by race or nationality or possessions as by personal merit. Otherwise, how could a Booker Washington, born a Virginia slave, have 'stood before kings,' and associated for the greater part of his life with the earth's greatest and best?" (Dec. 4, 1910, E2.) Two days later it published a letter to the editor from John C. Bankett, a black man who repudiated BTW's leadership and criticized his silence on civil rights. (Dec. 6, 1910, 8.)

[2] Scott did not believe the New York *Times* would take an article, since it had not taken cognizance of the Du Bois appeal, but he arranged for friends to write letters to the New York *World* and *Sun*. (Scott to BTW, Dec. 9, 1910, Con. 50, BTW Papers, DLC.)

To Oswald Garrison Villard

Hotel Manhattan, New York. December 11, 1910

Personal

My dear Mr. Villard: Please do not take time to answer this letter. When I return to Tuskegee, which will be within a few days, I shall hope to be writing you about some matters which I should like for you to reply to when you can find the time.

I have just had a long talk with Mrs. Terrell, and she tells me that your committee did not send out that circular regarding my supposed utterances when I was in Europe. This I was very glad to hear. Of course I do not question the right of your committee to send out any kind of circular that it chooses to send out, but what was contained in this circular was so far at variance with what you first wrote me regarding the purposes of the committee that I confess I was greatly surprised when I saw it as coming from your committee as I suppose. If you have not seen the circular itself, I hope you will see it, and after reading it I think you will agree with me that it was very natural that any one should feel that it was a document sent out by your committee. At the head of the circular (quoting from memory as I have not a copy of it before me) I think you will find these words: "Headquarters of the National Negro Committee, 20 Vesey St." The person who sent out these circulars signs himself as "Secretary National Afro-American Committee."

Enclosed I send you a clipping from the New York Sun which published the appeal, and states that "The National Association for the Advancement of Colored People" issued the circular, etc.

Under these circumstances I think you will agree with me that any person would be naturally misled, and of course the majority of the people have been. But more serious than sending out the circular by far, and I repeat that I do not question the right of anybody to send out any kind of circular he chooses, is the evident attempt at deception on somebody's part. The use of the word "Negro" and "Afro-American" instead of "Colored" is a mere attempt to play on words and deceive, and I cannot see how people who would thus try to deceive their friends and the public can be trusted with the larger interests of the race.

I have been questioned by several white people including Mrs. Warburg[1] since I have been in New York concerning the origin of this circular. I have never directly or indirectly connected your committee with the sending out of this circular except in one case; I did speak to Mrs. Baldwin and told her what I honestly believed; that it was sent out by your committee. I have, however, since seeing Mrs. Terrell conveyed to Mrs. Baldwin the information which Mrs. Terrell has given me.

When there is so much that is needed to be done in the way of punishing those who are guilty of lynching, of peonage, and seeing that the Negro gets an equitable share of the school fund, and that the law relating to the ballot is enforced in regard to black men and white men, it is difficult to see how people can throw away their time and strength in stirring up strife within the race instead of devoting themselves to bringing about justice to the race as a whole.

503

I shall be writing you about other matters from Tuskegee when I return there, which will be within a few days. Yours very truly,

Booker T. Washington

TLS   Oswald Garrison Villard Papers   MH.   A carbon is in Con. 51, BTW Papers, DLC.

¹ Nina J. Loeb (Mrs. Paul M.) Warburg (1870–1946), the daughter of Solomon Loeb of Kuhn, Loeb and Co., served for a number of years on the board of directors of the Henry Street Settlement.

To Emmett Jay Scott

Washington, D.C. December 12, 1910

Dear Mr. Scott: I confess that I am gradually coming around to the opinion that it is a valuable thing to have Mrs. Terrell connected with that committee. She made a speech in New York last week, and I am told by several people who heard her that she referred several times most complimentar[il]y to Tuskegee and to myself, but not to the other side at all. I had a long talk with her in New York, and she told me many things of interest. One of her values is in this direction. She gets on the inside of things and is always capable of stirring up trouble in any organization that she has a part in. Of course all this is strictly confidential, as I have told her that her name would not be used. I can keep in close touch with her if her name is not quoted. She tells me that she and Du Bois have absolutely nothing to do with each other; they scarcely speak, and she did not see him during her stay in New York, but more important than this, she says, the European circular was an imposition on the committee, that Villard, a white woman and all the head people are disgusted and considerably torn up that such a circular should have been sent out presumably under the guise of the committee. It seems that Du Bois was sharp enough to use the word "Negro" instead of "Colored," and in signing his own name used "Afro-American" instead of signing himself as secretary of the Colored Committee. This of course, is a mere quibble. At any rate they seem to be in a pretty big row among themselves, and the circular seems to have caused it. Mrs. Terrell appears to be very much disgusted with the whole affair, and I think she will make matters pretty lively from now on. Yours very truly,

Booker T. Washington

TLS   Con. 606   BTW Papers   DLC.

From Oswald Garrison Villard

New York   December 13, 1910

My dear Mr. Washington: I have yours of December 11th which comes as I was on the point of writing you to tell you what Mrs. Terrell has already conveyed to you. I regret that in an unauthorized way the envelopes of the National Association were used in sending out the protest of the thirty-two colored men. This mistake I have carefully investigated and find that it was absolutely accidental as far as this office was concerned (the letters were not mailed from 20 Vesey Street). Orders were also given to erase the words "headquarters of the National Negro Committee" on every copy. If you have one on which the words are not erased it is because the stenographer to whom they were submitted did not follow instructions. That this should have happened is, of course, humiliating, but it is one of the incidents, which, I suppose, happens to most every organization which has not yet had time or means to work out an absolutely effective organization. The matter will come officially before the Executive Committee at its next meeting.

So far as the circular is concerned, I am heartily of the opinion that the protest was a desirable one. I agree with you that when there is so much to be done for the colored people it is a pity that people should have to waste time and strength in presenting different views instead of being united upon one. I have, therefore, in this organization thrown my weight wholly against taking any notice of your, to me, often mistaken speeches and attitude on public questions. Sorry as I am to say it, I cannot but feel that your speeches abroad were a misrepresentation of actual conditions in this country. Your optimism is leading you astray. It goes without saying that I respect your sincerity and know that you are endeavoring to do what is right. I would never have stated that you were influenced, even unconsciously, by those who contribute to your school, but I do feel that, from my point of view, your philosophy is wrong, that you are keeping silent about evils in regard to which you should speak out, and that you are not helping the race by portraying all the conditions as favorable. If my grandfather had gone to Europe say in 1850 and dwelt in his speeches on slavery upon certain encouraging features of it, such as the growing anger and unrest of the poor whites, and stated the number of voluntary liberations and number of escapes to Canada, as evidences that the institution was improving, he never would have accomplished what he did, and he would have hurt, not helped, the cause of freedom. It seems to me that the parallel precisely affects your case. It certainly cannot be unknown to you that a greater and greater percentage of the intellectual colored people are turning from you and becoming your opponents, and with them a number of white people as well. I can only repeat, as I wrote to Major Moton, that so long as the National Association is guided by my advice it will not take official notice of your utterances; but the time may easily come when, in the judgment of a majority of the Executive Committee, it might become necessary to oppose publicly a position of yours. As the Association is self-governing and does not belong to Mr. Milholland, or Dr. Du Bois, or myself, or anybody else, it will make up its own mind on this point. From the bottom of my heart I hope that you will make no more such speeches as those you made in Europe, for I want to see you preserve your standing and reputation, precisely as I want to see your work at Tuskegee flourish and become more and more effective. As you know, I am at all times ready to help in it in any way that I can. Sincerely yours,

Oswald Garrison Villard

TLS Con. 413 BTW Papers DLC.

To Andrew Carnegie

[Boston, Mass.] Dec. 16, 1910

My dear Mr. Carnegie: For several years you have been kind enough to give us $2700 for the work of the Committee of Twelve, and $2700 for the work of the National Negro Business League. I do not believe that many sums of money which you have so kindly given to so many causes have been made to accomplish greater service in proportion to the amount than these two sums of money.

The Committee of Twelve has used this money in putting into the hands of the people all over the country, especially the Southern white people, definite facts indicating the Negro's progress. A year ago I gave you samples of the kind of work that this committee is doing.

In the year of 1913 the Negro will have been free in America fifty years, and the Committee of Twelve wants to begin now getting hold of definite facts indicating his progress during the half century of his freedom so that we can put them into the hands of people all over the country. We have used to good advantage the facts brought out in your Edinburgh address as well as many others.

The National Negro Business League has used a large portion of the money which you have given in employing an agent who has traveled among the colored people urging them to turn their attention to commercial and business enterprises as well as other lines of progress. As a result of this work, the race within the last ten years has made greater progress in the promotion of business enterprises than has ever been true. Let me give you two examples. Twenty years ago the colored people owned and controlled but four banks in the United States and they were small and insignificant. Today they own and control 52 banks. Twenty years ago they had only about twelve or fifteen drugstores in the United States; now they have about three hundred. They have made equal progress in establishing other lines of business. We have not, however, in either case depended wholly upon what you have given for the promotion of these two enterprises, because the colored people themselves have given generously.

I am writing to ask that you extend these gifts through another year if you can possibly see your way clear to do so.[1] The last payment for the Committee of Twelve will be made next January; after that there will be no other payment unless you authorize it. The last payment for the National Negro Business League has already been made. Yours very truly,

[Booker T. Washington]

TLc Con. 49 BTW Papers DLC.

[1] Carnegie contributed $2,700 to the NNBL for the year 1911, but he did not renew his contribution to the Committee of Twelve. (BTW to Carnegie, Dec. 29, 1910, Con. 38 new series, BTW Papers, DLC; BTW to Hugh Mason Browne, Jan. 7, 1911, below.)

To Emmett Jay Scott

Boston Mass Dec–17–10

Think good policy discreetly advise our friends stop complete-[ly] for considerable while giving attention to European circular and other matters bearing upon Dubois he is getting good deal of advertisement which he likes.

B.T.W.

HWIr Con. 596 BTW Papers DLC.

From Melvin Jack Chisum

Salisbury, Md. Dec 19th, 1910

My Dear Dr Washington: Just a word to say I have delivered the goods in 1910. Have founded two banks, in two states, representing a combined capital of $24,000. I am yours to command,

Chisum

ALS Con. 420 BTW Papers DLC. On stationery of the Houston Savings Bank, Salisbury, Md., Melvin J. Chisum, President.

From Monroe Nathan Work

Tuskegee Institute, Alabama December 20, 1910

Dear Sir: According to your request I send you the following information concerning prohibition and Negro crime in Alabama.

From the letters which you sent out to sheriffs, chiefs of police and recorders of city courts, seventeen replies were received. I thought it well to take the two answers that were given concerning the chief causes of Negro crime and the effect of prohibition on Negro crime. A tabulated statement of these replies you will find on the attached memoranda.

An analysis of these shows first, that strong drink is the chief cause of crime among the Negroes of Alabama. This conclusion is substantiated by the Biennial report of the Attorney General of the state for 1906–1908. The Attorney General in the year 1908 sent out letters to all the solicitors of the state and asked them to furnish him with data for the purpose of ascertaining the relation of murder to strong drink. These replies show that fifty-three per cent of all the murders in Alabama were due to strong drink; sixty-seven per cent of the murders in Alabama during this period were committed by Negroes. Although the report does not separate the whites from the colored with reference to strong drink, yet I think that we could conservatively estimate that from sixty to seventy-five per cent of the murders committed by Negroes were directly or indirectly due to strong drink.

With reference to the effect of prohibition on Negro crime the Recorder of the Selma Police Court reports that rapes, murders and crime generally have decreased since prohibition went into effect. The Recorder of the Montgomery Court reports that total police arrests and Negro arrests have both decreased since prohibition went into effect (The Recorder says that Negro arrests have increased, but his figures are the reverse).

The Sheriff of Jefferson County says: "I can say without hesitation, and the records in the Criminal Court will bear me out, that more crimes are committed by the Negro race on account of strong drink, than all other vices combined.

"80% of the colored men confined in the County Jail are there for crimes caused by whiskey, directly or indirectly, in these so-called innocent crap games, where whiskey flows freely. . . .

"Under Prohibition as it is now, a man has to violate the law [ninety?] nine times out of every hundred and [to] secure whiskey and in this way, a great many who would drink, cannot do so because they cannot buy it legally."

The Sheriff of Mobile County says: "In our County the Negroes are very temperate, very few cases of drunkenness reported, and in proportion to the population consisting of all other nationalities, it is my opinion that less drunkenness occurs amongst the Negroes than amongst the others. The prohibition law has had a good effect upon them."

The Sheriff of Colbert County reports that crime has decreased at least one-half since prohibition went into effect. The Sheriff of Jackson County reports that crimes of all nature have decreased materially and thinks that prohibition is the cause. The Sheriff of Macon County reports that crime has been reduced sixty per cent since prohibition went into effect in the County four years ago.

The Sheriffs of Randolph, Autauga and Bullock Counties were of the opinion that prohibition had made conditions worse; but, it seems that the increase in crime has been because the prohibition laws have not been enforced in these counties, this according to the statements of the sheriffs.

Taking everything into consideration I think you ought to base your letter to the legislature on the two points; first, that all the evidence from the solicitors of the various counties, the sheriffs and the police records go to show that drink is one of the most important factors in Negro crime and second, that prohibition has appreciably reduced Negro crime in Alabama. Therefore it would be to the interest of the state to maintain its prohibition laws and see that they are efficiently enforced.

No data with reference to rape were obtainable. Respectfully yours,

M. N. Work

TLS BTW Papers ATT.

To Rollo Walter Brown[1]

[Tuskegee, Ala.] December 22, 1910

My dear Mr. Brown: In reply to your letter of December 3rd, let me say that I have never since I was in school made any systematic attempt to learn to write. I have tried, to a certain extent, to improve my speaking vocabulary, but my efforts in that direction have not gone very far, and I have not produced, I fear, any very striking results. I always carry a notebook or a piece of paper with me, on which I jot down during the day such ideas as occur to me. If it is an important idea, I find it will turn up again and again in moments of leisure. Every time, however, the idea is likely to occur to me in some new form, and in this way it connects itself with other ideas and with the practical problems I have in hand; and by-and-by I find that I have by this means gathered material enough for an article or a speech.

As a usual thing I do not write my articles, but dictate them. I am more accustomed to speaking than to writing. After I have obtained a rough draft containing what I want to say, I turn it over to someone else to get his corrections and criticism. Whenever I have had anything very important to say or write I have found it good policy to hand over this first draft to the most critical person I could find, and in some cases to many different persons. In this way I have obtained valuable suggestions which have helped me to give form to what I wanted to say.

In all my speeches I invariably jot down briefly what I want to say, beforehand, and the order in which I propose to say it. That is about all the notes I ever use. I proceed the same way, of course, when I attempt to dictate an article.

I think this answers in a general way all the questions you have asked. If I have any method at all in my writing and speaking, it consists in thinking very hard about what I want to say and considering very carefully to whom I wish to say it. After I have done that, the words, sentences and paragraphs generally take care of themselves. Yours truly,

Booker T. Washington

TLpS Con. 903 BTW Papers DLC.

[1] Rollo Walter Brown (1880–1956), a graduate of Harvard University (M.A. 1905), taught rhetoric and English at Wabash College in Crawfordsville, Ind., from 1905 to 1920. He was co-author of a college text, *The Art of Writing English* (1913).

A News Item in the *Tuskegee Student*

Tuskegee, Alabama, December 24, 1910

INTERNATIONAL CONFERENCE

Principal Washington has formulated plans and has recently issued invitations for an international conference at Tuskegee of all persons in Europe or America who are directly interested in the education and improvement of the Negro peoples of Africa.

The purpose of this conference will be to bring together not only students of colonial and racial questions, but more particularly those who, either as missionaries, teachers or government officials, are actually engaged in any way in practical and constructive work, which seeks to build up Africa by educating and improving the character and condition of the native peoples.

This conference will meet at Tuskegee about the middle of January, 1912. Its purpose will be to get from the people who are on the ground a clearer and more definite notion of the actual problems involved in the redemption of the African peoples; to enable those who are engaged in work in Africa to see for themselves what is being done at Tuskegee in the way of educating black men, and to enable them to decide for themselves to what extent the methods employed at Tuskegee can be used to advantage in Africa.

For a number of years past missionaries from all parts of the world have been coming in increasing numbers to visit and study the methods of the Tuskegee Institute, and it is believed that this conference will prove a welcome opportunity to many others to do the same. It is expected that a permanent organization of "The Friends of Africa" may be effected as a result of this conference, which will aid in organizing, stimulating and directing the work of education and civilization in the Dark Continent.

Tuskegee Student, 22 (Dec. 24, 1910), 1. A typescript of the press release is in Con. 433, BTW Papers, DLC.

To Henry Jones Willingham[1]

[Tuskegee, Ala.] December 28, 1910

Dear Sir: I suppose that about this time you must be flooded with all kinds of advice from all parts of the state. For this reason, I hesitate to inflict a letter upon you.

Some time during the present month, preferably before the legislature meets, I want to go to Montgomery and have a conversation with you regarding Negro education in Alabama. Among other things, I want to discuss with you the possibility of getting a sum of money from the legislature that might be used by you in carrying on teachers' institutes during the summer. My own feeling is that the legislature would be much more likely to appropriate a lump sum which could be used at your discretion in carrying on institutes for colored teachers than it would be to appropriate any sum that might be used for any special institution for the same kind of work.

There are other matters that I also want to discuss with you. If it will suit your convenience, I should like to reach Montgomery at about 3:25 o'clock in the afternoon, and remain until 6:10 p.m., returning to Tuskegee that same night. Yours truly,

Booker T. Washington

TLpS Con. 414 BTW Papers DLC.

[1] Henry Jones Willingham (b. 1868), a former president of Lineville College and mayor of Lineville, Ala., for two terms. Willingham was secretary of the state board of examiners from 1907 to 1911, and Alabama superintendent of education from 1911 to 1914. From 1914 to 1939 he was president of the State Normal School at Florence, Ala.

To the Editor of the Montgomery *Advertiser*

Tuskegee, Ala., Dec. 29, 1910

I have seen considerable discussion in the Alabama papers bearing on the question as to why the majority of the "Black Belt" counties have, during the past ten years, lost population. An examination shows that it is the "Black Belt" counties that have no large cities that have decreased in population. Macon County, however, is an exception for instead of losing population it has during the past ten years increased in population. In my opinion there are reasons for this. I may not be able to state all the reasons, but I think I know, at least, one or two reasons why Macon County has gone forward in population instead of going backward.

So far as the negro race is concerned, I am quite sure that Macon County has gained in population because the County Board of Education has been wise enough to encourage and help the colored people to have good public schools in the country districts of the county. The average white man does not realize that no matter what else the average negro will do without, he wants education for his children. I am not taking time now to discuss the wisdom of all the wants of the negro, but to state why there are few negro families in Alabama who would be content to live from year to year in a country community that provides no public school or a school taught in a log cabin for three or four months only during the year and that with a very poor teacher at its head. This condition means that the negro family becomes restless, dissatisfied and seeks as soon as possible to better its condition, and to do this it moves to a community where school facilities are better.

LITTLE SCHOOL MONEY

I do not believe that the leading white people, and especially land owners of the "Black Belt" counties know how little money some negro schools receive. I actually know of communities where negro teachers are being paid only from $15 to $17 per month for services for a period of three or four months in the year. This, of course, means practically no schools. In making this statement, I am not overlooking the fact that even where the disposition exists to help the negro public schools the money is often lacking to a large extent, but I am stating facts so far as I know them. More money is paid for negro convicts than for negro teachers. About $46 per month is now being paid for first-class able bodied negro convicts, $36 for second-class and $26 for third-class, for twelve months in the year.

One other element in the situation that drives negroes from the farms of the "Black Belt" counties is this: In many of the "Black

Belt" counties when a negro is charged with a crime, a mob of wild, excited and often intoxicated people go scouring through the country in search of the negro. In many cases it happens, as former Governor Jelks frankly stated, that the wrong negro is caught and often lynched. There have been happenings of this kind in the country districts which have made many of the best colored people feel that the safest thing for them is to move to a large city where they will receive police protection in case they are charged with crime. The experience of the civilized world shows that even where the utmost care and deliberation is exercised on the part of lawyers, judges and jury innocent persons are sometimes punished. In the face of this experience, it is impossible for a wild, frenzied and excited mob of people to pass judgment upon the guilt or innocence of an individual.

In my opinion if the negroes understand that their public schools in the country districts are gradually going to be improved as fast as the state can do so and that they will receive police protection in case they are charged with crime in the country districts as they do in the cities, then the best colored farmers will cease moving from the country districts into the cities.

MACON COUNTY SCHOOLS

In Macon County there are good school houses and reasonably good teachers. This is true, I think I am safe in saying, for both races. Ask any white man in Macon County, and he will tell you, I think, that since Macon County has had good public schools it has a more orderly and law-abiding negro population; that labor is much easier to secure and that the colored people work better than they did before.

In addition to this, negro public schools in Macon County have teachers who teach about the things by which they are to earn their living. In addition to teaching the children with books and about the Bible, they teach them how to farm, how to grow vegetables, how to raise poultry, pigs, fruits, etc., they also teach the girls something of cooking, table service and sewing. The result is, the whole community, through the school, is taught to love country life and to respect labor.

Since the state of Alabama is going to spend money on the education of the negro child, I believe it will be better to see that this money is looked after closely and is wisely spent so as to produce good results.

Certainly, so far as "Black Belt" counties are concerned, if they would pursue the policy Macon County is pursuing, they would have a negro population that would be a continual source of usefulness and strength to the whole state.

Another reason why I think Macon County is in such good condition, is because the negroes have good sense enough to realize that they have certain duties to perform themselves — that all the responsibility does not rest with the white people. There are few negroes in Macon County who do not co-operate with the officers of the law in order to get rid of lawbreakers. There are few negroes in Macon County who would refuse to assist the sheriff in ferreting out crime and bringing criminals into a court of justice. And the negroes of Macon County also co-operate heartily with the school officials in building up and sustaining good public schools.

NO RACE PROBLEM

We have no race problem in Macon County. We have no race friction. In talking with the sheriff of Macon County, a few days ago, he told me that there is so little crime in Macon County that he can scarcely find enough to keep him busy.

As I have gone into Montgomery, Birmingham, Atlanta and other large cities, I have found colored people who formerly lived in rural communities, and have asked them why they moved to the cities and in nine cases out of ten they have told me that there were no public schools in the communities where they formerly lived.

I believe that the "Black Belt" counties of Alabama will continue to lose in population unless some attention is given to building up good public schools in rural districts. It is just as easy to have a negro population that is happy, contented and prosperous as to have one that is restless and dissatisfied because of poor schools and all such matters. I believe in this respect the two races can co-operate and in this way add to the happiness and prosperity of both.

Booker T. Washington

Montgomery *Advertiser*, Dec. 30, 1910, 2. A typescript is in Con. 909, BTW Papers, DLC.

To Charles William Anderson

[Tuskegee, Ala.] December 30, 1910

My dear Mr. Anderson: By this mail I send you a marked copy of the Montgomery Advertiser which has an article over my signature.

You will note that in my own way I have talked in a very plain way to the Southern white people concerning their duty to help educate the Negro and concerning the evils of lynching. If you read between the lines and on the lines you will see that I have stated the whole truth in a way to make the Southern white people think and to make them act. The other fellows would have said something to have made the white people mad, to have made them get up their bristles and do nothing. Putting it in this way in the first place makes them read what I say, and in the next place will incline them to act, in my opinion. Yours very truly,

Booker T. Washington

TLpS Con. 52 BTW Papers DLC.

To Samuel Gompers

[Tuskegee, Ala.] December 30th, 1910

My dear Sir: Your kind letter of December 27th[1] has been received, but you have doubtless already learned that I had anticipated you because before I received your letter I had written you one calling your attention to the fact that I had learned that you were misquoted and I had taken means to correct the impression in the colored papers. You can easily see how I was imposed upon. The next day after your speech, I received a telegram from the St. Louis Post Dispatch purporting to quote your direct words. That paper being published in the city where your address was delivered made me take for granted you were quoted correctly. I also received the same day a dispatch from the Boston Journal. Both the St. Louis Dispatch and the Boston Journal asked me to give an expression concerning your speech. I did, however, receive another telegram from the Post Dispatch the next day stating that they had learned you were misquoted and consequently would not use what I had said concerning your address. When I received this dispatch it was too late, however, for me to prevent the matter from appearing in the Boston Journal.

I shall send you this week the editorial which I have asked the editor of the New York Age, the leading colored paper in this country, to publish in order to put you in a correct position before the public. I am always most anxious to never do an injustice to a public man because I have suffered too much in the same way myself.

I hope at some time to have the privilege of meeting you and knowing you better.[2] Yours very truly,

Booker T. Washington

TLpS Con. 423 BTW Papers DLC.

[1] Gompers had written on Dec. 27, 1910, enclosing an editorial from the January issue of the *American Federationist* on "The Negro in the A. F. of L.," as an answer to charges that he advocated eviction of blacks from the union. (Con. 423, BTW Papers, DLC.)

[2] Gompers replied that he hoped to use BTW's statement in a further editorial reference to the race policy of the A. F. of L. He added a postscript: "I had the pleasure to meet you at the Peace Jubilee at Chicago in 1897 [actually 1898]." (Jan. 4, 1911, Con. 423, BTW Papers, DLC.)

An Article in a Book Edited
by William Newton Hartshorn[1]

1910

THE BIBLE IN NEGRO EDUCATION

The first schools for Negroes in this country were Sunday-schools, and the first school book the Negro knew was the Bible.

For many years after slavery was introduced into the United States the Negro slaves remained a heathen people, holding fast, for the most part, to the barbarous beliefs and practices they had known in Africa. But in 1701 a society was organized in England to carry the gospel to the Indians and Negroes in America, and in June, 1702, Rev. Samuel Thomas, the first missionary of this society, in reporting upon his work in South Carolina, said that he "had taken much pains, also, in instructing the Negroes and learned twenty of them to read."

From that day to this the Negro Sunday-school taught by southern white men and women, in spite of discouragements and of opposition and special difficulties, has continued to exist and has been a source of inspiration and a helpful, wholesome influence in the lives of both races in the South.

From the very first, then, the Bible has been associated with Negro education in the South. Even after the fear of a slave insurrection had made it seem dangerous to further educate the slaves, and when the laws of many of the states made it a crime for a master to teach his slaves to read, these Sunday-schools continued to teach the Bible orally, and there were always certain favorite slaves who were taught sufficiently to be able to read one great and good Book. These in turn passed on their knowledge to others, and so the tradition of learning, which was started in the Sunday-school, was kept alive all through the darkest days of slavery.

The result was that at the time slavery came to an end, the Bible was the one book that the slaves knew. Many a slave who could not read or write could repeat large portions of the Bible by heart.

When freedom came, it seemed as if all at once the whole race had started to go to school. On every plantation and in nearly every home, whether in the town or city, the hidden book that had been tucked away under the floor or in some old trunk, or had been concealed in a stump or between mattresses, was brought from its hiding place and put into use.

The thing that more than any other inspired this ambition to read among the freedmen — and this was particularly true of the older people — was the desire to read the Bible.

I recall the strange picture, which might have been seen in almost any part of the South directly after the war, of men and women, some of whom had reached the age of sixty or seventy, tramping along the country road, side by side with their own children, with a spelling book or a Bible under their arms.

It did not seem to occur to them that age was in any sense an obstacle to learning to read. With weak and unaccustomed eyes, old men and women would struggle along month after month in their effort to master the primer, in order to get, if possible, a little knowledge of the Bible. Some of them succeeded; many of them failed. The thought of passing from earth without being able to read the Bible was a source of deep sorrow.

One of the compensations to the Negro for the hardships of slavery was that he learned during this period of his servitude, as he could have learned in no other way, the meaning of the Christian religion. In spite of what has been said about the shortcomings of the religion of the slave, the Christianity that the Negro learned in slavery helped him to endure with resignation and without bitterness the hardships of his condition. It did this by teaching him to look forward with hope to a world where all the sorrow and trouble which the slave knew in this world would cease. It taught him to look forward to a day when he should lay aside the worn and ragged garments he had worn in the field and put on a long white robe and golden slippers; when he should leave the cabin in which he had lived down here and fly away to dwell in a great white mansion in the skies.

The favorite parts of the Bible to the Negro slaves were those mysterious passages that gave them pictures of that wonderful life after death when they should gain a sort of freedom and there should be no more work and no more sorrow. It was this thought and this vision that inspired the "freedom songs" which the slaves used to sing, in which the thought of freedom in the world hereafter was strangely and secretly mingled with the hope of freedom that was to come at some time in this world. In fact, the plantation hymns express in a very clear and definite way all the hopes and the consolations with which Christianity and the Bible cheered and lightened the heart of the slave.

I believe that a careful study of these old hymns, as well as of the other forms in which the Negro slave expressed his religious feeling, will show that the Negro worked out in slavery a pretty definite conception of Christianity of his own, and one that was peculiarly suited to his needs at that time. It is true that it was lacking in many elements that attach to the religion and particularly the morality of the white man. But it should be remembered that the Negro was a slave. He did not have occasion or opportunity to practice many of the virtues that are necessary to the success of a society of free men. If the Negro neglected some of the rules prescribed by the morality of his master, he put emphasis on those elements that permitted him to live, to endure, and to hope.

The first white people in America, certainly the first in the South, to exhibit their interest in the reaching of the Negro and the saving of his soul through the medium of the Sunday-school were Robert E. Lee and "Stonewall" Jackson. In the midst of the war a letter was received from Jackson by one of his friends in Lexington, Va., where he lived, and as this friend opened the letter, expecting that it would convey important news, there fell out a check for five dollars — the contribution of "Stonewall" Jackson for the expenses of his Negro Sunday-school. Where Robert E. Lee and "Stonewall" Jackson have led in the redemption of the Negro through the Sunday-school, the rest of us can afford to follow.

The teaching of the Bible is just as necessary to the Negro in freedom as it was in slavery, and it is one of the great losses of the race that, in recent years, the Negro Sunday-schools that were formerly taught by some of the best and greatest men and women in the South, have been so largely neglected. The Negro boys and girls of to-day need the help, the direction, and the personal sympathy and interest of the white people just as much as they ever did, if not more.

I shall never forget the first time that I had an opportunity of attending a Sunday-school. I was a poor boy. My mother had passed away. I was thrown out, literally, as a waif upon the street. There passed by where I was playing with other children one Sunday morning, a godly man. He called to me and said, "Sonny, I want you to go with me to Sunday-school." I did not know where he was leading me, but I had faith in him, and he led me, a poor, unknown Negro boy, into the Sunday-school, and I have been interested in the Sunday-school ever since.

There is no hope in the solution of the problems that confront us in the South except as the solution is based upon the teachings of the Bible. I am a busy man, and have many responsibilities in connection with the carrying on of a great institution, and in connection with the interests of ten millions of people, but years ago I formed one habit which still is with me, and no matter how busy my day, how exciting the problems, how pressing the responsibility, I never leave my house without taking my Bible and sitting down and reading a chapter or two. And I have found that it pays.

When the Negro in the schools or in his daily life parts company with the Bible and its teachings, he gives up the one great heritage that the fathers and mothers gained for him by blood and toil through all the years of their servitude; he gives up the inspiration, the hope, and the comfort of the Christian religion, without which I do not believe it possible for the Negro as a race to struggle on and upward to success.

Our progress does not stop with material possessions and education. In proportion as our people have the Sunday-school and the church and the day school and the college and the industrial school, they become more religious people. It is not true that the penitentiaries and jails are full of men and women who have been educated at colleges and universities. I ask any one to make the test. Go through the jails and penitentiaries of the South, and you cannot find fifty men and women with college diplomas or industrial diplomas. The people in the jails or in prison have had no chance; they are the ignorant, the ones who are away down, and it is our duty to take them by the hand through the church and Sunday-school and help to lift them up.

I believe the time has come in America, in the Southland, when the most cultured and influential white men and white women are making up their minds that it is just as much a part of their Christian duty to help to save the Negro at their doors through the medium of the Sunday-school and church as it is to help redeem the heathen in China or Japan or Africa.

William Newton Hartshorn, ed., *An Era of Progress and Promise 1863–1910* (Boston: Priscilla Publishing Co., 1910), 554–55.

[1] William Newton Hartshorn was president of the Priscilla Publishing Co. in Boston. He was a leader of the International Sunday School Association, serving as its president from 1911 to 1914.

The volume also contained a laudatory article on BTW by Hollis B. Frissell tracing the Tuskegean's rise from slavery to national prominence. "As really as Moses was chosen by God to help the people of Israel out of the and of Egypt," Frissell wrote, "so really has Booker T. Washington een chosen to lead the Negroes of America out into the light and into a life of self-supporting industry" (p. 412).

An Excerpt from a Book by William Archer

[1910]

Two Leaders

"People are always laying stress on the white blood in me," said Mr. W. E. Burghardt Du Bois, "and attributing to that anything I do that is worth doing. But they never speak of the white blood in Mr. Booker Washington, who, as a matter of fact, has a larger share than I have."

"How do you make that out?" I asked; and Mr. Du Bois gave me the story of his ancestry. The story went back two hundred years, for he comes of a New England stock, and has had no slave ancestors (I take it) for many generations. I could not follow his proof that more of Africa flows in his veins than in Mr. Booker Washington's; nor does it greatly matter; for if it be so in fact, Nature has taken great pains to conceal the fact, and the popular error of which he complains is practically inevitable.

Principal Booker T. Washington is a negro in every lineament, and not, one would say, of the most refined type. His skin is neither black nor copper-coloured, but rather of a sort of cloudy yellow, to which the other shades are, perhaps, aesthetically preferable. His hair, his ears, his nose, his jaw, all place his race beyond dispute; only his grave, candid, forceful eyes announce a leader of men. He is above middle height, and heavily built; seated, he is apt to sprawl. He has a curious trick of drawing back the corners of his mouth, so as to reveal almost the whole of his range of teeth. At first I took this for a slow smile, heralding some humorous remark; but humour is not Mr. Washington's strong point. His grin is a nervous habit, and scarcely a pretty one.* Altogether, in talking with him, you have no difficulty in remembering the race of your interlocutor, and if you make an untactful remark — if you let the irrepressible instinct of race-superiority slip out — you have all the more reason to be ashamed.

With Mr. Du Bois the case is totally different. His own demonstration notwithstanding, I cannot believe that there is more of

---

* Since writing this, I have heard Mr. Washington make a speech, and now conceive this grin to be partly, at any rate, a habit contracted in the effort to secure perfectly clear enunciation.

the negro in him than in (say) Alexandre Dumas fils. Meeting this quiet, cultivated, French-looking gentleman, with his pointed beard, olive complexion, and dark melancholy eyes, it is hard to believe that he is born, as he himself phrases it, "within the Veil." In appearance he reminded me a good deal of Gabriele d'Annunzio, only that D'Annunzio happens to be fair, while Mr. Du Bois has something more like the average Italian complexion. In speaking to this man of fine academic culture — this typical college don, one would have said — the difficulty was to feel any difference of race and traditions, and not to assume, tactlessly, an identical standpoint.

These two men are unquestionably the leaders of their race today; but their ideals and their policy are as different as their physique. Mr. Washington leads from within; Mr. Du Bois from without. Should he read this phrase he will probably resent it; but it may be none the less true. Mr. Washington could never have been anything else than a negro; he represents all that is best in the race, but nothing that is not in the race. Mr. Du Bois is a negro only from outside pressure. I do not mean, of course, that there are no negro traits in his character, but that it is outside pressure — the tyranny of the white man — that has made him fiercely, passionately, insistently African. Had there been no colour question — had the negro had no oppression, no injustice to complain of — Mr. Du Bois would have been a cosmopolitan, and led the life of a scholar at some English, German, or perhaps even American University. As it was, he felt that to desert his race would be the basest of apostasies; but it was because he could have been disloyal that he became so vehemently — one might almost say fanatically — loyal.

William Archer, *Through Afro-America: An English Reading of the Race Problem* (London: Chapman and Hall, Ltd., 1910), 45–47.

To James Hardy Dillard

[Tuskegee, Ala.] Jan. 3d, 1911

My dear Dr. Dillard: Enclosed I send you a copy of the Montgomery Advertiser of January 2d giving an account of a meeting which I held in Bullock County on January 1st. This meeting was packed with the best white people and colored people in the county. I talked straighter than I have ever done to the white people about the condition of the rural schools for Negroes, and they seemed to take it all right and I believe are going to act on my suggestion.[1] I am going to keep up this work of going straight to the white people throughout Alabama and talking to them regarding the condition of the Negro schools. I find that the white people in this state really like to be talked to in a frank way; that is, most of them do. Yours very truly,

Booker T. Washington

TLpS Con. 52 BTW Papers DLC.

[1] BTW spoke for two hours to a large crowd at Union Springs, Ala., on Jan. 1, 1911. Extracts from the speech indicate that it was less frank than he believed it to be. For example, he remarked that "the nine millions of Negroes residing in the Southern States enjoy some peculiar and gratifying advantages, though in making this statement no honest man can fail to recognize the fact that we have some disadvantages, but the advantages I believe are more than the disadvantages." He did say, however, that for black tenant farmers to remain in the rural districts, white owners needed to provide good dwellings, good schoolhouses, and personal encouragement. (Montgomery *Advertiser*, Jan. 2, 1911, 1–2. A typescript of part of the address is in Con. 957, BTW Papers, DLC.)

From Monroe Nathan Work

[Tuskegee, Ala.] January 3, 1911

Mr. B. T. Washington: I have been thinking about your proposed letter to the legislature concerning prohibition. The following has occurred to me as a way of putting the matter before the legislature:

The colored man has no voice in the matter of having or not having a prohibition law although he is the one that will be most affected by the law. Whether there is a prohibition law or not will probably not materially increase or decrease the number of users of strong drink among the white people, nor will it probably increase the amount that is used by them. The white people have attained a certain amount of self-control so that if a thing is thrown open to them they are not as likely to abuse their privileges.

On the other hand the colored man will abuse his privileges. Both the amount of strong drink consumed and the number of persons using strong drink among the colored people will probably be increased if the prohibition law is repealed.

From eighty to ninety per cent of the cases of drunkenness handled in the various courts of the state are colored. Also between eighty and ninety per cent of the persons in the penitentiary are colored and according to the information which we have obtained the majority of these have gone there because of strong drink.

The information which you have received from the various officials will substantiate the above. What is needed is not a repeal of the prohibition law, but its enforcement, especially in the country districts. Respectfully yours,

M. N. Work

TLS BTW Papers ATT.

To Harry Hamilton Johnston

[Tuskegee, Ala.] January 4, 1911

My dear Sir Harry Johnston: I have your letter of December 18th.

I am glad that you are pleased with the review[1] I have written of your book for The African Society, while taking exception to one remark therein. My statement that the Negro types used by you were exaggerated is, I find, confessed in your letter. Of course, it is a matter of one's personal judgment only as to whether he likes or does not like that kind of thing.

I reviewed your book for The African Society from the copy which you sent to me and so, for that reason, did not regard myself as having "ignored" the book.

Since, however, you feel disappointed that it has not been discussed in the columns of some of our school publications, I have arranged to have it reviewed in one of them at an early date.[2]

I am very much interested in the work you are now engaged upon in compiling "The Comparative Grammars of African Languages."

I wish to assure you of my keen appreciation of your very full and chatty letter.

With kindest regards always, I am   Yours truly,

Booker T. Washington

TLpS Con. 426 BTW Papers DLC.

1 See A Book Review in the *Journal of the African Society*, Jan. 1911, below.

2 See Monroe Work's review in the *Tuskegee Student*, 23 (Feb. 11, 1911), 1, 4. Work followed the same lines of praise and criticism as BTW's review. He approved of Johnston's commitment to industrial education of blacks, but disapproved of the racial stereotypes in both the illustrations and text.

To William Clarence Matthews[1]

[Tuskegee, Ala.] January 4, 1911

Personal

My dear Mr. Matthews: I shall be willing to help you in any way I can, but in order for me to be of service to you, I advise that you do not mention my name in any way to anybody as the men who represent your state in congress would naturally resent any outside interference. Yours very truly,

Booker T. Washington

TLpS Con. 430 BTW Papers DLC.

1 William Clarence Matthews (b. 1877), a Boston attorney, graduated from Tuskegee Institute in 1897 before attending Harvard (A.B. 1905) and Boston University (LL.B. 1907). On Dec. 28, 1910, Matthews asked BTW's aid in securing appointment as a U.S. attorney. (Con. 430, BTW Papers, DLC.) From 1912 to 1915 he was a special U.S. attorney in Massachusetts.

From Theodore Hazeltine Price[1]

New York City   January 4th, 1911

My dear Mr. Washington: A perusal of the article from your pen, appearing in the January number of the WORLD'S WORK, leads me to address you.

By way of introduction, I may mention that I am personally acquainted with Mr. Walter Page, of the WORLD'S WORK; Dr. Pritchett, of the Carnegie Foundation, and Dr. Charles W. Dabney, President of the University of Cincinnati, all of them men whom you know as in sympathy, as I am, with your purposes.

I am President of the Price-Campbell Cotton Picker Corporation, which is a company that has been formed for the commercialization of the first and only successful mechanical cotton picker that has even been invented.

You know as well as I do what a mechanical cotton picker means to the agricultural South. It is perhaps unnecessary to tell you that assuming the cost of picking the cotton crop by hand to be $1 per hundred of seed cotton — which is actually paid in Texas, and which directly and indirectly is paid in the older Atlantic states, that the total cost of harvesting the crop by hand is not far from $200,000,000.

As nearly as I can calculate, the Machine which my Company controls will harvest a crop of equal size for $20,000,000.

The potential economy of $180,000,000 will, therefore, in some way be added to the world's wealth derived from the cotton crop.

I enclose you reprint of an article with regard to the Cotton Picker which appeared in the December number of the WORLD'S WORK, which was written by Mr. Arthur W. Page,[2] son of Mr. Walter H. Page, who spent something over a week with the Machine in Texas during the past autumn.

I also enclose a Brown Pamphlet which contains a reprint of the written opinions of many thousands of eye witnesses with regard to the efficiency of the Machine during our recent operations in Texas.

We had some ten Machines at work in Texas during the past season. We hope to have a larger number of them at work next autumn.

One of the questions constantly asked me in connection with the Machine is — What effect would it have upon the negro labor which now finds one of its most important sources of income in the picking of the cotton crop?

My answer has invariably been: The Cotton Picking Machine will make a very much increased cotton crop possible in the South, and that, as the wealth of the South is thereby increased, the negro labor will find employment in a higher order of labor related to the various forms of constructive activity in which the increased wealth must find investment.

That in addition, he will to a great extent find employment in operating the Cotton Picking Machines, and that the mechanical education and greater intellectual activity resulting will greatly increase his industrial versatility.

Assuming this to be the case, the income of the adult and wage-earning negro men will be so increased that they can afford to send their children to school and keep their wives in the home.

As, however, I am only a business man and not a social philosopher, it has occurred to me to solicit an expression of your views upon the subject, with the thought that perhaps you might be induced to allow their publication in the WORLD'S WORK, where, it goes without saying, Mr. Page would be only too glad to give them a place.

I may say that the effect of the Cotton Picker upon the social, industrial and financial condition of the negro is for me a very practical question.

In order to make possible the prompt commercialization of the Cotton Picking Machine, it is necessary to raise a large amount of money. Some of the capitalists before whom I have put the subject, while recognizing the enormous financial value of the Machine, have hesitated to make the necessary investment, because they are philanthropists as well as capitalists and have thought that possibly the effect of the Machine upon the financial condition of the negro would be injurious.

To one of them — a man of large wealth — who seemed restrained by the considerations above named, I suggested, the other day, that the stock representing such an investment as he chose to make in the Cotton-Picking enterprise, be donated to your Tuskegee institution so that the earnings of the Cotton Picking Machine accruing to him should be devoted to the cause of educating the negro children who would be displaced by the Machine.

The idea seemed to appeal to him very strongly. I am not sure whether it will bear fruit or not. Of one thing, however, I am certain, and that is, that in America the time is very near at hand when it will be generally recognized that great wealth is but a trusteeship to be administered in the public interest.

Accepting this statement as a fact, it would seem to me ideal that the money devoted to the development of labor-saving machinery should be so placed that the income and profit from it should be used to defray the cost of industrial education.

If you are at any time in the near future in New York I shall be more than pleased to have an opportunity of meeting you, and meantime, remain, with great regard, Yours very truly,

Theo. H. Price

TLS   Con. 827   BTW Papers   DLC.

1 Theodore Hazeltine Price (1861–1935), a New York cotton broker who headed Price, McCormick and Co. from 1884 to 1900, before launching his own brokerage firm, was president of the Price-Campbell Cotton Picker Corp. beginning in 1910. He was also an editor and writer on various financial and economic topics and in 1918 published his own weekly, *Commerce and Finance*.

Price sought the endorsement of BTW and other prominent Americans for his cotton picker. BTW was invited to a New York dinner in January 1911 where Price planned to demonstrate the cotton picker. (Price to BTW, Jan. 13, 1911, Con. 827, BTW Papers, DLC.) BTW did not attend the dinner, but apologized a month later and promised to make an effort to see the machine. (BTW to Price, Feb. 13, 1911, below.) In March Emmett J. Scott wrote Price: "Dr. Washington understands from newspaper reports that Dr. John Graham Brooks is of the opinion that the cotton picking machine may complicate the racial question in the South. Dr. Washington, however, is of the opinion that it ought to help conditions." (Mar. 15, 1911, Con. 827, BTW Papers, DLC.) BTW finally spoke at a dinner in Boston on Apr. 12, 1911, and endorsed the cotton picker as a device that would help end racial friction in the South. Price paid BTW's expenses and then donated $500 to Tuskegee Institute. (See Price to BTW, Apr. 15, 1911, and BTW to Price, Apr. 22, 1911, below, vol. 11.)

2 Arthur Wilson Page (1883–1960), for many years an editor at Doubleday, Page and Co., was vice-president and editor of *World's Work* from 1913 to 1927. He later was an executive for several large firms such as AT&T, Continental Oil Co., and Westinghouse Electric Corp.

To Oswald Garrison Villard

Tuskegee Ala   Jan 5/11

Personal. Supreme court decision regarding Alonzo Bailey case is great victory for whole south. The most encouraging feature is some of the strongest and best southern white people worked with us unceasingly in securing this decision.

Booker T. Washington

TWSr   Oswald Garrison Villard Papers   MH.

To the Editor of the *Liberian Register*

Tuskegee, Alabama, Jan. 5, 1911

Editor The Liberian Register —

I read from time to time your paper with a great deal of interest and profit. I am glad to note the sane advice which you give to the people of Liberia from time to time.

No one, not even the citizens of Liberia, is more interested in the progress and success of the Republic than I am.

One thing I consider fundamental. It is this. No matter how much aid or encouragement Liberia may receive from outside sources whether in the form of money, advice or service, permanent success, and therefore permanent independence, cannot be achieved unless all the people in Liberia realize that it is with a nation as with an individual, the nation must earn more than it spends otherwise it will go into bankruptcy sooner or later. A nation must export more than it imports or financial disaster follows. This means but one thing, that the Liberian people should try to get their living out of the natural resources of their country instead of depending to any extent upon the resources of foreign countries. Every time a Liberian eats a tin of canned goods imported from any other country, it means poverty for the Liberians, it means that the Liberians are paying somebody else to manufacture the tin cans, paying somebody else to put the goods in the tin cans, are paying the freight upon the cans, and all this of course means money taken out of Liberia.

I very much wish that in Liberia there might be something of the old time New England spirit in regard to a consumption of home products. I wish that the leading Liberians might set the fashion and therefore create a public sentiment that would make it fashionable and desirable for Liberians to eat, with little exception, only that which they can produce in their own country. Here in Tuskegee our teachers and students are encouraged to have their meals composed as often as possible of things which are produced on our own farm and in our own county. I have frequently gone into our own dining room where we have over 1600 students and teachers boarding, and have found practically nothing upon the tables but what has been grown upon our own farm by the hands of our students. Personally nothing gives me more delight and satisfaction than to have on my own table poultry, vegetables and other products which I have raised with my own hands in my own garden. I value this much more highly than anything produced by the hands of others which I might purchase.

Liberians must in an increasing degree, it seems to me, go into the soil, go into the water, go into the forests, and get out the riches of nature and consume these riches and not depend upon outside nations to supply them with the necessities of life. All this means another thing, and that is, that a large proportion of the brightest men and women should receive scientific, technical and industrial education in order to enable them to understand and master these natural resources to the extent that these riches right about their feet can be gotten out and used in the markets of the Republic. No matter how many loans Liberia may secure, unless this policy is pursued financial and other embarrassment will be the result.

I am glad to note that in your paper as well as in other publications of Liberia that there is an increasing tendency in the direction to which I have referred.

Booker T. Washington

TLpS Con. 428 BTW Papers DLC. Sent to J. L. Morris, Editor, in Monrovia, Liberia.

To William Hayes Ward

[Tuskegee, Ala.] January 6, 1911

Personal.

My dear Dr. Ward: I wonder if you realize the significance of the recent decision by the U.S. Supreme Court bearing on the Alonzo

Bailey case taken up from Alabama. It is far-reaching in its importance as it makes null and void the labor contract laws of nearly every one of the Southern states. A number of us have been working quietly for a number of years to overthrow these unjust laws, and it is a matter of great satisfaction that we have succeeded. Yours very truly,

Booker T. Washington

TLpS Con. 445 BTW Papers DLC.

A Draft of a Letter to William Howard Taft[1]

Tuskegee Institute, Alabama Jan. 6th, 1911

Personal and Confidential
My dear Mr. President: I dislike very much to trouble you about a subject about which I know you have heard a good deal.

I am writing regarding Mr. W. S. Harlan,[2] of Lockhart, Ala. I am not attempting to pass judgment upon his guilt or innocence because regarding that I am sure the courts know more than I do, but I do know that there are few men anywhere in the South who have stood higher than Mr. Harlan or have done more for the development of the South than is true of Mr. Harlan. Sixty-five per cent of the people employed at his mill plant are colored, and without exception they tell me that he has treated them with the greatest degree of kindness. He has built a good school for the colored people which has kept in session eight or nine months every year at his company's expense. He has also put up a good church building for the colored people, and besides has manifested his interest in them in any number of ways. What he has done for the colored people he has also done for the white people. His industrial plant is a model.

In view of Mr. Harlan's high character and usefulness, I very much hope that you can see your way clear to let him off with a fine. I hope you will bear in mind, too, that he has already been severely punished in his feelings and reputation. In a small community such as Mr. Harlan lives in, it is hard for one to realize that even though he goes to the penitentiary for only a week that his reputation and usefulness in that community are blasted for all time. I believe that all the purpose of the law would be answered in his case in view of the punishment which he has already undergone and in view of his high reputation, by having him pay a fine without having him go to the penitentiary.

I hesitate very much to take your time in this matter, and should not do so except for the high and useful character of Mr. Harlan. Yours very truly,

[Booker T. Washington]

TLd Con. 7 BTW Papers DLC.

1 The letter, on BTW's personal stationery, apparently was never sent. After Taft decided not to pardon W. S. Harlan, BTW wrote to one of Harlan's supporters in Lockhart, Ala., refusing to bother Taft further in the matter, on the ground that it might so embitter the President that he would not do what BTW expected him to do, shorten the sentence after a certain time had expired. (BTW to R. H. Trammell, Jan. 11, 1911, Con. 443, BTW Papers, DLC.)

2 William S. Harlan, originally from Iowa, became manager of the Jackson Lumber Co. in Lockhart, Ala., in 1902. In 1906 he was convicted of peonage, fined $5,000, and sentenced to eighteen months in jail. After a series of appeals that ended in the U.S. Supreme Court, Harlan's conviction was upheld on Nov. 28, 1910. He eventually served four months behind bars. (For an account of the Harlan case and BTW's role in it, see Pete Daniel, *Shadow of Slavery*, 88–94.)

To Charles Dyer Norton

[Tuskegee, Ala.] January 6, 1911

Personal

My dear Mr. Norton: I wonder if you and the President have noticed the decision recently rendered by the U.S. Supreme Court in the Alonzo Bailey Case: Enclosed I send you a clipping regarding it. This I think is the most important decision in justice to the colored people — in fact to all working people — that has been rendered by the Supreme Court in many years, and the fact that almost the first decision rendered after a Southern Democrat was made Chief Justice in favor of the Negro is most encouraging.

Please tell President Taft that I am calling the attention of the colored people throughout the country to this phase of the decision. I am reaching them through the medium of the colored papers and otherwise. Yours very truly,

Booker T. Washington

TLpS Con. 249 BTW Papers DLC.

To Hugh Mason Browne

Tuskegee Institute, Alabama   January 7, 1911

Dear Mr. Browne: Mr. Carnegie has declined to continue the money for the work of The Committee of Twelve. I have written his Cashier, Mr. Franks, however, that there is due us the final payment of $1350 promised for last year's work.

It does seem that we shall not be able to get the money for circulating Mr. Weatherford's[1] book or in fact money beyond the $1350. Yours very truly,

Booker T. Washington

TLS BTW Papers ATT. Twenty-two press copies are in Con. 52, BTW Papers, DLC.

[1] Willis Duke Weatherford (1875–1970), a pioneer in interracial relations in the South, was international student secretary of the YMCA for colleges in the South and Southwest from 1902 to 1919. In 1919 he was founder of the Commission on Interracial Relations. Later, as a member of the board of directors of the American Cast Iron and Pipe Co. in Birmingham, he employed many blacks and instituted a profit-sharing plan for them. He served on the board of trustees of Berea College for fifty years. In 1962 he helped obtain funds for an important study of southern Appalachia. (See Dykeman, *Prophet of Plenty.*)

In his book *Negro Life in the South, Present Conditions and Needs*, published in 1910, Weatherford stated that disease, immorality, and ignorance among blacks limited the advancement of whites. He wrote of slavery as a civilizing influence, advocated industrial education, and criticized radical blacks like W. E. B. Du Bois, who, he said, could see no good in the white man. The book was prepared for use as a text for the home mission classes of the college YMCA. It was designed to appeal to white college men in the South and was published by the YMCA Press in New York.

To Albert Franklin Owens[1]

[Tuskegee, Ala.] January 7, 1911

Rev. Mr. Owens: I think it would be a good thing if the Bible School would get hold of the three or four families, who live in the cabins near Cassedy Hall and show those families how to improve themselves, not only in the general appearance of their houses and yards, etc., but in other directions. This would be good work and helpful work. We ought not to have within a stone's throw of the Bible School people living in the condition that those families are. A school ought to let its influence and power be felt first of all among the people who live nearest to it.

Booker T. Washington

TLpS   Con. 614   BTW Papers   DLC.

[1] Albert Franklin Owens, a black clergyman and former school principal in Mobile, Ala., played a leading role in the formation of the National Baptist Convention in 1880. He was dean of Phelps Hall Bible Training School at Tuskegee Institute from 1908 to 1912, and served on the Tuskegee faculty executive council in 1913, while directing the extension division of Phelps Hall Bible Training School. After 1913 he taught at Selma University.

From Charles William Anderson

New York, N.Y., January 7, 1911

Personal

My dear Doctor: Only a line about the Sumner meeting last night under the auspices of the N.A.A.C.P. Ahem! The small hall of the Ethical Culture rooms was about two-thirds filled — certainly no more than that. The addresses were all read from manuscript, and were intensely monotonous. There was distinctly something lacking in all of them. There was no thrill, nothing specific, no lesson from the life of Sumner, nothing to make one recall the past with pride, or look to the future with hope. It was the same old wail about hard conditions and cruel caste. Each speaker missed the higher meaning of the life and work and influence of Charles

Sumner. The applause was stinted. In short, the whole function lacked fire and heart and enthusiasm, and that dynamic force which goes out from a speaker and warms all hearts, and impels all hearers to care for higher things. The bugle call of the leader of a good cause, cheering men onward for their fight for larger liberty and more exact justice, was not heard. It was just such a little meeting as might have been held by the ladies of a sewing circle of a country Episcopal church. Poor Sumner, he must have turned over in his grave, when he learned that one hundred years after his birth, in the greatest city of the New world, only about one hundred negroes, and a like number of white theorists assembled to commemorate his birth, and review the beneficence of his public career. I am not so sure that as many of these were drawn thither because Mr. Burleigh was expected to sing, as for any other reason. I am sending you the program that you may note the list of Vice Presidents. I think it worthy of attention that only three or four names of negroes appear on the list. As you will see, they were not well enough acquainted with me to get my name right. Mr. Schieffelin and his mother were both there. He did not seem to think much of the meeting. As usual, the white men who permitted their names to be used as Vice Presidents did not attend, and of course, these same names could not attract a crowd of colored people. Hence, the slight attendance. Jacob Schiff sent a ringing telegram. He seems to be rather friendly to this movement. When have you seen him? Doubtless most of the white men felt, as I did, that they would not be justified in declining to allow the use of their names as Vice Presidents, although they were not particularly interested in, or sympathetic toward the organization under which the meeting was held.

You may be interested to know that the Chairman took occasion to ask for subscriptions for the movement. This is significant. I am afraid they need a little ready cash, and I shrewdly suspect that some one is getting tired of putting it up.

The colored people will celebrate Sumner at Ransom's church tomorrow. I shall have a few words to say, although up to date I have prepared nothing. I hope to be able to remind our folks that the best way to honor Sumner's memory is to prepare ourselves to go forth and build up and conquer in the face of opposition, and thereby demonstrate that we are not unworthy of the sacrifices made by Sumner in our behalf. If I succeed in emphasizing this, I think I will have accomplished more than was done last night. I also want to remind our people that hope is better than despair — better as a weapon against injustice and wrong, better to encourage all who are patiently striving for more exact justice and larger liberty.

Let me again advise you that I am in my "shirt-sleeves" these days, and am omitting no opportunity to say a positive word whenever and wherever it needs the saying. Yours very truly,

Charles W. Anderson

TLS Con. 52 BTW Papers DLC.

To Emmett Jay Scott

[Tuskegee, Ala.] Jan. 8th, 1911

Mr. Scott: I want to take up the following matter at the Executive Committee meeting:

I think we might as well face the fact that Mr. Carnegie is not likely to aid us longer than the present year, certainly, if he does so at all he is likely to reduce the amount given, therefore we should put on foot a plan at once by which the League will be self-supporting. We ought to consider how to use our present funds in order to bring about this result. With this in view, the following matter should be first:

We should put on foot a movement by which a League will be organized in every community in the U.S. where there are one thousand or more colored people.

We should have a man in charge as an organizer who has executive ability of a high order and who can devote himself wholly to the work of organizing Leagues and keeping up interest in those already organized. This man should have [central?] headquarters at some proper point and should by letters, circulars and travel keep in direct touch with all the Leagues and be sure they are kept actively at work.

It is important that we organize a scheme by which each Local League will contribute a small amount every month or every year toward the expense of keeping up headquarters and sustaining an organization. A very small amount contributed regularly from each League would pay all our expenses without having to call on Mr. Carnegie or anybody else.

Booker T. Washington

TLpS BTW Papers ATT.

From William Howard Taft

The White House   Washington   January 8, 1911

My dear Professor Washington: I have yours to Norton of January 6th, and agree with you that the decision in the Bailey case is most important. I had to consider another case, the Harlan case, on a question of pardon, and I presume you saw what my action was. Sincerely yours,

Wm H. Taft

TLS Con. 55 BTW Papers DLC.

To Gaston J. Greil[1]

[Tuskegee, Ala.] January 9, 1911

Dear Sir: Within recent weeks I have seen considerable in the papers concerning the high death rate among the colored people, and I have also noted with interest what you, the Mayor[2] and others have said and are doing regarding the matter of reducing the death rate among the colored people.

It occurs to me that this institution might be of service to you and your department in lowering the death rate among the Negroes of Montgomery. Of course, we should not like to do anything except through the co-operation and with the consent of the leading colored people, especially the physicians of Montgomery.

I believe that a thorough and stringent campaign among the

colored people would result in bringing about better conditions.

Without making any move in the matter, however, I should like to have the opinion of yourself and the Mayor concerning the advisability of our attempting to be of service in the matter. Yours truly,

Booker T. Washington

TLpS Con. 423 BTW Papers DLC.

[1] Gaston J. Greil (b. 1878), city physician of Montgomery, Ala., until 1909, was founder of the Montgomery Anti-Tuberculosis League.

[2] William Adams Gunter (b. 1872) was elected mayor of Montgomery in 1910.

To Oswald Garrison Villard

[Tuskegee, Ala.] January 10, 1911

Personal.

My dear Mr. Villard: I am very tardy in replying to yours of December 13, but I have had so many weighty matters to attend to recently that this is the first chance I have had to write in reply to your letter.

There has been much discussion of my speeches in Europe, but no one has pointed out to me any specific utterance to which objection is made.

Mr. Milholland's first circular of protest was issued October 6th, before I had made a single speech in London. I did not speak there until October 7. Before you get through with Mr. Milholland, you will finally agree with me that he is not a man whose word can be depended upon. For example, I quote this utterance from the first circular he issued in London: "The Sunday following his famous luncheon at the White House with President Roosevelt, when the consequent excitement — that exhibition of barbarism — was at its height, I gave a dinner in his honor at the leading hotel of New York. Not less than $50,000 was realized for his school on that occasion." Now, any man who would make a false statement of this character is not a man who could be trusted to report impressions. If Mr. Milholland can name a single human being who ever gave any cash or subscribed a single dollar to

Tuskegee at a dinner or banquet which he gave me, I will be willing to drop the whole contention. I simply give you this instance to show you that Mr. Milholland with his excitable and volatile nature is not a man whose word can be depended upon.

My speeches in Europe did not differ from my speeches in this country. When I am in the South speaking to the Southern white people, anyone who hears me speak will tell you that I am frank and direct in my criticisms of the Southern white people. I cannot agree with you, or any others, however, that very much or any good is to be gained just now by going out of the South and merely speaking about the Southern white people. I grant that there are times when something can be gained in that direction, but I do mean that it should not be the main line of procedure. I think it pays to do such talking to the people who are most responsible for injustice being inflicted upon us in certain directions rather than to spend much time, as I have already stated, in talking about them.

It seems to me that there is little parallel between conditions that your grandfather had to confront and those facing us now. Your grandfather faced a great evil which was to be destroyed. Ours is a work of construction rather than a work of destruction. My effort in Europe was to show to the people that the work of your grandfather was not wasted and that the progress the Negro has made in America justified the word and work of your grandfather. It seems to me that it would be an insult to the memory of your grandfather for me to have gone to Europe and told the people there that what he did had amounted to nothing when I could sincerely and honestly state that the race was making progress as a result of its freedom.

You, of course, labor under the disadvantage of not knowing as much about the life of the Negro race as if you were a member of that race yourself. Unfortunately, too, I think you are brought into contact with that group of our people who have not succeeded in any large degree, and hence are sour, dissatisfied and unhappy. I wish you could come more constantly into contact with that group of our people who are succeeding, who have accomplished something, and are not continually sour and disappointed.

I keep pretty closely in touch with the life of my race, and I happen to know that the very same group of people who are opposing me now have done so practically ever since my name became in any way prominent, certainly ever since I spoke at the opening of the Atlanta Exposition. No matter what I would do or refrain from doing, the same group would oppose me. I think you know this.

I should be very glad if you would send me any extracts from interviews or from speeches that I delivered in Europe to which you object. Unfortunately, I had to leave London the next day after I met the newspaper people in London, and was absent on the Continent for a month and did not see reports of my interviews. I spoke in London on October 6, and had to leave the next day, so that I did not have time to see the reports of my speeches, but at any rate, you can depend upon it that both in my interviews and in my speeches I said the thing which I thought was right and which from the bottom of my heart I believed in. For this, I am sure I will have your respect, even though you do not agree with what I had to say.

I cannot agree with you that there is an increasing number of intellectual colored people who oppose me, or are opposed to me. My experience and observation convince me to the contrary. I do not see how any man could expect or hope to have to a larger extent the good will and cooperation of the members of his race of all classes than I have, and it is this consciousness that makes me feel very humble.

I confess that I cannot blame any one who resides in the North or in Europe for not taking the same hopeful view of conditions in the South that I do. The only time I ever become gloomy or despondent regarding the condition of the Negro in the South is when I am in the North. When I am in the North, I hear for the most part only of the most discouraging and disheartening things that take place in the South, but when I leave the North and get right in the South in the midst of the work and see for myself what is being done and how it is being done, and what the actual daily connection between the white man and the black man is, then it is that I become encouraged.

You say that I ought to speak out more strongly on public questions. I suppose that means such questions as relate to our receiving justice in the matter of public schools, lynchings etc. In that regard, I quote you some sentences which I used only a few days ago in talking to the Southern white people here in Alabama concerning their duty toward the Negro.

"I do not believe that the leading white people, and especially land owners of the 'Black Belt' counties know how little money some Negro schools receive. I actually know of communities where Negro teachers are being paid only from $15 to $17 per month for services for a period of three or four months in the year."

·   ·   ·   ·

"More money is paid for Negro convicts than for Negro teachers. About $46 per month is now being paid for first-class able bodied Negro convicts, $36 for second-class, and $26 for third-class for twelve months in the year."

·   ·   ·   ·

"One other element in the situation that drives Negroes from the farms of the 'Black Belt' counties is this: In many of the 'Black Belt' counties when a Negro is charged with a crime, a mob of wild, excited and often intoxicated people go scouring through the country in search of the Negro."

·   ·   ·   ·

"The experience of the civilized world shows that even where the utmost care and deliberation is exercised on the part of lawyers, judges and jury, innocent persons are sometimes punished. In the face of this experience, it is impossible for a wild, frenzied and excited mob of people to pass judgement upon the guilt or innocence of the individual. In my opinion, if the Negroes understand that their public schools in the country districts are gradually going to be improved as fast as the state can do so, and that they will receive police protection in case they are charged with crime in the country districts, as they do in the cities, then the best colored farmers will cease moving from the country districts into the cities."

·   ·   ·   ·

"And then I repeat what I have said elsewhere, that the land owners in the 'Black Belt' of the South cannot expect the Negroes to remain in the rural districts on the farm, unless they have good schoolhouses and a good school term that is in session seven or eight months during the year."

·   ·   ·   ·

As I telegraphed you on the 5th instant, we are all rejoicing over the decision of the United States Supreme Court in the Alonzo Bailey case. Some of the Southern white people especially Judge Thomas of Montgomery, deserve the very highest credit for standing up most manfully in connection with this case.

I am always glad to hear from you. Yours truly,

Booker T. Washington

TLpS Con. 444 BTW Papers DLC.

From Gaston J. Greil

Montgomery, Ala. Jan. 10, 1911

Dear Sir: In reply to yours of Jan. 9th, 1911, I beg to state that the statistics that you have seen lately in the papers, were, unfortunately, correct, and that the death rate among the negroes of Montgomery is, indeed, alarming.

I have not been city physician here for the past two years, but I have been heading, and am still chairman of the executive committee of the Anti-Tuberculosis League, in which we endeavor to run an educational campaign, without regard to race, color, or creed. Our League employs the services of a secretary and a nurse. The nurse has at present from 15 to 18 negro patients, who we treat gratis, supply with what necessities we can, and furnish free with drugs. The secretary attends to the details of the office, and mails out educational literature, copies of which she is sending you under separate cover.

I have made several trips to New York and the East, in an effort to do something which I think is absolutely essential in decreasing our death rate; i.e. to obtain about $10,000 to form a camp for Tuberculosis negro patients.

You know as well as I do — in fact, I suppose better — the cramped and crowded conditions of negroes in the South, and how, when one of them becomes ill, or dies, the others crowd around. You also know of the uncleanly condition in which most of them live. Now, we with our League, are doing the best that we can to improve these conditions, but you can see just how little we can accomplish, no matter how great our efforts, with the conditions scattered as they are. You can also see, without my going into details, the enormous advantage that would accrue, not only to your race, but to the entire community, if we could establish such a camp, as it has been my aim and ambition to establish.

Just exactly what you can do, I can't say. I shall take the matter up with Mr. Gunter, and let you hear further from me. In the meantime, should you come to Montgomery at any time in the near future, if you would drop into my office between the hours of 1.00 and 1.45, or into the office of the Anti-Tuberculosis League, room 505 Bell Bldg, we will be glad to discuss the matter with you and see what can be done. I shall be glad to hear from you at any time, with any suggestions, and hope that you will take the opportunity to call.

G J Greil

TLS   Con. 423   BTW Papers   DLC.

To Charles William Anderson

[Tuskegee, Ala.] January 12, 1911

Personal.

Dear Mr. Anderson: I thought you would like to see from a disinterested source something of an official summing up of my London speech about which so much noise was made. Enclosed I send it to you. It was in the official organ of the organization before which I spoke.

You will also note that our friend Milholland is working over time in order to make a big man of our friend Du Bois. To do this he has got the hardest job on his hands he has ever tackled. It is rather interesting to know how he is trying to copy what I have attempted to do. Yours very truly,

Booker T. Washington

TLpS   Con. 52   BTW Papers   DLC.

From Ralph Waldo Tyler

Washington, D.C. January 13, 1911

Dear Doctor: I am in receipt of your letter suggesting a cash testimonial for Tim Fortune.

Really I think this too much goodness on your part. Tim has wasted every dollar in wine and women. He never was true to you, and is not today. There never was a time when he was not for sale, and never was a time when he would not rap you, and he will do so today, and almost immediately on receipt of such alms as you might give him. This is a case in which I would much prefer to buy flowers for the dead rather than the living. Tim has knocked you too much to me for me to pay him a premium on his ungratefulness.

However, if you are overly anxious about this fund being raised, I might reconsider and make a small contribution, tho I do not believe our erratic alleged friend is deserving of your consideration. Sincerely,

R W Tyler

TLS Con. 443 BTW Papers DLC.

A Sunday Evening Talk

[Tuskegee, Ala.] January 15, 1911

ON THE VALUE OF OBEDIENCE

Tonight for a few minutes I shall talk to you on a very old and commonplace subject, but the more one has experience in life, the more he is convinced that the oldest things, the most commonplace things, the things that are used most and talked about most, are the most valuable things in life.

I want to speak to you concerning the importance and value of obedience. I have no special reason for speaking to you as a school on this subject, because I feel that there are few large bodies of people, few large organizations anywhere in the world that are more subject to law and order and obedience than is true of the rank and file of those connected with this school, but this subject has such far-reaching value, not only to you while you are here, but especially after you leave here and go out into the world, that I am tempted to speak to you concerning it for a few minutes.

If you will study the history of people and of nations you will find that the great and fundamental difference between ignorance and intelligence — certainly one of the great fundamental differences — consists in the fact that ignorant people have not learned the value of respect for authority, have not learned the value of instant, unquestioned obedience to authority, while intelligent people, intelligent nations, intelligent and cultured individuals, have learned the value of unquestioned obedience and respect for authority.

The very foundation of all civilization that is worthy to be called by that name rests upon respect for authority and obedience to those whose duty it is to give orders or to utter commands. This applies to nations, to races, to communities, to schools, to churches, to industrial organizations, to shops, to farms, to housekeeping, to every department of life. All chances for success, whether it be an organization, in the shop, of a nation, or of a race, a community, a household, a farm, or anything, rest upon obedience, upon respect for authority.

In that regard, people must learn that they must often forget the individuals who happen to hold positions and have respect for the position. Sometimes the individual whose duty it is to give a command which you must obey, you do not like as an individual; you may not have any respect for that individual as an individual, but all civilization rests upon the idea that no matter what his name is, what his color is, what his race is, who may happen to occupy a position of respect and responsibility you should respect their authority. Respect the position, though you may not respect the individual, and that means that the individual's words of command must be obeyed. That means, further, that no people can succeed until they have got to the point where they not only obey promptly without question, without hesitation, but they must be guided by the decision of the majority. All governments — whether of nations, races, secular governments, church governments — all rest upon the individuals connected with that organization being ready and willing to follow the decision of the majority.

I have often said to you as individuals, and I repeat it here, that it is a great deal better for you, as students, to learn to obey an unwise order than it is to disobey, to even question such order. It is better for you to learn to obey an unwise order, an order that should not have been issued, than it is for you to get into the habit of hesitating, of questioning the wisdom of an order when a person gives that order who is in a position to give it. It means you are to learn here, that when you go out from here and you are connected with any organization — whether it is school, whether it is a farm or whether it is a shop — that without question, without hesitation, you should obey the order of the person who is in a position to give an order.

Obey first and complain afterward; obey first and get your explanation afterward. Let that be the motto of your lives. No organization can exist, can prosper, can have the respect of individuals, unless those connected with it follow the motto that I have referred to of obeying first, complaining afterwards. Get your explanation after you have obeyed an order.

There is another difference between the ignorant and the intelligent, the cultured person. The intelligent person does not count it a sign of degradation to obey an order, but in most cases, in many cases, at least, the ignorant person counts it a sign of degradation to obey an order. I repeat: you must get that — if you have it — out of your heads and hearts. The very highest sign of education, of intelligence, of culture, is for one to get to the point where without question, on the instant, he will obey an order and consider it a privilege to obey an order. Remember that if you wish to show your intelligence while here at Tuskegee, or after you go away from here — if you wish to show that you are educated, that you have got intelligence, manifest it by being ready and willing and anxious to respect authority. By being ready and willing to obey an order means that you have control of yourselves. That is what we mean by the slight military organization we have here. We mean to get you to the point where you shall have such discipline, such control over your minds, over your bodies, that you will obey on the instant. No person can succeed in life, unless he has control of himself. No person can obey in life so long as he is led away and governed by his passions, by his appetites, by his temper. He must get to the point where he is able to overcome passions, to overcome temper, to overcome every disposition to go wrong, and that means, when he has gotten to the point where he can obey an order from his superior, from one in authority, that he has gotten control over his mind and control over his body. It means, further, that he is becoming an educated, a cultured person, if you please.

One of the best examples of obedience is found in the army of the United States Government — in the army of most governments. One of the best things in connection with the training of an officer, in connection with the training of a soldier, is that he gets such discipline, such schooling, such education, that he never questions an order, does not stop to debate whether an order is wise or unwise, whether it should be given, or not be given. His only question is, does that order come from a proper source, does it come from a person who is in authority to give that order, and when he has made up his mind that the person issuing that order has a right to issue it, he never questions. It is a privilege, it is his delight, it is a part of his religion to obey such an order.

That is the kind of discipline that we want every student from Tuskegee Institute to go out into the world possessed of. It means, I repeat, self-control, and every one gets education in proportion as he is able to control himself, to control his passions, to control his tongue, to control his appetite, to say, "I will do this"; to say, "I will not do this," in proportion as it is right or as it is wrong.

You will find that persons who are entrusted with the greatest authority in the world are the persons who learned the secret of obedience. You will find that the people who are seldom trusted with any authority in school, in business, in any direction, are people who have not learned obedience, are seldom with authority in any department of human activity.

Take this institution: the officers, teachers, everyone, are under the authority and control of the Board of Trustees and we would not be worthy of occupying our places in this institution if we did not consider it a pleasure and a privilege to obey the orders, the wishes of the Trustees of this institution.

I want you to take this lesson away with you and put it into

549

practice everywhere you go, in your communities where you live, in the city or in the country where you work, in the schoolroom, or in the shop, or on the farm — take away the lesson with you that the very highest sign of education that you can exhibit will consist of the fact that you have learned to respect authority, that you have learned the fundamental lesson of obedience, and I repeat, that no person is worthy of being entrusted with much responsibility, unless that person has learned the lesson of obedience.

In a word, no one can command unless he has learned to obey. No one can command others unless he himself has learned to obey. That lesson I want you to put into practice every day of your life here on these grounds, and more important, put it into practice every day of your life after you leave this institution.

Tuskegee Student, 23 (Jan. 21, 1911), 1, 4. Stenographically reported.

To Charles William Anderson

[Tuskegee, Ala.] January 16, 1911

Very Personal

Dear Mr. Anderson: I find that there is a rather serious situation in Washington so far as you and I are concerned. It seems that Mr. Norton has been saying to several colored visitors that what the President said in his inaugural address concerning Negroes in the South had the approval of yourself and myself. This has gotten around to Chase and others and has made them rather bitter. You will notice the effect of this in the recent issue of Chase's paper.

Now of course both of us are placed not only in an awkward position but in a delicate position. No one with decency can explain to outsiders just what the President of the United States did say or did not say to him. Of course as we both discussed and decided at the time, the only decent way to treat the President of the United States was to find out what he wanted to say and then help him say it in the least harmful and most decent manner. You and I both know that if we had permitted the President to say what he had planned to say and in the way he wanted to say it, the effect would have been one hundred per cent worse than it has been. In fact, if the colored people really knew what a change we made in the message they would feel grateful to us, but, of course, we cannot tell them and will have to suffer in silence. And then, notwithstanding the utterances of the President, if he had stuck to the spirit and letter of his inaugural address things would not have come out very badly after all, but that he has not done.

I am simply writing to put you on your guard. If indirectly, you can influence Mr. Chase I wish you would try to do it, but I would not give him any opportunity to hold us up.[1]

I am glad you like my Villard letter.[2] I thought the time had come when I had just as well let him know I am not a child to be advised and guided by him. In fact, these men in the last analysis have more respect for one in proportion as he shows that he is not afraid of them. Yours very truly,

Booker T. Washington

TLpS Con. 5 BTW Papers DLC.

[1] Another of BTW's lieutenants, Ralph W. Tyler, wrote E. J. Scott two days later: "I saw him [Chase] and made a deal with him, tho no reference was made to either you or the Doctor. It is understood that I alone am the principal dramatis persona. I am to furnish editorials, and The Bee is to have its policy shaped by me. In return I am to pay him $20 per month." Tyler expected help from other Bookerites in Washington, D.C., namely, James A. Cobb and R. C. Bruce. Tyler told E. J. Scott: "Not even Cobb has any intimation of your communicating with me." (Ralph W. Tyler to E. J. Scott, Jan. 18, 1911, Con. 443, BTW Papers, DLC.)

[2] BTW to Villard, Jan. 10, 1911, above. Anderson wrote BTW: "Your reply to Mr. Villard is a corker." (Jan. 13, 1911, Con. 52, BTW Papers, DLC.)

To Ralph Waldo Tyler

[Tuskegee, Ala.] January 16, 1911

Personal

Dear Mr. Tyler: In connection with the report which I understand that Mr. Norton has unwittingly given currency to, I would state that any person who is fortunate, or unfortunate, enough to be called upon by the President of the United States for advice and opinion is placed in an awkward and defenseless position. One cannot come out and tell what the President said to him, neither can he state what he said to the President.

Of course the only way to be of service to the President in matters pertaining to public utterances is to find out what he has made up his mind to say, and then when he calls for you [to] advise him to say it in the least harmful and most helpful way.

I want to say to you for your own personal information and guidance that if the inaugural address had gone out in the form it was when Mr. Anderson and I first saw it, it would have startled and thoroughly discouraged the Negro one hundred per cent more than it did. Of course we cannot come out and say that the thing was pruned down and made many per cent less harmful than it was originally.

Of course the President thoroughly understood that it was our view that it should have been far better to have left the South entirely out of the discussion, but we had to bear in mind that he was the President and not we ourselves.

I think Mr. Anderson and I have demonstrated and are constantly demonstrating in a hundred ways our ability to stand up straight when some definite thing is to be done in the interests of the colored race. For example, a telegram went out from Washington lately which was published in practically every daily paper in the country to the effect that Speaker Cannon was opposing the appointment of Mr. Lewis for the position of Assistant Attorney General and I was standing up for him. It is strange that people who now seemed stirred up because of Mr. Norton's conversation should take no notice of these dispatches bearing upon the Lewis case. I am sure, however, that in your own way you can handle the whole matter and put both Mr. Anderson and myself right. Yours very truly,

Booker T. Washington

TLpS Con. 443 BTW Papers DLC.

An Editorial for the
Montgomery *Colored Alabamian*[1]

[Tuskegee, Ala.] January 16, 1911

Every colored man in Alabama who respects and values his citizenship should pay his poll tax and become a voter between now and February. If he does not it will be too late for him to vote. There are hundreds of colored people in Alabama who might register and become voters if they would exert themselves a little.

People cannot get something for nothing, and if our people are not willing to pay the small fee required to put their names on registration books, it would seem that they do not value their rights as citizens.

Although failure might have resulted in the past there is no reason why individuals should not keep trying until they become registered voters. Aside from this thought, every dollar we pay in poll taxes goes to the support of the Negro schools.

TLp   Con. 426   BTW Papers   DLC.

[1] BTW sent this to the editor, Robert Chapman Judkins, pastor of the Dexter Avenue Baptist Church in Montgomery, Ala., with the suggestion that he use it "in the form of an editorial."

From Charles William Anderson

New York, N.Y., January 19, 1911

(Personal)

My dear Doctor: Your good favor is before me. During my trip to Beverly last Fall with Mr. Scott, I learned (I think from Mr. Lewis) that Mr. Norton had been handing out the statement that you and I had looked over that "document" and were, therefore, responsible for what is in it. Of course, we are placed in the unhappy position of having to remain silent when, as a matter of fact, we saved the document from being a bomb-shell. I do not quite like the tendency to unload blame on other folks, especially when the other folks in question are forbidden by the decencies of the situation, to defend themselves. However, we shall see what we shall see.

I am enclosing herewith a copy of the invitation to the Black and White dinner.[1] You will be interested to note the subjects, as well as those who are to discuss them. The last half of the title of the subject assigned to Miss M. R. Lyons rather discloses the moral tendencies of the movement, in my judgment.[2] One needs only to glance over this invitation, printed as it is on yellow paper, and note the names of the speakers and the long-winded topics they are to discuss, to be convinced that they are a bunch of freaks. I shall do my best to see that the movement gets a full newspaper report.[3] I would suggest that you do something along that line also. Much good can be accomplished by having the Associated press, and other distributing news agencies send a full report of this meeting through the country. Yours very truly,

Charles W. Anderson

TLS Con. 52 BTW Papers DLC.

[1] The enclosed invitation to the annual dinner of the Cosmopolitan Society of America at the Cafe Boulevard, New York City, on Jan. 24, 1911, listed W. E. B. Du Bois and John E. Milholland among the speakers. For accounts of the dinner incident, see Kellogg, *NAACP*, 71–72; Harlan, "Secret Life of BTW," 413–15.

[2] Maritcha Remond Lyons (b. 1848), a Brooklyn schoolteacher, was scheduled to speak on "Social Progress of the Woman: 'The Fig Leaf' vs. 'The Hobble.' "

[3] *See* BTW to Anderson, Jan. 21, 1911, Anderson to BTW, Jan. 25, 1911, An Account of the Cosmopolitan Club Dinner in the New York *Press*, Jan. 25, 1911, Anderson to BTW, Jan. 26, 1911, and Scott to Anderson, Jan. 28, 1911, below.

From Oswald Garrison Villard

New York   January 19, 1911

Dear Mr. Washington: I beg to inform you that at the last meeting of the Executive Committee of the National Association for the Advancement of Colored People and the representatives of the Constitutional League, it was decided that the two organizations should not coalesce as had originally been planned, and that hereafter they would continue separate existences. Our Association is being incorporated under its own name, the National Association for the Advancement of Colored People, in the State of New York. I write this so that you may not in any way hold us liable for any actions taken by the Constitutional League.[1] Very truly yours,

Oswald Garrison Villard

TLS   Con. 55   BTW Papers   DLC.

[1] BTW sent this letter to Charles W. Anderson with the comment: "This indicates one of two things, either that he and Milholland have broken, or that they have agreed between them to let the Constitutional League do the dirty work and use the other organization to inveigle our friends into believing in their sincerity." (Jan. 23, 1911, Con. 52, BTW Papers, DLC.)

To Timothy Thomas Fortune

[Tuskegee, Ala.] January 20, 1911

Personal.

My dear Mr. Fortune: Your kind letter has just been received which I have read with deep interest. I am only answering it in part just now, as I shall take time to write you more at length later.

Du Bois did run away from Atlanta. All the time that the riot was going on, Du Bois was hiding at the Calhoun School in Alabama — a school which I was responsible for establishing some fifteen years ago. He remained there until the riot was over and then came out and wrote a piece of poetry bearing upon those who were killed in the riot.

There are some curious things going on. It seems strange that our friends Villard and John E. Milholland are attempting to run and control the destinies of the Negro race through Du Bois. I think they will have a tough time of it, as in my opinion, the Negro in New York like the Negro everywhere else is going to do his own thinking and own acting and not be second fiddle to a few white men, who feel that the Negro race belongs to them. I am glad that you went for Du Bois in the way that you did.[1]

Very confidentially, I am glad to say now that the funds for the tribute to you are coming in at an encouraging rate. Please use the enclosed in any way you may deem fitting.

It seems rather strange, too, that persons like Walling, who is a Russian and some white woman,[2] whose name I cannot recall, who is put down as the Secretary of the new organization, whom no one has ever heard of, should come in at this late date to take charge of our race. Yours very truly,

Booker T. Washington

TLpS Con. 607 BTW Papers DLC.

[1] Fortune wrote on Jan. 10, 1911: "I am after Du Bois and their business of tearing down everything and building up nothing. He writes the Amsterdam News this week denying that he ran away from Atlanta during the riots, but as to my other characterizations of him he is dumb." (Con. 607, BTW Papers, DLC.)

[2] Probably Frances Blascoer, a friend of Arthur B. Spingarn, who was secretary of the NAACP from about February 1910 to March 1911, when she resigned after a vehement controversy with Du Bois. (Kellogg, *NAACP*, 37, 93–94.)

To Charles William Anderson

[Tuskegee, Ala.] Jan. 21, 1911

Regarding black and white dinner be sure get hold of same reporter who reported for American year or two ago.[1] Would see that copies of printed announcement reach all city editors in advance. Think New York Times will work in harmony with you.

Booker T. Washington

TWpSr Con. 52 BTW Papers DLC.

[1] Anderson replied: "I am busy trying to secure suitable Press service for the forthcoming event. I would like to get hold of the man that handled it before, but unfortunately, I do not know his name. He was an artist. I shall leave no stone unturned to secure due publicity." (Jan. 23, 1911, Con. 52, BTW Papers, DLC.)

From Timothy Thomas Fortune

New York, N.Y. January 23, 1911

My dear Dr. Washington: Your letter of the 23rd instant was received, and I thank you for it and for the enclosure.

I have put Dr. Du Bois in a ragged hole in this town. In all public places, and the Amsterdam News goes everywhere in this town, the discussion hinges on the hole I have put him [in], as to the facts and suggestions raised by him, and as to the arguments pro and con. I have discussed with our Mr. Anderson[1] sometime ago the point you suggest that Du Bois is allowing himself to be used to put race leadership in the hands of white men, and we agreed that I should write a series of articles on that subject. But I felt that it was necessary to discredit Du Bois in the matters I have before taking up the other and more vital matter. I have done that now, and shall take up the main question in the near future. I attended a Socialist meeting at Lenox and 116th street Friday evening last to hear him speak on the race problem. It was a great meeting of long hairs and discontents and he had a glorious opportunity to present the Negro case for labor men so that it would do the most good, but he put the meeting in a fighting attitude on the race question.

I am so very much surprised that few of our newspapers have noticed the admission Du Bois was forced to make in the January Crisis that the National Association for the Advancement of Colored People was not responsible for the statement and appeal that I call your attention to it.

When we get done with Dr. Du Bois I am sure that he will have some trouble in handing over the leadership of the race to white men. Your view of that matter is entirely correct, and it is necessary to popularize it and to keep your name out of the discussion of it as much as the presentation of the case will allow of.

I am pleased to learn that the testimonial is doing well. I shall be glad to have a stake in a newspaper again, and the testimonial may serve as a stepping stone in that direction. The Amsterdam News people are willing and anxious to have me with them in that way, as they have confidence in me.

By the way, when you have anything (news) for the paper hereafter send it to Mr. James H. Anderson, and he and I will take care of it, as we are in accord as to the policy of the paper and as to our good will towards you.

With kind regards, Yours sincerely,

T. Thos. Fortune

TLS   Con. 607   BTW Papers   DLC.

[1] James Henry Anderson (b. 1868), editor and publisher of the *Amsterdam News* beginning in 1909.

To Frederick Randolph Moore

[Tuskegee, Ala.] January 24, 1911

Dear Mr. Moore: I do not like to trouble you unnecessarily, but I want to say to you that the Amsterdam News is fast out-distancing The Age in the matter of local news, and if the News continues to make inroads on The Age in the way it now is in collecting and publishing local news, you will find that The Age cannot hold its own in New York City. This is not only my opinion, but the opinion of some of your best friends. I advise that you give especial attention to holding your own in Greater New York.

Some one in your office ought to give more attention to the dates on your news items. For example, you published last week a letter from Montgomery dated January [18?] and the date of your publication was the 19th. In the same issue you published a letter from California dated January 15 and the date of your publication is January 19. Now everybody knows it is not possible for letters to reach The Age from these two points and be published so soon. If you are not careful in planning the matter of the dates, people will get the idea that nearly everything in The Age is faked. I hope you will find time to give attention to these matters. Yours very truly,

Booker T. Washington

TLpS Con. 54 BTW Papers DLC.

From Charles William Anderson

New York, N.Y., January 25, 1911

(Personal)
My dear Doctor: Please find enclosed the dinner clippings. The man who handled it last year could not be found, but a "good friend" on the Press took care of that end of it. I have only come upon these two notices in the morning papers, but doubtless the afternoon papers will handle it also. If they do, I will forward

you the clippings. I cannot account for the failure of the Times, Sun and Herald to handle it. They were all duly notified, as well as the Associated Press and the City News Association. The trouble is, that just now, nearly all of the dailies are running big stories about the Senatorial fights in New York and in New Jersey, and the demand for an extra session of Congress, together with the great Subway fight between McAdoo and the Belmont[1]-Ryan[2] people. It was probably cut out on this account. The Press, however, took good care of it, and I hope the Associated Press did likewise.

I quite agree with you concerning Moore. These difficulties may teach him a lesson. You may recall that I complained about his failure to support the Republican ticket last Fall, and especially Secretary Koenig,[3] who gave him the Concurrent Resolutions. Koenig was only defeated by seventeen hundred votes. Had he been elected Moore would again have had the Concurrent Resolutions, which would amount to twelve or fifteen hundred dollars. So you see, he was working against himself, when he doubled up with Lee and Langston.

Hoping you are very well, I remain, Yours truly,

Charles W. Anderson

Private

P.S. Dont forget to write to the Governor and others of our speaking friends to prepare and keep on hand, one or two good speeches on the race question, for delivery on short notice at any time. In this way we can monopolize the "speaking business" here, & shut out the opposition. The Gov. will not take the trouble to do this unless you direct him. He likes to socialize, but does not bother about the cause — political or otherwise — very much.

C. A.

TLS Con. 52 BTW Papers DLC. Postscript in Anderson's hand.

[1] August Belmont.

[2] Thomas Fortune Ryan (1851–1928), the New York street railway financier, was director or officer of more than thirty corporations.

[3] Samuel S. Koenig (b. 1872), a Hungarian immigrant, lawyer, and former New York secretary of state, was active in Republican politics in New York County and was a member of the New York State Republican Committee.

An Account of the Cosmopolitan Club Dinner in the New York *Press*[1]

[New York, Jan. 25, 1911]

THREE RACES SIT AT BANQUET FOR MIXED MARRIAGE

FASHIONABLE WHITE WOMEN AT BOARD WITH NEGROES, JAPS AND CHINAMEN TO PROMOTE THEIR "CAUSE" — YELLOW AND BLACK REPRESENTATIVES SHOW MOST ENTHUSIASM

COSMOPOLITAN SOCIETY ANNOUNCES MISSION

INTERMARRIAGE OF KINKY-HAIRED PEO-PLES WITH CAUCASIANS KEYNOTE OF BLOW-OUT AT CAFE BOULEVARD — AFRICANS HAVE TIME OF THEIR LIFE, BUT THE WAITERS ARE SORELY PUZ-ZLED

Whites, negroes and Japanese of both sexes sat side by side in the dining room of the Cafe Boulevard, Tenth street and Second avenue, last night, and talked of the abolishment of racial distinctions. The occasion was the annual dinner of the Cosmopolitan Society of America, the aims of which are to encourage social intercourse between men and women of different races.

Although there was no direct reference to marriage between whites and blacks, the speakers strongly intimated miscegenation was inevitable and not undesirable. It was remarked incidentally that the room in which this assemblage gathered would see on January 31 a dinner attended by President Taft.

White women, evidently of the cultured and wealthier classes, fashionably attired in low-cut gowns, leaned over the tables to chat confidentially with negro men of the true African type. Negresses in glittering frocks, their faces whitened with powder and touched with rouge, talked intimately with scholarly looking white men. Girls of both races laughed and sipped their wine and flirted with the younger cosmopolites, with the natural grace of the carefree debutante.

"The cosmopolitan chop suey," one of the waiters called the diners. "I wouldn't mind waiting on one of them African kings," he added, "nor even on Booker Washington, who's a king in his own way. But I don't like this black-and-white mixture at all. It leaves you guessing too much."

The representatives of the African and Mongolian races evidently were on their best behavior. When the chairman found it necessary to rap for order, it was always the white folk who were last to respond. To the casual observer, too, it was the latter race that appeared to realize most the incongruity of the affair. Only the broad smiles of the negroes as they leered surreptitiously across the room at their Caucasian friends made one feel their inner ecstacy over the unwonted social communion.

Josefus Chant Lipes, a small man with waving side whiskers, was toastmaster. As the banquet was the first of its kind held in the Boulevard, Lipes said he felt it his duty to explain the principles of the Cosmopolitan Society. To show that the association was "working for the true brotherhood of man in every possible way, leaving aside all distinctions of race as between the sexes," Lipes read the following excerpts from the society's constitution:

"The oneness of all human beings in the social and economic brotherhood of man may well be typified by the physiological truth that red blood courses the veins of all peoples of whatever race, creed or color. The real cosmopolite takes this physical fact for an entering wedge to ethically rend asunder the accumulated fallacies, rank injustices and racial and class prejudices that besmirch society at large to-day, and from the depths of his being there emanates an imperative call for a fraternity of all peoples of the earth to be nurtured, and in due time brought to a state of actuality. For this express purpose an organization with definite regulations must be established.

"The object of this society shall be to bring together under one fraternal order all the varied racial and social types of the peoples of the earth, regardless of the incidents of birth or station in life, where each may learn through an exchange of thought, of the inclinations and aspirations of others born and bred under different geographical and psychological environments — to the end that an extended and vigorous propaganda campaign shall be inaugurated for the mutual and common benefit of all mankind — the consummation of which noble and holy mission [is] to reach its fruition in the Universal Brotherhood of Man."

"In the furtherance of such a propaganda we undoubtedly will be subjected to repeated attacks by the press," Lipes added.

Having announced that Esther Remiz would play on the piano, the toastmaster began reading announcements. In the midst of this a young negro in fashionably cut evening clothes, leaned forward and whispered to Miss Remiz, who immediately advanced to the piano and plunged forthwith into the intricacies of the "Ronda Capriccioso," much to Lipes' discomfiture. All about the banquet hall the glistening ivories of the negroes and Japs showed their amusement at this melodious interruption.

After the song the president of the Cosmopolitan Society, James F. Morton, Jr.,[2] a young man with a thick shock of blond hair, delivered the address of welcome. "We are not a set of irresponsible persons bringing the races together to show our daring," Morton shouted. "We are here for a serious purpose. To affect the brotherhood of all nationalities we so greatly desire we must come into closer contact, much closer contact, with the psychologies of each other. We must banish all the idle prejudices we feel toward those of opposite color or race, and embrace them as we would those of our own flesh and blood. Only thus can all men become brothers in the most complete sense of the word!"

After Morton's speech there was much applause and a babel of comments. At most of the tables negro men had been placed beside white women, and in many cases these dinner partners smiled at one another and shook hands warmly in the enthusiasm that followed the Cosmopolitan president's words. Lipes, his whiskers fluttering like a dish of ferns in the wind, exclaimed:

"I'll ask you not to talk when I am speaking! You have no right to do it!" Instantly the blacks subsided, but their white associates simply laughed. A poem called "The Great Desideratum," which breathed the desires of mankind for brotherhood, was read by its negro author, William S. McKinney, secretary of the society.

The toastmaster apologized for the absence of Mrs. Alma Webster-Powell,[3] the Brooklyn singer and social reformer, who was to have spoken on "Social Progress in Dress Reform" and Maritcha R. Lyons, described as a "negress educator," whose theme was to have been "The Fig Leaf Versus the Hobble." He introduced Professor Masujiro Honda, associate editor of The Oriental Economic Review, as one of the greatest educators Japan has sent to this country.

Professor Honda told of American women in the Mikado's realm, and said the reforms inaugurated by them resulted in Buddhist priests being permitted to "marry and eat meat." The necessity for the education of the fair sex, the Japanese said, was ingrained in the minds of his countrymen, and the problem of improving the race by intermarriage also was being considered.

New York *Press*, Jan. 25, 1911, 1–2.

1 For an earlier example of adverse publicity see An Account of the Cosmopolitan Club Dinner in the New York *American*, Apr. 28, 1908, above, 9:515–20.

2 James Ferdinand Morton, Jr. (1870–1941), a Harvard graduate and New York lawyer, was active in the single-tax movement and later was counselor of the Universal Esperanto Association. He wrote *The Curse of Race Prejudice* (1906) in addition to magazine articles, poems, and several pamphlets.

3 Alma Webster Powell (1874–1930), a well-known soprano, was an activist in the Socialist party and a champion of women's rights. She received a Ph.D. from Columbia University in 1913.

From Charles William Anderson

New York, N.Y., January 26, 1911

My dear Doctor: The New York Evening World of yesterday carried a column's account (with proper sensational headlines of the dinner).[1] I did not send you the clipping, as it contained about the same report that was printed in the New York Press of yesterday, which I forwarded to you. Thus you see, the function was well handled by the papers.

I certainly hope Mr. Hilles will take the Secretaryship. Both he and Mr. Loeb are mentioned for it. I could be satisfied with either. Yours very truly,

Charles W. Anderson

TLS   Con. 52   BTW Papers   DLC.

¹ The New York *World* item carried the headline "MEN OF THREE SKINS WOULD BE ONE RACE" and had a sensational tone similar to that of the New York *Press* account above. (New York *World*, Jan. 25, 1911, 2.)

Emmett Jay Scott to Charles William Anderson

[Tuskegee, Ala.] January 28, 1911

Dear Mr. Anderson: Your "special representative" seems to have served up for the New York Press a particularly savory article and I am sending it forward to the Doctor at Hotel Manhattan today. I am sorry that the "artist" of The American was not also turned loose to describe this delectable function. Yours very truly,

Emmett

TLpS   Con. 52   BTW Papers   DLC.

To Helen Van Wyck Lockman

Hotel Manhattan, New York. January 30, 1911

My dear Mrs. Lockman: I have yours of January 23d. I am very sorry to hear that we are to be deprived of the use of the property next summer, but I am glad to hear that you are so improved in health that you can use the place yourself. I am sure you will enjoy it to the fullest extent.

I will take up with Mrs. Washington the matter of the furniture which has been left in the house.

I thank you very much for the information which you give regarding the property at Lawrence, Long Island. I should like further particulars regarding this property in case it is directly on the water. I should not like to invest in any property that is not directly on the water. I wish you would be kind enough to let me know.[1]

While writing I want to thank you and your family for all of your kindness to us while we were your tenants.

If you are in New York at any time this winter, I shall be glad to see you in case I am in the city at the same time. Yours very truly,

[Booker T. Washington]

TLc   Con. 428   BTW Papers   DLC.

[1] BTW informed Mrs. Lockman on Feb. 17, 1911, that he had purchased a house on a 1½-acre lot near Northport, L.I., about five miles from the Lockman place. "The surroundings at present," BTW wrote, "are not nearly so pleasant as at your place but we can improve these. The great advantage however that the place has is a good hard sandy beach right in front of the house." (Con. 428, BTW Papers, DLC.)

Margaret James Murray Washington
to Emmett Jay Scott

Tuskegee Inst. Jan. 31, 1911

Somewhat Confidential

Mr. Scott: On Saturday last, I met seven or eight *younger* looking white women coming toward Dorothy Hall with the Officer of the Day. There was no conversation what-so-ever going on. They were walking as if they were going into battle, and perhaps feeling that way. They looked it, at least.

The officer brought them inside this building, and said that he wanted to carry them through. After I had passed them I rang up Dorothy Hall, and got Mrs. Vivian,[1] who seems never to have "a chip on her shoulder" to take them through the building.

I write you this because I do not believe we should send those white women around with these young men students. I think that some person in the building where visitors are going should be notified of their coming, in order that some one may be ready in the building to carry them around. Some time it is necessary to show them special attention.

I always try to give Southern women special attention because they can be so *nasty*, and often they are won over to our side, because of the polite treatment they receive from us. Very truly yours,

Mrs W

TLI   Con. 616   BTW Papers   DLC.

1 Cornelia A. Vivian taught millinery at Tuskegee from 1902 until after BTW's death.

A Book Review in the
Journal of the African Society

Jan. 1911

THE NEGRO IN THE NEW WORLD

Sir Harry H. Johnston under the title "The Negro in the New World" has published a very interesting and in some respects a very remarkable book. It is the only book of its kind; that is, it is the only book that gives detailed information concerning the Negro in every part of the Western Hemisphere.

Until this book was published, there was no accurate statement concerning the number of Negroes in the New World. Even we in America are accustomed to think that the Negroes in the Western Hemisphere consist of the ten million in the United States and a few thousand in the West Indies. It is startling, therefore, for us to learn that there are 24,591,000 Negroes and Negroids in the New World. Their distribution according to Sir Harry's estimate is 30,000 in the Dominion of Canada; 10,000,000 in the United States; 12,500 in the Bermudas; 5,756,000 in the West Indies; 117,000 in Central America; 60,000 in Venezuela and Colombia; 225,500 in the Guianas; 8,300,000 in Brazil, and 90,000 in the remainder of South America.

When one has finished reading the book he knows how the Negroes were brought to the various islands of the West Indies, to the several countries of South America and to the United States. He also knows the conditions of the Negro during his enslavement in these various countries, how his emancipation was brought about, what he has done since his emancipation, what are his present relations with the whites and what is his outlook for the future. The author has shown a remarkable insight into the problem of racial adjustment and has been able to point out the weaknesses and the strong points of the Negro and the white people in contact with whom the Negro lives. The frankness with which Sir Harry Johnston has pointed out the weaknesses of the Negro and of the whites will tend to make the book unpopular. His remarkable powers of observation have enabled him to see practically everything in a country from beautiful landscapes to the women's costumes and he has criticised everything from the landscapes to the costumes.

I am sure that everyone who reads this book will have his outlook concerning the Negro problem broadened, and will also have learnt greater toleration with respect to the Negro.

Although I am not an anthropologist and for this reason cannot presume to discuss the first chapter of the book which deals with the anthropology of the Negro, yet it appears to me that in some instances much more representative types could have been given. For example, the picture of the Kru man from the Kru Coast, Liberia, as representing the typical Negro will, I am afraid, be misleading to the average reader, in that the type here shown does not represent that to which the present Negro race is tending, but rather that away from which it is tending. I think that the anthropological section, in fact the whole book, could have been made much more valuable, if there had been more pictures showing the types toward which the Negro is tending.[1]

I am pleased to note that the author takes a hopeful view of Haiti and says that this little nation is not quite so black as she has been painted. Sir Harry has, I think, correctly indicated what Haiti should do in order to become a progressive nation; which is that the blighting military despotism should be done away with or at least greatly minimized, that there should be great efficiency and justness in the administration of the customs and other public functions, that education should be put on a practical basis, and that instead of the students being taught distant and unpractical things, they should have instruction in "agriculture, forestry, zoology, botany, mineralogy, bacteriology — not a single Haitian interests himself in such pursuits. There are the magnificent pine forests of Alpine Haiti being recklessly destroyed year after year by ignorant peasants or hasty concessionaires. The Government of Haiti, from the President down to the lowest 'buraliste' in Port-au-Prince, does not care an iota.

"Haiti possesses one of the most magnificent floras in the world and a wonderful display of bird-life. Do you suppose any Haitian knows or cares anything about the trees, flowers, or fruit, beautiful or useful, of his own country; the birds, the fish, the butterflies, the rocks, minerals, rainfall, or wind force? Not one."

If Haiti should carry out the suggestions of Sir Harry Johnston, the Negroes of that country would take their rightful place as the leaders of all the black people of the New World; for, as he says, Haiti has it in her to become a wealthy and respected Negro community. "She has no enemies because the United States is her all-powerful friend."

My own experience with students who have come from the West Indies to attend Tuskegee Institute, and from letters which I have received from many of them after they have gone back to their homes, causes me to agree with the author that a much more universal and practical education should be aimed at. What Sir Harry Johnston says further on this point in the preface of the book is of such importance that I quote it in full: "And just as the British Government has in a very munificent way taken in hand the agriculture of the West Indies, and grouped its teaching round a Central Institute, and thereby contributed greatly to the revival of prosperity, so in like manner some system of universal, British-West-Indian, practical, collegiate education should be brought into being. Otherwise all intelligent Negroes in these islands, and in British Honduras and Guiana, will look to receive their twentieth-century education at the hands of the United States. A great deal more should be done in the future to unify the British administration of these remarkable West Indian Islands, not merely in the interest of the Black and the Yellow, but also of the White."

I have been very much impressed with the fact that the crime rate among the Negroes of the West Indies is so small. In speaking of Jamaica, the author says that the criminality of the Jamaican

Negroes is very slight. This is particularly true with reference to crimes of a serious nature. "Indecent assaults by Negroes on Negro women or children are not uncommon, a little more common, possibly, than they are among people of the same social status in England and in some Scotch towns. But it is scarcely too sweeping an assertion to say that there has been no case in Jamaica or any other British West Indian island of rape, or indecent assault or annoyance on the part of a black man or mulatto against a white woman since the Emancipation of the Slaves.

"There is not much serious crime in the Bahamas; such as there is, is more common, proportionately, among the indigenous white population than among the coloured. The Bahaman Negro bears a good reputation in this American Mediterranean. He is honest in big things, exceedingly good-tempered, brave, law-abiding, and hard-working."

There are probably many reasons why the crime rate among the West Indian Negroes is so low; but one of these reasons and a very important one, I think, is that policing and the administration of justice in the petty courts is to a large extent in the hands of the Negroes themselves. This causes them to have a greater respect for law and for the officers who are the representatives of the law. One of the greatest difficulties that we have in dealing with crime among the Negroes in the United States is, that so often the Negro does not think of the law as something made for his protection and designed to promote his welfare, but as something which is primarily to do him an injury. This is largely due to the fact that we as a people are so recently come out of slavery and have not yet been able to dis-associate law from slavery. I think, if there were throughout our Southland a system of Negro policing somewhat after the fashion of the Negro constabulary in the West Indies, that this would go a long way toward increasing the Negroes' respect for the law and tend to decrease our crime rate. In a few places in North Carolina, Alabama and Georgia this has already been tried with a fair degree of success.

With reference to the problem that confronts the Negro in the New World, it appears that the problem in Haiti is for an independent Black people to develop themselves and the great resources of their rich island. The problem in Cuba, where one-third of the population are Negroes, is to prevent an acute form of the race problem from developing. Since Sir Harry's visit to the island in 1908 a number of things have happened to indicate that a race problem similar to what we have in the United States is likely to arise there. It will be a surprise to many to find the author saying: "Altogether, socially and materially, in Cuba the American Negro appears at his best, so far as an average can be struck. Nowhere of course is there the intellectual development of the United States Negro in his higher types: on the other hand, I did not see any real squalor, stupid barbarity, aggressive noisiness, or ill manners. The country homes seemed better and neater than the worst class of Negro habitations in the Southern States; the town dwellings might not always be sanitary, but they had about them the dignity of Spain."

Nowhere in South America is there a race problem in the sense that we have it in the United States. It is very gratifying to know that Brazil with its very large Negro and Indian population is developing in such a way that all the races are living together with mutual goodwill toward each other. Nowhere in the New World is the race problem so acute as in the United States. There are a number of reasons for this. Among these are, first, the long and bitter agitation that preceded the emancipation of the slave; second, the fierce and prolonged civil war, by which emancipation was achieved; third, the further intensification of sectional and racial hatred engendered during what is known as the "Reconstruction Period," that is the period immediately following the close of the civil war; fourth, the injudicious use in recent years of the Negro as a political issue.

Since, however, it is agreed that the Negro is permanently to remain in the United States, the problem, then, is to bring about a better understanding between the races and so to adjust matters that the two races will be able to live side by side in peace and harmony, both developing, each mutually assisting the other and both working for the general development of the nation. It is by means of practical education that the Negro is to be developed and made a useful citizen. This, of course, applies to the Negro race everywhere and particularly to that part of the race which is yet in Africa.

Being myself an educator, I am of course especially interested in what the author has to say of education in the various countries in the New World which have large Negro populations.[2] In every instance the author thinks that the backwardness of the people is largely due to the lack of adequate educational facilities of the proper sort. He is, I think, very nearly correct in insisting that education is going a long way towards solving the race problem, not only in the New but in the Old World. It would be well if throughout the New World the Negro teachers, pastors and leaders of every sort would everywhere follow Sir Harry Johnston's advice and direct "their attention to the questions that are really vital: to theories and practices of disease-prevention and cure; to the correlation of intestinal worms and sanitary reform; to the inculcation of the chemistry of nature, of practical agriculture, beautiful horticulture, sound building, modern history, modern science, modern languages, modern religion."

Negro education, Sir Harry Johnston sets forth, should be of the kind that can be transmuted into money. "The one undoubted solution of the Negro's difficulties throughout the world is for him to turn his strong arms and sturdy legs, his fine sight, subtle hearing, deft fingers, and rapidly-developed brain to the making of Money, money being indeed but transmuted intellect and work, accumulated energy and courage."

Booker T. Washington

Journal of the African Society, 10 (Jan. 1911), 173–78.

1 Johnston took exception to this criticism after reading the proof of the article: "You call attention to my having given in the first chapter pictures of exaggerated negro types, exaggerated as regards their development of muscle and their homeliness of feature, and you seem to resent this a little. But my object was (as I think I explained in the text) not only to show the question in all its bearings, but to illustrate extreme features as well. For example, in my portraits of a typical Englishman and a typical Anglo-Saxon American, I selected faces altogether exceptional [and] remarkable for their beauty of outline or for the spirituality they conveyed, in order to show the White man at his best. I also wished to show the Negro at his worst, or, let us say, at his least developed; *not* from malice, but in some way to explain and partially excuse the White man's attitude of mind towards him in the unreasonable guise in which it often appears. Perhaps, also, I illustrated the best types of Anglo-Saxon to explain why the Negro has on the whole been so forgiving and so ready, over and over again, to 'put up with' the White man. But if you had looked through all my illustrations (though I marvel that you were able to devote as much time as you did to this, which is perhaps only one of the two or three thousand books you read in the course of a year) you would have seen that I strive over and over again, in regard to Africa as well as to America, to photograph the Negro and Negroid at their *best*. You will find in that same book some pictures of negroes or negroids which for physical beauty stand very nearly in rivalry with the White

man. Indeed, as I have written in another place, if one is to put aside questions of skin-colour (which are matters of local taste) the negroes as a whole may be regarded as being quite as comely as the entire mass of the White peoples; at least a sculptor would often think so." (Johnston to BTW, Dec. 18, 1910, Con. 426, BTW Papers, DLC.)

2 See Johnston's favorable account of Tuskegee and BTW after a visit to the school in 1908. (London *Times*, Jan. 15, 1909, 6.)

To Kelly Miller

New York City. February 1st, 1911

My dear Professor Miller: I have just had a conference with the Outlook staff. They have received protests from a Russian, a Japanese, a Chinaman and from yourself, and in an early issue of the Outlook they are going to feature those protests and give them to the public.[1]

One other thing that I accomplished during this interview will interest you. I have gotten the Outlook thoroughly committed to the use of the capital "N" for Negro in the future. Yours very truly,

[Booker T. Washington]

TLc Con. 430 BTW Papers DLC.

1 *Outlook* had favored the policy of restrictive immigration in its editorial pages. Four dissenting views, including one by Kelly Miller, were published in *Outlook*, 97 (Feb. 18, 1911), 357–60. Miller attacked *Outlook* for being dogmatic when its editorial declared that "no nation is large enough for two races." Miller wrote: "I am sure it will not be considered unmannerly to call attention to the inconsistency of your position. It is universally understood that The Outlook is a firm and enthusiastic supporter of Dr. Booker T. Washington, whose policy is based upon the harmonious adjustment of the races in the United States, each maintaining its separate and distinct racial identity. How can this be hoped for if 'no nation is large enough for two races'?"

From Theodore Roosevelt

New York   February 7th, 1911

Dear Dr. Washington: When I see you[1] I always have so many things to say that some of them are sure to remain unsaid. But I wish to write you now to tell you how really pleased I am at what you said of me in the World's Work.[2] It seems to me that taking into account what was said and who said it I could imagine nothing that I would prize more or desire more to have my children read. Of course a man ought not to concern himself over-much with either praise or blame, and I do not think that I do. Still, it is very pleasing to know that those whom you respect and whose judgment you value believe that you have acted well. For ordinary applause and ordinary blame I do not care a rap either way; but I do value the good opinion of the best citizens; and therefore I value yours. With regards, Always yours,

Theodore Roosevelt

TLS   Con. 438   BTW Papers   DLC.   On stationery of the *Outlook*.

[1] At a conference between BTW and the *Outlook* staff a few days earlier.

[2] BTW praised Roosevelt as "the highest type of all-round man that I have ever met." (*World's Work*, 21 [Feb. 1911], 14035.)

From Oswald Garrison Villard

New York   February 7, 1911

Dear Mr. Washington: I have been delayed in answering your letter of January 10th by illness at home and a great rush of work. I have perused it with the greatest interest and while I do not wish to continue the discussion in any detail, there are one or two things that I would like to say.

I realize, of course, that Mr. Milholland has his weaknesses, but he is a tried friend of human liberty and has worked unselfishly and still is working unselfishly according to his lights, to help on the race. You certainly used to find his friendship of value.

As to the analogy of the present situation with 1859, I should never have asked you to state in Europe that the race was not making progress as a result of its freedom, because we all know that it is making tremendous strides. But I do not think that bad conditions should be glossed over. I think every leader of the race, for instance, ought to come out and denounce in unmitigated terms the movement towards segregation in Baltimore, now happily temporarily checked by the courts; but it has already spread to Richmond and is likely to go elsewhere. The difficulty of your presentation as I see it is that you present but half the case — the pleasant side. For instance, you are delighted, like the rest of us with the Alabama peonage decision, but you are silent about the Berea court decision; you talk about prosperous negroes, but you say nothing about the Pink Franklin case; you record cases of friendliness, but are silent about the increasing prejudice and injustice and the retrogression of the public school system in the South. As I said to you in my earlier letter, it seems to me that where we differ is in the fundamental philosophy. You feel that this is the best way to aid the case; I feel that other ways are better, and that stressing the evils of the situation ought never to be neglected for a moment. I respect your position though I dissent from it.

I do resent, however, your saying that I am brought into contact with that group of your people "who have never succeeded in any large degree and hence are sour, dissatisfied and unhappy." I do not know one of this class who has seemed to you "sour, dissatisfied and unhappy." I know colored men and women who are achieving great things under very great difficulties and with very great cheerfulness; Mrs. Terrell, for instance, Leslie Hill, who has more than made good at Manassas; Lewis in Boston I only see occasionally, it is true, but I count him none the less a friend, and there are many others, like Benson, who is doing mighty well, to say nothing of the professional men, the successful ministers, lawyers and doctors, whom I meet in New York. And certainly there is nobody more successful than Dr. Du Bois. I trust, therefore, that you will quite revise your opinion as to my being in touch with people who are sour and disappointed; I should have very little interest in such persons. I think you are also under a mistaken comprehension as to what you call the opposition to yourself. The opposition is never to you personally as I have noticed it, but to the doctrines you advocate and the things you have said.

I am glad indeed to read the extracts from your speeches which you are good enough to enclose in this letter. They could not be improved upon as far as they go, but they do not go far enough to satisfy any Garrison. Perhaps this is the fault of the Garrisonian temperament, but it is a fact.

I am glad to know that Mr. Schiff is shortly to visit you, and am always pleased to hear of the advances of your work, because, for one thing, they make the task easier for those of us who are trying to do the same thing on a smaller scale, as we at Manassas.

With best wishes, as always, Sincerely yours,

Oswald Garrison Villard

TLS Con. 444 BTW Papers DLC. A carbon is in the Oswald Garrison Villard Papers, MH.

To Oswald Garrison Villard

Tuskegee Institute, Alabama   February 11, 1911

Dear Mr. Villard: There is, as you say in your letter of February 7th, no particular reason for continuing a futile correspondence.

You will permit me to say, however, that I am just a bit amazed to find how easily disposed you are to gloss over a piece of down-right misrepresentation, which seems to be one of the cornerstones of Mr. Milholland's special letter of complaint against me, namely, that he had proved his great friendship for me and the school by giving a dinner at which $50,000.00 was raised. This statement has not back of it even a semblance of truth, but I notice you dismiss such a statement with the simple remark that Mr. Milholland has his weaknesses. The only comment I would add is that if a man is capable of so thoroughly misrepresenting a matter by plausible argumentation in one respect, it is altogether possible for him, one may assume, to misrepresent by plausible argumentation other matters.

Of course, I can easily understand that it would be much more satisfactory in every way if I would do my work according as you and others direct or would direct, but I imagine I shall have to continue doing it in my own way, bringing about such results as I have been able to bring about, and helping as best I can in the general work of the uplift.

It is pleasing to learn that you endorse the extracts from the addresses which I have been making in the South, and that you find that they are "good as far as they go, but do not go far enough to satisfy a Garrison." You also refer to the "Garrisonian temperament." No one, as you know, has a higher respect or appreciation of the work done for the Negro by William Lloyd Garrison than I. I have on numerous and numberless occasions spoken my word of appreciation. But is it not possible that those possessing the "Garrisonian temperament" may be disposed to be more impatient with others because they do not as they would have them do, in contrast with what would probably be the attitude of Mr. Garrison himself if he were living?

I have found that when I am in the South, talking with Southern people, I say quite as frankly as I know how to say those things which will help conditions, and that is the attitude which I believe Mr. Garrison would endorse. I could deal in epithet and denunciation as many of my own detractors do, but somehow it has never seemed to me that they got very far with that kind of thing.

I am always glad to hear from you.

With best wishes always, I am, Sincerely yours,

[Booker T. Washington]

TL Con. 444 BTW Papers DLC. Possibly not sent, as it is on Tuskegee stationery.

To Roscoe Conkling Bruce

[Tuskegee, Ala.] February 11, 1911

Personal and confidential

Dear Mr. Bruce: I am writing you regarding a very confidential matter, and I hope you will not let this letter pass out of your hands.

It is important from my point of view that you have friendly support from colored newspapers as far as possible in Washington. This can be brought about without any sacrifice of principle or without doing anything any of us would be ashamed of. No matter how weak we may consider that the individual character of a newspaper editor or owner is, the public seldom considers this phase of it, seldom goes deeper. The editor and owner of the New York Times may be a very unprincipled man, but the public does not consider that, the public only considers what the New York Times says editorially and in its news columns and the public is more or less influenced by what the New York Times says.

If the white officials in Washington see that you are continually attacked by colored papers they gradually make up their minds, unconsciously, perhaps, that you are lacking in influence and are without friends among your own race in Washington.

Aside from this element, what the colored papers say in Washington is quoted all over the country, and we cannot discount that kind of influence.

I have thought it all over, and without going into details I wish you would have a good frank talk with Mr. Tyler at once and I think you will find that a change in the situation can be brought about. Yours very truly,

Booker T. Washington

TLpS Con. 418 BTW Papers DLC.

To Daniel M. Gerard[1]

[Tuskegee, Ala.] February 11, 1911

Dear Sir: Enclosed I send you a copy of a letter which I have sent Mr. Baylis.[2] I think you had better (telephone) instruct Mr. Baylis not to present this N.Y. draft to Mr. Snyder[3] in payment, but get the draft cashed and pay the currency because if Mr. Snyder sees the word "Tuskegee" on the draft he might balk.[4]

Also I hope you will see that Mr. Baylis carries out the plan which you suggested to me of not having the papers made direct to me by Mr. Snyder but to a third party,[5] and that party can transfer to me in the way you suggested. Yours very truly,

Booker T. Washington

Draft is made payable to Mr. *Bayliss.*

TLpS Con. 423 BTW Papers DLC. Postscript in BTW's hand.

1 A partner in the firm of Gerard and Hall Real Estate Brokers in Huntington, L.I.

2 Willard N. Baylis was a partner in the New York law firm of Baylis and Sanborn. Baylis maintained an office at Huntington, L.I., and handled the purchase of BTW's Long Island home. Baylis owned about 200 acres adjacent to BTW's property. (See Baylis to BTW, May 10, 1911, Con. 444, BTW Papers, DLC.)

3 Judson S. Snyder, president of Northport Estates on Long Island.

4 BTW's circuitous method of purchasing the 1½-acre J. Cornell Brown estate at Huntington, L.I., through several transfers of the property to others, was evidently to avoid public knowledge which might prevent the sale. (See A News Item in the New York *Times*, Apr. 2, 1911, below, vol. 11.)

5 Probably Benjamin H. Cozart, secretary-treasurer of Stony Brook Estates, mentioned in the New York *Times* account of the purchase of the home. (See A News Item in the New York *Times*, Apr. 2, 1911, below, vol. 11.) In Daniel M. Gerard to BTW, Feb. 16, 1911, Con. 423, BTW Papers, DLC, the third party mentioned is Frederick Cozart.

From George A. Myers

Cleveland, Feb. 11, 1911

Dear Dr. Washington: The publication of enclosure from the Plain Dealer of this date, in which you are quoted by Brascher[1] as favoring the establishment of a so styled Branch Y.M.C.A. (But in reality a Jim Crow Y.M.C.A.) for the negroes of Cleveland is regretted by your many friends.

Several were to see me yesterday after Brascher's paper came out and advised me to write to ascertain if Brascher properly quoted you.

The agitation of this matter by Brascher, Fleming,[2] Blue[3] and John P. Green has greatly stirred the community and I fear will do us irreparable injury — by causing discrimination in many avenues where it did not exist.

Personally I deplore Brascher's running into print. About every selfish negro, who has an ax to grind or his own interest to further, seeks to couple his name with yours. A certain man prayed to be delivered from his friends, I presume that you have many times done likewise, but added "fool friends and would be advisers." I am also inclosing a clipping from the Plain Dealer of Feb. 1st which will give you an idea of how we who are opposed to this feel and of the vigorous opposition.

Trusting the enlightenment sufficient, I am with best wishes to you and Mrs. Washington, Very truly yours,

George A. Myers

TLS   Con. 430   BTW Papers   DLC.

¹ Nahum Daniel Brascher, editor of the Cleveland *Journal* beginning in 1903. The newspaper was the voice of the younger black professionals and entrepreneurs of the city. His partners in the newspaper were Welcome T. Blue and Thomas W. Fleming. While Brascher and his associates were generally pro-BTW, they stressed BTW's racial solidarity themes but ignored the Tuskegean's emphasis on industrial education and avoidance of politics.

Brascher later moved to Chicago, where he became editor of the Associated Negro Press. (See Kusmer, *A Ghetto Takes Shape*; Gerber, *Black Ohio*; Davis, *Black Americans in Cleveland*.)

² Thomas Wallace Fleming (b. 1874), a lawyer and secretary of the Cleveland Association of Colored Men, was active in Ohio politics. He was a member of the Cleveland city council from 1909 to 1911, and served five terms on the Republican State Executive Committee. From 1915 to 1929 he again served on the Cleveland city council and held power in the black community based on his ability to dispense patronage. During World War I, he joined with Nahum Brascher, Welcome Blue, and others to form the Cleveland Realty, Housing, and Investment Co. (See Kusmer, *A Ghetto Takes Shape*; Davis, *Black Americans in Cleveland*.)

³ Welcome T. Blue, a black realtor in Cleveland, founded the Acme Real Estate Co., an enterprise designed to build low-cost housing for blacks. He later established other realty firms, and was a partner with Nahum Brascher and Thomas Fleming in the Journal Publishing Co.

A Sunday Evening Talk

[Tuskegee, Ala.] February 12, 1911

EDUCATION NOT EXCLUSIVE

During the past few days, one of the teachers here called my attention to a picture in some newspaper published in the West, or in the North, that represented a picture of a cow exhibited on the Commencement platform of a certain college or institution. That teacher also called my attention to the fact that we began having those same kinds of Commencement expositions or exhibits here nine or ten years ago. I call your attention to that fact because you will find it will be true of all races, and all countries, and under all circumstances, that if one sticks to nature in his educational methods and processes, he will come out all right.

It is true of education as it is with everything else: all that is artificial, all that is not based upon nature, all that is not based upon absolutely sound principles will disappear and people will come back or go forward to that which is founded upon nature and upon common-sense.

One great trouble with educational methods in the past has been that people have been trying to make education an exclusive thing — something that was for the few, something that was for the aristocratic, something that was far off, something that was, if not sublime, clothed in an atmosphere of mystery — and that element in the situation prevents a lot of people from doing good work as teachers, when they might otherwise.

Take the average man or the average woman, who goes out from any institution as a teacher. They often yield to the temptation of, first of all, impressing their own greatness upon their students, of impressing upon their students the fact that they know a great deal, that there is something hidden away back in their heads that may not come out for fear the world will be revolutionized: that is, they yield to the general temptation to surround education with an atmosphere of aristocracy, of exclusiveness, of mystery. Now all that is changing. The world is coming to understand and is forcing everybody to understand that education must be for the many, not for the few. It must concern itself with the ordinary things of life, not confining itself to the extraordinary things of life.

I have often called attention to the fact that a number of years ago, a certain religious sect was quite in evidence, was constantly before the public. It was known as the spiritualist denomination. The spiritualists of America have never made very much progress because when you heard of a spirit coming he always came at night, and if you asked what the spirit did you usually heard that the spirit took a lead pencil and made a mark on a piece of paper, or moved the leg of a table, or made a piano key move. The fact is, a spirit may come every night and do those three things and the world will never be made any better or any wiser by a mark on a piece of paper, by a table leg moving, or because a piano key is made to move. The spiritualists did not make any progress because the world was not interested in that kind of thing. When the spirits will come at four or five o'clock in the morning and make the fire and cook the breakfast and put it on the table, or when the spirits will come and plow the field and plant the cotton and work the cotton and harvest the cotton, then possibly people will believe in spiritualism, but hardly before.

The way to get people interested in education, I repeat, is to stick to nature, to common sense. This means if you are going out to teach a school in the country district, you should study the condition, the needs of the people in that community, in that township, in that county, or that state, and then lay out a course of study, a curriculum that can be adapted to the needs of the people in that community. There is more aping in regard to education than in almost any other subject. Go into the average school room, especially in many large institutions, and some of them that call themselves colleges and universities; pick up their catalogues, examine their course of study, and you will find, in the majority of cases, that the catalogue, or the course of study, has no relation whatever to the needs, to the condition of the people in that community. In too many cases, the catalogue is simply a copy of something that somebody has seen or heard of in a school a thousand miles away, having no relation whatever to the condition, the needs of the people in the immediate community.

In regard to education, there is entirely too much aping, without applying educational methods to conditions as they exist in the immediate community. Common sense teaches and nature teaches that if you are teaching a school in a farming community, and if you want to help those people, really help them and get them interested in your school, in your effort, you ought to emphasize in a practical way, inside of the school room and outside of the school room, farming, agriculture. Everything that grows out of the soil in that community should find a place in your work as a teacher there. That is following nature; that is common sense. Then, if you want to strike a common chord, you can do so in the matter of preparing and serving food — cooking; every farmer eats once, twice or three times a day.

Did you ever notice on Commencement Day how much attention the girl gets here who comes on the platform and puts a table cloth on a table and puts some flowers on the table and sets the table and puts some food on it? Did you ever notice how much attention that girl gets? She gets more attention than you would get or anybody else would get if he delivered an oration on "Beyond the Alps lies Italy." People used to be attracted by that kind of thing, but why are they now attracted to the girl who is giving an exhibition in the matter of the proper methods of setting the table? Simply because that girl is applying education to the ordinary things of life, not to the extraordinary things of life. People have gotten so into the habit in regard to education of expecting you to deal with the extraordinary things of life on Commencement Day, that they are really surprised when they see education applied to the ordinary things of life.

I remember a few years ago I attended a commencement, and I remember especially one oration. It was not very far from here. It was a description of a journey that each member of that class was to take through Europe the next year, or within the three years following. That did not create much interest because not many people there were interested in traveling through Europe, and all the people there knew that the members of that class would not travel through Europe, but if that individual had had an essay describing a trip through Macon County, or Bullock County, or Barbour County, then everybody would have been interested. He or she would have been applying education not to the extraordinary things of life, but to the ordinary things. If, when you go out to teach school, you will concern yourself with the proper method of preparing food and serving food, you will get the interest of every mother and every father, of every member of the family in your community; and so I repeat, that we have come to that period in our educational progress where everywhere people are demanding that in our methods we stick to nature, stick to common sense, that we use the things which are about us in promoting and carrying forward education.

That means again that we must teach the people how to be more comfortable in their homes, teach them to have more of the conveniences of life, more of the necessities of life because our school is in their midst. I repeat, that in five cases out of six a school, so far as reaching the condition of the people in the community where it exists might as well be 50 or 100 miles away from that community, because when you look through the catalogue, look through the curriculum of study, you will find in too many cases that there is not a thing in what is being taught that has any relation to the condition and needs of the people in that community.

The time has come, again, when the world is requiring that education should take account of the health of the pupils, of the health of the entire community. That means that education should concern itself with food, with dress, with proper methods of ventilation.

You read I suppose — I hope you do at least — the daily papers. If you do, you will find that every week there is a report in these newspapers to the effect that a large number of colored people die. Two and three times as many colored people as white people die in the city of Montgomery for instance in proportion to the number of each. That means, or should mean that every teacher in our cities should begin to examine his curriculum of study; should begin to find out in what degree he is teaching anything in his school which will help to change and better these conditions. Notwithstanding these figures have been published in daily newspapers for years, I will guarantee to suggest that if you will go into the public schools, and other schools of these cities, you would not find a thing mentioned in the daily course of study or in their printed curriculum that relates directly to these conditions.

If a school means anything, it means that it should at once take hold of those conditions and see that they are changed, and what I say in regard to education, I repeat with equal emphasis regarding moral and religious progress. The average man looks to the church, to the minister, for information, for guidance in those directions. The question is often asked why people in many places refuse to go to church as they used to go. In many cases you will find that people do not go to church because of the instruction and the inspiration they get there. They go because the church presents a convenient meeting place, a kind of club where people like to meet each other from different parts of the county, of the township. They come together, shake hands, ask how each other is. That is all right. Very few people go to church in many communities because they are interested in the sermon. Why? Simply because the minister never applies the Gospel to the things that are right about him in his community. He preaches about Heaven, about Jonah and about Peter and all those people, but very seldom a word that can be made of service to the people, that they can apply to their own daily lives, and you will find that the minister who does make the application, who does study conditions in his community and tries to apply the Gospel in the direction of helping the people to get land, building better houses, having more rooms in their houses, better food, better clothing, more books, more newspapers, more schools, that minister has a full church and does not go begging for want of pay.

You ask how can all of this be made of service in developing the mind? That is the great end in which the average educator is interested. There is scarcely a single thing that I have mentioned or that anyone can mention that concerns itself with farm life, with town life, with community life, with city life, that cannot be made the basis for the very best kind of academic training — training of the most practical, severe and highest kind in the direction of mathematics, in the direction of composition, in the direction of science. You can apply all the knowledge in academic branches that the average person gets, or can hope to get. He can dove-tail it into the kind of instruction that I have been trying to suggest to you.

For example: suppose you are teaching a country school. Instead of picking up a book in arithmetic, printed in Boston, or Chicago or somewhere up there — suppose the teacher just gets courage enough and summons common sense enough to say that Johnny Jones' father, who lives a quarter of a mile from the school has a pig, and instead of working out the old, dead, abstract problem in arithmetic which some fellow in Chicago wrote, she suggests going over to John Jones' father's house and weighing his father's pig. All the boys and girls will go with the teacher to weigh the pig. Get a pair of scales. Most of the pupils have never seen a pig weighed. Every pupil would be interested in that — intensely interested — and suppose they find out how many pounds that pig weighs, then after they have found out the number of pounds the pig weighs, then suppose the teacher will say: "What will this pig bring at the market price of meat today?"

That will mean that they will have to read the newspapers to find out what the market price is, and after they have found out what the market price of the pig is on that day, then they will multiply, or add, or subtract or divide, or whatever it calls for, and very soon the teacher with his pupils has found out what John

Jones' father's pig is worth in actual cash on that day and John Jones' father will scratch his head and say: "I did not know that this is what you mean by education, that my boy would come here and weigh my pig and tell how much my pig will bring.

"I always thought education meant what a pig in Chicago or New York would bring. I didn't think it would calculate the cost of my pig."

If you will apply your educational methods and processes to the thing that is right about you, you will find that in reference to the colored race, in reference to the white race, you will be supported, you will be encouraged.

What I say of the school, I emphasize with equal emphasis regarding the work of the Christian Church, and regardless of ignorance on the part of the colored race, on the part of the white race — when all the people of both races begin to see that we mean this kind of thing by education — money and sympathy and influence and support will be at your command.

Tuskegee Student, 23 (Feb. 18, 1911), 1, 2, 3, 4. Stenographically reported.

To Emmett Jay Scott

Tuskegee Institute, Alabama   February 13, 1911

Mr. Scott: I think it would be well for you to have at our expense, if necessary, 12 of the strongest colored papers sent regularly to Mr. Villard, personally.[1] Of course you will have to be very careful as to how this arrangement is made.

B. T. W.

TLI   Con. 608   BTW Papers   DLC.

[1] Scott sent, in BTW's name, letters to ten black newspaper editors asking them to send their papers to Villard regularly, without using BTW's name. These were Nahum D. Brascher, Cleveland *Journal;* W. Calvin Chase, Washington *Bee;* Nick Chiles, Topeka *Plain Dealer;* Benjamin J. Davis, Atlanta *Independent;* J. C. Gilmer, Charleston (W.Va.) *Advocate;* J. Thomas Harrison, Cambridge (Mass.) *Advocate;* D. A. Hart, Nashville *Globe;* George L. Knox, Indianapolis *Freeman;* Cary B. Lewis, Chicago *Chronicle;* and Christopher J. Perry, Philadelphia *Tribune.* (Letters dated Feb. 24, 1911, Con. 433, BTW Papers, DLC.)

To Theodore Hazeltine Price

[Tuskegee, Ala.] February 13, 1911

My dear Sir: I feel that in a way I owe you an apology.

I regret exceedingly that I could not serve you on the occasion to which you invited me, but I am writing to say that if at any other time in the future I can be of service, I shall be glad to be present at any function you may give, provided I have enough notice ahead, so that I can arrange my plans. It is very difficult for me to attend a meeting, unless I have a good many days notice ahead.

Mr. Ogden and many of my New York friends have written and spoken to me in the very highest terms of you personally and of the enterprise in which you are interested.

I also had the pleasure of talking with many people who attended the dinner and they spoke in the very highest terms of the work and the results of the cotton picker. Yours very truly,

Booker T. Washington

TLpS   Con. 827   BTW Papers   DLC.

To Loring Wilbur Messer[1]

[Tuskegee, Ala.] February 14, 1911

Dear Sir: I am writing regarding a matter about which I hope you will not misunderstand me.

Mr. W. Sidney Pittman is very anxious to get the work of drawing the plans for the Colored Branch of the Y.M.C.A. in your city. I ought to say in the first place that Mr. Pittman is my son-in-law, but I do not want this fact to weigh in his favor or against him. I want him to have the work if possible simply on his merits.

Mr. Pittman finished a course in architecture in this institution and later graduated at the Drexel Institute, of Philadelphia. He has had several years of active practice in Washington, but before going to Washington he drew the plans for several of our most important buildings at this institution. He has drawn the plans for important buildings in Washington and elsewhere. I hope you will give him a chance if possible.

I ought to add this: in my opinion it would serve as a great encouragement to the young colored men in Chicago and would be a part of broader education if they could know that a colored man drew the plans for the building.

At this institution, if I can give a colored man a chance to help make the bricks, to do the brickmasonry, or do the painting, or to put in the electrical wiring in connection with the completion of our buildings, I feel that I am helping to educate the race in a broad sense, and I think the influence of having a colored man draw the plans for the Chicago building will be more far-reaching than you realize.

Let me also add, that in case in the future you put in a course in mechanical drawing or architectural drawing in the night school, and this I hope you will do, the fact that a colored man drew the plans for the building in which the night school lessons are being given would be a constant source of inspiration to the young men to do their best.

Of course, in regard to Mr. Pittman, I should prefer that you get information from other sources regarding his ability, etc. Yours truly,

Booker T. Washington

TLpS Con. 430 BTW Papers DLC.

[1] Loring Wilbur Messer (1856–1923), a former dry-goods merchant in Reading, Mass., served as general secretary to YMCAs in Peoria, Ill., Cambridge, Mass., and, beginning in 1909, in Chicago.

To Portia Marshall Washington Pittman

[Tuskegee, Ala.] February 14, 1911

My dear Portia: I am sending you by today's express, prepaid, some presents for the children. I bought these in New York and hoped to give them to the children in person when I was to be in Washington for the Trustee meeting, but was disappointed.

I hope the children will enjoy the presents nevertheless. Your Papa,

B. T. W.

TLpI   Con. 436   BTW Papers   DLC.

To Philander Chase Knox

[Tuskegee, Ala.] February 15, 1911

My dear Mr. Secretary: The enclosed memorandum will give you some idea of the Conference bearing upon the methods of elevating the Negro in Africa and the West Indies to be held at this institution in April, 1912.

I am wondering if there is any way by which your Department could give publicity to this Conference, especially to the European governments.

I am constantly beset with letters, not only from missionaries, but from officials of European governments seeking information as to the methods used at Tuskegee Institute and I have been thinking of giving not only missionaries, but representatives of the European governments, who are at work in Africa and the West Indies, an opportunity to come here and see our methods and at the same time spend two or three days in forming the plans for better work. Yours very truly,

Booker T. Washington

TLpS   Con. 427   BTW Papers   DLC.

To Philip A. Payton, Jr.

[Tuskegee, Ala.] February 15, 1911

My dear Mr. Payton: I am writing you further concerning the subject which I telephoned you and Mrs. Payton about. After all I find that the demoralizing influence of New York City has gotten hold of me and I have yielded to the temptation of buying an "equity" in some New York property. I have just got a telegram from my lawyer stating that the papers have been passed and the transaction closed.

Tell Mrs. Payton that I have asked my lawyer to send the keys to the house to her, and sometime when you and Mrs. Payton get a chance I wish you would go down to Huntington or North-port and look the property over and let Mrs. Payton write Mrs. Washington a description of the rooms, etc., so she will know what to provide.

Until I get hold of the papers describing the property, I am afraid I cannot tell you how to reach it. The house is right on the Sound and about one-eighth of a mile from the post office Fort Salonga. You get off the steam cars at Northport and take the trolley to Northport Harbor and from there you have to take a team to the house. A party named Brown,[1] I think, occupied the house last summer. I think it is called the Snyder place. Yours very truly,

Booker T. Washington

TLpS Con. 436 BTW Papers DLC.

[1] J. Cornell Brown.

To George A. Myers

[Tuskegee, Ala.] February 17, 1911

Dear Mr. Myers: Please pardon my failure to answer your letter of December 14th. I thought I had done so, until your letter came reminding me of my failure to do so. I shall in this letter attempt to answer all of the various matters about which you have writ-ten me.

Mr. Cottrill is now of course confirmed, and I feel quite sure that he is going to give a good account of himself.

I have already expressed to you my appreciation of your kind-ness in emphasizing my own opinion of Mr. Cottrill's ability.

I agree with you fully in your statement that it well behooves our friends to look to 1912 if they are to have the support of the Negro people.

Your report of the meeting held in behalf of the N.A.A.C.P. interested me very much. It is probable that our friends will wake up to the futility of a program of obstruction and denunciation. Any cause that is based upon right principles can well withstand such opposition as that.

I thank you for your note regarding the trip through Ohio at some time in the future. I shall of course do nothing in the matter until I have had opportunity to confer with you and other of our friends.

With reference to the Y.M.C.A. matter:

Mr. Brascher wrote me a letter telling me of his efforts to secure a branch Y.M.C.A. I wrote him in reply the following: "The work you are planning in the way of extending the influence of The Cleveland Journal and of helping to establish a branch Y.M.C.A. should offer an opportunity for the greatest possible service to the colored people of Cleveland. I hope you may succeed in securing a Y.M.C.A. building." Of course, my reply to Mr. Brascher was based upon the assumption that the Negro people of Cleveland were interested in securing such a Y.M.C.A., based upon the Rosenwald[1] offer of $25,000.00 for any city which should raise $75,-000.00. I have not the slightest disposition to say or do anything that would even seem to outline a program for the Negro people of Cleveland. They are best able to decide as to their wants and needs. My letter was a courteous reply to a communication which had come from a friend in Cleveland.

With kindest regards to Mrs. Myers and yourself from Mrs. Washington and me, I am, Yours very truly,

Booker T. Washington

TLpS   Con. 430   BTW Papers   DLC.

1 Julius Rosenwald (1862–1932), the son of German Jewish immigrants, rose from poverty to wealth as a business entrepreneur and then devoted equal care to his philanthropic endeavors. Leaving high school in Springfield, Ill., before graduation, he learned the clothing business in New York for six years and then with a cousin founded the clothing firm of Rosenwald and Weil in Chicago. In 1895 he joined Sears, Roebuck and Co. as vice-president and one-third owner, and grew immensely wealthy when the company became the world's largest mail-order house. He was president from 1910 to 1925 and chairman of the board from 1925 to 1932.

Rosenwald shared with Rockefeller, Carnegie, and other large donors of his time a sense of the social responsibility of the philanthropist, who offered not only money but new ideas and stimuli for the improvement of the social order. (Rosenwald,

"Trend Away from Perpetuities," 748.) He aided hospitals, universities, and YMCAs, including controversial segregated black YMCA buildings in several major cities. His most important contribution, however, was to black education in partnership with BTW. He first met BTW in 1911 and became a trustee of Tuskegee Institute in 1912. Under BTW's tutelage he learned of the basic inadequacies of southern black public schools, and made money available to BTW for construction of black rural school buildings in the South. Rosenwald at first suggested the use of Sears, Roebuck prefabricated buildings, but BTW proved that with local material and donated labor, small rural school buildings could be constructed at about half the cost of a prefabricated mail-order building. He also recommended that Rosenwald match funds raised by the local patrons.

The Rosenwald schools built along these guidelines soon dotted the South, and in 1917, after BTW's death, the project was institutionalized as the Rosenwald Foundation, with headquarters in Nashville. It worked closely with the Jeanes Foundation. Rosenwald also aided some of BTW's other projects. He advanced money to BTW's friend Charles Banks, for example, to help him save the bank and cotton-oil mill of the all-black town of Mound Bayou, Miss. He frequently sent to Tuskegee consignments of shoes and hats from Sears, Roebuck to be sold to students at nominal prices. Even before the Great Depression gave poignancy to his views, Rosenwald opposed the "dead hand" of perpetual endowments, and suggested the spending of principal as well as interest of endowments. (Rosenwald, "Principles of Public Giving," 600.)

To Charles Dewey Hilles

[Tuskegee, Ala.] Feb. 21, 1911

Personal and Confidential

My dear Mr. Hilles: I hope you will not let this matter pass out of your hands. You have been so kind and generous I hate to impose upon you further, but as a matter of fact both Mr. Napier and his friends are being placed in a very awkward position regarding the delay in his name being sent to the Senate as Register of the Treasury. I know he has definite promises in writing from both the President and the Secretary of the Treasury that his appointment will be made within a few days, but yet nothing has been done. The giving out of this kind of thing and then having it fail to mature hurts all around.

I understand that Mr. Napier is being kept out while they are waiting to find something for Vernon. Now I want to tell you with the greatest frankness and in confidence that Vernon has no influence with anybody in this country whose influence counts for anything. I was recently in Kansas where Vernon lives, and I found that he is dead out there; he has no influence whatever. Aside from other matters, it is well known in Kansas that he was guilty of committing rape upon a woman out there and the people are in possession of the facts. This within itself makes him completely valueless and useless so far as the President is concerned or anybody else. It is a great deal better so far as the President's interests are concerned to have one good, strong, active friend with influence than to have one who has no influence.

If it is not asking too much of you, I very much wish that you would telegraph me on receipt of this letter after you have had time to look into matters. Yours very truly,

Booker T. Washington

TLpS   Con. 55   BTW Papers   DLC.

To James Carroll Napier

[Tuskegee, Ala.] Feb. 21, 1911

Think you better go to Washington at once see President, secretary of treasury and Hitchcock if necessary. Find out why being played with. Very much fear longer the delay greater chance of failure. Matter now reached point where you owe it not only to yourself but to friends to see that promises made are carried out.

B. T. W.

TWplr   Con. 431   BTW Papers   DLC.

To George Washington Carver

Tuskegee Institute, Alabama   February 26, 1911

Mr. Carver: After considering this matter carefully myself and going over it with other officers of the school, I am convinced that we owe it to you and to the school to state frankly the school's position and intention in regard to your work and relation of your work toward other instructors on the grounds.

Perhaps in the past we have done ourselves as well as you an injustice by pursuing a policy of trying to please everybody. This policy has not resulted in success; and such a policy seldom does result in success. The time has now come when the school must lay down a definite policy and state what it wishes you and others to do, and see that these requests or orders are carried out. We cannot stand any further or pursue a policy which permits you or anyone else to argue at length every order that is given, and to lay down the conditions upon which you will.

This school represents a large organization. The only way to bring about success when one has a large organization to deal with is to see that each individual has definite work laid out and that he does that work. Now it is perfectly possible and even true that where there is a large organization, individuals are working hard and are deeply in earnest, still results are not accomplished because each individual is working in a different direction from the other individual, and because there is lack of team work in the organization. That is the danger that we are approaching now. In fact, that is the weakness of our present attitude toward you.

From the first it has been the settled policy of this institution to give each individual head of a department all the liberty possible. We realize fully that it is not possible to keep in the employment of the school strong men and women unless we give them liberty of action. It is very rare that an order goes out from my office to any head of a department, stating in detail what policy we wish this or that head to pursue in any given case. Once in a while, however, such orders must be issued and when they are issued we expect them to be complied with without hesitation and in a sympathetic manner.

For example: You have had charge of the experiment station some twelve or fifteen years; during this time I think you will agree with me that the school has never suggested, except on two or three occasions, how the experiment station should be conducted; has never given you more than two or three orders as to what should be planted and what should not be planted in the experiment station. The rule has been to leave you in absolute

593

control. This does not mean, however, in your case nor in any case that the school abrogates its authority to give direct orders.

This year the school has thought it wise, on account of certain ends which it wishes to accomplish, to give you a definite order as to what should be planted in the experiment station during the next twelve months. Instead of complying with this order in a sympathetic and prompt manner you are dilly-dallying with it, and have tried in many ways to bring influences to bear through officers of the school and students to get us to change this order. This is not the proper way to act: and instead of gaining you lose in influence and power by such actions.

I think I ought to say to you again that everyone here recognizes that your great forte is in teaching and lecturing. There are few people anywhere who have greater ability to inspire and instruct as a teacher and as a lecturer than is true of yourself; that is your great forte.

When it comes to the organization of classes, the ability required to secure a properly organized and large school or section of a school, you are wanting in ability. When it comes to the matter of practical farm managing which will secure definite, practical, financial results, you are wanting again in ability. You are not to be blamed for this. It is very rare that one individual anywhere combines all the elements of success. You are a great teacher, a great lecturer, a great inspirer of young men and old men; that is your forte and we have all been trying as best we could to help you do the work for which you are best fitted and to leave aside that for which you are least fitted.

You also have great ability in original research in making experiments in the soil and elsewhere on untried plants. You have great ability in the direction of showing what can be done in the use of foods and the preserving of foods. In all that it is the policy of the school to give you the fullest liberty and the greatest encouragement, but once in a while we shall have to give you definite orders as to what we want done and what we do not want done.

I ought to say that I was greatly surprised in putting your report before the Executive Council to find that you wish a laboratory fitted up for your exclusive use and that you do not mean to give instruction to any students in this laboratory. This is a departure in the history of the school which we cannot permit. We have no right to expend so large a sum of money in the fitting up of a laboratory which is not to be used as frequently as possible in the instruction of students. We are all here to help the students, to instruct them, and there is no justification for the presence of any teacher here except as that teacher is to serve the students.

Again, you seem to have made up your mind that you are to give no instruction; that you are to teach no classes whatever. Here, again, the school cannot agree to have any person here in the capacity that you are serving unless he gives instruction to classes when the school requests that such instruction shall be given.

You do not help yourself when you assume the attitude that when you make a request that many hundred dollars shall be spent for fitting up a laboratory and so many hundred dollars shall be spent for chemicals that there must be no modification of your requisition[,] that the last dollar you request in the way of fitting up the laboratory shall be spent and that every dollar you request for chemicals, etc., shall be spent, nothing must be cut down[,] that you must have all or nothing; that is an attitude, again, which the school cannot comply with.

We do not encourage any teacher here in any such attitude. My own requests for supplies go before the Finance Committee the same as yours. Very often the Finance Committee refuses to give what I ask for. The same is true of every officer of the institution. We can make no exception in your case. However, we do mean to give you all that we possibly can give which in our judgment we think is necessary. In a word, I am simply trying to say that we have now reached the point where you will have to decide whether you intend to do the thing that the school wants done or whether you will stick to the policy of doing only that which you want to do.

Now, I do not mean to be unkind in making these statements. In fact, in putting the matter before you as I do, I am acting in the greatest charity and with the greatest degree of kindness. The longer we go on treating you as we are, the worse conditions are going to be. There is no officer in the institution who does not understand that he must obey orders when our orders are given. Further than this, I feel quite sure that if you will simply put yourself in the attitude that the other teachers put themselves in

— follow our orders and carry out our policy you will be much happier, much more successful and much more useful than you have ever been.

I repeat that all of us recognize your great ability, recognize your rare talents in certain directions, and we should all be sorry to part with your service, but the time has now come for perfect frankness and for definite action.

Nothing that I have said should be interpreted as meaning that we want you to work in a straight-jacket, that is to do what you are told to do and nothing else. We want to allow you the largest amount of liberty. But all this does mean that when an order is given it is to be complied with without objection and difficulty being thrown in the way to the extent that has been true in the past.

[Booker T. Washington]

TLc   Con. 255   BTW Papers   DLC.

To Charles William Anderson

[Tuskegee, Ala.] February 26, 1911

Personal

Dear Mr. Anderson: I think I ought to say to you that which I have said to Mr. Scott a dozen or more times recently, and that is this:

Of all the men that I have tried to serve in the matter of securing prominent, official positions, you are practically the only one who has ever been able to help himself after his name was discussed. The others lay completely down, and it is equal to carrying a load of lead as they seem to be absolutely helpless in the matter of self-help after their names are gotten before the public.

They not only are helpless in most cases, but many of them seem to say, in so many words, you have been responsible for naming me now you have got to push me on to success or the blame will be on you for failure. They do not put it in so many words, but you can feel and see that that is their attitude.

I have said to Mr. Scott that the next man I take up will be a fellow, without question, who will be able to help himself.

I shall write you about other matters soon. Yours very truly,

Booker T. Washington

TLpS Con. 61 BTW Papers DLC.

A Sunday Evening Talk

[Tuskegee, Ala.] February 26, 1911

TAKING ADVANTAGE OF OPPORTUNITIES

Two weeks ago, for the first time in my life I had the opportunity of attending a Socialist meeting in New York City. I had read a good deal about Socialists, but I had never before had the opportunity or privilege, of attending one of their meetings. I accepted the invitation to speak at this meeting, but before I spoke, they had some half-hour or more of preliminary discussion, and I was very much interested in hearing what they had to say; in hearing what they were talking about. I am not now, at least, expressing any opinion for or against the Socialists as an organization, because I confess I have not reached the point where I can understand them, so I am neither blaming nor praising them. I am simply reporting my own experience. I heard a good number of them speak and there were two things that impressed me.

In the meeting I attended everyone who spoke seemed to be dissatisfied with his surroundings, seemed to be dissatisfied with the world in general. Everything seemed to be going wrong, at cross purposes, so far as I could discover from their talk; nothing apparently was right, so far as their own experience or observation was concerned.

The second thing that impressed me was the fact that each individual who spoke, with a great deal of complacency, placed all the blame for his own failure in life upon somebody else. Not a single speaker seemed to have the idea that he himself was at fault for anything that was wrong with himself, or with his surroundings. Most of those who spoke found that the houses in which they lived were bad; the food they ate was bad; the work they were doing was not to their liking; the wages they received were too low; the hours were too long — something was wrong in every case, but in neither case was there anything wrong so far as I could discover with the men or women themselves. I confess it was not a very inspiring meeting. Those who spoke did not inspire me.

Here at Tuskegee, if we are trying to do anything above any other thing, it is to turn out men and women who will go out and inspire and lead somebody else; men and women who have such faith in themselves, such faith in their surroundings, such faith in their country, that they will go out and inspire other people to be successful. No people can be successful unless they possess the power of self-examination, the power to examine themselves, to hold themselves up day by day before a mirror, as it were, and find out their strong points and their weak points. No people can be successful and become leaders and become inspirers of others, unless they have faith in their surroundings, faith in their opportunities and above all, faith in the country they live in, faith in the opportunities that country offers to them. It is that kind of faith we want.

You, young men and women, who go out from Tuskegee, should go inspired with the idea that you have a mission, that you can lead somebody else, that you can get hold of people who are looking downward and make them look upward, that you can get hold of people who are discouraged and encourage them; that you can get hold of people who are failures and make them successful. Those are the kind of men and women we want at Tuskegee and I say to you frankly that we have no place here for any other kind of men and women.

Sometimes people, like individuals, races like individuals, look upon the gloomy, disappointing, dismal side of life to such an extent that they fail to see the opportunities, the privileges that are before them, and as I speak to you I am perfectly aware of the difficulties, of the discouragements, of the obstacles, which are often before us, but the man or woman who is going to succeed must turn his face in the direction of his opportunities, rather than toward his disadvantages.

Few races of people have had the opportunity of passing through such a tremendous change within a few years as is true of our race in this country, and especially here in the South. It is only within a few years ago, within a generation, as it were, that we have been permitted to own property anywhere we wish to own it. Exceptions, perhaps, there may be, but they are so few that these exceptions but emphasize the rule. How different is our condition from that of millions of our race in Africa; how different in that respect is our condition from that of millions of people in many parts of Russia, and in some other parts of the Old World.

We have then the fundamental right, the fundamental privilege of getting and holding and handing down to posterity property. This is one of the primary, one of the fundamental privileges that belong to every member of our race throughout this country.

Then we have with that another fundamental privilege, that of securing work, of working, with few exceptions, in any direction we have the talent. Here in the South we are peculiarly blessed in that respect. I have been talking with some gentlemen this afternoon from the North, and the problem they were discussing concerning our race is how to find employment for the men and women after they get education. Whether or not they could stick them into this little corner or this little hole; where they could find a niche here and there to stow them after they have secured their education. Here in the South this problem is turned around.

The constant problem that confronts us is to find men and women enough for the places that are waiting for them in every part of the Southland. There are few races, few people of any race, that have before them such great and constant and tempting opportunities for employment as is true of the educated men and women of our race, right here in the South.

Then, again, the opportunity to find work is a fundamental opportunity and we should think of that, not of the few isolated cases where individuals cannot find work that is exactly to their taste, but think of the prevailing condition, which is that we can find more work than we are able to do; and then it is only a few years ago that by law in many parts, if not in most parts of this country, we were not permitted to secure education. Today the Negro race is permitted to secure education everywhere. True, we do not get enough of it and sometimes not of the kind we think we ought to get, but there are few races in history that within the [two] generations, within 40 or 50 years, have had granted to them so many privileges in education as is true of our race, and I think I am safe in saying that never in the history of mankind has it been true when one race of another color has so liberally poured out its services and its substances in order to aid another race in getting education as is true of the white race in America in relation to giving the black people education in this country.

In regard to labor, there are many parts of the Old World where labor is restricted, where if a man's father is a shoemaker, his son is expected to be a shoemaker and his grandson and his great grandson is expected to be a shoemaker. There are many parts of the Old World today where members of certain races, notably the Jews, cannot work at certain employments, are restricted in their employments, restricted regarding the professions, restricted regarding skilled labor, restricted so far as responsibility is concerned, restricted in regard to the amount of education and the kind of education they shall receive. Few, if any of these restrictions hamper us here in this country.

Then we have the great privilege of owning and making a home, a home that we can call our own, one that we can hand down to our children and our children's children. We have the great privilege and opportunity in this country of making that home just as beautiful and surrounded with just as much culture, just as much of refinement as we wish, and of putting into it as many of the elements of high noble living as is true of any race under the sun.

In no part of this country can any Legislative body pass a law to prevent any young man or young woman, or any member of our race living every day in the year a clean, beautiful, useful, unselfish, upright life. These are the fundamentals for life among any race of people and when we consider it, we have much to encourage us and few things to permanently discourage us.

I want to inspire you with these ideas, with the thought of these privileges, and I want you to go out with these ideas in your minds and lead the people on to higher endeavors.

We have in a peculiar degree another opportunity and privilege — one not granted always to races or to groups of people, and that is, we have obstacles to overcome. I always pity the man or woman,

I always pity the race, that has no difficulties, that has no obstacles to overcome. In my opinion, neither individuals nor races can develop to their fullest extent, unless day by day, difficulties confront them. Instead of bowing our heads in discouragement, in despair, in disappointment, in the face of obstacles and difficulties, let us ask God for strength to meet them manfully; and we shall be strong in body, in mind, in spirit, and day by day we shall be broadened and lifted up into the atmosphere of the Christ.

A few days ago, we had a visit from Mr. Jacob H. Schiff, one of the half dozen great financiers of the world. Mr. Schiff belongs to the Jewish people. He is not ashamed or afraid to let the world know that he is by religion a Jew. Somewhere in the Bible you will find words to this effect: Overcome evil with good. Mr. Schiff could have gone about through the world with a chip on his shoulder, being insulted at every turn of the corner and continually putting up a "poor mouth," continually whining and crying because he is a Jew, and because his race is persecuted here and there, in this way and in that way, but instead of pursuing that course, Mr. Schiff mapped out a career for himself and seemed to say, "I will make myself so strong, so powerful, so successful in the world of finance that the world will forget that I am a Jew and only remember that I am a successful man"; he overcame evil with good.

So it is possible for us, all of us, to map out a career in finance, in farming, in skilled labor, in housekeeping, in teaching, in church work — we can make ourselves so strong, so successful in that work that when people think of us and talk of us, they will forget our race and think only of the good service we are rendering the world. It is possible everywhere for people to overcome evil with good.

Everywhere let us learn — and I want you to learn as you go out — to be leaders and inspirers of the people about us, teach them to be too big to notice the little insults, too big to notice the little things that too often make people miserable and blue and discouraged. Let us be so, that if others would be little, we must be broad and if others would be mean, we must remember that we can be greater than they by being good.

In this country we have great opportunities. Today, here in the South, only 45 years after being free, taking our race as a whole, we own more property, live in better houses, secure more work, get better wages, eat better food, get more education, grow faster in moral and religious directions than is true of any similar group of people anywhere in the world, and we are going forward faster in these directions than is true of any similar number of working people in the civilized world anywhere.

Let us not forget, then that each one of us has a place where we can serve, a place where we can inspire, where we can lead, a place where we can in some capacity be a great general, but remember no general ever won a victory who did not believe in himself, who did not believe in his army, who did not have faith in the country for which he was fighting.

Tuskegee Student, 23 (Mar. 11, 1911), 1, 3, 4. Stenographically reported.

An Article in *Metropolitan Magazine*

February 1911[1]

ROBERT C. OGDEN

It is impossible, I think, for any one to fully appreciate the impression that the first sight of a man of the physical, mental and moral build of Mr. Robert C. Ogden made upon me the first time I saw him.

I had gone from my home in the coal mines of West Virginia, walking the greater portion of the distance, to be a student at the Hampton Institute. Some months after I became a student at the Hampton Institute, Mr. Ogden, in company with a number of other gentlemen from the North, came to Hampton on a visit, to see for the first time and to come into contact with me, even though at a distance. To see a man with a strong, fresh, clean, vigorous physique, a man who is intensely practical and in earnest, a man who while deeply engrossed in business affairs was strong enough to turn aside and give a portion of his time to the elevation of an unfortunate race, was to me an experience which I had never before had, and the impression, as I have said, that the first sight of such a man as Mr. Ogden made upon me I shall never forget.

In this regard, I always associate him in my mind with the impression that Gen. Samuel Chapman Armstrong, the founder of Hampton, made upon me the first time I saw him.

I often hear Mr. Ogden remark in public and in private that he is not an educated man. I am quite sure, however, that few people who know Mr. Ogden will agree with him in this matter. Perhaps he has not got so much education in the usual formal, technical matter[2] out of books as some other people. But through the study of books, or men, or things, Mr. Ogden has secured the finest kind of education, and deserves to be classed with the scholars of the world. So far as I have studied Mr. Ogden's career, it is of interest and value to the public in three directions:

First: He has been a successful business man.

Second: More than any other one individual except Gen. S. C. Armstrong, he has been the leader in a movement to educate the whole South, regardless of race or color.

Third: In many important matters relating to moral and religious education in the North, Mr. Ogden is an important leader.

I know of few men in America whose life can be held up before young people as a model as can Mr. Ogden's life. When I told Mr. Ogden that I was going to prepare this little article, he wrote back as follows:

"There is very little material upon which to base such an article as you propose for THE METROPOLITAN MAGAZINE." In this I do not agree with Mr. Ogden, nor do I think the readers of THE METROPOLITAN MAGAZINE will agree with him.

To begin with, Mr. Ogden has back of him a successful business career covering a period of fifty-six years. If there were nothing else to his credit, here would be material enough to awaken the envy and awe of the thousands who have tried their hands at this great game and have lost, and to teach every American boy that genuine success can be gained and held through honest Christian principles. This fifty-six years of service has created and perfected one of the biggest and best known "houses" in New York. I refer to the John Wanamaker store in New York, a business palace in every detail, a monument which the public, the vast American public, will not soon let die. I never see this store (never think of its reliable mail order system, its quick and courteous clerks, its simple faith in the average man, everywhere, its perfect arrangement that affords one an education merely to pass through the various departments) but I feel that Mr. Ogden, like General Armstrong and many others, was a born educator, making whatever he touched lead to the elevation of the mind and spirit.

On learning that this great store is the work of Mr. Ogden's hands, the typical American would inquire why Mr. Ogden has not taken his place among the mighty capitalists of the nation. And truly it is remarkable. Yet one has only to know Mr. Ogden's position as touching capital and labor, seller and buyer, to realize that he is far too much of an idealist ever to be a great capitalist. His policies are too generous, his spirit too widely embraces all mankind in the distribution of favors to make him one of our moneyed men. During the whole period of his services as administrator, he stood for "strict justice toward both capital and labor." "The open shop," he declared, "is demanded by human rights." His motto toward the customer was always that "A good bargain is good to both buyer and seller," and "Success gained for one by pulling down another is not success in any true sense." "Money that is obtained by compelling another to lose is dishonestly obtained." These are some of the business watchwords that have dropped from Mr. Ogden's pen and that stamp him as an altruist in business and a model for every American boy who wishes to win success and at the same time keep his feet in the straight and narrow path of justice. It ought to be added that Mr. Ogden's policy in the Wanamaker business in New York was all in harmony with Mr. John Wanamaker's ideas.

This same generous policy of aggressive unselfishness has marked Mr. Ogden's work among both races of the South. I have often spoken of the impression he made upon me in my early days at Hampton. When I saw him there it never occurred to me that a man of his earnestness, with his vigor and sparkle of energy to make things go, could in any way be misunderstood! I thought how all the Southland must clap its hands and rejoice at the appearance of another such man as our own General Armstrong. But I later on learned that his actions were being questioned. It was not a question this time of race prejudice against the black man of the South, but rather against the white man of the South. Whispers of negro[3] social equality, negro political domination began to circulate as the possible cause of Mr. Ogden's deep interest in the education of this section of the country, the average white man in those early days finding it equally difficult to understand how a business man from the North would give such earnest effort merely for the cause of general education. But his unassuming personality, his willingness to lend a hand to help any cause that would advance intelligence soon put to rest any misgiving the South may have entertained about his intentions. How rapidly they learned to trust him is convincingly seen in his being the president and only Northern member of the Conference for Southern Education and the president of the Southern Education Board, and by the further fact that he has held his office in the Conference at the request of Southern people.

Instead of these offices rendering him estranged to my race, it seems only to have gained a firmer hold on him. At this writing he is president of the Board of Trustees of Hampton. He has been a Trustee of Hampton from the beginning, and so direct and personal has been his interest that he has seen all but two classes graduate from that Institution, these being my class and the class of 1907. In both cases serious illness was the cause of the absence. He has also been a trustee of the Tuskegee Institute from its founding, and his personal interest as well as his frequent visits here have been a constant source of inspiration. It is in connection with some of our work at Tuskegee that Mr. Ogden has exhibited much of his greatest genius for service, seeming to draw men and things into a constructive scheme for making human life better and happier. Nine years ago there was started near our Institution the Southern Land Improvement Company, whose purpose was to purchase large tracts of farm land and sell portions to colored people on reasonable terms. The company purchased about four thousand acres of this land. The founder, and until his death the president of the company was Mr. Alexander Purves, treasurer of Hampton and Mr. Ogden's son-in-law. At the death of Mr. Purves it became necessary to elect a new president. Few knew until then who was the senior stockholder and chief promoter, after Mr. Purves, in the company. But when the time for election came Mr. Ogden was elected over his protest because he was chief stock owner and promoter. Under him, following Mr. Purves, this company has done a lasting service for the colored people in this country. During these nine years, twenty-five colored families have bought and paid for farms with an average of forty acres each, and thirty families have bought and partly paid for their farms averaging about the same acreage. Mr. William V. Chambliss, a Tuskegee graduate, is the local superintendent for the company, and if you ask Mr. Chambliss how vital is Mr. Ogden's connection with the company, he will answer, "Oh, he's everything. He is president and leader, always looks into the life and condition of the people when he comes here." Mr. Chambliss is himself a stockholder and a farmer, owning about one thousand acres of land.

I have already referred to the fact that Mr. Ogden was not a great capitalist. In placing his money in this way, Mr. Ogden shows the reason far better than any words of mine can show why a man intimately conversant with all the business investments, stocks and bonds, and the great business men of a metropolis like New York, should come South and set his money to work on land to be sold to poor people, putting it out at a sort of missionary service for which, as far as this world goes, there are small returns; it can be explained only when we reflect that Mr. Ogden has a large heart as well as a wise head. Where the great capitalist has seen the place where he could make fifty or one hundred per cent. on his investment, Mr. Ogden has seen where he could bring life, comfort, intelligence and happiness to from fifty to one hundred human souls, and the good schools, the happy homes, the smiling faces of women and children are the returns on his capital down here in Macon County, Alabama.

In addition to the responsibilities I have already mentioned, Mr. Ogden is a trustee of the Anna T. Jeanes Fund, and a member of the General Education Board. These Boards — the Southern Education Board, the Southern Conference, the Jeanes Board, and the General Education Board — touch every phase of education and development in the South. They touch the public school, the private school, the college, the farm and farm industries, and most and best of all they reach and revitalize the teaching force in all these directions.

This service of educating the educators, of teaching and inspiring those who have in charge the training of the children of the South, cannot be too highly estimated. It came, too, at the time, one might almost say, of distress, when our methods in education were still crude, when one teacher knew very little about what another teacher was doing, and when there was prevalent the narrow conception that education was a very good thing for one class of people, but a very bad thing for another class. The Ogden parties at this time were exceedingly helpful in still another direction. They served not only to bring in contact educators of the same section, but teachers and educators of the whole nation. The principals and presidents of the schools in the North gained a wider education themselves and had thrown around them the bond of sympathy that embraced all people, regardless of race or color. They learned in the South that we were doing some things they in the North might attempt with profit to both teachers and pupils, while we in the South quickly caught the lessons of brevity, economy, and concentration of forces and of money which our Northern friends brought us. In these directions the South owes in all educational matters a great debt to Mr. Robert C. Ogden, greater indeed than to any one individual since Gen. S. C. Armstrong.

For all this, Mr. Ogden is not wholly Southern in the devotion of his service. His activities as president of the Board of Directors of Union Theological Seminary, of New York, as member of the Sage Foundation Board, and of the Presbyterian Board of Home Missions, show how broad and democratic are his sympathies. In all these directions he has stood for all that made for the good of the whole country, uttering at times in his annual addresses sentiments worthy of a great statesman. Speaking of the founding of the Education Conference, he said: "Its foundation is the proposition that every American child is entitled to an English education." Again he says: "This Congress was called by the voice of democracy," and, finally: "The note of democracy in catholic unison has ever resounded dominant and universal."

I have spoken of Mr. Ogden as a scholar. No man who ever saw him preside at a gathering or ever sat within the range of his voice could doubt this. His wealth of recollection of men and things, his bright, crisp style of speaking, surprising you continually by the delicious flavor of Scriptural passages and Scriptural ideas put in modern language make him one of the present day masters of the platform. Again it requires the finest kind of education to adjust yourself so as to be able to do your best with all classes of men. One trouble with the so-called scholar is that he cannot do this. He must live and talk and converse ever with books. That Mr. Ogden to-day presides over these various bodies I have mentioned — bodies of men different in training, in sentiments on religion, politics, education, and every practical subject — is to me a proof of scholarship of the highest order. Nothing short of the most liberal scholarship could have kept him unbiased in passing from one class and one race of people to another, and nothing smaller than the name of a patriot in no affected or canting sense can be applied to him when we consider the national scope and application of his business and educational ideals.

Metropolitan Magazine, 33 (Feb. 1911), 636–42. A typescript version with minor variations is in Con. 51, BTW Papers, DLC.

1 BTW received much of the information in the article directly from R. C. Ogden. See Ogden to BTW, July 15, 1910, above.

2 This was rendered "manner" in the typescript version.

3 Here and elsewhere in the typescript version "Negro" was capitalized.

To J. R. Barlow[1]

[Tuskegee, Ala.] March 1, 1911

My dear Mr. Barlow: Thank you for your kind letter of January [February] 9th.[2]

I am glad that you received the papers and the picture. I shall be interested to hear from you after you have talked matters over with our mutual friend, Mr. Harris.

As to the suggestion which you make for the land scheme, I am going to talk the whole matter over with Mr. Logan and by the time you have had a counsel with Mr. Harris and we can hear from you again, I think we may have reached some more definite conclusion.

I note what you say regarding Mr. Du Bois. He and I do not agree on most matters regarding the course to pursue in reference to our race in this country. In the first place, I do not think Dr. Du Bois understands conditions in the South. He was born in New England and has never been in the South among the rank and file of Southern white people and Southern colored people long enough to really understand conditions and to get hold of a true point of view. At present, he is living in New York and comes in little contact with the real problems of the South, but the most fundamental difference between us is in the following direction: I believe that the Negro race is making progress. I believe that it is better for the race to emphasize its opportunities than to lay over-much stress on its disadvantages. He believes that the Negro race is making little progress. I believe that we should cultivate an ever manly, straightforward manner and friendly relations between white people and black people. Dr. Du Bois pursues the policy of stirring up strife between white people and black people. This would not be so bad, if after stirring up strife between white people and black people in the South, he would live in the South and be brave enough to face conditions which his unwise course has helped to bring about; but instead of doing that, he flees to the North and leaves the rank and file of colored people in the South no better off because of the unwise course which he and others like him have pursued.

We are making progress as a race — tremendous progress — and I believe it is better to hold up before the colored people the fact that they are making progress than to continually hold up a picture of gloom and despair before them.

I say all this fully conscious of the wrongs suffered by my race. I say all this not with the idea of in any degree limiting or circumscribing the progress or growth of the race in any direction, but I want to lay a sure foundation for progress. In a word, the great weakness, in my opinion, of Dr. Du Bois' position is that he fails to recognize the fact that it is a work of construction that is before us now and not a work of destruction. Mr. Garrison and his followers had to destroy a great evil. Those of us who are now at work have got to build up the physical education and moral resources of the South and besides, have got to cement friendly relations between black people and white people, rather than tear the two races asunder.

Enclosed, please find receipt for the amount you sent to pay for the papers. Yours very truly,

Booker T. Washington

TLpS Con. 414 BTW Papers DLC.

¹ J. R. Barlow, of Greenthorne, Edgeworth, near Bolton, England, had met BTW at a gathering of the Liberal Club. He also accompanied BTW on some of his travels in England.

² Barlow had written BTW on Feb. 9, 1911, in reply to BTW's letter of Jan. 9, 1911, continuing discussion of a possible plan for black farmers to purchase land through a department of Tuskegee Institute. He incidentally asked BTW for his opinion of Du Bois, who was to come to England soon. (Feb. 9, 1911, Con. 414, BTW Papers, DLC.)

To Isaac Fisher

[Tuskegee, Ala.] March 1, 1911

Dear Mr. Fisher: Please pardon me for not writing you earlier. We have been unusually busy here the last week or ten days with the many Superintendents of Education, who have been coming to see us.¹

The letter to which you refer as receiving from Dr. Du Bois is a circular letter, which has been sent to a considerable number of colored men. I think you will find that this letter is a printed letter and we find that many persons have received similar ones. I am inclined to think that at the Congress to be held in London that an attempt will be made in some way to minimize the value of the program which we are pursuing in working out our problems in the South. For your confidential information, I beg to state that Dr. C. T. Walker of Augusta, Georgia, will be present at that meeting and will see that our cause is properly placed before it. Yours very truly,

Booker T. Washington

P.S. As a matter of straight fact, this organization is for the purpose of tearing down our work wherever possible and I think none of our friends should give it comfort.

B. T. W.

TLpS Con. 422 BTW Papers DLC.

¹ The Department of Superintendence of the National Educational Association held a conference in Mobile, Ala., in mid-February. Many of the educators, from all parts of the country, visited Tuskegee Institute both before and after the Mobile conference. On one day sixty-five superintendents were at the school. Later in the same week "three or four Pullman cars full of educators" from Pennsylvania and Ohio visited the school. (*Tuskegee Student*, 23 [Mar. 4, 1911], 1, 3.)

To James Carroll Napier

[Tuskegee, Ala.] March 1, 1911

My dear Mr. Napier: I shall be writing you about other matters soon, but one thing I have in mind at present.

Just so far as you and Mrs. Napier can use your influence in this direction, I very much hope you will see that no invitations are sent to Booker to attend social functions in the city of Nashville. I find that he is in danger of accepting too many of these invitations and in that way getting behind in his studies and having his mind taken off his real work. I should prefer that no invitations be sent him to attend social functions. Of course I know that it is impossible for you to control this matter wholly, but I thought you might be in a position to speak a word here and there. Yours very truly,

Booker T. Washington

TLpS   Con. 431   BTW Papers   DLC.

From Adam Clayton Powell

New York, March 1st, 1911

Personal

My dear Dr. Washington: I have been ill about six weeks and am still confined to the bed. For this reason my correspondence has been neglected.

Although late in answering, allow me to assure you that I very greatly appreciate your letter received a few weeks ago. When I was commending your work and leadership before my audience I did not expect my words to reach Tuskegee. They were intended for a class of men, most of whom are my friends, who were not only unjustly assailing you and your work, but were trying to get everybody who had the ear of the public to join them.

Perhaps you know that for ten years I was identified with a group of thinkers known as radical Negroes. While I still believe in a sane, intelligent and manly protest against the major wrongs from which the race is suffering, I am no longer a radical in the sense that the members of that group are radicals, for two reasons: First, because our radicalism has not accomplished any good thing. In the very places where the largest number of protest meetings have been held during the last ten years, as pointed out in a recent Age editorial, conditions have constantly grown more unfavorable. Secondly, because I have learned that the paramount object of this group is not so much to destroy race prejudice as it is to discredit you and your policies on both sides of the ocean. If this were accomplished, the race's loss would be a hundredfold greater than yours. I have been speaking of you and your policies not because you need me to defend either you or them, but because I have been forced to the conclusion that while your method of solving the problem by industry, education and an accumulation of property is a very slow one, after all it is the only theory that has advanced the race since the Emancipation, and I would not be honest to my convictions if I did not advise my people to follow you along the lines indicated.

With best wishes for your continued health and success, I am Sincerely yours,

A. Clayton Powell

TLS   Con. 436   BTW Papers   DLC.

To Albert Franklin Owens

[Tuskegee, Ala.] March 2, 1911

Dear Mr. Owens: Mr. Scott has spoken to me about the conversation he had with you a few days ago. In this connection I wish to say that I have just read your report in today's "Advertiser."[1] It is remarkable how you can get up so good a report and get it published in a typical Southern white paper.

While, as I said, I do not want to over-influence you one way or another, I want to leave the whole matter to your own conscience and judgment, but I will say this, that you will have to decide whether you can do more good in preaching to an audience of five or six million of White people in the South or by preaching to a few hundred colored people.

There is no greater work in connection with the future of the Negro than to bring a Southern white man around to the point where he believes in Negro education. When I say this, I do not mean the exceptional white man. The exceptional white man already believes in Negro education, but we must go further and reach and convert the average white man. You have a talent for doing this through your pen and through your ability to reach the white people through their own papers that no other colored man in the United States has. You have a talent in this respect that is equal to the call to preach.

Every time you can get a Southern white man to read anything about a Negro school, and in any degree be influenced to a broader conception of Negro education, you are helping in the highest sense to solve our problem.

Further than this, in doing this kind of work, you would be aiding Tuskegee as well as other institutions to get financial assistance from the North and elsewhere, because more and more every year the Northern white man and Southern white man are getting closer together, and the North will no longer help schools in the South in any large degree that have not the confidence and support of the Southern white people.

I repeat that I am not seeking to influence you unduly one way or the other, but I am simply putting an impression before you which is so strong that I cannot resist speaking out loud, especially after reading your very excellent report in today's "Advertiser." The kind of work you are doing as related in the "Advertiser" can be extended to 12 or 15 of the leading papers of the South, and in reaching and influencing white people through their press, you will be doing a work that no other colored man in the United States is doing or could do so well.

I repeat what Mr. Scott has said, that in this respect you will be of incalculable and invaluable service.

Booker T. Washington

TLpS Con. 614 BTW Papers DLC.

1 BTW was apparently mistaken about the date of the newspaper item. Owens's letter to the editor actually appeared a few days earlier. He had appealed for aid

to the black reformatory at Mt. Meigs, Ala., and urged passage of a bill to provide state funds for the institution. (Montgomery *Advertiser*, Feb. 27, 1911, 4.)

To Charles William Anderson

[Tuskegee, Ala.] March 3, 1911

Personal.

My dear Mr. Anderson: I believe you are keeping up with the case of Mr. Wm. English Walling. He is a great fellow to become the leader of the colored race, to advise them along moral lines. You know he is the chairman of the executive committee of the new "movement."

I wonder if you cannot get Moore to "burn Walling up" in an editorial in his paper.[1] Yours very truly,

B. T. W.

TLpI Con. 52 BTW Papers DLC.

[1] Walling was involved in a breach-of-promise suit that dragged through the courts from 1909 until early 1911. The scandal seriously affected his leadership role in the NAACP, and he resigned the chairmanship of the executive committee while the case was in trial in January 1911. Fred R. Moore had attacked Walling in an editorial in the New York *Age* in 1909, and, at BTW's suggestion, did it again in 1911. Moore said that it would be a disgrace for any black persons to invite Walling into their homes or to have him speak at a public meeting. (See Kellogg, *NAACP*, 32–33, 79–80.)

To Oswald Garrison Villard

Tuskegee Institute, Alabama   March 4, 1911

Dear Mr. Villard: I wonder if The Evening Post cannot be persuaded to begin using the capital N for Negro. You will be glad to know that The Outlook has recently decided to use the capital N in the future.

Whatever may be the historical reasons for not using the capital N, I believe you will agree with me that so far as present usage is concerned, there is just as much justification for using the capital

N for Negro as there is for using a capital J for Jews. Each name stands for a distinct class of people. Yours very truly,

Booker T. Washington

TLS   Oswald Garrison Villard Papers   MH.   A press copy is in Con. 55, BTW Papers, DLC.

To William D. Parkinson[1]

[Tuskegee, Ala.] March 8th 1911

My dear Mr. Parkinson: In reply to your letter of March 2nd, let me say that I fear we have no such systematic instruction in the matter of sex as your letter would indicate. The girl students are under the direct care of the Dean of the Women's Department. She is assisted by an assistant and four matrons, who have charge of the different dormitories. The discipline throughout the institution is very strict and in order to maintain it it is necessary for the Dean and her assistants to get pretty thoroughly acquainted with each individual student. The consequence is, there is very little formal instruction in the matter to which you refer. Once at least every week, the Dean brings together all of the girls and talks to them about matters of deportment and matters which concern their personal welfare. The same thing is done with the boys by the Commandant and his assistants.

Boys and girls recite, and frequently as in the tailor and the printing shops, they work together. Otherwise, the two sexes are kept apart except that in the upper classes, the young men may call upon the young women once a week, and occasionally during the year, they have sociables where the young men and young women meet in a formal sort of way. As a matter of fact, the members of the Senior class get pretty thoroughly acquainted with each other before they graduate. As nearly as we can learn, about ten percent of our graduates intermarry, though we have not as yet obtained accurate data on that point.

We have tried and are at present making an effort to keep up with every graduate and every former student to find out just what they are doing and how they are behaving themselves. With one possible exception as far as our investigation goes, none of our girl graduates have gone wrong.

Sorry I am not able to give you more definite information in reply to your questions. I appreciate all that you say about the school and wish to assure you that we have greatly profited by the visit of yourself and the other superintendents. Very truly yours,

Booker T. Washington

TLSr Copy Con. 436 BTW Papers DLC. Signature initialed by Emmett J. Scott.

¹ Superintendent of schools in Waltham, Mass.

Robert Heberton Terrell to Emmett Jay Scott

Washington, D.C., March 8, 1911

My dear Emmett, I am sending you herewith a money order for $1.15 for photo of the Doctor and as subscription to the Tuskegee Student. I couldn't think of trying to do without the Student. I have become thoroughly accustomed to it and I read it through religiously. I receive no paper which is more interesting to me than this one. It contains just the kind of matter that appeals to me, and I get certain information from this source that I cannot get elsewhere. Your system of reviewing all of the best and sanest books on the Negro question is a most commendable one and ought to be the means of making the paper attractive to all who are interested in the "problem." Then again, there are Doctor Washington's talks to the students, full of the soundest kind of advice both for young and old folks. It would be a splendid thing for our boys and girls if their teachers would from time to time read them to the assembled school.

How are you and the other more important Scotts? Well, I hope. Mention me kindly to them and tell *Mrs.* Scott to kiss my sister for me. We are preparing to welcome the distinguished additions to our crowd here. We did expect to meet them at the train with a band of music and flower girls, but the snow is nearly knee deep today and is still falling. We shall have to content ourselves with allowing Dr. Vernon to bring his successor from the depot in his own carriage. We know that the Assistant Attorney General will have a taxicab or two for himself and baggage.

I presume you have noted the nasty, *color* warfare that has been waged against Napier in certain sources. It is a despicable thing, and I believe that the "Sacred Bull" (that's my name for the reverend Register) is behind the whole contemptible business. In my opinion we are going to have our problem made more difficult of solution by this same question — the blackness of the black man as a predominant element in all matters touching the recognition of men of our race in public affairs. Are we to have the Haytian idea grafted on our system? It is a cloud no bigger than a man's hand today, but tomorrow it may be beyond our control both in size and portent.

I am mighty glad that the Doctor is trying to help Tim.

Drop me a line occasionally. I hope to get progressive enough to use a typewriter someday. Faithfully yours,

R. H. Terrell

ALS Con. 443 BTW Papers DLC.

Charles William Anderson to Emmett Jay Scott

New York, N.Y., March 10, 1911

(Personal) Confidential

My dear Emmett: As I predicted in my last two letters, the Fortune testimonial was very poorly attended. The lower part of the church was not one-third full, and the upper part completely empty. Both Wilford Smith and Rev. Bolden[1] referred to the small attendance in their speeches, and at the conclusion of the speechmaking, two of the deacons of the church asked permission to say a few words, and both stated that only on last Sunday were they notified that the church would be needed for the testimonial, and even then they were not given any of the facts — not even the names of the speakers. Thus you see Moore accomplished his purpose. However, I am enclosing clipping from the Amsterdam News

617

(which is out today) giving the whole story. During the course of Wilford Smith's speech, he mentioned that Fortune was a race champion who had never compromised, and Moore seized upon this to make a blatant defense of "the Doctor," and a bitter denunciation of those who talk about "compromise" and inferred that Booker T. Washington was a compromiser. I need not tell you that Smith did not so infer, for he took pains during the course of his speech to pay the Doctor a most generous and handsome tribute. The term compromise was used by Smith merely in referring to Fortune, without any thought of reflecting on any one else. Even Dodson[2] made a fairly good speech, without saying anything that could be twisted into criticism of the Doctor or his work. Yet Moore indulged in a blatant harangue of an half hour in defense of a man who was not assailed, either directly or by the remotest innuendo. He knew that he was guilty of making the meeting a frost, and he knew that everybody present was cognizant of that fact, and he felt that the only way out of it was to see something unfriendly to the Doctor in the meeting, and thereby excuse himself on the ground that he had to try to kill the meeting because he knew that its complexion would be unfriendly to the Doctor. Apart from this disagreeable feature, the meeting was a success. Fortune made a very sensible and discreet speech, and all the speakers, save Moore, praised him heartily, as the foremost editor the race has produced.

I do hope the Doctor will open his eyes to Moore. He can make enemies for the best cause that was ever defended by tongue or pen. The Guardian reporter was present, and left the church in company with Fortune. You can, therefore, look forward to a rotten report in the Guardian of next week. During the course of Moore's speech he spoke of circuitous as "circus," and he referred to me as having made an "exceptionable" Collector, instead of an unexceptionable one which, although intended to be complimentary, was exceedingly diverting, and especially so to the Guardian man in the audience. If we could only make people do the work they know something about, and leave the rest of it to others, what a blessing it would be. Yours very truly,

Charles

TLS Con. 52 BTW Papers DLC.

1 Richard Manuel Bolden (b. 1878), an occasional contributor to the New York *Age*, was an A.M.E. Zion clergyman and founder of Emmanuel Church in the World in New York City.

2 Nathaniel Barnett Dodson (b. 1870) attended Wayland Seminary in Washington, D.C., from 1891 to 1895. He was employed by the American Negro Press Association in New York beginning in 1897 as a messenger. He was a contributing editor to several black newspapers including the New York *Age* and the *Amsterdam News*. Later he was an executive of the National Negro Press Association, and was active in the Brooklyn branch of the NAACP.

Frederick Randolph Moore to Emmett Jay Scott

[New York City] 3/12/11

My dear Emmett, The testimonial came off and it was very nice — not a large crowd but an enthusiastic one. The addresses were very nice — and the whole thing passed off fine — $315.00 was handed him. I printed 1,000 circulars and had them distributed besides the notices in the Age. The notices were distributed in the principle churches. Fortune has acted nasty and I have done with him. Anderson and I had all we could do to pull it off.[1] I threatened to have the check returned to Mr Washington. Then his paper comes out and makes the meeting a frost. The people in N.Y. and Bklyn have no respect for the man. The Doctor deserves great credit — but is it appreciated[?] I am done old man. I'll serve my friends, but no more like this one.

I am send[ing] you check for $8.00 to hand to Mr. Stewart[2] on a/c of Nov note. Please ask him to credit it. This will leave a balance due $35.00.   Sincerely yours,

Moore

ALS   Con. 54   BTW Papers   DLC.

1 Emmett J. Scott informed BTW two days earlier that Moore had "tucked away in an unimportant portion of the paper" (New York *Age*) the notice of the Fortune testimonial dinner. "It does seem as Fortune and Anderson say," Scott wrote, "that Moore was more anxious to kill the meeting than he was to help it. He is not a very inspiring person to have to work with." (Mar. 10, 1911, Con. 422, BTW Papers, DLC.) Fortune described the dinner as "no music, no recitation, nothing but a cold blooded hand over of the money, with a charity flavor all over it." (Fortune to Scott, Mar. 17, 1911, Con. 607, BTW Papers, DLC.) The *Amsterdam News*, however, re-

ported BTW's warm letter of tribute and Anderson's testimonial to "one of the bravest champions the race has ever produced." (New York *Amsterdam News*, Mar. 11, 1911, reprinted in *Tuskegee Student*, Mar. 18, 1911, 1.)

2 Alexander Robert Stewart.

To Hamilton Holt

[Tuskegee, Ala.] March 13, 1911

My dear Mr. Holt: I should be very glad if you would be good enough to instruct the printer in the within article to use the capital N for Negro, instead of the small n. I very much dislike to have an article appear over my name where the term Negro is used as a race designation with the small n.

I return the proofs herewith and thank you for so promptly sending them to me. Yours very truly,

Booker T. Washington

TLpSr Con. 425 BTW Papers DLC. Signed in Emmett J. Scott's hand. BTW was en route to Battle Creek, Mich.

To George Washington Carver

[Tuskegee, Ala.] March 13, 1911

Personal and Confidential.

Mr. Carver: I am preparing an article on some five or six of the most distinguished black men that I know. I would like a few facts about yourself that I might use in the article and, if possible, I wish you would tell me some incident in your experience illustrating how, in spite of some difficulties, colored people and white people manage to get on pretty well with each other here in the South.

What I have in mind is some anecdote which will illustrate the contrast between what I may call the "official" relations between the races and the actual relations between individual white men and colored men. Officially, every white man is expected to act in such a way as to keep the races apart, and this he pretty generally does on all public occasions. But in spite of this fact, personal friendships, business relations and common interests constantly bring individuals together in friendly and helpful ways that make it easier than most people out of the South imagine to get on with the discrimination that we meet with.

If you can tell me some anecdote like this, I think I can use it in a way to make people realize that our handicaps in the South are not always as serious as people outside of the South frequently believe.

I hope you will let me have this material as soon as possible. Yours truly,

Booker T. Washington

TLpSr Con. 615 BTW Papers DLC. Signed in Emmett J. Scott's hand.

From Robert Ezra Park

Tuskegee Institute, Alabama, March 17, 1911

My dear Mr. Washington: I am sending you enclosed, the chapters for the book, "Chapters from my Experience," up to and including the 8th chapter, but with the exception of the first which, as you know, has not yet been written. It occurred to me that from these chapters, it would be possible for Mr. Page to make up the dummy that he wants without waiting for the completion of the first chapter. There still remain four chapters to be completed. They are as follows: Chapter I, LEARNING FROM MEN AND THINGS; Chapter IX, SOME THINGS I HAVE LEARNED FROM BLACK MEN; Chapter X, MEETING HIGH AND LOW IN EUROPE; Chapter XI, WHAT I LEARNED ABOUT EDUCATION IN DENMARK. Chapter XII, MISTAKES AND FUTURE OF NEGRO EDUCATION, is, as I understand it, already in the hands of the publishers. It will be necessary, however, to make some corrections before this chapter is put into the book, because a portion of the material, not very much, which I used there I have used elsewhere in reconstructing some of the earlier chapters.

You will want to read over Chapter III, SOME EXCEPTIONAL

MEN AND WHAT I LEARNED FROM THEM, because that has been almost entirely re-written. After reflection, I came to the conclusion that your suggestions for completing that chapter were better than my own and I have, therefore, not waited for the material you were to furnish in order to complete that chapter.

I am sending you the duplicate copy of My Experience with Reporters and Newspapers. The original, as you know, is in the hands of Mr. Hartley Davis[1] at 126 Waverly Place, New York.

I am now trying to get together material for the Chapter X: MEETING HIGH AND LOW IN EUROPE. I should be very glad to get from you some dictation of the material which you would like to put in this chapter, also I should like to get, as soon as possible, material for Chapter XI: WHAT I LEARNED ABOUT EDUCATION IN DENMARK.

I am sending you two copies of the Table of Contents of the book, Chapters from My Experience. One of these indicates, in red type, the condition in which each of these chapters will now be found. I am, Yours very truly,

Robert E. Park

TLS   Con. 54   BTW Papers   DLC.

[1] Hartley Cortlandt Davis (1866–1938), a newspaper and magazine editor who later was publisher of the Great Neck *News*.

BIBLIOGRAPHY

THIS BIBLIOGRAPHY gives fuller information on works cited in the annotations and endnotes. It is not intended to be comprehensive of works on the subjects dealt with in the volume or of works consulted in the process of annotation.

Archer, William. *Through Afro-America: An English Reading of the Race Problem.* London: Chapman and Hall, Ltd., 1910.

Bryce, James. *The American Commonwealth.* 2 vols. Revised ed. London and New York: Macmillan and Co., 1915.

Butt, Archibald. *The Letters of Archie Butt.* New York: Doubleday, Page and Co., 1925.

Chesnutt, Helen M. *Charles Waddell Chesnutt: Pioneer of the Color Line.* Chapel Hill: University of North Carolina Press, 1952.

Daniel, Pete. *The Shadow of Slavery: Peonage in the South, 1901–1969.* Urbana: University of Illinois Press, 1972.

Davis, Russell H. *Black Americans in Cleveland from George Peake to Carl B. Stokes, 1796–1969.* Washington, D.C.: Associated Publishers, [c. 1972].

Du Bois, W. E. B. *Dusk of Dawn: An Essay toward an Autobiography of a Race Concept.* New York: Harcourt, Brace and Co., 1940.

Dykeman, Wilma. *Prophet of Plenty: The First Ninety Years of W. D. Weatherford.* Knoxville: University of Tennessee Press, 1966.

Farr, Finis. *Black Champion: The Life and Times of Jack Johnson.* Greenwich, Conn.: Fawcett Publications, Inc., 1969. Originally published in 1964.

Gerber, David A. *Black Ohio and the Color Line, 1860–1915.* Urbana: University of Illinois Press, 1976.

Gilmore, Al-Tony. *Bad Nigger! The National Impact of Jack Johnson.* Port Washington, N.Y.: Kennikat Press, 1975.

Harlan, Louis R. "Booker T. Washington and the White Man's Burden," *American Historical Review,* 71 (Jan. 1966), 441–67.

———. "The Secret Life of Booker T. Washington," *Journal of Southern History,* 37 (Aug. 1971), 393–416.

Hartshorn, William Newton, ed. *An Era of Progress and Promise 1863–1910.* Boston: Priscilla Publishing Co., 1910.

Kellogg, Charles Flint. *NAACP: A History of the National Association for the Advancement of Colored People, 1909–1920.* Baltimore: Johns Hopkins University Press, 1967.

King, Kenneth James. *Pan-Africanism and Education: A Study of Race Philanthropy and Education in the Southern States of America and East Africa.* Oxford: Clarendon Press, 1971.

Kusmer, Kenneth L. *A Ghetto Takes Shape: Black Cleveland, 1870–1930.* Urbana: University of Illinois Press, 1976.

Lewinson, Edwin R. *Black Politics in New York City.* New York: Twayne Publishers, 1974.

Matthews, John Michael. "The Georgia 'Race Strike' of 1909," *Journal of Southern History,* 40 (Nov. 1974), 613–30.

Moton, Robert R. "The Washington Party in North Carolina," *Southern Workman,* 39 (Dec. 1910), 647–49.

Osofsky, Gilbert. *Harlem, the Making of a Ghetto: Negro New York, 1890–1910.* New York: Harper and Row, 1966.

Proceedings of the Conference on the Care of Dependent Children Held at Washington, D.C., January 25, 26, 1909, 60th Cong., 2nd Sess., Senate Doc. no. 721. Washington, D.C., 1909.

Proceedings of the National Negro Conference, 1909. Reprint. New York: Arno Press, 1969.

Rosenwald, Julius. "Principles of Public Giving," *Atlantic Monthly*, 143 (May 1929), 599–606.

———. "The Trend Away from Perpetuities," *Atlantic Monthly*, 146 (Dec. 1930), 741–49.

Ross, B. Joyce. *J. E. Spingarn and the Rise of the NAACP, 1911–1939*. New York: Atheneum Publishers, 1972.

Rudwick, Elliott M. *W. E. B. Du Bois: Propagandist of the Negro Protest*. Reprint. New York: Atheneum Publishers, 1968.

Scheiner, Seth M. *Negro Mecca: A History of the Negro in New York City, 1865–1920*. New York: New York University Press, 1965.

Stone, Alfred Holt. *Studies in the American Race Problem*. New York: Doubleday, Page and Co., 1908.

Washington, Ernest Davidson, ed. *Selected Speeches of Booker T. Washington*. Garden City, N.Y.: Doubleday, Doran and Co., 1932.

Weare, Walter B. *Black Business in the New South: A Social History of the North Carolina Mutual Life Insurance Company*. Urbana: University of Illinois Press, 1973.

Weatherford, Willis Duke. *Negro Life in the South, Present Conditions and Needs*. New York: YMCA Press, 1910.

INDEX

NOTE: The asterisk indicates the location of detailed information. This index, while not cumulative, does include the major identifications of persons annotated in earlier volumes of the series who are mentioned in this volume. References to earlier volumes will appear first and will be preceded by the volume number followed by a colon. Lawrence Fraser Abbott's annotation, for example, will appear as *5:409. Occasionally a name will have more than one entry with an asterisk when new information or further biographical detail is presented.

from, 129-30; provides BTW with information on W. L. Cohen, 129-30
Jones, Robert Lee, 211, *236
Jones, Thomas Jesse, *189-90; consults with BTW on use of terms "Colored" and "Negro" in U.S. census, 344-45; letters from, 189, 344-45; letters to, 351-52, 496-98; seeks accurate census of blacks, 189
Jones, Wesley Livsey, *252, 262
Jones, William C., *112
Josephs, James S., 451, *452
Journal of the African Society: publishes book review by BTW, 566-71
Judd, John Walters, *240
Judkins, Robert Chapman, *553
Justice, E. J., 459

Kealing, Hightower T., *5:130; accompanies BTW on tour of Mississippi, 62-63; advises E. J. Scott that he will not be led into any movement animated by bitterness and complaint, 334-35; cautioned about joining NAACP, 331; letter from E. J. Scott, 331; letter to E. J. Scott, 334-35
Kenna, John Edward, 485, *486
Kennaway, John Henry, 401
Kennedy, Alexander B., *6:486; 440
Kenney, John Andrew, *7:164-65; 428; letter from, 338-39; reports on Tuskegee Institute hospital, 338-39
Kenney, Mrs. John Andrew, 428
Kentucky: BTW tours state, 215-16
Keys, Thomas I., 266, 267, 268-69, 277
Keystone Aid Society (Philadelphia), 425
King, George H., 456, *469
King's College (Va.), 200
Knapp, Seaman Asahel, *9:122; 146
Knights of Labor: BTW once member, 475
Knights of Pythias, 62
Knox, George L., *5:463; 585
Knox, Philander Chase, *6:223; 6, 279, 281, 321; letter from M. F. Egan, 393-94; letter to, 588; promises aid to Liberia, 340, 341; shows interest in Liberia, 317, 318
Koenig, Samuel S., *559

Koenigin Luise, 82
Kroo: uprising in Liberia, 324-25, 326, 327
Kuntz, Emile, 81, *82

Labor: BTW apologizes to S. Gompers for criticism based on erroneous information, 517-18; BTW charges S. Gompers with racial discrimination, 475-77; BTW downplays friction between blacks and whites, 358; BTW once member of Knights of Labor, 475; BTW's notebook entries of conditions in Europe, 369-72, 374; BTW's views of black employment opportunities, 305-6; blacks and Italians compete for jobs in South, 278, 363-64; blacks and railroad unions, 149-50, 155; blacks win decision in Georgia railroad employment dispute, 155; discrimination on railroads, 182-83; on southern plantation, 346-48; seen as key to good health, 257-59; unions refuse blacks, 423; views of R. C. Ogden, 355-56
Landers, Edna Amelia Spears, *8:482; 430
Langston, Ralph, 559
Laveleye, Emile Louis Victor de, 422
Lawrence, William, *5:30; 85
League for Industrial Democracy, 435
Lee, Edward E. ("Chief"), *154, 304, 559
Lee, John Robert E., *5:399; 428, 430; letter to, 188
Lee, Mrs. John Robert E., 428, 493
Lee, Robert E., 37, 230, 521
Leopold II (King of Belgium), 349
Lewey, M. M., 277
Lewis, Cary B., *8:521; 585
Lewis, James, *5:239; 140, 154; loses office during Taft administration, 276
Lewis, William Henry, *4:229-30; 47, 140, 368, 386, 439, 440, 552, 553, 574; accompanies BTW on tour of Tennessee, 226; appointed assistant attorney general, 426; letters from, 45, 85-86, 141-42; letter from E. J. Scott, 54; letter to, 86; privately criticizes Taft for policy regarding appointment of blacks to office, 45; recommended for office by BTW, 328-29; retains appointment as

hiding during Atlanta Riot, 555; accuses W. E. B. Du Bois of not registering to vote, 324; accuses W. E. B. Du Bois of undermining work of Tuskegee Institute, 322; accuses W. E. B. Du Bois of preparing critical letter, 501-3; attacked by J. E. Milholland while on European tour, 394-400; attacked in open letter by W. E. B. Du Bois and others for being too optimistic about American race relations, 422-25; attacks letter of protest by J. E. Milholland, 478-79; C. W. Anderson undermines dinner planned for W. E. B. Du Bois, 127; cautions R. H. Terrell regarding M. C. Terrell's association with BTW's enemies, 323; chastises signer of protest letter, 471; claims he will not be threatened by defections to Du Bois camp, 421; claims never to personally abuse W. E. B. Du Bois, 322; critical of W. E. Walling, 556; criticized for being overly optimistic regarding American race relations, 505-6; criticized for failure to face black labor problem, 306; criticized for supporting black YMCA in Cleveland, 578-79; criticized for views on woman suffrage, 12, 23-24, 31-32; criticizes National Negro Conference membership, 333-34; defends European speeches, 540-43; describes differences between W. E. B. Du Bois and self, 608-9; disagrees that black intellectuals oppose him, 542; enemies active in Cleveland, 418-19, 434-35; hope expressed for rapprochement with W. E. B. Du Bois, 482; invites O. G. Villard to speak before NNBL, 329; leadership contrasted with that of W. E. B. Du Bois, 386; NAACP accused of undermining work, 472-73; not afraid of critics, 551; O. G. Villard claims his political activities harmful to blacks, 487-89; O. G. Villard says he does not go far enough in statements on racial injustice, 573-74; on Garrisonian temperament, 576; opinion of blacks and whites in NAACP, 454; orders unfavorable publicity for Cosmopolitan Club dinner, 556; plans to

control activities of W. E. B. Du Bois in New York, 355; political leadership criticized by W. E. B. Du Bois, 309-10; racial strategy criticized in New York *Evening Post* editorial, 308-11; receives report from R. R. Moton on NAACP officials, 498; sees advantages in having M. C. Terrell in NAACP, 504; sees critics as bitter and unhappy group, 479, 483, 541-42; sees J. E. Milholland as promoter of W. E. B. Du Bois, 545; sees W. E. B. Du Bois as tool of O. G. Villard and J. E. Milholland, 555; skeptical regarding motivations of NAACP and Constitution League, 555; urges O. G. Villard to speak mind at NNBL meeting, 335; uses protest letter by J. E. Milholland to influence O. G. Villard, 416-17; wants friends to ignore W. E. B. Du Bois, 508; William Pickens explains reasons for signing letter of protest, 477-78, 489-90. *See also* Cosmopolitan Club

—Early years: first impression of R. C. Ogden, 602; recalls first knowledge of Abraham Lincoln, 33; recalls first opportunity to attend Sunday school, 521; taught Bible lessons while at Hampton Institute, 44

—Family: aids son with small farm, 367; buys presents for grandchildren, 587-88; concerned about BTW Jr.'s active social life interfering with studies, 611; concerned about health of daughter and grandson, 106-7; daughter expresses pride in father, 437; inquires about health of grandson, 99; last will and testament, 112-16; plans to spend day with BTW Jr., 453; promotes career of son-in-law, 157-58, 586-87; receives letter from BTW Jr., 98-99; receives report on health of grandson, 111-12; spends summer on Long Island, 137-38; wants son to go through Fisk University on own merits, 319

—Fund-raising: appeals to H. H. Rogers, Jr., 133-34; philanthropy of H. H. Rogers described, 122-26; recommends distribution of school funds, 174-76; recommends schools to receive funds